"Bathroom reading: It's your right ...
and your responsibility."

W. C. Privy's
Original Big Fat
Bathroom Companion

EDITED BY ERIN BARRETT & JACK MINGO

BARNES
& NOBLE
BOOKS
NEW YORK

www.stmartins.com

ISBN 0-7607-7056-5

W. C. Privy's Original Bathroom Companion was
originally published by St. Martin's Griffin in 2003.

W. C. Privy's Original Bathroom Companion: Number 2 was
originally published by St. Martin's Griffin in December 2003.

This edition published for Barnes & Noble, Inc., by St. Martin's Press

First Edition: July 2005

10 9 8 7 6 5 4 3 2 1

Acknowledgments

To the *Bathroom Companion* staff members, our family and friends, thank you for helping us keep W. C. Privy's dream alive.

Heather Jackson Silverman
Lindy Settevendemie
Pam Suwinsky and Thalia Publishing Services
Kathie Meyer
Susan Shipman
Chris McLaughlin
Mary-Nell Bockman
Michele Montez
Oilville Goochland
Louisa Fernside
Georgia Hamner
Elana Mingo
Jackson Hamner
Eric "Stumpy Joe" Childs
Vera Mingo
Jerry & Lynn Barrett
Powell Hamner
Everyone at St. Martin's Press
The Honorable Mr. Doo-Wop
Ms. Deborah
Mark Hardin
Ray Davies
The BCOMPs (members of the W. C. Privy fan club—p. 478)
"Big Bob"
Ms. Fawcett
Shirley & Nigel Jest
Joe Mugs
Ed Zorn
Roxanne Barrett
The Univark Truckers

"Bugs: Everything You Wanted to Know About Insects," adapted from *Just Curious About Animals and Nature, Jeeves*, by Erin Barrett and Jack Mingo, Pocket Books, 2002. Adapted with permission by authors.

"Between Courses: Tricks for the Dinner Table," originally published in *How To Spit Nickels*, by Jack Mingo, McGraw Hill, 1993. Adapted with permission by author.

"Doctor Riots: The Mobs That Smashed Medical Schools," adapted from *Doctors Killed George Washington*, by Erin Barrett and Jack Mingo, Conari Press, 2002. Adapted with permission by authors.

"A Toast to Toasters: Bred for Bread ... and So Much More," "Full Metal Lunch Jacket: The Birth of the Cool Lunch Boxes," and "Anty Matters: How Uncle Milton Put the Ant in Ant Farm," "Toaster Foods: The Best Thing Since Sliced Bread," adapted from the *Whole Pop Magazine Online*. With permission from the editors.

Excerpts taken from *Just Curious, Jeeves* (Ask Jeeves, Inc., 2000) and *Just Curious About History, Jeeves* (Pocket Books, 2002) for "Presidential Trivia I & II: Presidents & Their Vices." With permission from authors.

Excerpts from *Cats Don't Always Land on Their Feet*, Conari Press, 2002, for "Cat Lovers: From the Ailurophiles," and "Cat Haters: Real-Life Ailurophobes." Permission granted by authors.

Excerpts from *Not Another Apple for the Teacher!*, Conari Press, 2002, for "More Deskware Trivia." Permission granted by authors.

Genius!

Mr. Privy, the Original

"There will be imitators, but no matter: 'Imitation is the sincerest form of plagiarism.' They can be nothing but pale counterfeits of the genuine Privy." **—W. C. Privy**

EXACTLY ONE CENTURY AGO, a remarkable thing happened in bathrooms across America. In the spring of 1903, W. C. Privy published *W. C. Privy's Original Bathroom Companion,* making him the foreflusher of bathroom reading. Composed of jokes, stories, quotations, facts, and other brief articles, the *Companion* made a big splash in the smallest room of the house.

And none too soon. For eons, the world had been waiting for bathroom reading. Reading, of course, had been around since 8000 B.C.; however, the real problem had been the bathroom. Before the approach of the twentieth century, bathrooms were not clean, well-lighted places suitable for reading. Instead, they were dark, smelly, uncomfortably hot or cold, and invariably infested with mosquitoes, horseflies, bats, and vermin. "Anyone who lingered to read in an outhouse was likely demented, addlepated, insensate, or drunk," Privy noted.

The simple fact was that bathroom reading required indoor plumbing, electric lights, a sturdy, locking bathroom door … and a visionary like W. C. Privy.

EARLY HISTORY

Admittedly it's not much, but here's what little we know about Mr. Privy. He was born in 1875 in either Cincinnati, Ohio, or the Szechwan Province of China. He spent the bulk of his childhood either studying in the Toledo (Ohio) Academy for Boys or working in a bootblack factory outside of London, England.

In 1893, Privy visited an elderly aunt in Iowa and experienced indoor plumbing for the first time in his life. According to the proud aunt's memoirs, Privy spent many long hours locked in her bathroom "with a book or magazine, and he wouldn't come out no matter how much I knocked." One such day, she heard splashes followed by her teenage nephew shouting "Eureka!" Seconds later, W. C. burst out of the bathroom.

W. C. told his aunt that he'd had a revelation about the importance of bathroom reading to digestion, health, happiness, and life in general. The 1890s were a time of many emerging beliefs about diet, meditation, sex, and self-improvement; even a young man of Privy's temperament was not immune. Privy began formulating a philosophy about the benefits of "filling the mind while evacuating the body." (Alas, his seven volumes of detailed philosophical observations have been apparently lost to time. No doubt they would have made fascinating reading.)

THE BOOK THAT LAUNCHED 2000 FLUSHES

"Bathroom reading: It's your right ... and your responsibility!"
–W. C. Privy

Philosophy aside, it's sufficient to say that the *Bathroom Companion* was a direct result of Privy's twin obsession with indoor plumbing and good reading. When enough homes had indoor plumbing to make it economically feasible, the twenty-eight-year-old Privy published the first volume of his *W. C. Privy's Original Bathroom Companion.*

Privy had a great deal of humor and curiosity, which he developed in his younger years by writing short books on the fads of the 1860s and the songs of popular stage shows. Neither prudish nor prurient, levelheaded but not unromantic, he had a healthy contempt for the publishers of his day "who issued volume after worthless volume of flowery prose, erroneous facts, and uplifting-sounding pablum." A look at his first *Bathroom*

Companion's Table of Contents shows the sorts of things he believed would transfix and transform his readers: humor, fiction, quizzes, wordplay, explanations of how things work, histories, puzzles, optical illusions, and trivia. He included pictures and rhymes so the young could also experience the joys of bathroom reading. Finally, he offered a limited number of advertisements (some of which are reproduced in this book as a curiosity).

W. C. Privy binding copies of ***Bathroom Companion* #6**

Privy apparently had a firm grip on what people wanted to read behind closed doors, and soon a grateful world beat a path to his bathroom door. Although some Victorian-era doctors and clergymen warned that bathroom reading was immoral and could lead to insanity, blindness, and unwanted hair growth, the first *Bathroom Companion* went through many printings, and the public began clamoring for more. For the next twelve years, W. C. Privy issued a *Bathroom Companion* annually, each more popular than the previous one. Thanks to his fame, "Going to see Privy" became a euphemism for a bathroom stop in the United States; in England, the phrase became, "Where's the W. C.?"

AFTERMATH

What happened to Privy? After thirteen editions of the *Bathroom Companion,* he was tired ... and rich beyond his dreams. In 1916, as World War I raged in Europe, W. C. Privy announced his retirement and disappeared into obscurity somewhere in the wilds of the Pacific Northwest.

What happened to all the copies of his books? That's the strange thing. Although Privy sold millions of copies of his *Bathroom Companion*, there are no known copies now in existence. All that's left of Privy's bestsellers are thirty-three loose and yellowed pages found in a long-abandoned outhouse near Beaverdam, Virginia, revealing a few articles, Privy's introduction, and the Table of Contents mentioned above.

How could it be that all those books just disappeared? Well, to put it delicately, the concept of store-bought toilet paper had caught on much slower than that of indoor plumbing. People had gotten used to "recycling" newspapers, catalogs, and even pages from books when they'd finished reading them. Under the circumstances, a book designed to reside in the bathroom was both Privy's folly (in that it was used on the posterior instead of saved for posterity) or genius (in that he sold more books that way).

(To save this book from a similar fate, we're depending that readers have an ample supply of store-bought paper ... but just to make sure, we've included an emergency stash in the back to be used only in dire circumstances.)

A HUNDRED YEARS LATER

Thanks to a dissolute Privy descendant and a lucky bar bet, we have obtained the rights to carry on W. C. Privy's formidable tradition. On this hundredth anniversary of its first edition, we're proud to present the rebirth of *W. C. Privy's Original Bathroom Companion.*

While sitting firmly on Privy's oval seat of wisdom and fun, we aim to let fly with all we've got. While we can't possibly hope to be as financially successful as Privy himself was, we'll at least aspire to his high standards in presenting (as he put it) "a mighty fine read." We hope you enjoy leafing through this book as much as we enjoyed putting it together. And W. C., wherever you are, we hope we've done you proud.

Jack Mingo

Erin Barrett

ABOUT BARRETT & MINGO

Erin Barrett and Jack Mingo are particularly well-suited for the task of reviving the *Bathroom Companion*, having written dozens of entertaining books including *Just Curious, Jeeves, Doctors Killed George Washington, Cats Don't Always Land On Their Feet, The Whole Pop Catalog,* and *How the Cadillac Got Its Fins.* Their fun fact column appears daily in newspapers around the country.

What's Inside...

Pop Culture History

Odd Lots of Trivia

All You Ever Wanted to Know

Aesop's Fables

Short Fiction

Stately Knowledge

Monopoly!

The World's Favorite Real Estate Game

Who came up with the idea for a game about buying and developing prime property? And how did a game like this become so popular? With a little digging, here's what we found.

According to Parker Brothers, Monopoly was invented by an out-of-work heating engineer named Charles Darrow. During the Great Depression, his family could no longer afford their trips to Atlantic City, so Darrow created the game to remind them all of happier times.

There's no doubt that Darrow created a game, but there's great controversy over how much of it was his original idea. At the time, there were at least eight similar real estate oriented games, including a popular one at Harvard Law School. There's evidence that Charles Darrow learned the game from a group of Quakers while in Atlantic City but that he added Chance cards and the Railroads before pitching his game to gaming companies.

Parker Brothers originally turned the game down. The company listed several reasons why the game was a failure: The rules were too complicated, the concept was too dull, the game was too long, and the players went around and around the board instead trying to reach a destination. When Darrow took his game to market on his own, though, it was a huge and instant success. Parker Brothers ate crow and bought the game. The company quickly snatched up earlier versions of the game and spread the Darrow-as-sole-inventor story.

The game has changed little over the years. The minor differences are in the game pieces. The original line up in 1935: race car, flat iron, cannon, pocketbook, lantern, baby shoe, top hat, racehorse, battleship and thimble

with "For a Good Girl" engraved on it. The hotels were made of wood instead of plastic and had "Grand Hotel" written on them. In 2002, a brand new token—the first one in over 40 years—was added to the line up. It's a sack full of money.

The streets in the game are real streets in Atlantic City. At least they were when the game was put out. You may be a little disappointed if you trek to see them today, though. All of the upscale places in the game are pretty run-down and seedy, and some, like Pacific Avenue, are hang-outs for hookers. Kentucky Avenue is lined with greasy burger joints. Marven Gardens, misspelled on the game board, is located so far out of town the trains don't even stop there anymore, and St. Charles Place is completely gone—wiped out by a parking lot for a casino. But one thing remains the same: there's always plenty of free parking at the jail.

Monopoly has continued to be a top seller over the years. It's published in over 23 languages, including Japanese, Russian, German, French, Chinese, and Spanish. The games are slightly changed to reflect the cultures of the people playing them. For instance, Boardwalk is "Rue de la Paix" in the French version, and different according to locale in other versions, like "Mayfair" (UK), "Kalverstraat" (Netherlands), and "Schlossallee" (Germany).

Over the years there have been specialty editions of the game. A gold set by Alfred Dunhill was offered in 1974 for $5,000, and Nieman-Marcus sold an all-chocolate set in the 1970s for $600. Other current and more affordable editions include the Braille edition, the Disney edition, the Power Puff girls edition, and the Pokémon Gold & Silver edition.

MONOPOLY FACTS & FIGURES:

• The spaces most frequently

landed on are, in order, Illinois Avenue, GO, B & O Railroad, Free Parking, Tennessee Avenue, New York Avenue, and the Reading Railroad.

• The smallest game of Monopoly ever played had an inch square board. The players looked through magnifying glasses during the 30-hour-long game.

• The longest game played underwater went for fifty days, or 1,200 hours. Divers in wet suits—1,500 of them—took turns playing in shifts.

• The largest outdoor game was larger than a city block—938 feet by 765 feet. Messengers on bicycles relayed plays to the participants.

• During World War II, Parker Brothers claims, "escape maps, compasses, and files were inserted into Monopoly game boards and smuggled into P.O.W. camps. Real money for escapees was slipped into the packs of Monopoly money."

• Parker Brothers annually produces more than twice the amount of money that the U.S. mint puts out each year. Despite this, you may be surprised to learn that a standard Monopoly game comes with a mere $15,140, total.

TIPS & TRICKS:

• Since there are only 32 houses available in each game, if you have low-rent properties, quickly build up four houses on each property to confront your opponents with a housing shortage.

• Jail can be a sanctuary later in the game when traveling around the board becomes monetarily dangerous. Get out of jail quickly early in the game when there's still property up for grabs.

• The rules don't allow for shuffling of the Chance and Community Chest cards. Therefore, remembering the order of the cards can work to your advantage.

• On average, you'll land on four properties each time around the board. To estimate the cost to you, count the unmortgaged properties that are owned by others in the game. Divide that number by 7 to get an estimate of the number of rents you can expect to pay on your next trip around the board.

Potty Pourri

Random Kinds of Factness

• Elvis Presley didn't believe in encores. A few moments after Elvis walked offstage, a voice on the PA would announce to the cheering fans, "Elvis has left the building," and that was that.

• Cats can drive even a genius crazy, what with that out-again, in-again thing they do. Sir Isaac Newton's cat kept interrupting his work on the laws of gravity, so he put his intellect to work. He invented that sanity-saving contraption, the cat door flap.

• Thirty-six dollars an ounce? No, don't call the vice squad, call the spice squad. Pickers pluck the stamens of nearly 5,000 blossoms to get just one ounce of saffron, making it the most expensive spice on your grocer's shelf.

• The Food and Drug Administration allows up to 210 insect fragments and seven rodent hairs in a regular 700-gram jar of peanut butter before considering the product too unsanitary for public consumption. The consuming public may have a differing opinion, of course.

• If you *deliberately* eat bugs, you're an "entomophagist."

• The very first American entrepreneur to be worth a billion dollars? Car mogul Henry Ford.

• That flavor we call "bubblegum" is a mix of vanilla, wintergreen, and cassia (a form of cinnamon).

• Experts say you should scrub with soap and water for at least 20 seconds if you want your hands to be sanitary.

• Douglas Engelbart invented the "X-Y Position Indicator for a Display System" in the late 1960s. "XYPIDS" didn't catch on as a name—early users first called it a "turtle," then a "rodent," then the cuter-sounding "mouse," the name that finally stuck to that computer thing that rolls, points, and clicks.

• When watching TV, you burn 1–2 calories per minute.

Apples & Oranges

JUICY TALES ABOUT FRUIT

Some fruitful incidents, fruitless accidents, and weird fruit facts from *Bathroom Companion* contributor Chris McLaughlin.

LET'S DO LAUNCH

Slipping on banana peels is a staple of silent films and clown acts. But it can really happen, as occasional lawsuits against produce markets show. However, the slippery peel phenomenon can also be a virtue. In 1995, owners wanted to launch the showboat *Branson Belle* into Missouri's Table Rock Lake without polluting the water with industrial grease. They covered the 160-foot-long launch ramp with 40 crates of unpeeled bananas.

REASON #12 FOR AVOIDING ITALY RIGHT BEFORE LENT

Every February, Ivrea, Italy, holds a Battle of the Oranges where thousands of people team up to lob surplus oranges at one another in mock battle. Although the combatants wear helmets and eyeguards, first-aid workers report hundreds of minor injuries from hard tosses, sprained throwing arms, and orange juice dripping in the eyes.

... BUT SPANISH TOMATOES ARE ANOTHER MATTER

Fewer injuries are reported each year at the Bunol, Spain, Tomato Festival, in which 30,000 partygoers attack each other with truckloads of ripe tomatoes. The tradition started in the

1940s with some teenagers tossing their lunches at each other in the city square. They had so much fun, they agreed to repeat the practice annually. Each year, more people joined in, and the event became one of Spain's most popular festivals.

DOLEFUL POLITICS

In an attempt to punish Senator Bob Dole for trying to block foreign aid to Turkey, the mayor of Izmir banned the sale of Dole bananas within his city. Only one problem with the boycott: the Senator had no connection with the company.

SGT. MANNERS

In San Bernardino, California, the county sheriff's department issued a book of etiquette that included an official way for an officer to eat a banana. No joke: You first must separate it into pieces, and then eat it with a fork.

GLAD TO SEE ME?

Two wild-and-crazy journalists from Slovakia were nabbed by security staff and stripped of potentially dangerous contraband at the 2002 Olympics in Salt Lake. Their offense? They were toting bananas in their pockets.

HAPPY GLOW IN THE DARK

If you ever get shipwrecked on Bikini Atoll, don't eat the fruit. The coconuts, oranges, lemons, bread fruit, and pandanus grow there as part of a United States Department of Energy experiment aimed at reducing radiation in the soil. Atomic testing from 1946 to 1958 left large quantities of radiactive cessium in the soil, and it still leeches into the fruit.

COCONUT CONCUSSION

If life hands you a coconut, look out below. A coconut dropped from 30 feet can cause concussions or more. In fact, beach towns in northern Australia decided to uproot their coconut trees in favor of "safer" fruits.

MORE COCONUT DANGERS

A couple in Albany, Georgia, was scared out of their Buick by a swarm of honeybees that were apparently attracted by a coconut-scented air freshener. An animal control officer said that the scent was so strong that it could be easily smelled by humans outside the car with the doors and windows shut. Bees, with an even stronger sense of smell, apparently found the odor irresistable.

EVEN MORE COCONUT DANGERS

Monkeys in Malaysia have been trained by growers to climb trees and twist the coconuts from them. One monkey in Kuala Lumpur, however, went severely off-task when it leapt onto the shoulders of a person passing by and tried to twist his head off. He was treated at a local hospital for a sprained neck.

DEATH BY DURIAN

People (and orangutans) are passionate about durians, which look like overinflated porcupines. They grow on 100-foot-high trees that bloom only at night and are pollinated by bats and fireflies. Death by randomly falling durian is not uncommon among those who farm them. Then again, you might just want to die when you encounter one: it smells like "civet cat, sewage, stale vomit, gasoline ... onions and moldy cheese." If that doesn't put you off, it tastes (we are told) like "custard, garlic, marshmallows, chicken pudding ... (and) butter-like custard with onion sauce imitations." The quotes are from a food critic, Fredric Paten-

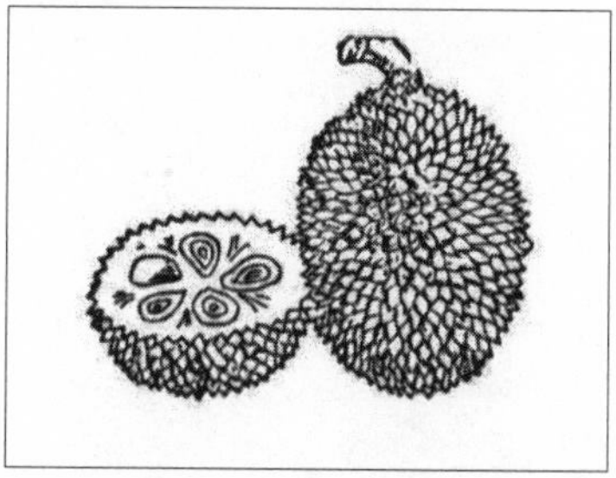

The stinky, sweet durian fruit

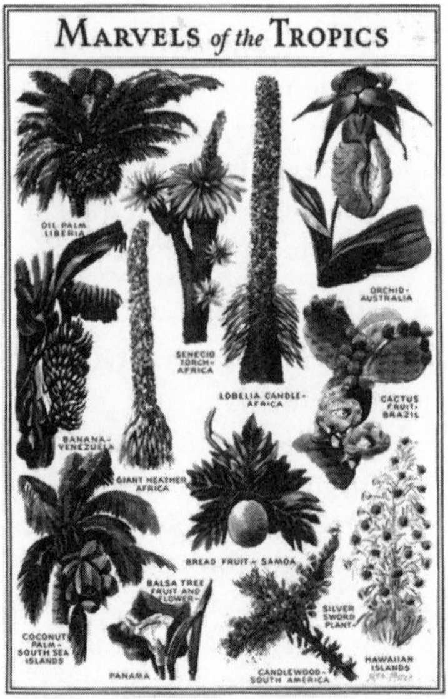

aude, who says, "It is simply the best thing there is!" We'll take his word for it.

CHEEKY LITTLE FRUIT BOWL

Sculptor Mark Maitre, of Woodland Hills, California, can turn castings of your body parts into a fruitbowl. He's done several for the rich and famous including one of a Hollywood star's rear end. The cost ranges from $1,000 to $4,000.

THIS JUST IN: BANANAS NOT FRUIT

Horticulturally, bananas are not a fruit. They grow on the tallest herb in the world—up to thirty feet high—that has no woody trunks or branches and dies after a growth season.

OUT, OUT, ORANGE SPOT

Orange growers are asking us all to stop using the name "blood oranges" when referring to the red-juiced citrus fruit. They believe that the name is unappetizing to consumers. They'd prefer that we use the term "Moro oranges" instead.

Type Your Password Here

- While many people use names of their spouses, children, or lovers, "God," "sex," and "money" are among the most popular computer passwords.
- Among middle-aged women, the most popular password is "love."
- About ten percent of male users have passwords that refer to obscenities or their masculinity.
- Younger users use self-laudatory terms more than any other group. Popular passwords among the under-25 crowd were "stud," "goddess," "cutiepie," and "hotbod."
- A surprisingly large number of people, no doubt trying to be clever, use the words "secret" or "password."

Aesop's Odds & Ends

AN ASSORTMENT OF FABLES

Here are some pretty obscure fables featuring stomachs, pots, and clouds, from the legendary Greek slave, Aesop.

THE BELLY AND THE MEMBERS

One fine day it occurred to the Members of the Body that they were doing all the work and the Belly was having all the food. So they held a meeting and, after a long discussion, decided to go on strike until the Belly consented to take its proper share of the work. So for a day or two, the Hands refused to take the food, the Mouth refused to receive it, and the Teeth had no work to do. But after a day or two the Members began to find that they themselves were not in a very active condition: the Hands could hardly move, and the Mouth was all parched and dry, while the Legs were unable to support the rest. So thus they found that even the Belly in its dull quiet way was doing necessary work for the Body, and that:

All must work together or the Body will go to pieces.

THE TREE AND THE REED

"Well, little one," said a Tree to a Reed that was growing at its foot, "why do you not plant your feet deeply in the ground and raise your head boldly in the air as I do?"

"I am contented with my lot," said the Reed. "I may not be so grand, but I think I am safer."

"Safe!" sneered the Tree. "Who shall pluck me up by the roots or bow my head to the ground?" But it soon had to repent of its boasting, for a hurricane arose that tore it up from its roots and cast it a useless log on the ground, while the little Reed, bending to the force of the wind, soon stood upright again when the storm had passed over.

Obscurity often brings safety.

THE TWO POTS

Two Pots had been left on the bank of a river, one of brass and one of earthenware. When the tide rose they both floated off down the stream. Now the earthenware pot tried its best to keep aloof from the brass one, which cried out: "Fear nothing, friend, I will not strike you."

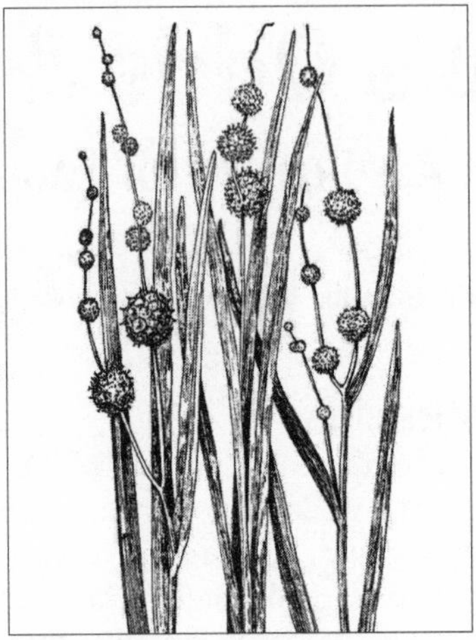

"I am contented with my lot."

"But I may come in contact with you," said the other, "if I come too close; and whether I hit you, or you hit me, I shall suffer for it."

The strong and the weak cannot keep company.

THE WIND AND THE SUN

The Wind and the Sun were disputing which was the stronger. Suddenly they saw a traveler coming down the road, and the Sun said: "I see a way to decide our dispute. Whichever of us can get the cloak off that traveler shall be regarded as the stronger. You begin." So the Sun retired behind a cloud, and the Wind began to blow as hard as it could upon the traveler. But the harder he blew the more closely did the traveller wrap his cloak round him, until at last the Wind had to give up in despair. Then the Sun came out and shone in all his glory upon the traveler, who soon found it too hot to walk with his cloak on.

Kindness has more effect than severity.

THE ROSE AND THE AMARANTH

A Rose and an Amaranth blossomed side by side in a garden, and the Amaranth said to her neighbor, "How I envy you your beauty and your sweet scent! No wonder you are such a universal favorite." But the Rose replied with a shade of sadness in her voice, "Ah, my dear friend, I bloom but for a time: my petals soon wither and fall, and then I die. But your flowers never fade, even if they are cut; for they are everlasting."

Greatness carries its own penalties.

Stately Knowledge

12 Reasons Why Ya Gotta Love Alabama

We've searched the vaults and come up with some pretty impressive facts about Alabama. Here are a dozen of our favorites.

1 Although New Orleans gets all the attention, it was Alabama, not Louisiana, that first introduced the Mardi Gras celebration to the Western world.

2 The first open heart surgery in the Western Hemisphere was performed in Montgomery in 1902. Dr. Luther Leonidas Hill sutured a stab wound in a young boy's heart.

3 George Washington Carver conducted most of his research at the Tuskegee Institute in Tuskegee, Alabama. He came up with over 100 new products from the sweet potato, and more than 300 from the peanut.

4 Other famous Alabamians include: home-run king Hank Aaron, actress Tallulah Bankhead, singer Nat King Cole, and author and blind-and-deaf educator Helen Keller.

5 The boll weevil is a terrible crop pest, yet there's a monument to the boll weevil in Enterprise, Alabama. Why? Well, when the boll weevil destroyed cotton crops, farmers in Alabama were forced to diversify into other crops, resulting in increased prosperity. In gratitude, they honored the little bugger with a statue.

6 Montgomery operated the very first electric trolley streetcars in the United States in 1866.

7 If you've ever irretrievably lost your luggage, you might be able to buy it back at the huge Unclaimed Baggage Center in Scottsboro, Alabama. Clothing, cameras, skis, radios, books, and CDs are all for sale, and the center even has a Web site where you can shop online.

8 Workers in Alabama built the first rocket booster that helped shoot man to the moon.

9 An Alabamian was the only American to ever get beaned by a meteorite. Mrs. E. Hulitt Hodge was in her sitting room in Sylacauga, Alabama, in 1954 when a meteorite crashed through the roof and hit her in the hip, bruising her, but otherwise leaving her unharmed. The meteorite is now housed in the Smithsonian in Washington, D.C.

10 A 56-foot statue of Vulcan, the Roman god of fire, stands near Birmingham. It was built in Birmingham as an exhibit for the 1904 World's Fair in St. Louis. It's not just the world's largest cast metal statue, but also the largest statue ever made in the United States. His hand holds a neon torch that is normally green, but turns red whenever there's a traffic fatality in the Birmingham area.

Vulcan being built in 1903

11 At the Bessemer Hall of History museum in Bessemer, Alabama, you can see a typewriter once owned by Adolf Hitler.

12 In 1864, when the Union Navy tried to enter Mobile Bay to take the city, "torpedoes" (mines) began going off. When Union Admiral David Farragut was warned of their presence, he issued his famous command: "Damn the torpedoes! Full speed ahead!" The Union Navy moved into the Bay, overtaking the Confederates at Mobile.

Slogos!

Try to match the slogan with the logo. This one's all about cereal and Saturday morning commercials. See if you can get them all.
Rated: Easy.

1. Which spokes-cartoon commanded a young television audience to "Follow your nose!"?
A. Sam the Toucan (Froot Loops)
B. L. C. Leprechaun (Lucky Charms)
C. Tony the Tiger (Frosted Flakes)
D. Sugar Bear (Golden Crisps)
E. Sonny the Cuckoo Bird (Cocoa Puffs)

2. "____ are for KIDS!" was always the answer to this poor, starving mascot.
A. Tony the Tiger (Frosted Flakes)
B. Sugar Bear (Golden Crisps)
C. Sonny the Cuckoo Bird (Cocoa Puffs)
D. Dig 'Em Frog (Smacks)
E. Trix Rabbit (Trix cereal)

3. Who claimed to be "Cuckoo for …" his cereal?
A. Sugar Bear (Golden Crisps)
B. Sonny the Cuckoo Bird (Cocoa Puffs)
C. L. C. Leprechaun (Lucky Charms)
D. Tony the Tiger (Frosted Flakes)
E. Dig 'Em Frog (Smacks)

4. Whose smoky voice sang out "Can't get enough of that ______"?
A. Tony the Tiger (Frosted Flakes)
B. L. C. Leprechaun (Lucky Charms)
C. Sugar Bear (Golden Crisps)

D. Captain Crunch (Captain Crunch)
E. Dig 'Em Frog (Smacks)

5. Which cartoon cereal mascot shouted, "They're gr-r-r-eat!"?
A. Dig 'Em Frog (Smacks)
B. Sonny the Cuckoo Bird (Cocoa Puffs)
C. Captain Crunch (Captain Crunch)
D. Tony the Tiger (Frosted Flakes)
E. L. C. Leprechaun (Lucky Charms)

6. Pick the cartoon logo that croaked "Dig 'Em!"
A. Tony the Tiger (Frosted Flakes)
B. Sonny the Cuckoo Bird (Cocoa Puffs)
C. Trix Rabbit (Trix cereal)
D. Dig 'Em Frog (Smacks)
E. Sam the Toucan (Froot Loops)

7. Who skipped and frolicked, singing "They're magically delicious!"?
A. Captain Crunch (Captain Crunch)
B. L. C. Leprechaun (Lucky Charms)
C. Sam the Toucan (Froot Loops)
D. Sonny the Cuckoo Bird (Cocoa Puffs)
E. Trix Rabbit (Trix cereal)

Answers: *1. A—Before he followed his nose, Toucan Sam talked in pig latin. Commercials got kids asking their moms for "Oot-fray Oops-lay!" 2. E—Trix Rabbit. The Trix Rabbit was allowed to eat Trix cereal just once in 1976 when kids voted (over 99 percent!) to let him indulge. 3. B—Sonny the Cuckoo Bird. 4. C—Sugar Bear. Originally, they were Super Sugar Crisps, but changed when "sugar" became a dirty word to health-conscious moms. 5. D—Tony the Tiger. 6. D—Dig 'Em Frog. Kellogg's Smacks is another cereal that lost its original too-sugary title "Sugar Smacks." 7. B—Lucky the Leprechaun. The little marshmallow shapes, called "marbits," were originally created by one John Holahan who worked for General Mills. Marbits debuted with Lucky Charms in 1963.*

Ripe Ol' Corn

"UNCLE JOSH AT THE OPERA"

"Uncle Josh," Cal Stewart's country bumpkin, had problems figuring out modern city life (circa 1901). Here he visits a metropolitan opera house.

WELL, I SAID TO MOTHER when I left home, "Now mother, when I git down to New York City I'm goin' to see a regular first-class theater. "

We never had many theater doin's down our way. Well, thar was a theater troop come to Punkin Centre along last summer, but we couldn't let 'em have the Opery House to show in 'cause it was summer time and the Opery House was full of hay, and we couldn't let 'em have it 'cause we hadn't any place to put the hay.

An then about a year and a half ago thar was a troop come along that was somethin' about "Uncle Tom's Home"; they left a good many of their things behind 'em when they went away. Ezra Hoskins, he got one of the mules, and he tried to hitch it up one day; Doctor says he thinks Ezra will be around in about six weeks. I traded one of the dogs to Ruben Hendricks fer a shot gun; Rube cum over t'other day, borrowed the gun and shot the dog.

Well, I got into one of your theaters here, got set down and was lookin' at it; and it was a mighty fine lookin' picture with a lot of lights shinin' on it, and I was enjoyin' it fust rate, when a lot of fellers cum out with horns and fiddles, and they all started in to fiddlin' and tootin', end all to once they pulled the the-

ater up, and thar was a lot of folks having a regular family quarrel. I knowed that wasn't any of my business, and I sort of felt uneasy like; but none of the rest of the folks seemed to mind it any, so I calculated I'd see how it come out, though my hands sort of itched to get hold of one feller, 'cause I could see if he would jest go 'way and tend to his own business thar wouldn't be any quarrel.

Well, jest then a young feller handed me a piece of paper what told all about the theater doin's, and I got to lookin' at that and I noticed on it whar it said that five years took place 'tween the fust part and the second part. I knowed durned well I wouldn't have time to wait and see the second part, so I got up and went out.

UNCLE JOSH'S PHILOSOPHY

"Those who hanker fer justice would be generally better off if they didn't git it."

"Suspicion—Consists mainly of thinking what we would do if we wuz in the other feller's place."

"Advice—Advice is somethin' the other feller can't use, so he gives it to you."

"Glory—Gittin' killed and not gittin' paid fer it." —Cal Stewart

Persons of the Tale

WHAT CHARACTERS DO BETWEEN CHAPTERS

Robert Louis Stevenson imagined what his characters did when he wasn't writing about them. Here is his fantasy of two of his characters conversing between chapters of *Treasure Island*.

AFTER THE 32ND chapter of *Treasure Island*, two of the puppets strolled out to have a pipe, and met in an open place not far from the story.

"Good-morning, Cap'n," said the first, with a man-o'-war salute, and a beaming countenance.

"Ah, Silver!" grunted the other. "You're in a bad way, Silver."

"Now, Cap'n Smollett," remonstrated Silver, "dooty is dooty, as I knows, and none better; but we're off dooty now; and I can't see no call to keep up the morality business."

"You're a damned rogue, my man," said the Captain.

"Come, come, Cap'n, be just," returned the other. "There's no call to be angry with me in earnest. I'm on'y a chara'ter in a sea story. I don't really exist."

"Well, I don't really exist either," says the Captain, "which seems to meet that."

"I wouldn't set no limits to what a virtuous chara'ter might consider argument," responded Silver. "But I'm the villain of this tale, I am; and speaking as one sea-faring man to another, what I want to know is, what's the odds?"

"Were you never taught your catechism?" said the Captain. "Don't you know there's such a thing as an Author?"

"Such a thing as a Author?" returned John, derisively. "The p'int is, if the Author made you, he made Long John, and he made Hands, and Pew, and George Merry and Flint; and he made this here mutiny; and he had Tom Redruth shot; and—well, if that's a Author, give me Pew!"

"Don't you believe in a future state?" said Smollett. "Do you think there's nothing but the present story-paper?"

"I don't rightly know for that," said Silver; "and I don't see what it's got to do with it, anyway. What I know is this: if there is sich a thing as a Author, I'm his favorite chara'ter. He does me fathoms better'n he does you—fathoms, he does. And he likes doing me. He keeps me on deck mostly all the time, crutch and all; and he leaves you measling in the hold, where nobody can't see you, nor wants to, and you may lay to that! If there is a Author, by thunder, he's on my side, and you may lay to it!"

"I see he's giving you a long rope," said the Captain. "But that can't change a man's convictions. I know the Author respects me; I feel it in my bones; when you and I had that talk at the blockhouse door, who do you think he was for?"

"And don't he respect me?" cried Silver. "Ah, you shoulda heard me putting down my mutiny, George Merry and Morgan and that lot, no longer ago'n last chapter; you'da seen what the Author thinks o' me! But come now, do you consider yourself a virtuous chara'ter clean through?"

"God forbid!" said Captain Smollett, solemnly. "I am a man that tries to do his duty, and makes a mess of it as often as not. I'm not a very popular man at home, Silver, I'm afraid!" and the Captain sighed.

"Ah," says Silver. "Then how about this sequel of yours? Are you to be Cap'n Smollett just the same as ever, and not very popular at home, says you? And if so, why, it's *Treasure Island* over again, by thunder; and I'll be Long John, and Pew'll be Pew, and we'll have another mutiny, as like as not. Or are you to be somebody else? And if so, why, what the better are you? and what the worse am I?"

"Why, look here, my man," returned the Captain, "I can't understand how this story comes about at all, can I? I can't see how you and I, who don't exist, should get to speaking here, and smoke our pipes for all the world like reality? Very well, then, who am I to pipe up with my opinions? I know the Author's on the side of good; he tells me so, it runs out of his pen as he writes. Well, that's all I need to know; I'll take my chance upon the rest."

"It's a fact he seemed to be against George Merry," Silver admitted, musingly. "But George is little more'n a name at the best of it," he added, brightening. "And to get into soundings for once. What is this good? I made a mutiny, and I been a gentleman o' fortune; well, but by all stories, you ain't no such saint. I'm a man that keeps company very easy; even by your own account, you ain't, and to my certain knowledge you're a devil to haze. Which is which? Which is good, and which bad? You tell me that!"

"We're none of us perfect," replied the Captain. "That's a fact of religion, my man. All I can say is, I try to do my duty; and if you try to do yours, I can't compliment you on your success."

"And so you was the judge, was you?" said Silver, derisively.

"I would be both judge and hangman for you, my man, and never turn a hair," returned the Captain. "But I get beyond that: it mayn't be sound theology, but it's common sense, that what is good is useful too—or there and thereabout, for I don't set up to be a thinker. Now, where would a story go to if there were no virtuous characters?"

"If you go to that," replied Silver, "where would a story be, if there wasn't no villains?"

"Well, that's pretty much my thought," said Captain Smollett. "The Author has to get a story; that's what he wants; and to get a story, and to have a man like the doctor (say) given a proper chance, he has to put in men like you and Hands. But he's on the right side; and you mind your eye! You're not through this story yet; there's trouble coming for you."

"What'll you bet?" asked John.

"Much I care if there ain't," returned the Captain. "I'm glad enough to be Alexander Smollett, bad as he is; and I thank my stars upon my knees that I'm not Silver. But there's the ink-bottle opening. To quarters!"

And indeed the Author was just then beginning to write the words: "CHAPTER XXXIII...."

Word Thieves I

Some Terms We've Borrowed from the French

Some of the world's citizens criticize Americans because we don't know much about other languages. However, it could be said that we speak dozens of languages a day.

barrage: From the French *tir de barrage,* which means "curtain of fire." It entered the English language during World War I.

Baton Rouge: The city in Louisiana got its name from a red marker that defined the boundary between two Native American tribes. It's French for "red stick."

cahoots: While there are other theories, our favorite is that it came from *cahute,* French for "cabin."

camouflage: Another World War I word, from the French *camoufler* ("disguise").

carry-all: It once was *carriole,* a light wagon, but during the 1700s got confused in translation.

clarinet: French word for "little bell." In French, though, the *t* doesn't sound.

Detroit: From *de troit,* "of the strait," describing the river that runs between Lake Erie and Lake St. Clair.

fruit: From *frut,* "means of enjoyment" in French.

mirror: From *mireor,* an old French word for "look at" or "wonder at."

oboe: Anglicized from *hautbois,* French for "high wood" (pronounced "oh-bwah").

pimp: First recorded in the diary of Samuel Pepys in 1666, it came from the French word *pimpant* ("speak seductively").

sashay: Corrupted from the French word *chasse* ("chase"), sashay originally referred to a sideways-shuffling dance step popular in the 1700s.

saloon: From *salon* ("hall").

Terre Haute: French fur traders named the future city after a flood in 1816. It means "high ground."

Hellish Neighbors

There Goes the Neighborhood

You think you've got it bad? Take a gander at some of these horror stories about naughty neighbors. This article was written by *Bathroom Companion* friend, Kathie Meyer.

YOUR FACE WILL SURELY SHOW IT

In the booming year of 1999, Denver logged 2,500 complaints against construction commotion, nearly a hundred percent increase from five years earlier. Neighbors understandably tended to get upset over debris, noise, and the steady stream of construction workers needed to complete remodeling projects. One contractor reported that while working on a deck project, a neighbor decided to retaliate. She blasted him with the children's song "When You're Happy and You Know It, Clap Your Hands" played loudly over and over for an entire week. "I asked her to turn it down, but she just said, 'It's my backyard,'" he recalled. "It took me a month to get that song out of my head."

BACK TO CLASS

Richard E. Clear ran a martial arts school in Tampa, Florida, that specialized in helping people effectively deal with stress. That, unfortunately, didn't stop Clear from getting a little overly stressed himself, shooting at a neighbor when the neighbor complained Clear's dog was barking too much.

IT KEEPS GOING, AND GOING, AND GOING....

In April 2002, Bo McCoy and his cousin, Ron McCoy, of Durham, North Carolina, filed suit against Hatfield descendent

John Vance and his wife Barbara. The McCoys complained that the Vances closed the only road to the McCoy family cemetery. The

Vances countered that the road was a private driveway and cited liability concerns as their reason for posting "No Trespassing" signs. Three McCoys buried in the cemetery were killed in a pawpaw patch ambush by Hatfields in August 1882. So are two other McCoys who were killed in another Hatfield-related incident in 1888. At least twelve people died as a result of the famous blood feud that began in 1860 with a fight over a pig. The battle apparently rages on.

NO PORKING ZONE

Neighbors of Ron Ripple in Crystal River, Florida, didn't much like the idea of seeing a mobile home parked in Ripple's yard. As a result, he was denied a permit to park one next to his home. In retaliation, he got permits and set up shop as a pig farmer instead. Lesson learned, we guess.

A LITTLE TO THE LEFT

It cost Stacy Ford of Stanwood, Washington, $40,000 to move her house three feet to the left. She had to either move it or tear it down—the result of complaints by a neighbor who cited an ordinance stating a house must be at least five feet away from property lines. Ford's was only two. She inherited the house from her uncle, Dennis Davis, the person with whom the neighbor was really at odds. The feud had started years earlier when the neighbor felled a tree in the wrong direction and destroyed Davis's storage shed.

CQ, CQ. NO 88 LOST BETWEEN THESE FELLOWS. OVER & OUT.

Charles Kissinger discovered another way to get in touch with his neighbor when he and Woodring Fryer began feuding over interference from ham radio signals. Since the two neighbors shared a wall between their apartments, Kissinger began early morning short-range broadcasts using a bull horn and a colorful vocabulary. Roger—over and out.

COLOR ME MAD

On the south side of his house, Michael Glick of Redington Shores, Florida, painted the siding purple and decorated it with yellow frowny faces to indicate his feelings about the neighbors next door. That's not all. He also included a troll in a mooning position and a stuffed pink panther displaying his middle fingers. On the other side lived neighbors who were in Glick's good graces. For them, he painted the side of his house orange with a large yellow smiley face. Glick, who ran an unsuccessful 1998 campaign for mayor, was visited by the police sixty times in in one decade for various complaints regarding actions against people he considers "mean." "There's no law that says I can't paint my house purple, and there's no law that says I can't have a stuffed animal on my roof," he said. "I'm maybe a little eccentric."

POLLY WANT A DEATH THREAT?

A longstanding feud between two women who lived next door to one another resulted in Maria Bruna Bortlussi laboriously training her blackbird to recite repeatedly, "Norina, I'm going to kill you."

LAY THAT PISTIL DOWN

In Painesville, Ohio, Robert Moore was arrested for taking a potshot at his neighbor Patrick Dial. It seems Dial's young children enjoyed picking the 75-year-old Moore's daffodils. That made Moore very grumpy indeed.

OH, WHAT A TANGLED WEB SITE

A feud between Julie and Keith Conrad and Tim and

Lori Gough of Fishing Creek Farm, a wealthy community near Washington, D.C., became so intense it spawned its own Web site: **www.fishingcreekfarm.com**. The feud began in 1997 when the Goughs received an anonymous letter accusing them of bad parenting. The Goughs believed one of the two Conrads had penned it. With these accusations, the fracas snowballed, sides were taken, and the Conrads were ostracized by the some of the neighbors. After losing a $2 million defamation lawsuit against the Goughs, the Conrads set up the Web site documenting the bickering in an attempt to clear their name. The feud has attracted media attention from as far away as Hong Kong.

NO LAWN ORDER

Kurt King of New Orleans, had pushed his lawn edger about three inches or so into his neighbor, Alfred Abadie's, yard. Abadie shot and killed him.

GOOD OFFENSES

If friends are sick of listening to you vent about your neighbor, you can post your frustrations on a special website set up for that purpose: http://www.youdontwantmyneighbor.com/

Neighborly Lexicon

- The word *neighbor* is a combination of the English words *nigh* or *neah* meaning "near" and *gebur* which means "dweller."
- *Neighborhood* dates from the 15th century, but was not used in the sense of indicating a district until the 17th century.
- The word *feud* originates from the Old French *fede* or *feide* and simply means "hostility."
- While the concept of a suburb seems relatively modern, the word is a derivative of *urban*, coming from the Latin *urbanus*, meaning "city." *Suburb* and *suburban* date back to the 14th and 17th centuries respectively, but *surburbia* did not appear until the 1890s.

In the Cards

A Hallmark Moment

Hallmark has dominated the greeting card market for nearly a century. Mix sweet sentiments with the economy of sending a card instead of a present, and you can see why the company's done so well.

The Hallmark Card style is instantly recognizable. This card inscription, featuring the world's cutest kittens on the front, is one of the company's all-time best sellers, written decades ago by the company's founder, Joyce C. Hall:

> **"These kittens feel important**
> **Cause here's what they get to do—**
> **They get to bring this birthday wish**
> **Especially 'fur' you."**

Hall was the youngest son of a devoutly religious Nebraskan woman who named him after a Methodist bishop, Isaac W. Joyce. Although mercilessly teased about his feminine first name, he didn't use his middle name—Clyde—because he thought it would be even worse. He finally settled on J. C.

Hall's father, a traveling preacher, abandoned his wife and children when J. C. was nine. The boy began taking on odd jobs selling perfume, sandwiches, and lemonade to help support the family. Eventually Hall and his two older brothers found a market in selling imported postcards, which had become popular for correspondence and seasonal greetings.

In 1910, Hall dropped out of high school a semester short of graduation and took a train to Kansas City, where he gambled on a desperate ploy to increase his postcard business. In the YMCA room that was both his home and office, he put together hundred-packs of postcards and mailed them unbidden with invoices to shopkeepers throughout the Midwest.

Some of the dealers sent

"And I Haven't Forgotten a Soul!"
"I HAVE learned my lesson. It is this. The people who always do the right thing at the right time—the people we come to love for their constant acts of kindness—who are always known for their thoughtfulness—these people aren't inspired. They don't act on the impulse of a moment. They simply use forethought. They are always thinking ahead about ways of showing their good will to others.
"It was last Christmas morning that this came over me, when the postman handed me dozens of Christmas cards from friends to whom I had entirely forgotten to send cards. I was so mortified that then and there I made a vow.
"And today, long before Christmas, I have made up my list of friends to send cards to this year. First, everyone who sent one to me last year, for I saved every card I got and on the back I wrote the name and address of the sender.
"Then I got out my old school class book for the friends of long ago. From the church list and the woman's club yearbook I got my acquaintances there, and from the local telephone book the correct addresses of my neighbors.
"I'm sure I haven't forgotten a soul. And what a relief it is to know that it's all done way ahead of time, that all the addresses are right, and that I can go out now and buy just the appropriate card for each person, with plenty of time to choose before the stores are crowded.
"And this year there won't be in my mail any cards from people I forgot to remember."
Send 10c for "Forget-me-nots"—a little book of days to remember
The Greeting Card Association
Scatter Sunshine with Christmas Cards

him back his postcards with blistering letters about his shady trick. Others just kept the cards without paying. But about one shopkeeper in three sent him a check, enough to have made the ploy worthwhile. Within a few months, Hall had socked away $200 in a local bank.

J.C. wrote to his brother, Rollie, who joined him in Kansas City. Acting as distributors for other companies' cards, they became successful enough to move out of the Y.

Things went well enough until January 1915, when their warehouse was full of Valentines ready to ship. All those passionate messages in one place apparently caused spontaneous combustion and the building went up in flames, leaving the brothers without inventory and $17,000 in debt.

After the disaster, the Halls decided to change the focus of the company. Rather than merely distribute cards, they were going to start manufacturing them as well. Somehow they convinced a banker to lend them enough money to buy an engraving company from one of their suppliers. They began designing and printing their own cards, shifting away from postcards and into the envelope variety. With syrupy inscriptions and sentimental pictures, they expressed the feelings of a tongue-tied nation. Hall Brothers became the biggest greeting card company in the world.

Today, Hallmark holds a fearsome share of the market, accounting for nearly half of all greeting cards sold in the United States (some are disguised as other lines, like Shoebox and Ambassador). Hallmark produces more than 11 million cards a day in 13,000 different designs (as well as 5,000 non-card products like gift wrap and Christmas decorations). The cards are generated by a staff of 700 writers and illustrators, and helped out by 70,000 unsolicited ideas that pour in from consumers every year.

A Little Latin Quiz

Food, Law, or Ailment?

What do they mean? Hey, it's all Greek to us, but maybe you can identify these Latin words and phrases. Circle the category that matches the meaning of the word or phrase.

1. Epistaxis	Food	Law	Ailment
2. Nemo est supra leges	Food	Law	Ailment
3. Kephalalgia	Food	Law	Ailment
4. Onus probandi	Food	Law	Ailment
5. Nolo contendere	Food	Law	Ailment
6. Apium graveolens	Food	Law	Ailment
7. Beta vulgaris cicla	Food	Law	Ailment
8. Aphthous stomatitis	Food	Law	Ailment
9. Habeas corpus	Food	Law	Ailment
10. Sarda ita fit	Food	Law	Ailment
11. Jus sanguinis	Food	Law	Ailment
12. Vulnus sclopeticum	Food	Law	Ailment
13. In vitulinam elixam	Food	Law	Ailment
14. Amicus curiae	Food	Law	Ailment
15. Aliter baedinam sive agninam excaldatam	Food	Law	Ailment

Answers: *1. Ailment: A nose bleed; 2. Law: "No one is above the law"; 3. Ailment: A headache; 4. Law: "The burden of proof"; 5. Law: "No contest"; 6. Food: Celery; 7. Food: Beet greens; 8. Ailment: A big canker sore; 9. Law: "Produce the body"; 10. Food: Tuna; 11. Law: Regarding children inheriting a parent's citizenship; 12. Ailment: A gunshot wound; 13. Food: Boiled veal; 14. Law: "A friend of the court"; 15. Food: Steamed lamb*

Unforgettable

DESCRIBING THE FACES OF HISTORY

You'd think big names in history like Anne Boleyn, Joseph Stalin, and Cleopatra would have faces that time could never forget. So much for that theory. Here are firsthand accounts of what these historical bigwigs really looked like.

SUBJECT: Cleopatra, Queen of Egypt
TIME PERIOD: 69–30 B.C.

OBSERVER: Plutarch, Greek biographer

DESCRIPTION: "Her actual beauty was not in itself so remarkable that none could be compared with her, or that no one could see her without being struck by it, but the contact of her presence, if you lived with her, was irresistible; the attraction of her person, joining with the charm of her conversation, and the character that attended all she said or did, was something bewitching."

Cleopatra, temptress of bewitching beauty

SUMMARY: Popularized by Hollywood, the image of Cleopatra as the beautiful temptress may have been far from the truth. At best, accurate depictions of her show an average-looking woman with buck teeth. At worst, she looked alarmingly like Robin Williams in drag. But Cleopatra spoke nine languages and had a way with words, not to mention a much-coveted kingdom. She was, in essence, irresistible.

SUBJECT: Abraham Lincoln, 16th U.S. president, reformer, orator, giver of good speeches

TIME PERIOD: 1861–1865

OBSERVERS: Contemporary writers Joshua Speed, William Herndon, and Abram Bergen

DESCRIPTIONS: "Mr. Lincoln's person was ungainly. He was six feet four inches in height; a little stooped in the shoulders; his legs and arms were long; his feet and hands large; his forehead was high. His head was over the average size. His eyes were gray. His face and forehead were wrinkled even in his youth. They deepened with age, 'as streams their channels deeper wear.'"

"Lincoln's voice was, when he first began speaking, shrill, squeaking, piping, unpleasant; his general look, his form, his pose, the color of his flesh, wrinkled and dry, his sensitiveness, and his momentary diffidence, everything seemed to be against him, but he soon recovered."

"Then involuntarily vanished all thought or consciousness of his uncouth appearance, or awkward manner, or even his high keyed, unpleasant voice."

SUMMARY: Honest Abe was lacking in beauty, but when he spoke, his face came alive and he was extremely animated. As a result, this made it difficult to catch his true "look" in a painting or photograph. Walt Whitman, who wrote "O Captain, My Captain" about the president, had this to say: "Though hundreds of portraits have been made, by painters and photographers (many to pass on, by copies, to future times), I have never seen one yet that in my opinion deserved to be called a perfectly good likeness: nor do I believe there is really such a one in existence."

Hun! I'm home!

SUBJECT: Atilla, powerful and vicious leader of the Huns, noted "Scourge of God"

TIME PERIOD: 5th century A.D., specifically A.D. 448.

OBSERVER: Priscus of Panium, a visiting Goth

DESCRIPTION: "He was haughty in his walk, rolling his eyes hither and thither, so that the power of his proud spirit appeared in the movement of his body.

He was indeed a lover of war, yet restrained in action, mighty in counsel, gracious to suppliants, and lenient to those who were once received into his protection. He was short of stature, with a broad chest and a large head: his eyes were small, his beard thin and sprinkled with gray: and he had a flat nose and a swarthy complexion showing the evidences of his origin."

SUMMARY: Atilla the Hun is a perfect example of the complexity of human beings. He popularized spearing the babies of the folks he was pillaging and plundering, but at the same time adored his youngest son and treated those he considered his friends to the finest food, drink, and entertainment. Not unlike some current world leaders, come to think of it. He died from a nosebleed on his wedding night.

SUBJECT: Alexander the Great, Greek Macedonian ruler and noted pretty boy

TIME PERIOD: 356–323 B.C.

OBSERVER: Plutarch, Greek biographer

Alexander, conqueror of the world

DESCRIPTION: "It is the statues of Lysippos which best convey Alexander's physical appearance (and he himself felt it proper that he should be modeled only by Lysippos). For it was this artist who captured exactly those distinctive features which many of Alexander's successors and friends later tried to imitate, namely the poise of the neck slightly turned to the left and the melting glance of the eyes."

SUMMARY: There are those who believe Alexander's well-known stance of right-tilted head and large-eyed glare were the result of a battle injury. A condition known as Brown's Syndrome causes the tendons in the eye to stiffen as a result of injury, causing a bug-eyed, glaring look. But most historians believe he was very good-looking (soft, curly hair, jutting jaw, fair complexion, perfectly proportioned lips), as well as extremely intelligent (he was educated by Aristotle himself) and charismatic. More than likely, Alexander spent a lot of time, in his youth and beyond, primping and practicing his steely gaze in a mirror.

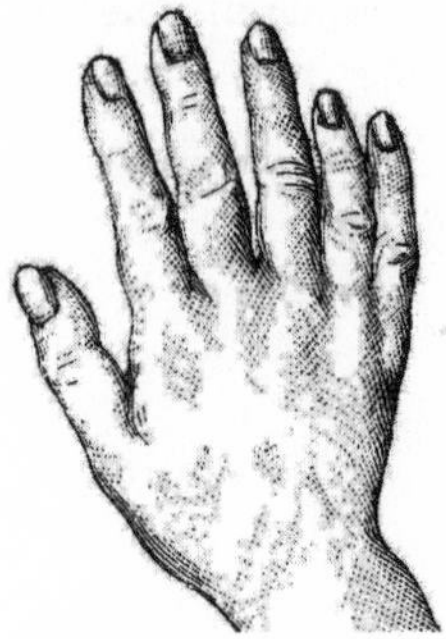
Among other oddities, it was claimed Anne had six fingers.

SUBJECT: Anne Boleyn, second wife of Henry VIII, rumored to be very ugly, and supposed bearer of several physical deformities

TIME PERIOD: Around 1532

OBSERVER: A visiting ambassador from Venice

DESCRIPTION: "[She's] not one of the handsomest women in the world. She is of middling stature, with a swarthy complexion, long neck, wide mouth, bosom not much raised, and in fact has nothing but the King's great appetite, and her eyes, which are black and beautiful."

SUMMARY: Henry VIII's first wife, Catherine of Aragon, had been a popular queen, and the king had managed to get an annulment from her in order to marry the young Anne Boleyn. Needless to say, this made Boleyn's marriage to the king more than a little unwelcomed by the people. As a result, there are no objective descriptions of Anne, and the rumors of her physical oddities are probably a result of the intense dislike the English felt for her. Ironically, it was probably her exotic dark eyes and skin—not a picture of popular beauty during the sixteenth century, when blond hair and fair skin were the epitome of loveliness—that attracted Henry to her. Anne was reportedly godly and fair, and tried hard to be a good queen. Because she didn't bear the king a son, however, she lost her most staunch defender in England—Henry—as well as her head. She did leave behind a daughter, though—Elizabeth, who would later become the famous (supposed) Virgin Queen of England.

SUBJECT: Iosef "Soso" Dzhugashvili, a.k.a. Joseph Stalin, ruthless Bolshevik leader

TIME PERIOD: Early twentieth century

OBSERVER: Tsarist police warrants; similar to modern-day

APBs

DESCRIPTION:

- 5′4″ male
- Sunken hazel eyes
- Soft voice
- Birthmark on left ear
- Pockmarked face
- Thick black hair and mustache (but no beard)
- Withered left arm
- Second and third toes of left foot grown together

SUMMARY: "Stalin" means "man of steel" in Russian. His physical description doesn't exactly match the overbearing, paranoid, and ruthless ruler image that his name usually conjures.

Got a favorite historical icon? Let us know and we'll see if we can find the down and dirty on what they really looked like.

Match the writer to the correct *nom de plume*:

1. George Orwell	a. Alissa Rosenbaum
2. Jack London	b. Howard Allen O'Brien
3. John le Carre	c. Charles Ludwidge Dodgson
4. Henry James	d. John Griffith Chaney
5. O. Henry	e. Patricia Neal
6. Ayn Rand	f. L. C. Kellenberger
7. Anne Rice	g. William Sydney Porter
8. Lewis Carroll	h. David Cornwell
9. Fannie Flagg	i. Eric Arthur Blair

Answers: *1. i; 2. d; 3. h; 4. f; 5. g; 6. a; 7. b (Mom and Pop wanted a boy); 8. c; 9. e*

Every Picture Tells a Story

Mona Lisa by Leonardo da Vinci

• There are only seventeen paintings attributed to Leonardo da Vinci, and about half of those are disputed. Of the few, two of them are big pop-art hits—*Mona Lisa* and *The Last Supper*.

• Da Vinci painted the mysterious portrait on pine wood, not canvas. He worked on it over a four-year period.

• Did you ever notice that Lisa doesn't have eyebrows? The stylish women of Florence in the early 1500s plucked their eyebrows, so Lisa Gherardini, the wife of Francesco Gioconda, was right in fashion.

• *Mona Lisa* was reportedly da Vinci's favorite painting.

• The painting was stolen in 1911 and wasn't found again until 1913. Some claimed afterward that it didn't quite look the same and wondered if maybe forgers had painted a copy and kept the real one. However, x-rays since then have pretty well knocked that theory down, and revealed two other paintings of the same woman underneath the one we see.

• It is the most-viewed painting of all in the Louvre. A few years ago, the museum moved it into its own separate room to better accommodate the crowds.

"Mr. Dullard"

The Quirky Life of Albert Einstein

The brainy guys are often a little bit strange. Take Al Einstein, the slow kid who befriended chickens. As a humble patents office clerk, he shook the world of physics.

EINSTEIN WASN'T CLEARLY A GENIUS early in life. As a child, little Albert was slow in learning to talk and walk. As he got older, his large feet made him waddle like a duck. He was extremely introspective, spending long hours watching ant colonies or trying to befriend the family's chickens. Most children in Ulm, Germany found him a dull companion.

• At school, he was inattentive and slow in everything but math and literature. Teachers called him "Herr Langweil," which roughly translates as "Mister Dullard."

• Although Einstein was Jewish, his family wasn't devout. Albert even attended a Catholic school. One traumatic year during Lent, his teacher held up three large rusty nails and told the students, "These were the nails the Jews used to crucify Jesus."

• As he grew up, Einstein was a lousy student who rarely took notes and often cut classes. He also had an attitude problem, preferring to work solutions out for himself instead of accepting the teacher's answer. "The problem is you don't think anyone has anything to tell you," scolded one teacher.

• When his father asked the headmaster what profession Albert should adopt, he got the answer, "It doesn't matter, he'll never make a success of anything."

• Einstein applied to the Polytechnic Academy in Zurich but flunked the entrance exam. One of the examiners noticed his brilliance in mathematics and recommended he go to a small liberal arts school; if he did well he could return to the Polytechnic in a year. Easy enough. A year later Einstein began a four-year course in physics.

• In college, he met Mileva Maric, who became his wife. She was a bright and independent women who was studying to become a math teacher. She and Einstein's best friend Marcel Grossman made sure that Albert, perpetually lost in the world of physics, remembered to take care of basics like eating and going to classes.

• After Einstein graduated in 1902, he couldn't find a teaching job, so he went to work in the Swiss patent office. Yet, he kept working on physics questions. Remarkably, in 1905, he published five papers that shook the physics world by explaining Brownian motion, photons, and relativity. This paved the way for a teaching position in Zurich in 1909.

• Albert and Mileva had two sons, the younger of whom was schizophrenic and spent most of his life living either with his mother or in an institution.

• Einstein's second wife, Elsa also had to protect him from his absentmindedness. Once when Einstein was sick and confined to his bed, Elsa banned paper and pencils from his room to keep him from working. She allowed a small group of students to visit him on the condition they not talk about physics or math. But after the students left, Elsa found equations scrawled all over Einstein's bed sheets.

• Einstein gave his eldest son the fatherly advice, "Don't get married." When his son married shortly after, Einstein warned him, "At least don't have children." His son ignored this advice, too, and had several children in a very happy marriage. Einstein grumbled, "I don't understand it. I don't think you're my son."

• Einstein charged people a dollar for his autograph, which he gave to charity. He made an exception when he met Charlie Chaplin, giving him an autographed photo for free.

• For many years Einstein thought of his work in physics as something of a hobby. He considered himself as something of a failure because what he really wanted to do was play concert violin.

• Einstein was uncharacteristically intense when playing his violin, cussing a blue streak whenever he made a mistake. One evening, while playing violin duets with Queen Elizabeth, Einstein suddenly stopped mid-piece and unceremoniously told her she was playing too loudly.

• Einstein was reluctant to give up his rarely used home in Germany until a friend convinced him that the Nazis would drag him through the streets by his famous hair if he returned. Einstein finally renounced his German citizenship and abandoned the country of his childhood forever.

• After the war, Einstein used his fame to support political ideas he favored, like Zionism and pacifism. He also remained an eccentric in other areas as well: For example, he gave up wearing socks as an unnecessary complication.

• Meanwhile he continued with his work. In 1949, at the age of seventy, he presented his Generalized Theory of Gravitation, the product of half a lifetime's work. Unfortunately, he had not yet been able to work all the mathematical proofs. His health was failing, and he knew he wouldn't live long enough to prove the theory either true or false.

• When asked about the proofs he would joke weakly, "Come back in twenty years." Four years later, he was dead. Since then his theory of a "unified field" in physics remains unsubstantiated.

• By his request, Einstein's brain was removed before cremation in 1955 so that it could be studied. For unknown reasons it got chopped into pieces and shelved in the study of Dr. Thomas Harvey, the doctor who removed it from Einstein's cranium.

• The brain spent three decades in Weston, Missouri, stored behind a beer cooler in a couple of Mason jars inside a box labeled "Costa Cider." It has since been found and has been made available to other scientists.

The Quotable Dr. Einstein

"Gravitation can not be held responsible for people falling in love."

"If we knew what it was we were doing, it wouldn't be called research."

"Put your hand on a hot stove for a minute, and it seems like an hour. Sit with a pretty girl for an hour, and it seems like a minute. THAT'S relativity."

"I have no particular talent. I am merely inquisitive."

"It's not that I'm so smart , it's just that I stay with problems longer."

"If I had my life to live over again, I'd be a plumber."

"As far as I'm concerned, I prefer silent vice to ostentatious virtue."

"The secret to creativity is knowing how to hide your sources."

"The faster you go, the shorter you are."

"The only reason for time is so that everything doesn't happen at once."

Home Sweet Home

Who Lives at These Famous Addresses?

Match the famous address with its most famous inhabitant. Answers appear below.

A. 1600 Pennsylvania Avenue
B. 221B Baker Street
C. 10 Downing Street
D. 17 Cherry Tree Lane
E. 32 Windsor Gardens
F. Bag End, Hobbiton
G. 1313 Mockingbird Lane
H. 742 Evergreen Terrace
I. 4 Privet Drive
J. 77 Sunset Strip

1. British prime minister
2. Bilbo Baggins
3. The Munsters
4. Gerald "Kookie" Kookson III
5. The Simpsons
6. Mary Poppins
7. Sherlock Holmes
8. Harry Potter
9. U.S. president
10. Paddington Bear

ANSWERS: 1600 Pennsylvania Avenue: U.S. president; 221B Baker Street: Sherlock Holmes; 10 Downing Street: British prime minister; 17 Cherry Tree Lane: Mary Poppins; 32 Windsor Gardens: Paddington Bear; Bag End, Hobbiton: Bilbo Baggins; 1313 Mockingbird Lane: The Munsters; 742 Evergreen Terrace: the Simpsons; 4 Privet Drive: Harry Potter; 77 Sunset Strip: Gerald "Kookie" Kookson III.

Potty Pourri

Random Kinds of Factness

• In 1932, Ole Kirk Christiansen needed a name for his new toy company. He took inspiration from *leg godt*, the Danish words for "play well," and called his company LEGO.

• Americans send over 3 billion Christmas cards each year.

• Ancient Egyptian doctors didn't use anesthesia, but they found an effective alternative—before operating, they whacked the patient on the head with a wooden mallet.

• Henry Ford's first car was named "Quadricycle Runabout."

• "The Pill" is known by (almost) the same name in most languages. For example, "la Pilule " (French), "die Pille" (German), "la Pildora" (Spanish), and "la Pillola" (Italian).

• The man who invented the birth control pill—Carl Djerassi—also invented an insect repellent based on similar principles: bug hormones that keep creepy crawlers from developing into mature, reproductive adults.

• Would it be fun to be a funambulist? Well, maybe. A funambulist is a tightrope walker.

• You may have heard of the herbal remedy for depression, St. John's Wort. It was first identified as a cure for the blues in the seventeenth century by a group of lawyers.

• Raisinettes, please! Movie theatre owners make the bulk of their money from selling snacks—more than $650 million in 2001 alone.

• Shoeless Joe Jackson still hasn't made it into baseball's Hall of Fame. However, his shoes are on display there.

• Like Elvis, Liberace had a twin who died during birth.

• In a poll, about half of all American Oreo consumers twist the cookies apart before eating them. Three times as many women as men engage in this twisted practice.

Family Feud

FRANKLIN'S SON: ENEMY OF THE STATES

America's Revolutionary War was supported by far less than a majority of the colonies' population. One of the Loyalists was Ben Franklin's son.

THE STRUGGLE ON THE BATTLEFIELDS of Revolutionary America was also even reflected within households, with Tories and revolutionaries facing off across the dinner table for spirited discussions that, in some cases, ripped families into opposing camps. This was true even among the most famous revolutionaries themselves: John Adams, George Washington, and John Hancock, for example, all had fervently Royalist in-laws. But few saw their families split apart as irrevocably as Benjamin Franklin's estrangement from his once-beloved son, William.

LIKE FATHER, LIKE SON

William Franklin is something of a mystery. Although he was clearly Ben's son, it is still not clear who his mother was. In his lifetime, Ben Franklin was a notorious womanizer—so much so that throughout much of the nineteenth century it was considered bad taste to mention Franklin's name in the presence of ladies. Although his reputation has been cleaned up and softened over the decades, Franklin was once referred to sarcastically as "the all-embracing Doctor Franklin, America's upstanding genius," grabbing, kissing, and propositioning anything in petticoats.

Despite the scandal behind William's conception, he was Ben's pride and joy. When his son was still a child, Ben provided him with a pony and plenty of books. As William grew older, he helped his dad with the *Poor Richard's Almanack* and acted as his secretary and assistant. For twenty-five years they were not just father and son, but partners, confidants, and friends. When Ben undertook his most famous scientific experiment with electricity, it was William who raced through cow pastures to get a kite to fly in a lightning storm. Benjamin sat dryly in a nearby shed.

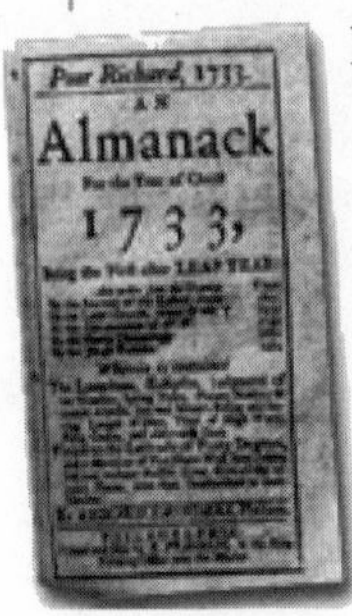

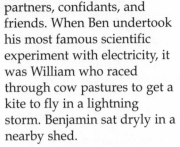

In 1757, Ben went to England to argue tax matters as a representative of the Pennsylvania Assembly. With the idea of saving William from what Ben considered an unfortunate engagement with the daughter of one of Ben's political enemies in Philadelphia, Ben convinced his son to come on the journey. That may have been a mistake.

Benjamin ended up staying for fifteen years, leaving his long-suffering, common-law wife Deborah back in Philadelphia. (She was terrified of transoceanic travel.)

REBEL DAD & ANGLOPHILE SON

In England, William began to emerge from his father's shadow and find an affinity with all things British. He studied law at the Inns of Court, was called to the bar in 1758, and slowly transformed himself from the bastard son of a colonial printer to an English gentleman. His skill at law favorably impressed some of King George's advisors. When Ben was ready to return to Philadelphia in 1762, William announced that he was ready to go, too—as the newly married, newly appointed Royal Governor of New Jersey.

Initially, Benjamin was a proud papa, writing to his sister, "I have no doubt but that he will make as good a Governor as Husband: for he has good principles and good Dispositions, & I think is not deficient in good Understanding." William Franklin at first busied himself with administrative concerns like upgrading roads and improving the debtors' laws, but he soon threw himself into representing the Crown with vigor. Ben worried that his son had become more English than American.

Ben and William in happier days

BEGINNING OF THE END

Meanwhile, Ben had become enough of a revolutionary troublemaker that he was removed from his royal position as colonial Postmaster General. He asked his son to resign his royal appointment, too. William refused, fretting that his aggravating papa was ruining his chance for his hoped-for promotion to Governor of Barbados. "You are a thorough courtier," Ben wrote accusingly, "and see everything with government eyes."

Ben returned to England in 1764, where he badgered William back home with letters demanding payment for a variety of moneys owed, including repeated references to the cost of a small quantity of Lapsang Souchong tea. William, in the meantime, attempted to mediate between the Crown and colonists, but slowly became one of the most vocal critics of American hopes of independence from Britain, even suggesting after the Boston Tea Party that the city's citizens should be heavily taxed to pay for the tea.

When Benjamin returned from England after eleven years in 1775, he found the colonies on the brink of outright revolution. He traveled to the Governor's mansion in Perth Amboy for one last-ditch attempt to convert his son to the rebel cause. The meeting did not go well. "I have lost my son," Ben wrote mournfully to his daughter's husband.

William Franklin, Ben's Tory son

AN ARREST

In June 1776, Ben was in Philadelphia, helping write the Declaration of Independence, when he got word that his monarchist son had been arrested by the New Jersey Assembly as "an enemy to the liberties of this country." It was a fate William might have escaped except for his predisposition, learned from his father, to practice what he believed.

"All over colonial America natural opponents of the rebellion were moving to their country houses and keeping quiet," wrote historian Willard Sterne Randall in *A Little Revenge: Benjamin Franklin & His Son.* "William Franklin might have suffered no worse fate than to sit out the Revolution in elegant comfort had it been his nature to acquiesce." Instead, he convened the loyalist New Jersey Assembly and began sending intelligence reports back to the British Army headquarters. One of his last letters, in fact, was a report on his father's rebellious activities, including the news that Benjamin had traveled to Canada to try to stir up rebellion there as well.

TOUGH LOVE

With his father's blessing William was thrown into a rat-infested hellhole of a jail in Litchfield, Connecticut. The floor was covered with straw, matted with the waste of previous occupants. The date, ironically, was July 4, 1776. Even George Washington urged Congress to have William moved to better quarters, but Ben used his influence to block a transfer. He also prevented William's son from seeing him, successfully working to alienate the boy from his father. He wrote to a friend about his grandson: "I have rescued a valuable young man from the danger of being a Tory...."

Meanwhile, William was discovered writing Tory diatribes that were being smuggled out of his cell, so the authorities confiscated all pen, ink, and paper.

During confinement, William lost his teeth, hair, health, and wife, Deborah. When she was on her deathbed, William sent a message to George Washington, requesting that he be allowed to visit her one last time. Washington was so moved that he wrote to Congress that "humanity and generosity plead powerfully in favor of his application." Congress looked to Ben for a sign of concurrence.

FREE AT LAST

William stayed confined for nearly three years until English authorities, alarmed at his conditions, won William's release in a trade for some rebel prisoners.

Intended lesson unlearned, William traveled to British-held New York, where he worked with new vigor to subvert the revolution, developing a network of informers and planning raids into rebel-held New Jersey. Finally, when it became clear that the cause was lost, he moved to London, never to return to the land of his birth.

Benjamin made an effort to erase all records of his son from his life. He expunged William's name from all diary entries and from his autobiography (the first draft of which had been dedicated to his "beloved son Billy" and had begun, "Dear son,..."). Ben not only disinherited him and forced him to give up his properties in the colonies, he even sent a bill for the "loan" of every farthing Ben had spent raising William from infancy.

Benjamin Franklin, unforgiving dad

ATTEMPT AT RECONCILIATION

The estrangement continued after the war. Finally, in July of 1784, William wrote to his father, who was on diplomatic mission to France: "Dear and Honoured Father, Ever since the Termination of the unhappy Contest between Great Britain and America, I have been anxious to write to you and to endeavor to revive that affectionate Intercourse and Connexion which till the Commencement of the late Troubles had been the Pride and Happiness of my Life.... I have uniformly acted from a sense strong of what I conceived my duty to my king and regard to my Country required....

"On a subject so disagreeable I have no Desire to say more, and I hope everything which has happened relative to it may be mutually forgotten.... I beg you to be assured of my constant Prayers for your Health and Happiness, and that I am, as ever, Your very dutiful and affectionate Son...."

His father's answer came back a month later: "I am glad to find you desire to revive the affectionate intercourse that formerly existed between us. It would be very agreeable to me; indeed, nothing has hurt me so much ... as to find myself deserted in my old age by my only son; and not only deserted, but to find him taking up arms against me in a cause wherein my good fame, fortune, and life were all at stake.

"Yet I ought not to blame you for differing in sentiment with me in public affairs. We are men, all subject to errors. Our opinions are not in our own power; they are formed and governed much by circumstances.... I will be glad to see you when convenient, but would not have you come here at present...."

Benjamin never did invite William to France. A year would pass before the father found it "convenient" to see his son, and only because he would be briefly stopping in England en route home. It was a brief and coolly formal meeting. Ben had spent most of his time in London meeting with old friends and associates, knowing that at near eighty, this was likely his last transatlantic trip. Finally, he arrived at William's door to present some financial documents to sign, and then sailed back to America as soon as a ship would take him away.

In 1788, two years before his death, Franklin wrote, "My son is estranged from me and keeps aloof, residing in England." When Benjamin Franklin died, he left the city of Philadelphia a large quantity of money, but provided little to William: It canceled Ben's claim to the sum that he believed William still owed him (including the cost of raising him) and left him a small parcel of land in Nova Scotia.

"Fish Eyes!"

A Translation of Diner Lingo

Mmm ... nothin' like a meal at an old-fashioned diner. But "nervous pudding"? "Adam and Eve on a raft"? What the heck is the waitress talking about?

BEVERAGES

"Adam's ale" = Water
"A cold spot" = Iced tea
"Mug of murk" = Coffee
"A brunette with sand" = Coffee with sugar
"Cow juice" = Milk
"Belch water" = Soda water
"Sinkers and suds" = Doughnuts and coffee

BREAKFAST

"An order of down with mama" = Toast with marmalade
"A bowl of birdseed" = Cereal

"Adam & Eve on a raft" = Two poached eggs on toast
"Deadeye" = Poached egg
"Wrecked hen fruit" = Scrambled eggs
"Warm a pig" = Ham
"Looseners" = Prunes (they loosen things up a bit)

BLUE PLATE SPECIAL

"Betsy in a bowl with cow feed and mystery in the alley" = Beef stew with salad and hash on the side

ENTREES

"First lady" = Spareribs (Eve was made with Adam's spare rib)
"Bowl of red" = Chili
"Pig between the sheets" = Ham sandwich
"Radio sandwich" = Tuna (a pun on "tuner")
"Burn one" = Grill a burger
"Jack" = spelled "GAC," or Grilled American Cheese sandwich
"Put out the lights and cry" = Liver and onions
"Bun the pup" = Hot dog
"Irish turkey" = Corned beef and cabbage
"Noah's boy" = Ham (in the Bible, Noah had a son named Ham)

EXTRAS

"Mike and Ike, the twins" = Salt and pepper
"Axle grease" = Butter

AS YOU LIKE IT

"Keep off the grass" = No lettuce
"On the hoof" = Rare
"All the way" = With everything
"High and dry" = Plain
"Breath" = With onion

JUST DESSERTS

"Nervous pudding" = Jell-O

"Eve with a lid on" = Apple pie (folklore has Biblical Eve tempted with an apple)

"Fish eyes" = Tapioca pudding

Y'all come back now, y'hear!

Etiquette from 1290 A.D.

While you're out dining, here are a few good rules from an old book of table etiquette. From *Fifty Table Courtesies* by Bonvieino da Riva, written in A.D. 1290.:

- "A number of people gnaw a bone and then put it back in the dish. This is a serious offense."
- "Refrain from falling upon the dish like a swine while eating, snorting disgustingly and smacking the lips."
- "Do not spit over or on the table in the manner of hunters."
- "When you blow your nose or cough, turn round so that nothing you expel falls on the table."

Escape Artist

How To Get Unstuck from a Quicksand Pit

Even though they're the stuff of B-grade movies, quicksand is real and can happen almost anywhere. Don't know what you'd do if you fall into a quicksand pit? Read on ... quickly!

Quicksand is the result when water mixes with sand or any grainy soil. Unless you happen to dive in head first, quicksand doesn't really have to be dangerous:

1. As with any frightening situation, don't panic. Stay calm and use your head. Most quicksand pits are rather shallow, and you probably won't sink over your head.

2. If it is deep, though, don't try to wriggle free or thrash about wildly. Even if it's shallow, it may be difficult to simply pull your feet out if the sand/water mixture is above your knees.

3. You are lighter than quicksand, so you have the capacity to float if you'll stay still. Slowly spread your arms and legs outward. Do not try to pull them up. This will cause a suction that will pull you deeper.

4. Lean backward and try to float on your back. Quicksand is essentially dense water. You'll float pretty easily.

5. Slowly "swim" and inch your way to the edge of the pit, without sudden movements.

6. Follow the slow-and-steady rule while getting out, too. Pulling parts of your body out too fast will create suction that can easily begin to pull you under again. Find some solid ground, and gently—ever so gently—pull each limb out one at a time until you're free.

Write On!

How Bic Got its Ball Rolling

The ballpoint pen seems pretty simple, but it took decades to make it work right. Here's the story of the ballpoint, and why you don't write with a "Bich pen."

LOOK CAREFULLY AT THE POINT of a ballpoint pen. There's a tiny little ball there, of course, which transports the ink from the ink reservoir onto the paper. It looks simple, and in theory it is. But actually developing a usable ballpoint pen was not as easy as it looks. Otherwise the pen in your pocket would be a Loud instead of a Bic, Parker, or Scripto.

John J. Loud of Massachusetts patented a "rolling-pointed fountain marker" on October 30, 1888. It used a tiny, rotating ball bearing that was constantly bathed on one side in ink. Over the next thirty years, 350 similar ballpoint patents were issued by the U.S. Patent Office. But none of the products appeared on the market. The main problem was getting the ink right. If it were too thin, the pens blotched on paper and leaked in pockets. If it were too thick, the pens clogged. Under controlled circumstances, it was sometimes possible to mix up a batch of ink that did what it was supposed to do ... at least until the temperature changed. The best they could do was a ballpoint that would (usually) work fine at 70° F, but would clog at temperatures below 64° and leak, blotch, and smear at temperatures above 77°.

At least that's how it was until the Biro brothers decided to take the challenge on. After World War I, eighteen-year-old Ladislas Biro, newly discharged from the Hungarian Army, tried out a number of career options. He studied medicine, art, and hypnotism, but nothing held his interest long enough to become a career. Eventually, he fell into newspaper work.

In 1935, Biro was editing a small newspaper and found himself cursing his fountain pen. The ink soaked into the paper's newsprint like a sponge, allowing the pen's sharp tip to shred it into soggy pulp. Even when he was working with a decent quality of paper, the ink left smudges on his fingers and clothes—and had to be refilled too often. He recruited his brother Georg, a chemist. The brothers Biro started designing new pens.

After trying dozens of new pen designs and ink formulations, Ladislas and Georg, unaware that it had already been done at least 351 times before, invented the ballpoint pen.

Vacationing at a resort on the shores of the Mediterranean, the two brothers began talking to an elderly gentleman about their new invention. They showed him a working model, and he was suitably impressed. It just so happened that the elderly gentleman was the president of Argentina, Augustine Justo, who suggested that the brothers open a pen factory in his country.

A few years later, World War II began, and the Biros fled Hungary. They remembered their old pal, the president of Argentina, and set sail for South America. They landed in Buenos Aires with $10 between them. Luckily, Justo remembered them. With his help, they lined up some investors. By 1943 had set up their manufacturing plant.

The results were spectacular. A spectacular failure, that is. They had made the mistake that all of their forerunners had made—they depended on gravity to move the ink onto the ball. That meant that the pens had to be held straight up and down at all times. Even then, the ink flow was irregular, leaving heavy globs.

The Biros returned to the lab and came up with a new design. This one depended on capillary action instead of gravity, siphoning the ink toward the point no matter what position it was held in. Within a year, the Biros had brought out their new improved model in Argentina, but the pens didn't sell very well. The Biros ran out of money and stopped production.

However, the U. S. Air Force came to the rescue. American flyers, sent to Argentina during the war, discovered that the ballpoints worked upside-down and at high altitudes without having to be refilled very often. The wartime U.S. Department of State attempted to get American manufacturers to manufacture a similar pen. The Eberhard Faber Company, in an attempt to corner the market, paid $500,000 for the United States rights, yielding the Biro brothers their first profitable year ever.

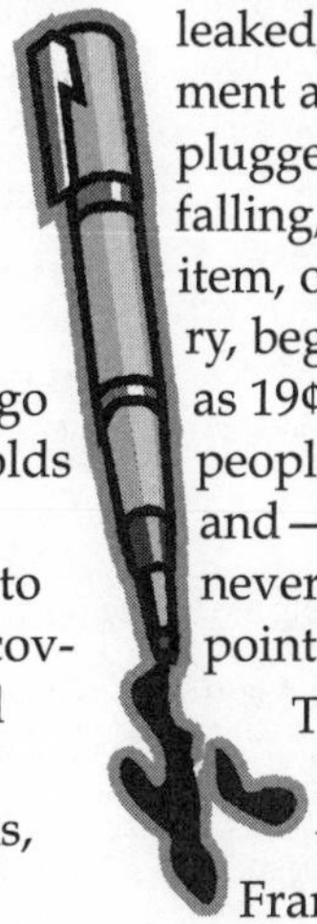

About this time a Chicago man named Milton Reynolds had seen the Biro pen in Argentina. He came back to the United States and discovered that similar pens had been patented by John J. Loud and other Americans, but that the patents had expired. He therefore figured he could get away with copying the Biro design. He began stamping out pens and sold them for $12.50 each through Gimbels department store in New York City. They were such a novelty that Gimbels sold out its entire stock the first day—a total of 10,000 pens.

Various manufacturers jumped on the bandwagon. Reynolds hired swimming star Esther Williams to show that the pen would write underwater; other manufacturers showed their pens writing upside-down or through stacks of a dozen pieces of carbon paper.

There was one problem, though: Despite the hoopla, the ballpoint pen still didn't work very dependably. They leaked, ruining many a document and good shirt. They plugged up. Sales started falling, as did prices. The item, once an expensive luxury, began selling for as little as 19¢. But even at that price, people bought one, tried it, and—frustrated—vowed never to buy another ballpoint as long as they lived.

The man who eventually change their minds was Marcel Bich from France. As a manufacturer of penholders and cases, he watched with professional interest as the ballpoint industry first took off and then began crashing to the ground. He was interested in the innovative design of the ballpoint pen, but was appalled at the high cost and low quality. He determined that he could take over much of the ballpoint market if he could come up with a dependable pen at a low cost.

The Biro brothers licensed their patents to Bich, who went to work. For two years, he bought every ballpoint pen on the market and systematically tested them, looking for their strengths and weaknesses. In 1952, Bich unveiled his triumph: a six-sided, inexpensive, clear plastic ballpoint pen that wrote smoothly and didn't leak or jam. Looking at the international market, he figured that his name would be a problem in America. Rather than risk having his product referred to as a "Bitch pen," he respelled his name on the pen so it would be pronounced correctly no matter where it was sold—"Bic."

The Bic ballpoint was an immediate hit all over the world. Billions of them, their style essentially unchanged in the years since, have been sold, used, misplaced, disassembled, lost, and disposed of. While Bic has expanded into other pen designs and even diversified into other products, the cheap but dependable Bic pen continues to be responsible for a large chunk of the company's year-

More Deskware Trivia

(From Erin Barrett's and Jack Mingo's book Not Another Apple for the Teacher!)

• Want to know what that distinctive crayon smell is? Maybe you don't. It's stearic acid, also known as beef fat.

• The first two crayons in a box to be worn down to nubs are usually first the black and then the red.

• The first paper clip was invented in 1899 by a Norwegian patent clerk named Johann Vaaler. A monument to him, shaped like a giant paper clip, stands near Oslo.

• Norwegians take pride in Vaaler and his wiry invention. During the Nazi occupation, Norwegians wore paper clips in their lapels as a sign of nationalism and resistance.

• Then how come we can never find one when we need one? The world generates more than 10 billion pencils every year. Two billion of these come from the United States. No, not all from Pencilvania.

• Pencils are the writing instrument of choice of astronauts, because unlike most pens, they write dependably in zero-gravity.

• Graphite, a carbon compound, has been used for writing since before pencils were invented. In 1789 geologist Abraham Werner named the mineral from a Greek word meaning "to write."

Potty Talk

Reading the Writing on the Stall

Here you sit brokenhearted in a public restroom without your *Bathroom Companion*. What do you do? Well, it may be a poor substitute, but you can always analyze the bathroom graffiti.

WALK INTO ANY PUBLIC RESTROOM and there's a chance you'll be bombarded with hand-written messages, some incoherent, some crude, and some even moderately funny. Believe it or not, scholars have spent time researching the writing on the stall walls, and have even give a name to it: *latrinalia.* Here's what they've found out.

WHERE IT ALL BEGAN

Many of us assume that the scrawlings on public stalls are a modern-day invention, but archeologists have learned that the practice isn't new. It seems even the ancient Romans expressed their ideas while sitting on the throne. When archeologists excavated the ruins of Pompeii that had been buried under ash since the eruption of Mount Vesuvius in A.D. 79, they found a treasure trove of artifacts from everyday life. Brushing ash from the walls of the public toilets, they uncovered a wealth of graffiti:

- *"Apollinaris, doctor to the Emperor Titus, had a crap here"*
- *"Artimetus got me pregnant"*
- *"The risen flesh commands, let there be love!"*
- *"Fortunatus made it with Anthusam"*

- *"Serena hates Isadore"*
- *"Daddy Colepius kisses the ladies where he shouldn't"*
- *"Hello, hello Mago, fare you well, you're obviously castrated"*
- *"Hello! We are wineskins!"*

There was even response graffiti. To the philosophical message, "Lovers, like bees, enjoy a life of honey" was a deflating zinger in a different hand: "Wishful thinking."

GRAFFITI FROM ANCIENT POMPEII. THE DRAWING IS A ROMAN SOLDIER. THE INSCRIPTION SAYS, "AUGE LOVES ARABIENUS."

The practice of writing on the walls of stalls didn't stop there, of course. And the study of bathroom graffiti didn't start in our time. *The Merry-Thought or The Glass-Window Bog-House Miscellany* is an 18th-century compilation of the writings from privy walls, put together by an early sociologist named Hurlo Thomas. One example of the earthy compositions he documented is this, which he found at "the bog house at the Nags'-Head in Bradmere":

You are eas'd in your Body
and pleas'd in your Mind
That you leave both a Turd
And some Verses behind—
But to me, which is worse,
I can't tell, on my Word:
The reading your Verses
Or smelling your Turd.

The walls of the Tower of London, too, bear messages, written by political prisoners awaiting execution. The graffiti was written in the only writing medium available—blood. Here's one:

Be frend to one
Be ennermye to none.

GRAFFITI, OR LATRINALIA?

Although all latrinalia is considered bathroom graffiti, not all bathroom graffiti is considered latrinalia (pronounced, in case you want to drop it casually into a conversation, *la-tri-NA-le-ah)*. Dr. Alan Dundes at the University of California (Berkeley) was the first sociologist to seriously study the fine art of stall scribbling. In his 1966 seminal thesis, "Here I Sit...." he defines the distinctive characteristic of latrinalia: It is universal enough to be found in many public restrooms. It's a piece of writing that is so memorable and universal that its readers spread it to other restrooms across the world.

For example, the familiar couplet *"Here I sit all broken hearted / Came to shit but only farted"* is classic latrinalia because it's been around since the 1920s. In that time it has spread from its first location to millions across the world (for example, it's been sighted in the girls' bathroom at Hong Kong International School). In contrast, *"Mr. Skinner stinks"* is mere graffiti because it is an individual statement that is specific to the few restrooms where Mr. Skinner would likely be known.

THE VARIATIONS

Dr. Dundes defined five categories of latrinalia:

• **Advertisements or solicitations.** For example: *"For a good time, call* [phone number]." Although the specific names, place, and phone number differ in each location, the phrases are so well known that Dundes includes them as latrinalia.

• **Requests or commands.** *"If you sprinkle when you tinkle, please be neat and wipe the seat."* Or the less serious request: *"Don't throw your cigarette butts in the urinal – it makes them soggy and hard to light."*

• **Facetious instructions.** *"In case of atomic attack, hide under this urinal. Nobody ever hits it."* Or the one found on a wall at Goddard Space Center: *"Look Up!"* On the ceiling it continued, *"You are now in launch position."*

• **Commentaries.** Above urinal: *"You are holding the future of America in your hands."* Or this three parter:

To be is to do – Friedrich Nietzsche
To do is to be – Immanuel Kant
Do be do be do – Frank Sinatra

• **Introspective musings / Personal laments.** *"Here I sit all tired and dirty, trying to hide until 4:30,"* wrote an employee at a sandwich shop.

THE CULPRITS

Research has shown that most latrinalia writers are men.

However, women write on bathroom walls as much as men or more, but their markings tend to be conversational and situation-specific (*"I'm bored because my friend left me here"*).

So why is there a gender difference? Well, researchers aren't totally sure. Some argue the practice is a leftover from the pre-civilization days of marking territory. Others argue that men are more driven to leave something significant of themselves behind, so are more likely to scribble things in public places. Whatever the reason, though, sociologists say that after the advent of the women's movement in the 1970s, more true latrinalia was found in women's rooms.

We're still a culture that's embarrassed about bodily functions. When that's gone, experts say, much of the writing on the stalls will decrease. We hope we stay uptight, then, because latrinalia makes good reading.

Stalling For Time

- On the stall door: *"Congrats! You've won a free game of Toilet Tennis! Now look left."* On the left wall: *"Look right."* On the right: *"Look left...."*
- *"Please do not throw cigarette butts in our urinal. We don't use your ashtrays as toilets!"*
- *"If PRO is opposite of CON, then what's the opposite of progress? CONGRESS."*
- *"Patrons are requested to remain seated thruout entire performance."*
- On an **Employees Must Wash Hands** sign, some soul scribbled, *"I waited and waited, but I finally gave up and washed them myself."*
- *"My wife follows me everywhere,"* complained one bathroom patron. In a different handwriting below it: *"I do not!"*
- *"Beauty is only a light switch away."*
- *"Fart for Jesus!"*
- *"Make love, not war. Hell, do both – get married."*
- *"Beer: Helping ugly people have sex since 3472 B.C."*

Giving Blood

Centuries of Confusion about Transfusion

Have you given blood? It's an easy way to save lives and be a hero. But it took hundreds of years, many deaths, and a bunch of monkeys before doctors figured out how to do it right.

IT'S A STRANGE THING, if you think about it—taking blood from one person and injecting it into another. Nobody really knows when the first successful blood transfusion took place. Some historians believe that it might've been in the time of the Incas, who were fairly advanced medically. The interesting thing is that transfusions between Incas would've worked out just fine because Incas were all the same blood type (O+).

INNOCENT BLOOD

The first documented attempt at giving a blood transfusion took place in Rome in 1492. Pope Innocent VIII was dying, and his doctor thought giving him some new blood would help. It didn't. This is a 1492 account from *Diareo della Citta 'di Roma* by Stefano Infessua, complete with shades of the antisemitism of the time:

> **Three ten-year-old boys, from whose veins a certain Jewish physician (who had promised that the pope would be restored to health) extracted blood, died without delay. The Jew had told them he could heal the pontiff, if only he could have a certain quantity of young human blood. He ordered it to be extracted from the three boys, to whom he gave a ducat for each. Shortly after they died. The Jew fled, and the pope was not healed.**

The deaths of the pope and the boys put a damper on further experimentation for a few centuries.

ARTERY & SCIENCE

Finally, in 1665, Dr. Richard Lower of England successfully transfused blood back and forth between two dogs using feather quills as hypodermic needles. It took some trial and error—at first he tried hooking the dogs up vein to vein, but the blood didn't go anywhere; it just clotted in the quills. Finally, Lower figured out that he needed to plug into the artery of the donor and the vein of the donee to set up an imbalance of pressure, and his dog-and-aorta show was off and running.

So far, so good. However, like many scientists, Lower didn't know when to quit. He tried what seemed to be the next logical step—a lamb-to-man transfusion. At about the same time in France, another doctor tried a calf-to-man transfusion. Both patients died. Because of the public outcry, research on blood transfusions again stopped.

YOUR BLOOD
CAN SAVE HIM
SIGN UP NOW!

In 1818, James Blundell tried a person-to-person transfusion in Guy's Hospital in London. Not only was he successful, but he was able to save his patient's life with the procedure. His success on the first try was a lucky fluke, however, since the mystery of compatible blood types had not yet been figured out. His first smashing success was soon shattered by a string of unexplained sudden deaths, and Blundell abandoned his research.

THANK YOU, RHESUS

Finally in 1900, Dr. Karl Landsteiner discovered the problem. He discovered the A, B, and O blood groups, and further figured out that mixing incompatible blood types creates a curdled mess of small red dumplings floating in yellowish liquid.

Landsteiner discovered, however, that blood within the same blood group could be successfully mixed without getting dumplings. To honor the research monkeys that gave their blood and lives to his research, Landsteiner coined the term *rh factors* — "rh" being short for "rhesus."

The good doctor's discoveries won him a Nobel Prize and led to a quick succession of breakthroughs. As World War I broke out, other doctors learned that sodium citrate kept blood from clotting without harming the blood recipient, allowing the storage of blood outside the donor's body. As a result of this discovery, the first blood bank opened in Chicago in 1937.

DR. DREW BLOOD

Pioneer hematologist Dr. Charles Drew was the first to realize that blood plasma—the straw-colored liquid that remains when you remove the red cells, white cells, and platelets—would store longer than whole blood, yet was just as useful in emergency applications. In 1940, he opened New York's first blood bank and set up a drive to raise 5,000 units of blood plasma for England's fight against the Nazis.

After the United States entered the war, Dr. Drew was offended and exasperated by the U.S. military's requirement in World War II that blood be sorted by the race of its donors. For one

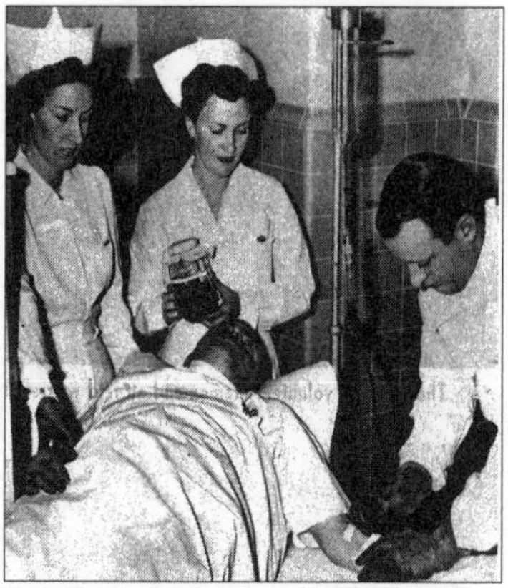

thing, he knew that it didn't make any medical difference and suspected that waiting for the right "race" of blood would result in the unnecessary deaths of countless injured troops. For another, military segregation—even reaching down to blood supplies—must have been personally galling, because Drew was an African American. Eventually, that restriction fell as the army became fully integrated.

Nowadays, there are about 5,000 blood banks in the United States alone. All are regulated by the United States Food and Drug Administration.

Escape Artist

How to Evade an Alligator

We know there aren't many chances to get chased and eaten by an alligator in the U.S., but what about when you visit Papua New Guinea? It's always best to be prepared, to borrow a phrase.

ALMOST ALL ALLIGATOR ATTACKS happen because the alligator's been fed by humans. Rule #1: Don't feed alligators. If you run into one, though, here's what to do:

1. You've probably heard you should run in a zigzag pattern if you find yourself chased by an alligator. This may sound like it makes sense, but trust us: it doesn't. Although an alligator can run up to 30 mph, it can't do so for long. The best escape route you have is running fast; the best way to do that is by running straight ahead.

2. So the above didn't work and the alligator's got your leg, and what you need to do is keep it from rolling you under water or shaking you—these things will cause more damage. Hold the alligator's jaw clamped shut on your limb. This will keep it focused on its jaw, not on pulling you under.

3. If you have access and can do this while in its clutches, cover the alligator's eyes. Reptiles often become docile if the light is blocked from their eyes.

4. Punch its snout. Although alligators have been known to open their mouths when touched lightly, if your leg or arm is in its clutches and you don't have time to spare, punch hard. This should open the alligator's mouth long enough for you to escape.

5. An alternative? Go for its eyes. A quick punch or hard slap to the eyes will often produce a similar jaw-opening reaction.

Ben's Naughty Advice

On Taking an Older Mistress

Ben Franklin was a brilliant man who didn't hesitate to write about a wide range of subjects. Here he offers a marriage-shy New Yorker named Caldwallader Colden some tongue-in-cheek advice.

June 25, 1745

My Dear Friend:

I know of no Medicine fit to diminish the violent natural inclination you mention; and if I did, I think I should not communicate it to you. Marriage is the proper Remedy. It is the most natural State of Man, and therefore the State in which you will find solid Happiness. Your Reason against entering into it at present appears to be not well founded. The Circumstantial Advantages you have in View by Postponing it, are not only uncertain, but they are small in comparison with the Thing itself, the being married and settled. It is the Man and Woman united that makes the complete Being. Separate she wants his force of Body and Strength of Reason; he her Softness, Sensibility and acute Discernment. Together they are most likely to succeed in the World. A single Man has not nearly the Value he would have in that State of Union. He is an incomplete Animal. He resembles the odd Half of a Pair of Scissors.

If you get a prudent, healthy wife, your Industry in your Profession, with her good Economy, will be a Fortune sufficient.

But if you will not take this Counsel, and persist in thinking a Commerce with the Sex is inevitable, then I repeat my former Advice that in your Amours you should *prefer old Women to young ones.* This you call a Paradox, and demand my reasons.

They are these:

1. Because they have more Knowledge of the world, and their Minds are better stored with Observations; their Conversation is more improving, and more lastingly agreeable.

2. Because when Women cease to be handsome, they study to be good. To maintain their Influence over Man, they supply the Diminution of Beauty by an Augmentation of Utility. They learn to do a thousand Services, small and great, and are the most tender and useful of all Friends when you are sick. Thus they continue amiable. And hence there is hardly such a thing to be found as an old Woman who is not a good Woman.

3. Because there is no hazard of children, which irregularly produced may be attended with much inconvenience.

4. Because through more Experience they are more prudent and discreet in conducting an Intrigue to prevent Suspicion. The Commerce with them is therefore safer with regard to your reputation; and regard to theirs, if the Affair should happen to be known, considerate People might be inclined to excuse an old Woman, who would kindly take care of a young Man, form his manners by her good Councils, and prevent his ruining his Health and Fortune among mercenary Prostitutes.

5. Because in every Animal that walks upright, the Deficiency of the Fluids that fill the Muscles appears first in the highest Part. The Face first grows lank and wrinkled; then the Neck; then the Breast and Arms; the lower parts continuing to the last as plump as ever; so that covering all above with a Basket, and regarding only what is below the Girdle, it is impossible of two Women to know an old from a young one. And as in the Dark all Cats are gray, the Pleasure of Corporal Enjoyment with an old Woman is at least equal and frequently superior; every Knack being by Practice capable by improvement.

6. Because the sin is less. The Debauching of a Virgin may be her Ruin, and make her for Life unhappy.

7. Because the Compunction is less. The having made a young Girl miserable may give you frequent bitter Reflections none which can attend making an old Woman happy.

8. 8th & lastly. They are so grateful!!!

Thus much for my Paradox. But still I advise you to marry immediately; being sincerely

Your Affectionate Friend,

Benj. Franklin

So You Think Your Child's a Musical Genius?

• **Mozart.** Wolfgang Amadeus Mozart started playing harpsichord at age 4 and a year later was giving concerts for royalty. The first pieces he published at age 6 are still played today.

• **Michael Jackson.** Okay, maybe he hasn't been that great as an adult, but did you know he got his first gold record (for "I Want You Back") at age 11?

• **Chopsticks.** A 16-year-old girl wrote the musical piece that is the one most performed on the piano. Yes, it's "Chopsticks," that percussive little melody that is the bane of piano owners everywhere. Euphonia Allen was an English girl who published her only known musical endeavor under the name of "Arthur de Lulli" in 1877. The title had nothing to do with Chinese eating utensils, but told how the piece was to be played: "with both hands turned sideways, the little fingers lowest, so that the movement of the hands imitates the chopping from which this waltz gets its name."

• **"Blind Tom."** Thomas Wiggins was born in 1845 with many strikes against him: he was blind, autistic, and a slave. At age 4, he began sneaking to the master's parlor piano and reproducing music he'd heard. He could play any piece after hearing it once. By age 8, he performed all over the world and had a repertoire of 7,000 pieces. As a stage gimmick, he sometimes played with his hands reversed and his back to the piano.

Listen Up

Life Advice From The Rich and Famous

"Do not allow children to mix drinks. It is unseemly and they use too much vermouth." – Fran Lebowitz

"First wipe your nose and check your fly." – Alec Guinness

"People disappoint you. Lovers disappoint you. But theatrical memorabilia stays with you, as long as you keep it under clear plastic." – Sylvia Miles

"Don't do anything you wouldn't be willing to explain on television." – Arjay Miller

"If your house is really a mess and a stranger comes to the door, greet him with, 'Who could have done this? We have no enemies!'" – Phyllis Diller

"The hardest years in life are those between ten and seventy." – Helen Hayes

"Brown shoes don't make it." – Frank Zappa

"No day is so bad it can't be fixed with a nap." – Carrie Snow

"Do not use a hatchet to remove a fly from your friend's forehead." – Chinese proverb

"Be honest with yourself until the end of your life. Then listen to the slow movement of the Schubert Quintet and kick the bucket." – Nathan Milstein

"The secret to success is to know something nobody else knows." – Aristotle Onassis

"Success usually comes to those who are too busy to be looking for it." – Henry David Thoreau

Bats, Clubs & Racquets

Inventing the Wild World of Sports

Before sports became big business, games were just games, and people invented them and changed them as they saw fit. Here are the stories behind some of our favorite sports.

GOLF

Who invented golf? We could say the Scots, but that wouldn't be telling the whole story. The simple fact is that hitting a rock into a hole in the ground is such an obvious concept for whiling away the hours that the basic game was "invented" in every corner of the world.

The ancient Romans, for instance, played a golf-like game called *paganica,* using a bent stick and a leather ball filled with feathers. The Visigoths—known for their plundering and overall pillaging—for sure played paganica after they overthrew ancient Rome on August 4, 410, but may have played a golf-like game even before then. It's been documented in writing and art that the Chinese played *Chuiwan* ("hitting ball") as early as the tenth century, but the French swear that golf came from their ancient game *jeu de mail.* Golf also might've come from an early British game called *knur and spell,* Belgium's *chole* that goes back to the 1300s, or the Dutch game of *kolven.*

The truth is that no one knows the origins for sure. Whatever the game's early roots, though, linguists agree that the word "golf" comes from an ancient Scottish word *gowf,* that meant "to strike."

And everyone agrees, as well, that the Scottish did love their golf. In 1744, the Company of Gentlemen Golfers of Leith

(Scotland) created the earliest known written golf code, consisting of thirteen rules. Ten years later, Scotland's St. Andrews golf club formed.

At the end of the nineteenth century golf really began to take off. In 1873, the Royal Montreal Golf Club opened, making it the first permanent golfing club in the Western Hemisphere. The first golf book in America, *Golf In America: A Practical Manual*, was published in 1895. Still, most Americans were terribly confused by the game, as evidenced by this explanation in the *Philadelphia Times*:

> **"It is sometimes agreed that the game shall be won by him who makes the largest number of holes within a given number of minutes, say 20 or 30.... Each player places his ball at the edge of a hole designated as a starting point. He then bats it ... toward the next hole. As soon as it has started he runs forward ... and his servant, who is called 'caddy,' runs after him...."**

BASEBALL

Despite a myth spread enthusiastically by early promoters, baseball was not really invented by Abner Doubleday in Cooperstown, New York. In fact, it wasn't exactly invented at all—instead it

TAKE ME OUT TO THE BALLGAME

Vaudevillian Jack Norworth wrote the words to "Take Me Out to the Ballgame" before he'd ever even seen a baseball game. He was inspired to put the new sport fad to verse in 1908 after seeing a sign on a bus advertising "Baseball Today—Polo Grounds." His friend Albert von Tilzer wrote the music. It wasn't until after the song became a hit that either of them actually went to "root root root for the home team."

While almost everybody knows the sing along chorus, almost nobody knows the verses. Here's the one to get you started:

"Katie Casey was baseball mad
Had the fever and had it bad.
Just to root for the hometown crew,
Every sound, Katie blew,
On a Saturday her young beau
Called to see if she'd like to go
To see a show but Miss Kate said, 'No
I'll tell you what you can do—
Take me out to the ball game....'"

evolved from the British games of cricket and rounders which, early on, were sometimes called "base ball."

By the early 1800s, Americans had already begun adapting the games into new variations called "town ball" and "one old cat—two old cat—three old cat." In 1845, Alexander Cartwright drew up some rules for the New York Knickerbocker Base Ball Club, arbitrarily fixing the diamond size at ninety feet square, and putting the batter at home plate instead of in a batters' box nearby. He also ruled out the deadly practice of "plugging" base runners—hitting them with a thrown ball to get them out. But still, the game had quite a bit of evolving to do in the coming years before it became the game we know today.

TENNIS

The French originated tennis during the twelfth century. They called it *jeu de paume,* ("game of the palm") because, in the beginning, players used their hands to bat the ball back and forth over the net. Rackets came later, and the name changed to *tenetz* ("get and hold").

The father of modern tennis is Major Walter Clopton Wingfield of England, who in 1873, introduced the modern sport with the idea of playing it on grass courts. Wingfield wasn't quite as good at coining names—he called the game *sphairistike,* Greek for "playing ball."

Most went back to the French name, and tennis soon replaced croquet as England's most popular outdoor sport, and in 1874, Mary Ewing Outerbridge, an American sportswoman, purchased tennis equipment from British army officers in Bermuda and introduced the sport to America.

BADMINTON

Badminton was invented in the 1860s by the daughters of the Duke of Beaufort. It was based loosely on an ancient game called *battledore and shuttlecock,* and used the same equipment.

They named the game after their dad's Badminton House in Gloustershire, England, where they first played it. The dimension of the modern official badminton court (44 feet long and 17 feet wide) report-

edly matches those of the room where the young women developed the game.

Badminton has been an Olympic event since 1992, and it's Malaysia's official national sport.

LACROSSE

Native Canadian tribes played a game like lacrosse hundreds of years ago. By the 1800's, French pioneers had begun to play, too. In 1867, Canadian George Beers standardized the game—setting field dimensions, team size, and rules.

JAI ALAI

Jai alai originated in the Basque regions of Spain and France during the 1600s. The name in the Basque language means "merry festival." It may well be the only game in which lefthanders are specifically banned from playing.

A Word to the Wise

"The roots of education are bitter, but the fruit is sweet." —Aristotle

"Soap and education are not as sudden as a massacre, but they are more deadly in the long run."—Mark Twain

"No man who worships education has got the best out of education. Without a gentle contempt for education, no man's education is complete." —G.K. Chesterton

"If you think education is expensive, try ignorance." —Derek Bok

"Education is a form of self-delusion." —Elbert Hubbard

"He that increaseth knowledge increaseth sorrow." —Ecclesiastes

"Education is what remains when we have forgotten all that we have been taught."—George Savile

"Education seems to be in America the only commodity of which the customer tried to get as little he can for his money." —Max Forman

"Education is the process of casting false pearls before real swine." —Irwin Edman

Presidential Trivia I

PRESIDENTS & THEIR VICES

From the question-and-answer books *Just Curious, Jeeves* and *Just Curious About History, Jeeves*, by Jack Mingo and Erin Barrett, we found some juicy little bits of gossip on some United States Presidents and Veeps.

How many U.S. presidents have been divorced?

Just one: Ronald Reagan.

Wasn't JFK pretty sick during his presidency?

He was sick. He suffered from two serious problems: Addison's disease, in which the body can't produce sufficient amounts of the crucial hormone cortisol, and a degeneration of the spine, probably due to repeat injuries. He also suffered the physical complications of having contracted malaria during World War II.

During his childhood, back problems, jaundice, and other ails kept Kennedy scrawny and weak. When he was serving in Congress he underwent steroid shots and back surgeries. There were at least four incidents prior to his death in 1963 where he had last rites administered by priests.

During the time of his presidency, though, Kennedy was healthier than he'd been in a while. Because so much of his appeal was based on his boyish good looks and athleticism, he went to great lengths to conceal his illnesses from the public.

Which president said he believed the Earth was flat?

Andrew Jackson. Ol' Andy never did cotton much to book larnin'.

Have there been any unusual pets in the White House?

It hasn't all been just cats and dogs. Calvin Coolidge had a raccoon. Teddy Roosevelt had a badger. Herbert Hoover had a horned toad. Woodrow Wilson had a ram named Old Ike that visitors fed so much chewing tobacco to that it became hopelessly addicted. Tad Lincoln had a pet turkey, and Andrew Jackson had a parrot with language so foul that the bird had to be removed from Jackson's funeral. But probably the most unusual pet was an alligator that John Quincy Adams kept around because he said he enjoyed "the spectacle of guests fleeing from the room in terror."

Were any of the United States presidents gay?

It's impossible to prove for sure. However, our only bachelor president, James Buchanan, had that reputation in his lifetime. His longtime roommate, Senator and later Vice President William Rufus De Vane King of Alabama, also never married. According to historians, the two had an inseparable relationship for nearly twenty-five years until King's death—in fact, King was called "Buchanan's better half," "James's wife," and "Miss Nancy" by some of his colleagues. When the two were temporarily separated after King was appointed minister to France in 1844, King wrote Buchanan, "I am selfish enough to hope you will not be able to procure an associate who will cause you to feel no regret at our separation." Buchanan wrote to a Mrs. Roosevelt, "I am now 'solitary and alone,' having no companion in the house with me. I have gone a wooing to several gentlemen but have not succeeded with any one of them. I feel that it is not good for man to be alone; and should not be astonished to find myself married to some old maid who can nurse me when I am sick, provide good dinners for me when I am well, and not expect from me any very ardent or romantic affection."

But that's not all. Hang onto your stovepipe hats, because a few rogue historians also claim that Abraham Lincoln was homoerotically involved with a lifelong friend named Joshua Speed. They shared private thoughts, fears, desires, and a bed for four years. Lincoln biographer Carl Sandberg wrote that their relationship had "a streak of lavender and spots soft as May violets."

Were any U.S. presidents not Christians?

If you judge them by their fruits, you could argue a number of them were not. However, Abraham Lincoln was one who specifically rejected Christianity, even writing a pamphlet called "Infidelity" that sought to disprove the Bible generally and the idea of Jesus being the son of God specifically. Later, as a politician, he succumbed to pressure to mention God in speeches but pointedly did not mention Jesus.

Thomas Jefferson attended an Episcopal church, but refused to discuss his religious beliefs during his election campaign and so was accused by rabble-rousing preachers of being ungodly and in league with Satan. Actually, he believed in the moral teachings of Jesus, but not in his divinity.

How old was George Washington when he chopped down the cherry tree?

Sorry to burst your bubble, but the cherry tree story's just a myth. (Where've you been, my friend?) It doesn't mean he wasn't ethical as a child, however. As a matter of fact, there's evidence George was extremely moral in his formative years. As a schoolboy he wrote rules of behavior for himself into his exercise book that still survives today. What's not clear is whether it was his own idea or that of his mother or schoolteacher. Decide for yourself. Following are some of them (rendered in his own boyhood spelling, capitalization, and punctuation):

- Turn not your Back to others especially in Speaking, Jog not the Table or Desk on which Another reads or writes, lean not upon any one.
- Use no Reproachfull Language against any one neither Curse nor Revile.
- Play not the Peacock, looking every where about you, to See if you be well Deck't, if your Shoes fit well, if your Skokings Sit neatly, and Cloths handsomely.
- While you are talking, Point not with your Finger at him of Whom you Discourse nor Approach too near him to whom you talk especially to his face.
- Be not Curious to Know the Affairs of Others neither approach those that Speak in Private.
- It's unbecoming to Stoop much to ones Meat Keep your Fingers clean & when foul wipe them on a Corner of your Table Napkin.

How many U. S. presidents have resigned from office?

One. Richard Nixon.

How many U.S. vice presidents have resigned from office?

Two: John Calhoun resigned in a policy dispute with the president; Spiro Agnew resigned after it was discovered he'd been taking bribes.

We've Got Your Number

We'll give you a number, abbreviated words, and a clue. Tell us what the famous phrase is. Answers below. (Don't cheat!)

1. 2001 A S O (Apes and spacecraft)
2. A B & T 40 T (Baghdad tale)
3. 1 L T L (Llanview soap opera)
4. 5 L M J O T B (Doc said: no more jumping!)
5. J & T 12 A (Attendees at a final dinner)
6. 3 L F & A M F T (1940s aqueous novelty song)
7. 2 B, 4 B, 6 B, A D (On your feet and cheer)
8. 1 P, 2 P, 3 P, 4 (You're it!)
9. 5 4 3 2 1, W H I, W H L-O (I'm a rocket man)
10. T 2 A & C M I T M (Telephone prescription)
11. 52 P-U (Wanna play a card game?)
12. 4 S & 7 Y A (An address in Pennsylvania)
13. P 6-5000 (Big band hit)
14. I L O A 4-L C (Don't overlook lucky tokens)
15. 1 R T R T A (Makes for a very bad hobbit)
16. 3 S & Y O (Baseball and harsh sentencing)
17. T G O 4 (Chinese clique)
18. 40 D & 40 N (Didn't it rain, children)
19. 88 K O T P (Flats, sharps, and naturals)
20. 99 B O B O T W (Endlessly annoying song)

Answers: *1. 2001: A Space Odyssey; 2. Ali Baba & the 40 Thieves; 3. One Life to Live; 4. 5 Little Monkeys, Jumping on the Bed; 5. Jesus & the 12 Apostles; 6. 3 Little Fishes & a Momma Fish Too; 7. 2 Bits, 4 Bits, 6 Bits, a Dollar; 8. 1 Potato, 2 Potatoes, 3 Potatoes, 4; 9. 5-4-3-2-1, We Have Ignition, We Have Lift-off; 10. Take 2 Aspirins & Call Me in the Morning; 11. 52 Pick-up; 12. 4 Score & 7 Years Ago; 13. Pennsylvania 6-5000; 14. I'm Looking Over a 4-Leaf Clover; 15. 1 Ring to Rule Them All; 16. 3 Strikes & You're Out; 17. The Gang of 4; 18. 40 Days & 40 Nights; 19. 88 Keys on the Piano; 20. 99 Bottles of Beer on the Wall*

Myth-Making

Her Life ... According to Calamity Jane

Martha Canary, known as "Calamity Jane," created quite a legend for herself. Unfortunately, most of it was not true. So, with several grains of salt ready, we present "The Life & Adventures of Calamity Jane by Herself," as published in a promotional pamphlet.

MY MAIDEN NAME was Marthy Cannary. I was born in Princeton, Missouri, May 1st, 1852. As a child I always had a fondness for adventure and out-door exercise and especial fondness for horses which I began to ride at an early age and continued to do so until I able to ride the most vicious and stubborn of horses.

In 1865 we emigrated from our homes in Missouri by the overland route to Virginia City, Montana, taking five months to make the journey. While on the way the greater portion of my time was spent in hunting along with the men and hunters of the party, in fact I was at all times with the men when there was excitement and adventures to be had. By the time we reached Virginia City I was considered a remarkable good shot and a fearless rider for a girl of my age.

Joined General Custer as a scout at Fort Russell, Wyoming, in 1870, and started for Arizona for the Indian Campaign. Up to this time I had always worn the costume of my sex. When I joined Custer I donned the uniform of a soldier. It was a bit awkward at first but I soon got to be perfectly at home in men's clothes.

Was in Arizona up to the winter of 1871 and during that time I had a great many adventures with the Indians, for as a scout I had a great many dangerous missions to perform and while I was in many close places always succeeded in getting away

safely for by this time I was considered the most reckless and daring rider and one of the best shots in the western country.

After that campaign I returned to Fort Sanders, Wyoming, until spring of 1872, when we were ordered out to the Muscle Shell or Nursey Pursey Indian outbreak. In that war Generals Custer, Miles, Terry, and Crook were all engaged. This campaign lasted until fall of 1873.

It was during this campaign that I was christened Calamity Jane. It was on Goose Creek, Wyoming, where the town of Sheridan is now located. Capt. Egan was in command of the Post. We were ordered out to quell an uprising of the Indians, and were out for several days, had numerous skirmishes during which six of the soldiers were killed and several severely wounded. When on returning to the Post we were ambushed about a mile and a half from our destination. When fired upon Capt. Egan was shot. I was riding in advance and on hearing the firing turned in my saddle and saw the Captain reeling in his saddle as though about to fall. I turned my horse and galloped back with all haste to his side and got there in time to catch him as he was falling. I lifted him onto my horse in front of me and succeeded in getting him safely to the Fort. Capt. Egan on recovering, laughingly said: "I name you Calamity Jane, the heroine of the plains." I have borne that name up to the present time.

We were afterwards ordered to Fort Custer, where Custer city now stands, where we arrived in the spring of 1874; remained around Fort Custer all summer and were ordered to Fort Russell in fall of 1874, where we remained until spring of 1875; was then ordered to the Black Hills to protect miners, as that country was controlled by the Sioux Indians and the government had to send the soldiers to protect the lives of the miners and settlers in that section. Remained there until fall of 1875 and wintered at Fort Laramie. In spring of 1876, we were ordered north with General Crook to join Gen'ls Miles, Terry, and Custer at Big Horn river. During this march I swam the Platte river at Fort Fetterman as I was the bearer of important dispatches. I had a ninety mile ride to make, being wet and cold, I contracted a severe illness and was sent back in Gen. Crook's ambulance to Fort Fetterman where I laid in the hospital for fourteen days. When able to ride I started for Fort Laramie where I met Wm. Hickock, better known as Wild Bill, and we started for Deadwood, where we arrived about June.

During the month of June I acted as a pony express rider carrying the U.S. mail between Deadwood and Custer, a distance of fifty miles, over one of the roughest trails in the Black Hills country. As many of the riders before me had been held up and robbed of their packages, mail and money that they carried, for that was the only means of getting mail and money between these points. It was considered the most dangerous route in the Hills, but as my reputation as a rider and quick shot was well known, I was molested very little, for the toll gatherers looked on me as being a good fellow, and they knew that I never missed my mark. I made the round trip every two days which was considered pretty good riding in that country. Remained around Deadwood all that summer visiting all the camps within an area of one hundred miles. My friend, Wild Bill, remained in Deadwood during the summer with the exception of occasional visits to the camps.

On the 2nd of August, while setting at a gambling table in the Bell Union saloon, in Deadwood, he was shot in the back of the head by the notorious Jack McCall, a desperado. I was in Deadwood at the time and on hearing of the killing made my way at once to the scene of the shooting and found that my friend had been killed by McCall. I at once started to look for the assassin and found him at Shurdy's butcher shop and grabbed a meat cleaver and made him throw up his hands; through the excitement on hearing of Bill's death, having left my weapons on the post of my bed. He was then taken to a log cabin and locked up, well secured as every one thought, but he got away and was afterwards caught at Fagan's ranch on Horse

Creek, on the old Cheyenne road and was then taken to Yankton, Dak., where he was tried, sentenced and hung.

I remained around Deadwood locating claims, going from camp to camp until the spring of 1877, where one morning, I saddled my horse and rode towards Crook City. I had gone about twelve miles from Deadwood, at the mouth of Whitewood creek, when I met the overland mail running from Cheyenne to Deadwood. The horses on a run, about two hundred yards from the station; upon looking closely I saw they were pursued by Indians. The horses ran to the barn as was their custom. As the horses stopped I rode along side of the coach and found the driver John Slaughter, lying face downwards, he having been shot by the Indians. When the stage got to the station the Indians hid in the bushes. I immediately removed all baggage from the coach except the mail. I then took the driver's seat and with all haste drove to Deadwood, carrying the six passengers and the dead driver.

I left Deadwood in the fall of 1877, and went to Bear Butte Creek with the 7th Cavalry. During the fall and winter we built Fort Meade and the town of Sturgis. In 1878 I left the command and went to Rapid City and put in the year prospecting.

In 1879 I went to Fort Pierre and drove trains from Rapid City to Fort Pierre for Frank Witc then drove teams from Fort Pierce to Sturgis for Fred Evans. This teaming was done with oxen as they were better fitted for the work than horses, owing to the rough nature of the country.

In 1881 I went to Wyoming and returned in 1882 to Miles City and took up a ranch on the Yellow Stone, raising stock and cattle, also kept a way side inn, where the weary traveler could be accommodated with food, drink, or trouble if he looked for it. Left the ranch in 1883, went to California, going through the States and territories, reached Ogden the latter part of 1883, and San Francisco in 1884. Left San Francisco in the summer of 1884 for Texas, stopping at Fort Yuma, Arizona, the hottest spot in the United States. Stopping at all points of interest until I reached El Paso in the fall. While in El Paso, I met Mr. Clinton Burk, a native of Texas, who I married in August 1885. As I thought I had travelled through life long enough alone and thought it was about time to take a partner for the rest of my days. We remained in Texas leading a quiet home life until

1889. On October 28th, 1887, I became the mother of a girl baby, the very image of its father, at least that is what he said, but who has the temper of its mother.

When we left Texas we went to Boulder, Colorado, where we kept a hotel until 1893, after which we travelled through Wyoming, Montana, Idaho, Washington, Oregon, then back to Montana, then to Dakota, arriving in Deadwood October 9th, 1895, after an absence of seventeen years.

My arrival in Deadwood after an absence of so many years created quite an excitement among my many friends of the past, to such an extent that a vast number of the citizens who had come to Deadwood during my absence who had heard so much of Calamity Jane and her many adventures in former years were anxious to see me. Among the many whom I met were several gentlemen from eastern cities who advised me to allow myself to be placed before the public in such a manner as to give the people of the eastern cities an opportunity of seeing the Woman Scout who was made so famous through her daring career in the West and Black Hill countries.

An agent of Kohl & Middleton, the celebrated Museum men, came to Deadwood, through the solicitation of the gentleman who I had met there and arrangements were made to place me before the public in this manner. My first engagement began at the Palace Museum, Minneapolis, January 20th, 1896, under Kohl and Middleton's management.

Hoping that this little history of my life may interest all readers, I remain as in the older days,

Yours, Mrs. M. BURK

BETTER KNOWN AS CALAMITY JANE

THE TRUTH

The truth of Calamity Jane's life is harder to dig up, in part because she and Wild West writers tirelessly lied about it. She did wander the West working as a cook, dancehall girl, and prostitute. In spring 1876, she drove ox carts to outlying camps. If she ever actually met Wild Bill Hickok, it was only briefly, because he died shortly after her arrival. She didn't capture his killer, never was on the Army's payroll, didn't barely miss being massacred at Little Big Horn, didn't really ride with the Pony Express.... From 1895 on she appeared in Wild West shows and exhibitions, but in 1901 was fired for erratic behavior and alcoholism. She died in poverty in 1903.

Potty Pourri

RANDOM KINDS OF FACTNESS

• A survey in 1978 by PEN, an international literary organization, found that the median annual income earned by published writers was $4,700, with 68 percent making less than $10,000, and 9 percent earning nothing. The results were so depressing to its members that the organization didn't bother updating the survey in subsequent years.

• In the United States, more gold is used to make class rings than any other piece of jewelry.

• How many O's in a can of SpaghettiOs? About 1,750.

• Ever see "carragenan" on an ingredients panel and wonder what it is? It's a thickener used in lots of things like dairy products. It's an extract made from red seaweed.

• What is it called when you're unnaturally afraid of machines? Mechanophobia.

• Wedding cake was originally provided at weddings as something to throw at the new bride and groom. Unfrosted, luckily.

• Why are they called "sardines"? Because the process of canning small herrings was invented on the Italian island of Sardinia.

• Competent writers know that "e.g." means "for example" and "i.e." means "that is" and never confuse the two in their writing. However it's a sure bet that few know that the abbreviations stand for *exempli gratia* and *id est*.

• A researcher asked kids which season is most boring. 53 percent said, "Summer."

• When troublemaker Henry David Thoreau graduated from Harvard, he refused to take his diploma. "It isn't worth five dollars," he said, complaining that Harvard taught "all the branches of learning, but none of the roots."

• Cheetahs are fast, reaching speeds of about 71 miles per hour.

Putting on the Dog

Facts About "Man's Best Friend"

Groucho Marx said it best when he said, "Outside of a dog, a book is a man's best friend: and inside a dog, it's too dark to read."

• People have been breeding dogs for at least 10,000 years. Evidence of the oldest known breed—the saluki, a Middle Eastern dog—appeared on artifacts from about 7000 B.C. Before 1500 B.C., Egyptians were breeding hunting dogs that resemble large mastiffs. The irresistible, fluffy Maltese also dates back to ancient Egypt, sometime around 500 B.C. Not surprisingly, they were worshiped as gods alongside members of the royal family.

• The American Kennel Club recognizes 150 breeds of dog in seven main categories: sporting dogs, hounds, working dogs, terriers, toy dogs, non-sporting dogs, and herding dogs.

• The American foxhound is descended from English hounds, brought to the United States in 1650, and a French hound that was given as a present to President George Washington. He is credited with introducing this classic hunting dog to the world

• The chihuahua, highly regarded by the Aztecs, was possibly first bred to be a hand warmer for royals in drafty palaces. The little dogs could easily fit inside the sleeves of robes, after all. Priests also used them as afterlife amulets for the dead (believing their presence warded off evil spirits), sacrificing them in burial rituals. Aztec commoners, however, merely kept them as house pets and sometimes for food.

• Jack Russell terriers were bred in the 1800s using fox terriers. They got their names from the man who originally bred them: the Rev. John ("Jack") Russell. As old as this English breed is, it wasn't officially recognized by the AKC until 1997.

• Although it looks nothing like a bull, bulldogs were so named because they were especially bred for bull baiting. This was a "sport" in which a bull was chained to a pole and dogs were let loose to tear the bull to bits while spectators watched and cheered. The sport was made illegal in 1835, and breeders successfully bred the traits of viciousness and fearlessness from these dogs so they could live on as house pets.

• Ever hear of a Staffordshire terrier? That's what the AKC called the American pit bull until 1936.

• The wrinkly skinned shar-pei is named with the Chinese word for "sharkskin."

• Great Danes originated in Germany, bred by mixing Irish wolfhounds and English mastiffs. French dog breeders were under the impression that the dog came from Denmark, so they gave the dog its inaccurate name; Germans, however, call them *Deutsche dogges* ("German dogs").

• So what do the Germans call the German shepherd, then? *Deutscher schaferhund,* meaning "German Shepherd hound."

• It's not just in cartoons, St. Bernard dogs really did save lives in the Alps—more than 2,500 over the last 200 years alone. During the Middle Ages, a monk named Bernard founded a travelers' hospice in Valle d'Aosta on the border of Switzerland and Italy. His monks bred and trained the large shaggy dogs for search and rescue missions. The hospice is still operating there, and so are the big furry dogs.

These days, however, they're there more for sentimental reasons than for rescue since technology is more effective at rescuing stranded people than big sloppy dogs. And, yes, the St. Bernards really did wear casks of Brandy on their collars. It helped give rescuees an illusion of being warmer until real help arrived.

- The ten most intelligent breeds are the border collie, poodle, German shepherd, golden retriever, doberman pinscher, Shetland sheepdog, Labrador retriever, papillon, rottweiler, and Australian cattle dog. The ten least intelligent breeds are the shih-tzu, basset hound, mastiff, beagle, Pekingese, bloodhound, borzoi, chow chow, bulldog, basenji, and Afghan hound.
- Forget the "one year equals seven dog years" formula.

Seeing Eye Dogs

After World War I, a school to train guide dogs first opened in Pottsdam, Germany, but closed due to lack of funding. Before it failed, one of its visitors was a wealthy American named Dorothy Harrison Eustis, who wrote about it for the *Saturday Evening Post.*

A blind man named Morris Frank heard about Ms. Eustis's article. Tired of depending on others to get around, the Nashville, Tennessee, native wrote to her that he was eager to see if he could become more self-sufficient by means of a dog companion. Eustis agreed to fund his training with a dog if, in return, Frank would start his own guide dog training school in the United States.

Frank called his school The Seeing Eye, from a Bible verse: "The seeing eye, the hearing ear; The Lord hath made them both." (Prov. 20:12). In its first year, the school graduated seventeen people and dogs. Now, after decades of success (as well as incorporating and having the term "Seeing Eye" trademarked), the school is located in New Jersey and still functions to train dogs and their blind companions.

The first year of a dog's life is equal to about nineteen or twenty human years. In that first year, the dog will go through infancy, young childhood, puberty, and teen rebellion. By the time it hits its second year, it's a young adult. From that point on, you can figure about four dog years for every human year.

• There is a precise word for the poop of domesticated dogs: *scumber.* If you're speaking of wild dog poop, though, the word is *lesses.*

• The main ingredient in chocolate is a caffeine-related chemical called *theobromine.* The better or darker the chocolate, the more theobromine. Because dogs metabolize theobromine more slowly than humans, the chemical can be highly toxic to them. Get your dog medical attention immediately if it gets into your Halloween stash.

• French-speaking trappers and explorers, using sled dogs to make their way across the frozen Canadian tundra, shouted "*Marchons!*" ("Let's go!" in French). English speakers heard it as "Mush on!" Eventually it was shorted to just "Mush!"

• A good sled with six to eight good working dogs should get you blazing through snow in excess of 20 miles per hour.

• Dogs aren't completely colorblind. They can see color, just not all color. Canines have a type of colorblindness called *deuteranopia,* meaning they don't the green spectrum. While they can recognize shades of the red spectrum, they're best at detecting blue.

• According to Disney, animators painted a total of 6,469,952 dog spots in *101 Dalmations.*

Two Little Ones

• Orchids got their name from *orkhis*, the Greek word for "testicles," which is what its root system looks like.

• The word *testimony* comes from the old Roman practice of cupping the genitals when swearing an oath.

Creepy Tales

Aesop Fables Featuring Insects

What can you learn from a bug? The story of the ant and the grasshopper is as well-known as any fable. Here it is, and several more.

THE ANT AND THE GRASSHOPPER

In a field one summer's day a Grasshopper was hopping about, chirping and singing to its heart's content. An Ant passed by, bearing along with great toil an ear of corn he was taking to the nest.

"Why not come and chat with me," said the Grasshopper, "instead of toiling and moiling in that way?"

"I am helping to lay up food for the winter," said the Ant, "and recommend you to do the same."

"Why bother about winter?" said the Grasshopper; we have got plenty of food at present." But the Ant went on its way and continued its toil. When the winter came the Grasshopper had no food and found itself dying of hunger, while it saw the ants distributing every day corn and grain from the stores they had collected in the summer. Then the Grasshopper knew:

It is best to prepare for the days of necessity.

THE BEE AND JUPITER

A bee from Mount Hymettus, the queen of the hive, ascended to Olympus to present Jupiter some honey fresh from her combs. Jupiter, delighted with the offering of honey, promised to give whatever she should ask. She therefore besought him, saying, "Give me, I pray thee, a sting, that if any mortal shall approach to take my honey, I may kill him." Jupiter was much displeased, for he loved the race of man, but could not refuse the request because of his promise. He thus answered the Bee: "You shall have your request, but it will be at the peril of your own life. For if you use your sting, it shall remain in the wound

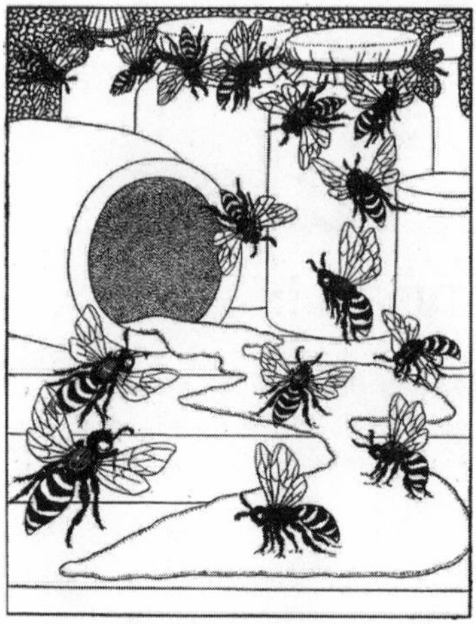

"I pray thee, a sting...."

you make, and then you will die from the loss of it."

Evil wishes, like chickens, come home to roost.

THE BALD MAN AND THE FLY

There was once a Bald Man who sat down after work on a hot summer's day. A Fly came up and kept buzzing about his bald pate, and stinging him from time to time. The Man aimed a blow at his little enemy, but WHACK! His palm landed on his head instead; again the Fly tormented him, but this time the Man was wiser and said:

"You will only injure yourself if you take notice of despicable enemies."

THE ANT AND THE CHRYSALIS

An Ant nimbly running about in the sunshine in search of food came across a Chrysalis that was very near its time of change. The Chrysalis moved its tail, and thus attracted the attention of the Ant, who then saw for the first time that it was alive. "Poor, pitiable animal!" cried the Ant disdainfully. "What a sad fate is yours! While I can run hither and thither, at my pleasure, and, if I wish, ascend the tallest tree, you lie imprisoned here in your shell, with power only to move a joint or two of your scaly tail." The Chrysalis heard all this, but did not try to make any reply. A few days after, when the Ant passed that way again, nothing but the shell remained. Wondering what had become of its contents, he felt himself suddenly shaded and fanned by the gorgeous wings of a beautiful Butterfly. "Behold in me," said the Butterfly, "your much-pitied friend! Boast now of your powers to run and climb as long as you can get me to listen." So saying, the Butterfly rose in the air, and, borne along and aloft on the summer breeze, was soon lost to the sight of the Ant forever.

"Appearances are deceptive."

Every Picture Tells a Story

Self-Portrait with Bandaged Ear **by Vincent Van Gogh**

• Vincent Van Gogh painted sixty-two self-portraits—more than any other major painter. He had good reason: while institutionalized for insanity, he didn't have models or landscapes available.

• He painted *Self-Portrait with Bandaged Ear* while confined after his most notorious bit of performance art. Trying to impress a local prostitute named Rachel, he cut off his ear lobe on Christmas Eve 1888, and presented it to her, telling her, "Guard this object carefully."

• When she unwrapped his lobe offering, she fainted, and the police were called. They found the artist catatonic, lying in a fetal position. It was the first of several attacks of madness until Van Gogh killed himself a year and a half later.

• His loss of sanity was the art world's gain. Of his 850 known works, about two-thirds were painted in the last two years of his life. Unfortunately, he sold only two paintings in his life, in sales arranged by his brother, Theo. Worse, even that degree of success—and a positive review from an influential art journal—seemed to disturb and unhinge him further. He shot himself in 1890.

Foodonyms

Ask for It by Name

Ever wonder how some of your favorite snacks or dishes got their names? Was Fig Newton named after Sir Isaac Newton? You might be surprised by some of these origins.

Melba Toast: Named for the Australian operatic singer, Nellie Melba. The dessert Peach Melba was also named for her. Both were invented by the French chef Auguste Escoffier, who seemed to have a little crush on Miss Melba.

Ritz crackers: In 1934, the National Biscuit Company made a cracker with a lot more shortening so it glistened, and shined.The name is glommed from that grand hotel, the Ritz.

Waldorf salad: A famous maitre d' named Oscar Tschirky at New York's Waldorf-Astoria Hotel created this salad of apple, nuts, and mayonnaise sometime around 1900. He named it the Waldorf salad, which was probably wise. It might not have lasted had he called it the Tschirky salad.

Graham crackers: Graham flour is just whole wheat flour. The name comes from the health nut, Rev. Dr. Sylvester Graham, who in the early 1800s preached that eating altered foods was a sin. Graham believed that altered food led to sexual desires.

Chicken à la king: Nobody really knows, but one of more than eight supposed origins for this dish is that King Edward VII really liked the recipe, hence the "à la King."

Fig Newton: Like all of the Boston-based Kennedy Biscuit Company's cookies and crackers, the Fig Newton was named after a nearby town. Other company products like the Beacon Hill, the Brighton, and the Quincy are lost to history, but Newton, Massachusetts, will always be remembered.

Cubical Sounds

How Muzak Invented Mood-Elevator Music

When's the last time you listened to Muzak? Do you remember what song was playing? No? That's good—you're not *supposed* to remember. In fact, if it's working "right," you're not really supposed to notice that it's there at all.

If you want to make Muzak's 174 franchisers and 350,000 subscribers mad, call it "background music" or "elevator music." They call it "environmental music," and it's all tied into a theory called "Stimulus Progression." To quote company literature: "Each segment plays music on an ascending curve during descending periods of the industrial work curve." In other words, they play peppy music at the times when people usually feel fatigued, and relaxing music when people usually feel tense.

ELECTRICITY KILLED THE RADIO STAR

Muzak began with Maj. Gen. George Owen Squier, a retired Army officer born at the end of America's Civil War. He was a pioneer in military radio work, discovering in 1907 that a live tree could be tapped into and used as a radio antenna ("tree telephony" he called it). In 1922 Squier came up with an idea he called "line radio" or "wired wireless," in which music, news, lectures, entertainment, and advertising would be transmitted into homes through power lines, not unlike modern cable.

He pitched the idea to a public utility holding company in New York City. They liked it. Squier always liked the brand name "Kodak." So, to name his product, he wedded "music" and "Kodak," ending up with "Muzak."

Wired Radio first began broadcasting through electrical wires in Cleveland, offering four different channels. With a low-cost receiver, people could listen to music and news by plugging into the electrical outlets that brought their power and light. In 1934, the company switched to telephone lines instead of power lines to transmit the music, but they were losing ground to the radio stations that broadcast over the air for free.

POP (AND JAZZ) PSYCHOLOGY

Finally, Muzak found a reason for existing. Two British industrial psychologists published a study on the benefits of music in the workplace. They said that music programming could increase productivity; and second, that the music must be "rationed" into segments—music played continuously creates as much monotony as having no music at all. Based on this study, Muzak executives decided to begin programming music for the work environment: soothing yet invigorating, and "rationed" into segments. Its sales reps convinced enough business owners to try it out, and Muzak, as we know it, was born.

Success in New York led to a franchise system in other cities, operated under the firm rule that franchises would play, without variation, all programs exactly as they originated from Muzak headquarters.

With technological advances, Muzak began using satellite and radio channels as well as phone lines to get music to its subscribers, which now included hotels, churches, mental institutions, corporate offices, prisons, secret military installations, and even a whorehouse in Germany.

GIVING YOU THE BUSINESS

Here's how it works: The songs come from all over. A repertoire manager listens to the radio to find music to rerecord for the channel. At any given time, Muzak has an active library of 5,000 titles.

Every song played on the channel is custom-recorded.

In the 1980s, a Czech radio orchestra recorded 75 percent of their songs, but now Muzak uses a number of instrumental configurations. But the basic workplace package allows no singers.

Voices are eliminated for the same reason Muzak favors violas over violins, French horns over trumpets, and muted percussion over drum solos—because Muzak is to be "felt and heard," but not listened to.

Each song is given a "stimulus value" score which denotes how stimulating it is, determined mathematically by measuring the song's tempo, rhythm, instrumentation, and orchestra size. Muzak arranges the songs into 15 minute sets of five songs each, customized for each specific time of day by a computer. The music reaches peaks of liveliness at 10 A.M. and at 2 P.M.—both lull times for most workers.

MUSIC HATH CHARMS?

Despite claims, "environmental music" doesn't work the same way with everybody. It is supposed to put shoppers in the mood to linger and buy, yet convenience stores in the Northwest began using it for the opposite effect: to chase away loitering teens who couldn't take another strings-and-piano rendition of "You Light Up My Life" or "Killing Me Softly With His Song."

The company dismisses anti-Muzak critics out of hand. "You know," says a spokesperson, "pollsters have done research of the electorate, and they found that there's a certain percentage that is just anti-everything. You have a hard core that's against everything, a vocal 10 percent, and I suspect that we're hearing from that vocal fringe group many times. If a business person is considering Muzak for an office and is going to be swayed by the 10% that always complains about something, then he'll have a big problem running his business."

MUZAK FACTS

• Twice the human voice was heard on the Muzak channel: in 1981, to announce that American hostages had been released from Iran, and Good Friday, 1985, when it joined thousands of radio stations around the world in a broadcast of "We Are the World."

• Muzak now has sixty channels of all musical styles for telephone on-hold music and store ambiance.

Potty Pourri

RANDOM KINDS OF FACTNESS

• Women could not legally practice law in the United States until 1872.

• Ever hear of the "lawyer bird"? The North American black-necked stilt is called that because one of its identifying features is "a big bill."

• Despite the name, a Venus flytrap most often eats ants.

• How's this for election reform? Ancient Athens chose its 500 lawmakers by lottery. They served a year, and then were replaced by the next year's winners.

• Before she was a master chef, Julia Childs was a spy. This was in India and China during World War II.

• The Pentagon has twice as many bathrooms as necessary, because it was built during a time when Virginia law required separate facilities for blacks and whites.

• Sculptor Frédéric-Auguste Bartholdi used his mother as the model for the Statue of Liberty's face and his girlfriend as the model for her body.

• On TV, CPR works most of the time to restart a heart. In real life, alas, it's not that often—only about 15 percent of the people survive.

• Author Anthony Trollope worked for the British post office for thirty-three years. During that time he produced four dozen novels by rising at 5:30 A.M. and writing a thousand words before trudging off to work. Within postal circles his biggest claim to fame is that he invented the street-corner mailbox.

• A good batch of cider will not just contain one kind of apple, but a blend of three to five varieties.

• Where's the much-maligned town of Podunk? Massachusetts.

Stately Knowledge

12 Reasons Why Ya Gotta Love Colorado

We've searched the vaults and come up with some pretty impressive facts about Colorado. Here are a dozen of our favorites.

1 Colorado means "red colored" in Spanish, referring to its reddish rocks. A reddish-colored marble, dubbed "Beulah red," gives the state Capitol its unique shade. Unfortunately, all of the known Beulah red marble in the world was used during its six-year construction, meaning it can't ever be replaced.

2 Penrose, Colorado, has a rocking chair that's 21 feet high and 14 feet wide, big enough for more than fifty people to rock on at a time.

3 The highest incorporated city in the United States is Leadville, Colorado, standing 10,430 feet above sea level.

4 When Denver was offered a shot at hosting the 1976 Winter Olympics, it became the first city in history to ever turn it down. The voters decided the Olympics would bring unwanted crowds, pollution, and urban growth.

5 Farmers trying to prepare Sunday dinner have long known that chickens can run around without heads for several minutes. But four and a half years? Fruita, Colorado, every year celebrates Mike the Headless Chicken Day to commemorate the bird who lost his head in 1945 but didn't actu-

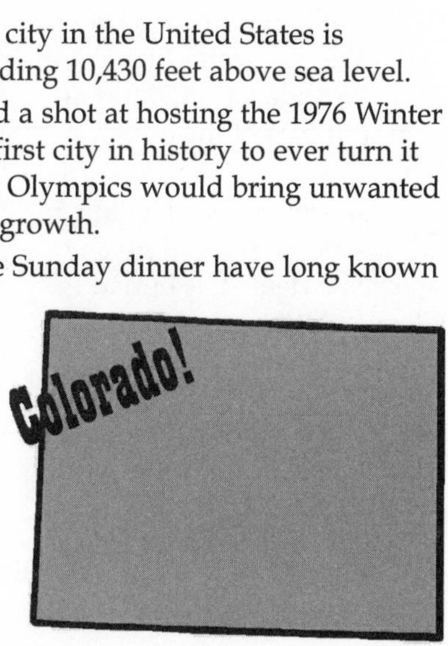

ally die until he choked on a piece of corn in 1950.

6 How romantic is this? Loveland, Colorado, has such a great name that hundreds of thousands of Valentines are sent to the post office there every year to be remailed with the LOVELAND postmark and a cupid. Awwww!

7 The Pinto Bean capital of the world is Dove Creek, Colorado. If you decide to go, be sure to pack a good supply of Bean-o.

8 The largest sand dunes in America are in the Great Sand Dunes National Monument near the town of Alamosa, Colorado. The 700-foot dunes were the result of ocean tides and winds more than a million years ago back when Western states like Utah, Nevada, and California were still part of the ocean floor.

9 Gunslinger Doc Holliday, friend of Wyatt Earp and practicing dentist, is buried in Glenwood Springs, Colorado. The epitaph on his grave? "He Died in Bed." He and Wyatt Earp ended up here for a while when hiding out from an arrest warrant from Arizona. Other Western legends who spent some time in Colorado include Calamity Jane, Bat Masterson, and Frank James.

10 "Rocky Mountain Oysters" came from the Denver area. They're not really from the sea. They go to prove the truism: "If you don't know what they are, don't order them." In case you didn't know, Rocky Mountain Oysters are fried bull testicles. Yum.

11 Alferd Packer was convicted of murder and cannibalism in 1874. He and five others got stuck in the snow and their provisions ran out. When authorities came upon the scene, the five others had been killed and one of them had been partially roasted and eaten. Packer served seventeen years and lived out the rest of his life as a recluse (and, some say, a vegetarian). More than fifty years later, the students at Boulder University voted to name the school cafeteria the "Alferd Packer Memorial Grill." It's most popular dish is the *"El Canibal"* burrito.

12 At the southwest corner of Colorado you'll find the only location in the United States where four states come together in one place. The states are Colorado, Arizona, Utah, and New Mexico.

Cat Haters

REAL-LIFE AILUROPHOBES

An ailurophobe is someone who hates cats, or is frightened by them. Here are a few examples from the book *Cats Don't Always Land on Their Feet*, by Erin Barrett and Jack Mingo.

• In his dictionary, Noah Webster had little good to say about cats, calling them "a deceitful animal and when enraged extremely spiteful."

• Cats were once used as torture devices in eighteenth-century America. Punishment involved the bareback of the accused and a fearful, angry cat dangling by its tail, just within reach of his or her back. The cat was then pulled back by its tail, across the victim's back. Inhumane on both counts, we'd say.

• Ever wonder why a cat plays a fiddle in the old nursery rhyme Hey Diddle Diddle? It's not that cats were thought to be musical—it's a rhyme of mismatches: the heavy cow flying; the tined fork and the bowled spoon, for instance. The word *fiddle* is a variation of the French word *fidele,* or "faithful one." The cat, to the author anyway, was considered the opposite embodiment of faithfulness.

• *"I just spent four hours burying the cat."*
" Four hours to bury a cat?"
"Yes—it wouldn't keep still." —Monty Python's Flying Circus

• Dwight Eisenhower loathed cats. He ordered his staff to shoot any found on the grounds of his Gettysburg home.

• Napoleon was deathly afraid of cats. He was once found cowering in his tent with a little kitty mewing at him. His guards quickly removed little Fluffy for the emperor so he could carry on with his war.

• The spread of the Black Plague in Western Europe can be attributed to a lack of available cats. Eradicated during a witch scare or two, the cat population was so low that rat numbers increased. So did their fleas and with them, the Plague.

• *Larousse Gastronomique,* the authoritative French cookbook, suggests choosing a young cat for cooking, as younger ones tend to be more stringy. It goes on to say that cooking cat like you would rabbit is your best bet: fricasséed or braised.

• Adolf Hitler was a known ailurophobe. Not that he feared them, per se, but he hated them.

• During the European witch hunts from 1560 to 1700, simply owning cats was sometimes enough evidence necessary to burn a person at the stake. This was especially true if you were an older woman who fit the stereotype of being a "witch." For example, in the St. Osyth witch trials of 1582 in Essex, England, one Alice Mansfield was accused of harboring satanic entities named Robin, Jack, William, and Puppet "all like unto black cats." She and the cats were put to death.

• How did lullaby composer Johannes Brahms spend his leisure time away from his keyboard? Sitting at an open window with a bow and arrow, shooting at the neighbors' cats.

• Percy was a homing pigeon that won the France-to-Sheffield race in 1993. Or would have, anyway. The moment Percy landed, a cat attacked and ate him. Percy's owner attempted to retrieve Percy's tag to show the judge, but by the time she could wrench it away from the cat, two other pigeons had flown in ahead. The deceased Percy never got his day, and his owner, now likely an ailurophobe, took home a third place ribbon.

• Ivan the Terrible lived up to his terrible name even as a youngster, throwing cats and other animals out of high windows of the palace for sport.

• In the 1700s, French apprentices, protesting working conditions, hideously tortured and killed their masters' cats "in a mood of great jollity and high good humor," according to one account.

• *"Cats are intended to teach us that not everything in nature has a purpose."* —Garrison Keillor

The Devil's Dictionary: A

Ambrose Bierce mysteriously disappeared in Mexico in 1914. Before that, he wrote a sardonic dictionary that present-day commentators still regularly steal from. We decided to do the same.

ABORIGINES, *n.* Persons of little worth found cumbering the soil of a newly discovered country. They soon cease to cumber; they fertilize.

ABSTAINER, *n.* A weak person who yields to the temptation of denying himself a pleasure.

ABSURDITY, *n.* A statement or belief manifestly inconsistent with one's own opinion.

ACCORDION, *n.* An instrument in harmony with the sentiments of an assassin.

ACQUAINTANCE, *n.* A person whom we know well enough to borrow from, but not well enough to lend to. A degree of friendship called slight when its object is poor or obscure, and intimate when rich or famous.

ADMIRATION, *n.* Our polite recognition of another's resemblance to ourselves.

ADMONITION, *n.* Gentle reproof, as with a meat-axe.

ALLIANCE, *n.* In international politics, the union of two thieves who have their hands so deeply inserted in each other's pockets that they cannot separately plunder a third.

ALONE, *adj.* In bad company.

AMBITION, *n.* An overmastering desire to be vilified by enemies while living and made ridiculous by friends when dead.

AMNESTY, *n.* The state's magnanimity to those offenders whom it would be too expensive to punish.

ANOINT, *v.t.* To grease a king or other great functionary already sufficiently slippery.

ANTIPATHY, *n.* The sentiment inspired by one's friend's friend.

APHORISM, *n.* Predigested wisdom.

APOLOGIZE, *v.i.* To lay the foundation for a future offense.

APPEAL, *v.t.* In law, to put the dice into the box for another throw.

APPLAUSE, *n.* The echo of a platitude.

APRIL FOOL, *n.* The March fool with another month added to his folly.

AUCTIONEER, *n.* The man who proclaims with a hammer that he has picked a pocket with his tongue.

Barrymorisms

The Barrymore dynasty—Ethel, Lionel, John, Drew—is legendary in Hollywood. Here are a few words of wisdom from the late, great actor, John Barrymore.

ON MORALS
"The good die young, because they see it's no use living if you have got to be good."

ON FINANCES
"Why is there so much month left at the end of the money?"

ON WOMEN
"Love is the delightful interval between meeting a beautiful girl and discovering that she looks like a haddock."

ON SEX
"Sex: the thing that takes up the least amount of time and causes the most amount of trouble."

ON MARRIAGE
"In Genesis, it says that it is not good for a man to be alone; but sometimes it is a great relief."

ON DIVORCE
"You never realize how short a month is until you pay alimony."

ON AGING
"A man is not old until regrets take the place of dreams."

ON HAPPINESS
"Happiness sneaks through a door you didn't know that you left open."

DYING WORDS
"Die? I should say not, dear fellow. No Barrymore would allow such a conventional thing to happen to him."

Ripe Ol' Corn

"Uncle Josh and the Liar's Club"

"Uncle Josh Weatherby," Cal Stewart's country bumpkin, lived in the bucolic town of Punkin Centre. Here's a scene of classic rural codgerism.

Well, sometimes a lot of us old codgers used to git down to Ezra Hoskins' grossery store and we'd set 'round and chaw terbacker and whittle sticks and eat crackers and cheese and prunes and anything Ezra happened to have layin' 'round loose, and then we'd git to spinnin' yarns.

Well, one afternoon we was all settin' 'round spinnin' yarns when Deacon Witherspoon said that echos was mighty peculiar things, 'cause down whar he was born and raised thar was a passell of hills come together and you couldn't git out thar and talk louder 'n a whisper on account of the echo. But one day a summer boarder what was thar remarked as how he wasn't afraid to talk right out in front of any old lot of hills what was ever created; so he went out and hollered jist as loud as he could holler, and he started an echo a-goin' and it flew up against one hill and bounced off onto another one and gittin' bigger and louder all the time 'til it got back whar it started from and hit a stone quarry and knocked off a piece of stone and hit that feller in the head, and he didn't come to fer over three hours.

Well, we thought that was purty good fer a Deacon. None of us said anything fer a right smart spell and then Si Pettingill remarked that he didn't know anything about echos, but he calculated he'd seen some mighty peculiar things; said he guessed he'd seen it rain 'bout as hard as anybody ever seen it rain. Someone said, "Well, Si, how hard did you ever see it rain?" and he said, "Well one day last summer down our way it got to rainin' and it rained so hard that the drops jist rubbed together comin' down, which made them so all-fired hot that they turned into steam; why, it rained so gosh-dinged hard, thar was a cider barrel layin' out in the yard that had both heads out'n it and the bung hole facing up; well, it rained so hard into that bung hole that the water couldn't run out of both ends of the barrel fast enough, and it swelled up and busted."

Well, we all took a fresh chew of terbacker and nudged each other; and Ezra Hoskins said he didn't remember as how he'd ever seen it rain quite so hard as that, but he'd seen some mighty dry weather; he said one time when he was out in Kansas it got so tarnation dry that fish a-swimmin' up the river left a cloud of dust behind them. And hot, too; why, it got so all-fired hot that one day he tied his mule to a pen full of popcorn out behind the barn, and it got so hot that the corn got to poppin' and flyin' 'round that old mule's ears and he thought it was snow and laid down and froze to death.

Well, about that time old Jim Lawson commenced to show signs of uneasiness, and someone said, "What is it, Jim?" and Jim remarked, as he shifted his terbacker and cut a sliver off from his wooden leg, "I was a-thinkin' about a cold spell we had one winter when we was a-livin' down Nantucket way. It was hog killin' time, if I remember right. Anyhow, we had a kettle of boilin' water settin' on the fire, and we set it out doors to cool off a little, and that water froze so durned quick that the ice was hot."

Ezra said, "Guess it's 'bout shuttin' up time."

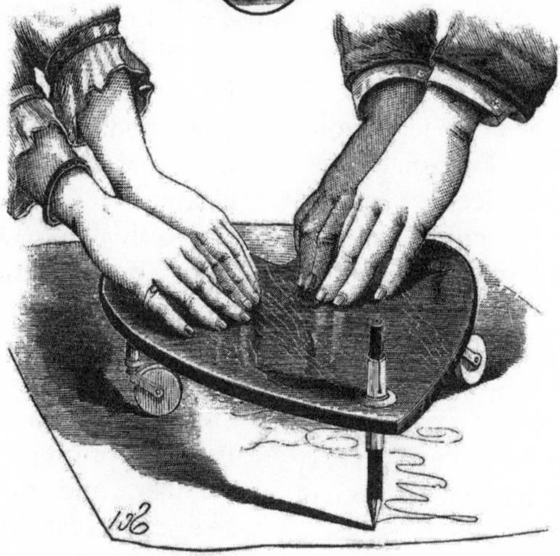

Piercing the Veil

Ouija or Won't Ya?

Is Ouija an ancient fortune-telling device that will connect you with the Other World or a mirror of your own subconscious mind? Is it (as some psychics and fundamentalist Christians claim) a spiritually dangerous brush with satanic spirits, or a harmless party game? Here's the story; you decide.

Ouija is not, as some have claimed, an ancient fortune-telling device that was first used thousands of years ago by ancient Egyptians or Sumarians. And while its inventors *might* have believed in its powers, the manufacturer, William Fuld, was by all accounts completely cynical about it.

GHOST WRITERS

The first Ouija rolled off the assembly line a little more than a hundred years ago. Its roots go back a few decades earlier to France, where interest in spiritualism was at the peak of a cyclical revival. In the 1850s, someone in France—tired of depending on channelers and mediums to supposedly bring forth spirits from the Other World—invented a device that was meant to let anyone have a direct long-distance line. That device was called a *planchette,* which means "little plank" in French. (Legend has it that the inventor's name was also Planchette, but that seems too coincidental to be true.)

The planchette was an easy-rolling, heart-shaped piece of wood with, at the heart's point, a pencil. The way it worked was that one or two people placed their hands on it. When their hands mysteriously moved, the pencil traced the path, handwriting a message from Beyond.

The earliest messages were all in French, but as the device spread to other countries, spirits began speaking other languages, too. When planchettes arrived in the United States in 1868, they became an immediate sensation as a parlor game, and millions were made by toy manufacturers. Many people took their messages seriously, but still complained at the slowness and illegibility of the writing.

Some business partners at the Kennard Novelty Company came up with the idea of a spiritual typewriter from Beyond. Rather than trying to interpret the shaky writing of disembodied hands, they figured that messages would be clearer if you gave the spirits the equivalent of a computer mouse and a menu that they could click-and-point to. The partners kept the planchette, but got rid of the pencil and created a lap tray with a helpful array of preprinted letters, numbers, and common words like *yes* and *no*. Suddenly, the spirits could communicate with speed and clarity. The new board was poised to revolutionize the spiritual medium.

But what to call it? The chief partner, Charles Kennard, came up with the brilliant idea of consulting the board itself for the name. The board gave him "Ouija," which it said was the Egyptian word for "good luck." Even though that turned out to be untrue, the name stuck. However, the Spirits from Beyond played an even worse trick on poor Kennard. Despite his frequent use of the board, they neglected to warn him that his company was about to be taken away from him. His partners suddenly forced him out and turned the company over to his shop foreman, William Fuld.

Fuld immediately began rewriting the history of the Ouija, representing himself as the inventor and claiming that the name actually came from the French and German words for "yes," *oui* and *ja*. Fuld ran the company for thirty-five years, until he was struck by his own unforeseen tragedy—while supervising the replacement of a flagpole at the top of his headquarters, he fell several stories and died.

Fuld's heirs ran the company until 1966, when they sold out to Parker Brothers. Sales continue to hold steady, but the boards sell especially well during times of crisis, especially during wars, when believers are willing to try any method to keep track of loved ones in battle.

TIPS AND TRICKS

So how *do* you tell the future using a Ouija board? A good beginning is the instructions printed on the back of Ouija boards and written by William Fuld in 1902. Those who believe in the Ouija add some more hints. Some are downright scary, depending on how much you believe in the power of the board. Here's a distillation of what they say:

• Why just "channel" spirits of the dead? Some Ouijaists say they also connect with angels and even extraterrestrials.

• If you're afraid of accidentally invoking evil spirits, visualize a protective white light of energy coming from your mind and completely surrounding yourself, the board, and everybody in the room. This will protect you.

• Using the Ouija is like meeting people on the Internet: Get a new entity's name and its reason for coming to talk to you, and check it out carefully before trusting too much. In your session, ask a few simple questions about things you'll know the answer to in the next few days, to determine if your informant is reliable for more important, long-range questions. If it seems that spirits are telling you to do weird things (like send your money to Satan or Jerry Falwell), just walk away from the Ouija and try again later.

• "Don't ask spirits to do harm to others. Do not use the board to control others. Do not let others use your board when you are not using it. Don't get addicted to the board." —Advice from a Ouija Web site.

WHAT DOES IT MEAN?

In the best of all worlds, all good spirits would have good spelling and grammar skills. But despite people who have claimed that spirits dictated entire books to them in perfect English, Ouija doesn't usually work that way.

Let's say you and a friend are using the board and you ask, "Who will I marry?" The indicator starts moving as if by a force from Beyond, and laboriously begins stopping on letters: M R S N O.

"Mrsno"? What the devil does that mean? Before you give up in disgust, look at the letters and try to figure out what a dyslexic spirit might be trying to say. (This, some say, is where the *real* power of the Ouija lies—how you interpret the cryptic message tells what your unconscious mind is thinking.)

So what are the possibilities?

MRSNO—Is it shorthand for someone you know? Mark Snott? Marsha Nobbins? Are they the first letters of a name? Or (sob!) are the spirits saying you'll never get married ("Mrs? No!")

Mr. SNO—Are they initials (Mr. Scott Nevil Orson)? Or maybe the "snow" indicates someone who has so far treated you coldly.

As you can see, there are a number of ways to interpret a message.

HOW IT WORKS

There are three theories as to why a Ouija board works (when and if it does):

1. The Spiritualist Theory. Forces or spirits from beyond our world are contacted by your use of the board, and they're moving the planchette. *Evidence for:* It sure seems like the thing is moving by itself, sometimes giving answers you don't expect. *Evidence against:* Try using the board with both people blindfolded and see how well the "all-seeing spirits" do.

2. The Ideomotor Theory. You are moving the indicator,

but don't consciously know it. It may be a mild form of self-hypnotism in which your hands move as if they're not in your control. So some say that the Ouija board can be used as a shortcut to knowing your unconscious mind. *Evidence for:* While people are often surprised at what comes from it, they are just as often not at all surprised when they get the message they expected. *Evidence against:* It's hard for people to imagine that you wouldn't "know" you're moving the indicator.

3. The Other Person's A Big Fat Liar Theory. This theory holds that both partners will usually deny manipulating the planchette, and that at least one is lying. *Evidence for:* How many Ouija sessions have ended with the two partners struggling as if arm wrestling to spell out the answer each wants? *Evidence against:* Very trustworthy people have sworn convincingly that they hadn't deliberately cheated, yet still got messages.

STRANGE OUIJA STORIES

• One woman in the early twentieth century claimed that she had contacted the spirit of Mark Twain. Although in his life he preferred a typewriter for writing (in fact, was the first published writer to use one), she said that she wrote a novel that he dictated by Ouija board. However, the book, called *Jap Heron,* was clearly inferior to the mortal Twain's works (one reviewer sniffed that apparently "Twain left more than his body when he passed over to the other side").

• The Ouija has also been tried on the other end of the criminal justice system with equally disastrous results. Four jurors in a murder trial in England allegedly used a Ouija board to ask the victim who had killed him. They convicted the accused murderer ... and their use of the board became the basis for an automatic appeal.

• Although many have tried this with no good results, at least one person, Iris

Maloney, won $1.4 million in a state lottery after consulting a Ouija board.

• Ghosts, high spirits, or mass hysteria came into play when ten Alberta teenagers went berserk while playing with a Ouija board, striking at "something in the air" with their fists. Worried parents called a local minister who performed a "spiritual cleansing" on the teens, and everything returned to normal.

• While most adults believe Ouija to be a harmless game, some fundamentalist Christians believe the Ouija is, as one put it, "the quickest and easiest way to become possessed by demons." One fundamentalist Web page earnestly warns of "spirit possession, insanity, financial ruin, adultery and divorce, criminal acts (including murder), and other tragedies" from using the Ouija board.

• This sort of fearmongering isn't new. Some mediums—perhaps not wanting the competition—have also issued grave warnings about Ouija dangers. One "Dr. Curry from the State Insane Asylum of New Jersey" was quoted in the 1930s as predicting that "insane asylums will be flooded with patients if interest in Ouija boards continues."

That was seventy years, and millions of boards ago. By some accounts, the Ouija continues to outsell all other games besides Monopoly. Which game is more injurious to mental health and the soul—the ghosts of the Ouija or the unforgiving capitalism of Monopoly—has yet to be determined.

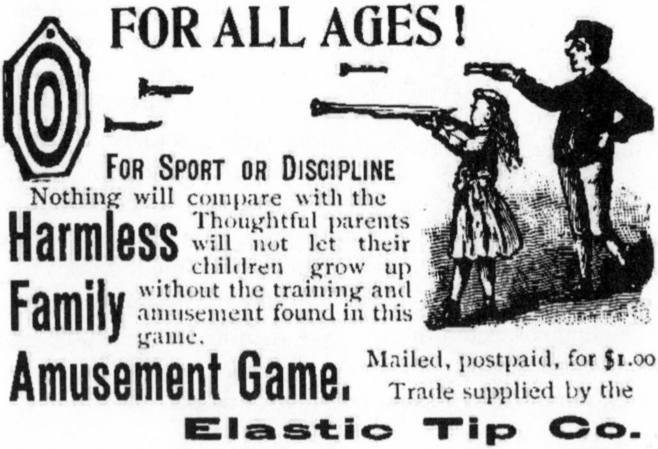

The Last Leaf

A Story of Love & Sacrifice by O. Henry

After being jailed for embezzling from his employer, William Sydney Porter borrowed the name of a prison guard named Orrin Henry and began writing stories about life in New York. This is one.

In a little district west of Washington Square the streets have run crazy and broken themselves into small strips called "places." So, to quaint old Greenwich Village the art people soon came prowling, hunting for north windows and 18th-century gables and Dutch attics and low rents.

At the top of a squatty, three-story brick Sue and Johnsy had their studio. "Johnsy" was familiar for Joanna. One was from Maine; the other from California. They had met and found their tastes so congenial that the joint studio resulted.

That was in May. In November, Pneumonia stalked about the colony, touching one here and there with his icy fingers. A little woman with blood thinned by California zephyrs was hardly fair game for the old duffer. But Johnsy he smote; and she lay, scarcely moving, on her painted iron bedstead, looking through small Dutch window-panes at the blank side of the next house.

One morning the busy doctor called Sue into the hall. "She has one chance in—let us say, ten," he said, as he shook down the mercury in his clinical thermometer. "And that chance is for her to want to live. Your little lady has made up her mind that she's not going to get well. Has she anything on her mind?"

"She wanted to paint the Bay of Naples some day," said Sue.

"Paint?—bosh! Has she anything on her mind worth thinking about twice—a man, for instance?"

"A man?" said Sue, with a jew's-harp twang in her voice. "Is a man worth—but, no, doctor; there is nothing of the kind."

"Well, it is the weakness, then," said the doctor. "I will do all that science can accomplish. But whenever my patient begins to count carriages in her funeral procession I subtract 50% from the curative power of medicines. If you will get her to ask about the new winter styles I will promise you a one-in-five chance for her, instead of one in ten."

After the doctor had gone Sue went into the workroom and cried a Japanese napkin to a pulp. Then she swaggered into Johnsy's room with her drawing board, whistling ragtime.

Johnsy lay, scarcely making a ripple under the bedclothes, with her face toward the window. Sue stopped whistling, thinking she was asleep. She arranged her board and began a pen-and-ink drawing to illustrate a magazine story. Young artists must pave their way to Art by drawing pictures for magazine stories that young authors write to pave their way to Literature.

As Sue was sketching the figure of the hero, an Idaho cowboy, she heard a low sound, several times repeated. She went quickly to the bedside. Johnsy's eyes were open wide. She was looking out the window and counting—counting backward.

"Twelve," she said, and a little later "eleven"; and then "ten," and "nine"; and then "eight" and "seven," almost together.

Sue looked solicitously out the window. What was there to count? There was only the blank side of the brick house twenty feet away. An old ivy vine climbed half up the brick wall. Its skeleton branches clung, almost bare, to the crumbling bricks.

"What is it, dear?" asked Sue. "Tell your Sudie."

"Leaves. On the ivy vine. When the last one falls I must go, too. I've known that for three days. Didn't the doctor tell you?"

"Oh, I never heard of such nonsense," complained Sue, with magnificent scorn. "Don't be a goosey. Why, the doctor told me this morning that your chances for getting well were ten to one! Why, that's almost as good a chance as when we ride on the street cars. Try to take some broth now, and let Sudie go back to her drawing, so she can buy port wine for her sick child, and pork chops for her greedy self."

"You needn't get any more wine," said Johnsy, keeping her eyes fixed out the window. "There goes another. No, I don't want any broth. That leaves just four. I want to see the last one fall before it gets dark. Then I'll go, too."

"Johnsy, dear," said Sue, bending over her, "will you promise me to not look out the window until I am done working? I don't want you to keep looking at those silly ivy leaves."

"Tell me as soon as you have finished," said Johnsy, lying still as a fallen statue, "because I want to see the last one fall. I went to turn loose my hold on everything, and go sailing down, down, just like one of those poor, tired leaves."

"Try to sleep," said Sue. "I must call Behrman up to be my model for the old hermit miner. I'll not be gone a minute. Don't try to move 'till I come back."

Old Behrman, past sixty and with a Michelangelo's Moses beard, was a failure in art. Forty years he had been always about to paint a masterpiece, but had never yet begun it. For several years he had painted nothing except now and then a daub in the line of commerce or advertising. He earned a little by serving as a model to those young artists in the colony who could not pay the price of a professional. He drank gin to excess, and still talked of his coming masterpiece, and regarded himself as mastiff-in-waiting to protect the two young artists in the studio above.

Sue found Behrman smelling strongly of gin in his dimly lighted den below. In one corner was a blank canvas on an easel that had been waiting there for 25 years to receive the first line of the masterpiece. She told him of Johnsy's fancy, and how she feared she would, indeed, light and fragile as a leaf herself, float away when her slight hold upon the world grew weaker.

Old Behrman, with his red eyes, plainly streaming, shouted his contempt and derision for such idiotic imaginings.

"Vass!" he cried. "Is dere people mit der foolishness to die because leafs dey drop off from a confounded vine? Ach, dot poor lettle Miss Johnsy. No, I will not bose as a model for your fool hermit-dunderhead."

"The fever has left her mind full of strange fancies," said Sue. "Very well, Mr. Behrman, if you do not care to pose, you needn't. But I think you are a horrid old flibbertigibbet."

"You are just like a woman!" yelled Behrman. "Who said I will not bose? Go on. I come mit you. Gott! dis is not any blace in which one so goot as Miss Yohnsy shall lie sick. Some day I vill baint a masterpiece, and ve shall all go away. Gott! yes."

Johnsy was sleeping when they went upstairs. Sue motioned Behrman into the other room. In there they peered out fearfully at the ivy vine. A cold rain was falling, mingled with snow. Then they looked at each other without speaking. Behrman took his seat as the hermit miner on an upturned kettle.

When Sue awoke from an hour's sleep the next morning she found Johnsy with dull, wide-open eyes staring at the drawn green shade. "Pull it up; I want to see," she whispered.

Wearily Sue obeyed. But, lo! after the beating rain and fierce gusts of wind through the night, there yet stood out against the brick wall one ivy leaf. Still dark green near its stem, but with its serrated edges tinted with the yellow of decay, it hung bravely from a branch some twenty feet above the ground.

"It is the last one," said Johnsy. "I thought it would surely fall during the night. It will fall today, and I shall die with it."

"Dear!" said Sue, leaning down to the pillow, "think of me, if you won't think of yourself. What would I do?" But Johnsy did not answer. The lonesomest thing in the world is a soul making ready to go on its mysterious, far journey.

The day wore away, and even through the twilight they could see the lone ivy leaf clinging to its stem against the wall. With the night the north wind was again loosed, while the rain pattered down from the low Dutch eaves. When it was light enough Johnsy commanded that the shade be raised.

The ivy leaf was still there.

Johnsy lay for a long time looking at it. And then she called to Sue, who was stirring her chicken broth over the gas stove.

"I've been a bad girl, Sudie," said Johnsy. "Something has made that last leaf stay there to show me how wicked I was to want to die. You may bring me broth now, and some milk with a little port in it, and I will sit up and watch you cook."

An hour later she said, "Sudie, some day I hope to paint the Bay of Naples."

The doctor came in the afternoon, and Sue had an excuse to go into the hallway as he left.

"Even chances," said the doctor, taking Sue's thin, shaking hand in his. "With good nursing you'll win. And now I must see another case downstairs. Behrman, his name is—some kind of an artist, I believe. Pneumonia, too. He is an old, weak man, and there is no hope for him; but he goes to the hospital today to be made more comfortable."

The next day the doctor said to Sue: "She's out of danger. You've won. Nutrition and care now—that's all."

And that afternoon Sue came to the bed where Johnsy lay, contentedly knitting a very blue and very useless woolen shoulder scarf, and put one arm around her, pillows and all.

"I have something to tell you, white mouse," she said. "Mr. Behrman died of pneumonia today in the hospital. He was ill only two days. The janitor found him on the morning of the first day in his room downstairs helpless with pain. His shoes and clothing were wet through and icy cold. They couldn't imagine where he had been on such a dreadful night. And then they found a lantern, still lighted, and a ladder that had been dragged from its place, and some scattered brushes, and a palette with green and yellow colors mixed on it, and—look out the window, dear, at the last ivy leaf on the wall. Didn't you wonder why it never fluttered or moved when the wind blew? Ah, darling, it's Behrman's masterpiece—he painted it there the night that the last leaf fell."

LOOKING BACK AT GREENWICH VILLAGE

There was a time when Greenwich Village really was a village, back when New York City was just a small city at the southern tip of Manhattan. Once a swamp, Greenwich became first a tobacco farm, then a small town miles from the big city. It became a refuge for the rich, then eventually a writers' and artists' haven as the rich moved to more fashionable parts of the city.

Some literary highlights:

• O. Henry got his inspiration for his story "The Last Leaf" from the gate at 10 Grove Street.

• Louisa May Alcott wrote *Little Women* while living at 130 MacDougal Street.

• Thomas Paine reportedly wrote *Common Sense* at 59 Grove Street.

• Edgar Allen Poe wrote *The Raven* at a club at 83 West 3rd Street while living at 49 East 9th Street.

• The ever-mobile Thomas Wolfe wrote *Look Homeward, Angel* in three different Greenwich Village apartments.

Word Thieves 2

Some Terms We've Borrowed from the Dutch

Here's some confusion: The "Pennsylvania Dutch" were really German ("Deutsch"). However, real Dutch did come to North America, and added some words to our language.

aardvark: Dutch for "earth pig," which is what settlers called any animal that lived in the ground and looked vaguely pig-like. The African animal kept the name; Americans translated *aardvark* into "groundhog."

booze: From the Middle Dutch *busen,* meaning "drink heavily."

boss: From the Dutch *baas,* meaning "master."

cole slaw: It has nothing to do with "cold" or somebody named "Cole." It came from *koolsla,* meaning "cabbage" and "salad."

cookies: From *koekje,* meaning "little cake."

cruller: From *kruller,* meaning "to curl."

dope: From *doop,* which was a Dutch dipping sauce made of suspiciously murky ingredients.

easel: From *ezel,* meaning "ass," as in beast of burden.

hunky-dory: In tag games, Dutch children try to reach what they call *honk,* the safe base where they can't be tagged. So the word came to mean, "safe, fine."

mannequin: From *mannekijn* ("little man").

poppycock: From *pappekak* ("soft dung").

Santa Claus: From *Sinter Klaus* ("Saint Nicholas"), we got both the name and the general idea of what the holiday gift-bringer looks and acts like from the Dutch.

snoop: From the word *snoepen,* which means to secretively eat sweets.

waffle: From the Dutch word *wafel,* which came in turn from the French *gauffre* ("honeycomb"), so named because of the pastry's pattern.

Flornithology I

How to Tell the Birds from the Flowers

We now present this helpful field guide by Robert Williams Wood (1868–1955) for those who may have trouble seeing the difference.

The Clover The Plover

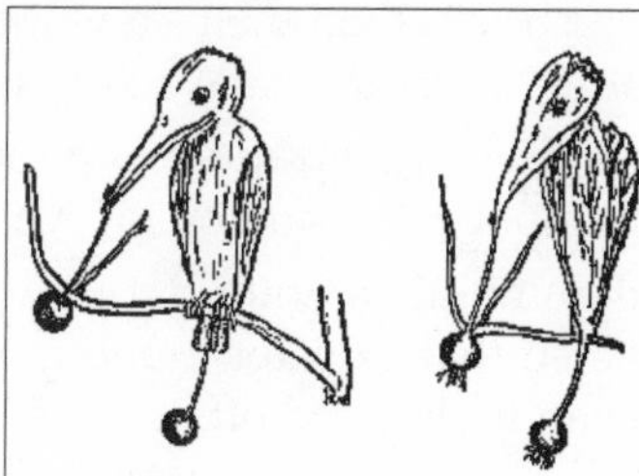

The Crow The Crocus

The Rue The Rooster

The Pelican The Panicle

The Pea The Pewee

The Parrot The Carrot

Potty Pourri

Random Kinds of Factness

• Listen up, architects: Women take nearly twice as long to use the restroom than men—a whopping 34 seconds longer. Women should, therefore, have nearly twice as many facilities.

• The U.S. organization with the most members is the American Automobile Association, or AAA.

• Hammurabi's Code of Law, enacted in 1780 B.C. in Babylon, dictated that a doctor found guilty of malpractice was to have his hands chopped off.

• Even though they may happen to have an orangy glow, the name orangutan actually comes from the Malay language and means "person of the forest."

• According to Gillette, if you're male and didn't shave your face for sixteen years, you'd theoretically gain an extra pound in hair—a beard that runs about 30 feet long.

• In Egypt, where cats were sacred, citizens followed a rule of thumb in a house fire: Save the cat first.

• Afraid of picking up the latest infection while out in public? You're suffering from mysophobia.

• You may know red herrings are smoked herrings, and that they're pretty stinky. But did you know that escaped prisoners once used them to throw tracking dogs off their scent? That's how "red herring" came to mean "diversionary tactic."

• Christmas, plum pudding, and mince pie were made illegal in England and its American colonies in 1647. Blame Oliver Cromwell and the Puritans.

• Confused about the difference between molybdomancy and myomancy? We're not surprised. Molybdomancers tell the future by dropping melted lead into water; myomancers tell the future by watching the behavior of mice.

Warts and All

Sure, we have more effective ways to get rid of warts today, but they involve knives and chemicals. Here are some creative cures for warts from days gone by.

• Folk remedies from the Appalachian Mountains were plenty. One involved spit, heavy with tobacco juice, and an incantation. The other used fatty meat rubbed on the wart, then bound in white cloth and buried under running water.

• In Mongolia they used red thread. After tying the wart with the thread, the string was then hung over a door hinge. The wart was expected to be cured within days.

• Russians believed that smearing bear or beaver fat directly onto a wart would heal it quickly. This is still touted today among some country folk as a legitimate cure.

• In an old Native American cure, a pepper pod was tied around the wart daily until the wart disappeared.

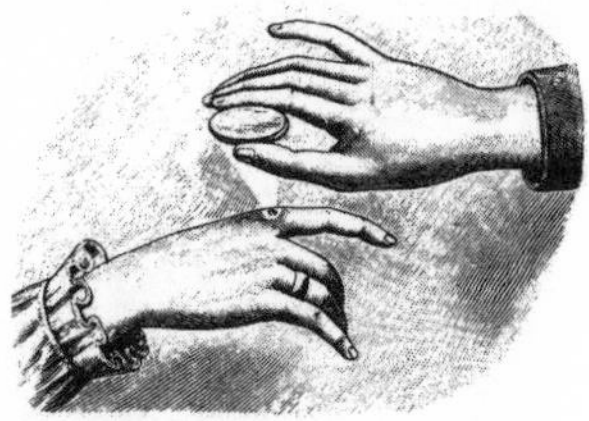

The magnifying glass treatment

• In nineteenth century America, it wasn't uncommon to burn off a wart using the sun and a magnifying glass. A less painful way was to find someone who would be willing to "buy" the wart. Still another was to secretly rub the wart against somebody who had fathered a child out of wedlock.

• In Merry Ol' England, *De Morbis Cutaneis* by Daniel Turner prescribed extracts from various medicinal herbs, but if that didn't work, patients were treated to a dose of corrosive brimstone, or went under the knife.

• Another folk cure of the same place and time counseled folks to rub an apple on the wart and feed it to a pig.

• A traditional folk cure in Western Europe involved sprinkling a snail with salt, then rubbing the juices on the wart.

• Explorer and writer Francis Bacon rubbed pork fat on his warts, then hung the fat in the sun to rot. He swore by this method, which was especially apt, considering his name.

• In ancient Rome, at least one doctor was known for his unique method of curing warts. He bit off the skin that stuck out, then sucked on the place where the wart had once been.

• The Irish had a unique ceremony for wart removals: While rubbing the wart with a dirty washcloth, you must say, "Away, away, away," then bury the washcloth.

• A variation on this was to "conjure" the wart into a snail, then skewer the creature with a thorn and leave it there to die. As the snail dries up, so should the wart.

• Swiss misses once believed that if they rubbed their warts on stones and left them at an intersection, the next person to come along would contract the wart.

• "Take an sticke of greene oke woode laie that in the fier to burne and keepe the water therof which wil ishew out at the ends and therwith anoint the wartes. Use and follow that well twisse or thrisse a daie rubbing the warts well therwith and that will take them cleane awaie for ever as cleare as if youe never haid had any." —17th century wart-removing recipe from the National Archives of Scotland

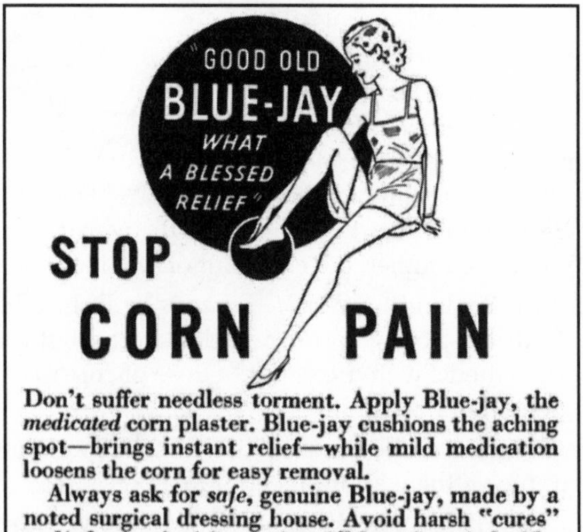

He Said/She Said

All's fair use in love and war.

"As long as a woman can look ten years younger than her own daughter, she is perfectly satisfied." —Oscar Wilde.

"Making coffee has become the great compromise of the decade. It's the only thing 'real' men do that doesn't seem to threaten their masculinity. To women, it's on the same domestic entry level as putting the spring back into the toilet-tissue holder or taking a chicken out of the freezer to thaw." —Erma Bombeck

"A woman's place is in the car." —Vinnie Barbarino, *Welcome Back, Kotter*

"Men read maps better than women because only men can understand the concept of an inch equaling a hundred miles." —Roseanne Barr

"Women: Can't live with 'em, can't stuff 'em in a sack." —Larry, *Newhart*

"The male is a domestic animal which, if treated with firmness and kindness, can be trained to do most things." —Jilly Cooper

"Direct thought is not an attribute of femininity. In this, women are now centuries behind man." —Thomas Edison

"Men are nothing but lazy lumps of drunken flesh. They crowd you in bed, get you all worked up, and then before you can say, 'Is that all there is?' that's all there is."
—Latka's mother, *Taxi*

"Women's intuition is the result of millions of years of not thinking."
—Rupert Hughes

"Men are such idiots and I married their king." —Peg Bundy, *Married ... with Children*

"When a woman becomes a scholar there is usually something wrong with her sexual organs."
—Friedrich Nietzsche

"What are the three words guaranteed to humiliate men everywhere? 'Hold my purse.'"
—Francois Morency

"Nature intended women to be our slaves. They are our property."
—Napoleon Bonaparte

"Whatever women do they must do twice as well as men to be thought half as good. Luckily, this is not difficult."
—Charlotte Whitton

"Men are superior to women. For one thing, men can urinate from a speeding car."
—Will Durst

"The only time a woman really succeeds in changing a man is when he's a baby."
—Natalie Wood

"Go see a girl? I'd rather smell a skunk!" —Beaver Cleaver, *Leave It to Beaver*

Clerk: *"You know what the fastest way to a man's heart is?"*
Roseanne: *"Yeah, through his chest!"* —Roseanne Conner, *Roseanne*

"If women didn't exist, all the money in the world would have no meaning."
—Aristotle Onassis

"I married beneath me. All women do." —Nancy Astor

"I'll never understand women if I live to be thirty!"
—Richard Harrison, *The Patty Duke Show*

"Don't accept rides from strange men, and remember that all men are strange." —Robin Morgan

"A dame is like a bottle of milk: If she hangs around long enough, she turns sour."
—Bluto, *Popeye Cartoon Show*

"Men are simple things. They can survive a whole weekend with only three things: beer, boxer shorts and batteries for the remote control."
—Diana Jordan

"Women are like elephants. Everyone likes to look at them but no-one likes to have to keep one." —W. C. Fields

Strange Bible Tales

Mighty Odd Stories from the Good Book

There are a lot of Bible verses you won't necessarily hear your preacher using as a text. In fact, most believers haven't even run across them.

GOD ADMITS MAKING A MISTAKE. THEN HE CONTEMPLATES WIPING ALL LIFE OFF THE EARTH (GENESIS 6:5–7)

And God saw that the wickedness of humanity was great in the world, and that every imagination of his thoughts and heart were continuously evil.

And the Lord regretted that he had made people, and it grieved him in his heart. And the Lord said, "I will destroy man, whom I have created, from the face of the earth; man, and beast, and every creeping thing, and the fowls of the air; for I am sorry that I made them."

GOD SAYS YOU DIE IF YOU SMART OFF TO YOUR MOM (EXODUS 21:15)

"And he that curses his father, or his mother, shall surely be put to death."

GOD SANCTIONS OWNING SLAVES, DIVIDING THEIR FAMILIES, AND BEATING THEM (WITHIN REASON) (EXODUS 21:2–6, 20–21)

"If you buy an Hebrew servant, six years he shall serve: and in the seventh he shall go out free for nothing. If he came in by himself, he shall go out by himself: if he were married, then his wife shall go out with him. If his master has given him a wife, and she have born him sons or daughter, the wife and her children shall be her master's, and he shall go out by himself.

"And if the servant shall plainly say, I love my master, my wife, and my children; I will not go out free: Then his master shall bring him unto the judges; he shall also bring him to the door, or unto the door post; and his master shall bore his ear through with an awl; and he shall serve him for ever.

"However, if a man sells his daughter as a female slave, she is not to go free as the male slaves do.

"If a man smite his servant, or his maid, with a rod, and he die under his hand; he shall be surely punished. However, if the slave survives a day or two, the master shall not be punished, for he is his property."

EARTH GIRLS ARE EASY FOR THE SONS OF GOD (GENESIS 6:2–4)

Now it came about, when men began to multiply on the face of the land, and daughters were born to them, that the sons of God saw the daughters of men that they were fair; and they took them wives of all which they chose. And the Lord said, "My spirit shall not always strive with man, for that he also is flesh: yet his days shall be an hundred and twenty years."

There were giants in the earth in those days; and after the sons of God came in to the daughters of men, they bore children with them also, which became mighty men of renown.

GOD GOES TO AN INN TO KILL MOSES FOR NOT CIRCUMSIZING HIS SON, BUT HIS WIFE SAVES HIM WITH A QUICK CUT (EXODUS 4:23–26)

And it came to pass by the way in the inn, that the Lord met him, and sought to kill him. Then Zipporah took a sharp stone, and cut off the foreskin of her son, and cast it at his feet, and said, "Surely a bloody husband you are to me." So he let him go: then she said, "A bloody husband thou art, because of the circumcision."

GOD KILLS ONE OF JUDAH'S SONS FOR WICKEDNESS, THEN ANOTHER FOR PRACTICING COITUS INTERRUPTUS WITH HIS BROTHER'S WIDOW. MEANWHILE, JUDAH UNKNOWINGLY IMPREGNATES THE SAME WOMAN (HIS DAUGHTER-IN-LAW), & DECIDES TO BURN HER ALIVE... (GENESIS 36:2–27)

Judah saw there a daughter of a certain Canaanite whose name was Shua. And he took her, and went in unto her. And she conceived, and bare a son; and he called his name Er. And she conceived again, and bare a son; and she called his name Onan. And she yet again bare a son, and called his name Shelah: and he was at Chezib, when she bare him.

And Judah took a wife for Er his firstborn, and her name was Tamar. And Er, Judah's firstborn, was wicked in the sight of Jehovah. So God killed him.

And Judah said unto Onan, "Go in unto thy brother's wife, and perform the duty of a husband's brother unto her, and raise up seed to your brother."

But Onan knew that the seed would not be his; and it came to pass, when he went in unto his brother's wife, that he spilled his seed on the ground, lest he should give seed to his brother. And the thing which he did was evil in the sight of Jehovah. God killed him also.

Then Judah said to Tamar his daughter-in-law, "Remain a widow in thy father's house, till Shelah my son be grown up, lest he also die, like his brethren." And Tamar went and dwelt in her father's house.

And in process of time Shua's daughter, the wife of Judah, died; and Judah was comforted, and went up unto his sheep-shearers to Timnah, he and his friend Hirah the Adullamite.

And it was told Tamar, saying, "Behold, thy father-in-law goes up to Timnah to shear his sheep." And she put off from her the garments of her widowhood, and covered herself with her veil, and wrapped herself, and sat in the gate of Enaim, which is by the way to Timnah; for she saw that Shelah had grown up, but she was not given unto him to wife.

When Judah saw her, he thought her to be a harlot; for she had covered her face. And he turned unto her by the way, and said, "Come, I pray, let me come into you," for he knew not that she was his daughter-in-law. And she said, "What will you give me, that you may come in unto me?"

And he said, "I will send you a kid from my goat flock." And she said, "Will you give me a pledge, until you send it?" And he said, "What pledge shall I give you?" And she said, "Your seal, your cord, and your staff." And he gave them to her, and came in to her, and she conceived by him.

And she arose, and went away, and put off her veil from her, and put on the garments of her widowhood. And Judah sent the his friend Adullamite to deliver the kid of the goats and retrieve the pledge: but he found her not. Then he asked the men of her place, saying, "Where is the temple prostitute, that was at Enaim by the wayside?" And they said, "There has been no prostitute here." And he returned to Judah, and said, "I have not found her; and also the men of the place said, 'There has been no prostitute here.'" And Judah said, "Let her keep them before we become a laughingstock: I sent this kid, but you did not find her."

About three months later, Judah was told, "Tamar your daughter-in-law hath played the harlot; and moreover, she is with child by whoredom." And Judah said, "Bring her forth, and let her be burnt!" When she was brought forth, she sent to her father-in-law, saying, "By the man, whose these are, am I with child," and she said, "Look and see, whose are these, the seal, the cords, and the staff?"

And Judah acknowledged them, and said, "She is more righteous than I; considering that I gave her not to Shelah my son." And he did not have sex with her ever again.

GOD KILLS THE FIRSTBORN CHILDREN OF EGYPTIANS ... AND FOR GOOD MEASURE, THE FIRSTBORN CATTLE, TOO (EXODUS 12:29)

And it came to pass, that at midnight the Lord smote all the firstborn in the land of Egypt, from the firstborn of Pharaoh that sat on his throne unto the firstborn of the captive that was in the dungeon; and all the firstborn of cattle.

GOD COMMANDS GENOCIDE AND LIVESTOCK KILLING; THE ISRAELIS KILL THE PEOPLE, BUT KEEP THE LIVESTOCK (I SAMUEL 15:2–9)

Thus said the Lord of hosts, "I remember that which Amalek did to Israel, how he laid wait for him in the way, when he came up from Egypt. Now go and smite Amalek, and utterly destroy all that they have, and spare them not; but slay both man and woman, infant and suckling, ox and sheep, camel and ass."

And Saul gathered the people together, and numbered them in Telaim, 200,000 footmen, and 10,000 men of Judah.... And Saul took Agag the king of the Amalekites alive, and utterly destroyed all the people with the edge of the sword. But Saul and the people spared Agag, and the best of the sheep, and of the oxen, and of the fatlings, and the lambs, and all that was good, and would not utterly destroy them: but every thing that was vile and refuse, that they destroyed utterly.

Gone Today...
Hair Tomorrow

You say Rogaine hasn't done the trick? Consider some of these old folk remedies for baldness.

• Medieval doctors from Western Europe would've prescribed an ointment made of oil and the ashes of burned bees.

• Another medieval cure consisted of rubbing goose pellets directly onto the scalp.

• Globe-topped citizens in the West Indies still rub the oils of hot chili peppers onto their scalps until they feel the tingle. (The main chemical in chilis is capsicum—the same tingling ingredient in the dandruff shampoo Denorex. It doesn't cure baldness and it doesn't get rid of dandruff, but it sure feels like it's doing *something* up there.)

• Native Americans also used chili pepper oil, but they mixed it with yucca root. This mixture (or variations) were sold to balding men well into the twentieth century. The silent movie director D. W. Griffith had an early career as a traveling salesman, hawking this very remedy under the name "Yuccatone."

• Doctors in ancient Egypt mixed up a quick solution of hedgehog hairs, human fingernails in hippo, lion, or crocodile fat to bring back hair.

• In America in the 1800s, cantharidine and rosemary were used in hair tonics to cure baldness. Cantharidine is a burning chemical derived from crushed beetles, also known as Spanish Fly.

• As tea is the cure to all ills in England, it's not surprising that balding Englishmen in the 1600s used a combination of lemon with tea imported from India.

• It pays to be a famous doctor. When ancient Greek Hypocrites was going bald, he used flower oil, dove poop, and opium to stop the hair loss. It didn't work, but hey, he was happy, although stinky.

• If you can't beat 'em....When the usual ancient Roman cure of boiled snake tonic didn't work, they just painted curls right onto their heads.

• When treating hair loss in thirteenth-century Hungary, nothing short of a rosemary and wine ointment would do.

• From an early eighteenth-century course on Herbalism, held at the Royal College of Physicians and Surgeons of Glasgow, Scotland: "Some choice medices fo the fulling of the heir from the head: 1. Beat linseeds very well: and mix them with sillet oyl and when you have well mixed them anoint the head therwith and in three or four times rinsing it: it will help you. 2. For the falling of the haire by reson of a scald head warm a litle oil of tartar that which is made by deliguium and rub your head with it and in a litle the heare will come again. 3. For beldiness in the head Anoint with the oil of Lizeards and the beldness will grow once again."

• As recently as the early 1900s, such methods as electric hair brushes were used to cure baldness. It was believed to shock hair follicles into producing again. At the same time, scalp vacuuming came into vogue. Charlatans hawking this service claimed the vacuum would unclog blocked pores.

***"The tenderest spot in a man's makeup is sometimes the bald spot on top of his head."* —Helen Rowland**

Razor's Edge

A Man Who Would Be King Gives a Close Shave

You can measure success by how close you come to your aspirations. King C. Gillette became an inventor of a new way to remove hair. But what he *really* wanted was to be president of the world.

King Camp Gillette was an eccentric who wanted to be leader of the world, but at least he came by his eccentricity honestly. First of all, there was his name, given in honor of his father's friend, Judge King (that was his given name—just as King Gillette wasn't really a king, Judge wasn't really a judge).

Then there was his mom, Fanny Lemira Camp, who was author of *The White House Cookbook,* a classic cookbook that made its debut in 1887; for most of King's childhood, his mom served up experimental recipes like Georgia Possum Pie or Rattlesnake Filet and took post-dinner polls on whether to include them in her cookbook.

Gillette's father, George, was a postmaster and part-time inventor whose hardware supply business had been wiped out by the Chicago Fire in 1871. In 1872, seventeen-ear-old King followed his father's footsteps and joined a hardware supply business as a traveling sales rep. While on the road, King filled his spare time by inventing things. In 1879, he patented a combination bushing and valve for faucets. Ten years later he patented two new types of electrical conduits. None of his inventions made him any significant money, but he continued his tinkering.

One of his bosses understood his drive to invent. He was William Painter, president of the Baltimore Seal Company, himself a successful inventor. One of Painter's money-making inventions was a soft rubber valve used in emptying cesspools and privy pits. But the one that made him rich beyond dreams was the Crown Cork, the cork-lined metal bottle cap still in use today.

Painter adopted Gillette as a protégé and personal friend. In 1885, he gave Gillette a piece of advice that eventually changed his life: "Why don't you try to come up with something like the Crown Cork, which, when used, is thrown away? The customer keeps coming back for more; with each additional customer you get, you are building a foundation of profit."

"That sounds simple enough," replied King, "but how many things are there like corks, pins, and needles?"

Painter paused, thoughtfully. "You don't know. It isn't probable that you will ever find anything that is like the Crown Cork, but it won't do any harm to think about it." King did, to a point of obsession. He kept his mind constantly busy, watching life around him and waiting for inspiration to hit. He went through the dictionary, compiling page after page of things people needed, but for the longest time, he couldn't think of anything that people would want to use once and then throw away.

That's when a different kind of revelation hit. It had nothing to do with inventing things. It was bigger than that, *much* bigger. Gillette's revelation had to do with reinventing humanity's place in the entire social and economic system.

It came to him in a hotel room in Scranton, Pennsylvania. A heavy storm was raging and the rain fell in torrents. Normally dependable to a fault, Gillette decided to cancel his appointments for the day. He sat in his room, looking out at the rain-snarled traffic below his window. In the wind and rain, a disorganized mess of horses, buggies, and pedestrians had achieved a pre-auto state of gridlock.

First, Gillette tried to figure out ways that the snarl could have been avoided; then his mind was blown far adrift. Looking down on the disabled grocery wagon that had caused the snarl, he began imagining what was inside and where it came from, tracing coffee back through grinding and roasting to plantations in Brazil, sugar back to the cane fields of Cuba, and spices back to Asia.

Until that point, he wrote later, he had always thought of the world's industries as separate, independent entities. But suddenly "came the thought that is destined to change man's conception of industry. THE THOUGHT—Industry as a whole is one vast operative mechanism. Included in it are the governments of every country, and

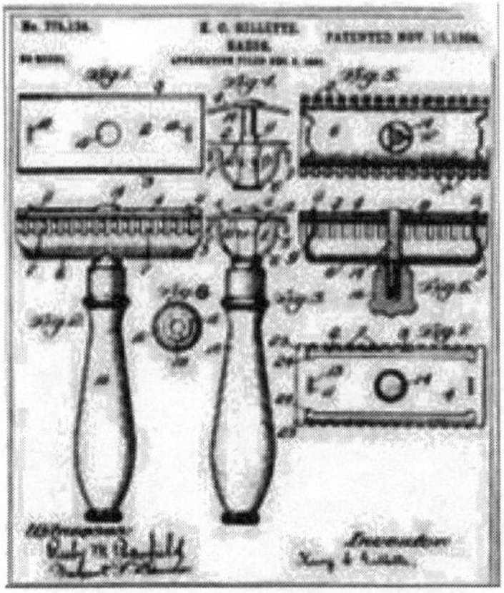

our combined system of social, political and industrial economy." He began seeing the whole world as one giant machine. But that machine was running inefficiently and needed someone who could put it back in order through "the displacement of governments and the amalgamation of all the people in the world into one corporate body, with one corporate brain."

Gillette decided that he was that someone. He decided to write a book: a practical, step-by-step guide to centralize the entire world into one gigantic corporation. He put away the idea of inventing gadgets and began reinventing the world.

In the summer of 1894, he finished his book, *The Human Drift,* and got it published. He sat back and waited for the world to see the rightness of his cause and began readying himself to take over as head of the worldwide Twentieth Century Company. His book began getting glowing reviews in utopian and socialist publications. Letters of support started filling his mailbox, some of them containing money to buy shares in Twentieth Century.

But, as he waited to become the world's chairman of the board, the next revelation struck, the one that would sidetrack him from his world-saving goals.

It happened while doing his morning ablutions in a hotel room. "On one particular morning when I started to shave, I found my razor dull, and it was not only dull, but was beyond the point of successful stropping and it needed honing, for which it must be taken to a barber or a cutler," he wrote years later. "As I stood there with the razor in my hand, my eyes resting on it lightly as a bird settling down on its nest...the thought occurred to me that no radical improvements had been made in razors, especially in razor blades, for several centuries, and it flashed through my mind that if by any possibility razor blades could be constructed and made cheap enough to do away with honing and stropping and permit the user to replace dull blades by new ones, such improvements would be highly important in that art.... The Gillette razor was born."

Well, not quite. It took another eight years for Gillette to work out the practical details, assisted by an engineer with the name William E. Nickerson (can you imagine the marketing difficulties if the razor had been named after him?). Expert cutlers and metallurgists said that it couldn't be done, but Gillette continued trying new metals and various designs. He finally worked out all the bugs and made the razor available to the public in 1903.

His company sold only 51 razors and 168 blades that year. Gillette continued to earn his living as a traveling salesman for Crown Cork and Seal. In September that year, he was assigned to a selling route in England, giving him a raise he couldn't afford to turn down. He went across the sea, reluctantly leaving the Gillette Razor Company in the hands of its board of directors.

While he was gone, the company seemed about to go under and the board considered selling its assets and going out of business. But suddenly sales figures began to climb, helped along by good word-of-mouth and an extremely modest level of advertising. The company sold 91,000 razors and 123,000 blades in 1904. In November of that year, Gillette resigned his sales position and returned home.

But he was still interested in utopian politics. He wrote more books. He put his name and picture on each package of blades to increase his fame, still hoping to be made leader of the world by public acclaim. Later, when it became clear that the world was not buying his leadership role, he offered the former president, Teddy Roosevelt, $1 million to serve as the head of the "World Corporation." But Teddy declined, and when Gillette died in 1931, the world revolution he dreamed about still had not come about. To his profound disappointment, Gillette didn't become renowned for having *saved* humanity; instead, he became famous for having *shaved* it.

Escape Artist

How to Avoid a Tiger Attack

Tigers attack humans often. Not because they like the way we taste (we're pretty bony and bland) but because they're ultimately lazy animals that will take what they can get.

Although it probably won't happen often at your local zoo, tigers munch down on dozens of humans a year. Here are a few ways to avoid being a tiger's next lunch:

1. When you're out in the wild, be aware of your surroundings. Is there dense jungle where something could hide without being noticed? Are you near a river that's a known watering hole for wild animals? If so, stay clear of these places.

2. But say your route must take you through the jungle. Then what? Use your nose. Tigers are solitary creatures like our house cats, and spray their scent to mark their territory. Their urine smells very similar to buttered popcorn. So if you start smelling something in the jungle that smells like a movie snack bar, watch out. You could be in a tiger's territory.

3. People swear this works: wear a mask on the back of your head. Tigers only pounce from behind. If you're not offering them a behind, they've been known to get confused and give up. Many natives in India have tried this method and found the tigers eventually slink off into the jungle, thoroughly demoralized.

4. But say your stalking tiger is smart and your mask fails you. Then what? Well, you can't outrun a tiger, so the only chance you've got is to face the tiger—again, taking away the option of attacking from behind—and stand your ground. Showing fear will be your downfall, so stand your ground. Good luck!

Lemming Aid

TRACKING THE MYTH OF LEMMING SUICIDE

The metaphor of lemmings following the crowd to their death is such an irresistible story. Too bad it's not true.

HOW DID THE MYTH BEGIN that lemmings commit suicide *en masse*? They don't, you know. Not even the really, really depressed ones. Yet, people still want to believe the story and use it as a metaphor for everything from the behavior of stock market investors to religious cult members to the peer group behavior of teens.

Not that many would care if lemmings really did have a tendency for mass suicide. They're nasty little things that look like voles. They reproduce like rabbits, popping out as many as thirteen babies every three weeks.

While there are other breeds, including an American variety, the most famous is the Norway lemming that lives in the tundra and grasslands of Scandinavia. These are the ones that are allegedly suicidal. In reality, though, that's wishful thinking, because lemmings are actually *homicidal.* As we said, they're nasty little things.

WHY LEMMINGS ARE SO DARNED NASTY

In the warm spring when grass is plentiful, the lemming population rises at an alarmingly unsustainable rate. By summer, desperation kicks in, and things turn ugly. Adults fight to the death for breeding territory; lemming moms raid the nests of their neighbors and kill their young, no doubt laughing maniacally while they do so.

Since all this carnage isn't enough to solve the population problem, the animals disperse from their nesting grounds in search of food and living space. They don't formally migrate in a huge mass; it just looks that way. "A booming population of near-sighted, physically clumsy rodents stumbling down Norway's numerous funnel-shaped gullies is what produced the massive migration look," reported an article in *Canadian Geographic.* True, a number of lemmings may accidentally fall over the edge of a narrow mountain path or get washed away while fording fjords and streams, but they don't intentionally kill themselves. Actually, most of the lemmings that die along the way are eaten by predators taking advantage of the free protein that's ambling by.

THE DISNEY CONNECTION

Which brings up another layer of lemming-suicide myth: that a Disney film crew simply made up the suicide myth and then shot phony footage to document it.

Granted, the Disney people have a lot to answer for in spreading the story. Disney cameramen filming lemmings for *White Wilderness* (1958) were instructed by the producers to "throw them over the cliff by the bucketful if necessary" to create the spectacle of lemmings plunging into the ocean to drown.

While that is despicable on humanitarian grounds, the Disney producers didn't *create* the myth, but were in fact victims of it as well. In their cruel and dubious shenanigans, they were merely trying to capture on film an ancient story that they themselves believed to be true.

RAINING CATS & LEMMINGS

In reality, the myth goes back long before Disney. Lemming suicide stories emerged centuries earlier in Scandinavia, where people had witnessed masses of the clumsy animals falling and drowning. Over time, these myths became even more bizarre. In 1555, Swedish archbishop Olaus Magnus, in *The History of Northern Peoples,* speculated that that the only explanation for the sudden explosions of lemming populations was that they rained from the sky. This echoes an Inuit myth about the collared lemming, which they call Kilangmiutak ("that which falls from the sky").

Too bad Disney didn't show that!

Edward Lear

Landscape artist Edward Lear (1812–1888) wrote and illustrated limericks. His Book of Nonsense *is considered a masterpiece of children's literature. Just for fun, here are some excerpts.*

There was an Old Man with a beard,
Who said, "It is just as I feared!
Two Owls and a Hen,
Four Larks and a Wren,
Have all built their nests in my beard!"

There was an Old Man with a nose,
Who said, "If you choose to suppose,
That my nose is too long,
You are certainly wrong!"
That remarkable Man with a nose.

There was a Young Lady whose bonnet,
Came untied when the birds sat upon it;
But she said: "I don't care!
All the birds in the air
Are welcome to sit on my bonnet!"

There was an Old Man in a boat,
Who said, "I'm afloat, I'm afloat!"
When they said, "No! you ain't!"
He was ready to faint,
That unhappy Old Man in a boat.

There was a Young Lady of Portugal,
Whose ideas were excessively nautical:
She climbed up a tree,
To examine the sea,
But declared she would never leave Portugal.

There was a Young Lady whose eyes,
Were unique as to colour and size;
When she opened them wide,
People all turned aside,
And started away in surprise.

The was a Young Lady of Bute,
Who played on a silver-gilt flute;
She played several jigs,
To her uncle's white pigs,
That amusing Young Lady of Bute.

There was a Young Lady whose nose,
Was so long that it reached to her toes;
So she hired an Old Lady,
Whose conduct was steady,
To carry that wonderful nose.

There was an Old Lady whose folly,
Induced her to sit on a holly;
Whereon by a thorn,
Her dress being torn,
She quickly became melancholy.

There was an Old Man of Cape Horn,
Who wished he had never been born;
So he sat on a chair,
Till he died of despair,
That dolorous Man of Cape Horn.

There was an Old Man of the Nile,
Who sharpened his nails with a file,
Till he cut out his thumbs,
And said calmly, "This comes
Of sharpening one's nails with a file!"

Believe It's Not Butter

Things You Didn't Know about Margarine

Have you ever wondered what that stuff is as you spread it on your bread? We give you the sometimes unsavory story behind margarine.

WHAT'S IN A NAME?

"Margarine" comes from margaric acid—an acid rendered from fat. A man named Michael Chevreul managed to isolate it almost fifty years before anyone found a use for it. Since the acid forms in shiny droplets, Chevreul named it "margaric" from the Greek word *margarites*, meaning "pearl."

THE CREATOR

Margarine itself was originally created by a man named Hippolyte Mege-Mouries in 1870. Napoleon's wars were costing the French a lot of money, and butter was in short supply. The emperor called for someone to find a substitute that could meet the demands of the people. Mege-Mouries did a little research and realized that even starving cows could produce milk that had milk fat in it. He deduced that this fat must be coming not from food intake, but from the fat of the cow itself. To test his theory, he squeezed out the fatty acids from beef fat, mixed it with milk and created oleomargarine (*oleo* being French for "beef fat"). It was a big success, and Mege-Mouries won a prize from Napoleon.

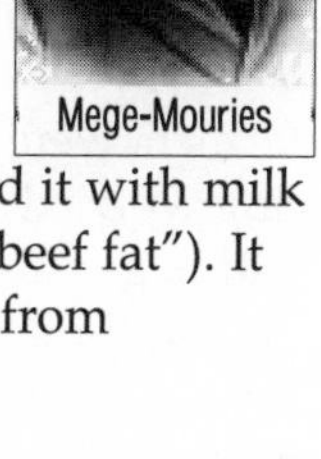
Mege-Mouries

MARGARINE COMES TO NORTH AMERICA

When the war ended in 1873 Mege-Mouries found himself with a margarine factory and zero demand for his product. He applied for a patent in the United States and moved across the Atlantic to set up shop. Things didn't pan out as he'd hoped for his company there, either, and he died in relative poverty and obscurity.

However, in 1874, the U.S. Dairy Company had bought the rights from Mege-Mouries for his invention. It built factories all over the country and began using left-over beef by-products to manufacture their "artificial butter." By 1882, the company was manufacturing more than 50,000 pounds of margarine a day. Meanwhile in Europe, the Lever Brothers and the Dutch Margarine Union also began marketing Mege-Mouries's spread.

DAIRY TRIES A SQUEEZE PLAY

With cheap margarine sweeping the Western world, dairy farmers were naturally getting worried. By 1877 they had begun using their clout to pass anti-margarine laws. In several states, for example, margarine manufacturers became subject to a $100 fine and 30 days in jail if their labels didn't clearly state that the product was margarine and not butter.

Fair enough. Unfortunately, the law didn't have the desired effect of reducing demand for margarine, so dairy interests convinced Congress to pass the Margarine Act of 1886, which mandated hefty fees for anyone making, distributing, or selling margarine. On top of that, the law levied a special tax of 2¢ for every pound of margarine consumers bought. However, margarine was still cheaper than butter, and sales didn't slow. Finally in 1902, the butter lobby got another federal tax levied: a 10¢ tax on yellow-colored margarine. Since margarine had been selling for 20¢ a pound, the tax increased the price fifty percent and made it more expensive than butter.

COLOR ME LEGAL

Dairy farmers lobbied state governments to pass more restrictive margarine laws. When consumers continued to buy the white product, states passed laws requiring margarine manufacturers to color their product an unappetizing pink. This time the dairy interests went to far: the Supreme Court ruled that the "pink margarine" law was unconstitutional.

Margarine manufacturers finally started fighting back against the restrictive laws. For example, manufacturers discovered that there was nothing in the law that prevented them from selling margarine inside a cellophane bag with a pellet of yellow food dye. Consumers could get yellow margarine by simply kneading the bag for a few minutes. Manufacturers also started making margarine from vegetable oil instead of animal fats. For years, the dairy industry had had a field day with lurid tales of diseased animals being made into margarine—vegetable oils not only preempted that campaign, but also produced a margarine with a naturally yellow hue.

A WINNING SPREAD

Dairy farmers kept fighting (and usually winning) legal battles on state and federal levels. However, the Great Depression and two World Wars solidified margarine's position in the marketplace, when consumers turned to margarine because butter was too expensive or rationed. Margarine producers teamed with the makers of vegetable oils and got the national tax on yellow margarine rescinded in 1950. Within five years every state except Minnesota and Wisconsin had repealed the laws against coloring margarine yellow (Minnesota repealed the law in 1963; Wisconsin, "The Dairy State" held out until 1967.)

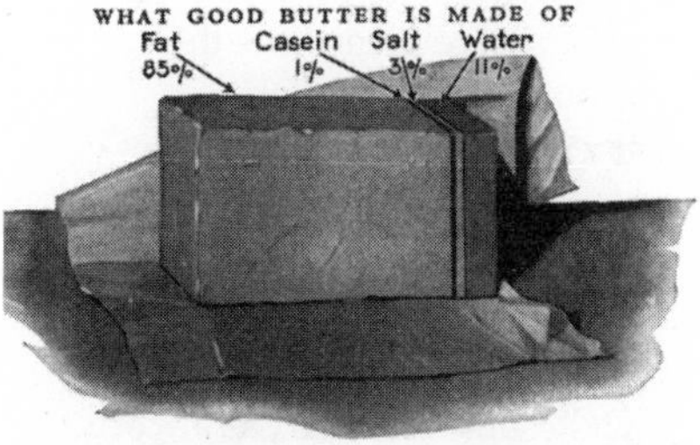

Pretty much the same: Margarine is 80% fat. Butter is 85%.

QUICK FACTS

- In the year 1930, consumers in the United States ingested about 2.6 pounds of margarine per capita, and 17.6 pounds of butter. Now butter's down to 4.2 pounds per capita while margarine's up to 8.3 pounds.
- To be called "margarine" in the United States, a spread must contain at least 15,000 IUs of vitamin A. Oil must make up eighty percent of the spread.
- If it's called a "spread" instead of "margarine," it just means that it doesn't meet the above legal standard.

The Devil's Dictionary: E

More of *The Devil's Dictionary* by Ambrose Bierce (1842–1914?)

ECCENTRICITY, *n.* A method of distinction so cheap that fools employ it to accentuate their incapacity.

ECONOMY, *n.* Purchasing the barrel of whiskey that you do not need for the price of the cow that you cannot afford.

EDIBLE, *adj.* Good to eat, and wholesome to digest, as a worm to a toad, a toad to a snake, a snake to a pig, a pig to a man, and a man to a worm.

EDUCATION, *n.* That which discloses to the wise and disguises from the foolish their lack of understanding.

EFFECT, *n.* The second of two phenomena which always occur together in the same order. The first, called a Cause, is said to generate the other—which is no more sensible than it would be for one who has never seen a dog except in the pursuit of a rabbit to declare the rabbit the cause of a dog.

EGOTIST, *n.* A person of low taste, more interested in himself than in me.

ELOQUENCE, *n.* The art of orally persuading fools that white is the color that it appears to be. It includes the gift of making any color appear white.

EMBALM, *v.i.* To cheat vegetation by locking up gases upon which it feeds. Many a dead man who ought now to be ornamenting his neighbor's lawn as a tree, or enriching his table as a bunch of radishes, is doomed to a long inutility.

ENTERTAINMENT, *n.* Any kind of amusement whose inroads stop short of death by injection.

ENTHUSIASM, *n.* A distemper of youth, curable by small doses of repentance in connection with outward applications of experience.

EPAULET, *n.* An ornamented badge, serving to distinguish a military officer from the enemy—that is to say, from the officer of lower rank to whom his death would give promotion.

EPITAPH, *n.* An inscription on a tomb, showing that virtues acquired by death have a retroactive effect.

ERUDITION, *n.* Dust shaken out of a book into an empty skull.

EXHORT, *v.t.* In religious affairs, to put the conscience of another upon the spit and roast it to a nut-brown discomfort.

EXILE, *n.* One who serves his country by residing abroad, yet is not an ambassador.

One Hump or 2?

THINGS YOU MIGHT NOT KNOW ABOUT CAMELS

They may be the Ships of the Desert, but most people don't know much about camels beyond their humps, bad tempers, and ungainly walk. Here's a quick primer.

WHAT'S IN THOSE HUMPS

Despite legend, camels don't really store water in their humps. The humps are big chunks of fat, which makes it possible for camels to go weeks without food in the desert. Why isn't their fat distributed over their bodies, like other animals? Well, ask any polar bear and you'll learn that fat is not just stored energy, it also makes a really good insulating jacket. It's why polar animals tend to look more like sumo wrestlers than ballerinas and why even penguins have a thick layer of fat on the bottoms of their feet. The last thing you'd want in the desert would be a warm layer of fat, so camels have evolved to a point where they've localized their fat in one (if Arabian) or two (if Asian) high-cholesterol lumps on the top of their bodies.

As a camel uses the stored fat in its hump, the hump gets floppy and bounces around from side to side.

HOW THEY GO WITHOUT WATER

There are other unusual heat-coping features that make camels the preferred ship of the desert. For starters, their kidneys are designed to absorb a high level of moisture from their urine. Also, their body temperature rises with the heat from 95° F. at night to more than 104° during the day—not an unusual thing with fish and amphibians, but almost never seen in mammals. It's only at the higher temperature that camels begin to sweat, and they're unusual in that they lose moisture evenly from all tissues of the body instead of just from the blood like most mammals. This allows a camel to lose 40 percent of its body weight in water loss before its life is endangered. Camels make up this water loss with binge drinking, staggering into an oasis and sucking down as much as 50 gallons at a time.

OPERATING ON A CAMEL

Camels can't lie flat on their backs, so how do veterinarian surgeons operate on them? In the Dubai Camel Hospital, it's done on a slab with a hole in the center. The operating slab tilts so that it fits down over the hump of an upright camel. After the camel is anesthetized, the table tilts back, allowing what camels can't normally do in nature: lie with all four legs in the air.

MANGY CAMELS

In the spring and summer, camels shed their winter coats in huge ugly patches—about 5 pounds total. It looks alarming, as though the large beast were falling apart. Believe it or not, though, this matted wool is valued as clothing fiber around the world. What looks grotesque when falling off the camel looks good when woven into a coat or a kicky little beret.

CAMEL HAIR BRUSHES

Are the bristles of a "camel hair brush" really made from camel hair? Usually not. The cheap ones come from a pony's tail or mane. Better ones come from an ox, ferret, goat, or squirrel.

THE EYE OF A CAMEL

Camels have a double set of eyelashes to keep the sand out of their eyes, and an inner eyelid that blinks to wash away any stray grains. Its eyebrow protrudes over the eyeball, shading it from the glaring sun. All of these things combined give the camel's eye a deceptively gentle look. Don't go up and try to squeeze its cute little cheeks, though. (Keep reading.)

SPITTING IMAGE

Camels are very territorial, and if they feel threatened, they spit. If you do get caught in the crossfire, it can get pretty vile, since the camel launches stomach bile mixed with saliva. Contrary to popular myth, camel spit is harmless—it won't burn or blind you. If one does spit, it's the camel's way of saying, "Get out of my way, or I'll really

hurt you." Best to heed the spit and split.

AMERICAN ROOTS?

Camels in America? Many natural history experts believe that camels originated in North America 40 million years ago and migrated through Alaska and into Asia prior to the Ice Age.

PACKING A HUMP

Camels were used as pack animals in the western parts of the U.S. deserts. In 1855, then-Secretary of War Jefferson Davis gave the Army $30,000 for the purchase of seventy-seven camels. They arrived in Texas from the Middle East, along with a native fellow named Hadji Ali to help lead the camel caravans. When Davis requested more funds from Congress in 1858 for 1,000 more camels, it looked like the camel might become a fixture of the American West. However, because of brewing Civil War tensions, the funds were never appropriated, and the Army camel experiment died a quiet death.

ROCKY RIDE

Camels move their legs on each side of their body together. Unlike most animals, their two right legs step forward, and then their two left legs. The rocking motion can be very hard for new riders. Many travelers have tales of "seasickness" upon their first few rides behind the hump of the desert ship.

THIS JARGON'S A BEDOUIN

The Bedouin name for the camel is *ata Allah*, or "God's gift." The Bedouins have over 160 specific words in their language to describe camels and their traits.

CAMEL RACES

Camels have been clocked upward of 40 miles an hour. This pace slows considerably as a race progresses, however. The average speed of a racing camel is about 25 miles per hour. In 1892, a horse and a camel competed in a famous one-day, 109.4-mile race in Australia. The horse won by a hair, then promptly collapsed and died. The camel, though second, crossed the finish line relatively unfazed by the experience.

NAR WAY!

Can one-hump and two-hump camels mate? Yes. You get what's called a "Nar" with one elongated hump.

1776 TERRORISM: TAR AND FEATHERS

Before the American Revolution, attacking Crown-appointed officeholders became a tactic used again and again to terrorize them into resigning their posts. Tarring and feathering added both insult and injury to the mix. The practice was not invented by the Americans—British mobs had used it against tax collectors and other pests back in the days of Richard the Lionhearted.

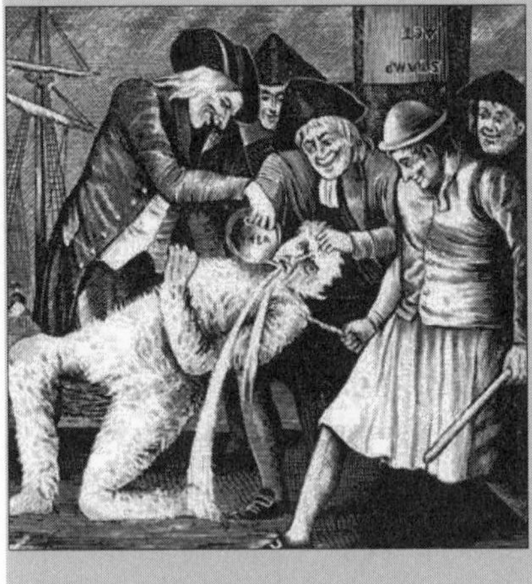

The idea was simple: to cover the victim with tar and then pour feathers on him to make him look like a large chicken. It sounds humiliating, and it was. It also could cause great injury, because the pine tar had to be burning hot to get the right consistency. Afterward, it was difficult and painful to get off.

Mob violence got rougher with time. After tarring and feathering a Loyalist minister, the mob hanged him and burned his body. A Loyalist physician was blistered by the tar, and hog dung was forced into his mouth. The Revolutionary leaders finally decided things had gotten out of hand and began reining in the practice.

Smoke Screen

Quotes from the Tobacco Industry

What if you were selling an addictive product that you knew was killing your customers? How would you justify that to yourself and explain it to the rest of the world? Not like this, we hope.

• "Cigarettes are not addictive." —Brennan Dawson, Tobacco Institute, 1994

• "I think we overuse the word 'addictive.' I think smoking can be a habit." —Brennan Dawson, Tobacco Institute, 1991

• "If I saw or thought that there were any evidence whatsoever that conclusively proved that, in some way, tobacco was harmful to people, and I believed it in my heart and my soul, then I would get out of the business and I wouldn't be involved in it. Honestly, I have not seen one piece of medical evidence that has been presented by anybody, anywhere that absolutely, totally said that smoking caused the disease or created it. I believe this. I'm sitting here talking to you with an extremely clear conscience." —Gerald H. Long, president of R. J. Reynolds Tobacco Company, May 19, 1986, as quoted in *The Washington Times*

• "Gosh, we're awed at how a story can be told and retold by the anti-cigarette people, and how little attention is given in the press to claims *for* cigarettes." —James C. Bowling, assistant to the president of Philip Morris

• "It's part of the whole anti-business movement, the Green Movement. If you think it's bad here, it's even worse in Europe. People have more time to think these days, and so they're more and more critical of everything. Look how critical they are of governments. And there's this health-consciousness movement running through the world." —John Dollisson, vice president of corporate affairs of Phillip Morris, explaining the anti-smoking movement

• "I think that if it were ever conclusively shown that there was some connection between smoking and, say, lung cancer, most ad agencies would not be advertising cigarettes. But it's easy to get stampeded, and the tobacco industry is being very much maligned.... The fact is that I have never met a finer group in my life than the people in the tobacco industry ... and tobacco has given pleasure to an awful lot of people. You should never act on hunches, suspicions, and stir-ups." —Henry Pattison, account executive for Philip Morris at the Benton and Bowles Agency, 1969

•"Just what the doctor ordered." —Ad, L & M cigarettes, 1956

• "If it was legal to sell to 'em, we'd be glad to. But it's not." —Walker Merryman, Tobacco Institute, August 5, 1992, discussing tobacco use by minors

"It's always been our policy that young people shouldn't smoke." —Brennan Dawson, Tobacco Institute, 1991

• "Realistically, if our company is to survive and prosper, over the long term, we must get our share of the youth market. In my opinion, this will require new brands tailored to the youth market." —In-house memo by Claude Teague of R. J. Reynolds, February 2, 1973

• "There is no science behind the accusation that advertising causes smoking initiation." —Thomas Lauria, Tobacco Institute, 1991

• "This attempt to ban smoking is an example of social engineering on a vast scale. Such massive intervention in the private lives and choices of one quarter of our adult population recalls the extremism of Prohibition, the last national crusade against a supposed social evil." —Charles Whitley, Tobacco Institute, 1990

• LAST WORD ON THE SUBJECT: "Tobacco is lothesome to the eye, hatefull to the Nose, harmfull to the braine, dangerous to the Lungs; and in the stinking fume thereof nearest resembling the horrific Stigian smoke of the pit that is bottomless." —King James I, banning tobacco in 1604

Penguin Love

THEIR SECRETS LAID OUT IN BLACK & WHITE

Penguins mate for life, and the fathers take an active role in their chicks' upbringing. Are these little waddlers a role model for us all, or what?

FIRST OF ALL, penguins are not particularly lusty birds. True, they mate for life, but they typically have sex only once a year.

They are, however, good parents. Yes, even the mothers, despite the rumors you might've heard. It's true that penguin moms don't look good in a straight retelling of the facts: they lay eggs, immediately go AWOL, and don't come back until after the eggs are hatched. But to come to the moms' defense, there are extenuating circumstances. Let's start at the beginning.

NORTH, SOUTH, EAST ... THEN NEST

Penguins don't normally spend much time on land because all of their food is in the water. However, nesting changes the rules. The penguins take to the same land where they were born, colonies of thousands of the birds walking single file in the same, often absurdly circuitous path that their forepenguins walked for untold generations. (How do we know this? Because scientists have found penguin paths worn into soil, ice, and rocks from the feet of millions of birds waddling through over time.)

Nest styles differ. Penguins in warmer regions may dig shallow burrows for nests; because of the hardness of the earth, many Antarctic penguins build nests of pebbles. Emperor and king penguins, though, don't build nests at all. Instead, they balance the eggs on the tops of their feet and keep them warm by covering them with their ample bellies.

With few exceptions, typically the penguin love schedule goes like this: In the same way that human lovers tune into each other over the hubbub of a crowded room, the two penguin mates find each other in the nesting areas by the sound of the other's voice. They mate, and the male stakes out a nesting area. He spends weeks defending it from interlopers, neither parent leaving the nesting area to find food. Finally, Mom lays the eggs.

She, more depleted than the father after manufacturing the eggs, immediately makes a rush to the sea to binge eat, replenish her famished self, and stave off post-ovum depression. The father stays around to keep the eggs warm.

DAD LOVES HIS EGGS

Of course, keeping eggs warm in Antarctica is harder than it sounds. The eggs have to be constantly heated at body temperature for 30 to 65 days, which requires extraordinary paternal efforts. For example, the male emperor penguin spends weeks standing stationary 24 hours a day with an egg cradled on his feet in the dead of winter. To keep warm in weather that stays close to –40° is nearly impossible for a single dad, but they've found a solution. Thousands of emperor penguin dads huddle together in a tight group, the penguins on the outside of the crowd rotating in toward the center to share the warmth and keep from freezing. Other types of penguin dads spend a lonely vigil sitting on a pebbly nest.

Shortly before the eggs are supposed to hatch, the prodigal mother penguin returns. She typically takes over the egg tending, and her exhausted, hungry mate takes off. He heads to the sea and replenishes his blubber in a remarkably short time, returning shortly after the eggs hatch with food for the baby. After that, the parents continue to alternate between taking care of the young and eating until the chicks are old enough to fend for themselves.

To the Pillory!

Cruel but Usual Punishment in America

Changing the hearts, minds, and behaviors of lawbreakers has long been the goal of criminologists. Unfortunately, their attempts have often been ineffective and sometimes just plain criminal.

ANYBODY WITH ANY HONESTY would admit we don't do a great job dealing with criminals. America has a larger percentage of its citizens locked up in prisons than any other country in the world, including Russia, China, and Iraq. It is one of the few advanced countries that still has the death penalty. And yet, despite being increasingly "tough on crime," America continues time after time to lead the lists of serious violence and crime in industrialized countries.

But as ineffectually inhumane as the present system is, it could always be worse. In fact, it *was* worse, back in a time that we romanticize now—the time when Pilgrims and Puritans ruled the new settlements in America. Justice in the New World was based on England's justice, which was not just at all. Different punishments were given to gentlemen, common people, and slaves. Brutality and death were common for even minor crimes, such as belonging to the wrong religious denomination, writing a book without authorization, or criticizing the authorities. Pain and public scorn were powerful weapons, and the civil/religious authorities used them creatively and often.

STOCKS & BONDAGE

Public humiliation was the point of the stocks. They descended from England's *bilboes,* which were heavy metal bars with foot shackles, designed to keep a prisoner from moving from the spot.

Bilboes were impractical in the New World because of a shortage of skilled metal workers, but America had plenty of trees, so a wooden version became common. (In fact, judges sometimes demanded that the prisoner provide wood and make stocks to bind himself.) Being stuck sitting with feet imprisoned between wooden slats on a Sunday between the morning and evening services was considered a suitable punishment for such things as drunkenness, mild profanity, breaching the Sabbath, and the like. Besides the discomfort and boredom, prisoners in stocks had to put up with the censure, jibes, and jests of other townspeople.

THE PILLORY

Also known as the "stretchneck," the pillory was for more serious crimes. It was more painful than the stocks and made the prisoner subject to much worse than jibes and jests. Standing uncomfortably with hands and head immobilized allowed every ruffian in town the sport of pelting the prisoner with rotten eggs, garbage, offal, and dung. Sometimes, to drive the point further, city officials nailed the prisoner's ears to the wood on either side of the head hole. The pillory—sometimes in conjunction with branding, mutilation, fines, and other penalties—was a one-size-fits-all punishment for treason, sedition, arson, blasphemy, witchcraft, perjury, wife-beating, cheating, forging, gaming, quarreling, lying, slander, drunkenness, begging, speculating in commodities futures, impudence, and general mischief.

THE DUCKING STOOL

The ducking stool was a milder punishment, used mostly for scolding and nagging women, but sometimes also for men a little too loose in their tongues: rumor mongers, whiners, and slanderers. The punishment was to repeatedly duck offenders under water until they emerged choking and thoroughly dispirited. A poem written in 1780 explained:

> There stands, my friend, in yonder pool
> An engine called the ducking stool....
> If noisy dames should once begin
> To drive your house with noisy din,
> Away you cry, you'll grace the stool;
> We'll teach how your tongue to rule....
> No brawling wives, no furious wenches
> No fire so hot but water quenches.

BRANKS, GAGS, & SPLIT STICKS

If the ducking stool didn't work on chronically harping women, there were more direct behavior modification techniques. Branks were a type of iron headgear with a sharp protrusion into the mouth that would injure the tongue if the wearer spoke.

A similar punishment was the "cleft stick"—cutting a split into a wooden stick and forcing it onto the tongue of a person deemed guilty of nagging, scolding, complaining, or criticizing the authorities.

SCARLET LETTER

Anybody who read *The Scarlet Letter* in school knows about this one: a person forced to wear a letter to advertise to the world his or her dire depravity. Hester Prynne had to wear an *A* for adultery. Other letters included *B* for blasphemy, *V* for viciousness, and *D* for drunkenness. To prevent poor people from receiving charity from more than one church parish, they had to wear letters to indicate where they lived.

WHIPPING

Like most of the early colonial punishments, whippings were likely to be given on Sabbath days in conjunction with church services, in order teach a moral lesson. A good whipping, each lash causing deep injury and permanent scars, was meant to correct serious offenses. Whippings were meted out for stealing a loaf of bread, shooting fowl on the Sabbath, sleeping in church, falling in love with an unsuitable suitor, and complaining about the government. To avoid killing the prisoner, judges generally limited the

whippings to a maximum of 39 lashes at a time; for modesty's sake, women were sometimes whipped behind walls instead of in public.

THE WOOD HORSE

Riding the wooden horse was a military punishment in both the British and American armies: Rule-breaking soldiers were forced to straddle a sharpened wooden rail, sometimes with cannonballs tied to their feet, sometimes for hours or days at a time.

BRANDING & MAIMING

Being subjected to permanent injury (including death) was the punishment for more serious crimes. For example, here's an account of the punishment given a man who was convicted of the "crime" of being a Quaker in New Haven, Connecticut:

> The Drum was Beat, the People gather'd, Norton was fetch'd and stripp'd to the Waste, and set with his Back to the Magistrates, and given in their View Thirty-six cruel Stripes with a knotted cord, and his hand made fast in the Stocks where they had set his Body before, and burn'd very deep with a Red-hot Iron with H for Heresie.

In Massachusetts, Quakers were banished from all settlements. If they returned, read a 1657 law, "a Quaker if male for the first offense shall have one of his eares cutt off; for the second offense have his other eare cutt off; a woman shall be severely whipt; for the third offense, he or she shall have their tongues bored through with a hot iron."

In early Virginia, a first-time hog thief might be heavily fined and have his ears cropped; if he repeated the crime, he might pay the same fine and have *H* branded on his forehead; the third time, he would be put to death.

Maryland law required that all towns have a set of branding irons for burning the cheeks of criminals: *SL* for "seditious libel" (criticizing the authorities); *M* for manslaughter; *T* for thief; *R* for rogue or vagabond; *F* for forgers, and so on.

Someone convicted of a misdemeanor might have his nose or ears slit or cut as a lesson to the miscreant and a warning to others.

A Toast to Toasters

Bred for Bread ... and So Much More

Stoves are unwieldy; microwaves have no soul. But a toaster is like a small, tabletop hearth; the smells and foods that emerge from it seem to whisper, "Home!"

CONSIDER THE TOASTER: Its function is modest—to singe both sides of a slice of bread to just the right temperature—yet that function is considered so crucial that 88 percent of all American households have at least one toaster.

Despite the ascendency of fad kitchen gadgets and microwave ovens, the toaster continues to hang on to its counter space in a way that lesser appliances have not. Of course, it's not just all about the bread. Thanks to the ingenuity of the food industry, a toaster can prepare main courses from waffles to pizza, exotic faux-international foods like bagels and English muffins, and even desserts, thanks to that class of foods known as "toaster pastries."

THE RISE OF BREAD

To understand the toaster, you have to begin with bread. And not just any bread, but fluffy bread. Even before the beginning of agriculture, people baked a flat, hard bread made from the seeds of grasses. As the varieties of these grains were recognized and purposely planted, breadmaking continued, but it was still flat, unleavened bread totally unsuited for toasting (and barely suitable for eating).

About 6,000 years ago, Egyptian bakers changed all that when they invented fluffy bread.

It was most likely an accident: If you've ever made bread from scratch, you can imagine the difficulty of kneading huge quantities of dough day in and day out. We can surmise that one of the bakers had a brilliant thought to save the constant strain on his arms, shoulders, and back: "If winemakers find it easier to crush grapes with their feet, why don't we try the same thing to knead our bread?"

Ancient Egyptian breadmakers kneading bread dough with their feet

PEDICUREAN DELIGHT

It wasn't a time of great cleanliness in food preparation. While it's true that their feet weren't particularly clean, their hands may have been just as bad or worse. One key difference between the two, though, was the yeast between the bakers' toes. We've all got it—it's the stuff that makes your feet smell cheesy. Wine and beer need yeast to ferment. Bread needs yeast to rise. And sure enough, the first batches of foot-kneaded bread came out of the oven radically different from what had ever come out before: they were light, fluffy, and chewy. (One "foot" note to think about next time you're having grilled cheese sandwiches: The yeast used in cheesemaking has a similar toejam pedigree.)

The bakers didn't have a clue why their foot-kneaded bread came out fluffy, but they did know that it was easier to make and that their customers seemed to like it. So they kept kneading bread that way, and the practice spread.

Despite its downtrodden origins, this softer bread became so valued that Egyptian workers accepted it as payment at the end of the workday, making them the first "breadwinners" in history.

ROMAN MEAL

It took the ancient Romans to take bread to its next logical step: toast! Toasting was first used as a way of preserving bread longer for the Roman Army, but it became popular as a tasty side dish among

Romans. who gave it its modern name (*tostum* means "scorch") and spread toast from Africa to Britain.

In the first millennia of toast, "toasters" were primitive things—often simply a stick to hold bread to within browning distance of a fire's flames. However, human ingenuity resulted in other solutions as well. For example, toasters in the 1800s consisted of bread-holding wire racks that stood next to the fireplace. Like all pre-electric toasters, they required constant monitoring to avoid burning the bread.

The first successful electric toaster didn't appear until 1909. Made by the General Electric Company, it plugged into a lightbulb socket (wall outlets weren't a common thing yet), toasted one side of bread at a time, and wasn't automatic—when the toast looked good to you, you unscrewed the plug.

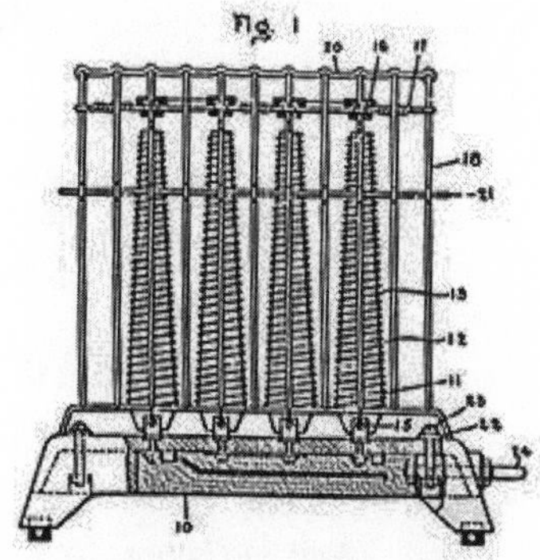

Patent drawing for General Electric's 1909 toaster. Note that it's just four electric coils with a wire bread stand.

Ten years later, Charles Strite finally got it right. He invented the modern, timer-activated, pop-up toaster. The innovation of pre-sliced bread from Wonder in 1930 advanced toasting technology even further.

MORE TOAST FACTS

• The optimal temperature for making toast is about 310°.

• Chemical changes occur when you make toast—the bread's starches and sugars caramelize into intense new flavors. It's even got a name: "the Maillard Reaction" in honor of L. C. Maillard, the chemist who identified it in 1912.

• Maybe you've heard "milktoast" used as an insult, but do you know what it is? It's a British concoction: toast in a bowl covered with milk and flavored with butter, salt, and pepper.

• Our favorite toaster? A yellow one from the early 1970s with Charlie Brown's dog on it and the inscription: "Happiness is a Snoopy Toaster." Awww!

Life Lessons

How to Milk a Cow

Say you're out in the middle of dairy country with nothing on you but the shirt on your back. What are you going to do—eat tumbleweed? Well, we're here to help with a quick primer on how to milk a cow. It could save your life.

If you can ignore the potentially lethal kicking legs and the shifting half ton of weight, it's really not so hard to milk a cow. Here we go step by step:

1. The pail of milk should be protected. It'll help if you can find a neck and leg harness for Bossie in order to keep her still. If you have no idea what these things are, you're on your own.
2. Hay is a good distracter. It'll keep the cow's interest off kicking you as you begin.
3. If you've got it, use anti-bacterial soap to wash your hands and the teats. Cows aren't the cleanest things, and you likely don't want invisible germs swimming around in your milk.
4. In order for the milk to "let down" (begin to flow), the cow's teats need to be stimulated. This isn't foreplay; you use your thumb and forefinger on each of the cow's teats to squeeze out a little milk before the official milking begins.
5. Now the fun begins. Take your forefinger and wrap it around an individual teat while pressing your thumb from the opposite side. Roll your forefinger in a downward motion, apply pressure as evenly as possible. If you're having trouble with this, visualize your fingers as a calf's mouth sucking like a baby.
6. This will take a while, so sit back and enjoy the process and the exercise. It'll take about 350 squirts to fill your typical five gallon bucket. A cow produces enough milk to fill one of these a day. That's a heap of milk for one body, so start dreaming up creamy recipes.

Snow Business

How to Build an Igloo

For most kids, building an igloo on snow days was a continuously unrealized goal. But it's not that hard ... if you learn from an expert.

THE PROBLEM BUILDING AN IGLOO is getting that round shape without having the roof cave in. At least, that's what doomed our childhood attempts so thoroughly we never even considered building one as we got older. So we were glad to run across an account of igloo building by native Canadians in a book called *The Igloo* by David and Charlotte Yue (Houghton-Mifflin, 1988). We learned enough from their observations to be able to put together our own igloo.

SOME THINGS WE LEARNED ALONG THE WAY

• *Iglu* is a native word meaning any kind of house.

• Not all native groups in the Arctic used snow igloos; some never used them, while others used them only as temporary shelter while traveling.

• A good builder can build a basic igloo in a little over an hour.

• The dome structure is energy efficient, offering the minimum amount of surface area, and snow is a great insulator. As a result, a good igloo can be 65° warmer inside than it is outside.

• Domes built by a competent builder were strong enough that native kids used to slide down them for fun.

WHAT YOU'LL NEED

- A 3-foot-deep drift of packed snow as big as your intended igloo. (If necessary, make one: pile some snow, pack it down, and let it sit.)

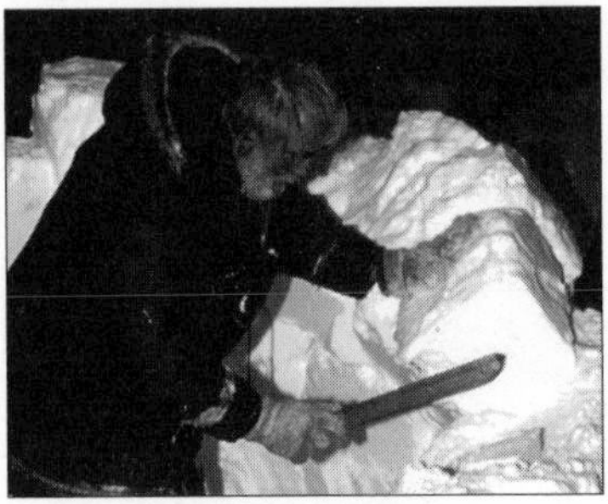

- A large kitchen knife. A curved blade made of caribou antler is traditional, but few homes stock them any more. If kids are involved in your project, keep them away from the knife.

HOW YOU DO IT

1. Draw a circle in the snow as a guideline. For sleeping 4 or 5 people, make it about 9–12 feet in diameter (but smaller igloos are possible).

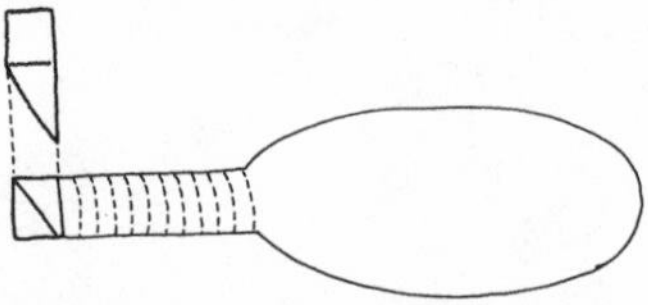

2. Draw the entrance passageway—two 6 foot parallel lines about 30–40 inches apart.

3. Cut 1–2 feet deep into the end of your two parallel lines. Remove and discard a wedge-shaped block from the end to give your igloo a ramped entrance and allow you room when cutting blocks.

4. Start cutting some building blocks from between your two cuts. Make them "curving rectangles" for the circle shape of the igloo, 1–2 feet deep, 4–6 inches thick, and as wide as your passageway. Cut and dig up to and then through the circle you've drawn.

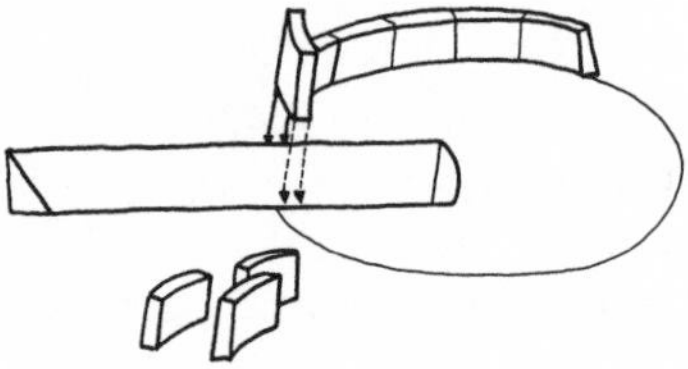

5. When you've accumulated a dozen blocks and cut out some working room inside the circle, jam one of the blocks back into the trough exactly where the opening of the igloo will go.

6. Next arrange your blocks in a layer around your circle, shaving a wedge off the bottom and sides of each so it leans inward. Each will support the others so that your walls should stay in place without additional props.

7. Before you add the next

layer of blocks, take your knife and cut two standing blocks in a diagonal from the far lower corner of one to the far upper corner of the other (see below). This allows you to place the rest of the blocks in an upward spiral.

8. From here on, you'll work

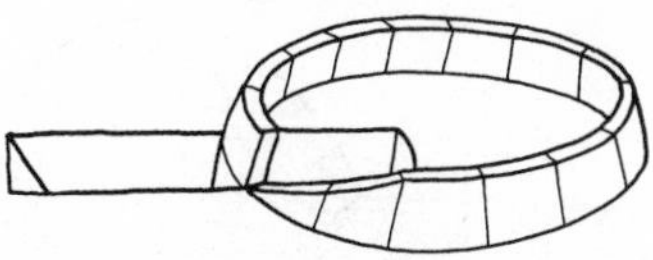

from the inside of the igloo, cutting blocks out from the "floor," shaping them, and positioning them on the spiral. After you place a block, run your knife along where it touches the other blocks. This softens the snow and smooths out irregularities, allowing for an airtight fit.

9. As you get closer to the top, you need to make your blocks more and more trapezoidal, so each layer will lean a little more toward the center.

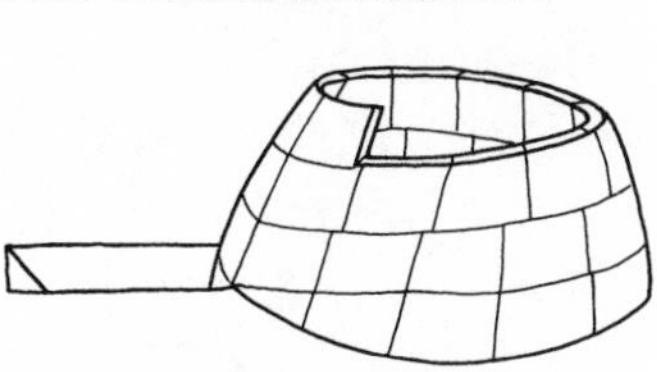

10. When your hole at top is too small for a full block, cut a custom-shaped block slightly bigger than the hole. From the inside, tilt it so you can slide it out through the opening. Standing inside the igloo, lower it into the hole while shaving it with your knife until it settles snugly in place.

11. You're now inside a fully enclosed dome. There shouldn't be any holes in the walls—if you see any, patch them with soft snow.

12. For ventilation and light, cut a small hole (up to 6 inches in diameter) into the top. If windy, put it slightly off-center, away from the wind.

13. Find the temporary block you put in the passageway, and cut a hole big enough to crawl through.

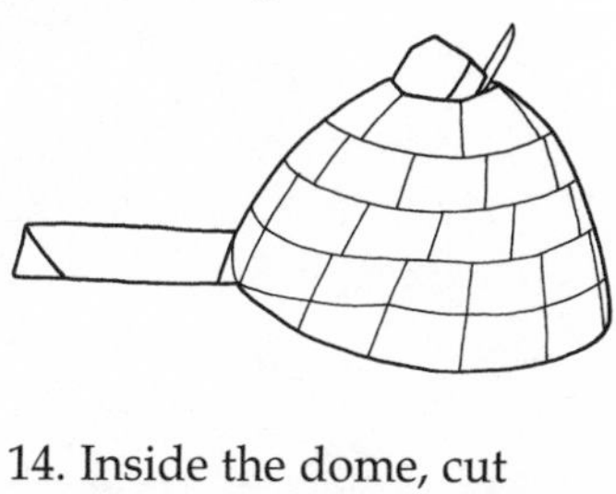

14. Inside the dome, cut blocks to enclose the passageway, creating ledges for sitting, lying, and working on. Shape the blocks so they'll curve inward, and arch them over your passageway. Save a big block for a door.

15. A candle or small lamp inside will give you light, and it will also melt a thin layer of snow, sealing the igloo walls and making it warmer.

16. ***IMPORTANT SAFETY WARNING: Never use a fire or heater inside your igloo—even with a vent hole—because you will suffocate. If using a lamp or candle, make sure that you have the doorway open and an adequate vent hole on top.***

17. If the igloo gets too stuffy from having people inside, enlarge the vent hole up to 8 inches. If it gets too cold, stuff a rag or mitten loosely into it. Don't seal it completely, though, because you want some ventilation.

18. When your igloo melts away, don't feel bad. Even in the Arctic, people use an igloo for a only month or so before abandoning it and starting over again with new snow (sure beats housecleaning).

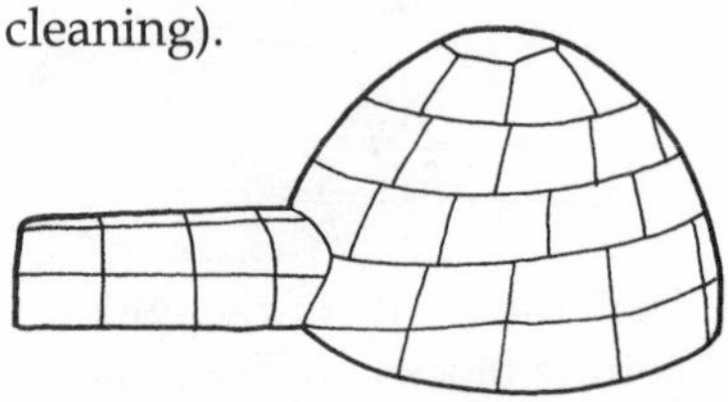

Great Danes

Here's a question people ask: Why didn't any of the countries conquered by Hitler refuse to go along with the Holocaust? The answer is, one did, and in a big way: Denmark.

Outgunned and vulnerable on the northern border of Germany, Denmark surrendered to the Nazis in 1940. However, unlike many other conquered countries, the Danes had no tradition of antisemitism for the Nazis to tap into. In fact, the government so strongly objected to singling out the Jews that the Nazis didn't make them wear Stars of David as in other occupied countries. (The story that they did and the King of Denmark wore one too is heartwarming, but a myth.)

When, in 1943, the Nazis did try to round up Denmark's Jews, they met with little success. Thousands of Danes banded together into a widespread conspiracy called the Freedom Council. Within days they began smuggling Jews to Sweden using fleets of cars, taxis, trucks, and fishing boats. Of the 7,500 Danish Jews, 7,000 were smuggled to safety. Meanwhile, the Danish government objected loudly about the 500 Jewish Danes who were sent to concentration camps, and probably saved lives: Of the 500, only 51 died.

Tom's Whitewash

A Classic Tale for Kids of All Ages

Mark Twain was a great observer of the best and worst of humanity. He lays out a sly lesson in psychology in this funny story from *The Adventures of Tom Sawyer*.

SATURDAY MORNING WAS COME, and all the summer world was bright and fresh, and brimming with life. There was a song in every heart; and if the heart was young the music issued at the lips. There was cheer in every face and a spring in every step. The locust-trees were in bloom and the fragrance of the blossoms filled the air. Cardiff Hill, beyond the village and above it, was green with vegetation and lay just far enough away to seem a Delectable Land, dreamy, reposeful, and inviting.

Tom appeared on the sidewalk with a bucket of whitewash and a long-handled brush. He surveyed the fence, and all gladness left him and a deep melancholy settled down upon his spirit. Thirty yards of board fence nine feet high. Life to him seemed hollow, and existence but a burden. Sighing, he dipped his brush and passed it along the topmost plank; repeated the operation; did it again; compared the insignificant whitewashed streak with the far-reaching continent of unwhitewashed fence, and sat down on a tree-box discouraged.

He began to think of the fun he had planned for this day, and his sorrows multiplied. Soon the free boys would come tripping along on all sorts of delicious expeditions, and they would make a world of fun of him for having to work—the very thought of it burnt him like fire. He got out his worldly wealth and examined it—bits of toys, marbles, and trash; enough to buy an exchange of work, maybe, but not half enough to buy so much as half an hour of pure freedom. So he returned his straitened means to his pocket, and gave up the idea of trying to buy the boys. At this dark and hopeless moment an inspiration burst upon him! Nothing less than a great, magnificent inspiration.

He took up his brush and went tranquilly to work. Ben Rogers hove in sight presently—the very boy, of all boys, whose ridicule he had been dreading. Ben's gait was the hop-skip-and-jump—proof enough that his heart was light and his anticipations high. He was eating an apple, and giving a long, melodious whoop, at intervals, followed by a deep-toned ding-dong-dong, ding-dong-dong, for he was personating a steamboat. As he drew near, he slackened speed, took the middle of the street, leaned far over to star-board and rounded to ponderously and with laborious pomp and circumstance—for he was personating the *Big Missouri*, and considered himself to be drawing nine feet of water. He was boat and captain and engine-bells combined, so he had to imagine himself standing on his own hurricane-deck giving the orders and executing them:

"Stop the stabboard! Ting-a-ling-ling! Stop the labboard! Come ahead on the stabboard! Stop her! Let your outside turn over slow! Ting-a-ling-ling! Chow-ow-ow! Get out that headline! Lively now! Come—out with your spring-line—what're you about there! Take a turn round that stump with the bight of it! Stand by that stage, now—let her go! Done with the engines, sir! Ting-a-ling-ling! Sh't! s'h't! sh't!" (trying the gauge-cocks).

Tom went on whitewashing—paid no attention to the steamboat. Ben stared a moment and then said: "Hi- yi ! You're up a stump, ain't you!"

No answer. Tom surveyed his last touch with the eye of an artist, then he gave his brush another gentle sweep and surveyed the result, as before. Ben ranged up alongside of him. Tom's mouth watered for the apple, but he stuck to his work. Ben said: "Hello, old chap, you got to work, hey?"

Tom wheeled suddenly and said: "Why, it's you, Ben! I warn't noticing."

"Say—I'm going in a-swimming, I am. Don't you wish you could? But of course you'd druther work—wouldn't you? Course you would!"

Tom contemplated the boy a bit, and said: "What do you call work?"

"Why, ain't that work?"

Tom resumed his whitewashing, and answered carelessly: "Well, maybe it is, and maybe it ain't. All I know, is, it suits Tom Sawyer."

"Oh come, now, you don't mean to let on that you like it?"

The brush continued to move. "Like it? Well, I don't see why I oughtn't to like it. Does a boy get a chance to whitewash a fence every day?"

'AIN'T THAT WORK?

That put the thing in a new light. Ben stopped nibbling his apple. Tom swept his brush daintily back and forth—stepped back to note the effect—added a touch here and there—criticized the effect again—Ben watching every move and getting more and more interested, more and more absorbed. Presently he said: "Say, Tom, let me whitewash a little."

Tom considered, was about to consent; but he altered his mind: "No—no—I reckon it wouldn't hardly do, Ben. You see, Aunt Polly's awful particular about this fence—right here on the street, you know—but if it was the back fence I wouldn't mind and she wouldn't. Yes, she's awful particular about this fence; it's got to be done very careful; I reckon there ain't one boy in a thousand, maybe two thousand, that can do it the way it's got to be done."

"No—is that so? Oh come, now—lemme just try. Only just a little—I'd let you, if you was me, Tom."

"Ben, I'd like to, honest injun; but Aunt Polly—well, Jim wanted to do it, but she wouldn't let him; Sid wanted to do it, and she wouldn't let Sid. Now don't you see I'm fixed? If you was to tackle this fence and anything was to happen to it—"

"Oh, shucks, I'll be just as careful. Now lemme try. Say—I'll give you the core of my apple."

"Well, here—No, Ben, now don't. I'm afeard—"

"I'll give you all of it!"

Tom gave up the brush with reluctance in his face, but alacrity in his heart. And while the late steamer Big Missouri worked and sweated in the sun, the retired artist sat on a barrel in the shade close by, dangled his legs, munched his apple, and planned the slaughter of more innocents. There was no lack of material; boys happened along every little while; they came to jeer, but remained to whitewash. By the time Ben was fagged out, Tom had traded the next chance to Billy Fisher for a kite, in good repair; and when he played out, Johnny Miller bought in for a dead rat and a string to swing it with—and so on, and so on, hour after hour. And when the middle of the afternoon came, from being a poor poverty-stricken boy in the morning, Tom was literally rolling in wealth. He had besides the things before mentioned, twelve marbles, part of a jews-harp, a piece of blue bottle-glass to look through, a spool cannon, a key that wouldn't unlock anything, a fragment of chalk, a glass stopper of a decanter, a tin soldier, a couple of tadpoles, six fire-crackers, a kitten with only one eye, a brass door-knob, a dog-collar—but no dog—the handle of a knife, four pieces of orange-peel, and a dilapidated old window sash.

He had had a nice, good, idle time all the while—plenty of company—and the fence had three coats of whitewash on it! If he hadn't run out of whitewash he would have bankrupted every boy in the village.

Tom said to himself that it was not such a hollow world, after all. He had discovered a great law of human action, without knowing it—namely, that in order to make a man or a boy covet a thing, it is only necessary to make the thing difficult to attain. If he had been a great and wise philosopher, like the writer of this book, he would now have comprehended that Work consists of whatever a body is obliged to do, and that Play consists of whatever a body is not obliged to do. And this would help him to understand why constructing artificial flowers or performing on a tread-mill is work, while rolling ten-pins or climbing Mont Blanc is only amusement. There are wealthy gentlemen in England who drive four-horse passenger-coaches twenty or thirty miles on a daily line, in the summer, because the privilege costs them considerable money; but if they were offered wages for the service, that would turn it into work and then they would resign.

The boy mused awhile over the substantial change which had taken place in his worldly circumstances, and then wended toward headquarters to report.

THINGS JUST SOUND SMARTER IN LATIN

"Accipere quam facere praestat injuriam." (It is better to suffer an injustice than to do an injustice.) –Marcus Tullius Cicero (106–43 B.C.)

"Nec quicquam insipiente fortunato intolerabilius fieri potest." (Nothing's more insufferable than a successful fool.) –Ibid

"Amor est melle et felle est fecundissimus." (Love is rich with both honey and venom.) –Titus Maccius Plautus (250–184 B.C.)

"Bene qui latuit, bene vixit." (One who lives well, lives unnoticed.) –Publius Ovidius Naso (43 B.C.–17 A.D.)

"Crescit amor nummi, quantum ipsa pecunia crevit." (The love of wealth grows as wealth grows.) –Decimus Junius Juvenalis (A.D. 60–135)

"Facilius est multa facere quam diu." (It is easier to do many things than to do one for a long time.) –Marcus Fabius Quintilianus (A.D. 35–100)

"Hoc tempore obsequium amicos, veritas odium parit." (Nowadays friends are won through flattery, truth gives birth to hate.) –Ibid

Expert Advice

THINGS TO NEVER, EVER DO

"Never wear anything that panics the cat." – P. J. O'Rourke

"Never jog while wearing wingtips …unless you are attending the Nerd Convention in Atlantic City." – Mark Russell

"Never eat in a restaurant that's over a hundred feet off the ground and won't stand still." – Calvin Trillin

"Never eat Chinese food in Oklahoma." – David Bryan

"Never slap a man who chews tobacco." – Willard Scott

"Never commit yourself to a cheese without having first examined it." – T.S. Eliot

"Never eat anything with suction cups." – Alf

"Never touch your eye but with your elbow." – English proverb

"Never run after your own hat – others will be delighted to do it; why spoil their fun?" – Mark Twain

"Never put a razor inside your nose, even as a joke." – Jake Johansen

"Never drop your gun to hug a bear." – H. E. Palmer

"Never face facts; if you do you'll never get up in the morning." – Marlo Thomas

"Never kill a boy on the first date." – Buffy, the vampire slayer

"Never trust a computer you can't throw out a window." – Steve Wozniak

Slogos 2!

Test your knowledge of slogans and logos in this big "O" Slogo quiz. We're going to give you pictures of distinctive "O's" from the packaging of well-known products. match the "O" with the right slogan. Rated: Medium difficulty.

1

A. "And I helped"

B. "Shot from guns"

C. "They plump when you cook 'em"

D. "Uh-Oh!"

E. "dot–dot–dot, dash–dash–dash, dot–dot–dot!"

2

A. "Uh-Oh!"

B. "Do the Twist"

C. "Strong enough for a man"

D. "... not in your hand"

E. "Built Ram Tough"

3

A. "Do the Twist"

B. "And I helped"

C. "Watch it Wiggle"

D. "Shot from guns"

E. "dot–dot–dot, dash–dash–dash, dot–dot–dot!"

4

A. "Honey of an O"

B. "It's a meal in itself"

C. "They plump when you cook 'em"

D. "Strong enough for a man"

E. "... not in your hand"

5

A. "It's a meal in itself"

B. "dot-dot-dot, dash-dash-dash, dot-dot-dot!"

C. "Do the Twist"

D. "Built Ram Tough"

E. "They plump when you cook 'em"

6

A. "Strong enough for a man"

B. "Shot from guns"

C. "... and she knows how to use them"

D. "I love what you do for me!"

E. "It's a meal in itself"

Answers: 1. D: You remember the old SpaghettiOs jingle: "Uh-oh, SpaghettiOs!" and "The neat new spaghetti you can eat with a spoon!" 2. B: In 1990, Nabisco signed creator of "The Twist," Chubby Checker, to a series of commercials in which he urged tv veiwers to "do the twist!". 3. C: "Watch it wiggle; see it jiggle." It's Jell-O! 4. A: "It's a honey of an "O," Honey Nut Cheerios." 5. B: S.O.S scouring pads. Some people mistakenly think that the last period after the second "S" in the logo is missing by accident. Not so. The Morse code distress symbol—S.O.S.—can't be trademarked. By removing the last dot, the company was able to register the name. 6. E: Oh Henry candy bar ads once claimed "It's a meal in itself." If you're counting calories and fat, that'd be about right.

Fat Free Diet

From* The Odd Index *by Stephen Spignesi, here are the foods that are most laden with cholesterol:

1. 3 oz. of cooked pork brains (2,169 mg)
2. 3 oz. cooked beef brains (1,746 mg.)
3. 6 oz. cooked beef sweetbreads (thymus) (1,560 mg.)
4. 1 cup egg salad (1,124 mg.)
5. 7 oz. braised lamb sweetbreads (932 mg.)
6. 1 cup stewed chicken liver (884 mg.)
7. 1 cup stewed turkey liver (876 mg.)
8. 6 oz. braised pork spleen (856 mg.)
9. 1 cup scrambled eggs (854 mg.)
10. 1 whole chicken, batter dipped and fried (810 mg.)

Corporate Tags

How Much for a Successful Logo?

"Repetition means remembrance," says logo designer Saul Bass. A successful corporate logo can be worth billions of dollars in Pavlovian response from consumers. So how much did companies pay the designers? You may be surprised....

FedEx

Company: Federal Express
Cost of logo: Almost $5,000,000

In 1992, Federal Express hired Landor & Associates, a "corporate identity" company, to update its image. After two years of tests, Landor designed a purple and orange logo featuring the company's nickname and a subliminal arrow between the E and X. The cost? "Less than $5 million," said a company official, adding that it's worth the money because the mark on all those double-parked trucks is the equivalent of $160 million in outdoor advertising.

Company: Nike
Cost of logo: $35

When Nike was trying to get a foothold in 1971, the founders decided that their shoes needed a distinctive marking like the Adidas stripes, so they hired Carolyn Davis, an art student from Portland State. The founders were at first unenthusiastic about her design but didn't have time to revise it. Since then, the "swoosh" has graced a zillion pieces of sporting equipment. For her work, Davis got $35, which doesn't sound like much, but it's a fortune compared to the 20–30¢ an hour that Nike pays its workers in Third World countries.

Coca-Cola®

Company: Coca-Cola
Cost of logo: $0

The lifespan of a logo is typically fifteen to twenty years, but good ones can last much longer. In 1887, Coke's advertising director, Frank Robinson, had an annual budget of only $150. Robinson, who had named the drink a few years earlier, saved money by drawing the logo himself. His reward? Robinson believed that he was an owner in the fledgling company, but his "partners" sold the company to tycoon Asa Candler and ran. Robinson, now broke, continued on as advertising director, making Coke the most successful soft drink ever. However, when Candler's nephew decided he wanted the ad director job in 1906, Robinson was moved into a meaningless position until he retired in 1913.

Company: MTV
Cost of logo: $1,000

A rock music channel was an unlikely joint venture of American Express and Warner Communications. They wanted to call it "TV-1," but the name was already taken. Second choice was TV-M (Television Music), until programming director Steve Casey suddenly blurted out, "Don't you think that MTV sounds better than TV-M?" They sent the name out to several designers, but especially liked one from a small shop called Manhattan Design. For their efforts, the designers walked away with a measly grand.

Company: Stussy
Cost of logo: $0

Californian beach boy Shawn Stussy first designed surfboards, but later branched out more successfully into clothes.The graffiti-like logo has umlauts to give it that heavy-metal band look and to increase the chance that people pronounce the name right. "It's his real signature," insists a Stussy spokesman. "He even signs his checks with it."

Company: Lucent
Cost of logo: Secret, but more than FedEx

AT&T hired Landor & Associates to provide a new identity for its new spinoff. Landor winnowed fifty names from a list of 700 possibilities and screened them for obnoxious connotations in nine countries and thirteen languages. They used a similar process with logo designs. Several million dollars later, Landor came up with a name that means "clear" or "glowing" in English, and a logo that's been compared to a coffee stain. Lucent Technologies launched itself with a $50 million ad campaign.

Company: Playboy
Cost of logo: $0

When Hugh Hefner launched *Playboy* in the early 1960s, he chose the rabbit as his mascot because of its reputation as an unusually sexual creature. As part of his regular duties, art director Arthur Paul sketched out a simple black and white design that would look good as a tiny dingbat at the bottom of stories, but the image's size grew as its popularity grew, making its way to every cover for four decades. Playboy licensed it to manufacturers, and it has appeared on everything from pinball machines to air fresheners.

Company: Ben & Jerry's
Cost of logo: $6 an hour

When Ben Cohen and Jerry Greenfield began packaging their ice cream, they needed a logo and package design but didn't have much money. Vermont designer Lyn Severance came up with a homemade look that fit their philosophy as well as their budget, using hand lettering and hand-drawn lines. This was fine with Jerry and Ben because it was cheaper to put her on staff at $6 an hour than buy typesetting and border tape.

Hot & Culinary

• "The hymn 'Onward Christian Soldiers,' sung to the right tune and in a not-too-brisk tempo, makes a very good egg timer. If you put the egg into boiling water and sing all five verses and chorus, the egg will be just right when you come to Amen." —Letter to the *London Daily Telegraph*

• "If you intend to tap a sugar maple tree for syrup, keep in mind that it should be at least 40 years old, 60 feet tall, and a foot wide. Each tree will yield about 10 gallons of sap; when boiled down, these 10 gallons will become one quart of syrup." —*American Farm Companion*

Pot Shots

Some of our favorite bathroom shots. Send us yours! (See page 478.)

Fee dollars
at work
UserFee
project:
new
Sweet Smelling
toilet

a. Straddle toilet in Kenya (note feet)
b. Nevada ghost town outhouses
c. Outhouse at Anchor Bay, Malta
d. Sign at Glacier National Park
e. Extra-tall in Brazil
f. Rustic outhouse in Baja, Mexico

Vrooom!

How the Harley Became America's Bike

Whether a Hells Angel or a mild-mannered desk jockey, for many motorcyclists only a noisy, rough-riding Harley can fuel their outlaw dreams.

Most motorcyclists live a certain contradiction: They swear they're just law-abiding folk who like to ride ... but at the same time cherish the biker image that transforms mild-mannered CPAs and computer nerds into weekend outlaws. And outlaws drive Harleys; that's the way it is. Even Sonny Barger, longtime head of the Hells Angels, told a reporter that he likes Japanese bikes better, but drives a Harley because of pressure from the other members of the club.

But it wasn't always so. Motorcycles were once just a cheap way of getting around town, and Harley-Davidson was once just a small start-up in a Milwaukee shack.

WHEEL-LIFE ADVENTURES

Putting a motor on a bicycle seemed like a logical idea from the early days of steam engines. The problem was getting the engine small enough to fit on a bike and powerful enough to move it. When that first happened still isn't clear, but the earliest known attempt is pictured in an 1818 drawing of a steam-powered "Velocipedraisiavaporianna" being tested in Paris's Luxembourg Gardens. In 1869, both a French team and American

French steam velocipede, 1869

Sylvester Roper successfully built "steam velocipedes" that could go faster than a horse.

However, there were some problems with the steam-powered bikes. They didn't have much power, for one. For another, they had a tendency to explode now and then. And even at their best, you had to continuously add water and coal into the hissing, smoking engine between your legs. Inventors looked for other approaches. For example, the "Cynosphere," invented by M. Huret of Paris in 1875, was powered by two dogs running on the wheels.

Dogs on hogs: The Cynosphere

Finally, in 1876, the internal combustion gasoline engine came into being, thanks to N. A. Otto of Germany. Nine years later, his former assistant, Gottlieb Daimler, fathered the first modern motorcycle. Not that it was perfect—the spark plug had not yet been invented, and so to ignite the gas and air mixture, Daimler provided a Bunsen burner to heat up a metal tube that extended into the engine's cylinder. The problem, of course, was that the flame occasionally blew out in the wind. Worse, it would occasionally catch the rider's pants on fire or, in the event of dumping the bike, ignite spilled gasoline. Then came 1895, a year that brought the twin miracles of electrical ignition and inflatable tires.

Motorcycles began evolving away from being merely bicycles with motors strapped to them. In 1901, a French company designed a motorcycle in which the engine was not just a clip-on, but an integral part of the design. The designers were so confident that their motor would dependably propel the cycle that they even left off the bicycle pedals. This design was the true forerunner of the modern motorcycle, the one the world copied ... including some young guys in a shack in Milwaukee.

HARLEY-DAVIDSON-DAVIDSON ... In 1901, Arthur Davidson, a twenty-year-old pattern maker, teamed up with a twenty-one-year-old draftsman named Bill Harley. Inspired by the European motorcycles, they decided to tinker after work hours on their own design.

The two partners recruited a second Davidson brother (Walter, a railroad machinist) and then a third (William, a toolmaker). Rounding out the team with ideas and advice was a friend named Ole Evinrude (who later went off and started his own company that made Evinrude outboard boat motors).

SCARING THE HORSES

Needing a place to work, the Davidson boys convinced their father, a cabinet maker, to build a shed in their backyard. They put together a two-horsepower engine from scrounged scraps (including a tomato-can carburetor) and attached it to a bicycle. Eventually they worked out the bugs and began tooling around town at 25 mph on motorized bicycles, amazing the citizens and scaring the horses. Pretty soon, people started asking if the bikes were for sale. The company sold three motorcycles in its first year.

The after-hours business grew slowly. From three motorcycles in 1903, the company increase its output 66 percent the following year, assembling five motorcycles, and then again 60 percent the following year, making eight.

This dizzying growth curve convinced the partners to build a new, 28-by-80-foot headquarters next to a rail spur. Unfortunately, they discovered afterward that they'd

World headquarters, 1903

built it dangerously close to the track. Rather than dismantle it, they got together a dozen of their huskiest friends and had them lift the building a legal distance away. (The company headquarters still stands on this site, a safe distance from the tracks.)

Meanwhile, the partners decided they needed some capital so they could quit their day jobs. They turned to another Davidson, who the boys called their "honey uncle" because he was a bee-keeper, and borrowed enough to get serious about manufacturing their bikes.

Ironically, Harley's first model was designed to be unobtrusive and quiet. The partners had decided that people hated the noise and flash of the new contraptions, so William designed a grey motorcycle and an effective muffler. The result was dubbed "The Silent Grey Fellow." While the company sold all they could make, the silence was short-lived. It turned out that motorcyclists *liked* making a disturbance.

In 1907, when annual production was up to 150 units, William Harley accidentally created Harley's distinctively

The Silent Grey Fellow

rough staccato "potato-potato" engine sound. It was the result of taking a fairly inept design shortcut while trying to increase engine power. Rather than designing a two-cylinder engine from scratch, he merely welded a second cylinder to his one-cylinder design, using a forked connecting rod to join both pistons to a single crankshaft "throw." The result was an engine that ran rough and produced an excessive amount of vibration ... which, for better or worse, has become the famous sound and feel of a Harley.

Despite the odd engine design, Harleys became the heavyweight bike of choice for American motorcyclists, accounting for more than half of U.S. sales.

In the century since its founding, the company walks a tightrope between keeping its traditional outlaw biker market happy and also selling hogs to the rebel dentists, lawyers, and CPAs who make up a large part of their customer base now. Whether they can keep pleasing everybody without ending up pleasing nobody remains to be seen. Still, the Harley mystique continues, even as their owners cheerfully complain about them. For example: "Harleys leak oil, they vibrate bad, and you can't turn the things," groused one biker to *Forbes*. So why does he keep buying them? "You get laid."

Change Your Looks

A Spy Manual from 1944 Tells How

This not-so-politically-correct manual from the Office of Strategic Services (forerunner to the CIA) suggests that all you really need to disguise yourself are newspapers, spirit gum, make-up, rubber tubing, and a couple of pencil erasers. Here's how to use them.

One main point should be stressed again and again: **Disguise must be to a great extent an *internal* matter. The less there is of it on the outside, the better.** First: You must study yourself and check up on your habits. Each individual has peculiar mannerisms. They must be analyzed and eliminated. Second: You must know your cover story thoroughly. Keep in mind that if you tell a lie often enough you believe it yourself.

The type of clothes you will be wearing will determine, to some degree, the amount of change you can make. It will be much easier to switch from a bank clerk to a tramp, for example, than vice versa. Consider also the district you have to pass through in making your escape. If it is the wharves, you will be less noticeable as a seaman or a stevedore. If it is the financial district, become the most typical of clerks. Be one of the crowd.

SHAPE OF BODY

To make yourself taller, $2\text{–}2^{1}/_{2}$ inches can be quickly added to your height by folding a newspaper to form a ramp in the heels of your shoes. Such ramps offer an added advantage in that they also change your walk and posture. Restyle the crown of your hat, using its complete height. Hoist your trousers way up and tighten the belt. This will make your legs look longer. Pull your collar down, showing as much neck as you can.

To appear shorter, the reverse of everything above should be done. Also, slump down and bend your knees a bit.

FACE, HAIR, AND HANDS

Pick out your most prominent features. These are the ones to disguise. Wads of cotton or paper between the teeth and cheeks will change a thin face to a fuller one. Under the upper or lower lip, or both, will radically change the profile.

A nose can be narrowed by shadowing it on both sides and highlighting the top down its length. A narrow nose is widened or twisted by the use of nose plugs. These can be made of rubber tubing, approximately one-half inch in outside diameter and cut into half-inch lengths. Place them in the nostrils just up out of sight, being careful not to let them slip into the nasal cavity. The firm upper part of a baby's rubber nipple can be used.

If you are wearing a mustache, remove it or cut it down to a stubble so that it loses its previous character. If you don't have one, it is possible to make one on the spot in a few minutes, using your own body hair, provided you have taken the trouble to carry with you a small vial of liquid adhesive or spirit gum. If you have glasses put them on or remove them.

A good swarthy or dirty skin color can be had by wetting your hands and rubbing them on an old piece of rusty iron. Its advantages are readily apparent when one realizes that when white officers and men go in with native troops, it is usually the white faces that the Japs shoot at first. Don't forget the hands. They too much match.

Soot from inside a water heater or stove pipe can darken the eyebrows and hair. Try using a little of the black mixed with the rust to accentuate "bags" under the eyes, hollows in cheeks, or even a broken nose effect.

For graying hair, mustache, or eyebrows, try grey ashes powdered by rubbing them in the palm of the hand; try talcum powder, flour, or shoe-white. The effect of a stubble beard is best put on by using a dark thick grease and a rough sponge.

POSTURE AND GAIT

If you have round shoulders, a "figure eight" cord around both arms and crossed in the back, will serve as a reminder to throw out your chest and stand up straight. Tying your suspenders together high up in the back will do the same thing to a lesser extent.

If you want round shoulders, cross the figure eight cord in front. Try the old trick of buttoning your pants to your vest to acquire a stoop. Another way is a strip of adhesive plaster stuck from just above the navel up to the hair on the chest, applied while slouched over. Then try to straighten up!

Even without making a clothes change, a student can assume a completely different cover merely by changing his gait and switching to the exact opposite of the tempo used in the first cover. Start now to observe how men of different classes of society and age sit, stand and walk. One section of the crowd will move with a purpose, preoccupied with their own important little lives. Another group will slouch or waddle along, like dully curious animals. Any little object catches their interest for a fleeting moment. They have no goals in life and every movement and line of their bodies show it.

Building up the inside of one shoe-heel will give a "short-leg" limp. With the same device it is easy to assume the walk of someone who has been paralyzed on one side. Build up your left heel about $1^1/_2$ inches, crook your right arm into a useless set, drop the right shoulder, and swing the right half-dead leg forward. Be sure your face has that drooped, dull, set expression of one who has had a stroke. The eyes are usually all that move, with a bewildered, anxious expression as though the person does not quite know what has happened to him. This cover, if not overplayed, has a good psychological angle because one's natural impulse is to look away from such cripples.

A small stone in one sock heel will produce a convincing limp. Slightly larger ones in the arch of each foot will produce a "fiat foot" walk. Detachable rubber pencil erasers are best for this because they do not bruise the foot so much over a period of time. Putting them inside the sock helps keep them in place. For an "old age" gait, try a tight bandage around the calf of your leg with something under it to hurt the muscle as the weight is put on that foot.

Try the "lost arm," which is best done when wearing a double-breasted coat. Take the left arm from the coat sleeve. Tuck the empty sleeve in the coat pocket. Hold the elbow close to the waist at the side front and put your forearm around your waist with the left hand resting on the right hip.

WOMEN STUDENTS

While many of the suggestions outlined in this volume are applicable to both men and women students, the following section is written solely for the women.

A change of hair style is one of the most simple and effective aids in changing a woman's appearance. The style chosen should be one that a woman can arrange herself without recourse to a beauty parlor. An important point to remember is that the most unbecoming hair style will probably change the wearer's appearance more than any other.

It should be borne in mind that in many parts of the world women do not get or use much make-up. If lipstick is used, however, making a different lip line will alter the appearance greatly, as will changing the shape of the eyebrows.

If a woman does not want to be noticed, she should strive to look mousy or old or dumpy. If the work calls for glamour, an expert on make-up should be consulted. A woman who normally chooses bright and colorful clothes should change to something darker, say a grey dress or suit. The point is to achieve a complete contrast from the clothes usually worn.

Before

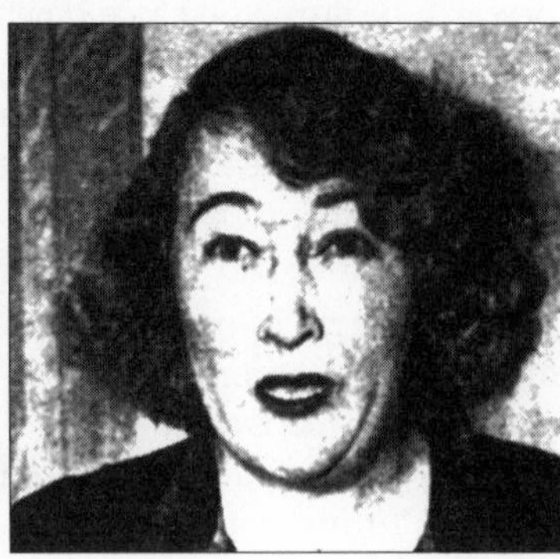

After

A woman of 30–40 years of age can easily add 10–15 years to her apparent age. She should clean off all make-up, wrinkle up her face, and with a very sharp brown eyebrow pencil lightly line all of the creases. Rub these down to the point where they are only soft shadows. A very thin application of the brown pencil mixed with Max Factor's No. 6 blue-grey liner, close to the bridge of the nose and accentuating circles under the eyes, will add to the effect. Next, a light-colored make-up should be used on all the high spots—the cheek bones, nose, chin and the tops of all wrinkles, care being taken to blend all edges out. If any lipstick is used at all, it should be thin and light-colored and blotted off. Next, the lips should be puckered and powder added on top of the lipstick. If the student wears dental plates or removable bridges, she should take them out. The neck and hands must not be overlooked; all must tie in together. A little hair white should be combed in at the temples or streaked through the whole head and the hair done up in an older style.

PERMANENT DISGUISE

Permanent disguise requires the services of a plastic surgeon. Its use has been successfully employed on a particularly noticeable feature, such as a prominent nose, ears that stick far out, or an easily remembered scar, that might be recognized on returning to the field.

Surgery has been used to alter the racial characteristics of Jewish students. Broken, bulbous and sharp Roman noses have also been successfully changed to shapes less eye-catching.

Prominent ears are dealt with by pinning them back. This leaves a small inconspicuous scar where the skin joins the ear to the head.

Scars should always be eliminated if possible. They can be removed surgically by a specialist without requiring hospitalization. An operation lasting two to three hours and removal of stitches after seven to ten days are all that are necessary.

Tattoo marks are extremely difficult to remove. The process is long and painful and is not recommended. A more satisfactory treatment is re-tattooing with a larger, more elaborate design. Skillful blending can achieve very satisfactory results. It has the advantage of speed and there is much less discomfort to the subject.

Listen Up

More Life Advice from the Rich & Famous

"You can't be happy with a woman who pronounces both Ds in Wednesday." – Peter DeVries

"Money is better than poverty, if only for financial reasons." – Woody Allen

"All Southern literature can be summed up in these words: 'On the night the hogs ate Willie, Mama died when she heard what Daddy did to sister.'" – Pat Conroy's mother (according to Pat)

"Don't tap your foot, it makes your arms get tired." – Thelonious Monk

"When in doubt, sing loud." – Robert Merrill

"Eat cereal for breakfast and write good prose." – Raymond Carver

"When you are smashing monuments, save the pedestals. They always come in handy." – Stanislaw Lec

"Cynicism is more than a pose; it's also a handy time saver. By deflating your companion's enthusiasm, you can cut conversations in half." – Lisa Birnbach

"Live each moment as if your hair is on fire." – Suzannah B. Troy

"I've always wanted to be somebody. But now I see I should have been more specific." – Jane Wagner

"I don't know the key to success, but the key to failure is to try to please everyone." – Bill Cosby

"The thermometer of success is the level of jealousy from the malcontents." – Salvador Dali

Elephant Jokes

Why Do Elephants Have Flat Feet?

Elephant jokes were a fad in the mid-1960s. Their surreal humor—half non-sequitur, half Zen koan—matched the tone of the times perfectly.

How do elephants communicate? *They talk on the elephone.*

How can you tell if an elephant's been in your refrigerator? *His footprints are in the Jell-O.*

How can you tell if two elephants have been in your refrigerator? *There are two sets of footprints in the Jell-O.*

How can you tell if three elephants are in your refrigerator? *The door won't close.*

How many hippos will fit in the refrigerator? *None. There are too many elephants in there.*

How do you make an elephant float? *Two scoops of ice-cream, a bottle of cola, and one elephant.*

Why do elephants paint their toenails red? *So they can hide in the strawberry patch.*

But there aren't any elephants in the strawberry patch! *See? It's working.*

How do you get an elephant to the top of an oak tree? *Plant an acorn under him and wait fifty years.*

How do you get an elephant down from an oak tree? *Tell him to sit on a leaf and wait until fall.*

What's the difference between an elephant and an egg? *You don't know? I guess I'm not sending YOU to the store!*

What do you do with a blue elephant? *Cheer him up.*

How do you keep an elephant from charging? *Take away his credit cards.*

Why were the elephants kicked off the beach? *They were walking around with their trunks down.*

Why do ducks have flat feet? *From stomping out forest fires.*

Why do elephants have flat feet? *From stomping out burning ducks.*

How do you get down from an elephant? *You don't – you get down from a duck.*

I Curse Thee!

"Ye little gayle hather mammothrept!" Jeffrey Racirk, author of the *Long Lost Insults Knowledge Cards*, has compiled an extensive list of long-forgotten English slurs. Test-marketed on our siblings and friends, here are some of our favorites.

GUDDLER: "A greedy drinker, one who is fond of liquor: [from] guddle, to drink much and greedily." —James Jennings's *Dialect of Somersetshire*, 1869

MUNZ-WATCHER: "One of those sneaks that makes a practice of watching the movements, etc., of sweethearts on their nightly walks, and if any impropriety is witnessed, demanding hush-money to keep the matter secret." —Joseph Wright's *English Dialect Dictionary*, 1896–1905

RUM-DAGGER: "A cheat who tells wonderful stories of his sufferings at sea to obtain money." —Admiral William Smyth's *Sailor's Word-book*, 1867

SHEEP-BITER: "A poor, sorry, sneaking, ill-lookt fellow." —B.E.'s *Dictionary of the Canting Crew*, 1698–1699

SLACKUMTRANCE: "A slovenly or dirty woman." —W. H. Long's *Dictionary of the Isle of Wight Dialect*, 1886

THEOLOGASTER: "A quack in theology; a shallow or pretended theologian." —William Whitney's *Century Dictionary*, 1889

ZOUNDERKITE: "Usually applied to one whose stupid conduct results in awkward mistakes." —C. Clough Robinson's *Dialect of Mid-Yorkshire*, 1876

Fabled Humans

Aesop Tales with People in Them

Most Aesop fables use animals to tell a story and deliver a lesson, but they occasionally include humans, sometimes at their worst and sometimes at their best.

THE WOODMAN AND THE SERPENT

One wintry day a Woodman was tramping home from his work when he saw something black lying on the snow. When he came closer he saw it was a Serpent to all appearance dead. But he took it up and put it in his bosom to warm while he hurried home. As soon as he got indoors he put the Serpent down on the hearth before the fire. The children watched it and saw it slowly come to life again. Then one of them stooped down to stroke it, but the Serpent raised its head and put out its fangs and was about to sting the child to death. So the Woodman seized his axe, and with one stroke cut the Serpent in two. "Ah," said he,

"No gratitude from the wicked."

THE WOLF AND THE KID

A Child was perched up on the top of a house, and looking down saw a Wolf passing under him. Immediately he began to revile and attack his enemy. "Murderer and thief," he cried, "what do you here near honest folks' houses? How dare you make an appearance where your vile deeds are known?"

"Curse away, my young friend," said the Wolf.

"It is easy to be brave from a safe distance."

THE MAN AND THE WOOD

A Man came into a Wood one day with an axe in his hand, and begged all the Trees to give him a small branch which he wanted for a particular purpose. The Trees were good-natured and gave him one of their branches. What did the Man do but fix it into the axe head, and soon set to work cutting down tree after tree. Then the Trees saw how foolish they had been.

Don't give an enemy the means to destroy you.

"But a Wolf actually did come..."

THE SHEPHERD BOY

There was once a young Shepherd Boy who tended his sheep at the foot of a mountain near a dark forest. It was rather lonely for him all day, so he thought upon a plan by which he could get a little company and some excitement. He rushed down toward the village calling out "Wolf, Wolf," and the villagers came out to meet him, and some of them stopped with him for a considerable time. This pleased the boy so much that a few days afterward he tried the same trick, and again the villagers came to his help. But shortly after this a Wolf actually did come out from the forest, and began to worry the sheep, and the boy of course cried out, "Wolf, Wolf," still louder than before. But this time the villagers, who had been fooled twice before, thought the boy was again deceiving them, and nobody stirred to come to his help. So the Wolf made a good meal off the boy's flock, and when the boy complained, the wise man of the village said:

"A liar will not be believed, even when he speaks the truth."

THE THIEF AND HIS MOTHER

A young Man had been caught in a daring act of theft and had been condemned to be executed for it. He expressed his desire to see his Mother, and to speak with her before he was led to execution, and of course this was granted. When his Mother came to him he said: "I want to whisper to you," and when she brought her ear near him, he nearly bit it off. All the bystanders were horrified, and asked him what he could mean by such brutal and inhuman conduct. "It is to punish her," he said. "When I was young I began with stealing little things, and brought them home to Mother. Instead of rebuking and punishing me, she laughed and said: 'It will not be noticed.' It is because of her that I am here today."

"He is right, woman," said the Priest; "the gods hath said:

"Train up a child in the way he should go; and when he is old he will not depart therefrom."

THE MAN AND HIS TWO WIVES

In the old days, when men were allowed to have many wives, a middle-aged Man had one wife who was old and one who was young; each loved him very much, and desired to see him like herself. Now the Man's hair was turning grey, which the young Wife did not like, as it made him look too old for her husband. So every night she used to comb his hair and pick out the white ones. But the elder Wife saw her husband growing grey with great pleasure, for she did not like to be mistaken for his mother. So every morning she used to arrange his hair and pick out as many of the black ones as she could. The consequence was the Man soon found himself entirely bald.

Yield to all and you will soon have nothing to yield.

TWO FELLOWS AND A BEAR

Two Fellows were traveling together through a wood, when a Bear rushed out upon them. One of the travelers happened to be in front, and he seized hold of the branch of a tree, and hid himself among the leaves. The other, seeing no help for it, threw himself flat down upon the ground, with his face in the dust. The Bear, coming up to him, put his muzzle close to his ear, and sniffed and sniffed. But at last with a growl he shook his head and slouched off, for bears will not touch dead meat. Then the fellow in the tree came down to his comrade, and, laughing, said "What was it that Master Bruin whispered to you?"

"He told me," said the other,

"Never trust a friend who deserts you at a pinch."

THE MILKMAID AND HER PAIL

Patty the Milkmaid was going to market carrying her milk in a Pail on her head. As she went along she began calculating what she would do with the money she would get for the milk. "I'll buy some fowls from Farmer Brown," said she, "and they will lay eggs each morning, which I will sell to the parson's wife. With the money that I get from the sale of these eggs I'll buy myself a new dimity frock and a chip hat; and when I go to market, won't all the young men come up and speak to me! Polly Shaw will be that jealous; but I don't care. I shall just look at her and toss my head like this." As she spoke she tossed her head back, the Pail fell off it, and all the milk was spilt. So she had to go home and tell her mother what had occurred.

"Ah, my child," said the mother,

"Do not count your chickens before they are hatched."

THE MAN BITTEN BY A DOG

A man who had been bitten by a Dog went about in quest of someone who might heal him. A friend, meeting him and learning what he wanted, said, "If you would be cured, take a piece of bread, and dip it in the blood from your wound, and go and give it to the Dog that bit you." The Man who had been bitten laughed at this advice and said, "Why? If I should do so, it would be as if I should beg every Dog in the town to bite me."

Benefits bestowed upon the evil-disposed increase their means of injuring you.

OLD WOMAN AND THE WINE JAR

You must know that sometimes old women like a glass of wine. One of this sort once found a Wine Jar lying in the road, and eagerly went up to it hoping to find it full. But when she took it up she found that all the wine had been drunk out of it. Still she took a long sniff at the mouth of the Jar. "Ah," she cried,

"What memories cling 'round the instruments of our pleasure."

"Go, give it to the Dog that bit you."

Stately Knowledge

12 Reasons Why Ya Gotta Love Rhode Island

We've searched the vaults and come up with some pretty impressive facts and stories about Rhode Island. Here are a dozen of our favorites.

1 It's the smallest state in the country. It has the shortest slogan of all the states: "Hope." But it has the longest official name: "State of Rhode Island and Providence Plantations."

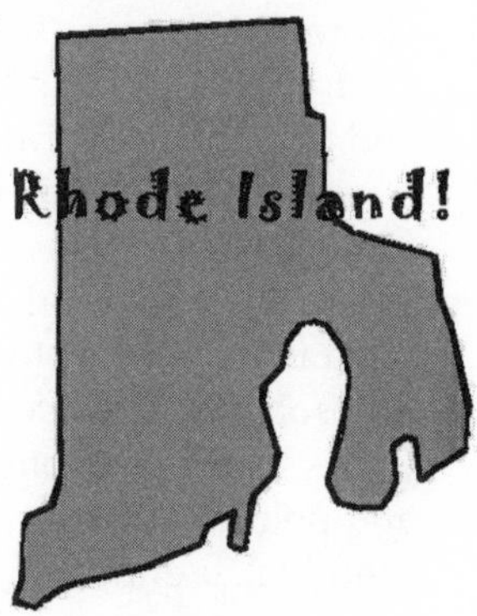

2 Rhode Island would fit inside the state of Alaska 483 times.

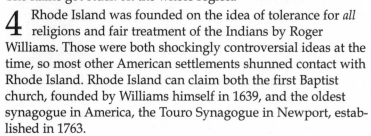

3 Despite the name, Rhode Island is not an island like Hawaii. It does, however, have thirty-six islands along its coast. In 1524, explorer Giovanni da Verrazzano decided that one of them looked like the island of Rhodes in Greece, and so he called it Rhode Island. The name got stuck on the whole region.

4 Rhode Island was founded on the idea of tolerance for *all* religions and fair treatment of the Indians by Roger Williams. Those were both shockingly controversial ideas at the time, so most other American settlements shunned contact with Rhode Island. Rhode Island can claim both the first Baptist church, founded by Williams himself in 1639, and the oldest synagogue in America, the Touro Synagogue in Newport, established in 1763.

5 You'll have a problem, though, if you want to see Roger William's gravesite. His earthly remains were eaten by an apple tree. Centuries after his death, the Rhode Island Historical Society wanted to bury him in a better resting place, but when they dug up his grave they discovered that Williams was completely gone, bones and all. An apple tree's roots had entered his coffin near his head and—apparently liking what it found—grew down his spine, even branching into his legs and arms.

6 Famous Rhode Islanders include songwriter George M. Cohan, (he wrote "You're a Grand Old Flag" and "I'm a Yankee Doodle Dandy"), painter Gilbert Stuart (his portraits of Washington are on the dollar bill and quarter), actors Van Johnson, Harry Anderson, James Wood, Anthony Quinn, and political commentator John McLaughlin.

7 More silverware is produced in Providence, Rhode Island, than anywhere else on Earth.

8 Rhode Island's state bird is a common chicken—the Rhode Island Red, bred in the village of Adamsville in Little Compton. You can see a granite monument with an image of the chicken on it. How can you tell if your morning eggs are from a Rhode Island Red? The shells are brown instead of white.

9 Newport, Rhode Island firsts: First game of polo played in America (1876). First jail sentence for speeding in an automobile (August, 1904). First circus in the United States (1774). The country's oldest tavern (the White Horse, 1673). And the first street illuminated by gas lights (Pelham Street, 1806).

10 Rhode Island's Official State Drink is "Coffee Milk"—half coffee, half milk, heavily sugared.

11 You may have been to Disney World, but how about Dairy World? It's really just the Nature's Best Dairy plant—featuring factory tours and dairy museum—in Cranston, Rhode Island.

12 The world's largest toy company, Hasbro, is headquartered in Pawtucket, Rhode Island. One of their bigger selling toys, Mr. Potato Head, was named the state's Official Travel Ambassador by the governor.

Dotty Detours

W. C. Privy's "Don't Miss" Attractions

Next time you head out to visit the Grand Canyon, Niagara Falls, or Disney World, don't forget to add these places to your Must-See list.

BEAN FEST & CHAMPIONSHIP OUTHOUSE RACE

Mountain View, Alaska

Cost: Free admission, cornbread, and beans

This event takes place on the last Saturday in October. Lots of beans and fast-rolling outhouses; the winner gets a gold-painted toilet seat.

THE HAIR MUSEUM

In the office of Lelia Cohoon, College of Cosmetology, Independence, Missouri

Cost: $3, but you get a discount on a hair cut

Lelia opened The Hair Museum to honor the old artistic tradition of hair art, which reached its height of popularity at the turn of the twentieth century. At this museum you'll find wreaths, butterflies, bracelet, and flower arrangements, among other things.

THE TOILET SEAT ART MUSEUM

239 Abiso, Alamo Heights, Texas

Cost: Free

"Doc" Barney Smith—a lifelong plumber and artist—has painted well over 650 toilet seats, and displayed them in his garage for folks to come and take a gander at. None are for sale. Open most afternoons, but call first: 210-824-7791.

TOILET ROCK

City of Rocks, New Mexico

Cost: No fee for daytime use, small camping fee

The name says it all: It's a rock shaped like a giant toilet.

LINGERIE MUSEUM AND CELEBRITY LINGERIE HALL OF FAME

Behind Frederick's of Hollywood store, Hollywood, California

Cost: Free

Here you'll see negligees once owned by Mae West and Loni Anderson, Madonna's bustier, and bras worn by Cher, Phyllis Diller, and Natalie Wood. Also a pair of Robert Redford's striped boxers, and other celebrity scanties.

THE DONNER PARTY MUSEUM

Donner Memorial State Park, Truckee, California

Cost: $1

Today it's called the Emigrant Trail Museum and Statue, dedicated to the pioneering spirit. However, that's been a recent change. The museum still heavily features the Donner Party's badly planned journey that ended up in misery, wintry deaths, and cannibalism.

THE MUSEUM OF QUESTIONABLE MEDICAL DEVICES

Science Museum of Minnesota, St. Paul, Minnesota

Cost: $7 adults, $5 kids and seniors

Here's a blurb from the museum's Web site: "The world's largest display of what the human mind has devised to cure itself without the benefit of either scientific method or common sense."

THE SPAM MUSEUM

1937 Spam Blvd., Austin, Minnesota

Cost: Free

Austin is the hometown of George A. Hormel's first meat-processing plant (opened in 1891). You enter the museum through a huge Spam can, and are greeted with case after case of packaging, old advertisements, and artifacts.

THE TESTICLE FESTIVAL

Just outside Clinton, Montana

Cost: $10 for five-day pass

In mid-September the Rock Creek Lodge hosts a Testicle Festival, honoring the eating of bull testicles ("Rocky Mountain Oysters").This one may not be fit for the kids, since public nudity, drinking, and general acting out seems to be a large part of the celebration. "In addition to 'nuts,'" says the Web site, "the festival provides chicken, music, group games and a little bit of 'crazy.'"

Tales of Gods

AESOP'S FABLES ABOUT DEITIES

Considering how much the ancient Greeks valued their gods, it's surprising there aren't more in Aesop's fables. We searched heaven and earth for these.

AVARICE AND ENVY

Two neighbors came before Jupiter and prayed him to grant their hearts' desire. Now the one was full of avarice, and the other eaten up with envy. So to punish them both, Jupiter granted that each might have whatever he wished for himself, but only on condition that his neighbor had twice as much. The Avaricious man prayed to have a room full of gold. No sooner said than done; but all his joy was turned to grief when he found that his neighbor had two rooms full of the precious metal. Then came the turn of the Envious man, who could not bear to think that his neighbor had any joy at all. So he prayed that he might have one of his own eyes put out, by which means his companion would become totally blind.

Vices are their own punishment.

HERCULES AND THE WAGONER

A Wagoner was once driving a heavy load along a very muddy way. At last he came to a part of the road where the wheels sank halfway into the mire, and the more the horses pulled, the deeper sank the wheels. So the Wagoner threw down his whip, and knelt down and prayed to Hercules the Strong. "O Hercules, help me in this my hour of distress," quoth he. But Hercules appeared to him, and said:"Tut, man, don't sprawl there. Get up and put your shoulder to the wheel:

"The gods help them that help themselves."

MERCURY AND THE WOODMAN

A Woodman was felling a tree on the bank of a river, when his axe, glancing off the trunk, flew out of his hands and fell into the water. As he stood by the water's edge lamenting his loss, Mercury appeared and asked him the reason for his grief. On learning what had happened, out of pity for his distress, Mercury dived into the river and, bringing up a golden axe, asked him if that was the one he had lost. The Woodman replied that it was not, and Mercury then dived a second time, and, bringing up a silver axe, asked if that was his. "No, that is not mine either," said the Woodman. Once more Mercury dived into the river, and brought up the missing axe. The Woodman was overjoyed at recovering his property, and thanked his benefactor warmly; and the latter was so pleased with his honesty that he made him a present of the other two axes. When the Woodman told the story to his companions, one of these was filled with envy of his good fortune and determined to try his luck for himself. So he went and began to fell a tree at the edge of the river, and presently contrived to let his axe drop into the water. Mercury appeared as before, and, on learning that his axe had fallen in, he dived and brought up a golden axe, as he had done on the previous occasion. Without waiting to be asked whether it was his or not, the fellow cried, "That's mine, that's mine," and stretched out his hand eagerly for the prize: but Mercury was so disgusted at his dishonesty that he not only declined to give him the golden axe, but also refused to recover for him the one he had let fall into the stream.

Honesty is the best policy.

THE OLD MAN AND DEATH

An old laborer, bent double with age and toil, was gathering sticks in a forest. At last he grew so tired and hopeless that he threw down the bundle of sticks, and cried out: "I cannot bear this life any longer. Ah, I wish Death would only come and take me!"

As he spoke, Death, a grisly skeleton, appeared and said to him: "What wouldst thou, Mortal? I heard thee call me."

"Please, sir," replied the woodcutter, "would you kindly help me to lift this bundle of sticks onto my shoulder?"

We would often be sorry if our wishes were gratified.

THE MAN AND THE SATYR

A man and a Satyr once drank together in token of a bond of alliance being formed between them. One very cold wintry day, as they talked, the Man put his fingers to his mouth and blew on them. When the Satyr asked the reason for this, he told him that he did it to warm his hands because they were so cold. Later on in the day they sat down to eat, and the food prepared was quite scalding. The Man raised one of the dishes a little towards his mouth and blew in it. When the Satyr again inquired the reason, he said that he did it to cool the meat, which was too hot. "I can no longer consider you as a friend," said the Satyr:

"A friend should not with the same breath blow hot and cold."

THE MAN AND THE WOODEN GOD

Long ago men used to worship sticks, stones and idols, and prayed to them for luck. It happened that a Man had often prayed to a wooden idol he had received from his father, but his luck never changed. He prayed and prayed, but still he remained unlucky. One day in a great rage he went to the Wooden God, and with a blow swept it down from its pedestal. The idol broke in two, and what did he see? An immense number of coins that had been inside all the time.

Having no god is better than one that does no good.

Juno refused the peacock's request.

THE PEACOCK AND JUNO

A Peacock once placed a petition before Juno desiring to have the voice of a nightingale in addition to his other attractions; however, Juno refused his request. When he persisted, and pointed out that he was her favorite bird, she said:

"Be content with your lot; one cannot be first in everything."

Potty Pourri

Random Kinds of Factness

• July, for some reason, is the most dangerous month for fatal auto accidents. February's next.

• Most barns in the 1800s really were painted red. Why was that? Red paint hid dirt well and was easy to make without having to resort to expensive store-bought paint. Here's the recipe: Mix skim milk with some linseed oil and lime. Add rust.

• The Hebrew word *musar* means both "education" and "corporal punishment."

• Put a Twinkie snack cake in a microwave oven, and in about 45 seconds, the Twinkie will explode.

• Your average cat usually has twelve whiskers on each side of its face.

• In Tudor-era England, doctors were expected to move in with the patient until they were nursed back to health.

• The term "freelancing" dates from the twelfth century when knights who lost employment with royal houses offered themselves as mercenaries.

• Because of "Blue Laws" forbidding such things on the sabbath, pro baseball didn't start playing Sunday games until 1933. Not that the laws changed—the baseball leagues just decided to ignore them.

• Ant queens never leave the ground except to mate. They do so after shooting straight up in the air. When they come back down, their minions pull off their wings and they never fly again.

• Roll out those lazy, hazy, crazy days of summer: A disproportionate number of people are admitted into mental institutions during the summer months.

• Watch out for cherry trees. Even though the fruit is divine, eating the leaves and limbs can be fatal.

Empty Soles

How Nike Turned Tennies into a Status Item

In the old days sports shoes were called tennies and cost a few bucks. Both of these things changed with the Nike Air sports shoe lines. Here's the story.

Did you know that the first air sole was patented in 1882? Since then, more than seventy different air-filled shoes have been registered with the U.S. Patent Office. Almost all of them, however, failed because of technical or commercial problems. It was Nike that made the air sole practical ... and sold it first for sports, and then status.

BIRTH OF THE NOTION

In 1969, Frank Rudy left a director-of-new-products job in the aerospace industry and started thinking about ski equipment. He decided to design an improved ski boot, since most of the current models were unnecessarily uncomfortable. He was joined in his quest by another aerospace industry guy named Bob Bogert, who had been a designer.

In a few years, they had come up with a practical air-filled boot liner. They took it to Howard Head, owner of Head Skis, who licensed the design. He began manufacturing boots with air soles inside. Unfortunately, not long afterward, he sold Head Skis to the AMF company. AMF decided to discontinue the line.

Meanwhile, the recreational running trend began taking hold. Rudy and Bogert decided to design a running shoe model of their air sole, figuring that the air would absorb some of the pavement shock that long-distance runners suffer from. After many attempts, they successfully designed a thin polyurethane air bag for the inside of running shoes and convinced the Bata shoe company to try them out.

A HURDLE OR TWO

The first prototypes worked great. The company ordered fifty more. Unfortunately, the oil embargo of 1974 was in full swing, and their supplier, without telling them, changed the formula for its polyurethane to use less oil. The new formula wasn't as strong as the old one. When the soles warmed up, the air inside expanded ... and the sole exploded with a bang. Bata suddenly lost interest.

Nearly broke and desperate, Rudy flew to France to meet with executives at Adidas. But talks broke down over terms and whether it was technically possible to mass produce shoes with air inside. Then a fortuitous thing happened: While hanging around the offices, Rudy overheard an Adidas employee mention a new little company named Nike that was selling a lot of running shoes in the United States. Rudy made some calls, found out that there was a running shoe trade show going on that weekend in Anaheim, and caught the next flight back to Southern California.

Nike, Greek goddess of Victory

He stopped by the booth in Anaheim just as it was closing and found out the name of the company's president, Phil Knight. Rudy found a pay phone and called Knight at headquarters in Oregon. Knight listened to Rudy's story and invited him up to Nike headquarters.

KNIGHT IN SHINING SNEAKERS

Knight had started Nike a few years before as Blue Ribbon Sports, distributing Tigers, an inexpensive Japanese running shoe. With time, Knight decided to manufacture his own shoes. An associate suggested the name Nike, after the winged Greek goddess of victory. Knight didn't like it much, but it was better than other names they'd come up with (among them Falcon, Bengal, and Dimension 6). Besides, it fit on the shoes and complemented the winged logo design.

After years of struggling, Nike was finally making strides in the recreational shoe business. Knight, an amateur runner, had seen the jogging boom coming and recognized the need for specialized shoes. He took Rudy's air-filled shoes for a run. They slowly deflated as he ran, but he saw the potential. "It was a great ride while it lasted," he told Rudy, and put him on six-month retainer to see if he could make something out of his idea.

Not long after, Nike decided that air soles were impractical. Sure, the air cushioned the road, but the friction from running heated the air to a level of discomfort and caused blisters. They tried putting an inflated midsole between a traditional sole and the runner's foot, which worked better.

They rushed the design into production. When the new shoe, called the Tailwind, hit the market, problems immediately started showing up. First of all, its price was $50, higher than any mass-produced running shoe up to that time. Then a last-minute fabric switch resulted in a shoe that fell apart quickly, infuriating customers. Just about half of the shoes were returned as defective.

Air Jordans' logo

But serious runners quickly saw some potential. An in-house study found that the air midsoles reduced impact by about 10 percent and decreased energy use by 2.8 percent. Some runners patched their shoes with duct tape and kept on running. The company eventually got the bugs out and prepared to promote them.

THE BOTTOM LINE

Up until this point, Nike had been signing up pros for between $8,000 and $100,000, each to wear and endorse their shoes. They "owned" about half of the players in the NBA (and all-in-all, about 2,000 expensive athletes from various sports) at a cost of millions of dollars a year.

For the new shoe models, they decided to find one promising rookie who had the potential to become a superstar and put all their eggs in his basket early, before he had a chance to get pricey. Charles Barkley was one candidate. Patrick Ewing was another. But the company finally settled on 20-year-old college junior named Michael Jordan. They decided that they would design a brand new shoe for him, push it hard, and tie the product to the man and vice versa, so that when consumers saw the player, they thought "shoes!"

Nike offered Jordan $2.5 million for a five-year contract, plus royalties on every Air Jordan shoe sold (they thought about calling them Jordan Airs, but decided it would cause too much confusion with the Mid-East airline and Elvis Presley's longtime backup group).

Nike came up with a proposed shoe, a logo, and an advertising campaign. There was only one stumbling block: Jordan didn't particularly like Nike shoes. He tried to work out a deal with Adidas, but they weren't willing to give even a fraction of what Nike offered him.

So in August 1984, Jordan signed with Nike. Nike came up with the distinctive black and red design for him. It was so distinctive, in fact, that NBA Commissioner David Stern threatened to fine him $1,000 if he wore the shoes during a game because they violated the NBA "uniformity of uniform" clause. He wore them anyway, creating an uproar in the stands and in the press ("Michael Jordan is not the most incredible, the most colorful, the most amazing, the most flashy, or the most mind-boggling thing in the NBA," wrote *Chicago Journal* sportswriter Steve Aschberner the next day. "His shoes are.")

IN THE END

Nike gladly paid Jordan's fine. It was the beginning of a brilliant PR and advertising campaign—a win-win situation for both parties. The Air Jordans endorsement went on to become the most successful in athletic history Over $100 million in shoes sold in the first year alone. The dark side: It became dangerous to wear the shoes in some cities as kids began killing other kids for their $110 sneakers. Meanwhile, despite the inflated price for the inflating shoes, Nike's workers in foreign plants were still being paid pennies an hour in sweatshops....

Despite the name, Nike Air soles don't have air in them. Instead, they contain a gas that has larger molecules than air so it don't leak through the airbag material as easily as air molecules would.

Stately Knowledge

12 Reasons Why Ya Gotta Love Maryland

We've searched the vaults and come up with some pretty impressive facts about Maryland. Here are a dozen of our favorites.

1 You may know that the state slogan is "Maryland is for Crabs!" But the state motto is downright dated for these nonsexist times: *Fatti masdhii, parole femine,* which means "Manly deeds, womanly words."

2 Sea Monkeys—the "pet" that is simply reconstituted brine shrimp—come from Bryans Road, Maryland, near the salty Atlantic Coast.

3 Back in 1988, Bob Rivers, a DJ at Baltimore, Maryland's WIYY radio station, vowed to stay on the air until the baseball team, the Baltimore Orioles, won a game. He didn't know what he'd gotten himself into. After ten losing games, and Rivers making the pledge, the Orioles continued to lose, keeping the DJ on the air 24 hours a day. Rivers took quick naps during songs, news, and commercial breaks. Finally, after eleven more losses in almost that many days, the Orioles beat the Chicago White Sox 9–0. Rivers played "I'm Free" by the Who and then went home to a well-deserved rest.

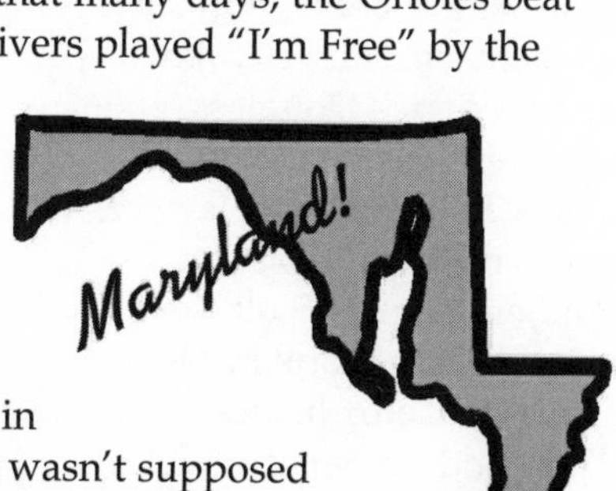

4 Maryland has more doctors per thousand people than any other state.

5 The first airmail flight in the United States landed in a cow pasture in Maryland. It wasn't supposed to. When the mail plane was launched with great ceremony in 1918, its scheduled route was supposed

to be from Washington, D.C. to New York. Unfortunately, the pilot discovered shortly after takeoff that somebody had forgotten to fill the plane's fuel tank.

6 There's something wrong about the sculpture of champion baseballer Babe Ruth at Baltimore's Oriole Park. Ruth grew up in Baltimore, so the 9-foot statue was supposed to be perfect, and it was, except for one thing: The Babe is shown leaning on a bat and clutching a right-handed fielder's glove. The real-life Babe Ruth was a lefty.

7 Boring, Maryland. It's not necessarily a description, it's the name of a town.

8 Maryland has no natural lakes. All of its lakes were made by humans digging and damming.

9 Famous Maryland residents include assassin John Wilkes Booth, anti-slavery activists Harriet Tubman and Frederick Douglass, polar explorer Matthew Henson, singer Billie Holiday, lawyer and writer of the National Anthem Francis Scott Key, chicken man Frank Perdue, Supreme Court Justice Thurgood Marshall, athletes Babe Ruth and Cal Ripken, Jr., authors H. L. Mencken, Upton Sinclair, Tom Clancy, and Leon Uris, weird musician Frank Zappa, and the first American-born saint of the Roman Catholic church, Elizabeth Seton.

10 Here's a fact for a rainy day: The world's first umbrella factory was opened in Baltimore in 1828, boasting the catchy slogan, "Born in Baltimore—Raised Everywhere." Get it?

11 Camp David, near Thurmont, Maryland. It was called Shangri-La until Dwight D. Eisenhower decided to rename it Camp David in honor of his grandson and his father—both named David.

12 Maryland was a leader in naming an official state sport—jousting. Several tournaments are held during the year, but, alas, it's the wimpy kind where they spear rings, not each other.

The Five Senses

A Few Sensory Notes

***Bathroom Companion* correspondent Kathie Meyer has found some intriguing tidbits and odd stories on the things we use to navigate the world—the five senses.**

NOSING AROUND AT THE OLFACTORY

• At the upper end of each nostril are the olfactory regions, a yellow, moist, fatty substance. Heredity determines the shade of yellow of this body part, and the richer the color of yellow, the more acute one's sense of smell. People with darker skin have more sensitive noses than those with lighter skin. Albinos have an especially poor sense of smell.

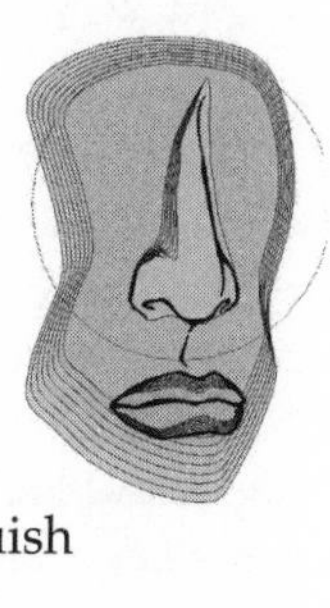

• There are odor technicians in the perfume trade who reportedly have the olfactory skills to distinguish 20,000 odors at twenty levels of intensity.

• Harry "the Nose" Jongen is a "remains identification expert" in the Netherlands. He's won worldwide attention for his ability to smell out the dead, even buried underground, and his skills are usually used for police work. However, not always. A Jewish man asked Harry if he would help him find an available plot in an old Jewish graveyard where he wanted to be buried. The problem was that the graveyard had been left untouched for more than 300 years, and the Jewish faith precludes graves from being disturbed. "We knew Harry only needs a stick to poke in the earth and, by the look and the odor of the ground, he can find out if someone has been buried there before," said a spokesman of the Jewish community. Sure enough, Harry found an empty grave site for the guy.

OPTICAL ALLUSIONS

• A newborn baby's eye is remarkably close to its full adult size. At birth the length of the eye is around 17 mm, growing to full adult size of 23 mm. This explains why so many babies are admired for having such "big, beautiful eyes." Your ears and nose, on the other hand, continue to grow throughout your entire life.

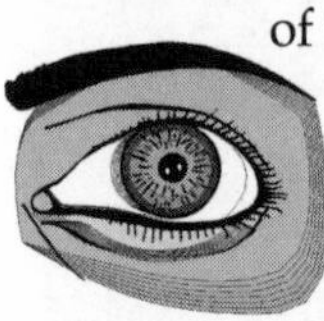

• A bird's eye takes up about fifty percent of its head; a human's eyes take up about five percent of the head.

• Humans can't perceive color in bright moonlight. "Get up on a dark moonlit night and look around," suggests David Hubel of Harvard Medical School, Nobel prizewinner for his vision research. "Although you can see shapes fairly well, colors are completely absent. It is remarkable how few people realize that they do without color vision in dim light."

• Anton's Syndrome is characterized by a person's complete blindness coupled with a firm belief that they can still see. Medically, it is a cortical blindness associated with dementia and delirium, and otherwise downright weird.

• George Edgar Lizarralde, a legally blind man, failed to gain a California driver's license the first three times he took the test. On the fourth try, even though he failed the vision test, the DMV granted him the much coveted license. Five years later, Lizarralde plowed into a woman in a crosswalk, and a court ruled it was the DMV's negligence.

• The average human eye can distinguish about 500 different shades of gray.

• There are 1,200,000 fibers in a human optic nerve.

• The average person's field of vision encompasses a 200-degree wide angle.

YOU GOT SOME NERVE, PAL!

• Electrical impulses travel from the skin to the spinal cord at a rate of up to 425 feet per second.

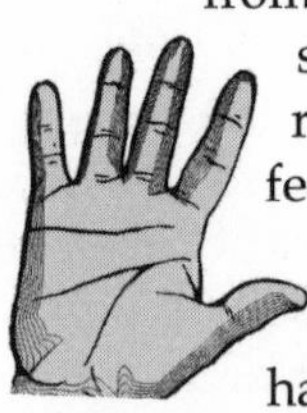

• The star-nosed mole is said to have the most delicate sense of touch in the animal kingdom. This nosey beast boasts twenty-two pink tentacles on its snout.

• Heel, boy! Although the benefits of stroking your pet are widely documented in touch research, *The New England Journal of Medicine* revealed one unexpected detriment. A woman's mysterious, chronic heel pain was found to be due to an accumulation of dog hairs embedded in her skin over the Achilles tendon. The woman had a long history of using her bare heel to pet her Scottish terrier. We wonder who had the worse end of that deal....

• Babies who are frequently touched gain weight fifty percent faster than unmassaged babies and cry less often.

• Here's something to rub you the wrong way: Massage therapy is covered by only eleven percent of all HMOs.

EARS LOOKIN' AT YOU, KID

• A New York judge dismissed a lawsuit by Clifford Goldberg against the heavy metal group, Motley Crüe. Goldberg said the music gave him a "searing pain" through his ears. The judge ruled that Goldberg had no case—everyone at a Motley Crüe concert knows it's going to be loud.

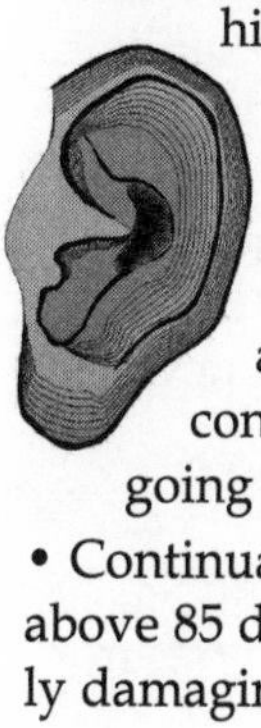

• Continual exposure to noises above 85 decibels is potentially damaging to your hearing. Sixty decibels is normal conversation. Exposing yourself to 90 decibels (a lawnmower) for more than eight hours, 100 decibels (a chainsaw or snowmobile) for more than two hours, 115 decibels (a rock concert or auto horn) for more than 15 minutes per day, or 140 decibels (a gun blast or jet engine) will most assuredly cause damage.

• In 1995, Carty Finkbeiner, mayor of Toledo, Ohio, came up with a politically tone deaf solution for the homeowners in the neighborhood nearest the airport: If they didn't like the noise, they could just sell their homes to the deaf. Several days later, the mayor issued an apology for this idea, which, as you might suspect, never really got a fair hearing.

• During World War I, before radar, birds were used in aerial warfare. Because of their acute hearing, the Army kept parrots on the Eiffel Tower to squawk out a warning of approaching enemy aeroplanes long before they could be seen or heard by humans.

• The first electrical hearing aid was invented in 1901 by Miller R. Hutchinson. It was a rather large appliance, too large to carry comfortably—in fact, it worked best to build it into a chair.

• American deaf people have better driving records than their hearing counterparts.

THE BETTER TO TASTE YOU WITH, MY DEAR

• Taste buds can perceive four things: salt, bitter, sour, and sweet. Some experts believe there's a fifth taste category, known as *umami,* found in soy products.

• Humans have approximately 9–10,000 taste buds. Cats have only 473.

• Eat your favorite foods when you're young, because by the age of seventy half of your taste buds will be gone.

• There are people known as "supertasters" who may have more than 1,000 taste buds per square centimeter on their tongues, as opposed to the average person who has fewer than forty.

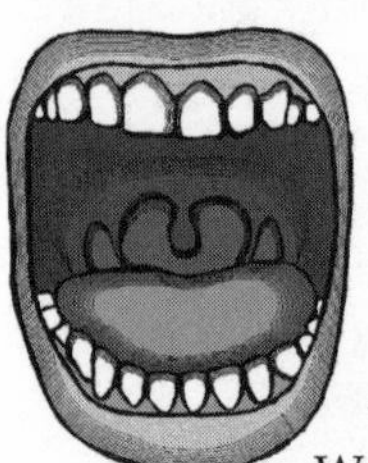

Women are more likely to be "supertasters" than men, and hormones such as estrogen are thought to play an additional role in taste perception. For instance, during the first trimester of pregnancy, many women are more sensitive to bitter flavors. This may explain the whole pickle-and-ice-cream thing.

• The official taste tester for Dreyers and Edy's Ice Cream, John Harrison, had his taste buds insured for a cool $1 million.

• If you're a supertaster and don't care for ice cream, there still may be a place for you as a professional tea taster, wine taster, beer taster ... in fact, you can probably name your food group, because the food and drink industry employs professional tasters in a variety of categories.

• New York gourmet chef Howard Schaeffer believed a traffic accident caused him to lose his senses of smell and taste. He sued for $1.1 million. When asked later why he still ate well enough to weigh over 200 pounds, he said he found other ways to enjoy his food, explaining, "It's amazing how quickly you can get into texture." He was awarded the money.

Dear Sir or Madame

"I regret the American public is not interested in anything on China."—an editor's 1931 rejection of Pearl S. Buck's now-classic *The Good Earth.*

The Eyes Have It

THINGS ARE A LITTLE DOTTY

Are the dots really flashing, or are your eyes playing tricks?

Stare at the black dot. What happens to the haze around it?

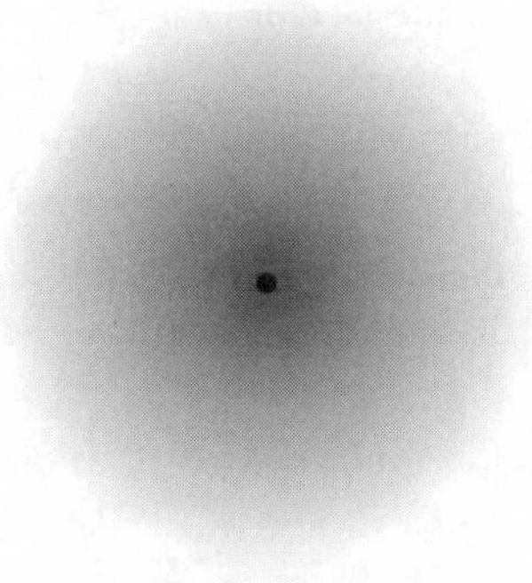

Every Picture Tells a Story

Washington Crossing the Delaware **by Emanuel Gottlieb Leutze**

• It is perhaps the most lasting image of the Revolutionary War, although it was painted eighty-five years later in Germany using the Rhine to stand in for the Delaware. Ironically, it commemorates a minor victory in the war, in which Americans made a sneak Christmas morning attack and captured 900 German troops, hired by the British.

• The painting is huge, about 21 feet long.

• The black man half-standing behind the flag bearer represents Prince Whipple, a slave emancipated during the war who served as bodyguard for his former master, Gen. William Whipple, a signer of of the Declaration of Independence and an aide to Washington.

• Nitpickers like to point out some problems with the painting:

1. Standing up in a boat in icy water is a really stupid idea.
2. The boat is too small for that many people (Washington's troops really used 30-footers).
3. The ice is all wrong.
4. The flag pictured wouldn't exist for another six months.
5. The sky shows a clear dawn, but the Americans crossed at 3 AM in a driving storm.

Shell Games

Aesop's Tales about Things with Shells

You know the Tortoise and the Hare, but perhaps these more obscure fables will also delight you. Shell-related, they're everything they're cracked up to be.

THE HARE AND THE TORTOISE

The Hare was once boasting of his speed before the other animals. "I have never yet been beaten," said he, "when I put forth my full speed. I challenge any one here to race with me."

The Tortoise said quietly, "I accept your challenge."

"That is a good joke," said the Hare; "I could dance round you all the way."

"Keep your boasting till you've beaten," answered the Tortoise. "Shall we race?"

So a course was fixed and a start was made. The Hare darted almost out of sight at once, but soon stopped and, to show his contempt for the Tortoise, lay down to have a nap. The Tortoise plodded on and plodded on, and when the Hare awoke from his nap, he saw the Tortoise just near the winning-post and could not run up in time to save the race. Said the Tortoise:

"Plodding forward steadily wins the race."

THE GOOSE WITH THE GOLDEN EGG

One day a countryman going to the nest of his Goose found there an egg all yellow and glittering. When he took it up it was as heavy as lead and he was going to throw it away, because he thought a trick had been played upon him. But he took it home on second thoughts, and soon found to his delight that it was an egg of pure gold. Every morning the same thing occurred, and he soon became rich by selling his eggs. As he grew rich he grew greedy; and thinking to get at once all the gold the Goose could give, he killed it and opened it only to find nothing.

Greed oft o'er reaches itself.

Seizing the Tortoise by the shell with her talons, she soared aloft

THE TORTOISE AND THE BIRDS

A Tortoise desired to change its place of residence, so he asked an Eagle to carry him to his new home, promising her a rich reward for her trouble. The Eagle agreed and seizing the Tortoise by the shell with her talons soared aloft. On their way they met a Crow, who said to the Eagle: "Tortoise is very good eating." "The shell is too hard," said the Eagle in reply. "The rocks will soon crack the shell," was the Crow's answer; and the Eagle, taking the hint, let fall the Tortoise on a sharp rock, and the two birds made a hearty meal of the Tortoise.

Never soar aloft on an enemy's pinions.

THE TWO CRABS

One fine day two Crabs came out from their home to take a stroll on the sand. "Child," said the mother, "you are walking very ungracefully. You should accustom yourself to walking straight forward without twisting from side to side."

"Pray, mother," said the young one, "do but set the example yourself, and I will follow you."

Example is the best precept.

THE BOY AND THE FILBERTS

A boy put his hand into a pitcher full of filberts. He grasped as many as he could possibly hold, but when he tried to pull out his hand, he was prevented from doing so by the neck of the pitcher. Unwilling to lose his filberts, and yet unable to withdraw his hand, he burst into tears and bitterly lamented his disappointment. A bystander said to him, "Be satisfied with half the quantity, and you will readily draw out your hand."

Do not attempt too much at once.

Stately Knowledge

12 Reasons Why Ya Gotta Love Texas

We've searched the vaults and come up with some pretty impressive facts and stories about Texas. Here are a dozen of our favorites.

1 Dr Pepper was invented in Waco, Texas, but not by a guy named Dr Pepper. The guy who invented the drink, Wade Morrison, named it after his former boss, a Virginia druggist named Dr. Kenneth Pepper.

2 You can visit a lot of the solar system without leaving Texas, because it has towns named Earth, Mercury and Pluto.

3 In 1987, Gene Gordon of Fort Worth, Texas, was in his backyard when he heard a loud bang in his house. He ran inside and found a large hole in his roof and smelly, bright blue ice melting in his attic. What do you suppose happened? He finally figured it out: A plane had a leaky toilet tank. The contents of the tank, including the bright blue liquid that flushes the toilet bowl, had dripped out and frozen on the bottom of the airplane. After a while, the blue ice let go ... right above Gordon's house. Yech!

4 Our favorite Texan? "Country" Bill White, who lived 341 days in a coffin more than six feet underground. His only connection to the outside world was a four-inch wide tube used for feeding and oxygen. Why'd he do it? Just to prove it could be done.

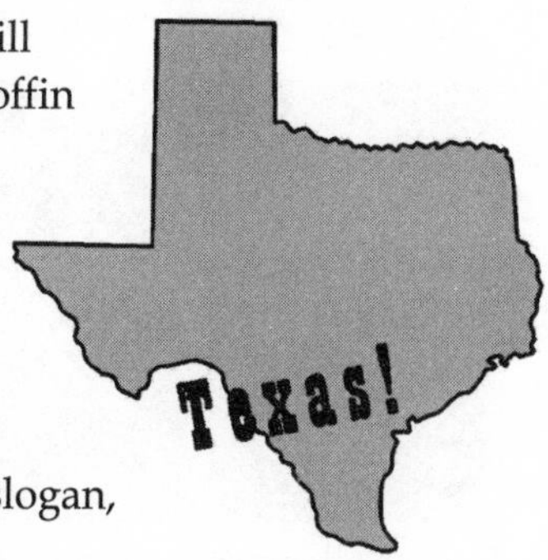

5 Texan Gail Borden invented condensed milk. He also coined the slogan, "Remember the Alamo!"

6 The King Ranch in southern Texas can lay claim to developing the very first new breed of beef cattle in the Western hemisphere—the Santa Gertrudis Cattle.

7 The first laundromat opened in Fort Worth, Texas, in 1934.

8 The largest tumor removed from a person's body came from a woman in Galveston, Texas, in 1905. It weighed 328 pounds.

9 The gas found in blimps and balloons is a natural substance that helium drillers drill for. Most of the world's helium comes from the ground under Texas. The largest helium well is in Amarillo, Texas.

10 There are not one but two statues of Popeye in Crystal City, Texas. They're there to celebrate Crystal City's main crop. Guess what that leafy vegetable might be?

Fire ants swarming toward the Festival

11 Under the 1845 annexation treaty that brought Texas into the Union, the state has what's called the "Right to Divide." That means at any time the state can legally divide into as many as five separate states.

12 Our favorite city in the lone star state is Marshall, located near the eastern border near Louisiana. It has a rich history and culture that embodies the Texan spirit. For starters, during the Civil War, Missouri governor Thomas Reynolds, running from Union forces, holed up in Marshall and made the Texas city the capital of Missouri. As far as we know, Marshall is the only city to be used as another state's capital. More recently, Marshall has played host to the annual Fire Ant Festival. In case you've never experienced a fire ant up close and personal, the little buggers are sort of like killer bees without wings; they're mean. The people of Marshall decided that since they can't seem to get rid of them, they might as well have some fun with them. They have fire ant calling contests, fire ant roundup competitions, and even a fire ant cook-off, featuring recipes made with fire ants.

Cosmic Pekoe

Tea Reading to the Great Beyond

Today it's virtually unheard of, but it used to be common. In tearooms and coffee houses across the land, a dark, mysterious stranger would approach when you'd reached the end of your cup and offer to read your future for a few coins. After a mysterious ritual of stirring and dumping the cup's dregs, the reader would point out pictures in the leaves and tell you what they meant.

THE HISTORY OF TEALEAF READING

Telling the future with tea leaves (called tasseography, by the way) goes so far back that there's no way to trace its history. Suffice it to say that reading coffee grounds and tea leaves has been around for thousands of years in a number of cultures. (A similar technique appears in Genesis 44:5, in which Joseph reads wine dregs from a special silver cup to foretell the future.)

Sadly, reading tea leaves and coffee grounds has nearly died out in our time. The reasons are simple and concrete: tea bags and coffee filters. But we can work around that. In the really old days, people drank hot beverages through clenched teeth to strain out loose leaves and coffee grounds. Get used to the idea, because it's something you'll need to do when telling fortunes.

HOW DOES IT WORK?

Interpretation is a lot like inkblots in a psychiatrist's office. This is especially true when you start realizing that it's awfully hard to differentiate between, for example, a tea-leaf dog ("faithful friends") and a wolf ("jealous friends"), or between a toad ("unknown enemy") and a frog ("arrogant French person"). So, in this way, tea-leaf reading can be a reflection of your subconscious mind.

Throw in a reader who is also a good and intuitive judge of people, which many tea-leaf readers have proven to be, and you can see how effective fortunetelling with tea can be.

The best thing about tea and coffee reading, though, is that it can be done anytime you stop and have a cup of something, so it allows a relaxing moment by yourself or a social, self-revealing one when you're with friends.

READING THE LEAVES

- Use a cup with a wide opening, the kind that comes with a saucer, not a mug. The inside of the cup should be light-colored and patternless so that you can see the leaves clearly.
- Use loose tea if you can find it in the store, preferably with big leaves. Otherwise, simply cut open a tea bag or two and dump the contents into a cup. If you're making coffee, dump the loose ground coffee (instant coffee won't work) right into the cup, add hot water, and wait for a few minutes before adding cream or sugar.
- The room should be peaceful, if possible, and the light dim with one spot of light—either artificial or a ray of moonlight—illuminating the cup. Clear your mind and relax, concentrating on your future and asking whatever power is involved for an accurate reading.

1. Don't drink to the last drop. Instead, save the leaves or grounds with a little liquid in the bottom (not too much, one or two teaspoonsful).
2. Take the cup in your left hand and spin it three times clockwise. (At least, that's what most tea leaf readers say, although we found one source that said you should do it *counter*clockwise. So, either this one is wrong, or it doesn't really matter which way you turn it ... or, perhaps

this advice is for leaf readers in the Southern Hemisphere.)

3. Immediately after swirling it, turn the cup over on a saucer or plate. After all the liquid drains out, set it back up upright, with the handle pointing toward you.

INTERPRETING

• The handle is like a YOU ARE HERE arrow on a map—it represents you and your sphere of influence and home, and a symbol found near the handle indicates something that will literally strike close to home. Leaf configurations stuck near the rim represent your present; the walls, your immediate future; and the bottom, the distant future.

• Look carefully into the cup, tipping it and noting all walls and the bottom, noting the leafs or grounds stuck to them from all angles. At first they may look like random clumps and glops, but see if their shapes remind you of anything. This will take some imagination, like when you were a kid and looked for pictures in the clouds. Also notice their size and relative positioning, because two images next to each other can influence each other.

• The bigger and clearer an image is, the more significant it is. A small or blurry image has substantially less significance. If all the images are blurry, it indicates that you'll be troubled by delay and disturbance before the events come to pass. If the cup itself is blurry, too, it signifies that you'll soon be receiving bad news from your optometrist.

• You may see just a few symbols, or dozens, in one cup. The idea is to note all of them in a big picture and see how they interact with each other instead of trying to isolate each one as a separate thing. As in life, each component influences and is influenced by each of the other components.

• Your message doesn't lie in any one symbol, but within the unique relationship of all the elements. Bad omens may be weakened or canceled out by nearby good omens and vice versa. For example, something that looks like a snake ("bad luck") that appears near something looks like the letter M may indicate that you should be on guard against an enemy whose name begins with M. A number 6 next to a travel symbol may mean you'll be gone for that many days, weeks ... or even years (no matter what the Skipper and Gilligan promised about it being "a three-hour tour").

• Start with the images near the rim ("the present"), then work your way inward into the future.

Below are some of the images you might see.

SYMBOL KEY

Acorn: Good health, good luck (especially if you're reading for a squirrel)

Ants: Bad news, hard work (perhaps a disastrous picnic)

Apple: Long life, gain in business (may be incompatibility with other PCs)

Arch: Trip abroad (or maybe to McDonalds); if blurred, a bad trip

Bat: Fruitless endeavor (unless it's a fruit bat, perhaps)

Boat: Friendly visitor (howdy, sailor!)

Cat: Treachery, insincere friends

Comet: Unexpected visitor (or maybe clean sinks)

Cross: Trouble (if your father was a god and your mother a virgin, *big* trouble)

Crown: Success

Desk: Prosperity (or at least a cubicle of your own)

Dog: Faithful friends (some of whom perhaps will gladly hump your leg)

Dragon: Sudden change

Egg: Some say good fortune; others, that you'll lose your savings

Fan: Good luck with the opposite sex

Frog: Beware of excessive pride, arrogance (or French people ... but I repeat myself)

Goat: You're surrounded by enemies

Grasshopper: A friend will leave, maybe not return (or perhaps you'll be cast in the remake of *Kung-Fu*)

Hen: New addition to family

Hourglass: Danger nearby

Monkey: Success

Mountain: Friends in high places

Mouse: Thief nearby

Owl: Failure, sickness, poverty, maybe death (but have a nice day anyway)

Square: Peace, or no marriage (actually, the two may go together)

Violin: Excessive vanity

Wolf: Jealous friends

Worms: Secret enemies

ONE LAST ODD FACT

In China, a country full of both divination and tea, reading tea leaves is all but unknown.

Foodonyms

A Bunch of Fruits and Nuts

Did you know that there's a reason we call it a Bartlett pear or a macadamia nut? The origins of some of these names may surprise you as much as they did us.

Granny Smith apple: In the 1860s, Australian grandmother Maria Ann Smith created this tart apple by mixing a late-ripening crabapple with her regular orchard apples.

McIntosh apple: John McIntosh immigrated to Canada in the 1700s. He found a grove of wild apple trees growing near his farm. Word soon spread of their flavor and the McIntosh Red apple was born. The trees were probably cultivated by an earlier Indian settlement.

filbert: The filbert, also known as the hazelnut, got its name from St. Philbert. In Greece, Italy, and Turkey, where the plant is native, the bush blooms around the Catholic saint's feast day.

loganberry: This berry from the raspberry family was cultivated in the home garden of California lawyer James Logan in 1881.

boysenberry: Using the loganberry, raspberry, and blackberry, botanist Rudolph Boysen developed this hybrid in the 1920s and '30s.

macadamia: This nut, native to Australia, was discovered by European settlers in the 1800s. It was named in 1859 by Australian botanist Ferdinand Von Mueller in honor of his friend, Scottish scientist Dr. John Macadam. Macadam died at 38 without ever tasting the nut that bore his name.

Bartlett pear: In the 1600s, an English schoolteacher named John Stair created a pear variety. A horticulturist named Williams did some further breeding and named the result after himself. Massachusetts nursery owner Enoch Bartlett became known for selling this variety. Locals called the pear "Bartlett," and this time the name stuck.

Potty Pourri

RANDOM KINDS OF FACTNESS

• Dr. Pearl Zane Grey was only a moderately successful dentist. He did much better as "Zane Grey," writing Western novels between patients.

• Mexican jumping beans jump because there's a caterpillar inside. The "bean" is from a shrub that grows south of the border, and the caterpillar eats out the inside, jerking now and again to scare away birds and other seed-eaters. Eventually the caterpillar grows up and emerges from the seed as a butterfly.

• When he was a desperately poor child, Charles Dickens was forced to work at a shoe polish factory in London.

• How many ridges are there around the edge of a United States dime? 118. Don't believe us? Count 'em yourself.

• The oldest letter in our alphabet is *o*, first used by the Egyptians in about 3000 B.C.

• The newest letters are *j* and *v*. *J* was derived from *i* in about 1600. *V* had double-duty as vowel and consonant until someone got the bright idea to round the bottom and create a separate letter, *u*. This happened during the Renaissance.

• A 216-minute movie with a cast of thousands, yet not a single woman in a speaking role: That's one way of describing *Lawrence of Arabia*.

• In a poll, American speech teachers came up with the ugliest sounding words in the English language. The list included "plump," "gripe," "sap," "jazz," "crunch," "treachery," "cacophony," "phlegmatic," "plutocrat," and "flatulence."

• If you're dealing in Polish currency, just remember that it takes 100 groszy to make one zloty.

• Each of your eyeballs weighs about an ounce.

• In ancient China, the color of your fingernail polish was an indicator of your rank and position.

The Stalled Ox

A Short Story by Saki (Hector Monro)

Before he was killed in World War I, Hector Monro wrote short stories with a twist under the pen name "Saki." In this one, a bull in a garden inspires a major career change....

THEOPHIL ESHLEY WAS AN ARTIST by profession, a painter of cattle by force of environment. Not that he lived on a ranch or a dairy farm, in an atmosphere pervaded with horn and hoof, milking-stool, and branding-iron. His home was in a villa-dotted district that only just escaped being suburban. On one side of his garden there abutted a small, picturesque meadow, in which an enterprising neighbor pastured some small picturesque cows of the Channel Island persuasion.

In summertime the cows stood in meadow-grass under walnut trees with sunlight falling in dappled patches on their mouse-sleek coats. Eshley had executed a dainty picture of two reposeful milk-cows in filtered sunbeam, and the Royal Academy had duly exposed the same in its Summer Exhibition.

As he had begun, so, of necessity, he went on. His "Noontide Peace," was followed by "A Mid-day Sanctuary," a study of a walnut tree with two dun cows under it. In due succession there came "Where the Gad-Flies Cease from Troubling," "The Haven of the Herd," and "A-dream in Dairyland," all studies of walnut trees and dun cows. His two attempts to break away from his own tradition were signal failures: "Turtle Doves Alarmed by Sparrow-hawk" and "Wolves on the Roman Campagna" came back to his studio as abominable heresies, until Eshley climbed back into grace and the public gaze with "A Shaded Nook where Drowsy Milkers Dream."

On a fine late-autumn afternoon he was putting finishing touches to a study of meadow weeds when his neighbor, Adela Pingsford, assailed the door of his studio with loud knockings.

"I paint dairy cows, certainly," admitted Eshley, "but I cannot claim any experience in rounding-up stray oxen."

"There is an ox in my garden," she announced, in explanation of the tempestuous intrusion.

"An ox," said Eshley blankly; "what kind of ox?"

"I don't know what kind," snapped the lady. "A common or garden ox, to use the slang expression. It is the garden part of it that I object to. My garden has just been put straight for the winter, and the chrysanthemums are just coming into flower."

"How did it get into the garden?" asked Eshley.

"I imagine it came in by the gate," said the lady impatiently; "it couldn't have climbed the walls, and I don't suppose anyone dropped it from an aeroplane. The immediately important question is not how it got in, but how to get it out."

"Won't it go?" said Eshley.

"If it were anxious to go," said Adela Pingsford rather angrily, "I would not have come to chat with you about it. I'm practically all alone; the housemaid is out and the cook is lying down with neuralgia. Anything that I may have learned at school or life about how to remove a large ox from a small garden seems to have escaped my memory. All I could think of was that you were a cattle painter, presumably familiar with the subject, and that you might be of some assistance. Possibly I was mistaken."

"I paint dairy cows, certainly," admitted Eshley, "but I cannot claim any experience in rounding-up stray oxen. I've seen it done in a cinema film, of course, but there were always horses and lots of other accessories; besides, one never knows how much of those pictures are faked."

Adela Pingsford said nothing, but led the way to her garden. It was a fair-sized garden, but looked small in comparison with the ox, a huge mottled brute, dull red with shaggy ears and large blood-shot eyes. It bore about as much resemblance to the dainty paddock heifers that Eshley painted as the chief of a Kurdish nomad clan would to a Japanese tea-shop girl. Eshley stood very near the gate while he studied the animal's appearance and demeanor. Adela Pingsford continued to say nothing.

"It's eating a chrysanthemum," said Eshley at last, when the silence had become unbearable.

"How observant you are," said Adela bitterly. "You seem to notice everything. As a matter of fact, it has got six chrysanthemums in its mouth at the present moment."

The necessity for doing something was becoming imperative. Eshley took a step or two in the direction of the animal, clapped his hands, and made noises of the "Hish" and "Shoo" variety. If the ox heard them it gave no outward indication of the fact.

"If any hens should ever stray into my garden," said Adela, "I should certainly send for you. Meanwhile, do you mind trying to drive that ox away? That is a *Mademoiselle Louise Bichot* that he's begun on now," she added in icy calm, as a glowing orange head was crushed into the huge munching mouth.

"Since you have been so frank about the mum's variety," said Eshley, "I don't mind telling you that this is an Ayrshire ox."

The icy calm broke down; Adela Pingsford used language that sent the artist nearer to the ox. He picked up a pea-stick and flung it with some determination against the animal's mottled flanks. The mashing of the flowers into a petal salad was suspended for a long moment, while the ox gazed with concentrated inquiry at the stick-thrower. Adela gazed with equal concentration and more obvious hostility at the same focus.

As the beast neither lowered its head nor stamped its feet, Eshley threw another pea-stick. The ox seemed to realize that it was to go; it gave a hurried final pluck, and strode swiftly up the garden. Eshley ran to head it towards the gate, but only succeeded in quickening its pace to a lumbering trot. With no real hesitation, it pushed its way through an open French window into the morning-room. Some chrysanthemums and autumn herbage stood about the room in vases, and the animal resumed its browsing; Eshley fancied that a hunted look had come into its eyes, a look that counseled respect. He discontinued his attempt to interfere with its choice of surroundings.

"Mr. Eshley," said Adela in a shaking voice, "I asked you to drive that beast out of my garden, but I did not ask you to drive it into my house. If I must have it anywhere on the premises I prefer the garden to the morning-room."

"Cattle drives are not in my line," said Eshley; "if I remember I told you so at the outset." "I quite agree," retorted the lady, "painting pretty pictures of pretty little cows is what you're suited for. Perhaps you'd like to do a nice sketch of that ox making itself at home in my morning-room?"

The worm had turned; Eshley began striding away.

"Where are you going?" screamed Adela.

"To fetch implements," was the answer.

"Implements? I won't have you use a lasso. The room will be wrecked if there's a struggle."

But the artist marched out of the garden. In minutes he returned with easel, sketching-stool, and painting materials.

"Do you mean to say that you're going to sit and paint that brute while it's destroying my morning-room?" gasped Adela.

"It was your suggestion," said Eshley, setting canvas in place.

"I forbid it; I absolutely forbid it!" stormed Adela.

"I don't see what say you have in the matter," said the artist. "You can hardly pretend that it's your ox, even by adoption."

"You seem to forget that it's in my morning-room, eating my flowers," came the raging retort.

"You seem to forget that the cook has neuralgia," said Eshley. "Your outcry will waken her. Consideration for others should be the guiding principle of people in our station of life."

"The man is mad!" exclaimed Adela. A moment later it was Adela herself who appeared to go mad. The ox had finished the vase-flowers and the cover of *Israel Kalisch,* and appeared to be thinking of leaving its restricted quarters. Eshley noticed its restlessness and promptly flung it some bunches of Virginia creeper as an inducement to continue the sitting.

"I forget how the proverb runs," he observed. "Something about 'better a dinner of herbs than a stalled ox where hate is.' We seem to have all the ingredients for the proverb at hand."

"I shall go to the Public Library and get them to telephone for the police," announced Adela, and, raging, she departed.

Some minutes later the ox, awakening probably to the suspicion that oil cake and chopped mangold was waiting for it in some appointed barn, stepped with much precaution out of the morning-room, stared with grave inquiry at the no longer obtrusive and pea-stick-throwing human, and then lumbered heavily out of the garden. Eshley packed up his tools and followed the animal's example.

The episode was the turning-point in Eshley's artistic career. His remarkable picture, "Ox in a Morning-Room, Late Autumn," was one of the sensations of the next Paris Salon, and when it was subsequently exhibited at Munich it was bought by the Bavarian Government, after spirited bidding among three meat-packing firms. From then on his success was assured, and the Royal Academy was thankful, two years later, to give a conspicuous position on its walls to his large canvas "Barbary Apes Wrecking a Boudoir."

Eshley presented Adela Pingsford with a new copy of *Israel Kalisch,* and a couple of finely flowering pots of *Madame Andre Blusset,* but nothing in the nature of a real reconciliation has taken place between them.

Would "Little Worms" by Any Other Name Taste as Good?

Sometimes food just sounds better in a foreign language. For example, would pasta taste nearly as good if we translated the word from the Italian ("dough paste")? And how would you feel about eating these pastas translated?

- "large reeds" (cannelloni)
- "butterflies" (farfalle)
- "small ribbons" (fettucine)
- "small muffs" (manicotti)
- "small twists" (tortellini)
- "little strings" (spaghetti)
- "little worms" (vermicelli)
- "little turnips" (ravioli)
- "little tongues" (linguine)

Word Thieves 3

Some Terms We've Borrowed from the Africans

When African natives were kidnapped and enslaved they brought remnants of their cultures and languages with them. Some of their words ended up as part of American English.

banana: First a West African word, may have been borrowed by them from a word in the Arabic language, pronounced *banayna, and* meaning "fingers" or "toes."

banjo: Probably from the Kimbundu word, *mbanya,* which refers to a stringed instrument.

chigger: First used to indicate any biting insect, the word came from the Wolof language's *jiga* ("insect").

cooter: Most famous as a nickname for the box turtle in Alabama and Georgia. It most likely came from the West African word *kuta* or the Kongo tribe's *nkuda* meaning "turtle."

goober: This alternative name for a peanut comes from the Bantu *nguba.*

gumbo: *Kingombo* means "okra" in the Bantu language, and so the name got generalized to mean a thick stew made from okra pods.

juke: The word that goes into "juke joint" and "juke box" comes from the Wolof word *dzug,* which means leading a chaotic or wicked life.

Sambo: A common name among African American males in previous centuries, and now notorious because of a story called *Little Black Sambo.* Still, the name came from the Hausen people of Nigeria, and it means "second son."

tote: From the Western Congo word *tota* or *tuta* ("carry").

voodoo: From the Ewe tribe's *vodu* ("spirit").

yam: From the Vai *djambi* or the Sengal *nyami,* both of which mean "eat."

Lloyd's of London

How It Got Out of Coffee & Into Hot Water

What would you think if Starbucks started selling insurance? Lloyd's of London started out as a dockside coffee shop where professional gamblers hung out. "Insurance" was just another bet you could make. Maybe it's not that different from today, actually....

Lloyd's of London is the most famous insurance syndicate in history. Its willingness to insure things like Betty Grable's legs and Bruce Springsteen's voice have made it a risk taker's heaven and a press agent's dream. It appears in the news whenever an unlucky disaster breaks. An unlucky streak in recent decades—including the collapse of the World Trade Center (the biggest single loss in the company's long history), the *Exxon Valdez* oil spill, the 1989 San Francisco earthquake, and Hurricane Hugo—has pushed some of its investors and underwriters to the edge of bankruptcy.

If Lloyd's doesn't survive as an insurance provider, though, maybe it can go back to the business where it began three centuries ago: a coffee house.

London was the major player in the maritime business in the seventeenth century, with merchant ships coming and going constantly from its bustling harbor. At the same time, coffee-drinking was becoming popular across Europe. Dutch colonists had recently established coffee plantations on the island of Java. In 1688, a man named Edward Lloyd opened a coffee house on Tower Street near the docks. Unlike taverns, where drunken revelry reigned, coffee houses were sober places where business people went to do serious wheeling and dealing.

Because of its location Lloyd's coffee house attracted a clientele of ship owners, captains, merchants, and insurance brokers. The concept of marine insurance had been introduced to England earlier in the century, allowing owners of ships and cargos to mitigate the financial hit they took if a ship went down.

But, although insurance in the modern sense existed, insurance companies did not (Lloyd's today is still a peculiar hybrid, as noted below). A merchant with ship or cargo hired a broker to go from one wealthy individual to another, selling a share of the risk in return for a share of the premium. It was essentially betting that a ship would make it safely: If nothing happened, the insurers got to keep the hefty premium; if disaster struck, they were personally liable for their share of the claim ... to the full extent of their personal fortunes, if necessary. Clearly, it was a field for gamblers with a lot of money they could afford to risk.

ONE LUMP OR TWO?

Because of the amount of ship talk he heard, Edward Lloyd gained a reputation for being a trustworthy source of shipping news and gossip. His coffee house became recognized as the place to go to arrange for marine insurance. Lloyd himself was never directly involved in the insurance business, but he provided a congenial business atmosphere, semi-enclosed booths, and even writing materials for his patrons.

Lloyd's coffee house continued on after his death in 1713, and merchants continued to gather there. For decades, little separated those underwriters offering coverage in "respectable" marine underwriting from those betting on other things, like who would win a particular sports contest or war, or when the current king would die. Wanting to disassociate from their seamier brethren, a number of the respectable brokers broke away in 1769 to set up a coffee house in nearby Pope's Head Alley. They called it the "New Lloyd's Coffee House" and allowed business dealings in marine insurance only.

The building proved too small, and so a committee was formed to find new premises. Seventy-nine brokers, underwriters, and merchants each chipped in £100 to finance the move. When they moved, they left the coffee business behind. Nonetheless their new headquarters was still called "Lloyd's

Coffee House" for decades afterward.

THE "NAMES" ARE THE SAME

Over the following century, the Lloyd's society of underwriters evolved into its modern incarnation. They expanded to other kinds of insurance. In the 1990s, Lloyd's had 32,000 members (called "Names" because they put their "name," or full reputation and fortune, behind the risk), grouped into approximately 350 underwriting syndicates varying in size from a handful to a thousand. Each syndicate is managed by an agent and hires experts who determine the betting odds (and thereby the premium) for each insurance policy. As was the case three centuries ago, the Names are personally liable for claims, meaning that they can make money if things go well, but can lose their shirts if things go wrong. (There have been moves in recent years to limit this personal liability).

When Coffee came to England
COFFEE HOUSES were the haunts of men of wit and fashion, and from these gatherings comes the proverb—"a good talker is a connoisseur of coffee."
The popularity of really fine coffee is unquestioned. That it promotes good fellowship and inspires to mental and physical effort, there is no question. But —we are speaking about "really fine" coffee such as is our splendid
"WHITE HOUSE" COFFEE
and if YOU would glean from coffee drinking not only the pleasurable satisfaction to the palate but the invigorating effects which promote energetic action, don't, we beg of you, allow your grocer to substitute something else. Be sure and ask for "White House" coffee and GET it.
Sold only in 1, 2 & 3-lb Sealed Tin Cans
DWINELL-WRIGHT Co.
PRINCIPAL COFFEE ROASTERS
BOSTON & CHICAGO GUARANTEE IT

Over time, Lloyd's developed a reputation for fairness, holding to a rule that no policyholder with a legitimate claim went unpaid. For example, after the disastrous San Francisco earthquake of 1906 that destroyed most of the

city, every insurance company but one—Lloyd's—defaulted on their policies. In fact, when Lloyd's discovered that many of their policyholders had either fire insurance or earthquake insurance, but not both, Lloyd's leading underwriter cabled an unequivocal message to the company's San Francisco agent: "Pay all of our policyholders in full, irrespective of the terms of their policies."

Silly Policies from Lloyd's of London

Over the years, PR agents discovered that frivolous insurance policies with Lloyd's made for good publicity and that Lloyd's was a good sport about insuring just about anything. For example:

- Kid-show host Pinky Lee's lisp (a $50,000 policy)
- Jamie Lee Curtis's legs ($1,000,000 pair)
- Fred Astaire's legs ($150,000 each)
- Jimmy Durante's nose ($50,000)
- Bruce Springsteen's voice ($6,000,000)
- Dolly Parton's breasts ($600,000)
- A grain of rice with a tiny portrait of the Queen and the Duke of Edinburgh ($20,000)
- That Elvis wouldn't be found alive ($1,000,000)
- The beards of the "Whisker's Club" in Derbyshire against fire and "theft" (£20 each)
- A comedy troupe, against the risk of having members of the audience laugh themselves to death ($1,000,000)
- Skylab's disintegration and return to earth (£2,500,000 property damage, £500,000 for deaths)
- The world's largest cigar (£17,933.35)
- The body of underwear model Suzanne Mizzi (£10,000,000)
- That the Loch Ness monster wouldn't be captured (£1,000,000)
- Actress Kerry Wallace, who had to shave her head for a *Star Trek* movie, against the possibility that her hair wouldn't grow back right ($100,000)
- However, there are limits. Mr. Methane, a British entertainer who farts out melodies such as "Twinkle, Twinkle Little Star," sought to buy insurance against losing his talents. He was refused.

Crazy Like a Foxglove

Some touching, and some horrible, here's a sampling of the remedies used for insanity throughout the ages.

• To cure insanity, medieval kings and queens might've used a bag full of buttercups slung around the neck.

• The Welsh during this same time period preferred daisies—particularly daisy tea—as a remedy.

• The Irish buried their crazies up to their necks in dirt. After three days, they'd take them out, and if they weren't cured, they'd beat them until they couldn't move.

• In a special lake in Scotland, the insane were tied and dragged behind a boat. Once they reached an island, they were plunged into an icy well. This treatment apparently worked on more than one occasion.

• Ancient Mongolians boiled old animal bones that were found out on the steppes and collected the remaining juices. The prescription was to bathe in the juices for seven days to remove the affliction.

• Pearls were used for more than mere adornment by Europeans and Persians in the late Middle Ages. Wearing them was supposed to chase off insanity.

• Mayan priests were known to use the testicles of a black rooster to make an insanity-curing breakfast elixir.

• Early Arabians swore by *Vitex agnus castus*—Chasteberry—to cure crazy people. It was an herb also used to squelch sexual desire. It's still sold in Egypt for various purposes.

• Ancient Greeks used Hellebore, aka Christmas Rose, to cure insanity. Hellebore has strong purgative properties, is very poisonous, often causing violent reactions in those who come in contact with it. It's also a potent narcotic, which may explain its success with helping the mentally ill.

• The ancient Greeks as well as the Egyptians also used dance, song, and drama therapy in treating the mentally ill. In many temples, there were rooms set aside for the insane to sleep, believing that the holy place would ease their suffering.

• Later Greek medical cures included poisons and narcotics, donkey milk and bland foods.

• As religion invaded the medical profession of Western Europe, cures for insanity included beating, torturing, and starving. Trepanning—the practice of drilling a hole in the skull of the afflicted—soon became the preferred method of treatment, the belief being that the demons could escape the patient's body through the hole.

• But fennel, too, was believed to help the mentally ill.

• By the mid-1800s anesthesia was all the rage, so lobotomies were used to solve the problem—often altogether.

"The distance between insanity and genius is measured only by success."
—Bruce Feirstein

STOPS
SHOPPING SICKNESS
and the exhaustion, faintness, nausea and dizziness caused by travel motion. Journey by Sea, Train, Car, Auto or Air in perfect comfort with Mothersill's.
32
75c. & $1.50 at Drug Stores or direct
The Mothersill Remedy Co., Ltd.
New York
Paris
Montreal
London
MOTHERSILL'S
SEASICK
REMEDY
25 Years
In Use

Family Feud

THE GRAPES OF WRATH

You would think that the gentility of wine would have a civilizing effect on the people who make it. The Ernest & Julio Gallo wine dynasty proved that idea wrong.

GIUSEPPE ("JOE") GALLO was a moody, violent man. He'd owned a saloon until Prohibition put him out of business. Since Prohibition still allowed individuals to bottle 200 gallons of "nonintoxicating cider and fruit juices exclusively for use in the home," Gallo shifted his business to growing wine grapes, which he sold all over the country to thirsty home winemakers. Most of his buyers, however, were bootleggers, making a lot more than the legal allotment.

Joe's oldest sons, Ernest and Julio, were drafted into working long, thankless hours on the family grape farm. Their younger brother, Joseph, Jr., wasn't old enough to help, and was able to enjoy the childhood that his older brothers had never had. Like his biblical namesake, Joseph was heartily resented by his brothers, and he paid for his favored position later.

Meanwhile, Joe, Sr.'s brother, Mike, was finishing up prison time he'd served for bribery and fraud. When he was released in 1918, he opened the San Pablo Bottling Shop in Oakland as a cover for an alcoholic distribution system. In addition to growing Mike's grapes, Joe was hired to supervise his production of brandy and wine. In 1922, Joe was arrested for running an illegal brandy still. Mike made a few calls to friends in high places and the charges were mysteriously dropped.

By 1925, Joe had accumulated enough money to move to Modesto and build an $8,000 home on the edge of 70 acres of prime vineyards he paid for with cash. He began shipping grapes on a much larger scale. He also apparently continued winemaking: one night in total darkness, young son Joseph woke up to find his father digging a wide, deep hole with his tractor for a 32,000-gallon underground liquor-storing tank.

CHANGE OF FORTUNE

By winter of 1929, Big Joe was doing well enough to buy 160 more acres across the street from his house, this time paying $25,000 in cash. Julio and Ernest, full of late-teen contempt for their father, graduated from high school and went to work for him full-time, arguing with him over their $30 a month pay and for shares of the business. In 1933, anticipating the end of Prohibition, Ernest applied for a license to open a bonded wine storeroom in San Francisco, but his application was turned down because he didn't own a winery—it was all in his father's name.

That changed suddenly the next day. His parents were found shot to death on the family farm. After a hasty inquest, in which Ernest testified that maybe they'd had a financial reverse or something, their deaths were ruled a murder-suicide.

The three brothers were supposed to inherit equal thirds of the business, but Ernest immediately began maneuvering, according to author Ellen Hawkes in his book *Blood and Wine.* "While his two brothers mourned ... Ernest received permission from the probate court to continue his father's business." He applied for a winery permit twelve days after his parents' death in the name of himself and Julio, effectively cutting their younger brother out of his one-third inheritance. Little Joe essentially became their employee. He was soon chastised and fired for "an unwillingness to work hard" after he took a week's vacation.

NASTY, BRUTISH, AND SHORT

Neither brother knew much about making wine, so they learned what they could from a "how to make wine" pamphlet they found at the Modesto public library. Julio took over wine manufacturing and Ernest the marketing. "Ernest is the embodiment of the Hobbesian view of the world," one ex-employee was quoted as saying: "Nasty, brutish, and short." Ernest had a favorite saying: "Remember, people aren't led—they're driven."

The Gallo brothers built a successful company using hard-nosed competitive tactics. Its sales force was notorious for sabotaging the competition with tricks like counterscrewing their bottle caps tightly so that they couldn't be gotten off, or puncturing the caps with icepicks so the wine would go bad, or spraying light oil on the bottles so dust would collect, making them look like they weren't selling. They deliberately littered ghetto neighborhoods with empty Thunderbird bottles to "advertise" the brand.

Building an empire on a foundation of cheap, flavored alcohol-fortified wines deliberately designed to appeal to heavy drinkers in low-income neighborhoods, the Gallo company eventually moved up the class chain to $60 Cabernets. Their winery factories in Modesto and Livingston are the size of oil refineries, pumping out 40 percent of all wine made in California, one-quarter of all wine sold in the United States—about 70 million cases a year.

NO GALLO CHEESE WITH WINE

Years later the two brothers successfully sued Joseph, Jr. for using his own last name on a line of cheese. Joe sued them unsuccessfully for a percentage of the Gallo winery. The judge, who had been a partner in the Fresno law firm that represented Ernest and Julio, ruled that Joseph hadn't actually proved that his brothers had overtly defrauded him out of his

Flornithology 2

How to Tell the Birds from the Flowers

More entries from this helpful field guide by Robert Williams Wood (1868–1955) for those who may have trouble seeing the difference.

The Cowbird

The Cowslip

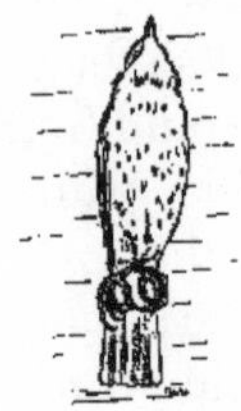

A Sparrow

Asparagus

The Tern

The Turnip

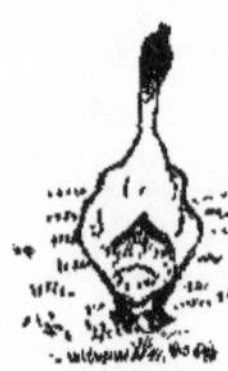

The Old Gander

The Oleander

Mountain Lory

Morning Glory

The Quail

The Kale

Strange Bible Tales

More Odd Stuff from the Good Book

There are a lot of Bible verses you won't necessarily hear your preacher using as a text. Here are some of the strange things we found while thumbing through.

SEAFOOD'S OUT (LEVITICUS 11:10–11)

"And all that have not fins and scales in the seas, and in the rivers, of all that move in the waters, and of any living thing which is in the waters, they shall be an abomination unto you: They shall be even an abomination unto you; ye shall not eat of their flesh, but ye shall have their carcasses in abomination."

NO HAIRCUTS, SHAVES, OR TATTOOS (LEVITICUS 19:27–8)

"Ye shall not round the corners of your heads, neither shall you mar the corners of thy beard. Ye shall not make any cuttings in your flesh for the dead, nor print any marks upon you: I am the Lord."

BIBLICAL CURE FOR LEPROSY (LEVITICUS 14:1–7)

And the Lord spoke to Moses, saying, "This shall be the law of the leper in the day of his cleansing: He shall be brought unto the priest: And the priest shall go forth out of the camp; and the priest shall look, and, behold, if the plague of leprosy be healed in the leper; then shall the priest command to take for him that is to be cleansed two birds alive and clean, and cedar wood, and scarlet, and hyssop: And the priest shall command that one of the birds be killed in an earthen vessel over running water: As for the living bird, he shall take it, and the cedar wood, and the scarlet, and the hyssop, and shall dip them and the living bird in the blood of the bird that was killed over the running water: And he shall sprinkle upon him that is to be cleansed from the leprosy seven times, and shall pronounce him clean, and shall let the living bird loose into the open field."

DAUGHTERS OF MINISTERS, BEWARE (LEVITICUS 21:9)

"And the daughter of any priest, if she profane herself by playing the whore, she profanes her father: she shall be burnt with fire."

NO PRIEST CAN HAVE GLASSES, A HANDICAP, A FLAT NOSE, OR CRUSHED TESTICLES (LEVITICUS 21:16–24)

And the Lord spoke unto Moses, saying, "Speak unto Aaron, saying, Whosoever he be of thy seed in their generations that has any defect, let him not approach the altar: a blind man, or a lame one, or he that has a flat nose, or any thing superfluous, or a man that is broken-footed, or broken-handed, or crookbacked, or a dwarf, or that has a defect in his eye, or be scurvy, or scabbed, or has his testicles crushed; no man of the seed of Aaron the priest who has a blemish shall come forward to offer the offerings of the Lord.

"He may eat the bread of his God, both of the most holy, and of the holy, only he shall not go in unto the veil, nor come near the altar, because he has a blemish, that he profane not my sanctuaries: for I the Lord do sanctify them."

GOD REALLY, REALLY DOESN'T LIKE WHINERS (NUMBERS 11:1–35)

And when the Israelis complained, it displeased the Lord: and the Lord heard it; and his anger was kindled; and he sent the fire of the Lord among them, and consumed the outskirts of the camp. And the people cried unto Moses; and when Moses prayed to the Lord, the fire died out.

And the children of Israel wept again, and said, "Who will give us meat to eat? We remember the fish, which we ate in Egypt freely; the cucumbers, melons, leeks, onions, and garlic. But now there is nothing at all except this manna."

The anger of the Lord was kindled greatly; Moses also was displeased. And Moses said to God,..."Whence should I have meat to give unto all this people? For they weep unto me, saying, 'Give us meat, that we may eat.'"

And the Lord said to Moses, "Say to the people,...'The Lord will give you meat, and you shall eat. You shall not eat one day, nor two days, nor five days, neither ten days, nor twenty days; but a whole month, until it comes out of your nostrils, and it be loathsome unto you, that because you have despised the Lord who is among you, and have wept in front of him, saying, 'Why did we ever leave Egypt?'"

And God brought forth a wind, and brought quails from the sea, and let them fall by the camp ... about two cubits high on the face of the earth. And the people stayed up all day and night, and they gathered the quails and they spread them out for themselves round about the camp.

And while the meat was yet between their teeth, before it was chewed, the wrath of the Lord was kindled against the people, and the Lord struck the people with a very great plague. So the name of that place became *Kilbroth-hattaavah* (Grave of the Greedy).

NO CROSS-DRESSING, SEED-MIXING, POLYESTER BLENDS, OR FRINGES (DEUTERONOMY 22:5–12)

"The woman shall not wear a man's clothes, neither shall a man put on a woman's garment: for all that do so are abomination unto the Lord thy God....

"You must not sow your vineyard with two kinds of seeds: or the fruit of your vineyard will be defiled.

"You shall not plow with an ox and an ass together.

"You shall not wear a garment of two fabrics, such as of wool and linen together.

"You shall not make fringes on your garment on the part that covers you."

IF RAPED, YOU MUST MARRY THE RAPIST (DEUTERONOMY 22:25–29)

"If a man finds a girl who is a virgin, who is not engaged, and forces her to have intercourse with him, and they are discovered, then the man shall give to the girl's father 50 shekels of silver, and she shall become his wife because he has violated her; he cannot divorce her all his days."

SORRY JOHN BOBBITT (DEUTERONOMY 23:1–2)

"No one who is emasculated, or has his male organ cut off, shall enter the assembly of God. No one of illegitimate birth shall enter the assembly; none of his descendants, even to the tenth generation, shall enter the assembly of the Lord."

JESUS DRIVES OUT DEMONS, KILLS A HERD OF PIGS, GETS RUN OUT OF TOWN (MATTHEW 8:28–32)

And when Jesus came into the country of the Gergesenes, he met two possessed with demons who were exceeding fierce, so that no man might pass by that way. They cried out, saying, "What have we to do with you, Jesus, you Son of God? Did you come here to torment us before the time?"

And there was a good way off from them an herd of many swine feeding. So the devils besought him, saying, "If thou cast us out, suffer us to go away into the herd of swine."

And he said to them, "Go." And when they left the men, they went into the herd of swine: and, behold, the whole herd of swine ran violently down a cliff into the sea, and perished in the waters. The sheepherders ran to the city and reported everything and the whole city came out to meet Jesus to send him away.

EYEWITNESS DESCRIBES GOD: "AMBER, FIERY FROM THE LOINS DOWN" (EZEKIAL 8:1–2)

And it came to pass in the sixth year, in the sixth month, in the fifth day of the month, as I sat in mine house, and the elders of Judah sat before me, that the hand of the Lord God fell there upon me. Then I beheld a likeness as the appearance of fire: from the appearance of his loins even downward, fire; and from his loins even upward, as the appearance of brightness, as the color of amber.

JESUS' BROTHERS AND SISTERS (MARK 6:3)

Is not this the carpenter, the son of Mary, the brother of James, and Joses, and of Juda, and Simon? And are not his sisters here with us?

GREAT EXPECTORATIONS (MARK 8:22–4)

They brought a blind man to him, and begged Jesus to touch him. And he took the blind man by the hand, and led him out of the town; and when he spat on his eyes and put his hands upon him, he asked him if he saw anything. And he looked up, and said, "I see men as trees, walking."

’Roos Clues

A Pocketful of Kangaroo Facts

Everyone loves kangaroos, right? It’s no wonder. Here are just a few of the amazing reasons why kangaroos fascinate us so.

BEST HOPS FOR THE FUTURE

Kangaroos hop 33 feet per jump, for a maximum speed of about 40 miles per hour. Kangaroos couldn’t run even if they wanted to, because their legs are completely unsuited for doing so. Centuries ago, when the lush Australian rain forests dried into deserts, kangaroos needed to be able to travel great distances to find the quantities of food they needed to stay alive. It turned out that hopping requires about 25 percent less energy than running. To add to its energy efficiency, its digestive organs bounce backward and forward with each hop, saving the energy that kangaroos normally have to expend breathing in and out.

BEANY BABIES

When a kangaroo baby’s newly born, it’s larger than a lima bean but smaller than a full-sized peanut. It’s not at all cute, either, unless you’re the kind of person who can love something that looks like a slimy pink intestinal worm. Marsupials give birth to tiny, hairless, helpless, blind, nearly larval young after a gestation that lasts only 30–40 days. Looking like undeveloped fetuses (which is essentially what they are), the young are instinctively capable of only two things: crawling up the fur of their mom to the safety of her *marsupium* (pouch) and finding a nipple there to suck upon.

The little joey stays attached to the mother’s teat for six or seven months. After that time, the baby finally becomes a miniature version of its parents, leaving Mom's pouch for short hops before returning for protection and food.

TWO HEADS BETTER THAN ONE?

Like all marsupials, kangaroos have bifurcated (forked) penises, and their testicles lie in front of their penises instead of in back like other mammals. Female marsupials have two uteri and two vaginas that share a common fork-shaped opening. The birth canal forms from an opening in the connective tissue between the two vaginas.

WALLABIES AND WANNABES

People wonder if wallabies and wallaroos are the same as kangaroos, or are they just kangaroo wannabes? The truth is that they're all members of one big happy family (*Macropodidae* or "big foot"), which has fifty-five different species. Differences among them are not particularly apparent—what they're called is largely determined by their size and where they live:

• Kangaroos are generally bigger—up to 185 pounds for the red kangaroo—and they prefer congregating in large groups on open, dry, grassland plains.

• Wallaroos are not quite as tall, but they're stocky and they live in small groups in hilly country.

• Wallabies are much smaller, some as small as rabbits, which works out pretty well since they hang out in places without much traveling space—in dense forests and thick vegetation along rivers and lakes. They also live in small groups.

Be warned, though, that even with these distinctions, there are exceptions. For example, the "tree kangaroo" lives in the forest and is smaller than most other kangaroos, which should arguably make it a "tree wallaby."

CLIMBING UP THE FAMILY TREE

All kangaroos once lived in trees, but as the Australian rain forests turned to desert, Kangaroos adapted into land-based animals. At some point in history, though, the tree kangaroo reversed course and climbed back into the trees, where it now spends most of its time, climbing instead of hoping.

RAT KANGAROOS

Rat kangaroos are not to be confused with kangaroo rats. The former live in the swamps and deserts of northeastern Australia; the latter, in the southwestern deserts of North America.

More Lear

More rhymes and drawings from Edward Lear's classic children's book, *The Book of Nonsense* (published 1846).

There was an Old Person of Rheims,
Who was troubled with horrible dreams;
So, to keep him awake,
They fed him with cake,
Which amused that Old Person of Rheims.

There was an Old Person of Troy,
Whose drink was warm brandy and soy;
Which he took with a spoon,
By the light of the moon,
In sight of the city of Troy.

There was an Old Person of Tring,
Who embellished his nose with a ring;
He gazed at the moon
Every evening in June,
That ecstatic Old Person in Tring.

There was an Old Man of Calcutta,
Who perpetually ate bread and butter,
Till a great bit of muffin,
On which he was stuffing,
Choked that horrid Old Man of Calcutta.

There was an Old Man of Coblenz,
The length of whose legs was immense;
He went with one prance
From Turkey to France,
That surprising Old Man of Coblenz.

There was an Old Man who said, "How
Shall I flee from that horrible cow?
I will sit on this stile,
And continue to smile,
Which may soften the heart of that cow."

There was a Young Lady of Hull,
Who was chased by a virulent bull;
But she seized on a spade,
And called out, "Who's afraid?"
Which distracted that virulent bull.

There was an Old Person of Dutton,
Whose head was as small as a button,
So, to make it look big,
He purchased a wig,
And rapidly rushed about Dutton.

There was an Old Man of the coast,
Who placidly sat on a post;
But when it was cold
He relinquished his hold
And called for some hot buttered toast.

There was an Old Man of Kamschatka,
Who possessed a remarkable fat cur;
His gait and his waddle
Were held as a model
To all the fat dogs in Kamschatka.

There was an Old Man who said, "Hush!
I perceive a young bird in this bush!"
When they said, "Is it small?"
He replied, "Not at all!
It is four times as big as the bush!"

Life Lessons

How To Use a Cricket as a Thermometer

Have you ever been surprised by the weather outside? After all, how are you supposed to just know how cold it is without actually getting out of your bed or chair? Well, we've got a little trick that just may help.

True, you could go to the trouble of mounting a thermometer outside of your bedroom window.Or we suppose you might even step outside and try to estimate the temperature. But if you'd rather not go to such extreme efforts, you can depend on Nature's Thermometer, the cricket. Here's how:

1. Make sure you have a watch or clock handy that can calibrate seconds.

2. You'll need quiet for this one, so quiet your snoring partner, uproarious neighbors, and overactive children.

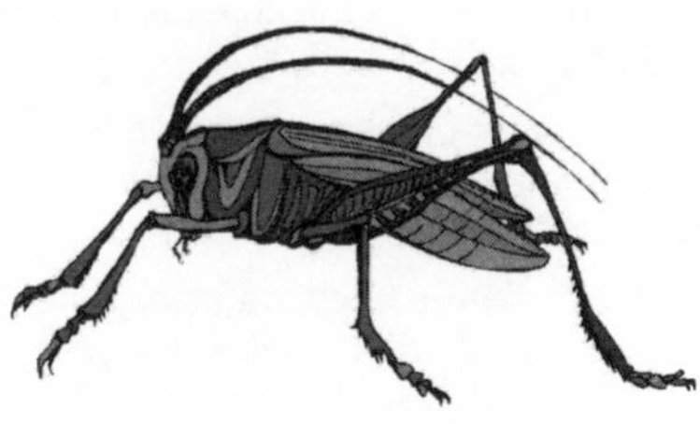

3. Sit perfectly still and listen to the outside ambiance through your windows and walls. Find one clear, crisp cricket chirp that's loud enough for you to keep track of its call.

4. Watch your watch and count the number of chirps you hear from your cricket within 14 seconds.

5. Add 40 to your chirp number, and you'll get the approximate number of degrees Fahrenheit outside. Dress accordingly.

H. L. Mencken vs. the World

H. L. Mencken (1880–1956) was a controversial curmudgeon who penned "Those who can't do, teach" and "No one ever went broke underestimating the taste of the American public."

• "Puritanism: The haunting fear that someone, somewhere may be happy."

• "Imagine the Creator as a low comedian, and at once the world becomes explicable."

• "The only really happy folk are married women and single men."

• "A cynic is a man who, when he smells flowers, looks around for a coffin."

• "We must respect the other fellow's religion, but only in the sense and to the extent that we respect his theory that his wife is beautiful and his children smart."

• "The kind of man who wants the government to adopt and enforce his ideas is always the kind of man whose ideas are idiotic."

• "For every problem, there is one solution which is simple, neat, and wrong."

• "Every failure teaches a man something; to wit, that he will probably fail again."

• "Women have simple tastes. They can get pleasure out of the conversation of children in arms and men in love."

• "On one issue at least, men and women agree: they both distrust women."

• "Conscience is the inner voice that warns us that somebody is looking."

• "God is the immemorial refuge of the incompetent, the helpless, the miserable. They find not only sanctuary in His arms, but also a kind of superiority, soothing to their macerated egos: He will set them above their betters."

• "Men become civilized, not in proportion to their willingness to believe, but in proportion to their readiness to doubt."

• "There are two kinds of books: those that no one reads and those that no one ought to read."

• "Democracy is the art and science of running the circus from the monkey cage."

• "Under democracy one party always devotes its chief energies to trying to prove that the other party is unfit to rule—and both commonly succeed, and are right."

• "The older I grow, the more I distrust the familiar doctrine that age brings wisdom."

• "Always remember this: If you don't attend the funerals of your friends, they will certainly not attend yours."

The Open Window

A Short Story by Saki (Hector Monro)

Before he was killed in World War I, Hector Monro wrote short stories with a twist under the pen name "Saki." In this one, a nervous man is confronted by the supernatural....

"MY AUNT will be down presently, Mr. Nuttel," said a very self-possessed young lady of fifteen. "In the meantime you must try and put up with me."

Framton Nuttel endeavored to say the correct something which should duly flatter the niece of the moment without unduly discounting the aunt that was to come. Privately he doubted more than ever whether these formal visits on a succession of total strangers would do much toward helping the nerve cure which he was supposed to be undergoing.

"I know how it will be," his sister had said when he was preparing to migrate to this rural retreat; "you will bury yourself down there and not speak to a living soul, and your nerves will be worse than ever from moping. I shall just give you letters of introduction to all the people I know there. Some of them, as far as I can remember, were quite nice."

Framton wondered whether Mrs. Sappleton, the lady to whom he was presenting one of the letters of introduction, came into the nice division.

"Do you know many of the people round here?" asked the niece, when she judged that they had had sufficient silent communion.

"Hardly a soul," said Framton. "My sister was staying here, at the rectory, you know, some four years ago, and she gave me letters of introduction to some of the people here."

He made the last statement in a tone of distinct regret.

"Then you know practically nothing about my aunt?" pursued the self-possessed young lady.

"Only her name and address," admitted the caller. He was wondering whether Mrs. Sappleton was in the married or widowed state. An undefinable something about the room seemed to suggest masculine habitation.

"Her great tragedy happened just three years ago," said the child; "that would be since your sister's time."

"Her tragedy?" asked Framton; somehow in this restful country spot tragedies seemed out of place.

"You may wonder why we keep that window wide open on an October afternoon," said the niece, indicating a large French window that opened on to a lawn.

"It is quite warm for the time of the year," said Framton; "but has that window got anything to do with the tragedy?"

"Out through that window, three years ago to a day, her husband and her two young brothers went off for their day's shooting. They never came back. In crossing the moor to their favorite snipe-shooting ground they were all three engulfed in a treacherous piece of bog. It had been that dreadful wet summer, you know, and places that were safe in other years gave way suddenly without warning. Their bodies were never recovered. That was the dreadful part of it." Here the child's voice lost its self-possessed note and became falteringly human. "Poor aunt always thinks that they will come back some day, they and the little brown spaniel that was lost with them, and walk in at that window just as they used to do. That is why the window is kept open every evening till it is quite dusk. Poor dear aunt, she has often told me how they went out, her husband with his white waterproof coat over his arm, and Ronnie, her youngest brother, singing 'Bertie, why do you bound?' as he always did to tease her, because she said it got on her nerves. Do you know, sometimes on still, quiet evenings like this, I almost get a creepy feeling that they will all walk in through that window—"

She broke off with a little shudder. It was a relief to Framton when the aunt bustled into the room with a whirl of apologies for being late in making her appearance.

"I hope Vera has been amusing you?" she said.

"She has been very interesting," said Framton.

"I hope you don't mind the open window," said Mrs. Sappleton briskly; "my husband and brothers will be home directly from shooting, and they always come in this way. They've been out for snipe in the marshes today, so they'll make a fine mess over my poor carpets. So like you men-folk, isn't it?"

She rattled on cheerfully about the shooting and the scarcity of birds, and the prospects for duck in the winter. To Framton it was all purely horrible. He made a desperate but only partially successful effort to turn the talk on to a less ghastly topic; he was conscious that his hostess was giving him only a fragment of her attention, and her eyes were constantly straying past him to the open window and the lawn beyond. It was certainly an unfortunate coincidence that he should have paid his visit on this tragic anniversary.

"The doctors agree in ordering me complete rest, an absence of mental excitement, and avoidance of violent physical exercise," announced Framton, who labored under the tolerably wide-spread delusion that total strangers and chance acquaintances are hungry for the least detail of one's ailments and infirmities, their cause, and cure. "On the matter of diet they are not so much in agreement," he continued.

"No?" said Mrs. Sappleton, in a voice which only replaced a yawn at the last moment. Then she suddenly brightened into alert attention—but not to what Framton was saying.

"Here they are at last!" she cried. "Just in time for tea, and don't they look as if they were muddy up to the eyes!"

Framton shivered slightly and turned toward the niece with a look intended to convey sympathetic comprehension. The child was staring out through the open window with dazed horror in her eyes. In a chill shock of nameless fear Framton swung round in his seat and looked in the same direction.

In the deepening twilight three figures were walking across the lawn toward the window; they all carried guns under their arms, and one of them was additionally burdened with a white coat hung over his shoulders. A tired brown spaniel kept close at their heels. Noiselessly they neared the house, and then a hoarse young voice chanted out of the dusk: "I said, Bertie, why do you bound?"

Framton grabbed wildly at his stick and hat; the hall-door, the gravel-drive, and the front gate were dimly-noted stages in his headlong retreat. A cyclist coming along the road had to run into the hedge to avoid an imminent collision.

"Here we are, my dear," said the bearer of the white mackintosh, coming in through the window; "fairly muddy, but most of it's dry. Who was that who bolted out as we came up?"

"A most extraordinary man, a Mr. Nuttel," said Mrs. Sappleton; "could only talk about his illnesses, and dashed off without a word of good-bye or apology when you arrived. One would think he had seen a ghost."

"I expect it was the spaniel," said the niece calmly; "he told me he had a horror of dogs. He was once hunted into a cemetery somewhere on the banks of the Ganges by a pack of pariah dogs, and had to spend the night in a newly dug grave with the creatures snarling and grinning and foaming just above him. Enough to make anyone lose their nerve."

Romance at short notice was her speciality.

THE HISTORY OF THE HAWAIIAN SHIRT

THE HAWAIIAN SHIRT, that overly colorful garb favored by American tourists and extroverted college-age guys, is the result of missionaries sent to Hawaii in the 1800s. Scandalized by the overabundance of naked flesh, they introduced large, colorless, one-size-fits-all shirts and muumuus. The natives decided that if they had to wear clothes, they at least should be colorful, so they took the plain cotton garments and decorated them with bright Polynesian designs.

The 1920s brought a tourist boom to Hawaii. Tourists carried the gaudy, tropical shirts back to the mainland as souvenirs. Later, during World War II, soldiers and sailors on leave discovered that Hawaiian shirts made a cheap and colorful replacement for the drabness of their uniforms.

After two decades of depression and war, there was another big Hawaii tourist boom in the 1950s, followed by a faddish interest in the islands after they became an American state in 1959.

Cursed Opera

Is Tosca an Overture to Disaster?

According to theater folklore, certain productions are staged only at the risk of great peril.

THE HISTORICAL OPERA *TOSCA* is about intrigue and treachery in the Vatican. According to backstage legend, it's also cursed, and terrible things may happen to those who dare perform it. Well, we're not so sure about that, but we're impressed by the string of bad-luck stories, even though some of them may only be legendary.

• In the first night of a 1995 production in Rome, tenor Mario Cavaradossi was injured after debris fired from blanks punctured his leg. The script called for Tosca (Raina Kabaivanska) to rush to his fallen body; when she did so, his fallen body whispered to her, "Call an ambulance...." Kabaivanska promptly passed out onstage at the sight of his blood, stopping the show.

• But the show must go on. After recuperating in the hospital, Cavaradossi returned to the show hobbling and on crutches. His first night back, he made it through most of the first act. While waiting in the wings, his crutches slipped and he fell, breaking his *other* leg in two places. "Could it be that I am destined to never leave this theater on my own two feet?" he complained as he was carried away on a stretcher.

• The same scene has caused problems before. In a 1965 production in Rome, the gunfire scorched the face of tenor Gianni Raimonde. And, according to legend, another tenor in an early production was killed in the same scene.

• However, *not* having the guns go off proved fatal to yet another tenor. He was nonplussed when the guns failed to go off as scheduled, and promptly died of a heart attack.

• Professionalism under pressure: During a production in Covent Garden, Maria Callas's hair caught on fire during a scene with Scarpia, a villain played by Tito Gobbi. Gobbi improvised a lecherous lunge, embracing her while patting out the fire. Callas responded in character by recoiling from from the villain, whispering, "Thank you, Tito," as her character followed the script and stabbed his character to death.

Composer of the cursed opera, Giacomo Puccini

• In the 1920s, another performance at the Metropolitan Opera in New York ended during the same scene. A trick blade failed to retract, and Tosca (Maria Jeritza) stabbed Scarpia (Antonio Scotti) for real. He survived and continued in the role for another decade.

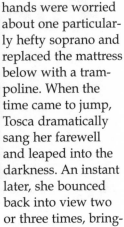

• Not surprisingly, a scene where Tosca flings herself off a parapet is another one where mishaps can happen. In 1993, Elisabeth Knighton Printy jumped off the wrong side of the stage in St. Paul, Minnesota, and fell more than 30 feet, breaking both legs.

• Legend has it that stagehands were worried about one particularly hefty soprano and replaced the mattress below with a trampoline. When the time came to jump, Tosca dramatically sang her farewell and leaped into the darkness. An instant later, she bounced back into view two or three times, bringing down the house.

• Another incident, perhaps apocryphal, turned the same dramatic scene into an incident of mass suicide. In one rushed production, the "supers"—extras hired to stand around in costume onstage—weren't in on the rehearsals, so the director gave them the opening night instructions to "exit with the principals." When Tosca leaped, the supers, seeing no other principal players on stage, shrugged and leaped after her.

SHUT UP AND DEAL

Do the math—there are 635,013,599,600 possible hands of bridge.

After You Flush

What Happens to the Stuff in the Bowl?

You flush. Waste and water whirlpool down the drain and out of your life. Where does it go? What happens to it? We sent one of our intrepid staff members—Oilville Goochland—to find out. Here's his report.

As soon as you flush the toilet, you start a process that is a modest miracle. One day, with the help of sewer and sanitation workers, I traced the path of waste from my home near Oakland, California. Its system is typical of that of most modern cities.

Flushing the toilet sends body waste surfing on several gallons of water down through an S-shaped stink trap and into a pipe that threads through the walls and under the floor. A small pipe beneath the house leads to a pipe under the street and eventually to an 18-inch-wide sewer main, headed on a 3-hour, 7-mile trip toward a sewage treatment plant near Oakland's Bay Bridge.

The sewer system here has 1,800 miles of sewer pipes serving more than 600,000 people in eight cities covering 83 square miles. After meandering through sewer mains for a few hours and about 5 miles, coaxed along by gravity and pumping stations, my flush reaches the interceptor main, so-called because it intercepts the waste that once flowed freely into the open waters. Until 1951, the sewage dumped right into the San Francisco Bay. It was so bad that health agencies in the 1930s prohibited all recreational water activities, and motorists driving along the shore made a habit of raising their windows and holding their noses at the stench. Finally, the East Bay Municipal Utility District (EBMUD) built huge "interceptor mains" paralleling the shoreline.

The mains are huge, 9 feet across—easily big enough to drive a car through. My flush has become completely indistinguishable from the rest of a fast-moving sewage river rolling and tumbling into the sewage treatment plant—urine, fecal matter, toilet paper, and waste water have dissolved into a brown, smelly soup.

An average of more than a million gallons of sewage arrive here every hour, about 80 million gallons a day. The river peaks at about 10 A.M. (when the morning showers and flushes arrive) and 10 P.M. (from the evening's baths, laundry, and dish washing). The plant can handle up to 320 million gallons a day, with temporary storage of another 95 million gallons, which sometimes becomes necessary during storms when rainwater seeps into ancient, broken pipes upstream.

STRAINING AT STOOL

At the plant, a walk down a flight of stairs lets you see and smell the river of sewage flowing in. Here treatment begins with a pipe spewing chlorine to kill bacteria.

Each step in the sewage treatment process removes a specific class of material from the water waste. The first step strains out what they call "rags," whether made of cloth or not, which just means the really big stuff. The sewage runs through two grates of vertical bars. The first has bars set 4 inches apart to catch the really big stuff: shoes, dead animals, rocks, ropes, and other large things that have inexplicably found their way into the pipes. The bars on the second grate are a half-inch apart to catch the smaller stuff. A long rake continually moves along the bars, pulling things like feminine hygiene products, baby wipes, condoms, string, dental floss, and unidentifiable

A tour group gets a glimpse and whiff of the incoming sewage.

clumps of paper onto a conveyor belt headed for a landfill truck.

An engineer tells me that sometimes they find paper money caught among the "rags." So what do you do, I ask? He pauses with a half-smile, choosing his words carefully. "We take it out, wash it off, and put it back into circulation."

SHOWING A LITTLE GRIT

The water moves next into one of the eight grit aeration tanks. "Grit" is used to mean anything that sinks. This includes sand, gravel, coffee grounds, eggshells, and much of the stuff that people grind up in kitchen garbage disposals. The method is simple: Air jets bubble up lighter stuff and allow heavier stuff to hit bottom. There's a giant screw in the bottom of the tank that constantly pushes the grit out of the tank for disposal in a landfill.

Bubbling in the air, explains my guide, also "keeps anaerobic bacteria from smelling up the place. It strips out gasoline, diesel fuel, and hydrogen sulfide, the gas that smells like rotten eggs. And it floats the scum—your basic oils and greases—so we can deal with it in the sed tanks."

SEDIMENTARY JOURNEY

After degritting and floating the scum, the sewage flows into one of sixteen sedimentation tanks. There it sits for about 2 hours, allowing sludge solids to settle to the bottom of the tank. What look like extra-long bicycle chains glide bars across the tank to skim off scum. A similar system is working unseen at the bottom of the tank, scraping sludge to a low spot on one end, where a pump sucks it out and sends it to the digesters (which we'll visit later).

AN INFUSION OF CULTURE

In the next tank, the wastewater gets dosed with tons of oxygen—about 140 tons a day. The plant manufactures its own supply, cooling compressed air down to –175° C until it becomes a liquid, and separating the oxygen out by distillation.

While a huge blender blade stirs the oxygenated mixture, the plant adds "activated sludge" enriched with microorganisms. It acts like yeast in bread dough, multiplying like microscopic rabbits in the oxygen-rich water and gobbling up most of the remaining pollutants.

Staff microbiologists have to

When an uncultured biomass takes over, it looks like "a huge chocolate mousse."

watch this phase closely. "Certain troublesome microorganisms can take over if we don't constantly balance out the system," says my guide. What happens then? "With an unhealthy biomass, we see excessive flotation and foaming—sometimes enough to come right over the handrails. When that happens, it looks like a huge chocolate mousse."

SEEKING CLARIFICATION

After its 2 hours in the oxygenation tank, the water moves into a big round pool called a secondary clarifier, 17 feet across and able to hold 1.5 million gallons of water.

As the water flows through, giant scrapers rotate constantly along the bottom, moving solids out of the tank. Most of those solids are microorganisms from the previous step, which are shipped back to the oxygenation tank to culture the next batch of wastewater.

The water—now clear and smelling like water—continues on through a flow control system that looks a lot like a large-scale decorative water sculpture in a hotel lobby.

Before the water leaves the plant, it's again dosed with chlorine to kill pathogens, then dosed with sulfur dioxide to neutralize the chlorine's negative effects on wildlife. The water travels 3 miles into the San Francisco Bay before being released. To minimize its impact on the bay, the water comes out of dozens of small holes, like a giant garden soaker hose, instead of one large opening. A little of the water is recycled for use on the grounds, but EBMUD has elaborate future plans for recycling this virtually clean waste water back to customers for irrigation, landscaping, and toilet-flushing.

SLUDGE FEST

As we wave good-bye to the reclaimed water, only the sludge remains.

After it was pumped out of the sedimentation tanks and clarifiers, the sludge traveled to one of twelve huge white silo-shaped tanks called digesters. As the name implies, a digester works like a stomach, holding the sludge with

no air circulation at 95° F, allowing anaerobic bacteria to do its smelly thing. Much gas is produced in the process, and it's about 60 percent methane. It's piped to the plant's power station and burned, generating about 40 percent of the plant's electrical needs.

After 25 to 30 days, the sludge emerges as a wet, soil-like humus. It travels to one of three perpetually howling centrifuges to remove excess water. The sludge no longer smells like an outhouse, but sort of fishy, like the beach at low tide. The sludge flows in at a rate of a thousand gallons per minute, gets spun at 1,600 RPMs, and then flows out the other end.

Despite the days of digestion, there's still a lot of it. What do they do with it? Some sludge gets used by landfills to cover up the day's trash. Some is trucked into rural areas and spread on farmland as a soil conditioner for crops. And for a little irony, some is composted and sold to fertilizer companies that, in turn, sell it back to the same consumers who flushed it down the toilet months earlier.

WINGING IT

According to the Catholic Church, angels have ranks and hierarchies, just like the employees of a well-run utility company. Let's start from the bottom:

Third Choir

1. Angels: Your basic winged guardians who watch over us all.
2. Archangels: Angelic equivalent of foremen or sergeants.
3. Principalities: Supervisors of the archangels and angels.

Second Choir

4. Powers: Lower middle-management angels that report to Virtues.
5. Virtues: Middle middle managers that report to Dominions.
6. Dominions: Upper middle managers, not much more known about them.

First Choir

7. Thrones: Seem to be high-ranking administrative assistants to higher-ups.
8. Cherubim: Executive VPs with wings, human head, and an animal's body.
9. Seraphim: Notable by their six wings, Seraphim are the only beings allowed in the presence of God.

Secrets of '76

Things You Didn't Know about the Revolution

You know everything about the American Revolution, right? We thought so, too, but here are some things that might surprise you about that part of history.

THERE WERE TWO BOSTON TEA PARTIES

Well, okay, sequels never get the same attention as the original. Which is why we don't hear much about the second one. The first time the Sons of Liberty snuck aboard British ships and dumped tea in the harbor took place on December 16, 1773; the second one, on March 7, 1774. Both were meant to protest a tax of 3¢ per pound on tea; between the two parties, the little stunt cost British monopoly the equivalent of $3 million in modern money.

JOHN ADAMS DEFENDED THE BRITISH IN COURT ... AND WON

The Boston Massacre was used well by revolutionary propagandists, who portrayed the incident as a case of British soldiers killing four Americans with little provocation. In fact, the soldiers were under attack. One was being beaten with a board and pelted with rocks and ice when other British soldiers ran to his defense. They came under attack as well, and eventually they fired their guns at the crowd. Despite his sympathy for the rebels, John Adams figured they deserved a fair trial. He did a good job, too—two of the four defendants were found innocent, the other two guilty of manslaughter ... but that sentence was commuted to making penance (under the plea of "benefit of clergy") and having their thumbs branded with a C.

THE REVOLUTIONARY WAR SAW THE FIRST SUBMARINE ATTACK

This was in New York Harbor on September 6, 1776. A Connecticut inventor named David Bushnel got his design inspiration from a tortoise and created a one-man, hand-propelled submarine of two rounded shells that he called (sensibly enough) the Turtle. Late that autumn night, the Turtle submerged and snuck up on the HMS *Eagle*, the flagship of the British Navy. Alas, it had to surface before it could fulfill its mission of securing a cask of gunpowder to the *Eagle's* hull. To speed the retreat, the Turtle dropped its cask, which exploded with a harmless 'though deafening explosion, and high tailed it back to shore.

BENEDICT ARNOLD WAS A DAMNED FINE GENERAL

For the three years before he turned traitor, Benedict Arnold was the best general the Continental Army had. He nearly captured Canada, fought the British Navy to a standstill on Lake Champlain, and captured a large contingent of the British Army at Saratoga. Ironically, this last victory convinced the French to send troops to help the revolutionaries against their ancient enemies, the British. It was an alliance that Arnold strongly deplored—so much so, that he decided to switch sides, instead of fight alongside the hated French. As a British officer, he led expeditions that burned Richmond, Virginia, and New London, Connecticut. After the war, he moved to London, England.

ONE IN SEVEN CONTINENTAL SOLDIERS WAS BLACK

It was an idea that made George Washington nervous—giving arms to volunteer slaves and freemen. However, when a battalion of African Americans distinguished themselves at the Battle of Bunker Hill, he changed his mind. The much-decorated First Rhode Island Regiment consisted of 33 freedmen and 92 slaves who were promised freedom if they served. They distinguished themselves in the Battle of Newport. However, not many of the enslaved soldiers lived long enough to be freed—the regiment was all but wiped out in a British attack.

MORE AMERICANS JOINED THE BRITISH SIDE

About a third of Americans supported the revolution. About a third supported the king. The rest just wanted to be left alone. The British recruiting efforts were better than the Continental

Army's. In a 1779 count, there were 6,500–8,000 Americans in the British Army, and only 3,468 with the revolutionaries.

IF IT WEREN'T FOR THE FRENCH, THE PATRIOTS WOULD'VE LOST
The French had reason to want to screw things up for the British in the New World, so they dived in to help the Americans. Their Navy blockaded much of the coastline, and their Army fortified the small American force. At the battle that won the war, Yorktown, there were nearly three French soldiers and sailors for every one American. Washington's Army had grown to 11,000, but it was the 29,000 French troops that turned the redcoated tide.

THE SITE OF THE BOSTON TEA PARTY IS NOW ON SOLID GROUND
The city has filled in so much of the Boston Harbor that the site is several hundred yards inland, near a freeway.

PAUL REVERE DIDN'T MAKE IT TO CONCORD AND LEXINGTON
If Paul Revere didn't make it to warn the Minutemen, then why is he famous? Maybe because "Listen my children and you shall hear/Of the midnight ride of Dr. Samuel Preston" doesn't rhyme. In fact, three men rode out on the journey. Revere and Richard Dawes got turned back by the British. Prescott, though, slipped around the enemy. He was the guy shouting, "The British are coming!" as he rode to Concord.

A SIGNER OF THE DECLARATION CHANGED HIS MIND ... TWICE
After signing the Declaration of Independence and agreeing to "mutually pledge to each other our Lives, our Fortunes and our sacred Honor," Richard Stockton of Princeton, New Jersey, changed his mind. He had had qualms in the first place, and when he got captured by the British during the war, he decided to sign an oath disavowing the document and swearing allegiance to the king. However, after the war ended, he changed his mind again and publicly supported the winning side.

KING GEORGE III NEARLY RESIGNED AFTER THE LOSS OF AMERICA
After Parliament refused to keep fighting after the British loss at Yorktown, George III drafted a letter of abdication, but didn't follow through. He did keep his hopes high, however, that the Americans would beg to have him as king again.

The Devil's Dictionary: K–L

More of *The Devil's Dictionary* by Ambrose Bierce (1842–1914?)

KILL, *v.t.* To create a vacancy without nominating a successor.

KILT, *n.* A costume sometimes worn by Scotchmen in America and Americans in Scotland.

KING, *n.* A male person commonly known in America as a "crowned head," although he never wears a crown and has usually no head to speak of.

KLEPTOMANIAC, *n.* A rich thief.

LABOR, *n.* One of the processes by which A acquires property for B.

LAP, *n.* One of the most important organs of the female system—an admirable provision of nature for the repose of infancy, but chiefly useful in rural festivities to support plates of cold chicken and heads of adult males.

LAUGHTER, *n.* An interior convulsion, producing a distortion of the features and accompanied by inarticulate noises. It is infectious and, though intermittent, incurable.

LAWFUL, *adj.* Compatible with the will of a judge having jurisdiction.

LAWYER, *n.* One skilled in circumvention of the law.

LAZINESS, *n.* Unwarranted repose of manner in a person of low degree.

LEXICOGRAPHER, *n.* A pestilent fellow who, under the pretense of recording some stage in the development of a language, does what he can to arrest its growth, stiffen its flexibility and mechanize its methods.

LIBERTY, *n.* One of Imagination's most precious possessions.

LIFE, *n.* A spiritual pickle preserving the body from decay. We live in daily apprehension of its loss; yet when lost it is not missed.

LINEN, *n.* A kind of cloth the making of which, when made of hemp, entails a great waste of hemp.

LITIGATION, *n.* A machine which you go into as a pig and come out of as a sausage.

LOQUACITY, *n.* A disorder which renders the sufferer unable to curb his tongue when you wish to talk.

LOVE, *n.* A temporary insanity curable by marriage.

LUMINARY, *n.* One who throws light upon a subject; as an editor by not writing about it.

Cold Comfort

How the Popsicle Got on the Stick

It's a sugary, fruity drink, frozen on two sticks so you can split it with a friend. Here's the story behind this comforting childhood treat.

HOW MANY THINGS have been invented by eleven-year-old boys? Lots, no doubt. But how many of them would you want to stick in your mouth?

Eleven-year-old Frank Epperson, the story goes, accidentally left a glass of soda pop mix and water on his back porch. The stirring stick was still in it. That night the temperature got well below freezing. Absentminded Frank went out and found the stick emerging from a frozen block of soft drink. His friends and family were amazed. On that night in 1905, the Popsicle was invented.

You could question the details of the story. On a cold winter's day, after all, how many people take a cold drink outside to enjoy? How often do eleven-year-olds mix up a soft drink and then forget to drink it? Isn't it more likely that Epperson had figured out what would happen and left the glass outside on purpose? Or, even more likely, that he simply made up the story years later when his patent application came under question? Hmmm.

Well, regardless, a decade or two later, the very same Frank Epperson was running a lemonade stand at an amusement park in Oakland, California. When a man has to stand and squeeze lemons all day, he starts thinking philosophically. Epperson decided that when life hands you lemonade, you should make Popsicles. He remembered that cold winter night years earlier and decided to blow that lemonade stand and go into the business of selling fruity frozen confections.

Epperson started making his frozen drinks at home and transporting them each morning to the the amusement park to sell. He called them Epsicles, after his name and "icicles." Nobody seemed too excited by the name, including his own children, who took to calling them "Pop's cycles." Eventually, that name more or less stuck. Popsicles it was.

Epperson later admitted that he had heard about ice cream on a stick not long before he'd begun making Popsicles. A few years earlier, a man named Harry Burt had figured out a way to keep the ice cream from falling off. He called the product "Good Humor." However, Burt went into a decidedly bad humor when he heard that Epperson was trying to patent Popsicles, figuring the similarity was more than coincidental. Burt protested Epperson's patent in 1923. The two eventually reached a compromise: Epperson agreed to make only sherbet and water ice products and leave the dairy-based concoctions to Burt. (Many years later the two companies merged.)

Popsicles grew very popular in outdoor summer events in the 1920s. When the Great Depression hit, however, the company's profits slipped fast. In response, the company designed the two-sticked Twin Popsicle we know today, so that two kids could share one nickel Popsicle.

At first, Epperson froze each Popsicle in a large test tube using a several-hour process. Nowadays, though, it takes only about eight minutes. The molds sit in a pool of supercooled brine, and the liquid formula is squirted into them. After a few minutes, the sticks are stuck in when the liquid is half-frozen and thick enough to hold them up. At the end, the mold is lifted out of the brine and heated slightly. Machines pull the hardened Popsicle out of the molds and dip them in water. A thin layer of the water freezes, smoothing the surface and giving the Popsicle a glossy sheen.

Millions of Popsicles are sold in about three dozen different flavors. But the top three best-selling flavors are the traditional orange, cherry, and grape.

Between Courses

Tricks for the Dinner Table

These are tricks that will endear you to everyone at the table ... except perhaps the person who owns the fine crystal that you're trying to flip spoons into.

LOOKING FOR A WAY TO AMUSE YOURSELF, your friends, or small children at a restaurant or between courses at a family dinner? Then we've got some amusing stunts for you. Just one word of caution: Try these tricks at home first ... with your own dishes.

WINE GLASS BALANCE

This one looks downright scary, but is mostly harmless. You pick up a wine glass and hold it on the top edge of the plate. Subtly adjusting it, like you're trying to find the balance point, you suddenly let go. It wobbles a little, but people are amazed when the wine glass stays put.

How you do it. As you're holding the dinner plate with your hand, you sneak your thumb up to support the glass.

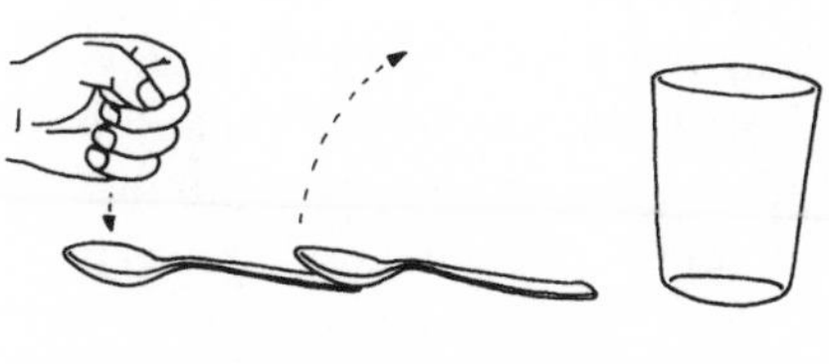

TIDDLY SPOONS

Let's do launch! Whaddya say, best of 10 tries, or until we break the glass ... whichever comes first?

SUPPORTING THE MIDDLE GLASS

Place four glasses in a square pattern and challenge those present to suspend a fifth glass in the center of the pattern using just four dinner knives, with neither glass nor knives touching the table.

How you do it. Temporarily put the fifth glass in the center of the pattern as a support. Lay the knives down in the overlapping pattern below. If you do it right, you can move the middle glass to the top of the knife blades, where it will stay suspended in midair. Violà!

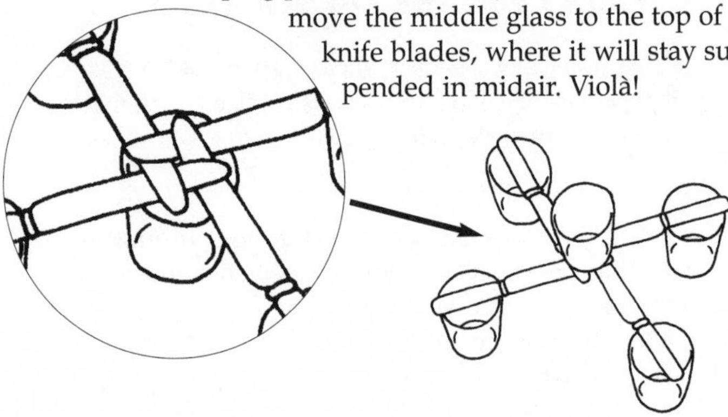

CHANGING SEASONS

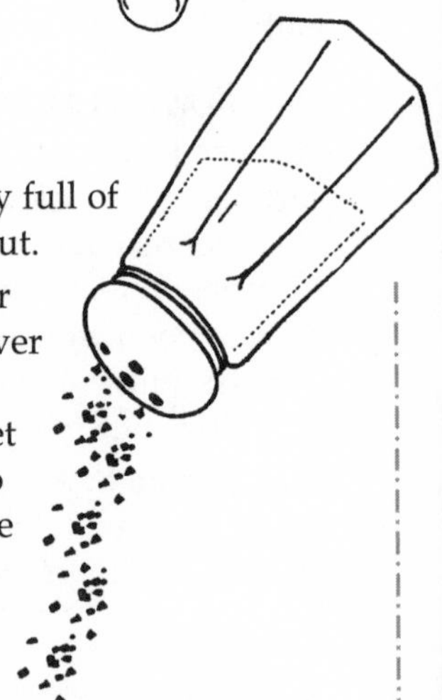

You take a clear glass shaker, very obviously full of salt, and when you pour it, pepper comes out.

How you do it. Unscrew the cover of a clear glass salt shaker and lay a paper napkin over the top. Push the napkin into the shaker, creating a shallow pocket. Fill this pocket with pepper. Screw the cover back onto the shaker, being careful not to tear the napkin inside. If you don't see flecks of pepper falling into the salt, you're okay. Carefully tear away the excess paper from the napkin that's sticking out from around the edge of the cover. Now, when someone shakes the salt, pepper will come out. Now do the reverse to the pepper shaker.

A BIG JERK AT THE DINNER TABLE

What's the classic stunt that's infamous for disastrous results? Ah yes, the old jerk-the-tablecloth bit.

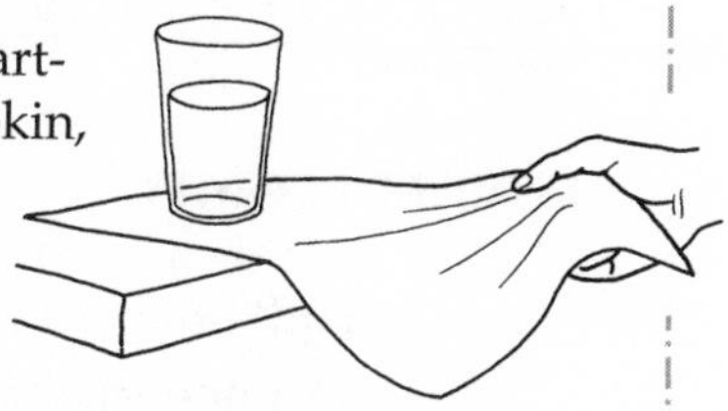

How to do it. We don't recommend starting with a full china set—maybe a napkin, a glass, and water-tolerant carpet. Grasp the napkin firmly, and slide it swiftly from under the glass. Don't jerk it hard, but don't pull too softly, either. If you do it right, the glass will remain on the table and not a drop will spill. If you do it wrong ... well, at least you have a napkin on hand.

UNIDENTIFIED FLYING SAUCERS

This is another stunt involving skill, dexterity, and jeopardy to place settings. We suggest trying it on a soft couch first.

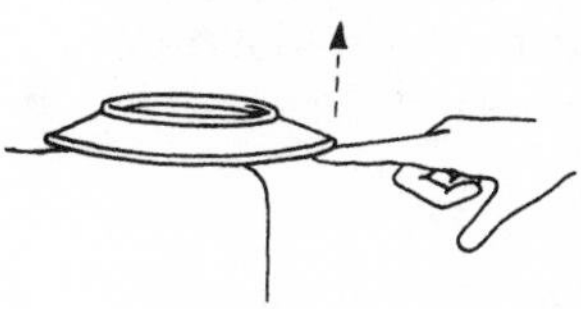

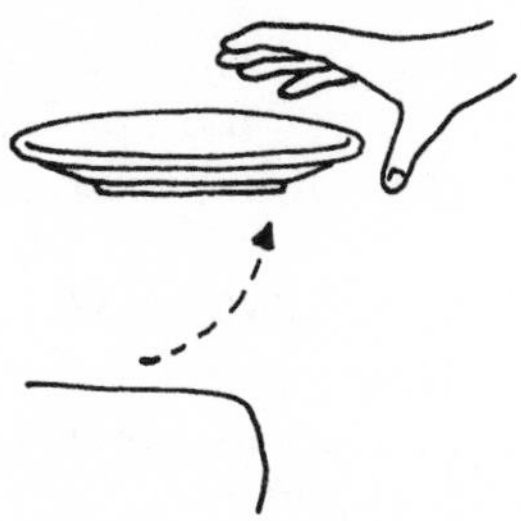

How to do it. Place a saucer upside down with its lip extending beyond the edge of the table. Point your index finger under the overhanging lip of the saucer. Now, flip the saucer into the air with your finger and catch it between your thumb and middle finger before it lands again on the table. Simple!

FRUIT ON THE REBOUND

You suddenly bounce an apple off the floor, nearly to the ceiling. You catch it nonchalantly and take a bite out of it.

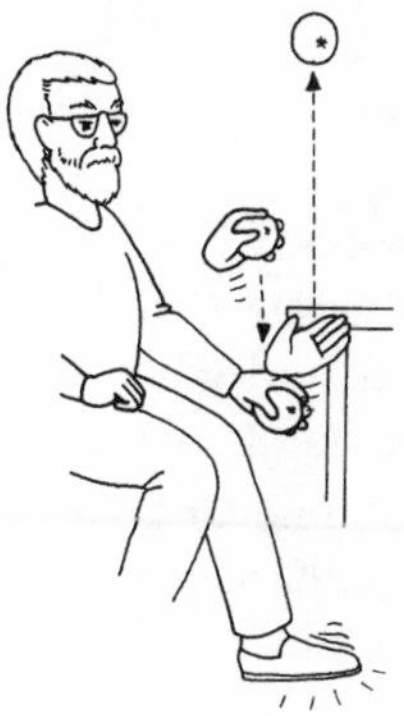

How you do it. Without warning, lift a fruit or baked potato above shoulder level and pitch it at the floor, as hard as you can. (Nobody can see that you didn't actually let go, because your hand has gone below table level.) At exactly the same time, tap your foot loudly against the floor and follow the apple's presumed path with your eyes. For the "rebound," flip the apple straight into the air with your hand and wrist only, without moving your arm.

A TIME FOR LEVITATION

There is no time like mealtime for revealing your awesome hidden powers of levitation. Please use these secrets only for good, not for evil.

ASSAULT ON GRAVITY

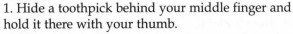

1. Hide a toothpick behind your middle finger and hold it there with your thumb.

2. Announce that the secrets of levitation have been taught you by your esteemed guru, A. Baba Reba. Place your middle finger on the top of the salt shaker. Craftily wedge your hidden toothpick into one of the shaker's holes.

3. Command the salt shaker to rise. Slowly lift your hand a few inches off the table as your hand and brow tremble with the psychokinetic effort.

4. Bring the shaker back to earth and dislodge the toothpick. Announce: "You have just witnessed a miracle!" Ditch the toothpick in your lap; don't repeat the trick.

SELF-RISING BREAD

This is an old trick; but if somebody claims to know it there's even a variation to confound them.

1. Hold a breadstick in your left fist. Turn your hand toward you and away from your companions.

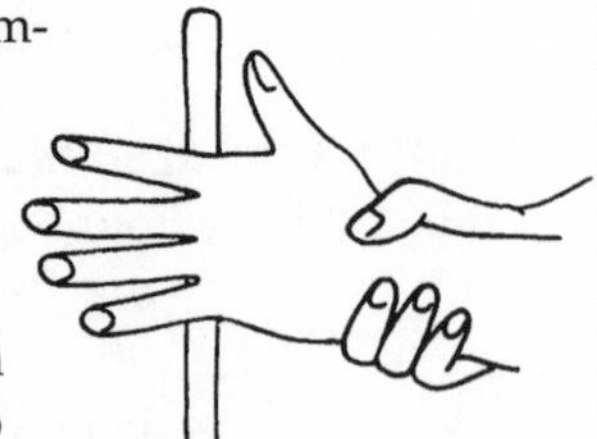

2. Grasp your wrist with your right hand. Sneak your unseen right index finger up into your hand and rest it on the breadstick to hold it in place. Slowly open your fist—the breadstick stays attached to your hand!

3. That's the trick. But since this is an old one, somebody may say they can do it, too. If so, challenge them to demonstrate. As they do, secretly slip a knife under your watchband, and when you do the trick again, wedge the breadstick under its blade.

4. Say: "One thing Guru Baba Reba taught me was to never take the other hand away." With that, you pull your right hand away from your wrist. The breadstick will stay in place. Ooh!

CORPORATE AMERICA SPEAKS

Protecting consumers is not something that comes naturally to the people who run corporations. Seat belts? Air pollution standards? What seems like common sense now was once derided as "radical" and "absurd." Here are some examples.

• *"Hell, there's more nitrates in a kiss than in a ton of bacon."* – Larry Lee, National Pork Producers' Council

• *"If no changes are made, either by Congress or the EPA, we will not be able to build cars after late 1974 because we will not be able to meet the standards."* – Henry Ford II, whining about clean air mandates

• *"All this concern about auto safety ... it's of the same order as the hula hoop – a fad. Six months from now, we'll probably be on another kick."* – W. B. Murphy, president of Campbell's Soup Company, commenting on fickle consumers and their concerns

• *"I find it difficult to believe that the seat belt can afford the driver any great amount of protection over and above that which is available to him through the medium of the safety-type steering wheel if he has his hands on the wheel and grips the rim sufficiently tight to take advantage of its energy absorption properties and also takes advantage of the shock-absorbing action which can be achieved by correct positioning of the feet and legs."* – Howard Gandelot, vehicle safety engineer for General Motors, 1954

• *"We should not fall prey to the beautification extremists who have no sense of economic reality."* – Fred L. Hartley, president of Union Oil

• *"Uninterrupted scenery, too, can get pretty monotonous. Billboards are only a way of humanizing what is still an overwhelming landscape."* – June Martino, McDonald's executive, 1959

A Name in Common?

It's easy, really—we'll give you a series of first or last names and you tell us what name goes with all of them. For example, number 1 is "Irving." Now try the rest.

1. Washington, Berlin, Julius.
2. Washington, Lloyd, Sand, Custer, Clooney.
3. Woody, Hesse, Melville, Wouk, Pee-wee.
4. Brooks, Laird, Harold, Ott, Gibson.
5. Patrick, Ford, O., John, VIII.
6. Kennedy, Billy, Pete, MacGowan, Bowl.
7. Kennedy, Jay, Adams, Elton.
8. Eddy, Palmer, Benedict, the Pig.
9. Bowie, Henry, Brown, P. D., Jesse.
10. Danny, Aquinas, Clarence, Jefferson.
11. George, Ness, T. S.
12. Hal, Camp, Garrick, Niven, Letterman.
13. James, Brothers, Kilmer, Oates.
14. Meredith, Henry, Spike, Jason, Oswald, Marvin.
15. King, Hardy, North, Cromwell, Twist.
16. Joe, St., Armstrong, L'Amour, XIV.
17. Mary, Van Buren, Dean, Luther, Purple.
18. Jones, John, Dizzy, Jimmy, James, Rusk.
19. Mrs., Simon, Peter, Les, Ru, Revere.
20. Ives, Ray, Prince, Nick & Nora, Schultz, Dickens.

ANSWERS: *1. Irving; 2. George; 3. Herman; 4. Melvin; 5. Henry; 6. Rose; 7. John; 8. Arnold; 9. James; 10. Thomas; 11. Eliot; 12. David; 13. Joyce; 14. Lee; 15. Oliver; 16. Louis; 17. Martin; 18. Dean; 19. Paul; 20. Charles.*

Oscar Who?

The Names behind the Awards and Prizes

Who is Nobel and could he have ever won a Peace Prize? Did Pulitzer embody excellence in journalism? For that matter, were Ryder, Heisman, and Stanley even athletes?

THE AWARD: NOBEL PEACE PRIZE
WHAT IT'S FOR: PEACEMAKERS
NAMED FOR: THE INVENTOR OF DYNAMITE

The Nobel Peace Prize is something of an irony, in that it was funded by the inventor of dynamite. It's said that Alfred Nobel was shocked when a newspaper mistakenly printed his obituary. It essentially called Nobel a merchant of death and said that his invention of high-powered explosives triggered an escalating arms race of mass destruction. To salvage his reputation and the family name, Nobel decided to will $9,000,000 to establish prizes for chemistry, literature, medicine, physics, and peace.

THE AWARD: PULITZER PRIZE
WHAT IT'S FOR: JOURNALISM
NAMED FOR: A TABLOID PUBLISHER

In the 1890s, Joseph Pulitzer became involved in an ugly newspaper war that inspired the term "yellow journalism." No headline was too tasteless, no crime too bloody in the battle for readers between Joseph Pulitzer's *New York World* and W. R. Hearst's *New York Journal*. When Pulitzer died in 1912, he willed money for an annual prize that would award excellence in journalism.

THE AWARD: OSCAR
WHAT IT'S FOR: MOVIE MAKERS
NAMED FOR: AN EMPLOYEE'S UNCLE

The Oscar statuette is meant to look like a knight holding a crusader's sword, standing on a reel of film. However, on first see-

ing it, an Academy employee named Margaret Herrick blurted out, "It looks like my Uncle Oscar!" Academy staffers began to informally refer to the award by that name, and Herrick's quip spread through the film community. In 1934, Walt Disney publicly called it an "Oscar" during an acceptance speech, but the Academy didn't officially use the nickname until 1939. Ms. Herrick later became executive director of the Academy. We don't know what became of her uncle.

THE PRIZE: NEWBERY MEDAL
WHAT IT'S FOR: CHILDREN'S BOOKS
NAMED FOR: A BRITISH BOOKSELLER

The foil medal embossed on the front of some kids' books indicates the book has won the Newbery Award. It was established in 1921 by Frederic G. Melcher, publisher of *Library Journal* and *Publishers Weekly*. The Newbery was named for John Newbery, who owned London's Bible & Sun bookstore in the 1700s. He was the first person to print and sell books specifically for children. His titles included *A Little Pretty Pocket-Book* (1744) and *Goody-Two-Shoes* (1765).

THE PRIZE: MACARTHUR FELLOWSHIP
WHAT IT'S FOR: TALENTED, SMART "GENIUSES"
NAMED FOR: A COUPLE OF SKINFLINTS

The John D. and Catherine T. MacArthur Foundation gives grants of $500,000 paid out over five years to two dozen creative folks every year. Who were the MacArthurs? While they lived, John D. and wife Catherine T. were notoriously thrifty tycoons who lived in an apartment in a rundown motel that they'd bought in Florida, running their insurance and real estate holdings from a booth in the motel's coffee shop. John died in 1978 and Catherine in 1981, and their stinginess paid off, in a way—the foundation they founded as a tax dodge is now the sixth largest in the United States, with $4.2 billion in assets.

THE PRIZE: EMMY
WHAT IT'S FOR: TELEVISION
NAMED FOR: A NOW-OBSOLETE TV TUBE

The Emmy Award statuette consists of a winged woman holding a globe over her head. However, Emmy has no human counterpart—the name's a garbled variation of "Immy,"a nickname for the *image orthicon*, a tube once used in television cameras until it was replaced by the more advanced *vidicon* in the 1960s.

THE PRIZE: CLIO
WHAT IT'S FOR: ADVERTISING
NAMED FOR: A GREEK MUSE

The Clio Awards are named after the Greek muse of history, whose name comes from the Greek *kleos* ("glory"). Why it's named for the muse of history instead of something more appropriate—for example, the Sirens, whose sweet songs led sailors to their doom—we don't know.

THE PRIZE: STANLEY CUP
WHAT IT'S FOR: HOCKEY
NAMED FOR: A BUREAUCRAT

Lord Stanley without his cup

Frederick Arthur, known officially as "Lord Stanley of Preston, England," was the governor-general of Canada in the late 1800s, when it was still a British colony. His son played a newly invented Canadian game called hockey, and Lord Stanley became a fan. Before Lord Stanley returned to England in 1893, he paid a silversmith $50 for a gold-plated silver bowl for the National Hockey Association's amateur hockey champions. When the NHA went pro and became the National Hockey League, the Stanley Cup went pro, too.

THE PRIZE: RYDER CUP
WHAT IT'S FOR: GOLF
NAMED FOR: A SEED MERCHANT

The Ryder Cup was started in 1926 by Samuel Ryder, a wealthy English businessman who made his fortune from selling penny packets of flower seeds. Samuel Ryder's idea of good prize money? "I'll give $5 to each of the winning players," he offered. "And I'll give a party afterwards, with champagne and chicken sandwiches." Eventually he was convinced to put up $250 for a gold trophy instead.

THE PRIZE: CY YOUNG AWARD
WHAT IT'S FOR: BASEBALL PITCHERS
NAMED FOR: EARLY PITCHER

Over twenty-two seasons, Denton True "Cy" Young won more games than any other pitcher in history: 511, almost 100 more than any other pitcher, out of a career total of 906. Young retired in 1911, and the award was established in 1956, the year after his death.

THE PRIZE: HEISMAN TROPHY
WHAT IT'S FOR: COLLEGE FOOTBALL
NAMED FOR: EARLY PLAYER & COACH

Football player and coach John W. Heisman wasn't just the inspiration for the Heisman trophy, he also invented the center snap in the game and coined the term "hike." He also invented the hand-off, the hidden ball trick, the double lateral, and the "flea flicker." Heisman coached at a number of colleges from 1892 to 1927, including Auburn, Clemson, Georgia Tech, and Rice. His most memorable game: a record-breaker in 1916 in which his Georgia Tech team squeaked past Cumberland University of Tennessee, 222 to 0.

THE PRIZE: DAVIS CUP
WHAT IT'S FOR: TENNIS
NAMED FOR: NE'ER-DO-WELL HARVARD BOY

In 1899, four members of the Harvard tennis team decided to challenge the best and brightest tennis players of Britain. One of the four, Dwight Filley Davis, paid $700 for a trophy. By 1905, all available spaces on it were filled with names, so he shelled out $500 more for a silver tray to go with the cup. For that contribution, the award was named for Davis after he died in 1945.

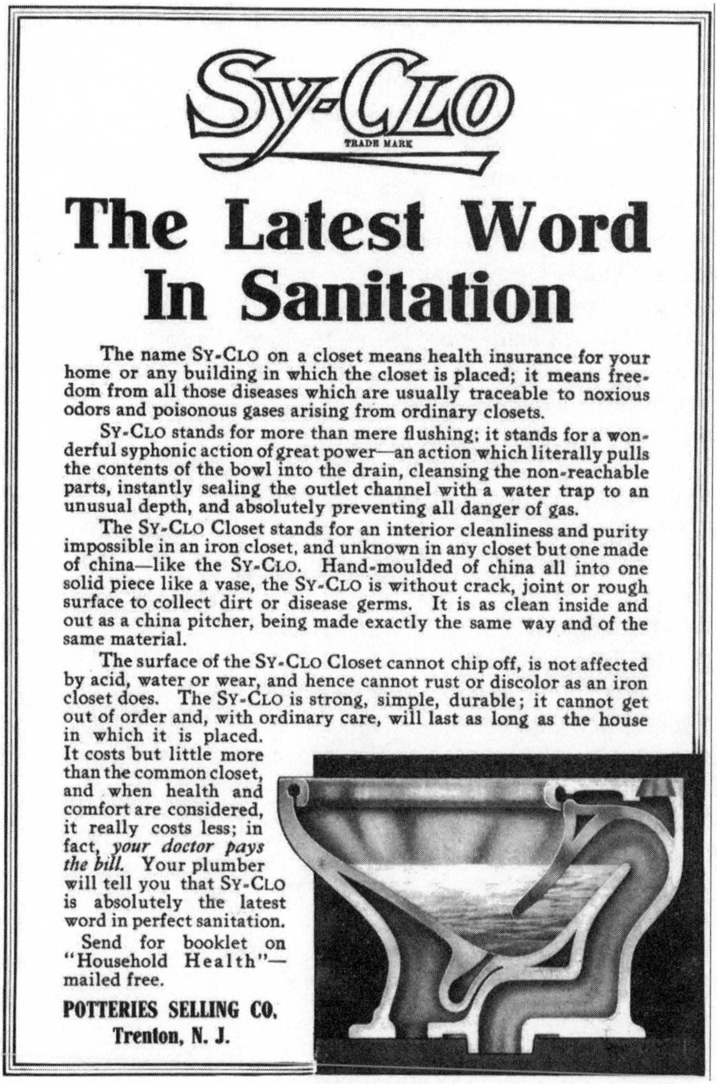

Get a Job!

Careers Your Guidance Counselor Never Mentioned

Slapper: Prepares clay for potters.
Advertisement Conveyancer: Wears sandwich board.
Devil: Assists a printer.
Shrager: Prunes trees.
Wabster: Weavers cloth.
Intelligencer: Spies on people, armies, or governments.
Pricker: Makes clothes patterns.
Skinker: Bartender in an ale house.
Back Washer: Cleans wool before it's turned into yarn.
Dykeman: Digs ditches.
Jagger: Sells fish.
Pugger: Mixes clay for ceramics.
Bagniokeeper: Manages a brothel or bath house.
Dripping Man: Buys and sells secondhand fat.
Purefinder: Collects animal poop for use in making leather.
Jongler: Travels and entertains people.
Skelper: Sells bees.
Bal Maiden: Works surface mines (female).
Quister: Bleaches cloth.
Dry Stane Dyker: Builds stone walls.
Xylographer: Carves wooden blocks for printing.
Zincographer: Etches designs in zinc plates for printing.
Kisser: Makes helmets.
Wet Nurse: Suckles the infant of another.
Ratoner: Catches rodents.
Ant Catcher: Collects ants for ant farms.
Baller: Rolls balls of clay for potters.
Slaymaker: Carves wooden pegs for looms.
Palister: Maintains the grounds of parks.
Earth Stopper: Fills holes made by gophers and badgers.
Batman: Acts as personal assistant to a military officer.
Faggotter: Bundles sticks and firewood.

R_x: Drain His Blood!

How Doctors Killed George Washington

How did the best minds of medicine come up with the outlandish theory that draining your blood would be the best medicine?

THIS IS A STORY OF HOW DOCTORS started with a sore throat and ended up with a dead patient. It illustrates the dangers of trusting what "everyone knows is true" instead of learning from your own observations.

When George Washington retired from the presidency in 1797, he was sixty-five years old and as healthy as an ox. Although the former general complained to Thomas Jefferson that he felt he was "growing old" with "bodily health less firm," he was fit enough to ride on horseback for several hours on daily inspections of his farms and fields.

On December 12, 1799, Washington went out as usual, despite snow, wind, and freezing rain. Five hours later, he returned home with a sore throat. He was kept awake that night by a violent cough, and so he sent for his doctor, Dr. James Craik.

Craik did standard doctorly things of the time: he had Washington gargle with a mix of vinegar and sage tea. Then he wrapped the former president's throat with *cantharides* – now known as "Spanish fly," an extract of dried beetles that raises painful blisters on the skin – to "draw the inflammation to the surface." That treatment may have been painful and unnecessary, but at least it wasn't fatal. However, that was about to change: he next drained a half-pint of Washington's blood.

DOESN'T WORK? GIVE HIM MORE OF THE SAME

Hard to believe, but none of these things seemed to help. Washington still didn't feel any better. In fact, he was doing worse—in pain and feeling weaker. Go figure.

Perhaps the doctor should have taken a cue that blistering and bleeding was not helping. Instead, he decided that the patient needed even more of the same. Craik took another half-pint of blood.

DISCREDITED THEORIES

How was it that doctors came to believe that draining a patient's blood would somehow help heal them? Well, blame it on the Greeks. They had a theory that went something like this: The body's essence is made up of the "Four Humours": blood, yellow bile, phlegm, and black bile. In order for your body, mind, and character to be healthy, these four fluids need to be in perfect balance. If something goes seriously wrong, you can take out some of the person's blood and the other fluids will magically adjust themselves back into balance, restoring health, sanity, and moral fiber.

It was a crazy idea ... and it didn't work. Doctors in the more scientific parts of the world like the Far East and Middle East had abandoned bleeding as ineffective and dangerous centuries earlier, but doctors in Europe and America continued "balancing the humours" of their patients with knives and leeches well into the nineteenth century.

MEANWHILE, BACK AT MT. VERNON

After two bleedings in one morning, Washington was in anything but "good humour." The doctor waited for a few hours to see if Washington would perk up. He did not, so the afternoon Craik set about bleeding him again. Later that afternoon, his colleague Dr. Elisha Dick arrived, and the two bled Washington one more time. This time, the blood was thick and came slowly. No wonder—he was dehydrated and

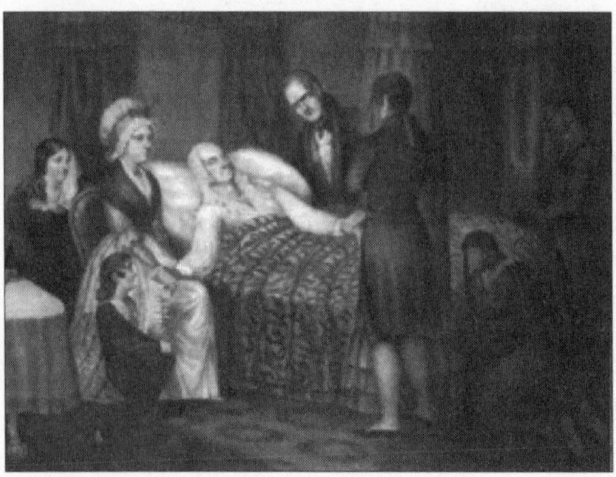

George Washington's life draining away

anemic after losing two pints of blood in one day.

Martha Washington tried to intervene to have the bleeding stopped, according to an eyewitness account by Tobias Lear, Washington's secretary: "Mrs. Washington, not knowing whether bleeding was proper or not in the General's situation, begged that much might not be taken from him, lest it should be injurious, and desired me to stop it; but when I was about to untie the string the General put up his hand to prevent it, and as soon as he could speak, said—'More, more.'"

Washington's condition worsened even more. The former president sunk slowly into stupor and then death, killed by his doctors and a misplaced faith in their skills. During a millennium of medical malpractice, Washington was only one of the thousands of patients who were doctored to death.

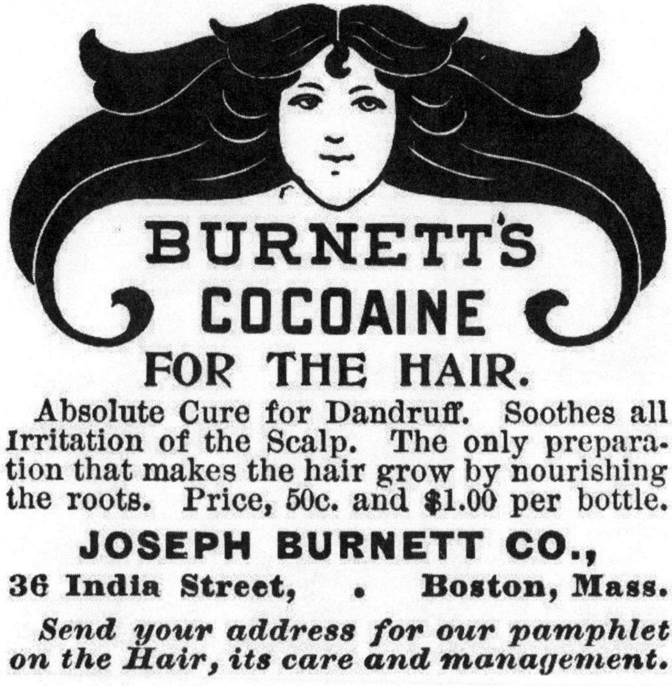

More Pot Shots

Some favorite bathroom shots. Send us yours! (See page 478.)

a. WC fields in Saudi Arabia
b. Shadow goes fishing
c. Great Smokey National Park outhouse
d. Italian train station squat toilet
e. Aussie outhouse
f. New Jersey outhouse

I Curse Thee, Too!

And more of our favorite long-forgotten insults from merrye old England.

BLOWMAUNGER: "A fat, blown-cheek'd person, as if blown up with fat by full feeding and juncketing: or perhaps it may be applied to one who puffs and blows while he is eating. Perhaps from the French blankmanger…a kind of flummery (a tasty but insubstantial dish)." —Frederick Elworthy's *Devonshire Glossary*, 1879

CRUMP: "One that helps solictors to affidavit men and swearers…who, for a small sum will be bound or swear for anybody, on that occasion putting on good cloaths to make a good appearance, that bail may be accepted." —B.E.'s *Dictionary of Canting Crew*, 1698–1699

FUSTILUGS: "A great foul creature. The foulness implies bad smelling. Used only in the plural." —Frederick Elworthy's *Devonshire Glossary*, 1879

GLOBSLOTCH: " A greedy, clownish person … apt to gobble his food." —William Holloway's *Dictionary of Provincialisms*, 1838

GONG-FARMER: "A night-man; a cleanser of privies or cesspools. From *gong*, a privy." —Robert Hunter's *Encyclopedic Dictionary*, 1894

GONGOOZLER:"An idle and inquisitive person who stands staring for prolonged periods at anything out of the common." —Joseph Wright's *English Dialect Dictionary*, 1896–1905

Barrymorisms II

The Barrymore family has a long relationship with Hollywood, from Lionel, John, and Ethel, down to Drew. Here are a few words of wisdom from the late, great actress, Ethel Barrymore.

ON THE AUDIENCE

"I never let them cough. They wouldn't dare."

ON SUCCESS

"For an actress to be a success, she must have the face of Venus, the brains of a Minerva, the grace of Terpsichore, the memory of a Macaulay, the figure of Juno, and the hide of a rhinoceros."

ON THE COMPETITION

"The face of Garbo is an Idea, *that of Hepburn an* Event.*"*

ON LIVING

"You must learn day by day, year by year, to broaden your horizons. The more things you love, the more you are interested in, the more you enjoy, the more you are indignant about – the more you have left when anything happens."

ON LAUGHTER

"You grow up on the day you have your first real laugh at yourself."

ON FAILURES

"Our achievements speak for themselves. What we have to keep track of are our failures, discouragements, and doubts. We tend to forget the past difficulties, the many false starts, and the painful groping."

ON FAITH

"When life knocks you to your knees – and it will – why, get up! If it knocks you to your knees again, as it will, well, isn't that the best position from which to pray?"

HER DYING WORDS

"Is everybody happy? I want everybody to be happy. I know I'm happy."

Gatorade

Inventing it Was No Sweat

This from a book we like called *How the Cadillac Got Its Fins*, which is—alas—currently out of print.

Is drinking a "sports drink" any more effective than drinking water while exercising? Several studies have suggested that the answer is no, unless you're involved in an extraordinary level of exertion, like running an ultra-marathon. On the other hand, Gatorade and the research that spawned it did one undeniable service for the sports community: It broke down a lethally misguided notion held by old-style coaches about the detriments of drinking liquids while exercising.

Idle questions from a coach brought James Robert Cade, a kidney researcher at the University of Florida, into sports research. In 1965, Florida Gator assistant coach DeWayne Douglas asked Cade, "How come football players never have to pee during games? Since players lose as much as 15 pounds during a game, where does all that weight go? And why do they seem to run out of gas during the fourth quarter?"

Cade did some research and found that players playing hard in the Florida sun sweated at an amazing rate, losing water, sodium and potassium. As a result, the players' kidneys shut down to conserve liquid, so players didn't have to pee. On the other hand, the loss of liquid was potentially dangerous, and led to fourth-quarter sag.

Cade analyzed sweat and came up with a liquid of similar composition. He added a lime flavoring to make it more palatable, but kept the flavor light, figuring it would inspire players to drink more of it. He mixed up a huge quantity of the stuff and presented it to the coach.

"TASTES LIKE PEE"

When the Gators started drinking Cate's concoction during play, they discovered that they didn't sag midway during the game—and that the heat didn't leave them as exhausted as before. They dubbed it "Gatorade" and even got used to the taste after a while. One player had complained that the concoction "tastes like pee"; Cade, ever the scientist, went back to his lab, took a sample of his own urine, chilled and sampled it, and reported back to the player that "urine doesn't taste a bit like Gatorade."

The big jug of Gatorade on the sidelines engendered a mystique of invulnerability among the Gators and eventually among the teams they played. In 1967, when Florida beat Georgia Tech 27–12 in the Orange Bowl, Tech's coach claimed they lost because "we didn't have Gatorade."

That year, Cade licensed the rights to Stokely-Van Camp, which began paying him a royalty on every drink sold. Jugs of Gatorade began appearing on the sidelines at professional football games, and coaches all over the country began changing a deeply held but completely erroneous belief. For decades, most had denied their athletes liquid during games and practices, thinking it would cause debilitating muscle cramps and worse. Athletes were allowed only damp towels to suck on when they got thirsty. As a result, about 50 school athletes died every year from heat stroke. Cade's research—and that highly visible jug on the sidelines—convinced coaches to rethink. Heat stroke deaths dropped to nearly zero.

When royalty money began pouring in, the University of Florida sued Cade, saying that it should own the rights to Gatorade because he was an employee at the time of his development. Cade countered that he had worked on Gatorade on his own time. In fact, early in the process, he had asked his department administrators to help him develop and patent the liquid, which would have given the university full rights to the drink, but they turned him down.

The final court settlement gave Cade and his researchers 80 percent of the profits and the rest—about $2 million a year—to the university.

Mad Tea Party

A Classic Tale for Kids of All Ages

If you've only seen the cartoon or the movie of Lewis Carroll's *Alice's Adventures in Wonderland*, you really must read the book. Let us get you started. Would you like some tea?

THERE WAS A TABLE SET OUT under a tree in front of the house, and the March Hare and the Hatter were having tea at it: a Dormouse was sitting between them, fast asleep, and the other two were using it as a cushion, resting their elbows on it. "Very uncomfortable for the Dormouse," thought Alice; "only, as it's asleep, I suppose it doesn't mind."

The table was a large one, but the three were all crowded together at one corner of it: "No room! No room!" they cried out when they saw Alice coming. "There's PLENTY of room!" said Alice indignantly, and she sat down at one end of the table.

"Have some wine," the March Hare said encouragingly.

Alice looked all round the table, but there was nothing on it but tea. "I don't see any wine," she remarked.

"There isn't any," said the March Hare.

"Then it wasn't very civil of you to offer it," said Alice.

"It wasn't very civil of you to sit down without being invited," said the March Hare.

"I didn't know it was YOUR table," said Alice; "it's laid for a great many more than three."

"Your hair wants cutting," said the Hatter. He had been looking at Alice with great curiosity, and this was his first speech.

"You should not make personal remarks," Alice said with severity; "it's very rude."

The Hatter opened his eyes very wide on hearing this; but all he SAID was, "Why is a raven like a writing-desk?"

"Come, we shall have some fun now!" thought Alice. "I'm glad they've begun asking riddles.—I believe I can guess that," she added aloud.

"Do you mean that you think you can find out the answer to it?" said the Hare.

"Exactly so," said Alice.

"Then you should say what you mean," the Hare said.

"I do," Alice hastily replied; "at least I mean what I say—that's the same thing."

"Not the same thing a bit!" said the Hatter. "You might just as well say that 'I see what I eat' is the same thing as 'I eat what I see'!"

"You might just as well say," added the Hare, "that 'I like what I get' is the same thing as 'I get what I like'!"

"You might just as well say," added the Dormouse, apparently talking in his sleep, "that 'I breathe when I sleep' is the same thing as 'I sleep when I breathe'!"

"It IS the same thing with you," said the Hatter, and here the conversation dropped. Alice thought over all she could remember about ravens and writing-desks, which wasn't much.

The Hatter was the first to break the silence. "What day of the month is it?" he said, turning to Alice: he had taken his watch out of his pocket, and was looking at it uneasily, shaking it every now and then, and holding it to his ear.

Alice considered a little, and then said, "The fourth."

"Two days wrong!" sighed the Hatter. "I told you butter wouldn't suit the works!" he added, looking angrily at the March Hare.

"It was the BEST butter," the Hare meekly replied.

"Yes, but some crumbs must have got in as well," the Hatter grumbled: "you shouldn't have put it in with the bread-knife."

The Hare took the watch and looked at it gloomily: then he dipped it into his cup of tea, and looked at it again: but he could think of nothing better to say than, "It was the BEST butter, you know."

Alice had been looking over his shoulder with some curiosity. "What a funny watch!" she remarked. "It tells the day of the month, and doesn't tell what o'clock it is!"

"The Dormouse is asleep again," said the Hatter, and he poured a little hot tea upon its nose. The Dormouse shook its head impatiently, and said, without opening its eyes, "Of course, of course; just what I was going to remark myself."

"Have you guessed the riddle yet?" the Hatter said, turning to Alice again.

"No, I give it up," Alice replied: "What's the answer?"

"I haven't the slightest idea," said the Hatter.

"Nor I," said the Hare.

Alice sighed. "I think you might do something better with the time," she said, "than waste it in asking riddles that have no answers."

"If you knew Time as well as I do," said the Hatter, "you wouldn't talk about wasting IT. It's HIM."

"I don't know what you mean," said Alice.

"Of course you don't!" the Hatter said contemptuously. "I dare say you never even spoke to Time!"

"Perhaps not," Alice cautiously replied: "but I know I have to beat time when I learn music."

"Ah! that accounts for it," said the Hatter. "He won't stand beating. Now, if you only kept on good terms with him, he'd do almost anything you liked with the clock. For instance, suppose it were nine o'clock in the morning, just time to begin lessons: you'd only have to whisper a hint to Time, and round goes the clock in a twinkling! Half-past one, time for dinner!"

("I only wish it was," the March Hare said to itself.)

"That would be grand, certainly," said Alice thoughtfully: "but then—I shouldn't be hungry for it, you know."

"Not at first, perhaps," said the Hatter: "but you could keep it to half-past one as long as you liked."

"Is that the way YOU manage?" Alice asked.

The Hatter shook his head mournfully. "Not I!' he replied. "We quarrelled last March—just before HE went mad, you know—" (pointing with his tea spoon at the March Hare) "—it was at the great concert given by the Queen of Hearts, and I had to sing 'Twinkle, twinkle, little bat! How I wonder what you're at!' You know the song, perhaps?"

"I've heard something like it," said Alice.

"It goes on, you know," the Hatter said, "'Up above the world you fly, Like a tea-tray in the sky. Twinkle, twinkle—'"

Here the Dormouse shook itself, and began singing in its sleep, "Twinkle, twinkle, twinkle, twinkle—" and went on so long that they had to pinch it to make it stop.

"Well, I'd hardly finished the first verse," said the Hatter, "when the Queen jumped up and bawled out, 'He's murdering the time! Off with his head!'"

"How dreadfully savage!" exclaimed Alice.

"And ever since that," the Hatter went on mournfully, "he won't do a thing I ask! It's always 6 o'clock now. It's always tea-time, and we've no time to wash the things between whiles."

"Then you keep moving round, I suppose?" said Alice.

"Exactly so," said the Hatter: "as things get used up."

"But what happens when you come to the beginning again?" Alice ventured to ask.

"Take some more tea," the March Hare said to Alice, very earnestly.

"I've had nothing yet," Alice replied in an offended tone, "so I can't take more."

"You mean you can't take LESS," said the Hatter: "it's very easy to take MORE than nothing."

"Nobody asked YOUR opinion," said Alice.

"Who's making personal remarks now?" the Hatter asked triumphantly.

This piece of rudeness was more than Alice could bear: she got up in great disgust, and walked off; the last time she saw them, they were trying to put the Dormouse into the teapot.

"At any rate I'll never go THERE again!" said Alice as she picked her way through the wood. "It's the stupidest tea-party I ever was at in all my life!"

Kicks, Spikes & Slapshots

Inventing the Wild World of Sports

Before sports became big business, games were just games, and people invented them and changed them as they saw fit. Here are the stories behind some of our favorite sports.

SOCCER

As early as 400 B.C., Chinese athletes played a soccer-like game. The Romans played a non-kick version in the third century. By the 1100s, London children played a form of soccer they called "football." Soccer moved into all English schools by the early 1800s, but each school interpreted the rules differently. In 1848, school representatives met at Trinity College in Cambridge and agreed upon a standardized set of soccer rules.

RUGBY

According to its legendary history, rugby was invented by a renegade schoolboy named William Webb Ellis at Rugby School in Warwickshire, England. One day in 1823, when his "football" (soccer) team was badly losing, Ellis picked up the ball and ran for the goal while onlookers watched in dumfounded amazement. He was heavily penalized on the field and forced to write a letter of apology afterward. However, his simple act of frustrated defiance inspired the idea of a game where you can kick, throw, or run with the ball, and "Rugby-styled football" eventually became just "rugby."

AMERICAN FOOTBALL

It's hard to believe, but football was once so deadly that it was nearly outlawed in the United States.

In 1874, a team from Montreal's McGill University visited Harvard and taught its soccer team how to play a variation of

Football in the good old days. Note the elbow in the face of the ball carrier.

rugby. Harvard then introduced it to other Eastern colleges. Walter Camp, who had played for Yale from 1876 to 1882 established a scoring system, downs, yards to gain, and the center's snap to the quarterback.

By 1900, football had become increasingly violent, but players still did not yet wear pads or helmets. In 1909 alone, 27 players died and hundreds more were permanently injured. Gunfighter-turned-sportswriter Bat Masterson, no stranger to mayhem, wrote, "Football is not a sport in any sense. It is a brutal and savage slugging match between two reckless, opposing crowds. The rougher it is and the more killed and crippled, the more delighted are the spectators, who howl their heads off at the sight of a player stretched prone and unconscious on the hard and frozen ground."

Woodrow Wilson, then president of Princeton University, convened an intercollegiate football rules committee to see if the game should be changed, or even outlawed. After five months, the committee issued its recommendations, prohibiting some of the most dangerous practices, like diving tackles, blocking with linked arms,

Worst Shut-Out in Football History

The most uneven game in football history took place in 1916. Georgia Tech had been humiliated in an earlier athletic contest, so its football team demanded that Cumberland University meet them on the football field to settle the score. Unfortunately, Cumberland had canceled its football program that year, but the school cobbled together a team of volunteers, some of whom had never even played the game before.

Georgia Tech, using the excuse of an earlier defeat to act with poor sportsmanship, piled on the points. The final score? 222-0.

picking up and carrying ball carriers, and interfering with pass receivers. Deaths and injuries went way down, however, some hardcore fans complained that the changes ruined the game forever.

BASKETBALL

"Basketball" could've easily been called "box ball" or even "trashcan ball."

In 1891, James Naismith invented a dribble, pass, and shoot game for bored, snowbound students at a YMCA in Springfield, Massachusetts. In designing the court, he had intended to use wooden boxes for his targets. Unfortunately, when he asked the custodian for boxes, he said there were none in any of the club's back rooms. "But," he added, "I have two old peach baskets down in the store room, if they'll do you any good."

Naismith shrugged and nailed the peach baskets on the balconies at either end of the gym. They just happened to be ten feet off the floor, which is why that came to be the regulation height for baskets. Later, when it became clear that the thin wood baskets weren't going to hold up for long, Naismith switched to wire trash cans, and then eventually to the hoop and netting combination we see today.

VOLLEYBALL, THE ALTERNATIVE

Volleyball was invented in Holyoke, Massachusetts by William Morgan in 1895 for sedentary businessmen who found the new sport of basketball too strenuous.

ULTIMATE FRISBEE

In 1967, high school student Joel Silver introduced his idea of a soccer-like Frisbee game to Columbia High School in Maplewood, New Jersey. In 1969, Silver formed a team at the school and they played in a parking lot.

The rules were revamped in 1970 by Silver and two friends. In 1975, Yale hosted the first organized tournament. That same year, World Frisbee Championships adopted Ultimate as a sanctioned game.

RODEO

Rodeo developed on ranches in the late 1800s. Cowboys

competed informally at bronco riding and steer roping. The first rodeo that offered prizes and attracted paying spectators was held in Prescott, Arizona, in 1888. Cowboys eventually formed the first professional rodeo organization in 1936.

HOCKEY

McGill University, which had an important role in the development of football, played an even more pivotal role in the invention of ice hockey. But the game itself was invented by unknown members of the British Army.

It's true that field hockey games—with balls and without the ice—were played by ancient Egyptians, Greeks, Arabs, Romans, and Persians. Irish played "hurley" more than 2000 years ago, and native South Americans had a similar game when Columbus arrived in 1492. However, the dubious genius of trying to play the basic game while sliding on ice skates took a special kind of crackpot genius you'd expect to find only among extremely bored soldiers in a wintry clime.

And so it was: British soldiers stationed in Canada in the mid-1850s came up with the basics of ice hockey. The rules were refined and set down by students at McGill University in Quebec in 1879.

The name comes from the French word for a shepherd's crook, *hoquet*. By the beginning of the twentieth century, the sport had spread into the U.S. and Europe. In late 1917, professional players formed the National Hockey League.

MUSICAL NOTES

• The difference between two notes that are an octave apart is that the higher note is vibrating twice as fast as the lower one.

• Our musical scale has twelve notes, of which we normally sing only seven (do-ra-mi-fa-so-la-ti). Chinese music uses five notes. Arabic uses seventeen. Indian, twenty-two. The Japanese use the same seven notes that we do, only "fa" is half a step higher.

Slogos 3!

It's pretty weird that beer companies use cute little forest creatures to hawk their alcoholic products. But hey, it makes a good Slogo quiz. We're going to give you slogans from well-known beers—past and present. Match the slogan to the right animal logo. Rated: Hard.

1. Which of the following animals was the logo for Molson—the beer company that claimed, "What beer's all about"?

A. Deer

B. A fox

C. A duck

D. An opossum

E. Horses

2. "Grab ____ by the neck!" suggested Weinhard's ads. Which animal was not only the company's logo, but the name of the beer, too?

A. A boar

B. An eagle

C. A goose

D. A moose

E. A bear

3. Which spokes-animal goofed off in Hamm beer ads that boasted, "Land of sky blue waters"?

A. An aardvark

B. A turtle

C. Rainbow trout

D. Frogs

E. A bear

4. This animal group sang back up for the "King of Beers," Budweiser.

A. Puppies

B. Raccoons

C. Deer

D. Bears

E. Frogs

5. "[Name] means great beer." This animal's decapitated head represents a beer by the same name.

A. A pig

B. A moose

C. A rhinoceros

D. A fox

E. A duck

6. "Follow your instincts," said this beer's slogan, but we wouldn't follow this red animal logo anywhere in the wild.

A. A wolf

B. A deer

C. An eagle

D. A mouse

E. A lion

7. In ads, this animal was featured with voice-overs claiming, "It's Miller time!"

A. An elephant

B. A beetle

C. A tiger

D. An eagle

E. A moose

Answers: *1. C: Three quacks for the Molson Duck. 2. A: Weinhard's Boar. 3. E: The Hamm bear skated on frozen lakes and otherwise goofed off and had a grand time in the old Hamm beer commercials. 4. E: The Budweiser Frogs—named Bud, Weis, and Er—proved to be Budweiser's most beloved ad campaign to date. 5. B: Consumers never have seemed bothered by drinking something named after a disembodied game animal. 6. A: Red Wolf beer. 7. D: The Miller Eagle, representing freedom and flight—two things made infinitely more difficult when intoxicated.*

Ripe Ol' Corn

"Uncle Josh Plays Golf"

"Uncle Josh," Cal Stewart's country bumpkin, had problems figuring out modern city life (circa 1901). Here he tries out the fad sport that was sweeping the nation—golf.

WELL, ABOUT TWO WEEKS AGO the boys said to me, "Uncle we'd like to have you come out and play a game of golf?"

Well, they took me out behind the woodshed where mother couldn't see us and them durned boys dressed your uncle up in the doggondest suit of clothes I ever had on in my life. I had on a pair of socks that had more different colors in 'em than in Joseph's coat. I looked like a cross atween a monkey and a cirkus rider, and a-goin' across the medder our turkey gobbler took after me and I had an awful time with that fool bird. I calculate as how I'll git even with him 'bout Thanksgiving time.

Well, the boys took me into the pasture, and they had it all dug up into what they called a "T," and they had a wheelbarrow full of little Injun war clubs. They called one a nibbler, and another a brassie, and a lot of other fool names I never heerd afore, and can't remember now. Then they brought out a little wooden ball 'bout as big as a hen's egg, and they stuck it up on a little hunk of mud. Then they told me to take one of them thar war clubs and stand alongside of the ball and hit it.

Well, I jist peeled off my coat and got a good holt on that war club and I jist whaled away at that durned little ball, and by gum I missed it, and the boys all commenced to holler "foozle." Well, I got a little bit riled and I whaled away at it again, and I

hit it right whar I missed it the first time, and I whirled round and sot down so durned hard I set four back teeth to achin', and I pawed round in the air and knocked a lot of it out of place. I hit myself on the shin and on the pet corn at the same time, and them durned boys was jist a-rollin' round on the ground and a-hollerin' like Injuns.

Well, I begun to git madder 'n a wet hen, and I swore I'd knock that durned little ball way over into the next county. So I rolled up my sleeves and spit on my hands and got a good holt on that war club and I whaled away at that little ball agin, and by chowder I hit it. I knocked it clear over into Deacon Witherspoon's paster, and hit his old muley cow, and she got skeered and run away, jumped the fence and went down the road, and the durned fool never stopped a-runnin' 'til she went slap dab into Ezra Hoskins' grocery store, upset four gallons of apple butter into a keg of soft soap, and set one foot into a tub of mackeral, and t'other foot into a box of window glass, and knocked over Jim Lawson who was settin' on a cracker barrel, and broke his durned old wooden leg, and then she went right out through the window and skeered Si Pettingill's hosses that was a-standin' thar, and they run away and smashed his wagon into kindlin' wood' and Silas has sued me for damages, and mother won't speak to me, and Jim he wants me to buy him a new wooden leg, and the neighbors all say as how I ought to be put away some place fer safe keepin', and Aunt Nancy Smith got so excited she lost her glass eye and didn't find it for three or four days, and when she did git it the boys was a-playin' marbles with it and it wuz all full of gaps, and Jim Lawson, he trimmed it up on the grindstane and it don't fit Nancy any more, and she has to sort of put it in with cotton round it to hold it, and the cotton works out at the corners and skeers the children and every time I see Nancy that durned eye seems to look at me sort of reproachful like, and all I know about playin' golf is, the feller what knocks the ball so durned far you can't find it or whar it does the most damage, wins the game.

Fore-Footed Friends

Uganda's Jinja Golf Course has some interesting house rules. For instance, if a ball lands near a crocodile and it's deemed unsafe to play it, you may drop another ball. If your ball lands in a hippopotamus footprint, you may lift and drop the ball without incurring penalty. (Don't try invoking these rules at most golf courses, however—we've tried and it doesn't seem to work.)

• Golfers in Australia report that crows and currawongs (an indigenous black bird) swoop down and steal balls. When one bird's nest was blasted with a water cannon, 40–50 golf balls came raining down.

• In 1994, a farmer in Germany sued because errant golfers were hooking balls into his field. After one of his cows suffered a sudden death, the vet discovered a golf ball lodged in its throat. Further investigation revealed that thirty cattle had a collective total of 2,000 balls lodged in their stomachs.

• At the Talamore Golf Course in Southern Pines, North Carolina, you have the option of renting an old-fashioned golf cart for $20 ... or a llama caddy for $100.

• How's this for a hole-in-one? In 1981, on a par-3 hole at Mountain View (California) Golf Course, amateur Ted Barnhouse hit a wayward ball over a fence into a cow pasture. The ball bounced off a grazing cow's head, ricocheted off a lawn mower, bounced off the flag and into the hole.

• Cattle's revenge? A herd of about fifty cattle invaded the eighteenth hole of the 1984 St. Andrews Trophy, menacing several golfers in their path. The stampede was driven back by officials and golfers waving 8-irons, averting cattleclysm.

• While playing a tournament in South America, Sam Snead was once attacked by an ostrich. The birdie bit him on the hand, rendering him out of commission for two weeks.

• On a golf course in Natal, South Africa, Molly Whitaker was about to hit a shot from a bunker when a monkey leaped from a tree and wrapped its arms around her neck. Her caddie chased it away, and the game continued.

Knock, Knock!

Who's There?

Knock knock jokes became a fad in the 1930s among grownups, but quickly made their way down to the youngest set. Here are some favorites of all age groups....

Knock knock.
Who's there?
Yule.
Yule who?
Yule never know.

Knock knock.
Who's there?
Dwayne!
Dwayne who?
Dwayne the bathtub, I'm dwowning!

Knock knock.
Who's there?
Wendy.
Wendy who?
"Wendy red red robin comes bob, bob bobbin' along...."

Knock knock
Who's there?
Sara.
Sara who?
Sara doctor in the house?

Knock knock.
Who's there?
Atch.
Atch who?
Gesundheit.

Knock knock.
Who's there?
Owl.
Owl who?
Owl you know unless you open the door?

Knock knock.
Who's there?
Boo.
Boo who?
Oh, don´t cry. It's only a knock-knock joke.

Knock knock.
Who's there?
Dishes.
Dishes who?
Dishes me. Who ish you?

Knock knock.
Who's there?
You.
You who?
Whaddya calling me for?

Presidential Trivia II

Presidents & Their Vices

From the question & answer books *Just Curious, Jeeves* and *Just Curious About History, Jeeves*, by Jack Mingo and Erin Barrett, we found some more juicy bits of gossip on some United States Presidents and Veeps.

How much older was Grover Cleveland than his wife Frances?

She was twenty-one and he was forty-nine. Cleveland was the first and only president to marry in the White House. The public went crazy over the couple. They saw her as the young gal who put the reins on an old codger, their bachelor president. However, the story has a twist: the couple had had a different type of relationship prior to their romance. She was his ward. When her father—Cleveland's former law partner, Oscar Folsom—died in a carriage accident when Frances was eleven, he left Cleveland his estate. Grover Cleveland spent the rest of Frances' childhood financially and emotionally supporting her and her mother.

***Who was the first presidential candidate to be endorsed by* TV Guide?**

That prestigious honor goes to Ronald Reagan. *TV Guide* can also be remembered as the first print venue to publish the conservative Republican coalition's "Contract With America" that helped Newt Gingrich capture the House of Representatives in the 1996 campaign.

Who was the most unpopular president in history?

Probably John Tyler. After he vetoed key points of his own Whig Party's program, his entire cabinet resigned except one member, an armed mob stormed the White House and threw rocks through its windows, and members of his party introduced an impeachment resolution in the House of Representatives. (It failed 127 to 83.) Spurned by both parties, Tyler retired after finishing his one partial term. Teddy Roosevelt summed him up 75 years later: "Tyler has been called a mediocre man, but this is unwarranted flattery. He was a politician of monumental littleness."

What happened in the duel between Alexander Hamilton and Aaron Burr?

America's most infamous duel took place on July 11, 1804 in Weehawken, New Jersey. Burr and Hamilton had become political rivals when Burr won a Senate seat that had belonged to Hamilton's father-in-law. When Burr left the vice presidency and ran an unsuccessful campaign for New York governor, he was the victim of a vicious smear campaign that he thought Hamilton might've had a hand in. Afterward, when Hamilton made some negative statements about him in the press, Burr challenged him to a duel. Hamilton was killed, but Burr's "victory" made him a political and social pariah, and murder charges hung over his head in New York and New Jersey.

A few years later Burr got himself even further in disgrace when he was caught putting together a private army with the hope of conquering parts of Louisiana and Mexico and creating his own kingdom. He was tried for treason, but escaped conviction on a technicality. After hiding out in Europe for a few years and piling up debt, he had to leave quickly to escape debtors' prison. Returning to New York, Burr managed to get the old murder charges dropped and began practicing law again. Still, after personal setbacks including the death of his beloved daughter and a disastrous late-life marriage and divorce, he lived a life "severed from the human race" (as he put it) and died forgotten in 1833 at the age of 80.

What United States president slept through most of his term?

President David Rice Atcheson. He was president for one day on March 4, 1849. James Polk's term ended then, but Zachary Taylor refused to be sworn in on a Sunday so the job went automatically to the senate president pro tem. "I slept most of that Sunday," he admitted, and Taylor was sworn in the next day.

Who was on his knees playing marbles when told he had become president?

John Tyler. William Henry Harrison had died a month

into his term and on April 6, 1841, Tyler was found deep in a game of aggies and given the news that he was the first vice president to succeed a dead president. Two decades later, Tyler apparently lost those marbles. He renounced his citizenship and joined the Confederacy.

When in American history was it a crime to criticize the president?

During the second half of John Adams' administration, which has become known as the Federalist Reign of Terror. Under the Alien and Sedition Acts, it became a crime to criticize the president. It got so bad that his vice president, Thomas Jefferson, stopped signing his letters, correctly assuming that government agents were reading his mail. More than twenty newspaper editors and a member of Congress were jailed. (Representative Matthew Lyon got four months in jail and a $1,000 fine for writing an editorial in a Vermont newspaper; his constituents re-elected him while he was in jail and paid his fine.) The law finally expired after Jefferson became president.

Who was on Richard Nixon's "Enemies List?"

Literally hundreds of people and organizations. The list was given to government agencies like the IRS with quiet presidential orders to harass the people on it. He wanted payback.

Some of the more famous names on the list included movie stars, politicians and media folks, including Carol Channing, Jane Fonda, Dick Gregory, Judith Martin ("Miss Manners"), Steve McQueen, Joe Namath, Paul Newman, Gregory Peck, Edward Kennedy, Edmund Muskie, Harold Hughes, Walter Mondale, William Proxmire, Jack Anderson, Rowland Evans, Julian Goodman, Marvin Kalb, Joseph Kraft, Dan Rather, James Reston, and Daniel Schorr.

Nixon's list also targeted an odd assortment of groups like the National Education Association, the American Civil Liberties Union, the National Organization for Women, National Cleaning Contractors, Philip Morris, the Urban League, MIT (Massachusetts Institute of Technology), the World Bank, and Harvard Law School.

What did Vice President Martin Van Buren always have beside him when he presided over the Senate?

A pair of pistols.

Just 15 Minutes *a Day*

But it will mean a tremendous difference in their positions and earning power fifteen years from now.

HERE are two men of equal position and business income. Which of them represents you?

They read about the same number of hours each week. But one has no plan for his reading; at the end of the year he has little or nothing to show.

The other talks like a man who has traveled widely, though he has never been outside of the United States.

He knows something of Science, though he had to stop school at fifteen. He is at home with History, and the best biographies, and the really great dramas and essays. Older men like to talk to him because he has somehow gained the rare gift of thinking clearly and talking interestingly.

What's the secret of his mental growth? How can a man in a few minutes of pleasant reading each day gain so much.

Dr. Charles W. Eliot, from his lifetime of reading, study and teaching, forty years of it as president of Harvard University, has answered that question in a free booklet that you can have for the asking. In it are described the contents, plan and purpose of

Dr. Eliot's
Five Foot Shelf of Books
The pleasant path to a liberal education

EVERY well-informed man and woman should at least know something about this famous library.

The free book tells about it—how Dr. Eliot has put into his Five Foot Shelf "the essentials of a liberal education," how he has so arranged it that even "fifteen minutes a day" is enough, how in pleasant moments of spare time, by using the reading courses Dr. Eliot has provided for you, you can get the knowledge of literature and life, the culture, the broad viewpoint that every University strives to give.

"For me," wrote one man who had sent in the coupon, "your little free book meant a big step forward, and it showed me besides the way to a vast new world of pleasure."

Think of it. The satisfaction of being a marked man or woman in any company. And all for a few minutes of pleasant reading each day.

This is the promise of the Five Foot Shelf. Two hundred thousand Americans have proved that promise; they have tested the value of Dr. Eliot's guidance.

Send for this free booklet that gives Dr. Eliot's own plan of reading

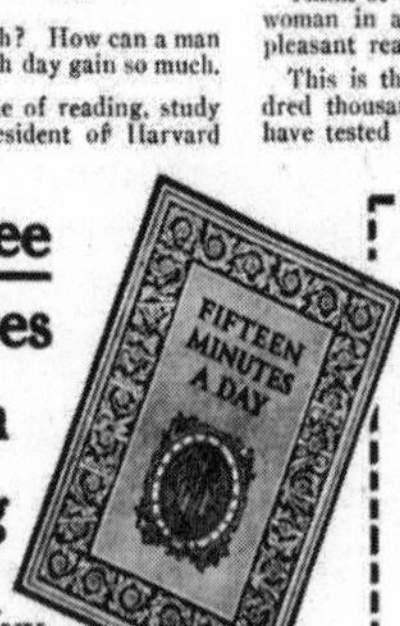

P. F. COLLIER & SON COMPANY
Publishers of Good Books Since 1875
Branches and Representatives Everywhere
New York

P. F. Collier & Son Company,
416 West 13th Street, New York:

Mail me the 32-page Free Book, "Fifteen Minutes a Day," telling about the Five Foot Shelf of Books and containing the two valuable articles by Dr. Eliot and Hamilton Wright Mabie, on what and how to read for a liberal education.

Name..

Address..

....

N.C. 11-20

Stately Knowledge

12 Reasons Why Ya Gotta Love Wisconsin

We've searched the vaults and come up with some pretty impressive facts and stories about Wisconsin. Here are a dozen of our favorites.

1 Look out below! In 1962, a 21-pound fragment of the Soviet space satellite *Sputnik IV* landed at the intersection of Park and North 8th streets in Manitowoc, Wisconsin. Nobody was hurt.

2 From 1884 to 1918, Baraboo, Wisconsin, was the headquarters of the Ringling Brothers Circus and six other circuses. Circus World Museum is housed in the original Ringling building and features circus acts, elephants, calliopes, magic shows, and about 200 restored circus wagons. Every year in mid-July, bands, horses, elephants, and circus wagons star in the world's biggest circus parade, marching from Baraboo to Milwaukee.

3 Harry Houdini was the best and most famous magician of all time. His real name was Erich Weiss and he was born in Budapest, Hungary. A son of a rabbi, he was brought as an infant to Appleton, Wisconsin, where he was raised. (In later years he would claim that he had actually been born there.)

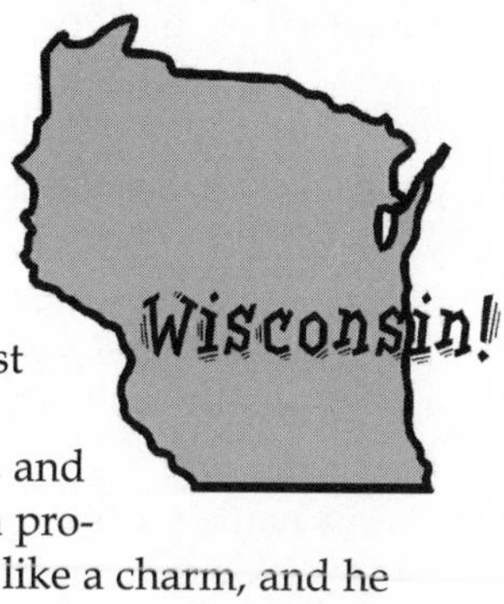

4 In 1902, Bill Harley and three Davidson brothers, all in their twenties, started building motorcycles in Milwaukee, creating the first American company to do so. In their first year of operation, they built only three motorcycles. Ole Evinrude helped them, and then decided that a similar motor with a propeller could move a rowboat. It worked like a charm, and he began selling his new invention, the Evinrude outboard motor.

5 Sayner, Wisconsin, lays claim to its own invention: the first snowmobile, invented by Carl Eliason in 1925. As far as we know, he wasn't affiliated at all with any of the Harleys, Davidsons, or the Evinrudes.

6 Milwaukee resident Christopher Sholes built the very first typewriter in 1873. Mark Twain bought one of the newfangled machines for $125 (a whole lot of money back then) and became the first author to submit a typewritten manuscript to a publisher (his book *Life on the Mississippi)*.

7 In the capital of Madison, Wisconsin, there are more bicycles that people living in the city. In fact, bicycles outnumber citizens by a ratio of 3 to 2.

8 Luck, Wisconsin, home of The Duncan Yo-Yo Company, has long advertised itself as the "Yo-Yo Capital of the World." We guess that's why people always keep coming back ... and back ... and back....

9 An inventor named Ben Hirsch was walking along Turtle Creek in Beloit, Wisconsin, in the early 1940s when a name for his new car polish suddenly came to him: Turtle Wax.

10 In 1856, in Watertown, Wisconsin, Mrs. Carl Schurz opened the first American kindergarten. She had been a pupil of Friedrich Froebel, who started the kindergarten movement in 1837. *Kindergarten*, by the way, is German for "children's garden." Froebel's first choice for a name had been *kleinkenderbeschaftigungsanstalt*, which means "institution where small children are occupied," but even Germans had trouble saying it, so he settled for "kindergarten."

11 Wisconsin produces more milk than any other state, which may explain why milk is its Official State Beverage and the cow is its Official State Domestic Animal. It's a little harder to figure out, however, why its Official State Dance its the polka.

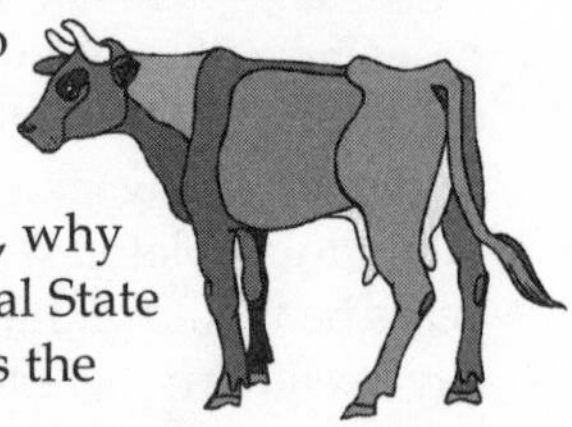

12 It's no wonder then, that many dairy "firsts" come from this state. In 1887, malted milk was invented by William Horlick in Racine, Wisconsin. And the ice cream sundae had first appeared six years earlier in Two Rivers.

Word Thieves 4

Terms We've Borrowed from the Spanish

Thanks to Spanish explorers, conquistadors to the New World, and Hispanic influences since then, more than 10,000 words have migrated from Spanish into American English.

alligator: From *el lagarto* meaning "the lizard."

bonanza: *Bonacia,* a Spanish word derived from Medieval Latin, meaning "calm sea."

breeze: From *brisa,* which translates to "northeast wind."

buffalo: When the Spanish saw American bison for the first time, they applied their name for a wild ox: *bufalo.*

cafeteria: It originally meant "coffee shop" as *café* means "coffee" in Spanish.

cockroach: From *cucaracha.*

Colorado: Meaning "rust-colored." It describes the red soil.

embargo: From the verb *embargar* ("arrest, impede").

Florida: Ponce de Leon landed in Florida on Easter in 1513. He named the land after the traditional Spanish Easter festival of the flower: *Pascua de Florida.*

mosquito: It means "little fly."

Nevada: Translates to "snow-capped."

patio: This is the Spanish word for "courtyard."

savvy: It's a derivation from the Spanish phrase *¿Sabe usted?,* meaning "do you know?"

serrated: This word comes from *serra* ("saw"). The name Sierra also comes from the same source, referring to peaks that are irregular and jagged.

tornado: An alteration of the Spanish word *tronada* meaning "thunderstorm."

vanilla: From *vainilla* ("little sheath"), describing the shape of vanilla pods. It descends from the Latin word *vagina* ("sheath").

Potty Pourri

Random Kinds of Factness

• After snoozing through a screening of *Gone with the Wind* at the White House, President Franklin D. Roosevelt complained, "No movie has a right to be that long!"

• One of Walt Disney's favorite hobbies was planning train wrecks on his half-mile of miniature train tracks.

• Would you buy a car called the Pastelogram, Piluma, Mongoose Cigique, or Utopian Turtletop? All of these names were considered for a futuristic car model in the late 1950s, but the company decided to play it safe and name the car after the company founder's late son. It didn't help, and the funny-looking Ford Edsel became a marketing laughingstock.

• Which song had the highest sheet music sales in history? No, it's not "Happy Birthday," "The Star Spangled Banner," or "Yesterday." It was "Yes, We Have No Bananas" by Frank Silver and Irving Cohn. It sold over half a million copies in its first few weeks of sale in 1923.

• Being called a twit isn't technically so bad. It's the name breeders use for a pregnant goldfish.

• In the 1930s, when Pepsi first came on the market, it cost a nickel for a 12-ounce bottle. That sounds really cheap, but it's about the same as today's price if adjusted for inflation: 60¢.

• You would expect a law against lawyers accepting bribes, but in 240 B.C., Rome passed a law against lawyers accepting fees.

• Peter the Great, working to modernize Russia, passed a law that men with long whiskers had to pay a special tax.

• The term "vaccine" comes from the Latin *vacca,* meaning "cows." There's good reason for this. The first successful smallpox vaccine in 1796 was derived from cowpox.

• To hard-boil an ostrich egg, set your egg timer for 40 minutes.

Fox Tales

Some Foxy Fables from Aesop

The Greek slave Aesop may or may not have really existed, but his fables have stood the test of time. Here are some about those wily foxes.

THE FOX, THE COCK, AND THE DOG

One moonlight night a Fox was prowling about a farmer's hen-coop, and saw a Cock roosting high up beyond his reach. "Good news, good news!" he cried.

"Why, what is that?" said the Cock.

"King Lion has declared a universal truce. No beast may hurt a bird henceforth, but all shall dwell together in brotherly friendship."

"Why, that is good news," said the Cock; "and there I see some one coming, with whom we can share the good tidings." And so saying he craned his neck forward and looked afar off.

"What is it you see?" said the Fox.

"It is only my master's Dog that is coming toward us. What, going so soon?" he continued, as the Fox began to turn away as soon as he had heard the news. "Will you not stop and congratulate the Dog on the reign of universal peace?"

"I would gladly do so," said the Fox, "but I fear he may not have heard of King Lion's decree."

Cunning often outwits itself.

THE FOX AND THE CAT

A Fox was boasting to a Cat of its clever devices for escaping its enemies. "I have a whole bag of tricks," he said, "which contains a hundred ways of escaping my enemies."

"I have only one," said the Cat; "but I can generally manage with that." Just at that moment they heard the cry of

"Just the thing to quench my thirst."

a pack of hounds coming toward them, and the Cat immediately scampered up a tree and hid herself in the boughs. "This is my plan," said the Cat. "What are you going to do?" The Fox thought first of one way, then of another, and while he was debating the hounds came nearer and nearer, and at last the Fox in his confusion was caught up by the hounds and soon killed by the huntsmen. Miss Puss, who had been looking on, said:

"Better one safe way than a hundred on which you cannot reckon."

THE FOX AND THE GRAPES

One hot summer's day a Fox was strolling through an orchard till he came to a bunch of grapes just ripening on a vine which had been trained over a lofty branch. "Just the thing to quench my thirst," quoth he. Drawing back a few paces, he took a run and a jump, and just missed the bunch. Turning round again with a One, Two, Three, he jumped up, but with no greater success. Again and again he tried after the tempting morsel, but at last had to give it up, and walked away with his nose in the air, saying: "I am sure they are sour."

It is easy to despise what you cannot get.

THE FOX AND THE STORK

At one time the Fox and the Stork were on visiting terms and seemed very good friends. So the Fox invited the Stork to dinner, and for a joke put nothing before her but some soup in a very shallow dish. This the Fox could easily lap up, but the Stork could only wet the end of her long bill in it, and left the meal as hungry as when she began. "I am sorry," said the Fox, "the soup is not to your liking."

"Pray do not apologize," said the Stork. "I hope you will return this visit, and dine with me soon." So a day was appointed when the Fox should visit the Stork; but when they were seated at table all that was for their dinner was contained in a very long-necked jar with a narrow mouth, in which the Fox could not insert his snout, so all he could manage to do was to lick the outside of the jar.

"I will not apologize for the dinner," said the Stork:

"One bad turn deserves another."

THE FOX WITHOUT A TAIL

It happened that a Fox caught its tail in a trap, and in struggling to release himself lost all of it but the stump. At first he was ashamed to show himself among his fellow foxes. But at last he determined to put a bolder face upon his misfortune, and summoned all the foxes to a general meeting to consider a proposal which he had to place before them. When they had assembled together the Fox proposed that they should all do away with their tails. He pointed out how inconvenient a tail was when they were pursued by their enemies, the dogs; how much it was in the way when they desired to sit down and hold a friendly conversation with one another. He failed to see any advantage in carrying about such a useless encumbrance. "That is all very well," said one of the older foxes; "but I do not think you would have recommended us to dispense with our chief ornament if you had not happened to lose it yourself."

Distrust interested advice.

THE FOX AND THE GOAT

By an unlucky chance a Fox fell into a deep well from which he could not get out. A Goat passed by shortly afterward, and asked the Fox what he was doing down there. "Oh, have you not heard?" said the Fox; "there is going to be a great drought, so I jumped down here in order to be sure to have water by me. Why don't you come down, too?" The Goat thought well of this advice, and jumped

"How well you are looking today."

down into the well. But the Fox immediately jumped on her back, and by putting his foot on her long horns managed to jump up to the edge of the well. "Good-bye, friend," said the Fox, "and remember next time,

"Never trust the advice of a man in difficulties."

THE FOX AND THE CROW

A Fox once saw a Crow fly off with a piece of cheese in its beak and settle on a branch of a tree. "That's for me, as I am a Fox," said Master Reynard, and he walked up to the foot of the tree.

"Good-day, Mistress Crow," he cried. "How well you are looking today: how glossy your feathers; how bright your eye. I feel sure your voice must surpass that of other birds, just as your figure does; let me hear but one song from you that I may greet you as the Queen of Birds."

The Crow lifted up her head and began to caw her best, but the moment she opened her mouth the piece of cheese fell to the ground, only to be snapped up by Master Fox.

"That will do," said he. "That was all I wanted. In exchange for your cheese I will give you a piece of advice for the future:

"Do not trust flatterers."

THE FOX AND THE MASK

A Fox had by some means gotten into the storeroom of a theatre. Suddenly he observed a face glaring down on him and began to be very frightened; but looking more closely he found it was only a Mask such as actors use to put over their face. "Ah," said the Fox, "you look very fine; it is a pity you have not got any brains."

Outside show is a poor substitute for inner worth.

THE FOX AND THE LION

When first the Fox saw the Lion he was very frightened, and ran away and hid in the wood. Next time however he came near the King of Beasts he stopped at a safe distance and watched him pass by. The third time they came near one another the Fox went straight up to the Lion and passed the time of day with him, asking him how his family was, and when he should have the pleasure of seeing him again; then turning his tail, he parted from the Lion without much ceremony.

Familiarity breeds contempt.

Blue Jeans

From a Miner to Major Fashion

What's more essential than blue jeans? Everyone has at least one pair. But for most of their history, they were considered working class garments, frowned upon by parents, educators, and other members of the bourgeoisie.

BLUE JEANS STARTED with a man named Levi Strauss, born "Loeb" in Bavaria in 1829. After his father died of consumption in 1845, his mother decided that there was no future for her children growing up Jewish in anti-Semitic Bavaria. In 1847, Loeb moved with his mother and two sisters to the golden promise of America, where he changed his name to Levi because it "sounded more American."

Strauss's two older brothers had arrived a few years earlier and started a business selling dry goods in New York City. Strauss began learning the business, and in 1848 traveled to Kentucky to earn his living as a traveling peddler, schlepping fabrics, threads, pins, needles, hooks, buttons, ribbons, combs, and scissors from town to town.

Strauss carried his goods on his back with the hope of someday joining the more established peddlers who used a horse-drawn wagon and eventually progressed to owning a store somewhere. (Sometimes this last transition happened when their wagons broke down or their horses suddenly died.)

He peddled his wares on foot for several years. Then he succumbed to gold fever. It was 1849, and gold had been discovered in California. Tens of thousands of laborers, lawyers, teachers, clerks, and farmers trekked and tried getting rich in the gold fields. Twenty-four-year-old Levi Strauss thought he could get rich, too, but not by digging. He knew that the influx of people had created shortages of everyday things and jacked prices up. Apples that would cost a nickel in New York sold for 50¢ in California. A $15 dollar wagon could fetch over $100. Strauss loaded merchandise from his brothers' store onto a ship bound west around South America.

THE MAKING OF A BUSINESS

At the end of the five-month journey, Strauss arrived in San Francisco. He found a great demand for the sewing supplies he brought. One account has it that his ship was met by eager merchants in rowboats who bought everything but a roll of tent canvas before the ship had even docked. When he tried to sell the roll, somebody told him, "Canvas, hell. You shoulda' brought pants. Pants don't wear worth a hoot in the diggin's," so Strauss brought the canvas to a tailor and had stiff but sturdy pants sewn from the brown fabric. They sold out in a flash.

Strauss sent word back to New York to send more canvas. Meanwhile, he salvaged sails from among the 700 ships in the harbor that sailors had abandoned to dig for gold. (The city eventually sank them into the mud and built boardwalks over them.)

"Eureka!"

Levi and his brother-in-law, David, opened a dry goods shop, and Levi continued making work clothes out of whatever materials came in on the latest merchant ship. Levi peddled pants and other dry goods in mining camps and towns with names like Rough and Ready, Bedbug, Henpeck City, and Groundhog's Glory. He saw firsthand how mining was particularly hard on trousers because of the miners' continuous squatting, kneeling, and stuffing pockets with ore. He learned from the miners that canvas chaffed unbearably (most miners didn't wear underwear); they preferred pants of a flexible yet sturdy cotton fabric from Nîme, France. It came in bundles labeled *serge de Nîme* which they read as "denim." Strauss also found that indigo was the most popular color because it hid dirt stains. In 1853, Strauss started Levi Strauss and Company to make denim pants.

A RIVETING STORY

But the company still hadn't licked the pocket problem. Complaints rolled in from miners that tools and ore samples ripped the seams too easily.

Strauss couldn't come up with a satisfactory solution, but a tailor in Reno, Nevada, did. Jacob Davis had been given an order for work clothes by a woman who complained that her husband's pockets always tore through. Davis had chosen his heaviest twill and then had an idea: Why not use rivets on the pockets to reinforce them? Sure enough, the rivets worked. Davis started making riveted work clothes, selling 200 pairs of pants in eighteen months.

Davis knew he had a good idea, and he wanted to file a patent on his idea. His wife, however, threatened to leave him if he spent $68 on a patent fee. So he wrote to the Levi Strauss Company and offered to share his idea if Strauss would finance the patent. He sent along two samples of his pants of duck and blue denim, with a letter explaining everything:

> **The secratt of them pents is the rivits that I put in these Pockets and I found the demand so large that I cannot make them up fast enough. I charge for the Duck $3.00 and the Blue $2.50 a pear. My nabors are getting yalouse of these success and unless I secure it by Patent Papers it will soon become a general thing. Everybody will make them up and thare will be no money in it.**
>
> **Therefore Gentlemen, I wish to make you a Proposition that you should take out the Latters Patent in my name as I am the inventor of it, the expense of it will be about $68 all complit.... The investment for you is but a trifle compaired with the improvement in all Coarse Clothing. I use it in all Blankit Clothing such as Coats, Vests and Pents, and you will find it a very salable article at a much advenst rate....**

While the idea was simple, it had a huge effect on sales. In the first year, Levi sold 21,600 riveted pants and coats to miners, cowboys, lumberjacks, and farmers throughout the West.

The rivet on the fly, by the way, was eventually removed after the company received dozens of hot, testy letters complaining about hot testes. It turned out that the rivet was a painfully good conductor of heat when the wearer crouched in front of a campfire. Later, because of complaints about scratched saddles and furniture, the back-pocket rivets were replaced with reinforced stitching.

COOL AND BLUE

Before the 1950s, jeans were

just for farmers and workers. But in the 1950s, consumers began seeing jeans in a new light. Thanks to Western movies and James Dean, blue jeans became cool within the teen set. During the proletariat-chic 1960s, groovy denims became a counterculture uniform (especially when worn, torn, and patched). The 1970s brought forth the oxymoron of "designer jeans" costing as much as dress slacks. Today, you'd be hard pressed to find anyone who owned fewer than two or three pairs of blue jeans.

Working Conditions

Levi Strauss grew into a large company with the reputation of good employee relations and moderately progressive social policies. But that wasn't always the case. In this country, demagoguery and hysteria seem to arise every few decades against immigrants. During an anti-Chinese frenzy of the 1800s, Levi Strauss advertised that "Our riveted goods are made up in our Factory, under our direct supervision, and by WHITE LABOR only."

The claim, used until the end of the century, was not only despicable, but untrue as well. While Levi's sewing was done by sixty white women working for $3.00 a day, the fabric cutting was done by a Chinese man. The company repeatedly tried to replace him, but could find no white laborer who was able to do the job.

But the company has improved on this score. During World War II, it was among the first to hire African American workers in its factories, and refused to keep black workers segregated or limited to low-paying jobs. The company has promoted women and minorities, and developed a reputation for treating employees better than most big corporations.

Potty Pourri

RANDOM KINDS OF FACTNESS

• If life hands you peanut plants, make peanut butter. You can make 30,000 peanut butter sandwiches from just one acre.

• Some researchers have claimed that green in office environments reduces headaches, stomach distress, and other stress symptoms.

• Cows, sheep, dogs, and goats are aplenty in the Bible, but cats are never even mentioned once.

• Never give up the dream. Why, even George Orwell faced rejection. A publisher turned down his future bestseller *Animal Farm* with, "It is impossible to sell animal stories in the U.S.A."

• Manhole covers aren't round because someone at city planning liked the shape. Nope, they're round because they're the only common shape that won't fall through the holes if they get tilted sideways.

• Although the stalk of the rhubarb is delicious, beware: Its leaves are toxic and can kill you.

• A cow consumes the equivalent of a bathtub full of water every day. Granted, some of the moisture comes from the grass it eats, but it all adds up to about 50 gallons.

• Pinball game designers kept this in mind when creating a new pinball game: An okay player should get an average of about 47 seconds of play per ball. Too much more time and the machine loses potential revenue; less, and players feel so defeated they'll likely stop playing.

• Lost childhood: It used to be that kids could use Silly Putty to lift pictures off newspapers and then stretch them this way and that for comical effect. Alas, that innocent pleasure is all gone now, a victim of advances in smear-proof ink and newsprint.

• Bovines are cattle, but what are ovines? Sheep.

The Eyes Have It

Can You Trust What You See?

What's wrong with the legs on this pachyderm?

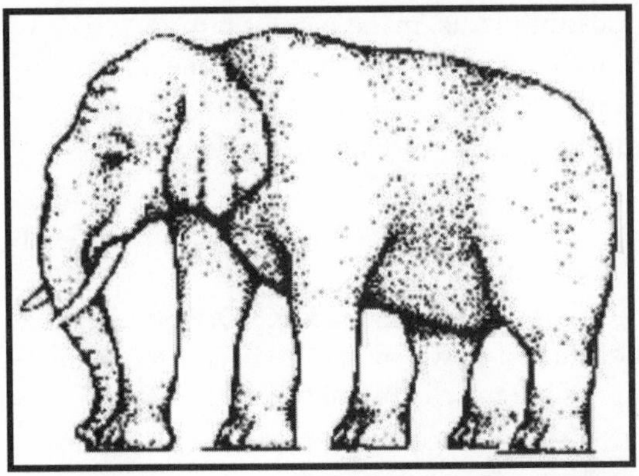

This picture was drawn in 1915 by W. E. Hill. It was titled *My Wife and My Mother-in-Law*. Can you tell why? (Hint: One is looking away. The other is looking down.)

Holey Food

How the Life Saver Got Its Hole

Why put a hole in the middle just for a catchy name? Well, that's not exactly how it all came to be, as you'll see.

IN 1913, CLARENCE A. CRANE, a candy manufacturer in Cleveland, Ohio, was having trouble with his line. The chocolates he sold didn't travel well during the hot summer months. Candy stores would order almost nothing from him between June and September. To stay in business, he decided to develop a line of hard mints.

His factory, however, was only set up for chocolates, so he jobbed the mints out to a pill manufacturer. Unfortunately, the pill maker's machine was malfunctioning—despite all efforts, it kept punching a hole in each mint's center.

The pill manufacturer presented the first batch apologetically to Crane, and told him that they'd try to fix the problem for the next batch. Crane looked at the candy and said, "Don't bother. Keep it the way it is. They looked like little life savers!" Suddenly, he had an irresistible name for the mints.

Crane advertised his "Crane's Peppermint Life Savers" as way of saving yourself from "that stormy breath." He designed a round paperboard tube and printed a label showing a crusty old seaman tossing a life preserver to a young woman swimmer. Still, he considered the product to be just a summer sideline and didn't push the idea any further.

Enter Edward John Noble, who made a living selling ad space on streetcars in New York City. One day he saw Crane's Life

Savers in a candy store and bought a roll on impulse. He was so impressed with the product that he jumped on a train to Cleveland to convince Crane that he should buy streetcar ads. "If you'd spend a little money promoting these mints," Noble told Crane, "you'd make a fortune!"

Crane wasn't interested. He still saw the mints as a sideline to his real product—chocolates. Noble persisted. Crane, to get rid of him, suggested sarcastically that he buy the Life Saver brand. He'd even throw in the defective pill machine for free. When Noble asked, "How much?" Crane was caught completely unprepared. He blurted out, "$5,000."

Noble thought the price was a steal, but he didn't have that kind of money. He returned to New York and was able to raise only $3,800. He went back to Cleveland and talked Crane's price down to $2,900, leaving $900 for his operating expenses.

Noble immediately started running into problems. It turned out that the roll Noble had tried tasted so good because it was fresh. After a week or two on the shelves, the candy started tasting like the paperboard it came in. Noble came up with a tinfoil wrapper that kept the flavor fresh, but, unfortunately, there were thousands of the old rolls sitting stale and unsold on candy store shelves. Store owners refused to order any more unless Noble exchanged the old rolls for new ones.

He made the exchanges, but the candy still wasn't selling very well. Noble started giving away free samples on street corners, to no avail. Luckily, he had kept his day job, but more and more of his weekly salary was going to propping up his company. He then came up with a brilliant marketing idea: Why sell his candy only in candy stores? He started convincing owners of drug stores, smoke shops, barber shops, restaurants, and saloons to carry Life Savers. He told them: "Put the mints near the cash register with a big 5¢ card. Be sure that every customer gets a nickel with his change, and see what happens."

It worked. With change in hand, customers impulsively flipped a nickel back to the clerk and pocketed a pack. Noble finally began making money from his product.

Other candy manufacturers

quickly discovered the magic of counter displays for impulse sales. The space around cash registers started getting overcrowded. To make sure he kept his counter space, Noble designed a large, segmented candy bin for store owners, leaving space for all the other candy products—but putting his Life Savers in the best position across the top. Life Saver counter displays can still be found next to checkout lines in supermarkets and drug stores everywhere.

Meanwhile, the company began expanding its line from the original Pep-O-Mint. Life Savers became the world's bestselling candy. Since 1913, the company has sold more than 44 billion of the familiar little tubular rolls.

IS THAT A SPARK IN YOUR MOUTH OR ARE YOU JUST GLAD TO SEE ME?

One of the three best in-the-dark revelations of adolescence is that if you crack a Wint-O-Green Life Saver between your teeth, tiny blue and green lights will flash in your mouth.

If you've never seen it happen, pick up a pack of Wint-O-Greens and wait until after dark. Turn out the lights and crunch one between your teeth while standing in front of a mirror. Besides feeling silly for standing in the dark in front of a mirror, you'll probably see a blue-green spark.

But how does it happen? Nabisco claims to get three or four queries about this phenomenon per month—enough to have a canned answer: It's "Triboluminescence resulting from crystal fracture" at work.

Huh? Simply put, when crystalline molecules of the candy are crunched and crushed, the free electrons run into the plentiful molecules of nitrogen in the air. The nitrogen molecules become excited and vibrate. They emit this extra energy in the form of mostly ultraviolet light; however a small bit of visible light is emitted as well. This is the spark you see in the mirror.

All hard candies that contain sugar create triboluminescence when cracked, though. So why do Wint-O-Greens produce a visible result when other flavors don't? Because oil of wintergreen has the special ability to take in light with short wavelengths (ultraviolet) and then spit out light with longer wavelengths (visible light). This is called fluorescence. That's right: Wintergreen oil is fluorescent. It takes in the ultraviolet rays from the vibrating nitrogen molecules and spits out visible light in a blueish-green shade.

Electrically speaking, *triboluminescence* is mini-lightning bolts in your mouth.

Bits to Fill in the Holes

• Francis Bacon was the first to seriously study triboluminescence reaction, some 400 years ago.

• Scotch tape also makes good fodder in the dark. Try ripping some tape quickly from the roll and see if you can see the glow.

• Seven hours and ten minutes is the record set for holding a Life Saver in the mouth, intact. It was set by Thomas Syta of Van Nuys, California.

• Pep-O-Mint is the most popular Life Saver flavor in the world.

• The top-selling flavors in the United States are orange, pineapple, cherry, lemon, lime, Wint-O-Green, Pep-O-Mint, and butter rum.

• There are fourteen candies in a roll of Wint-O-Green Life Savers.

• Life Savers come in twenty-five different flavors. The fruit flavor packs contain orange, lemon, lime, pineapple, and cherry flavored candies.

• Other roll varieties include Tropical Fruit, Tangy Flavors, Chill-O-Mint, and Wild Sour Berry.

• Besides Life Savers, RJR Nabisco (the tobacco/food company) also owns Bubble Yum, Trolli gummy candies, Bonkers, Carefree, and Terry's chocolates.

He Said/She Said

Part Deux

All's fair use in love and war.

"I don't have any buried anger against men, because my anger is right on the surface." —Camille Paglia

"It's not the frivolity of women that makes them so intolerable. It's their ghastly enthusiasm." —Horace Rumpole, *Rumpole of the Bailey*

"If men can run the world, why can't they stop wearing neckties? How intelligent is it to start the day by tying a little noose around your neck?" —Linda Ellerbee

"Women are nothing but machines for producing children." —Napoleon Bonaparte

"Men get their opinions as boys learn to spell: By reiteration chiefly." —Elizabeth Barrett Browning

"My wife is the sort of woman who gives necrophilia a bad name." —Patrick Murray

"I know what men want. Men want to be really, really close to someone

who will leave them alone." —Elayne Boosler

"Women should have labels on their foreheads saying, 'Government Health Warning: Women can seriously damage your brains, genitals, current account, confidence, razor blades, and good standing among your friends.'" —Jeffrey Bernard

"Men should be like Kleenex, soft, strong, and disposable." —Cher

"Love is the delusion that one woman differs from another." —H. L. Mencken

"If men were as great lovers as they think they are, we women wouldn't have time to do our hair." —Marlene Dietrich

"A woman is like an appendix ... she's something a man is better off without." —Popeye

"Give a man a fish and he eats for a day. Teach him how to fish and you get rid of him for the whole weekend." —Zenna Schaffer

"Men who don't understand women fall into two groups: Bachelors and Husbands." —Jacques Languirand

"If you never want to see a man again say, 'I love you, I want to marry you, I want to have children.' They leave skid marks." —Rita Rudner

"Women should be obscene and not heard." —Groucho Marx

"The difference between government bonds and men is that government bonds mature." —Debbie Perry

"Here's to woman! Would that we could fold into her arms without falling into her hands." —Ambrose Bierce

"When I eventually met Mr. Right I had no idea that his first name was Always." —Rita Rudner, again

"Perhaps crimefighting is better left to the men, Batgirl, perhaps not. But this isn't exactly women's work." —Batman

"I'm not denyin' that women are foolish; God Almighty made 'em to match the men." —George Eliot (Mary Ann Evans)

"Despite my thirty years of research into the feminine soul, I have not yet been able to answer the great question that has never been answered: What does a woman want?" —Sigmund Freud

"Ass, n.: The masculine of 'lass.'" —Unknown

Fables & Foibles

Odd Little Stories from R. L. Stevenson

You probably know Robert Louis Stevenson for books like *Treasure Island* and *Dr. Jekyll and Mr. Hyde.* But he also wrote a series of "fables" with a dark take on humanity and its foibles.

THE TWO MATCHES

One day there was a traveler in the woods in California, in the dry season, when the Trades were blowing strong. He was tired and hungry, and dismounted from his horse to smoke a pipe. But when he felt in his pocket he found but two matches. He struck the first, and it would not light.

"Here is a pretty state of things!" said the traveler. "Dying for a smoke; only one match left; and that certain to miss fire! Was there ever a creature so unfortunate? And yet," thought the traveler, "suppose I light this match—the grass might catch on fire, for it is dry like tinder; and they might evade me, and seize upon yon bush of poison oak; before I could reach it, that would have blazed up; over the bush I see a pine tree hung with moss; that too would fly in fire; and the flame—how would the trade wind take that through the flammable forest! I hear the joint voice of wind and fire, I see myself gallop for my soul, and the flying conflagration chase me through the hills; I see this forest burn for days, and the cattle roasted, and the springs dried up, and the farmer ruined, and his children cast upon the world. What a world hangs upon this moment!"

With that he struck the match, and it missed fire.

"Thank God!" said the traveler, putting his pipe in his pocket.

THE SICK MAN AND THE FIREMAN

There was once a sick man in a burning house, to whom there

entered a fireman. "Do not save me," said the sick man. "Save those who are strong."

"Will you kindly tell me why?" inquired the fireman, for he was a civil fellow.

"Nothing could possibly be fairer," said the sick man. "The strong should be preferred in all cases, because they are of more service in the world."

The fireman pondered a while, for he was a man of some philosophy. "Granted," said he at last, as a part of the roof fell in; "but for the sake of conversation, what would you lay down as the proper service of the strong?"

"Nothing can possibly be easier," returned the sick man; "the proper service of the strong is to help the weak."

Again the fireman reflected, for there was nothing hasty about this excellent creature. "I could forgive you being sick," he said at last, as a portion of the wall fell out, "but I cannot bear your being such a fool." And with that he heaved up his fireman's axe, for he was eminently just, and clove the sick man to the bed.

THE DEVIL AND THE INNKEEPER

Once upon a time the devil stayed at an inn, where no one knew him, for they were people whose education had been neglected. He was bent on mischief, and for a time kept everybody by the ears. But at last the innkeeper set a watch upon the devil and took him in the fact.

The innkeeper got a rope's end.

"Now I am going to thrash you," said the innkeeper.

"You have no right to be angry with me," said the devil. "I am only the devil, and it is my nature to do wrong."

"Is that so?" asked the innkeeper.

"Fact, I assure you," said the devil.

"You really cannot help doing ill?" asked the innkeeper.

"Not in the smallest," said the devil; "it would be useless cruelty to thrash a thing like me."

"It would indeed," said the innkeeper. He made a noose and hanged the devil.

"There!" said the innkeeper.

THE MAN AND HIS FRIEND

A man quarreled with his friend.

"I have been much deceived in you," said the man.

And the friend made a face at him and went away.

A little after, they both died, and came together before the great Justice of the Peace. It began to look black for the friend, but the man who had a clear character was in good spirits.

"I find here some record of a quarrel," said the justice, looking in his notes. "Which of you was in the wrong?"

"He was," said the man. "He spoke ill of me behind my back."

"Did he so?" said the justice. "And pray how did he speak about your neighbors?"

"Oh, he had always a nasty tongue," said the man.

"And you chose him for your friend?" cried the justice. "My good fellow, we have no use here for fools."

So the man was cast in the pit, and the friend laughed out aloud in the dark and remained to be tried on other charges.

THE CITIZEN AND THE TRAVELER

"Look round you," said the citizen. "This is the largest market in the world."

"Oh, surely not," said the traveler.

"Well, perhaps not the largest," said the citizen, "but the best."

"You are certainly wrong there," said the traveler. "I can tell you...."

They buried the stranger at the dusk.

THE DISTINGUISHED STRANGER

Once upon a time there came to this earth a visitor from a neighboring planet. And he was met at the place of his descent by a great philosopher, who was to show him everything.

First of all they came through a wood, and the stranger looked upon the trees. "Whom have we here?" said he.

"These are only vegetables," said the philosopher. "They are alive, but not at all interesting."

"I don't know about that," said the stranger. "They seem to have very good manners. Do they never speak?"

"They lack the gift," said the philosopher.

"Yet I think I hear them sing," said the other.

"That is only the wind among the leaves," said the philosopher. "I will explain the theory of winds: it is very interesting."

"I wish I knew what they are thinking," said the stranger.

"They cannot think," said the philosopher.

"I don't know about that," returned the stranger: and then, laying his hand upon a trunk: "I like these people," said he.

"They are not people at all," said the philosopher. "Come along."

Next they came through a meadow where there were cows.

"These are very dirty people," said the stranger.

"They are not people at all," said the philosopher; and he explained cows in scientific words which I have forgotten.

"That is all one to me," said the stranger. "But why do they never look up?"

"Because they are graminivorous," said the philosopher; "and to live upon grass, which is not highly nutritious, requires so close an attention to business that they have no time to think, or speak, or look at the scenery, or keep themselves clean."

"Well," said the stranger, "that is one way to live, no doubt. But I prefer the people with the green heads."

Next they came into a city, and the streets were full of men and women.

"These are very odd people," said the stranger.

"They are the people of the greatest nation in the world," said the philosopher.

"Are they indeed?" said the stranger. "They scarcely look so."

Three Facts about Robert Louis Stevenson

• It took Robert Louis Stevenson only six days to write *Dr. Jekyll and Mr. Hyde*, which runs about 60,000 words. That's an especially surprising output, since he was suffering from the advanced stages of tuberculosis. On the other hand, he fortified his night-and-day writing with lavish doses of medicinal cocaine.

• He had trained for engineering and then law, but decided to write instead.

• Stevenson spent his last years in Samoa, where the natives called him *Tusitala* (Teller of Tales).

Cowboy Country

Smile When You Say That, Pardner

The heyday of the American cowboy really lasted only about twenty years—from the late 1860s until the 1880s, when settlers' barbed wire put an end to the open ranges.

buckaroo: The first cowboys were *vaqueros* from Mexico. (*Vaca* is Spanish for "cow.") "Buckaroo" was what happened as Anglos attempt to pronounce the Spanish term.

cowpokes and cowpunchers: Cowboys got the name because they often had to poke or prod the cattle to get them to go into railroad cars.

Stetson: The classic cowboy hat came not from Texas or Wyoming, but from the John B. Stetson Hat Company in Philadelphia, Pennsylvania.

ten-gallon hat: Despite the name, it held only about 3 quarts. One theory is that it got its name from being big enough for "ten *galions*." (Galions are braids that decorated the hat's crown.)

chaps: Short for *chaparegos,* a vaquero invention that protected the legs from spiny vegetation and rope burn.

cowboy boots: There were two good reasons why cowboys wore high heels: to keep their feet from slipping out of the stirrups, and put some extra distance above the mud, muck, and cattle excrement.

cowboy demographics: The average cowboy was twenty-four, and he could expect a working career of about seven years. About half were white; about a quarter Mexican, and another quarter black.

corral: Spanish for "enclosed yard."

Every Picture Tells a Story

Arrangement in Gray & Black #1: The Artist's Mother **by James Whistler**

• The painting we call *Whistler's Mother* by Massachusetts-born James Abbott Lowell Whistler is the only American painting hanging in the Louvre in Paris.

• It's also the only painting that Whistler did of his mother.

• On this occasion, he painted his reluctant mom in a straight-backed wooden chair only because his scheduled model hadn't shown up.

• The painting has given people the impression that he was a sentimental Norman Rockwell sort of guy, but this wasn't his normal style. Whistler usually created more abstract art. He loved seeing himself as a shocking rebel against the art establishment, and presented himself and his work in ways that kept that image alive.

• Despite being a Yankee, Whistler throughout his life pretended to be a southern gentleman.

• He was later bankrupted by legal fees when he sued an art critic. Despite winning the lawsuit, he was awarded no money.

Even More Lear

More rhymes and drawings from Edward Lear's classic children's book, *The Book of Nonsense* (published 1846).

There was an Old Man of the West,
Who never could get any rest;
So they set him to spin
On his nose and chin,
Which cured that Old Man of the West.

There was an Old Person of Anerley,
Whose conduct was strange and unmannerly;
He rushed down the Strand
With a pig in each hand,
But returned in the evening to Anerley.

There was a Young Lady of Troy,
Whom several large flies did annoy;
Some she killed with a thump,
Some she drowned at the pump,
And some she took with her to Troy.

There was an Old Person of Berlin,
Whose form was uncommonly thin;
Till he once, by mistake,
Was mixed up in a cake,
So they baked that Old Man of Berlin.

There was an Old Man who said, "Well!
Will nobody answer this bell?
I have pulled day and night,
Till my hair has grown white,
But nobody answers this bell!"

There was an Old Person of Cheadle,
Who was put in the stocks by the beadle
For stealing some pigs,
Some coats, and some wigs,
That horrible person of Cheadle.

There was an Old Person of Chester,
Whom several small children did pester;
They threw some large stones,
Which broke most of his bones,
And displeased that Old Person of Chester.

There was an Old Person from Gretna,
Who rushed down the crater of Etna;
When they said, "Is it hot?"
He replied, "No, it's not!"
That mendacious Old Person of Gretna.

There was an Old Man of the Cape,
Who possessed a large Barbary ape,
Till the ape one dark night
Set the house all alight,
Which burned that Old Man of the Cape.

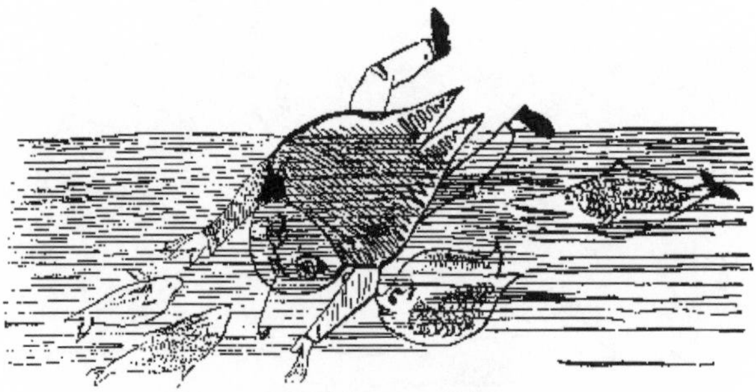

There was an Old Person of Ems,
Who casually fell in the Thames;
And when he was found
They said he was drowned,
That unlucky Old Person of Ems.

There was an Old Person of Ewell,
Who chiefly subsisted on gruel;
But to make it more nice
He inserted some mice,
Which refreshed that Old Person of Ewell.

Bugs!

Everything You Wanted to Know about Insects

...But were afraid to ask.

INSECTS, DRUGS, ROCK 'N' ROLL

What is the song "La Cucaracha" about, anyway? The song is beloved by children and hungry office workers waiting for the lunch truck, but few people have seen an accurate translation. There's a reason for that. Strike up the trumpets, guitars, and violins, because here are the lyrics, along with a singable translation.

La cucaracha, la cucaracha
Ya no puede caminar
Porque no tiene, porque le falta
Marijuana que fumar.

Ya la murio la cucaracha
Ya la lleven a enterrar
Entre cuatro zopilotes
Y un raton de sacristan.

Oh, there's a cockroach, yes, there's a cockroach—
His travel plans became a joke
Because he's missing, yes he's lacking,
Marijuana he can smoke.

Oh, it killed the poor old cockroach—
Brought him to the funeral house
He was carried by four buzzards
And the churchyard sexton's mouse.

¡Ole niños, magnifico! Yes, the song is about a pothead cockroach's wasted life, squalid death, and tawdry funeral.

FLY, FLY!

How fast can a fly fly? When you're trying to catch a housefly, it may seem like it can take off at supersonic speed. Really, though, you could easily outrun one, or even outwalk it.

Although its wings can flap 200 times a second, a housefly flies through the air at a speed of only about 4.5 miles per hour. That's nothing compared to the world's fastest insect. That would be the Australian dragonfly, which can blast through the air so fast the experts don't agree on its top speed: their estimates range from a remarkable 35 mph to an unbelievable 60 mph.

A TERRIBLE FINISH

In order to make shellac, you have to crush shellac beetles. A pound of shellac takes about 150,000 of them. The red dye called cochineal is also made from crushing beetles. In this case, a red-colored scale beetle that lives only on prickly pear cacti.

BEE FOR THE PILGRIMS

There were no honeybees in America before European settlers first brought hives to America in 1622. Over the following years, many bees fled human-made hives and sought freedom in their own colonies throughout the New Land. By the late 1700s, honeybees had settled along most of the eastern side of North America. During the 1800s, they spread across the continent.

OUTNUMBERED

Entomologists estimate that there are about 10,000 bugs for every human being on Earth, which is no surprise to anyone who has gone outside on a hot summer night. Over 1.5 million insect species are known to populate the world today, but there may be many more out there waiting to be discovered and classified.

BLOODSUCKERS

If you're an average-sized adult, it would take about 1,120,000 mosquitoes to completely drain your blood.

LADYBUG'S NOT FOR BURNING

Why do they call ladybugs ladybugs when half of the bugs ain't ladies? During the Middle Ages, these aphid-eaters were regarded by farmers as having been sent from heaven. French farmers called them *les betes du bon Dieu* ("creatures of the good God") and *les vaches de la Vierge* ("cows of the Virgin"). Germans called them *Marienkafer* or "Mary's beetles." And the English called them "Our Lady's beetles," which became shortened to "ladybugs."

Why did the farmer value them so? Well, an adult female can consume 75 aphids and scale bugs a day, while a male may consume 40. Even its larva, resembling tiny alligators, chomps about 350 aphids before becoming a ladybug.

YOU LIGHT UP MY LIFE

Glowworms are the larvae of fireflies (although in some species they are flightless females). Fireflies spend one or two years in the larval state, but only 5 to 30 days as adults. As larvae, they eat earthworms, snails, and the larvae of other insects, killing their prey by injecting poison into them. As adults, they eat nectar from flowers or, in some species, nothing at all. There are about 1,900 glowing members of the *Lampyridae* family – not a bad name for a bug that lights up the night.

HEY BIG BOY, GOT A LIGHT?

Why do fireflies glow? Sex, mostly. Males flash a pattern of dots and dashes that is specific to their species. Female

F is for Firefly
that shines in the dark
And lights up the woods
with its tiny white spark.

fireflies wait for the correct signal, then they flash back. They meet and make beautiful luminescence together.

Well, most of the time that's how it works. However, the females of some species prey on the males of other species, imitating their mating signals, and then eating the lovesick males that come close.

MULTIPLY BY DIVIDING?

If you cut an earthworm in half, will both halves live and grow back? Alas, no. While some worms can regrow a tail if they lose it, the tail part dies. True, the lopped-off tail end can wriggle around helplessly for a few hours, but that's just like a chicken running around with no head. Furthermore, the head end may well die from the injury,

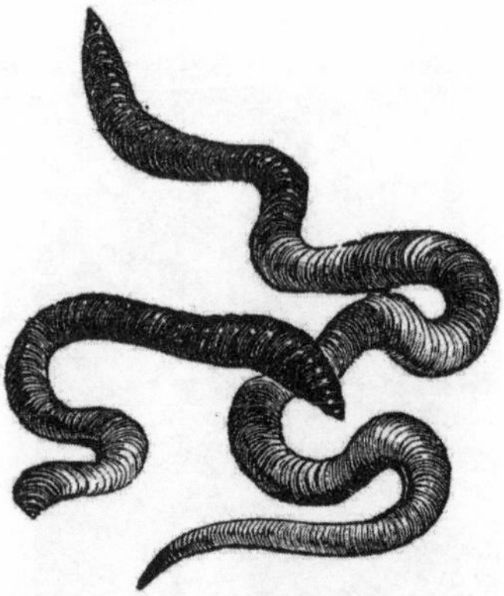

but it has a chance of surviving if its intestines and other vital organs are still intact.

Too bad. If worms could multiply by dividing, they could dispense with that messy, slimy worm sex. Worms are hermaphrodites (both male and female), so they can mate with any other worm of their species. They do that in a slimy sodden mess, writhing, putting together their clitella and exchanging sperm. Each partner ends up pregnant, laying an egg capsule a week later. After 14–21 days, one to five little squirmers hatch.

NO EATING IN THE LIBRARY

What did bookworms eat before there were books? After centuries of clay tablets and scrolls did they stand up and cheer in the fourth century A.D. when somebody got the bright idea of sewing and binding parchment? Well, no. "Bookworms" don't eat just book bindings and glue, but any number of things. There's not even a specific bug—"bookworm" is used to describe any moth or beetle larvae found infesting books.

Makes us wonder what eats audio books—"tapeworms," maybe?

LONG LIVE THE KING

Queen ants and queen bees live in a matriarchal society and mate with expendable male courtiers. However, not all social insects suffer from the tyranny of gender supremacy. Termites live up to our highest ideals of gender egalitarianism. Unlike ants and bees, their nests have workers of both sexes. Furthermore, they have a king and queen that are bound together in a monogamous relationship of a sort that's seldom seen in royalty of any species. The royals mate for life, and they do it lustfully and regularly, keeping a termite queen happily popping out an egg per second day after day.

Despite this, the termite is poisoned and maligned by a selfish human world unwilling to share its wood products with such a virtuous, family-values sort of bug.

Life Lessons

How to Charm a Snake

Just in case you fall on hard times, here's a career option you might not have ever considered. The tools are few, there's little competition, and the show is worth the price of admission. You'll have it made!

Charming a snake looks near-impossible, but the steps are pretty simple. Before you begin, you have to get your props in order. You'll need a basket, a cobra, and a pungi—an oboe-like Indian reed instrument. You also may want to acquire a turban, a loin cloth, and a certain panache to accompany your act.

1. Take the lid off the basket with much fanfare. The cobra will rise from the darkness of the basket into the light, with its hood flared defensively. The crowd will go, "Oooh!" and step back. This is your cue to also jump back slightly, and make a point of keeping your wide, wary eyes on your snake.

2. Play your pungi. Although having some basic knowledge of how to play the pungi may help in convincing your audience of the trick's authenticity, the snake has no ears and won't care if you can't tell a B-flat from an A-sharp.

3. Here's the key step: sway to your music, making sure the tip of the pungi is in front of the cobra. A cobra can't pivot its eyes, so will follow the tip of your instrument with its whole head and body. Practice this well in order to get down the movements that the snake can keep up with. If you keep swaying, there's a good chance the snake won't strike.

4. Keep your distance while you're moving to keep the cobra from lunging and biting you. If it does attack, let's hope you've done what the professionals do—had it defanged beforehand.

Flornithology 3

How to Tell the Birds from the Flowers

Even more entries from the field guide by Robert Williams Wood (1868–1955) for those who may have trouble seeing the difference.

The Pecan The Toucan

The Auk The Orchid

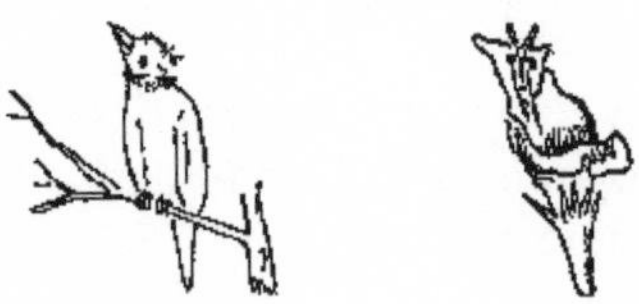

The Catbird The Catnip

The Ibis The Ibiscus

The Pipe The Snipe

The Roc The Shamrock

Forbidden Bible Tales

Mighty Strange Stories from the Good Book

There are a lot of Bible verses you won't necessarily hear your preacher using as a text. In fact, most believers haven't even run across them.

NOAH'S SON HAM SEES HIS DRUNK DAD NAKED, SO HAM'S SON IS MADE A SLAVE (GENESIS 9:20–6)

And the sons of Noah, that went forth from the ark, were Shem, and Ham, and Japheth: and Ham is the father of Canaan. These three were the sons of Noah: and of these was the whole earth overspread.

And Noah began to be a husbandman, and planted a vineyard: and he drank of the wine, and was drunken. And he was uncovered within his tent.

And Ham, the father of Canaan, saw the nakedness of his father, and told his two brethren without.

And Shem and Japheth took a garment, and laid it upon both their shoulders, and went backward, and covered the nakedness of their father. And their faces were backward, and they saw not their father's nakedness.

And Noah awoke from his wine, and knew what his youngest son had done unto him. And he said, "Cursed be Canaan; a servant of servants shall he be unto his brethren."

And he said, "Blessed be Jehovah, the God of Shem; And let Canaan be his servant. God enlarge Japheth, and let him dwell in the tents of Shem; and let Canaan be his servant. "

HEY, YOU GALS—SHUT UP! (I CORINTHIANS 14:34–5)

Let the women keep silence in the churches: for it is not permitted unto them to speak; but let them be in subjection, as also saith the law. And if they would learn anything, let them ask their own husbands at home: for it is shameful for a woman to speak in the church.

LOT OFFERS HIS VIRGIN DAUGHTERS FOR GANG RAPE, THEN GETS DRUNK & IMPREGNATES THEM WITHOUT PUNISHMENT ... BUT HIS WIFE LOOKS BACK AT THE WRONG TIME AND GETS TURNED TO SALT (GENESIS 19:1–38)

And the two angels came to Sodom in the evening as Lot was sitting at the gate and Lot saw them; and he bowed with his face to the earth; and he said, "My lords, turn aside into your servant's house tonight, and wash your feet, and then you may rise up early, and go on your way." And they said, "No; we will spend the night in the street."

Yet he urged them strongly and they entered into his house; and he made them a feast, and baked unleavened bread, and they ate.

But before they lay down, the men of the city surrounded the house, both young and old, all the people from every quarter; and they called to Lot, and said unto him, "Where are the men that came in to you this night? Bring them out unto us, that we may have sex with them."

And Lot went outside, and shut the door after him. And he said, "I pray you, my brethren, do not act so wickedly. Now behold, I have two daughters who are virgins; let me, I pray you, bring them out, and you can do to them whatever you like: only to these men do nothing, since they have come under the shelter of my roof."

And they said, "Stand back." And they said, "This one fellow came here as an outsider, yet he's acting like a judge: now will we deal worse with you than with them." And they pressed hard against Lot, nearly breaking down the door. But the angels reached out their hands and pulled Lot into the house with them, and shut the door.

And they struck the men at the door with blindness, both small and great, so that they tired of trying to find the door. And the men said unto Lot, "Whom do you have here? Sons-in-law, and your sons and daughters, and anyone else you have in the city, take them away, for Jehovah has heard the disturbance of this place and has sent us to destroy it."

But Lot hesitated; and the men told hold of him, and upon the hand of his wife, and upon the hand of his two daughters, Jehovah being merciful to him; and set him outside the city and said, "Escape for your life! Don't look behind you, don't stay in the valley—escape to the mountain, or you'll be consumed."

Then Jehovah rained upon Sodom and upon Gomorrah brimstone and fire from Jehovah out of heaven; and he overthrew those cities and all the valley, and all the inhabitants of the cities, and that grew upon the ground. And Lot's wife looked back from behind him, and she became a pillar of salt....

And Lot went up out of Zoar, and dwelt in a cave, he and his two daughters. And the firstborn said unto the younger, "Our father is old, and there is not a man in the earth to come in unto us after the manner of all the earth: let us make our father drink wine, and we will lie with him, that we may preserve the seed of our father." And they encouraged their father to drink wine that night: and the firstborn went in and lay with her father; and he knew not when she lay down, nor when she arose.

And it came to pass on the morrow, that the firstborn said unto the younger, "Behold, I lay last night with my father: let us make him drink wine this night also; and go in, and lie with him, that we may preserve seed of our father." And they encouraged their father to drink wine that night also: and the younger arose, and lay with him; and he knew not when she lay down, nor when she arose.

Thus were both the daughters of Lot with child by their father. And the firstborn bare a son, and called his name Moab: the same is the father of the Moabites unto this day. And the younger, she also bare a son, and called his name Ben-ammi: the same is the father of the children of Ammon unto this day.

JESUS CURSES A FIG TREE FOR NOT BEARING FRUIT OUT OF SEASON (MARK 11:13–4, 20–22)

And seeing a fig tree afar off having leaves, he went to see if it had anything on it: but when he came to it, he found nothing but leaves; for it was not the season of figs.

And Jesus answered and said unto it, "No man eat fruit of you hereafter forever!" And his disciples heard it.... And in the morning, as they passed by, they saw the fig tree dried up from the roots. And Peter said to him, "Master, behold, the fig tree which you cursed is withered away." And Jesus answered to them, "Have faith in God." (**Note:** In the Matthew version of this story, the fig tree withers instantly before their eyes.)

GOD COMMANDS THAT FARMERS LEAVE SOME CROPS IN FIELDS FOR TRAVELERS AND THE POOR (LEVITICUS 19:10–11)

"And when ye reap the harvest of your land, thou shalt not wholly reap the corners of thy field, neither shalt thou gather the gleanings of thy harvest. And thou shalt not glean thy vineyard, neither shalt thou gather every grape of thy vineyard; thou shalt leave them for the poor and stranger: I am the Lord your God."

GOD COMMANDS GENOCIDE, LOOTING, AND RAPE (NUMBERS 31:1–18)

And Jehovah spoke to Moses, saying, "Avenge the children of Israel of the Midianites: afterward you shall be gathered with your people."

And Moses spoke to the people, saying, "Arm yourselves for war, that you may go against Midian, to execute Jehovah's vengeance. Of every tribe a thousand, throughout all the tribes of Israel, shall you send to the war." So there were delivered, out of the thousands of Israel, a thousand of every tribe, twelve thousand armed for war....

And they warred against Midian, as Jehovah commanded Moses; and they killed every male.... And the children of Israel took captive the women of Midian and their little ones; and all their cattle, and all their flocks, and all their goods they looted. and they burned their cities.

And they brought the captives, and the prey, and the spoil, unto Moses....

And Moses said unto them, "Have ye saved all the women alive? ... Now therefore kill every male child, and kill every woman that hath known man by lying with him. But all the girl-children and virgins, keep alive for yourselves."

Now the prey, over and above the booty which the soldiers took, was 675,000 sheep, and 72,000 cattle, and 61,000 asses, and 32,000 women who were virgins.

The soldiers split an additional 337,500 sheep, 36,000 cattle, and 16,000 women.

Toaster Foods

THE BEST THING SINCE SLICED BREAD

Hey, if you've got a toaster, why not use it for everything?

WHO WOULD'VE THOUGHT that we'd have the crust to offer two different takes on the seemingly mundane subject of toasters? (If you missed the history of toast and toasters on page 167, you might want to go back and read it first. Or not.) Bear with us, though, because the subject of toaster foods—foods deliberately designed to be made in your toaster—is an amusing one, and their histories are more interesting than we even imagined possible.

So set the settings (not too dark!) and pull down the lever, here are the stories behind some of our most popular (and sometimes most disastrous) toaster foods.

POP-TARTS

Pop-Tarts are more than mere convenience food, they have become pure pop culture: an easy laugh for comedians, a cultural and general milestone for the rest of us. Sit down, have a Pop-Tart, and we'll tell you the story.

On September 14, 1964, Kellogg's first rolled out Pop-Tarts in Cleveland, Ohio with a stern admonition to retailers to put them in the baked goods, cookie, or cake mix section of their stores ... but nowhere near their cereals. The company's detailed display instructions spelled out, "IN NO WAY SHOULD THIS PRODUCT BE SOLD AS A SUBSTITUTE FOR CEREAL," capitalized and underlined for emphasis.

The funny thing is that Kellogg's did not invent the toaster pastry, arch-rival Post did. It's just that Kellogg's was the first to really do it right. After World War II, Post had put a team to work to come up with non-cereal products. Their first successful product was Tang, a powdered orange juice substitute that got launched into the stratosphere when astronauts drank it in space. Their next product was Gaines Burgers, a semi-moist dog food that didn't spoil quickly on the shelf. Using the same technology, they came up with a fruit-filled pastry that could be stored for months without refrigeration.

On February 16, 1964, Post unveiled its new toaster pastry to the press, sending the food industry into an uproar.

Post, however, made two fatal mistakes. The company announced the product too early, before it was ready for release. This gave their arch-rivals at Kellogg's time to come up with their own toaster pastry. Furthermore, Post named its toaster pastry "Country Squares." This was a time when "country" implied rural bumpkins and "square" was slang for completely unhip. "Country Squares" didn't sound wholesome and homegrown, as Post intended, it sounded like Barney Fife or Gomer Pyle.

Kellogg's rushed their pastry to the market in a scant six months, and its name was a double pun on the hippest thing happening at the time: "Pop Art," which Andy Warhol had made a household word with his giant soup cans and Brillo boxes. Pop-Tarts took the market by storm, advertised by an animated toaster named Milton; the company literally could not keep shelves stocked.

The first Pop-Tarts came out in four flavors: strawberry, blueberry, brown sugar cinnamon, and apple currant. The first three are still with us.

Through the years, the company developed innovations of its own including no-melt frosting and sprinkles that wouldn't dislodge in the toaster. Not that there haven't been some missteps along the way: Who still remembers Danish Go Rounds and such wish-we-could forget flavors as Chocolate Peppermint, Frosted Peanut Butter and Jelly, and Chocolate and Cherry Chip? Despite such missteps, heavy competition from other brands, and the fact that they don't microwave well at all, Pop-Tarts continue to control the lion's share of the toaster-pastry market.

EGGOS: WAFFLEY GOOD

"Hey, leggo my Eggo!" The name alone is a tip-off that the brand has been around a lot longer than most people suspect—the corporate fad of putting an *O* at the end of a brand name peaked at a time that brought us Jell-O, Grain-O, Zippo, Drano, Cheerios, Harpo, Groucho, Chico and sometimes even Zeppo.

In Depression-era 1935, Frank, Tony, and Sam Dorsa borrowed money to buy a waffle iron. Their idea was to build a better batter, which they'd sell premixed to restaurants; all they needed was a name. A fourth brother, George, piped up with a suggestion: It's got a lot of eggs in it, why not call it "Eggo"?

The Eggo batter started selling like hotcakes, and in 1937 the company opened a huge batter factory in San Jose, California.

After World War II, the brothers noticed that Americans were buying record amounts of pre-cooked frozen foods. They abandoned the batter business and switched over to ready-made waffles. Within a year, they were pouring out 10,000 waffles an hour to keep up with the demand.

In 1968, the brothers sold out to Kellogg's, which used the "Leggo my Eggo" slogan to raise waffle-consciousness in a hungry nation. Today, the brand covers more than half of the $500 million annual frozen waffle market.

LENDER'S BAGELS

It's hard to imagine, but twenty-five years ago, most Americans had never even tried a bagel. If you weren't Jewish, bagels were exotic and pretty much unknown; even if you were Jewish, bagels were hard to find if you were outside a major metropolitan area.

In 1927, Harry Lender immigrated from Poland and opened the first American bagel bakery outside of New York City. In New Haven, Connecticut, Lender sold retail from his own bakery, and also distributed bagels to jewish delis and grocery stores. Being that New Haven was a relatively small place, his "roll with a hole" spread into Italian, Irish, and Russian neighborhoods, too. However, bagels go stale fast and don't travel well. Lender's market was limited geographically by the bagel's short shelf life.

Trying to solve that problem, Harry's sons Murray and Marvin discovered that flash-freezing would keep bagels from going stale for months. The Lenders also decided to try to make the bagel more acceptable to mainstream America, softening the crunchy crust and chewy center that is the essence of genuine bagelhood. The strategy worked. Lender's frozen bagels converted gentiles across North America to their holey roll, even if purists grumbled.

The Lender family sold the business to Kraft in 1986, which seemed a perfect marriage, what with their Philadelphia Cream Cheese, but Kraft turned around and sold it to Kellogg's, making it the premiere player in toaster foods.

THOMAS' ENGLISH MUFFINS

There really was a guy named Thomas, and he really was born English. However, despite some hints that suggest otherwise from the company's advertising, Mr. Thomas was never a baker in England.

Samuel Bath Thomas was born in Plymouth, England in 1855. Looking for adventure and opportunities, the 21-year-old traveled to New York in 1876 and worked a number of menial jobs until he could speak the language. (Okay, so we're lying about that last part.)

Young Sam saved his money and in 1880 opened his own business, a bakery at 163 Ninth Avenue in Manhattan.

Perhaps he adapted the crumpet to American tastes, or perhaps it was the "Bara Maen," a Welsh bread cake baked on hot stones. No matter, he managed to create the prototype of the "English muffin" (still completely unknown in England)—a bread baked with a griddle instead of an oven.

His was just one of several thousand small bake shops in New York, but his muffin caught the fancy of hoteliers, in part because it was just as easy to prepare as toast (pop in toaster and butter), but it was a classy alternative to crunchy, browned bread. Thomas delivered his muffins in glass-domed cases with "S. B. Thomas" stenciled on them, which created enough brand awareness to allow him to begin selling his toaster crumpet through grocery stores, as well.

Thomas died in 1919 and the business was inherited by his daughter and nephews. It was bought by CPC, a food conglomerate that is also known as Bestfoods. Following British tradition, CPC expanded the yeast-meets-west empire, colonizing the United States and subjugating Third World breads (Thomas' Sahara Pita Bread, Thomas' Bagels) into the Thomas' commonwealth.

TOASTER LOSERS

Not every toaster food product has been a success. Here are some that weren't:

• **Downyflake Toaster Eggs**. It was just too strange an idea.

• **ReddiWip's Reddi Bacon**. Bacon grease tended to leak, creating a fire hazard.

• **Toaster Chicken Patties.** Different grease, same fire hazard.

• **Electric French Fries.** According to one critic, the toast-shaped slab of potatoes "looked like a picket fence; tasted like a picket fence."

• **Toaster Breaks**. You'd think a company as smart as the maker of Hot Pockets wouldn't coin a name that sounds like a prediction of doom for your toaster. When the product faltered, though, the Chef America company replaced the name with one that sounded just as ominous: "Toaster Melts." At this writing, the product line has dwindled down to just one flavor (ham and cheese).

Pop-Up Toaster-Food Facts

• Researching Toaster Strudel, Pillsbury studied the pop-ups of 2000 models of toasters. They determined that 1.8 ounces was most toaster-compatible.

• Toaster pastries don't microwave well. If your toaster breaks, you can toast a single layer on a cookie sheet at 400° F. for five minutes.

• Very few toaster pastries are consumed by people over fifty.

More H. L. Mencken

More quotes from H. L. Mencken, the controversial curmudgeon.

• "Say what you will about the ten commandments: you must always come back to the pleasant fact that there are only ten of them."

• "It is only doubt that creates. It is only the minority that counts."

• "School-days, I believe, are the unhappiest in the whole span of human existence. They are full of dull, unintelligible tasks, new and unpleasant ordinances, brutal violations of common sense and common decency. It doesn't take a reasonably bright boy long to discover that most of what is rammed into him is nonsense, and that no one really cares very much whether he learns it or not."

• "Any man who inflicts the human race with ideas must be prepared to see them misunderstood."

• "Criticism is prejudice made plausible."

• "Marriage is a wonderful institution, but who would want to live in an institution?"

• "Every decent man is ashamed of the government he lives under."

• "Injustice is relatively easy to bear; what stings is justice."

• "It is hard to believe that a man is telling the truth when you know that you would lie if you were in his place."

• "A jury is a group of twelve people who, having lied to the judge about their health, hearing, and business engagements, have failed to fool him."

• "Faith may be defined briefly as an illogical belief in the occurrence of the improbable."

• "A poet more than thirty years old is simply an overgrown child."

• "A man may be a fool and not know it—but not if he is married."

• "Truth would quickly cease to become stranger than fiction, once we got used to it."

• "A newspaper is a device for making the ignorant more ignorant and the crazy crazier."

• "A celebrity is one who is known by many people he is glad he doesn't know."

• "A misogynist is a man who hates women as much as women hate each other."

• "Love is the triumph of imagination over intelligence."

• "'Tis more blessed to give than to receive; for example, wedding presents."

Re: Ducks

THE WILD WORLD OF DUCKS IN THE NEWS

DOWNING THE DUCKS

One beautiful fall day in London, 10 Downing Street was besieged by a whole hoard of waddling ducks. A mother with her seventeen babes in tow left St. James's Park—their usual hangout—crossed at least one very busy road, and headed straight for the prime minister's house. They evaded police efforts to round them up until one bright officer used his helmet as a ducky scooper. They were returned to the park without further incident.

MUST BE DUCK SEASON

In 1992 in San Antonio, Texas, a forty-year-old man sat in a Bank One, listening to a loan officer explain why he'd been turned down on his application. In response, the man disrobed and began quacking like a duck. He continued to quack like a duck even as police came and hauled him away.

DADDY'S GONE A-HUNTIN', SON

In Des Moines, Iowa, Jay Knudsen offers an interesting service to the families of avid duck hunters. For a fee, Knudsen will take the ashes of the deceased, load them into duck decoys, and fire at them. He'll also put the ashes into shotgun shells along with the gunpowder and fire at whatever the deceased would've wanted to shoot at—loved ones excluded, of course.

MARRIAGE ... NOT ALL IT'S QUACKED UP TO BE

From a psychology journal comes the story of the woman in Oklahoma who was convinced Donald Duck was trying to marry her. After her neighbors installed a satellite television dish, she lingered around it for hours on end, until one day Donald's wooing worked: she disrobed and climbed into the dish. It was, said Mrs. Donald Fauntleroy Duck, their official wedding night and she was consummating the union.

A FOWL RAIN

During a cool Arkansas thunderstorm in December 2001, ducks began falling on White's Mobile Home Supply in Hot Springs, Arkansas. A flock of ducks had been toasted by lightning in the storm, and like manna from heaven, they had the makings of an early Christmas dinner for the employees. Owner Ron White said of the incident, "It was like tennis shoes falling out of the sky and then they realized they were ducks."

RUBBER DUCKY, YOU JUST WON

Listen up, because there are now official rules in Connecticut regarding those artificial duck races where proceeds go to charity. To list a few:

1. Every entrant must receive a map of the faux duckies' race route.

2. The race must be conducted on a stream or river with a steady current.

3. The start and finish lines must be clearly marked.

4. Organizers must provide means to prevent cheating by contestants guiding their duckies through the course.

5. All duck entrants must be put in a holding tank for inspection prior to the race.

6. No "counterfeit" fake ducks will be allowed to participate. (Isn't that an oxymoron?)

I SAID "DUCK!"

In November 2001, a man testing a jet-ski on a lake in Deerfield Beach, Florida, was smacked in the head by a flying duck and died. Traveling a speed of up to 55 mph, Leon Resnick didn't stand a chance against the 10–15 pound duck. A bystander said that the duck "might as well have been a cinder block."

Duck Down and Cover

- Eider down is insulating feathers that get shed in the spring by eider ducks. People collect it from their nests for jackets and comforters.
- *Eider* is German or Dutch in origin. It's a derivation of the word "duck."
- Eider ducks are the fastest horizontal flyers on Earth, reaching speeds of up to sixty miles per hour.
- A single comforter takes up to 85 nests of eider feathers.

Eyewitness

I Was There at the Boston Tea Party

George Hewes was one of hundreds who helped unload tea from the tea boats docked in Boston in 1773. Here's his retelling of the events.

THE TEA DESTROYED was contained in three ships, lying near each other at what was called at that time Griffin's wharf, and were surrounded by armed ships of war, the commanders of which had publicly declared that if the rebels, as they were pleased to style the Bostonians, should not withdraw their opposition to the landing of the tea before a certain day, the 17th day of December, 1773, they should on that day force it on shore, under the cover of their cannon's mouth.

THE DAY BEFORE

On the day preceding the seventeenth, there was a meeting of the citizens of the county of Suffolk, convened at one of the churches in Boston, for the purpose of consulting on what measures might be considered expedient to prevent the landing of the tea, or secure the people from the collection of the duty. At that meeting a committee was appointed to wait on Governor Hutchinson, and request him to inform them whether he would take any measures to satisfy the people on the object of the meeting.

To the first application of this committee, the Governor told them he would give them a definite answer by five o'clock in the afternoon. At the hour appointed, the committee again repaired to the Governor's house, and on inquiry found he had gone to his country seat at Milton, a distance of about six miles. When the committee

returned and informed the meeting of the absence of the Governor, there was a confused murmur among the members, and the meeting was immediately dissolved,

many of them crying out, "Let every man do his duty, and be true to his country"; and there was a general huzza for Griffin's wharf.

DRESSING LIKE INDIANS

It was now evening, and I immediately dressed myself in the costume of an Indian, equipped with a small hatchet, which I and my associates denominated the tomahawk, with which, and a club, after having painted my face and hands with coal dust in the shop of a blacksmith, I repaired to Griffin's wharf, where the ships lay that contained the tea. When I first appeared in the street after being thus disguised, I fell in with many who were dressed, equipped and painted as I was, and who fell in with me and marched in order to the place of our destination.

When we arrived at the wharf, there were three of our number who assumed an authority to direct our operations, to which we readily submitted. They divided us into three parties, for the purpose of boarding the three ships which contained the tea at the same time. The name of him who commanded the division to which I was assigned was Leonard Pitt. The names of the other commanders I never knew.

We were immediately ordered by the respective commanders to board all the ships at the same time, which we promptly obeyed. The commander of the division to which I belonged, as soon as we were on board the ship appointed me boatswain, and ordered me to go to the captain and demand of him the keys to the hatches and a dozen candles. I made the demand accordingly, and the captain promptly replied, and delivered the articles; but requested me at the same time to do no damage to the ship or rigging.

ORDERS GIVEN

We then were ordered by our commander to open the hatches and take out all the chests of tea and throw them overboard, and we immediately proceeded to execute his orders, first cutting and splitting the chests with our tomahawks, so as thoroughly to expose them to the effects of the water.

In about three hours from the time we went on board, we had thus broken and thrown overboard every tea chest to be found in the ship, while those in the other ships were disposing of the tea in the same way, at the same time. We were surrounded by British armed ships, but no attempt was made to resist us.

AFTERMATH

We then quietly retired to our several places of residence, without having any conversation with each other, or taking any measures to discover who were our associates; nor do I recollect of our having had the knowledge of the name of a single individual concerned in that affair, except that of Leonard Pitt, the commander of my division, whom I have mentioned. There appeared to be an understanding that each individual should volunteer his services, keep his own secret, and risk the consequence for himself. No disorder took place during that transaction, and it was observed at that time that the stillest night ensued that Boston had enjoyed for many months.

During the time we were throwing the tea overboard, there were several attempts made by some of the citizens of Boston and its vicinity to carry off small quantities of it for their family use. To effect that object, they would watch their opportunity to snatch up a handful from the deck, where it became plentifully scattered, and put it into their pockets.

One Captain O'Connor, whom I well knew, came on

board for that purpose, and when he supposed he was not noticed, filled his pockets, and also the lining of his coat. But I had detected him and gave information to the captain of what he was doing. We were ordered to take him into custody, and just as he was stepping from the vessel, I seized him by the skirt of his coat, and in attempting to pull him back, I tore it off; but, springing forward, by a rapid effort he made his escape. He had, however, to run a gauntlet through the crowd upon the wharf, each one, as he passed, giving him a kick or a stroke.

Another attempt was made to save a little tea from the ruins of the cargo by a tall, aged man who wore a large cocked hat and white wig, which was fashionable at that time. He had sleightly slipped a little into his pocket, but being detected, they seized him and, taking his hat and wig from his head, threw them, together with the tea, of which they had emptied his pockets, into the water. In consideration of his advanced age, he was permitted to escape, with now and then a slight kick.

The next morning, after we had cleared the ships of the tea, it was discovered that very considerable quantities of it were floating upon the surface of the water; and to prevent the possibility of any of its being saved for use, a number of small boats were manned by sailors and citizens, who rowed them into those parts of the harbor wherever the tea was visible, and by beating it with oars and paddles so thoroughly drenched it as to render its entire destruction inevitable.

Ripe Ol' Corn

"Uncle Josh at Coney Island"

"Uncle Josh," Cal Stewart's country bumpkin, had problems figuring out modern city life (circa 1901). Here he visits New York's famous amusement park.

I'D HEERD TELL A WHOLE LOT at various times 'bout that place what they call Coney Island, and while I was down in New York, I jist made up my mind I was a-goin' to see it, so one day I got on one of them cars what goes across the Brooklyn bridge, and I started out for Coney Island.

Settin' right along side of me in the car was an old lady, and she seemed sort of figity 'bout somethin' or other, and finally she said to me, "Mister, do these cars stop when we git on the other side of the bridge?" I said, "Well now, if they don't you'll git the durndest bump you ever got in your life."

Well, we got on the other side, and I got on one of them tra-la-lee cars what goes down to Coney Island. I give the car feller a dollar, and he put it in his pockit jist the same as if it belonged to him. Well, when I was gittin' purty near there I said, "Mister, don't I git any change?" He said, "Didn't you see that sign on the car?" I said, no sir. Well, he says, "You better go out and look at it." Well, I went out and looked at it, and that settled it. It said, "This car goes to Coney Island without change." Guess it did; I'll be durned if I got any.

Well, we got down there, and I must say of all the pandemonium and hubbub I ever heered in my life, Coney Island beats it all. 'Bout the fust thing I seen there was a place what they called "Shoot the Shoots." It looked like a big hoss trough stood on end, one end in a duck pond and t'other end up in the air, and they would haul a boat up to the top and all git in and then come scootin' down the hoss trough into the pond. Well, I allowed that it'd be right smart fun, so I got into one of the boats along with a lot of other folks I never seed afore and don't care if I never see agin. They yanked us up to the top of that trough and then turned us loose, and I jist felt as though the whole earth had run off and left us.

We went down that trough lickety-split, and a woman what was settin' alongside of me, got skeered and grabbed me round the neck; and I said, "You let go of me you brazen female critter!" But she jist hung on and hollered to beat thunder, and everybody was a yellin' all at once't, and that durned boat was a goin' faster'n greased lightnin' and I had one hand on my pocket book and the other on my hat, and we went "kerslap" dab into that duck pond.

That durned boat upset and we went into the water, and that durned female critter hung onto me and hollered, "Save me, I'm jist a drownin'!" Well, the water wasn't very deep and I jist started to wade out when along come another boat and run over us, and under we went. Well, I managed to get out to the bank, and that female woman said I was a base villain to not rescue a lady from a watery grave. And I jist told her if she had kept her mouth shut she wouldn't have swallered so much of the pond.

Well, they had one place what they called the Middle Way Plesumps, and another place what they called The Streets of Cairo, and they had a lot of shows a-goin' on along there. Well, I went into one of 'em and set down, and I guess if they hadn't shut up the show I'd be settin' there yet. I purty near busted my buttins a laughin'. They had a lot of gals a-dancin' some kind of a dance; I don't know what they called it, but it suited me first-rate.

When I got home, the more I thought about it the more I made up my mind I'd learn that dance. Well, I went out in the cornfield whar none of the neighbors could see me, and I'll be durned if I didn't knock down about four acres of corn, but I never got that dance right. I was the talk of the whole community; mother didn't speak to me fer about a week, and Aunt Nancy Smith said I was a burnin' shame and a disgrace to the village, but I notice Nancy has asked me a good many questions about jist how it was, and I wouldn't wonder if we didn't find Nancy out in the cornfield one of these days.

MOST POPULAR NAMES

BY YEAR OF BIRTH, ACCORDING TO THE SOCIAL SECURITY ADMINISTRATION

1900 Boys: John, William, James; Girls: Mary, Helen, Anna
1905 Boys: John, William, James; Girls: Mary, Helen, Margaret
1910 Boys: John, William, James; Girls: Mary, Helen, Margaret
1915 Boys: John, William, James; Girls: Mary, Helen, Dorothy
1920 Boys: John, William, James; Girls: Mary, Dorothy, Helen
1925 Boys: John, Robert, James; Girls: Mary, Dorothy, Betty
1930 Boys: Robert, James, John; Girls: Mary, Betty, Dorothy
1935 Boys: James, Robert, John; Girls: Mary, Shirley, Barbara
1940 Boys: James, Robert, John; Girls: Mary, Barbara, Patricia
1945 Boys: James, Robert, John; Girls: Mary, Linda, Barbara
1950 Boys: John, James, Robert; Girls: Linda, Mary, Patricia
1955 Boys: Michael, James, David/Robert (tie); Girls: Deborah, Mary, Linda
1960 Boys: David, Michael, John; Girls: Mary, Susan, Maria
1965 Boys: Michael, James, John; Girls: Lisa, Maria, Karen
1970 Boys: Michael, David, John; Girls: Jennifer, Lisa, Kimberly
1975 Boys: Michael, Christopher, Jason; Girls: Jennifer, Amy, Michelle
1980 Boys: Michael, Jason, Christopher; Girls: Jennifer, Jessica, Amanda
1985 Boys: Michael, Christopher, Matthew; Girls: Jessica, Ashley, Jennifer
1990 Boys: Michael, Christopher, Joshua; Girls: Jessica, Ashley, Brittany
1995 Boys: Michael, Jacob, Matthew; Girls: Emily, Ashley, Jessica

The Devil's Dictionary: P

More of *The Devil's Dictionary* by Ambrose Bierce (1842–1914?)

PAINTING, *n.* The art of protecting flat surfaces from the weather and exposing them to the critic.

PANTHEISM, *n.* The doctrine that everything is God, in contradistinction to the doctrine that God is everything.

PASSPORT, *n.* A document inflicted upon a citizen going abroad, exposing him as an alien and pointing him out for special reprobation and outrage.

PATIENCE, *n.* A minor form of despair, disguised as a virtue.

PATRIOT, *n.* The dupe of statesmen and the tool of conquerors.

PATRIOTISM, *n.* In Dr. Johnson's famous dictionary patriotism is defined as the last resort of a scoundrel. With all due respect to an inferior lexicographer I beg to submit that it is the first.

PERSEVERANCE, *n.* A lowly virtue whereby mediocrity achieves an inglorious success.

PESSIMISM, *n.* A philosophy forced by the disheartening prevalence of the optimist's scarecrow hope and unsightly smile.

PHILANTHROPIST, *n.* A rich old gentleman who has trained himself to grin while his conscience is picking his pocket.

PHILOSOPHY, *n.* A route of many roads leading from nowhere to nothing.

PIETY, *n.* Reverence for the Supreme Being, based upon His supposed resemblance to man.

PLAN, *v.t.* To bother about the best method of accomplishing an accidental result.

PLEASURE, *n.* The least hateful form of dejection.

POLITENESS, *n.* The most acceptable hypocrisy.

POLITICS, *n.* A strife of interests masquerading as a contest of principles. The conduct of public affairs for private advantage.

POSITIVE, *adj.* Mistaken at the top of one's voice.

PRAY, *v.* Ask that the laws of the universe be annulled in behalf of a single petitioner confessedly unworthy.

PREFERENCE, *n.* A sentiment, or frame of mind, induced by the erroneous belief that one thing is better than another.

PRESENTABLE, *adj.* Hideously appareled after the manner of the time and place.

PRESIDENCY, *n.* The greased pig in the field game of American politics.

Archetypal Blonde

The Quirky, Sad Life of Marilyn Monroe

Marilyn Monroe was more than a movie star. She was an icon who shook up the sexually repressed 1950s. We've sifted through her biographies to give you the juicy stuff.

• A star was born on June 1, 1926, with the unlikely name of Norma Jeane Mortenson. Her mother, Gladys Pearl Monroe Baker Mortenson, was an emotionally unstable film negative cutter. Marilyn spent her childhood carted around between foster homes.

• Norma Jeane vowed she would never get married—that she was going to become a schoolteacher and have lots of dogs. She concocted the idea that Clark Gable was her biological father.

• In high school, Norma Jeane wrote news features for the school paper, concluding in one that "53 percent of the gentlemen prefer blondes as their dream girl."

• Norma left school at sixteen to marry twenty-one-year-old Jim Dougherty. She tried unsuccessfully to negotiate an agreement that they would not have sex after marrying.

• In April 1944, Norma Jeane took a wartime job spraying varnish on fuselage fabric. She became a parachute inspector. Soon after, she was discovered by an Army camera crew doing a "girls of the war effort" spread for GI morale. Her career began to blossom.

• By spring of 1946 she had appeared on thirty-three magazine covers. She had an affair with at least one photographer, and in September was granted a divorce from Jim. She was signed by Fox Studio that same year.

• After one movie deal, Fox declined to renew her contract. Monroe spent her small income on acting classes, rent, and car maintenance. She filled the gaps by prostituting off Hollywood Boulevard.

• With roommate Shelley Winters, Monroe began compiling a list of men she wanted to have sexual relations with. At the top of the list was Albert Einstein. (Whether it happened, nobody knows for sure, but later Winters came across a photo of Einstein inscribed, "With respect and love and thanks.")

• The price of stardom was high: At Columbia Studios, her bleached hairline was permanently heightened. Her drama coach taught her an overexaggerated, breathy voice that became so habitual she would later have to go to another coach to get rid of it. Her voice teacher paid for the correction of an overbite and to have her teeth bleached. Her agent arranged plastic surgery to remove a small bump from the tip of her nose and insert a silicone implant into her jaw to give it a softer line. She lifted weights to improve her bustline, and jogged each morning—neither activity commonplace for women in 1950.

• Monroe had camera fright, often vomiting before going on the set.

• But she was tough: While filming in 1952, Marilyn was diagnosed with acute appendicitis. She asked them to give her antibiotics and delay the operation until after the movie was finished. She returned to work and didn't have her appendix removed until nearly two months later.

• She learned her seductive "swivel" while filming a movie where she had to walk down a cobblestone street in high heels. After she saw the reaction from onlookers, she used that walk from that day on. When asked if her walk was natural, she quipped, "I've been walking since I was six months old." The Tokyo press dubbed Marilyn "Honorable Buttocks-Swinging Actress."

• She didn't wear any underwear, a custom very rare in 1952. The dress she wore in *Gentlemen Prefer Blondes* was so tight that she had to be sewn into it.

• When she met Joe DiMaggio, she was 25; he was 37 and retired from baseball.

• At their wedding, Marilyn turned to Joe and asked him if she died before him, would he place flowers at her grave every week—just as William Powell had done at the grave of Jean Harlow? Joe promised, and even though they were divorced when she died, he did so for decades afterward.

• Marilyn told a friend that Joe didn't like her work on screen: "He didn't like the women I played—he thought they were sluts. He didn't like the actors kissing me, and he didn't like my costumes. He didn't like anything about my movies, and he hated all my clothes." The famous blowing skirt scene brought matters to a head, and Joe reportedly got violent, causing bruises on her shoulders that had to be covered up with makeup. Two weeks later, Marilyn filed for divorce.

• After returning from her honeymoon with Joe, Marilyn told a friend that she was next going to marry Arthur Miller, author of *The Crucible* and other plays.

• Monroe did marry the playwright in June 1956. At the last minute, Monroe told friends that she wan't sure she wanted to marry him, but that she would go through it because she didn't want to disappoint the already-assembled wedding guests.

• Miller had second thoughts as well. He wrote in his journal that he feared his writing would be threatened by her continuous emotional de-

Marilyn and wooly friend in April 1946—her very first national magazine cover mands. Sure enough, after the wedding he immediately sunk into a case of writer's block. Monroe convinced him to write a movie script for *The Misfits* for her. As their relationship deteriorated, he rewrote drafts of the script, making her character more and more unsympathetic.

• After *Some Like It Hot*, Tony Curtis said that kissing her was like "kissing Hitler."

• According to biographer Donald Spoto, best evidence suggests that Monroe had only one sexual encounter with John F. Kennedy and that she never slept with Bobby Kennedy—she reportedly wasn't attracted to him. She did find him a sympathetic listener, though, and would called his office repeatedly. The attorney general eventually started avoiding her calls.

• She started seeing a psychotherapist named Ralph Greenson, who relied heavily on drug therapy, routinely prescribing barbiturates and tranquilizers. He told her to visit at his house instead of his office, and convinced her that she needed to see him every day. Right before her death, Greenson was injecting her with drugs at least once a day, and had given her pre-

scriptions for strong sedatives.

• Although there are a number of conspiracy theories about her death, biographer Spoto suggests that her psychiatrist, Ralph Greenson, administered barbiturates or chloral hydrate as an enema (evidenced by the coroner's report), which, combined with sedative she had taken earlier, killed her. Greenson and a housekeeper he had hired to keep an eye on her then tried to cover up his error, says Spoto, resulting in various contradictory accounts that have fed the conspiracy theories.

• Persistent stories had it that DiMaggio and Monroe had been planning to get remarried at the time she died.

Eyewitness

I Saw Lincoln Assassinated

History books are fine, but there's always a sense that they're leaving out the good parts, the parts that help us see the events vividly. For that, you've got to go to the real people who were actually there.

THERE ARE STORIES WE ALL KNOW, yet in a way, we really don't. Sometimes details get lost in the retelling. For example, after Lincoln's shooting, did you know that mobs reigned and federal troops chased innocent playgoers out of Ford's Theater with bayonets? That John Wilkes Booth thought he'd be lionized as a hero? Let's listen to some of the voices of people who lived through the time.

THEATERGOER PETER DOYLE'S EXPERIENCES, AS TOLD BY HIS GOOD FRIEND WALT WHITMAN: The day, April 14, 1865, seems to have been a pleasant one throughout the whole land....The popular afternoon paper, the little "Evening Star," had spatter'd all over its third page, divided among the advertisements in a sensational manner, in a hundred different places, "The President and his Lady will be at the Theatre this evening...."

On this occasion the theatre was crowded, many ladies in rich and gay costumes, officers in their uniforms, many well-known citizens, young folks, the usual clusters of gas-lights, the usual magnetism of so many people, cheerful, with perfumes, music of violins and flutes.... The President with his wife witness'd the play from the large stage-boxes of the second tier, two thrown into one, and profusely draped with the national flag....

There is a scene in the play representing a modern parlor, in which two unprecedented English ladies are inform'd by the impossible Yankee that he is not a man of fortune, and therefore undesirable for marriage-catching purposes; after which, the comments being finish'd, the dramatic trio make exit, leaving the stage clear for a moment. At this period came the murder of Abraham Lincoln.

Great as all its manifold train, circling round it, and stretching into the future for many a century, in the politics, history, art, etc., of the New World, in point of fact the main thing, the actual murder, transpired with the quiet and simplicity of any commonest occurrence—the bursting of a bud or pod in the growth of vegetation, for instance. Through the general hum following the stage pause, with the change of positions, came the muffled sound of a pistol-shot, which not one-hundredth part of the audience heard at the time—and yet a moment's hush—somehow, surely, a vague startled thrill—and then, through the ornamented, draperied, starr'd and striped space-way of the President's box, a sudden figure, a man, raises himself with hands and feet, stands a moment on the railing, leaps below to the stage (a distance of perhaps fourteen or fifteen feet), falls out of position, catching his

Another Eyewitness

"When the second scene of the third act was being performed, and while I was intently observing the proceedings upon the stage with my back toward the door, I heard the discharge of a pistol behind me, and, looking round, saw through the smoke a man between the door and the President. The distance from the door to where the President sat was about four feet. At the same time I heard the man shout some word which I thought was 'Freedom!' I instantly sprang toward him and seized him. He wrested himself from my grasp, and made a violent thrust at my breast with a large knife. I parried the blow by striking it up, and received a wound several inches deep in my left arm, below the elbow and the shoulder. The orifice of the wound was about an inch and a half in length, and extended upward toward the shoulder several inches. The man rushed to the front of the box, and I endeavored to seize him again, but only caught his clothes as he was leaping over the railing of the box....I then turned to the President; his position was not changed; his head was slightly bent forward, and his eyes were closed. I saw that he was unconscious and, supposing him mortally wounded, rushed to the door for the purpose of calling medical aid." **—Major Henry Rathbone, who sat in the Lincolns' box with his wife-to-be. An odd footnote: 19 years later Rathbone would end up in a mental institution after stabbing his wife to death.**

boot-heel in the copious drapery (the American flag), falls on one knee, quickly recovers himself, rises as if nothing had happen'd, (he really sprains his ankle, but unfelt then)—and so the figure, Booth, the murderer, dress'd in plain black broadcloth, bare-headed, with full, glossy, raven hair, and his eyes like some mad animal's flashing with light and resolution, yet with a certain strange calmness, holds aloft in one hand a large knife—walks along not much back from the footlights—turns fully toward the audience his face of statuesque beauty, lit by those basilisk eyes, flashing with desperation, perhaps insanity—launches out in a firm and steady voice the words "*Sic semper tyrannis*"—and then walks with neither slow nor very rapid pace diagonally across to the back of the stage, and disappears. (Had not all this terrible scene—making the mimic ones preposterous—had it not all been rehears'd, in blank, by Booth, beforehand?)

A moment's hush—a scream—the cry of murder—Mrs. Lincoln leaning out of the box, with ashy cheeks and lips, with involuntary cry,

pointing to the retreating figure, "*He has kill'd the President.*" And still a moment's strange, incredulous suspense—and then the deluge!—then that mixture of horror, noises, uncertainty—(the sound, somewhere back, of a horse's hoofs clattering with speed)—the people burst through chairs and railings, and break them up—there is inextricable confusion and terror—women faint—quite feeble persons fall, and are trampled on—many cries of agony are heard—the broad stage suddenly fills to suffocation with a dense and motley crowd, like some horrible carnival—the audience rush generally upon it, at least the strong men do—the actors and actresses are all there in their play-costumes and painted faces, with mortal fright showing through the rouge —the screams and calls, confused talk—redoubled, trebled —two or three manage to pass up water from the stage to the President's box—others try to clamber up—etc., etc.

War Department, Washington, April 20, 1865.
$100,000 REWARD!
THE MURDERER
Of our late beloved President, Abraham Lincoln,
IS STILL AT LARGE.
$50,000 REWARD
$25,000 REWARD
$25,000 REWARD
EDWIN M. STANTON, Secretary of War.

In the midst of all this, the soldiers of the President's guard, with others suddenly drawn to the scene, burst in—(some two hundred altogether)—they storm the house, through all the tiers, especially the upper ones, inflamed with fury, literally charging the audience with fix'd bayonets, muskets and pistols, shouting *Clear out! clear out! you sons of bitches*! Such the wild scene, or a suggestion of it, inside the playhouse that night.

Outside, too, in the atmosphere of shock and craze, crowds of people, fill'd with frenzy, ready to seize any outlet for it, come near committing murder several times on innocent individuals. One such case was especially exciting. The infuriated crowd through some chance got started against one man, either for words he utter'd, or perhaps without

In His Own Words

"I struck boldly, and not as the papers say. I walked with a firm step through 1,000 of his friends, was stopped, but pushed on. A colonel was at his side. I shouted, 'Sic Semper' before I fired. In jumping, broke my leg. I passed all his pickets, rode 60 miles that night, with the bone of my leg tearing the flesh at every jump. I can never repent it, although we hated to kill. Our country owed all her troubles to him, and God simply made me the instrument of His punishment....I am here in despair. And why? For doing what Brutus was honored for—what made William Tell a hero. And yet I, for striking down a greater tyrant than they ever knew, am looked upon as a common cutthroat....I have too great a soul to die like a criminal. O may He spare me that, and let me die bravely!" —**John Wilkes Booth, 27-year-old actor, states rights fanatic, white supremist, and assassin, writing in his diary shortly before being killed in a Virginia tobacco barn**

any cause at all, and were proceeding at once to actually hang him on a neighboring lamppost, when he was rescued by a few heroic policemen, who placed him in their midst, and fought their way slowly and amid great peril toward the station house. It was a fitting episode of the whole affair. The crowd rushing and eddying to and fro—the night, the yells, the pale faces, many frighten'd people trying the vain to extricate themselves—the attack'd man, not yet freed from the jaws of death, looking like a corpse—the silent, resolute, half-dozen policemen, with no weapons but their little clubs, yet stern and steady through all those eddying swarms—made a fitting side-scene to the grand tragedy of the murder. They gain'd the station house with the protected man, whom they placed in security for the night, and discharged him in the morning.

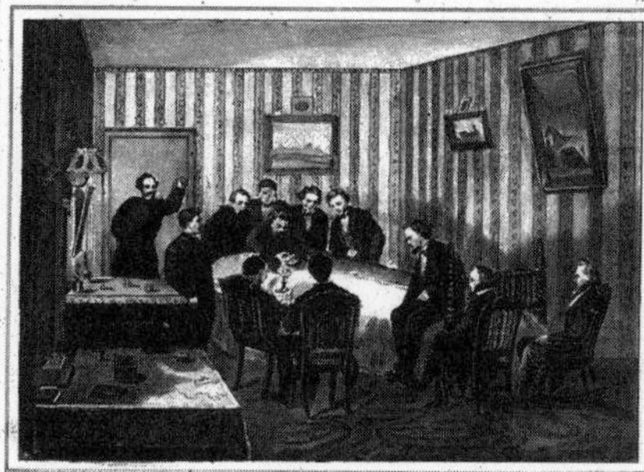

Lincoln's letzte Stunde. | Lincoln's last hour. | La dernière heure de Lincoln.

And in the midst of that pandemonium, infuriated soldiers, the audience and the crowd, the stage, and all its actors and actresses, its paint-pots, spangles, and gas-lights—the life blood from those veins, the best and sweetest of the land, drips slowly down, and death's ooze already begins its little bubbles on the lips.

Another Eyewitness

"The President had been carried across the street from the theater, to the house of a Mr. Peterson....I enquired of Dr. Hall as I entered the true condition of the President. He replied the President was dead to all intents, although he might live three hours or perhaps longer. The giant sufferer lay extended diagonally across the bed....His features were calm and striking. I had never seen them appear to better advantage than for the first hour....After that, his right eye began to swell and that part of his face became discolored....The respiration of the President became suspended at intervals,and at last entirely ceased at twenty-two minutes past seven. " **—Gideon Wells, Secretary of the Navy, writing in his diary**

We've Got Your Number

We'll give you a number, abbreviated words, and a clue. Tell us what the famous phrase is. Answers below. (Don't cheat!)

1. T F 2 & 2 F T (1920s song)
2. W I 64 (Fab 4 1920s-style song)
3. 3 S—L, M & C (Nyuk, nyuk, nyuk)
4. 50 S O T U (Last two were added in 1959)
5. 13 S & 50 S O T A F (Heavens to Betsy)
6. T 4 H O T A (Scary riders in the book of *Revelation*)
7. S W & T 7 D (Heigh-ho!)
8. H 57 V (Playing a catch-up game)
9. B & R 31 F (Rocky road, please)
10. 7 B F 7 B (Musical)
11. T 12 S O A A (Help yourself to a little self-help)
12. 5 G R, 4 C B, 3 F H, 2 T D & A P I A P T (Seasonal gifts)
13. R-A-D-D, 3 M I A T (One was a candlestick maker)
14. 1 L, 2 L, 3 L I (Kids' Native American census)
15. 3 B O G—L, E & J (Laws made, enforced, and interpreted)
16. T 9 P—M, V, E, M, J, S, U, N, P (Revolving and rotating)
17. 5 F 2, E O B (Another 1920s song)
18. P L I 1999 (1980s song)
19. G Y K O R 66 (1950s traveling music)
20. T 1812 O (Boom!)

Answers: *1. Tea for 2 & 2 for Tea; 2. When I'm 64; 3. 3 Stooges—Larry, Moe, & Curly; 4. 50 States of the Union; 5. 13 Stripes and 50 Stars of the American Flag; 6. The 4 Horsemen of the Apocalypse; 7. Snow White & the 7 Dwarfs; 8. Heinz 57 Varieties; 9. Baskin & Robbins 31 Flavors; 10. 7 Brides for 7 Brothers; 11. The 12 Steps of Alcoholic Anonymous; 12. 5 Golden Rings, 4 Calling Birds, 3 French Hens, etc. 13. Rub-A-Dub-Dub, 3 Men in a Tub; 14. 1 Little, 2 Little, 3 Little Indians; 15. 3 Branches of Government—Legislative, Executive, & Judicial; 16. The 9 Planets—Mercury, Venus, Earth, etc. 17. 5 Foot 2, Eyes of Blue; 18. Party Like It's 1999; 19. Get Your Kicks on Route 66; 20. The 1812 Overture*

Life Lessons

How to Whittle a Chain

Whittlin' a chain out of a single block of wood seems like it should be near impossible, but it's not. You can do it, too. Here's how.

WHITTLING has long been a therapeutic method of relaxation. All it takes is time and patience, and it's fun in a slow, rural sort of way. Carve a chain from a single block of wood? It's impressive, and it can be done. Let's start with a three-link chain, knowing we can go for more next time.

1. Get a piece of basswood (or another soft wood) measuring $1\frac{1}{2}$ x $1\frac{1}{2}$ x 6 inches.

2. Take a pencil and draw guidelines as pictured above, on all six sides of the board.

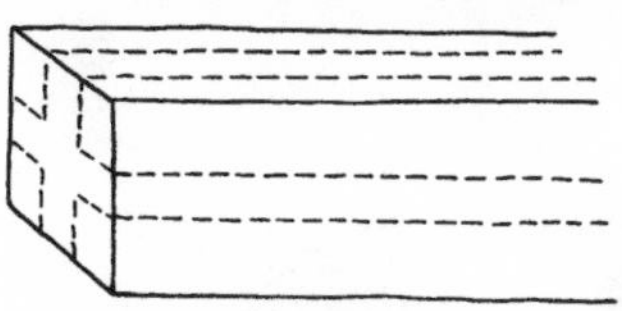

3. Begin cutting away the corner areas. Patiently slice a little at a time, or you'll split the wood. A good sharp knife and a meditative attitude will help a lot. You'll soon have a cross-shaped block that's 6 inches long.

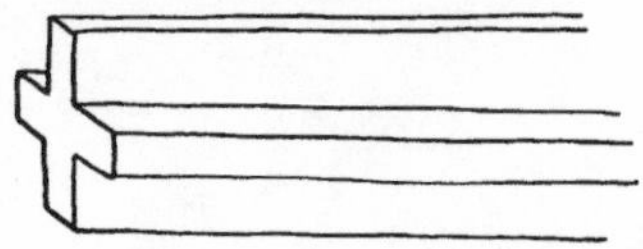

4. Take your pencil and draw two end chain links butted together and 3 inches long as pictured below. Draw the middle link centered on the "arms" of the cross, also 3 inches long.

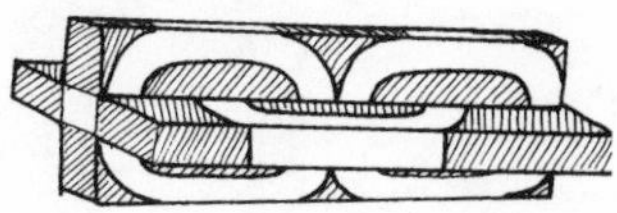

5. Start patiently whittling away the wood that doesn't belong to any of the links (dark areas, above).

6. Eventually the links will become individual pieces in a chain, linked but hanging free.

Congrats! You did it!

Even More Pot Shots

Some more favorite bathroom shots. Send us yours! (See page 478.)

a. Toilet on beach
b. Ancient public toilets in Turkish ruins
c. Discarded toilets
d. Dawson City, Yukon Annual Outhouse Race
e. Abandoned western site
f. Mt. Kilamanjaro pit stop

Time Capsules

ADVICE AND SEX AIDS FROM THE PAST

If you wanted to give a sense of life in our time, what would you put in a time capsule? The people of the future plead: "No more newspapers and city council minutes!"

TO BE FRANK, the contents of time capsules are usually pretty unimaginative things: newspapers, books, maps, photos, census results, puffery from local governments, self-important letters from industry leaders and elected officials—that sort of thing. Occasionally, though, some quirky items find their way in. Here are some examples of such items:

MIAMI COUNTY COURTHOUSE, KANSAS: 1898
A bottle of 1890 "Old Rye" whisky.

BALTIMORE MEMORIAL STADIUM: 1954
Business cards, baseball cards, and 36¢ in nickels and pennies.

RENTON, WASHINGTON: 2001
A commemorative mug, T-shirt, "static cling decal," and deck of cards. Also, an IKEA furniture catalog.

LIVERMORE, CALIFORNIA: 1969
A letter from President Nixon, two beer steins, and a program from a local production of *Up with People*.

UNIVERSITY OF MASSACHUSETTS: 2000
A list of university parking regulations, a video of the U.M. marching band, and the text of 100 student e-mails selected randomly from the university's server.

AKRON, OHIO: 1950

A package of flower seeds from a local garden club, a "B.F. Goodrich Tubeless Tire Demonstration Kit," and a Sears-Roebuck catalog.

SAN FRANCISCO, CALIFORNIA: 2001

A piece of the AIDS Quilt, a pack of Pokemon cards, a bolt from the Golden Gate Bridge, and a box of Rice-A-Roni.

CURIE HIGH SCHOOL, CHICAGO, ILLINOIS: 1976

A list of the year's top ten records, a bus transfer, a program from *You're a Good Man, Charlie Brown,* and a full-color poster of the Sweathogs from TV's *Welcome Back, Kotter.*

MCKEESPORT, PENNSYLVANIA: 1964

A 1964 telephone book, a model of a 1964 Ford Mustang, and a can of Royal Crown Cola (which leaked and ruined some of the paper goods in the time capsule).

ROCHESTER, NEW YORK: 1873

Opened in 2000, this capsule included an envelope tucked into a book. It bore two contradictory messages: "For the Person Who Opens this Box" and (in a different hand) "Not to go in." Inside the envelope was a 127-year-old condom. As described by the modern-day Rochester Museum & Science Center, which displayed the condom with the rest of the contents: "This condom appears to be made from a segment of animal intestine, probably sheep or goat. Nearly 8" long and 3" in diameter, it has a light blue drawstring-type ribbon closure on the open end."

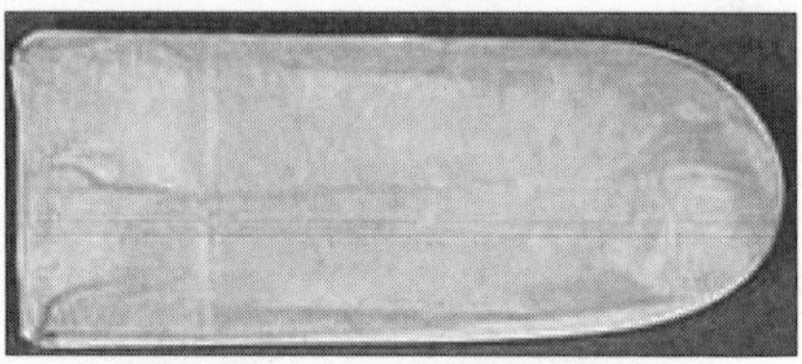

Uh, thanks, Great-great-great-granddad!

A CAVEAT

Whatever you decide to put in your own time capsule, heed this sobering observation from the International Time Capsule Society, which keeps track of such things: There are close to 10,000 time capsules that have been secreted around the world ... but most of them have already been lost or forgotten.

Month to Month

THE ROMAN ARTIFACT THAT RUNS OUR LIVES

Ever wonder where we got the names of our months? Blame the Romans. Legend has it that about 2,700 years ago, Numa Pompilius, the second emperor of Rome, invented the first Roman calendar. We're still stuck with it.

MARCH (MARTIUS)

"It's March 1—*Happy New Year!*" For centuries, Martius was the first month of the year, honoring the Roman god Mars. Although best known as the god of war, Mars was also the lord of agriculture and the mythical founder of Rome (thus making him first in war, first in peas, and first in the start of his countrymen).

Mars needs women, but women need Juno.

APRIL (APRILIS)

The month of April takes its name from the Latin word *aperere,* meaning "opening," as the buds and leaves are all doing about that time of year. The Greeks associated the goddess Aphrodite with this month; she represented beauty, love, and fertility. In ancient Rome, Miss April was Venus, the goddess of vegetation and defender of feminine chastity.

MAY (MAIUS)
The Roman poet Ovid wrote that the name of this month came from *maiores,* the Latin word for "elderly." However, more credible sources credit Maia, the Greek goddess of fertility and mother of the god Mercury. Ritual sacrifices were made to Mercury on the first day of Maia's month. The Romans passed the day on to the Anglo-Saxons, who exchanged messy sacrifices for more festive things like May Day feasts, May queens, and May poles.

JUNE (JUNIUS)
Juno was Jupiter's sister, and the head Roman goddess. She was the goddess of marriage and happy females, and watched over women during events like marriage and childbirth. As a result, June weddings became a common custom. (However, poet Ovid swore that June actually came from the Latin word *juniores,* loosely meaning "young folk." But who you gonna believe—tradition or some unreliable poet?)

JULY (JULIUS)
Originally July was called *Quintilis Mensis* ("the fifth month" in Latin). That was until Julius Caesar came along and did a lot of fidgeting with the calendar. In honor of all his hard work on what became known as the Julian calendar, he named this month after himself.

AUGUST (AUGUSTUS)
Caesar Augustus decided to follow Julius's example and renamed *Sextilis Mensis* ("month number six") after himself. Augustus had tweaked Julius's calendar a little, so thought he deserved his own month, too.

SEPTEMBER (SEPTEMBER MENSIS)
Although it's now the ninth month, September comes from the Latin *septem* meaning "seven." (It got its name before January and February got moved to the beginning of the calendar.) According to record, several Roman emperors attempted to insert their names into the calendar on this month, but none of them really took, so it remains "September."

OCTOBER (OCTOBER MENSIS)
October, originally the eighth month in the calendar, comes from *octo,* Latin for "eight."

NOVEMBER (NOVEMBRIS MENSIS)
November comes from *nonus* ("nine").

DECEMBER (DECEMBER MENSIS)
Decimus means "ten" in Latin. In the early days of the calendar there were only ten months. The Romans were farmers and just stopped counting after December, since farming wasn't possible anyway and keeping track of the days was meaningless. The calendar would start up again on March 1 as it became clear that the spring equinox was approaching. In about 700 B.C., as Roman culture diversified, two months were tacked on after December.

JANUARY (JANUARIUS)
The new month of Januarius was made the first month of the year in 153 B.C. It was named for the two-headed Roman god Janus, the god who guarded beginnings.

Janus on the proverbial two-headed coin

January originally had 29 days, but Julius Caesar changed it to 31 in 45 B.C., because among the ancient Romans, 31 was considered luckier than 29.

FEBRUARY (FEBRUARIUS)
At the end of the year, February marked the festival of Lupercalia, a time of *februar* ("purification") in ancient Rome. (One of the activities included beating barren women with thongs of goat leather by holy priests in the hope of making them fertile.)

The month had either 28 or 29 days until 450 B.C. when it was shortened to 23 or 24 days. However, Julius Caesar's calendar lengthened it again, and he added a leap day at the end of the year every four years to keep the years even. It turned out to be a pretty good way of making up the extra time, even if it isn't at the end of the year any more.

MERCEDONIUS
Before Julius Caesar, Mercedonius was the thirteenth month. It lasted a varying number of days at the end of the year and functioned to fill in the gaps of the calendar. The name came from the Latin word *merces* ("wages"), because it was the traditional time for year-end wages to be paid. When Julius Caesar lengthened some of the months and created the leap year, he was able to eliminate Mercedonius from the calen-

More Beer!

It's Good for What Ales You

"Those who drink beer will think beer," said Washington Irving. Have you ever wondered about the difference between an ale and a lager, or a porter and a pilsner? We can help.

ale: The main difference between beer and ale is that ale uses a yeast that floats to the top when it's done fermenting, and it isn't aged, which gives it a fruitier taste. Beer uses a yeast that sinks to the bottom and is aged.

lager beer: *Lager* means "storehouse" in German—in other words, aged beer. It's your basic, pale, highly carbonated standard American beer.

pilsner beer: The name comes from a beer made in the Bohemian town of Pilsen. It's any especially light, smooth beer.

stout: "Stout" once meant "strong" rather than fat, and that's why this dark, malty ale got the name in the nineteenth century.

porter: The name is short for "porter's ale," and supposedly came because produce carriers—or porters—of eighteenth century London preferred drinking it. In early America, this ale was served in what came to be known as "porterhouses"; one such tavern in New York City popularized the "porterhouse steak" in about 1814.

bock: A strong beer usually manufactured in fall or winter, bock may have as much as twice the alcohol as lager. The name comes from Einbeck (pronounced *Inebock*), Germany. In the United States, bock beer is sometimes made from the sediment left in beer-fermentation vats.

dark beer: It's dark only because brewers roast the malt before brewing with it.

malt liquor: For those who want to get wasted more efficiently, malt liquor is merely lager beer with a higher alcohol content, usually produced by adding sugar to the batch to give the yeast more to work with.

Another Little Latin Quiz

Food, Law, or Ailment?

Here we go again! Circle the category that matches the meaning of the Latin word or phrase.

1. In ovis apalis	Food	Law	Ailment
2. Mutatis mutandis	Food	Law	Ailment
3. Isicia omentata	Food	Law	Ailment
4. Pro tempore	Food	Law	Ailment
5. Icterus gravis neonatrum	Food	Law	Ailment
6. Acanthosis nigricans	Food	Law	Ailment
7. Vignan unguiculata	Food	Law	Ailment
8. Non compos mentis	Food	Law	Ailment
9. Trismus nascentium	Food	Law	Ailment
10. Pepones et melones	Food	Law	Ailment
11. Minutal marinum	Food	Law	Ailment
12. Septicemia	Food	Law	Ailment
13. Morbi cutis	Food	Law	Ailment
14. Ova sfongia exlacte	Food	Law	Ailment
15. Lapsus calami	Food	Law	Ailment

Answers: *1. Food: Boiled eggs; 2. Law: "Change must be accounted for"; 3. Food: An ancient Roman burger patty; 4. Law: "For the time being"; 5. Ailment: Extreme jaundice in a newborn; 6. Ailment: A skin disorder; 7. Food: Black-eyed peas/beans; 8. Law: "Not mentally competent"; 9. Ailment: Infant tetanus; 10. Food: Ancient Roman melon dish; 11. Food: Seafood fricassee; 12. Ailment: Blood poisoning; 13. Ailment: Serious skin disease; 14. Food: Pancakes made with milk; 15. Law: "A slip of the pen"*

Wisdom for Sale

Business Advice from the Sages of the Ages

"My rule always was to do the business of the day in the day." —The Duke of Wellington (1769–1852)

"No praying, it spoils business." —Thomas Otway (1652–1685)

"Who first invented Work—and tied the free
And holy-day rejoicing spirit down
To the ever-haunting importunity
Of business, in the green fields, and the town—
To plough-loom-anvil-spade-and, oh, most sad,
To this dry drudgery of the desk's dead wood?"
—Charles Lamb (1775–1834)

"No nation was ever ruined by trade." —Benjamin Franklin (1706–1790)

"He's happy who, far away from business, like the race of men of old, tills his ancestral fields with his own oxen, unbound by any interest to pay." —Horace (65–8 B.C.)

"Catch a man a fish, and you can sell it to him. Teach a man to fish, and you ruin a wonderful business opportunity." —Karl Marx (1818–1883)

"If a man can make a better mousetrap, though he builds his house in the woods the world will make a beaten path to his door." —Ralph Waldo Emerson (1803–1882)

"A financier is a pawnbroker with imagination." —A. W. Pinero (1855–1934)

"Finance is the art of passing currency from hand to hand until it finally disappears." –Robert W. Sarnoff (1918–1997)

"There is more credit and satisfaction in being a first-rate truck driver than a tenth-rate business executive." –Malcolm Forbes (1919–90)

Doctor Riots

The Mobs That Smashed Medical Schools

One of the strangest chapters in the history of medicine are the mobs that rioted against doctors and medical schools. On the other hand, knowing the story, we might've rioted, too.

WHAT COULD CAUSE OTHERWISE NORMAL PEOPLE to riot against doctors and smash up medical schools? In 1788, eight people were killed and scores wounded in three days of rioting against doctors in New York City. The riot didn't end until a militia fired into the mob, resulting in most of the reported deaths and injuries.

LEND ME A HAND, WILL YOU?

Here's how it started. Medical students at the New York Hospital were dissecting bodies in a second-floor laboratory, and a boy playing nearby climbed a ladder to see what was going on. One of the medical students, startled and annoyed by the face at the window, waved a disembodied arm at the boy and told him it had belonged to his mother.

Unfortunately, the kid's mother had died recently. He ran to get his father, who was laying brick at a nearby construction site. The enraged dad and his co-workers rushed the laboratory and discovered the mutilated corpses. In response, they wrecked the place and took the bodies off for burial. When people saw the bodies and heard the stories, civil outrage spread from there. Mobs roamed the streets, breaking into hospitals and the homes of doctors and vandalizing them. The semiliterate mob even looted the house of a man named Sir John Temple when they misread his name as "Surgeon Temple."

Wisely, many doctors left town until it all cooled down; those who didn't were taken into custody by police for their own protection. Outside a jail that harbored four doctors, a mob gathered, intending to lynch them. When they began throwing paving stones at the state militia, the soldiers fired into the crowd, killing seven and injuring dozens more.

Remarkably, no doctors or med students were injured or killed in the New York riots.

THE "RESURRECTIONISTS"

Animosity toward the medical profession had been brewing for years. In those years, few bodies were legally available for dissecting—only those of executed criminals—so medical schools got bodies any way that they could. It made sense from their point of view. The dead person wasn't using the body anyway, and dissecting corpses would help doctors save lives of the living.

In some cases, doctors paid others to come up with bodies, but oftentimes, they took care of the grave robbing by themselves. The practice was tacitly encouraged by medical societies. Calling themselves "Resurrectionists," teacher-student teams would raid local graveyards by night.

Digging out dirt above one end of the coffin, they'd drill a dotted line of holes to weaken the lid and pry up the exposed end until it broke. Using a hook, they'd slide the body out of the coffin, strip it bare, and toss the clothes back in the coffin before covering with dirt again. (A quirk in the laws made stealing things—even clothes—from a coffin a much more serious crime than stealing the body itself.) A good grave-robbing team could do the whole operation in about an hour.

STUDENT BODIES

In response to the epidemic of grave robberies, it became the custom in university towns to place iron bars on graves and post an armed guard on the site for two weeks until the body rotted enough to be unsuitable for dissection.

You'd think you could shrug off the Doctors Riots as a bizarre exception, but that wouldn't be true. Until 1852, when laws were changed to make it easier for medical schools to get cadavers, there were at least thirteen similar anti-doctor riots in Illinois, Maryland, Massachusetts, New York, Ohio, Pennsylvania, and Vermont.

Ripe Ol' Corn

"Uncle Josh in Wall Street"

Early in the twentieth century, humorist Cal Stewart wrote hundreds of "Uncle Josh" stories, about a country bumpkin coming up against the modern world. Here's one of them.

I USED TO READ in our town paper down home at Punkin Centre a whole lot about Wall Street and them bulls and bears, and one thing and another, so I jist said to myself—now Joshua, when you git down to New York City, that's jist what you want to see.

Wall, when I got to New York, I got a feller to show me whar it was, and I'll be durned if I know why they call it Wall Street; it didn't have any wall round it. I walked up and down it 'bout an hour and a half, and I couldn't find any stock exchange or see any place fer waterin' any stock. I couldn't see a pig nor a cow, nor a sheep nor a calf, or anything else that looked like stock to me.

So finally I said to a gentleman, "Mister, whar do they keep the menagery down here?" He said, "What menagery?" I said the place whar they've got all them bulls and bears a fightin'. Well, he looked at me as though he thought I was crazy, and I guess he did, but he said, "You come along with me, I guess I can show you what you want to see."

Well, I went along with him, and he took me up to some public institushun, near as I could make out it was a loonytick asylem. Well, he took me into a room about two acres and a half square, and thar was about two thousand of the crazyest men in thar I ever seen in all my life. The minnit I set eyes on them I knowed they was all crazy, and I'd have to humor them if I got out of thar alive.

One feller was a-standin' on the top of a table with a lot of papers in his hand, and a-yellin' like a Comanche injin, and all the rest of them was tryin' to git at him. Finally I said to one of 'em, "Mister, what are you a-tryin' to do with that feller up thar on the table?" And he said, "Well, he's got 5,000 bushels of wheat and we are tryin' to git it away from him."

LOOKED LIKE A LOONYTICK ASYLEM TO ME.

Well, the minnit he said that, I knowed for certain they was all crazy, 'cause nobody but a crazy man would ever think he had 5,000 bushels of wheat in his coat and pants pockits.

When they weren't a-looking I got out of thar, and I felt mighty thankful to git out. There was a feller standin' on the front steps; he had a sort of a unyform on; I guess he was Superintendent of the institushun; he talked purty sassy to me.

I said, "Mister, what time does the fust car go up town?" He said "The fust one went about twenty-five years ago."

I said to him, "Is that my car over thar?" He said "No sir, that car belongs to the street car company." I says, "Well, I guess I'll take it anyhow." He says "You'd better not, thar's bin a good many cars missin' around here lately."

I said, "Well now, I want to know, is thar anything round here any fresher than you be?" He said, "Yes, sir, that bench you're a sittin' on is a little fresher; they painted it about ten minnits ago."

Well, I got up and looked, and durned if he wasn't right.

The Fabled Frog

Frog Tales From Aesop

Clearly the frog played a role in ancient human life—the amphibian is the centerpiece for several of Aesop's fables. Here are but a few to keep you hopping.

THE FROGS WHO DESIRED A KING

The Frogs were living as happy as could be in a marshy swamp that just suited them; they went splashing about caring for nobody and nobody troubling with them. But some of them thought that this was not right, that they should have a king and a proper constitution, so they determined to send up a petition to Jove to give them what they wanted.

"Mighty Jove," they cried, "send unto us a king that will rule over us and keep us in order." Jove laughed at their croaking, and threw down into the swamp a huge Log, which came down splashing into the swamp.

The Frogs were frightened out of their minds by the commotion made in their midst, and all rushed to the bank to look at the horrible monster; but after a time, seeing that it did not move, one or two of the boldest of them ventured out towards the Log, and even dared to touch it; still it did not move. Then the greatest hero of the Frogs jumped upon the Log and commenced dancing up and down upon it, thereupon all the Frogs came and did the same; and for some time the Frogs went about their business every day without taking the slightest notice of their new King Log lying in their midst.

But this did not suit them, so they sent another petition to Jove, and said to him, "We want a real king; one that will really rule over us." Now this made Jove angry, so he sent among them a big Stork that soon set to work gobbling them all up. Then the Frogs repented when too late.

Better no rule than cruel rule.

THE HARES AND THE FROGS

The Hares were so persecuted by the other beasts, they did not know where to go. As soon as they saw a single animal approach them, off they used to run.

One day they saw a troop of wild Horses stampeding about, and in quite a panic all the Hares scuttled off to a lake hard by, determined to drown themselves rather than live in such a continual state of fear. But just as they got near the bank of the lake, a troop of Frogs, frightened in their turn by the approach of the Hares scuttled off, and jumped into the water.

"Truly," said one of the Hares, "things are not so bad as they seem:

"There is always someone worse off than yourself."

THE FROG AND THE OX

"Oh Father," said a little Frog to the big one sitting by the side of a pool, "I have seen such a terrible monster! It was as big as a mountain, with horns on its head, and a long tail, and it had hoofs divided in two."

"Tush, child, tush," said the old Frog, "that was only Farmer White's Ox. It isn't so big either; he may be a little

"Bigger, father, bigger."

bit taller than I, but I could easily make myself quite as broad; just you see." So he blew himself out, and blew himself out, and blew himself out. "Was he as big as that?" asked he.

"Oh, much bigger than that," said the young Frog.

Again the old one blew himself out, and asked the young one if the Ox was as big as that.

"Bigger, father, bigger," was the reply.

So the Frog took a deep breath, and blew and blew and blew, and swelled and swelled and swelled. And then he said: "I'm sure the Ox is not as big as this. But at this moment he burst.

Self-conceit may lead to self-destruction.

THE FROGS AND THE WELL

Two Frogs lived together in a marsh. But one hot summer the marsh dried up, and they left it to look for another place to live in: for frogs like damp places if they can get them. By and by they came to a deep well, and one of them looked down into it, and said to the other, "This looks a nice cool place. Let us jump in and settle here." But the other, who had a wiser head on his shoulders, replied, "Not so fast, my friend. Supposing this well dried up like the marsh, how should we get out again?"

Look before you leap.

THE BOYS AND THE FROGS

Some boys, playing near a pond, saw a number of Frogs in the water and began to pelt them with stones. They killed several of them, when one of the Frogs, lifting his head out of the water, cried out: "Pray stop, my boys: what is sport to you, is death to us."

One man's pleasure may be another's pain.

Who was Aesop?

Depending on who you ask, Aesop wrote between zero and several hundred fables in his lifetime. Some say that Aesop was a Greek slave who wrote down the folk tales that were popular at the time (620-525 B.C.), not unlike the Brothers Grimm. Tradition says that his owner finally freed him, but that he died at Delphi in 565 B.C.

It's a good story, but most now believe it to be just another story, that most of "Aesop's fables" came from two writers of the second century: Greek writer Valerius Babrius who mixed oral Greek tales with Indian ones, and the ancient Roman poet Phaedrus who translated them into Latin. This explains some the Roman influences in many of the popular fables from Aesop.

The word "Aesop" itself may very well have been invented by the ancient Greeks solely to denote this sort of tale with a moral from other kinds of stories. Regardless, it should be understood that Aesop was probably as mythical as the beasts in the stories.

Potty Pourri

Random Kinds of Factness

• The stink of onion was once thought strong enough to scare off illness. Oniony folk remedies have included onion tea to stop a fever, rubbing an onion on your head if you have a headache, and mixing turpentine with fried onions to smear on your chest to choke out a cold.

• The Jolly Green Giant began his career as a scary-looking ogre wrapped in an animal skin. With the help of an artist, he was given a kinder and gentler touch that bean eaters everywhere continue to appreciate.

• The milk of a cow that's been eating onions tastes oniony.

• Larger Than Life: The Statue of Liberty is about twenty times bigger than an average American woman. From her toes to the top of her head, she measures a bit over 111 feet.

• Thank Thomas Jefferson for French fries. He brought back samples of fried potato sticks from France and dubbed them "Potatoes fried in the French manner." Americans shortened the name to "French fries."

• If you've got a new box of crayons, expect the black one to get used up first, then the red. Those are the two colors that see the most wear.

• Thomas More is the patron saint of lawyers.

• Experts claim that the common, everyday headache annually loses U.S. businesses $25 billion in productivity.

• Switzerland didn't allow women to vote until 1971.

• Luckily, his acting and inherited real estate paid well, because the most William Shakespeare earned for writing a play was £8 ($1,325 in today's money), never making more than an annual income of £20 ($3,313) from his writing.

• The father of pro golfer Lee Trevino was a grave digger.

Bad Trip

How to Drive Your Tour Guide Crazy

A story in which Mark Twain and a group of fellow travelers get tired of the sights of Europe and decide to have some sadistic fun at the expense of their tour guides.

IN THIS PLACE I may as well jot down a chapter concerning those necessary nuisances, European guides. Many a man has wished in his heart he could do without his guide; but knowing he could not, has wished he could get some amusement out of him as a remuneration for the affliction of his society. We accomplished this latter matter, and if our experience can be made useful to others they are welcome to it.

All their lives long, tour guides are employed in showing strange things to foreigners and listening to their bursts of admiration. Think, then, what a passion it becomes with a guide, whose privilege it is, every day, to show to strangers wonders that throw them into perfect ecstasies of admiration! He gets so that he could not by any possibility live in a soberer atmosphere. After we discovered this, we never went into ecstasies any more—we never admired any thing—we never showed any but impassible faces and stupid indifference in the presence of the sublimest wonders a guide had to display. We had found their weak point. We have made good use of it ever since. We have made some of those people savage, at times, but we have never lost our own serenity.

The doctor asks the questions, generally, because he can keep his countenance, and look more like an inspired idiot, and throw more imbecility into the tone of his voice than any man that lives. It comes natural to him.

The guides in Genoa are delighted to secure an American party, because Americans so much wonder before any relic of Columbus. Our guide was full of animation—full of impatience. He said: "Come wis me, genteelmen!—come! I show you ze letter writing by Christopher Colombo!—write it himself!—write it wis his own hand!—come!"

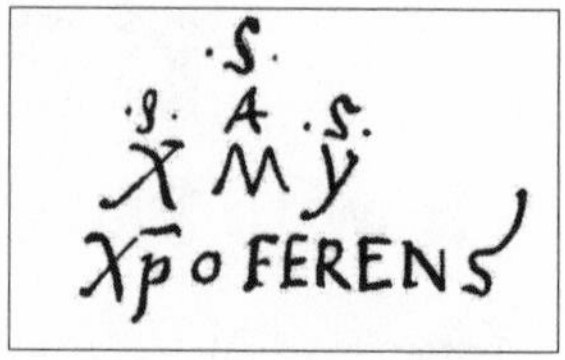

He took us to the municipal palace. After much impressive fumbling of keys and opening of locks, the stained and aged document was spread before us. The guide's eyes sparkled. He danced about us and tapped the parchment with his finger: "What I tell you, genteelmen! Is it not so? See! handwriting Christopher Colombo!—write it himself!"

We looked indifferent. The doctor examined the document very deliberately, during a painful pause. Then he said, without any show of interest: "Ah, what did you say was the name of the party who wrote this?"

"Christopher Colombo! ze great Christopher Colombo!"

Another deliberate examination. "Ah, did he write it himself; or—or how?"

"He write it himself!—Christopher Colombo! He's own handwriting, write by himself!"

The doctor laid the document down and said: "Why, I have seen boys only 14 years old who can write better than that."

"But zis is ze great Christo—"

"I don't care who it is! It's the worst writing I ever saw. Now you musn't impose on us because we are strangers. We are not fools. If you have got any specimens of penmanship of real merit, trot them out! If you haven't, drive on!"

We drove on. The guide was considerably shaken up, but he made one more venture. He had something which he thought would overcome us. He said: "Ah, genteelmen, you come wis me! I show you beautiful, O, magnificent bust Christopher Colombo!—splendid, grand, magnificent!"

He brought us before the bust—it was beautiful—and sprang back and struck an attitude: "Ah, look, genteelmen! Christopher Colombo! Beautiful bust, beautiful pedestal!"

The doctor put up his eye-glass, procured for such occasions: "Ah—what did you say this gentleman's name was?"

"Christopher Colombo!—ze great Christopher Colombo!"

"Christopher Colombo—the great Christopher Colombo. Well, what did he do?"

"Discover America!—discover America, Oh, ze devil!"

"Discover America. No—that statement will hardly wash. We are just from America ourselves. We heard nothing about it. Christopher Colombo—pleasant name—is—is he dead?"

"Oh, corpo di Baccho!—three hundred year!"

"What did he die of?"

"I do not know!—I can not tell."

"Small-pox, you think?"

"I do not know, genteelmen!—I do not know what he die of!"

"Measles, likely?"

"May be—I do not know—I think he die of somethings."

"Parents living?"

"Im-poseeeble!"

"Ah—which is the bust and which is the pedestal?"

"Santa Maria!—zis ze bust!—zis ze pedestal!"

"Ah, I see, I see. Happy combination, very happy, indeed. Is this the first time the gentleman was ever 'on a bust'?"

That joke was lost on the foreigner—guides can not master the subtleties of the American joke.

We have made it interesting for this Roman guide. Yesterday we spent four hours in the Vatican, that wonderful world of curiosities. We came very near expressing admiration—it was very hard to keep from it. We succeeded though. Nobody else ever did, in the Vatican museums. The guide was bewildered—non-plussed. He nearly walked his legs off, hunting up extraordinary things, and exhausted all his ingenuity on us, but it was a failure; we never showed any interest in any thing. He had reserved what he considered to be his greatest wonder till the last—a royal Egyptian mummy, the best preserved in the world, perhaps. He took us there. He felt so sure this time, that some of his old enthusiasm came back to him: "See, genteelmen!—Mummy! Mummy!"

The eye-glass came up as calmly, as deliberately as ever. "Ah, what did I understand you to say the gentleman's name was?"

"Name? He got no name! Mummy! 'Gyptian mummy!"

"Yes, yes. Born here?"

"No! 'Gyptian mummy!"

"Ah, just so. Frenchman, I presume?"

"No!—not Frenchman, not Roman!—born in Egypta!"

"Born in Egypta. Never heard of Egypta before. Foreign locality, likely. How calm he is, how self-possessed. Is he dead?"

"Oh, sacre bleu, been dead three thousan' year!"

The doctor turned on him savagely: "Here, now, what do you mean by such conduct as this! Playing us for fools because we are strangers and trying to learn! Trying to impose your vile second-hand carcasses on us!—thunder and lightning, I've a notion to—to—if you've got a nice fresh corpse, fetch him out!—or by George we'll brain you!"

We make it exceedingly interesting for this Frenchman. However, he has paid us back, partly, without knowing it. He came to the hotel this morning to ask if we were up, and he endeavored as well as he could to describe us, so that the landlord would know which persons he meant. He finished with the casual remark that we were lunatics. The observation was so innocent and so honest that it amounted to a very good thing for a guide to say.

There is one remark (already mentioned) which never yet has failed to disgust these guides. We use it always, when we can think of nothing else to say. After they have exhausted their enthusiasm pointing out to us and praising the beauties of some ancient bronze image or broken-legged statue, we look at it stupidly and in silence for five, ten, fifteen minutes—as long as we can hold out, in fact—and then ask:

"Is—is he dead?" That conquers the serenest of them. It is not what they are looking for—especially a new guide. Our Roman guide is the most patient, unsuspecting, long-suffering subject we have had yet. We shall be sorry to part with him. We have enjoyed his society very much. We trust he has enjoyed ours, but we are harassed with doubts.

Cat Lovers

From the Ailurophiles

An ailurophile is someone very fond of cats. Here are a few examples from the book *Cats Don't Always Land on Their Feet* by Erin Barrett and Jack Mingo.

• Mohammed the prophet had a cat named Meuzza who, like most cats, had a favorite sleeping spot—on Mohammed's robe. It's said that one day Mohammed was trying to dress quickly to get to an urgent task, so simply he cut the sleeve off his robe rather than disturb Meuzza, who was sleeping peacefully on it. Lucky kitty.

• *"With the qualities of cleanliness, affection, patience, dignity, and courage that cats have, how many of us, I ask you, would be capable of becoming cats?"* —Fernand Mery

• Charles I, the King of England from 1600 to 1649, got the idea that if he lost his beloved black cat, disaster would befall him, so he had the cat guarded constantly. Unfortunately, the cat got sick and died. Strangely enough, Charles had been right—the day after, Charles was arrested for treason, and, a few days later, beheaded.

• Never give up: The February 1, 1991, edition of the *Albuquerque Journal* ran this classified ad: "Lost since March 1983, tortoise shell female cat, reward."

• The Pennsylvania Dutch have a tradition that harks back to an ancient belief in Europe: If you place a cat on a cradle in a new married couple's home, the couple will be blessed soon with children.

• *"I gave my cat a bath the other day. They love it. He just sat there; he enjoyed it, it was fun for me. Sure, the fur would stick to my tongue, but other than that...."* —Steve Martin

• The Ernest Hemingway house and museum on Key West still hosts a population of about sixty cats, half of which are polydactyls, or six-toed, felines. Hemingway was given a polydactyl by an old sea captain and many of the current cat population are descendants of this original.

• Actor Billy Crystal swears his cat, Mittens, likes "fishing and computer programming."

• Winston Churchill would refuse to eat until his cat, Jock, was also at the table. He called the beloved cat his "special assistant." Jock was reportedly resting alongside Churchill in his bed when the ill statesman died.

• Martha Stewart named her cats Mozart, Beethoven, Verdi, Vivaldi, Teeney, and Weeney.

• In her lifetime, life saver Florence Nightingale had more than sixty cat companions. She named most of her cats after famous men of her day. Some examples are cute little Disraeli, petulant Bismarck, and fuzzy Gladstone.

• Researchers say that stroking a cat reduces heart rate and blood pressure. (In the human, that is.)

• John F. Kennedy's daughter, Caroline, had a pet kitty during her stay in the White House. Its name was Tom Kitten. Tom was the first cat in the White House since Theodore Roosevelt's cat, Slippers.

• Amy Carter had a male Siamese named, of all things, Misty Malarky Ying Yang.

• King Henry I was tough on kitty killers. In ninth-century England he declared the penalty for ending a cat's life would be a whopping sixty bushels of corn.

• Sir Isaac Newton, while taking a break from his laws-of-gravity tests, invented the first cat door for his kitty, Spithead.

• Confucius, Chinese philosopher extraordinaire, believed his cat was sent to him from the heavens to impart inspired wisdom. Cats are good for that, you know.

• *"Be suspicious of anyone whose clothes are immaculate and completely free of cat hairs. It means they either don't like cats or don't hug the ones they have."* —Leigh W. Rutledge

From Lady to Cowboy

The Marlboro Man Gets a Sex Change

From "mild as May" cigarette aimed at addicting women, Marlboro switched to macho themes to reassure men that filters weren't "unmanly." Here's a case study of how well people can be manipulated by the right images.

DID YOU KNOW that the idealized Marlboro smoker, now personified by rugged cowboys, was once a sophisticated woman? But it wasn't that the cowboys were transsexuals—it was the cigarettes.

Marlboro was born in 1924 as one of the first women's cigarette. In the decades before this, the idea of marketing cigarettes to women was more taboo than marketing them to twelve-year-olds is today (ask cartoony Joe Camel about the sticky problems with that one). But with the Suffragettes and the "Anything Goes" 1920s, women decided that there was no reason they couldn't develop the same filthy habits that men had (the health issues, although known to researchers, were not yet part of public consciousness).

Still, it was a tricky sell. Advertisers had to somehow convince women that stained teeth, foul breath, addictive cravings, and that dry, heaving morning cough were somehow genteel and ladylike. Philip Morris decided that their brand needed to have a classy, sophisticated name. Winston Churchill was in the news at the time, and it was being reported that he was related to the Earl of Marlborough. The marketers liked the sound of the Marlborough name, but didn't think it looked good on the pack. They lopped off the "ugh" and came up with "Marlboro."

In the 1920s, the Marlboro campaign was based around how "ladylike" the new cigarette was. The company printed a red band around the filter to hide those unattractive lipstick stains, calling them "Beauty Tips to Keep the Paper from Your Lips." They called Marlboro the "Mild as May" cigarette and added a tone of snobbishness: "Discerning feminine taste is now confirming the judgment of masculine connoisseurs in expressing unanimous preference for the Aristocrat of Cigarettes...." Marlboros developed a small following—enough to keep it alive, but not enough to be called a great success.

THE SWITCH

Two decades later, Philip Morris decided to "reposition" the brand to fit a new market niche—men who were afraid of lung cancer but who thought it unmanly to admit it. Here's what happened: In the early 1950s, scientists published a major, well-publicized study linking smoking to lung cancer. This was the "smoking gun" that the cigarette companies had been dreading for years. In 1953, for the first time ever, cigarette consumption dipped in the United States.

The cigarette companies moved fast. Then, like now, they pursued a contradictory strategy: claiming that the studies were "inconclusive" on cigarette safety, while simultaneously implying that their brands were somehow "safer" than other brands.

Unfiltered cigarettes suffered the biggest sales drop. Filtered cigarettes were perceived by smokers as "safer," but up to that point they had always been marketed to women. Men told marketers that they'd consider switching to a filtered brand, but were afraid they'd be subjected to ridicule if they smoked a "woman's cigarette."

Cigarette manufacturers had long resisted pushing filter cigarettes to men because filters implied that smoke was unpleasant or dangerous. Now, though, they started seeing some silver lining in doing so. Filtered cigarettes were more profitable because the filter material was cheaper than a comparable amount of tobacco. Besides, since filters screened out some of the smoke's harshness, manufacturers could use a cheaper grade of tobacco.

Philip Morris decided to give Marlboro a sex change

operation. The company hired Chicago advertising executive Leo Burnett to do the surgery.

Burnett's specialty was cute advertising characters like the Jolly Green Giant, the Keebler Elves, the lonely Maytag Repairman, Charlie the Tuna, Poppin' Fresh, and Morris the Cat. To defeminize Marlboros, he decided to use a series of the most testosterone-laced images he could think of.

He intended to present a lineup of muscled, sweaty sea captains, weight lifters, adventurers, war correspondents, construction workers, Marines, and the like. The cowboy was to be the first image of the series.

Philip Morris wasn't sure about the campaign. The company hired a research company that came back with the alarming report that there were only 3,000 full-time cowboys in the entire United States. How do you expect men working in a downtown office building to relate to an image like that? Burnett had to do some fast talking, but he eventually convinced the company to try the cowboy.

The campaign worked. In one year, Marlboro zoomed from a marginal presence with less than one percent of the market to the fourth best-selling brand. The company decided to forget the sea captains and soldiers and stick with cowboys.

MODEL COWBOYS

Burnett's first set of "cowboys" were professional models, some of whom had never been on a horse before. That led to a series of embarrassing gaffes that left cowpokes-in-the-know snickering. For example, an ad showed a cowboy's legs in close-up: his blue jeans were well worn, his hand-tooled boots were scuffed in all the right places ... but he had his spurs upside-down. After that, the agency started recruiting real cowboys from Texas and Montana for their ads.

In 1955, the agency added a trademark tattoo to their cowboy's hand. One model mused after a photo shoot that they had spent three minutes making up his face—and three hours painting the tattoo. In 1962, Burnett's agency bought the rights to *The Magnificent Seven* theme and added words ("Come to

where the flavor is, come to Marlboro Country").

The Marlboro Man has been one of the most successful advertising campaigns ever, keeping the cigarette at or near the top of the heap for years. When cigarette ads were banned from television in 1971, the cowboy made a smooth transition to print and billboards, since he never said anything anyway. He continued squinting off into the distance with that self-absorbed expression that addicts have when contemplating their next fix.

Everyone seems to love the cowboy. The image works as well at convincing women to smoke Marlboros as it does men. It also works well with blacks and Hispanics. (That's ironic, since even though many real cowboys were and are black or Hispanic, all the Marlboro Men have been Caucasian.) Best of all for the company (which has to replace all those dying customers), the cowboy has worked as a role model for kids and teens as well, making Marlboro the number one starter brand.

The popularity of the cowboy image has led to anti-smoking parodies as well. In France, Philip Morris sued an anti-smoking group that used a cowboy model to deliver an anti-smoking message, claiming trademark infringement. PM won a pyrrhic victory—a judgment of 1 franc instead of the $3 million they had asked for—but at least the company got the ads off the air.

The real cowboy models, meanwhile, periodically embarrass the company by dying like desperadoes from smoking-related diseases like lung cancer, emphysema, and strokes.

A Little Yiddish Quiz

Kiss or Curse?

The Yiddish words below are either a compliment or an insult. Circle the nature of the meaning of each word.

1. Mensch	Kiss	Curse
2. Chazzer	Kiss	Curse
3. Chamoole	Kiss	Curse
4. Meiskeit	Kiss	Curse
5. Schmoe	Kiss	Curse
6. Haimish ponem	Kiss	Curse
7. Berye'h	Kiss	Curse
8. G'vir	Kiss	Curse
9. Noodge	Kiss	Curse
10. Shiker	Kiss	Curse
11. Maiven	Kiss	Curse
12. Zhlub	Kiss	Curse
13. Yente	Kiss	Curse
14. Chavver	Kiss	Curse
15. Shlump	Kiss	Curse

Answers: *1. Kiss: A nice guy; 2. Curse: A pig; 3. Curse: A jackass; 4. Curse: Ugly person; 5. Curse: A naive or goofy person; 6. Kiss: A friendly face; 7. Kiss: A good and competent housewife; 8. Kiss: A rich man; 9. Curse: A pest; 10. Curse: A drunk; 11. Kiss: An expert or connoisseur; 12. Curse: A crude person; 13. Curse: A gossip; 14. Kiss: A friend; 15. Curse: A slob.*

Another Little Yiddish Quiz

Are You a Mensch or a Schmoe?

Can you tell which of these is an insult and which is a traditional Yiddish greeting? Match the phrase to its definition.

1. Mazel tov!	"Drop dead."
2. Kush meer in toches.	"Bless you."
3. Vee geyts?	"Hello, peace be with you."
4. Zay gezunt!	"Kiss my tushy."
5. Farshtinkener!	"Have a lousy life."
6. A shvarts yor!	"You rotten, stinky person!"
7. Sholem aleycham.	"How's it going?"
8. Ver derharget.	"Congratulations!"
9. A broch tsu dayn lebn.	"You deserve a lousy year!"
10. Le' chaim!	"To life!"

Answers: 1. *Mazel tov!*("Congratulations!"); 2. *Kush meer in toches.* ("Kiss my tushy."); 3. *Vee geyts?* ("How's it going?"); 4. *Zay gezunt!* ("Bless you."); 5. *Farshtinkener!* ("You rotten, stinky person!"); 6. *A shvarts yor!* ("You deserve a lousy year!"); 7. *Sholem aleycham.* ("Hello, peace be with you."); 8. *Ver derharget.* ("Drop dead."); 9. *A broch tsu dayn lebn.* ("Have a lousy life."); 10. *Le' chaim!* ("To life!")

More Fables & Foibles

Odd Little Stories from R. L. Stevenson

You probably know Robert Louis Stevenson for books like *Treasure Island* and *Dr. Jekyll and Mr. Hyde*. But he also wrote a series of "fables" with a dark take on humanity and its foibles.

THE TADPOLE AND THE FROG

"Be ashamed of yourself," said the frog. "When I was a tadpole, I had no tail."

"Just what I thought!" said the tadpole. "You never were a tadpole."

THE PENITENT

A man met a lad weeping. "What do you weep for?" he asked.

"I am weeping for my sins," said the lad.

"You must have little to do," said the man.

The next day they met again. Once more the lad was weeping. "Why do you weep now?" asked the man.

"I am weeping because I have nothing to eat," said the lad.

"I thought it would come to that," said the man.

THE YELLOW PAINT

In a certain city there lived a physician who sold yellow paint. Those bedaubed with it from head to heel were set free from the dangers of life, and the bondage of sin, and the fear of death forever. So the physician said in his prospectus; and so said all the citizens in the city; who took care to be properly painted themselves, and took delight in seeing others painted.

There was in the same city a young man of a somewhat reckless life, who had reached the age of manhood, and would have nothing to do with the paint: "Tomorrow was soon enough," said he; and when the morrow came he would still put it off.

He might have continued to do until his death; only, he had a friend who, taking a walk with not one fleck of paint upon his body, was suddenly run down by a water-cart and cut off in his heyday. This shook the young man to the soul; and on the very same evening, in the presence of all his family, to appropriate music, and himself weeping aloud, he received three complete coats of paint and a touch of varnish on the top. The physician (who was himself affected even to tears) protested he had never done a job so thorough.

Some two months afterwards, the young man was carried on a stretcher to the physician's house.

"What is the meaning of this?" he cried, as soon as the door was opened. "I was to be set free from all the dangers of life; and here have I been run down by that self-same water-cart, and my leg is broken."

"Dear me!" said the physician. "This is very sad. But I must explain to you the action of my paint. A broken bone belongs to a class of accident to which my paint is quite inapplicable. It is against sin that I have fitted you out; and when you come to be tempted, you will give me news of my paint."

"Oh!" said the young man, "I did not understand that, and it seems rather disappointing. But I have no doubt all is for the best; and in the meanwhile, I shall be obliged to you if you will set my leg."

"That is none of my business," said the physician; "but if your bearers will carry you round the corner to the surgeon's, I feel sure he will afford relief."

Some three years later, the young man came running to the physician's house in a great perturbation. "What is the meaning of this?" he cried. "Here was I to be set free from the bondage of sin; and I have just committed forgery, arson, and murder."

"Dear me," said the physician. "This is very serious. Off with your clothes at once." And as soon as the young man had stripped, he examined him from head to foot. "No," he cried with great relief, "there is not a flake broken. Cheer up, my young friend, your paint is as good as new."

"Good God!" cried the young man, "and what then can be the use of it?"

"Why," said the physician, "My paint does not exactly prevent sin; it extenuates instead the painful consequences. It is not so much for this world, as for the next; it is not against life; in short, it is against death that I have fitted you out. And when you come to die, you will give me news of my paint."

"Oh!" cried the young man, "I had not understood that, and it seems a little disappointing. But there is no doubt all is for the best; and in the meanwhile, I shall be obliged if you will help me to undo the evil I have brought on innocent persons."

"That is none of my business," said the physician; "but if you will go round the corner to the police office, I feel sure it will afford you relief to give yourself up."

Six weeks later, the physician was called to the town jail.

"What is the meaning of this?" cried the young man. "Here am I literally crusted with your paint; and I have broken my leg, and committed all the crimes in the calendar, and must be hanged tomorrow; and am in the meanwhile in a fear so extreme that I lack words to picture it."

"Dear me," said the physician. "This is really amazing. Well, well; perhaps, if you had not been painted, you would have been more frightened still."

THE FOUR REFORMERS

Four reformers met under a bramble bush. They all agreed the world must change. "We must abolish property," said one.

"We must abolish marriage," said the second.

"We must abolish God," said the third.

"I wish we could abolish work," said the fourth.

"Do not let us get beyond practical politics," said the first. "The first thing is to reduce men to a common level."

"The first thing," said the second, "is to give freedom to the sexes."

"The first thing," said the third, "is to find out how to do it."

"The first step," said the first, "is to abolish the Bible."

"The first thing," said the second, "is to abolish the laws."

"The first thing," said the third, "is to abolish mankind."

Flornithology 4

How to Tell the Birds from the Flowers

We bring you more of the field guide by Robert Williams Wood (1868–1955) for those who may have trouble seeing the difference.

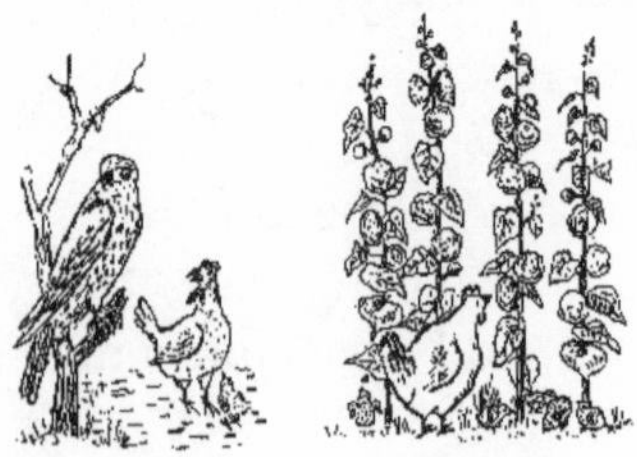

The Hawk — The Hollyhock

The Hen — The Lichen

The Butterball — The Buttercup

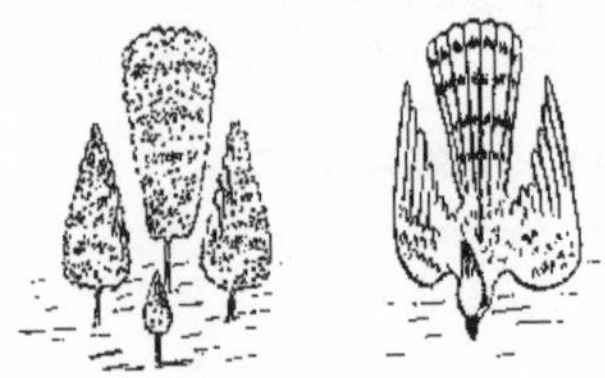

The Bay — The Jay

The Lark — The Larkspur

Puffin — Nuffin

Family Feud

THE KELLOGG BROTHERS' FLAKY CEREAL WAR

"John Harvey Kellogg and W. K. Kellogg were like two fellows trying to climb up the same ladder at the same time," observed a man who knew them both. Like Jacob and Esau or Cain and Abel, it's a classic tale of a long-suffering younger brother conniving against his overbearing older brother.

YEAST-FREE DIETS? Megavitamins? Colon cleansing? If you think today's food faddists are eccentric, you should have been around during the last half of the 19th century. There were hundreds of health regimens, some sensible, some just plain crazy. It was from those roots that Kellogg's cereals grew and thrived.

One popular health guru of the time was Sylvester Graham, who inspired the whole wheat flour and cracker that still bear his name. He had a fanatical belief in the benefits of fresh air exercise in all weather, whole grain foods, and complete sexual abstinence to retain "vital bodily fluids." He believed that whole grains with bland flavorings suppressed sexual desire and that meat, salt, and spices are dangerous aphrodisiacs.

One of Graham's disciples was Ellen Harmon White, founder and head prophet of the Seventh Day Adventist Church. In 1855, she convinced her New England congregation to emigrate to western Michigan, where she established the world headquarters of her apocalyptic religious movement, and wrote books about diet and the evils of sex. Eleven years later, she decided to build the Western Health Reform Institute, a health spa to give the world a taste of her medicine.

Dr. John Harvey Kellogg, the older brother

ENTER THE FAMILY KELLOGG

John Harvey Kellogg's was two years old in 1852 when his family traveled to Michigan with the Adventists. Eight years later, William Keith Kellogg was born. The two brothers, it turned out, were as different as could be: John was the golden boy who could do little wrong in his parents' eyes, while Will could do little right. While John was sent off to school, his parents figured a formal education for Will would be wasted since the Lord's apocalypse was still just around the corner. Besides, nearly everyone thought him a little dimwitted. (Actually, he was just nearsighted, but his health-faddist parents decided that a regimen of food and water cures would do more good than eyeglasses.) Will stayed home and worked in his father's broom factory.

DOCTOR AND CLERK

After graduating, John Harvey Kellogg became a school teacher in Ypsilanti, sixty miles away. Sister Ellen White offered to pay his tuition to Dr. Russell Trall's Hygeio-Therapeutic College in Florence Heights, New Jersey. A few years later, in 1876, the 24-year-old "Dr." Kellogg returned to Michigan to become the superintendent of the sanitarium. In a case of nepotism that he would live to regret, he hired his brother, Will, as his much put-upon chief clerk.

William would become embittered over the years as older brother John bullied him, took him for granted, and tried to hog full credit for mutual discoveries. Years later, Will would bite back.

Like White, John Kellogg was a believer in health food and complete sexual abstinence. He spent his honeymoon writing *Plain Facts for Old and Young,* a tract warning against the evils of sex. "Its effects upon the undeveloped person is to retard growth," he wrote, "weaken the constitution, and dwarf the intellect." Not surprisingly, Kellogg's marriage was apparently never consummated, which he believed made his wife very grateful. He wrote, "I should say that the majority of women, happily for them and for society, are not very much troubled with sexual feelings of any kind."

To suppress his patients' sexual desire, he used zwieback until a patient broke her dentures on it and demanded $10 to fix them. This prompted the notoriously tight-fisted doctor to begin looking for an alternative.

THE DREAM OF A FLAKE

John and Will decided a cold cereal would be the best thing. In 1885, John claimed that a dream showed him a way to make cereals into light and crispy flakes. Divinely inspired or not, his first attempts were failures. The brothers tried soaking wheat kernels and forcing them between steel rollers. The kernels were not flat enough for their purposes, so they began boiling them for longer and longer periods, trying to soften them enough to make an easily chewed flake. But even that didn't do the trick.

Will Keith Kellogg, the younger brother

One night while they were boiling a batch, an emergency came up, so they left the kernels soaking and didn't come back to them for a day or two. By the time they returned, the kernels had grown moldy, but they decided to run them

The Battle Creek Sanitarium in its heyday

through the rollers anyway. It turned out that the extra time of soaking was just what the doctor ordered, resulting in very thin flakes that toasted up nicely, each individual kernel becoming a well-formed, albeit moldy, flake. After experimentation, they discovered that soaking the wheat in a tin container suppressed much of the moldiness, so they began rolling out wheat flakes.

John had intended to grind the flakes into a powder, but Will convinced him to keep the flakes whole instead. Unfortunately it didn't make much difference, since no one wanted to eat them. The unflavored wheat flakes tasted like sawdust.

Finally, in 1902, the brothers discovered that corn flakes tasted better than wheat flakes, especially when flavored with barley malt. Realizing that the flakes had commercial possibilities, the brothers set up their own private corporation, the Battle Creek Toasted Cornflake Company.

CEREAL DRAMAS

In their first year, the brothers sold 100,000 pounds of the new breakfast cereal. With success, however, they ran into problems. First of all, Sister White was furious that the Kellogg brothers had desecrated her divine institution with commercialism—and that she wasn't even getting a cut. Also, competitors and imitators began jumping onto the bandwagon (the company later changed its name to Kellogg's to distinguish it from its imitators).

Worst of all for the brothers' partnership, William Kellogg started adding sugar to the flakes to make them more palatable. When John Kellogg found out, he was livid. He believed that sugar would reverse the cereal's sex-suppressing effects. Will countered that sugar was necessary if they wanted people to eat the stuff.

Matters quickly worsened between the two brothers, culminating in a series of lawsuits over who owned the rights to the process and even the Kellogg's name. William eventually won the lawsuits and took full control of the Kellogg's Corn Flake Company, with Dr. John retaining shares. It became a huge success, in large part because of William's innovative advertising, promotion, giveaways, and sponsorships. One ad, considered positively risqué at the time, told women to wink at their grocers and see what they got (in most cases, by pre-arrangement with the company, a free sample box of Corn Flakes). The company also aimed advertising directly toward children, knowing that they had a disproportionate power over cereal purchases in a household.

THE END COMES

Will and John each separately lived to be ninety-one, but they after all the lawsuits were over, they met only a few times for quick business. John continued to preach his gospel, even after medical findings soundly disproved most of his theories. Not surprisingly, he and his wife Ellen had no children, but they adopted and fostered forty-two children over the years. In later years, his wife became a virtual recluse and Dr. Kellogg took to strolling the hospital grounds in white clothes, carrying a white cockatoo on his shoulder.

Shortly before John died in 1943, he sent a message of brotherly reconciliation to Will. Will's staff, however, withheld the message from him, figuring it would just stir up trouble. Someone finally told him about it in 1951 while he was on his own deathbed. "My God," he reportedly cried out, "why didn't anybody tell me before this?"

Every Picture Tells a Story

American Gothic **by Grant Wood**

• Grant Wood studied art in Europe before returning to Iowa to paint his friends and neighbors. *American Gothic* is a sly mixture of the two influences: the farm couple is portrayed in the naturalistic Gothic style of fifteenth-century Flemish and German art, in front of a house with Gothic windows.

• Built in an 1880s style called Carpenter Gothic, the house—which still exists—inspired the idea of the painting. Wood recognized the similarity to its European counterparts and visualized the Gothic-like painting. He quickly sketched his idea on scrap paper and had a friend take a photo of the house so he could use it in the studio.

• Wood, painting in 1930, wanted a timeless feel, so he researched nineteenth-century clothes before bringing in his models: his sister and his dentist. Each posed in separate sittings.

• Is this mean to portray a couple, or a farmer guarding his daughter from the world? No one knows for sure, but her faraway gaze and a loose strand of hair imply he's already lost her.

• The painting was controversial. Some locals, especially farm women, believed that Wood was mocking them.

The War Prayer

Mark Twain's Take on Religion & Patriotism

Mark Twain wrote "The War Prayer" during the Philippine-American War and couldn't get it published then. Unfortunately, it's still timely.

IT WAS A TIME of great and exalting excitement. The country was up in arms, the war was on, in every breast burned the holy fire of patriotism;

The drums were beating, the bands playing, the toy pistols popping, the bunched firecrackers hissing and spluttering;

On every hand and far down the receding and fading spread of roofs and balconies fluttering flags flashed in the sun;

Daily the young volunteers marched down the wide avenue gay and fine in their new uniforms, the proud fathers and mothers and sisters and sweethearts cheering them with voices choked with happy emotion as they swung by;

Nightly the packed mass meetings listened, panting, to patriot oratory which stirred the deepest deeps of their hearts and which they interrupted at briefest intervals with cyclones of applause, the tears running down their cheeks the while;

In the churches the pastors preached devotion to flag and country and invoked the God of Battles, beseeching His aid in

The Philippine-American War

What was the Philippine-American War about? After fighting the Spanish for Cuba and other colonies America wanted, Spain gave up and sold the Philippines for $20 million. The Filipinos who had helped fight believed they'd been promised independence, but the United States decided it wanted to keep the colony. After defeating the the Filipinos, America set up a colonial government, and American businesses bought up much of the country.

our good cause in outpouring of fervid eloquence which moved every listener.

It was indeed a glad and gracious time, and the half-dozen rash spirits that ventured to disapprove of the war and cast a doubt upon its righteousness straightway got such a stern and angry warning that for their personal safety's sake they quickly shrank out of sight and offended no more in that way.

Sunday morning came—next day the battalions would leave for the front; the church was filled;

The volunteers were there, their young faces alight with martial dreams—visions of the stern advance, the rushing charge, the flashing sabers, the flight of the foe, the tumult, the smoke, the fierce pursuit, the surrender!—then home from the war, bronzed heroes, welcomed, adored, submerged in glory!

With the volunteers sat their dear ones, proud, happy, and envied by the neighbors and friends who had no sons and brothers to send forth to the field of honor, there to win for the flag or failing, die the noblest of noble deaths. The service proceeded; a war chapter from the Old Testament was read; the first prayer was said; it was followed by an organ burst that shook the building, and with one impulse the house rose, with glowing eyes and beating hearts, and poured out that tremendous invocation—

"God the all-terrible! Thou who ordainest, Thunder thy clarion and Lightning thy sword!"

Then came the "long" prayer: that an ever-merciful and benig-

On Publishing "War Prayer"

To Dan Beard, who dropped in to see him, Clemens read the "War Prayer," stating that he had read it to his daughter, Jean, and others, who had told him he must not print it, for it would be regarded as sacrilege. He submitted it to his publisher, who rejected it as unsuitable for the times.

"Still, you are going to publish it, are you not?"

Clemens, pacing up and down the room in his dressing-gown and slippers, shook his head. "No," he said, "I have told the whole truth in that, and only dead men can tell the truth in this world."

"It can be published after I am dead."

—*Mark Twain, A Biography* by Albert Bigelow Paine, Harper & Brothers, 1912

nant Father would watch over our noble young soldiers and aid, comfort, and encourage them in their patriotic work; bless them, shield them in the day of battle, bear them in His mighty hand, make them strong and confident, invincible in the bloody onset; help them to crush the foe, grant to them and to their flag and country imperishable honor and glory—

An aged stranger entered and moved with slow and noiseless step up the main aisle, his eyes fixed upon the minister, his long body clothed in a robe that reached to his feet, his head bare, his white hair descending in a frothy cataract to his shoulders, his seamy face unnaturally pale. With all eyes following him and wondering, he made his silent way; without pausing, he ascended to the preacher's side and stood there, waiting. With shut lids the preacher, unconscious of his presence, continued his moving prayer, and at last finished it with the words, uttered in fervent appeal,

"Bless our arms, grant us the victory, O Lord our God, Father and Protector Of our land and flag!"

The stranger touched his arm, motioned him to step aside—which the startled minister did. During some moments he surveyed the spellbound audience with solemn eyes in which burned an uncanny light; then in a deep voice he said:

"I come from the Throne, bearing a message from Almighty God!" The words smote the house with a shock; if the stranger perceived it he gave no attention. "He has heard the prayer of His servant and will grant it if such shall be your desire after I, His messenger, shall have explained to you its full import. For it is like many of the prayers of men, in that it asks for more than he who utters it is aware of.

"God's servant and yours has prayed his prayer. Is it one prayer? No, it is two—one uttered, the other not. Both have reached the ear of Him Who heareth all supplications, the spoken and the unspoken. Ponder this—keep it in mind. If you would ask a blessing upon yourself, beware, lest without intent you invoke a curse upon a neighbor at the same time. If you pray for the blessing of rain upon your crop which needs it, by that act you are possibly praying for a curse upon some neighbor's crop which may not need rain and can be injured by it.

"You have heard your servant's prayer—the uttered part of it. I am commissioned by God to put into words the other part of it—that part which the pastor, and also in your hearts, fervently prayed silently. And ignorantly and unthinkingly? God grant that it was so! You heard these words: 'Grant us the victory, O Lord our God!' That is sufficient. The whole of the uttered prayer is compact into those pregnant words. When you have prayed for victory you have prayed for many unmentioned results which follow victory—must follow it, cannot help but follow it. God the Father commandeth me to put the unspoken part of the prayer into words. LISTEN!

"O Lord our Father, our young patriots, idols of our hearts, go forth to battle—be Thou near them! With them, in spirit, we also go forth from the sweet peace of our beloved firesides to smite the foe. O Lord our God, help us to tear their soldiers to bloody shreds with our shells; help us to cover their smiling fields with the pale forms of their patriot dead; help us to drown the thunder of the guns with the shrieks of their wounded writhing in pain; help us to lay waste their humble homes with a hurricane of fire; help us to wring the hearts of their unoffending widows with unavailing grief; help us to turn them out roofless with their little children to wander unfriended the wastes of their desolated land in rags and hunger and thirst, broken in spirit, worn with

travail, imploring Thee for the refuge of the grave and denied it—for our sakes who adore Thee, Lord, blast their hopes, blight their lives, protract their bitter pilgrimage, make heavy their steps, water their way with their tears, stain the white snow with the blood of their wounded feet! We ask it, in the spirit of love, of Him Who is the Source of Love, and Who is the ever-faithful refuge and friend of all that are sore beset and seek His aid with humble and contrite hearts. Amen."

After a pause:

"Ye have prayed it; if ye still desire it, speak! The messenger of the Most High waits."

It was believed afterward that the man was a lunatic, because there was no sense in what he said.

Bathrooms through History

• In 1596, Queen Elizabeth I allowed her godson, Sir John Harrington, to install a flush toilet of his own invention in her living quarters. She lived to regret it when he published a small promotional booklet about it, making the queen's toilet the butt of many popular jokes.

• In 1775, Alexander Cumming improved Harrington's design by adding a "stink trap" to keep the sewer smells out of the house. Still, it would take another century before the toilet replaced the chamber pot and became a popular fixture in the house.

• In 1825, John Quincy Adams installed the first toilet in the White House, leading to much commentary, many jokes, and the adoption of "Quincy" as a slang word for toilet.

• In 1857, Joseph Gayetty invented the first packaged toilet paper—a packet of individual sheets—but the product sold poorly and Gayetty quickly discontinued it.

• For centuries, bathing was considered unnecessary, unhealthful, and even immoral. English diarist Samuel Pepys (1633–1703) noted with surprise that his wife had taken one bath in her life and was considering taking another!

• Benjamin Franklin started a lonely campaign to convince people that there were benefits to bathing. By the 1830s, the tradition of a once-a-week Saturday night bath started taking hold. By 1865, Vassar College required that all of its students bathe twice a week.

• By the 1880s, about 15 percent of all city dwellers in America had an indoor bathroom of one sort or another.

Foodonyms

A Toast to Drink Names

What the heck is the Maxwell House, and why is Mary bloody? Here are some drink name origins that quenched our thirst for knowledge. Drink up!

Maxwell House: Joel Cheek, the grocer who invented this smooth blend of coffee in 1886, named it after a popular Nashville hotel. The Maxwell House was one of Cheek's big clients of the day.

Tom Collins: This drink's origin isn't exactly clear. Britain, the U.S., and Australia all lay claim to the bartender—one Tom Collins—who invented it sometime in the 1800s.

Bloody Mary: Named for Queen Mary I who ruled England from 1553 to 1558. Her violent repression of Protestants earned her the nickname "Bloody Mary."

Gimlet: Sir T. O. Gimlette, a British naval surgeon, developed this lime and gin drink in 1890 as a health beverage.

Grog: In 1749, British admiral Edward "Old Grog" Vernon ordered his sailors to drink rum and water daily to prevent scurvy. (It didn't.)

Martini: The martini is a variation of an earlier, sweeter drink named the Martinez after a mysterious stranger from Martinez, California, who ordered one in San Francisco's Occidental Hotel bar in the early 1860s.

Gibson: This martini variation is most likely named after the illustrator Charles Dana Gibson (creator of the "Gibson Girl"). He liked his martinis extra dry with an onion.

Rob Roy: This drink is named "Rob Roy" after the Scottish version of Robin Hood, since the Rob Roy is simply a Manhattan made with Scotch whiskey.

Tom & Jerry: Named after Jerry Hawthorne and his pal Tom, characters from an 1821 book by British sportswriter Pierce Egan. The two buddies liked to drink this mix of hot milk, egg, rum, and brandy.

Zen of the Clay Boy

The Mystical (But True) Origin of Gumby

He has a strange bump on his head, googly red eyes, and green skin. He's not just a cartoon character, but also a Zen Buddhist spiritual master. He's Gumby.

In 1953, Art Clokey, a former seminary student, started playing with a movie camera and colorful plasticine clay. He laboriously made a four minute animated art film he called *Gumbasia* in honor of Disney's *Fantasia* which featured geometric shapes rolling and dancing to a jazz score. "Suddenly I saw a kinetic force at work, what I call the Phi Phenomenon, which is an impact on the nervous system brought about by images and the way they're edited," says Clokey.

Sam Engel was a film producer at 20th Century-Fox who had a teenage son that Clokey was tutoring in English and Latin. When Clokey showed him *Gumbasia*, Engel said, "That's the most fantastic thing I've ever seen!" and asked if Clokey could come up with some kid films for the emerging medium of TV.

FEATS OF CLAY

He went home and started experimenting immediately, molding hundreds of shapes in different colors. He found that clay characters didn't last very long under constant handling or the heat of movie lights. Clokey came up with a simple character that could be cut out of clay with a homemade cookie cutter and be replaced every few hours.

He made his clay character with a protrusion on one side of his head, modeled after a photo he had of his father as a teenager with a huge cow-lick hair lump. His friend, American Zen philosopher, Alan Watt, suggested that it was the "bump of wisdom that the Buddhists have." In that spirit, Clokey made the new character green with a touch of blue to suggest a field of grass under a blue sky. To provide *yin* for his character's *yang*, he created a down-to-earth horse sidekick colored an earthy orange-brown.

CHARACTERS UP THE YIN-YANG

Remembering that his father used to call the sticky, muddy clay around their farm in Michigan "gumbo," the Latin teacher in Clokey knew that the diminutive of *gumbo* would be *gumby*. "That was the first and last significant use I made of my seven years of Latin in school," he observed later. Based on Watts's observation that there are two kinds of people in the world, the prickly and the gooey, Clokey created two more characters, a dinosaur named Prickle and a tear-drop-shaped "what's-it" named Goo. Finally, for Gumby and sidekick Pokey, Clokey created a miniature hangout called the Zen Cafe.

Each character was moved a fraction of a millimeter per frame, again and again, 24 times for each second of cartoon. The series began as standalone, six-minute Gumby episodes, but they were eventually picked up by NBC to be shown during *The Howdy Doody Show*. Gumby proved so popular there he was spun off into his own show, which was hosted by comedian Pinky Lee.

WHERE'S THE MONEY?

Gumby started generating a lot of money. The problem was that Clokey wasn't getting much of it. He was paid a straight salary of $200 a week to write and produce the Gumby episodes. (That went up to $350 a week shortly before *The Gumby Show* was canceled in 1957.)

For eight years he refused to license the Gumby image for merchandising. "I was a very idealistic person," he says, "and I didn't want to exploit children." That attitude changed after Gumby's show left NBC and Clokey bought all rights back from the network. His Prema (Sanskrit for "universal love") Toy Corporation started manufacturing Gumby dolls and toys in 1964, the year that Gumby found new life in syndication and Clokey started getting rich.

THE SOUND OF ONE MAN FLOPPING

Not long afterward, however, Clokely's personal life fell apart, and so did his fortune. He went through a painful and expensive divorce with his wife of eighteen years in 1966, about the time that TV stations began dropping Gumby in favor of newer and slicker kid shows. Clokey invested his last dollars in a new venture—a flexy-faced doll called Moody Rudy—that bombed. His house went into foreclosure. In 1974, his daughter died in a car crash. Clokey went into heavy therapy and began "looking at various gurus" before adopting the teachings of Indian Swami Muktananda.

DEATH & REBIRTH

Clokey remarried in 1976, and three years later, he and his new wife Gloria traveled to Bangalore, India to visit a guru named Sathya Sai Baba, who supposedly had amazing magical powers. For some reason, Clokey brought a Gumby doll along to their audience with the guru. "I stood there with Gumby and he did this circular motion with his arms," Clokey says. "Out of nowhere he materialized this sacred ash. He plopped it right on top of Gumby. When we came home again, things started to happen." Gumby toy sales began to pick up, and then Eddie Murphy started doing a continuing Gumby skit on *Saturday Night Live.* The phone started ringing, and Gumby became hip again. Clokey received an $8 million contract with Lorimar for a new Gumby series. He started work on *Gumby – the Movie.*

Since then, the popularity of Gumby has been an ever-changing cycle of ebbs and flow. "Gumby is a symbol of the spark of divinity in each of us, the basis of the ultimate value of each person. Eddie Murphy instinctively picked up on this when he asserted, 'I'm Gumby, dammit!'" wrote Clokey in 1986. "When people watch Gumby, they get a blissful feeling. Gumby loves you. We love you. That's about all I can say."

Get a Job!

MORE JOBS YOUR GUIDANCE COUNSELOR NEVER MENTIONED

Knacker: Buys and sells animal carcasses and old horses.
Slubber: Operates a machine that prepares cotton for spinning.
Bead Piercer: Drills the holes in beads.
Faker: Hand-colors black and white photos.
Knocker-Up: Wakes up workers on the early shift.
Bellowfarmer: Maintains and repairs church organs.
Snobscat: Repairs shoes.
Feller: Cuts down trees.
Knoller: Rings bells.
Belly Builder: Puts together piano interiors.
Streaker: Mortician.
Tallow Chandler: Makes and sells candles.
Fewterer: Trains hounds and keeps them in hunting trim.
Linkerboy: Guides people through dark and unfamiliar streets.
Besom Maker: Makes brooms.
Ponderator: Inspects weights and measures.
Car Chaser: Controls movement of railway cars.
Flauner: Makes candy.
Loblolly Boy: Assists a ship's surgeon.
Birdboy: Scares crows away from crops.
Foot-Straightener: Assembles clock dials.
Scagiolaist: Makes imitation marble.
Blentonist: Finds water with a dousing rod.
Malster: Brews beer.
Trugger: Makes baskets.
Fripperer: Buys and sells old clothes.
Bodger: Carves chair legs.
Mudlark: Cleans out sewers.
Frobbisher: Polishes metal.
Topman: Sits as a lookout at the top of a sailing ship mast.
Bookholder: Prompts stage actors who have forgotten lines.
Muggler: Cares for pigs.

Dental Telepathy

A Magic Trick For Your Party

... with a minty-fresh theme!

Here's a card trick that has a surprise twist. "Oh, swell, another card trick," you say. But rest assured, this one not only entertains small groups of people, but can reduce cavities by up to 23 percent. The card trick involves a toothbrush and its psychic friend, a very gifted tube of toothpaste. "Maybe you've heard of mental telepathy," you announce, "but this is a case of DENTAL telepathy." Your friend squeezes out a ribbon of toothpaste ... and imbedded in it, discovers the name of the chosen card!

THE SET-UP

- Before you do the trick, get a tube of gel toothpaste. We like Crest® for kids because the little sparkles make it seem more magical.
- Cut a tiny strip of clear plastic (clear plastic packing tape glued to itself will do) and write an 8 with a spade symbol on it with a waterproof marker. Push the strip into the toothpaste just inside the tube.

• Find the eight of spades and put it on the top of the deck. Now you're about ready to begin.

THE OPENER

Assemble your friends and tell them a breathless story about how you've always felt "incredibly aware" whenever you brush your teeth with this toothbrush and its spiritual guide, the Psychic Toothpaste Tube. "I want to demonstrate their incredible affinity," you say, mysteriously. "I'm sure you'll be as amazed as I was at their minty-fresh powers."

Have a volunteer step forward, and ask her to choose a number between ten and twenty. Get ready to do the next steps quickly, matter-of-factly, and without hesitation, because you don't want your audience to think too much about it.

THE "HELPER"

Let's say she chooses seventeen. Take the deck and start counting out loud, slapping the cards onto the table into a neat pile as fast as you can, until you get to seventeen.

Hand the pile to your volunteer and say, "Would you count these again to make sure I counted right?" Most likely she'll count exactly as she saw you do. If she doesn't, though, stop her and make sure she does—counting out loud and dealing the cards into a neat pile.

"Seventeen cards, right?" you say. "Great. Okay, now what I want you to do is gently brush the back of the top card with the Incredible Psychic Toothbrush. Gently! Now lay the toothbrush on top of the card to increase the psychic connection."

THE BIG SQUEEZE

Have her get the toothpaste tube from the bathroom. "Keep it away from the toothbrush, though—I don't want them whispering to each other." Ask her to open it and squeeze a ribbon of toothpaste onto her finger. "What does it say?" you ask.

Turn over the card. If you did the trick right, it's the eight of spades. If you have no shame, you might pun: "Careful not to drop the toothpaste or you'll be Crest-fallen."

Nothing But the Tooth

• Before the invention of the modern toothbrush, folks used twigs, leaves, sand, fingers, animal bristles, and quills—anything that would work to brush off plaque.

• Early versions of toothpaste were made from a mixture of abrasives and astringents, like wine and pumice or urine and burned bone ash.

• Before modern dentistry, people prized white teeth more than we do today. Before the twentieth century, "dentists" would often unwittingly cause dental decay in their wealthier patients. By filing away the enamel of the tooth, and applying a corrosive bleaching solution, they would allow decay to set in.

• George Washington's false teeth were made from hippopotamus bone and human teeth—but never from wood, as legend had it.

• The first toothbrush, as we know it, popped up in China and was made from coarse hog hair, set in bamboo or ivory.

• Crest was the first toothpaste to add flouride.Other toothpastes eventually followed suit.

Potty Pourri

RANDOM KINDS OF FACTNESS

• Ian Fleming was an avid birdwatcher. When he was casting around for "an ordinary-sounding name" for his new spy hero, his eyes landed on his favorite bird identification book: *Birds of the West Indies* by ornithologist James Bond.

• Watch for oranges in The Godfather. Whenever they appear on the screen, it's a signal that someone is about to die.

• Better do some studying between games: Only 8 percent of college baseball, basketball, and football players even make the draft for their pro sport. Only 2 percent actually make it onto a professional team.

• Cats have 32 muscles surrounding their ears, allowing them to turn each ear independently.

• When Pablo Picasso tried his hand at writing a play, he had all of his characters die at the end from inhaling the fumes from fried potatoes. The few friends who attended a performance of *Desire Caught by the Tail* had just one piece of advice: "Stick with painting, Pablo."

• Are you deathly afraid of a lawsuit? Then you're liticaphobic ... just like the rest of us.

• In case you were wondering, there are three good reasons why male walruses have those big, white tusks: (1) As weapons in fights with polar bears, (2) To give the big blubbery beasts some traction on ice when pulling themselves out of the water, and (3) Because lady walruses think they're sexy.

• Hoping to get a positive answer from your Magic 8-Ball? "CHANCES ARE GOOD." Of the twenty possible answers, only five are negative. Ten indicate "YES." The remaining five? They tell you to "ASK AGAIN."

• Don't age your rice wine. Unlike most other wines, sake is best when served fresh. Bonzai!

Silly Putty

Bouncing Back from Oblivion

Bend me, shape me, bounce me off the wall. Silly Putty has been a fixture of childhood for fifty years. Here's how it happened.

SOMETHING FUNNY HAPPENED when the government began seeking an inexpensive rubber substitute during World War II. At General Electric's New Haven laboratory, chemical engineer James Wright was working on that problem. He combined silicone oil and boric acid into a gooey pink polymer. Excitedly, he tossed some down on the counter.

Boing! To his surprise, it bounced right back at him.

With high hopes, GE sent glops of the substance to scientists around the world, challenging them to find practical uses for it. They couldn't come up with any. Not that they didn't try. One scientist, noting that it retained its strange properties down to -70° F., tested it to see if it would work as an insulating or caulking material in Arctic climes. No such luck.

"Bouncing putty," as GE dubbed it, languished in limbo. Still, fun-loving GE scientists started mixing up small batches for parties. At one such affair in Connecticut in 1949, a chunk was passed to Peter Hodgson, Sr., high school dropout, advertising consultant, and bon vivant. As he fingered and massaged the chunk, the phrase "silly putty" suddenly came to him. Although he was already $12,000 in debt, he borrowed $147 more and bought 21 pounds of the polymer from GE at $7 a pound, which he packed into little plastic eggs and began selling as an adult toy at an incredible markup ($2 per half-ounce).

He was doing pretty well, selling as many as 300 eggs a day at a few outlets, when the *New Yorker* featured the putty in a small story. Within days, he received orders for 230,000 eggs.

Silly Putty, "the toy with one moving part," was on its way to becoming a national mania.

Originally, adults were the target market. Hodgson believed that kids wouldn't appreciate the putty's richness and subtlety: "It appeals to people of superior intellect," he told a reporter. "The inherent ridiculousness of the material acts as an emotional release to hard-pressed adults."

That marketing strategy worked initially, but, after about five years, the initial ratio of eighty percent adults to twenty percent children had inverted to twenty percent adults to eighty percent children.

Kids loved the stuff well, but not wisely—so much so that the manufacturer had to go back to the labs to reformulate it. The problem was complaints from parents about Silly Putty getting into hair, clothing, upholstery, and carpeting. The Silly Putty of today is less sticky than that made forty years ago, and the company now has a toll-free line that offers advice on how to get Silly Putty unstuck from things.

And, finally, the world has discovered practical uses for Silly Putty. It has been used by astronauts to hold tools in place while in zero-gravity, in physical therapy clinics to reduce stress and help people strengthen their hands and wrists, and at the Cincinnati Zoo to make casts of the hands and feet of its gorillas, and smoking cessation groups recommend Silly Putty to people trying to quit.

MORE NUTTY PUTTY FACTS

• American consumers buy more than 2 million eggs of Silly Putty every year.

• Silly Putty varieties include glitter, glow-in-the-dark, fluorescent colors and the original plain beige.

• When set on fire, Silly Putty produces a bright white flame. The charred remains crumble to bits.

• If Silly Putty is microwaved up to 3 minutes, it will begin to melt. If allowed to cool, it will return to its original consistency.

• Baked Silly Putty (450° oven for 15 minutes) not only stinks, it dries and gets gooey on the pan.

• Dropped from several stories up, a ball made of 100 pounds of Silly Putty will bounce about 8 feet. However, the ball will become somewhat misshapen upon impact.

Full Metal Lunch Jacket

The Birth of the Cool Lunch Boxes

There was a time not so long ago that, for school kids, the lunchbox was the ultimate in personal expression.

MORE THAN A MERE CARRYING CASE for peanut butter and bologna sandwiches, your lunchbox once showed who you were and who you aspired to be. The pretty-in-pink girls carried Barbie or the Monkees; tomboys brought Charlie's Angels; boys carried Roy Rogers; little kids carried Disney or the Jetsons ... and the completely clueless carried generic plaid. During the golden age (1950–1980), lunch boxes were a way to advertise your favorite band, TV show, movie star, or cartoon character.

Most people don't realize, though, that lunch boxes went through many stages of evolution. Let us tell you the story of how they came about.

WORKING-CLASS ROOTS

Before the popular lunch box, there was the working-class lunch pail. (And before the lunch pail, there were oiled goatskins, but let's not go *that* far back.) The lunch pail wasn't really a pail; it was a latching case of toolbox-grade metal that protected your noontime meal from just about anything up to a small bomb. And they weren't chic; on the contrary, they showed that you didn't have the time, freedom, or money for a decent meal for lunch.

Still, working-class children in the 1880s wanted to emulate Daddy, so some created their own school "lunch pails" out of colorful tin boxes that once housed biscuits, cookies, or tobacco. From there, it was a small step to a box specifically made for that purpose, and in 1902 the first true kids' lunch box came out. No, it didn't feature turn-of-the-century pop culture idols like P. T. Barnum, Buffalo Bill, or the Sousa Band—shaped like a picnic basket, it sported pictures of children playing.

BEYOND THE PAIL

True, there were forerunners, but it wasn't until 1950 that lunch boxes really entered their prime. It was an act of desperation by a company called Aladdin. Although the postwar market had created a demand for all kinds of consumer goods, metal lunch boxes were so durable that once a schoolkid bought one it could last until high school graduation.

Staring at charts of slumping sales, Aladdin execs started throwing around ideas:

"We've got these plain boxes—why don't we jazz them up with decals?" "Kids seem to like cowboys and Indians. How about using a TV cowboy? Maybe Hopalong Cassidy?"

And that's how Aladdin stumbled into the ethos of "planned obsolescence" that drove the American economy for decades thereafter—convincing customers to habitually replace perfectly good products for the sake of novelty and style. Aladdin hired a designer to sketch the cowboy star onto decal material that they slapped onto the side of a red lunchbox. On the strength of that crude prototype, they convinced a big department store chain to

make an advance order of 50,000, and the box took off like bad guys hightailing it to their hideout.

Meanwhile, back at the ranch, another cowboy star became jealous. Roy Rogers wanted his own box, but Aladdin had turned him down with: "One cowboy is enough." So Roy saddled up and rode north to American Thermos in Connecticut. Like Aladdin, Thermos had seen sales slump in its sets of lunch boxes and thermos bottles, made even more acute by

Aladdin's success. Thermos decided to do Aladdin's cowboy box one better by using bright, full-color lithography on all sides of the box instead of a decal on just one face. It worked: the company sold 2.5 million Roy Rogers & Dale Evans boxes in 1953, increasing their total sales 20 percent in one year.

Aladdin retooled to also use full-box lithography for their 1954 line. So did newcomers ADCO Liberty and Universal, as well as another old-style lunch pail manufacturer, Ohio Art (which later diversified into making toys like Etch-A-Sketch). In 1962, Aladdin added another trademark feature: designs stamped into the metal, giving a 3-D effect.

Lunchbox manufacturers began bidding for rights to hot new movies and TV shows. From 1950 until 1987, lunchbox manufacturers issued about 450 different designs.

The classic steel lunch boxes had a good run, selling about

The Disney Schoolbus was the biggest seller of all time—9 million total.

120 million between 1950 and 1970. Manufacturers in 1972 began switching to plastic to cut manufacturing costs. Meanwhile, concerned mothers and pandering state legislators banned metal lunch boxes as dangerous assault weapons. Ironically, the last metal lunch box of the classic era hailed the violent hero, Rambo, in 1987.

Life Lessons

Swirling & Sniffing Through a Wine Tasting

Follow these simple instructions and you'll be able to participate in a wine tasting without the least bit of embarrassment.

PEOPLE MAY LOOK PRETENTIOUS at a wine tasting, but there's a reason for everything they do. Step by step, here's what to do if you want to look like you belong there:

1. Hold the glass of wine up to your eyes and look at it. Enjoy the rich clear colors.

2. If you see anything suspicious, put it down and move on to another wine. What to look for: cloudiness (means wine isn't ready to drink), brownish hue (wine is too old), or pieces of glass or other residue. Pieces of cork won't hurt you.

3. Swirl your glass. Coat the inside edges with a thin layer of wine. The wine glass should be slightly curved inward at the top, to capture the smell of the wine (and decrease the chance of swirling the wine out of the glass), but you may also want to place your hand over the glass to capture the aroma.

4. Smell the wine. Place your nose deep into the glass to get a good whiff. A good wine should have a pleasant "bouquet." Wine that's going bad will smell like old sherry. Wine that's already gone bad will smell like vinegar. Other bad signs are wine that smells like rotten eggs (too much sulfur) or mildew (the cork has gone bad).

5. Swish the wine over your mouth and teeth. Clench your teeth and suck in air over your tongue and the wine to get the full aroma and taste at the same time.

6. If you're a "serious" taster, use the bucket provided to spit out the wine you've just tasted so you won't dull your senses. Otherwise swallow. Take notes of your observations about the wine. Eat a cracker to cleanse your palate and grab another glass.

Step Right Up!

How Incubator Babies Became a Popular Sideshow

Can't get funding to develop an invention that would save millions of babies? Well, how about doing what this doctor did—create a sideshow carnival exhibit? Here's the whole curious story.

Coney Island in its heyday: If early last century you joined the teeming crowds on the New York subway and traveled to the amusement parks on Coney Island, you'd experience things you couldn't do anywhere else. For example, you could ride one of the roller coasters, a thrill that was pretty much invented here in the ocean breezes off the tip of Brooklyn. You could gawk at sideshow freaks and a miniature town filled with 300 midgets, go on an elaborate trip "to the moon," or see a reenactment of the San Francisco earthquake or the Bible's Great Flood. If you were in search of racier stuff, you could see hoochy-koochy dancers or even visit an elephant-shaped hotel, where it was whispered you could find, for a price, an incredibly easy date.

However, in the center of Coney Island's crowds, noise, smells, lights, and excitement was perhaps the strangest exhibit of all was the Incubator Babies.

GIVING UP PREMATURELY

Until the 1940s, few maternity hospitals wanted to go to the expense of providing special facilities to handle premature babies. The thought was that such babies were too weak to survive anyway, so why bother going to any great effort beyond preparing the parents for the inevitable? The theory was a self-fulfilling prophecy: the death rate for preemies in most hospitals approached 85 percent.

In France, a doctor named Alexandre Lion thought this was a wasteful tragedy. In the 1890s, France's population was actually falling as birth rates fell and infant mortality remained high.

Because their bodies cannot yet regulate their temperature, premature babies often died from hypothermia. In 1891, Lion built a contraption with a cylindrical water boiler on the side to provide steady heat, and with a fan system that provided filtered air. The Lion incubator's effect on reducing mortality rates immediately proved remarkable, and the doctor sought hospital interest and funds to build more.

To his shocked surprise, neither funds nor interest were forthcoming. To try to drum up interest in his incubators with his limited funds, Lion decided to display them in exhibitions and international fairs. But simply showing them wasn't getting the idea across, so he took a bold step. He solicited premature infants from local hospitals. The hospitals, believing the preemies would die anyway, were happy to provide them. Lion hired medical personnel and wet nurses, and set up an exhibit behind glass of the preemie hospital of the future, with live babies.

The good doctor didn't anticipate that the medical establishment would continue its indifference to his invention. On the other hand, he was flabbergasted by how much interest ordinary citizens took in his exhibit. There were so many people who wanted to gawk through the glass at the tiny babies and the newfangled machines that many of the fairgoers had to be turned away.

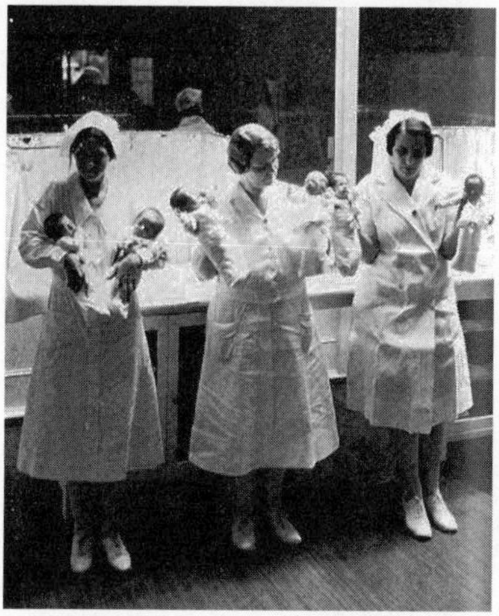

Lion came up with a way that he hoped would reduce the crowds and also help pay some of his expenses. He started charging admission. To his surprise, the crowds didn't diminish at all, and he finally started making money from his life-saving invention.

Lion's first exhibition success led to a flurry of invitations from other fairs. It also led to another pediatrician entering the field. Dr. Martin Couney also began exhibiting the life-saving devices at public expositions in Germany, then was invited to exhibitions in the United States.

He set up his first American exhibit in 1898 at the Trans-Mississippi Exposition in Omaha, Nebraska. After doing several incubator exhibitions, he decided to find a place where he could set up a permanent display, and where could be better than Coney Island? In 1904, Couney opened his first permanent exhibit in Luna Park under a sign announcing, "ALL THE WORLD LOVES A BABY." It was Coney Island's longest-running show, closing in 1943 when New York City hospitals finally opened their own preemie centers.

The exhibit at Coney Island was unusual in more ways than you'd expect. For one thing, the parents of the babies paid nothing for the extensive services provided. The 24-hour-a-day machines, nurses, and wet nurses were all paid for by the quarters of the curious spectators who stopped by. (Parents of the babies—as well as former patients as they grew up—got free passes to the exhibit.)

"... dozens of faces peered at her curiously"

Also, the excellent care was open to babies of all economic classes and races, which was unusual at the time. Finally, the results Couney achieved were nothing short of a medical miracle. Reported the *Minneapolis Daily Star*: "It is a matter of statistical record that previous to the use of the incubator that only 15% of the prematurely born lived. By use of the incubator, 85% are saved." Of the 8,000 babies raised in the Coney Island incubators, more than 6,500 survived.

To the credit of the medical profession, they did eventually take note of Dr. Couney's success rate, and despite the carney atmosphere, began coming to see and learn from his experience. By the 1940s, hospitals around the country had finally caught up with the Coney Island sideshow exhibit by opening their own preemie wards. Couney, now quite old and modestly affluent, finally retired.

How Short Was Napoleon?

Despite his reputation as a puny guy, Napoleon Bonaparte wasn't really that short. True, he was only five-foot-two, but for a French person of the time, that was a pretty average height. True, in comparison to other leaders of the time he was short. And of course, *le Petite Corporal* was shorter than most men today. (Most women too, for that matter.)

Despite his shortcomings, Napoleon managed to conquer 720,000 square miles of territory during his years of making war, much more than any of the leaders who towered over him.

Still More H. L. Mencken

More quotes from H. L. Mencken, the controversial curmudgeon.

• "It is inaccurate to say I hate everything. I am strongly in favor of common sense, common honesty, and common decency. This makes me forever ineligible for public office."

• "A judge is a law student who marks his own examination papers."

• "Nature abhors a moron."

• "Conscience is a mother-in-law whose visit never ends."

• "The Christian Church, in its attitude toward science, shows the mind of a more or less enlightened man of the Thirteenth Century. It no longer believes that the earth is flat, but it is still convinced that prayer can cure after medicine fails."

• "It is often argued that religion is valuable because it makes men good, but even if this were true it would not be a proof that religion is true. Santa Claus makes children good in precisely the same way, and yet no one would argue seriously that the fact proves his existence."

• "The liberation of the human mind has been best furthered by fellow who heaved dead cats into sanctuaries and then went roistering down the highways of the world, proving to all men that doubt, after all, was safe—that the god in the sanctuary was a fraud."

• "Sunday: A day given over by Americans to wishing that they themselves were dead and in Heaven, and that their neighbors were dead and in Hell."

• "Suicide is a belated acquiescence in the opinion of one's wife's relatives."

• "Do not overestimate the decency of the human race."

• "A courtroom is a place where Jesus Christ and Judas Iscariot would be equals, with the betting odds favoring Judas."

• "A dachshund is a half-dog high and a dog-and-a-half long."

• "He marries best who puts it off until it is too late."

• "One horse-laugh is worth ten-thousand syllogisms."

• "I believe it is better to tell the truth than to lie. I believe that it is better to be free than to be a slave. and I believe that it is better to know than to be ignorant."

• "Life may not be exactly pleasant, but at least it's not dull."

We've Got Your Number

We'll give you a number, abbreviated words, and a clue. Tell us what the famous phrase is. Answers below. (Don't cheat!)

1. 7 W O T W (See the pyramids along the Nile)
2. T 3 F O E (Multiple-personality movie)
3. 5 G L — H O M E S (Water, water everywhere)
4. 7 D S (Gluttony's one of them)
5. 10 P O E (Locusts, boils, frogs, etc.)
6. F 451 (Bradbury book-burning book)
7. 12 K O T R T (The gal I had liked to lance a lot)
8. 3 PC — R, Y, B (Meet my colorful friend, Roy G. Biv)
9. Y 16, Y B, & Y M (1950s song)
10. 76 T I T B P (Friends, you've got trouble)
11. 666 — T M O T B (Another from *Revelation*)
12. 6 O O, H A D O T O (Either way's the same)
13. 50 W T L Y L (Paul Simon song)
14. A S I T S 9 (An old saying that's sew true)
15. A C H 9 L (Ask Morris, he'll tell you)
16. 30 D H S, A, J, & N (The rest have 28 or 31)
17. 2 I C, 3 A C (So says Jack Ritter)
18. 101 D (Disney doggies)
19. 10,000 L U T S (Disney dives)
20. 1-E ,1-H, F P P E (1950s novelty song)

Answers: *1. 7 Wonders of the World; 2. The 3 Faces of Eve; 3. 5 Great Lakes—Huron, Ontario, Michigan, Erie, Superior; 4. 7 Deadly Sins; 5. 10 Plagues of Egypt; 6. Fahrenheit 451; 7. 12 Knights of the Round Table; 8. 3 Primary Colors—Red, Yellow, & Blue; 9. You're 16, You're Beautiful, & You're Mine; 10. 76 Trombones in the Big Parade; 11. 666—The Mark of the Beast; 12. 6 of One, Half a Dozen of the Other; 13. 50 Ways to Leave Your Lover; 14. A Stitch in Time Saves 9; 15. A Cat Has 9 Lives; 16. 30 Days Hath September, April, June, & November; 17. 2 Is Company, 3's a Crowd; 18. 101 Dalmations; 19. 10,000 Leagues Under the Sea; 20. 1-Eyed, 1 Horned, Flying Purple People Eater*

Wicked Jim

Mark Twain's Satire about Kid Stories

In Mark Twain's time, children's stories had heavyhanded morals at the end. It's a tradition that lamentably survives in kids' books even today, despite Twain's attempt to stomp it to death with this parody from 1865.

STORY OF THE BAD LITTLE BOY

ONCE there was a bad little boy whose name was Jim—though, if you will notice, you will find that bad little boys are nearly always called James in your Sunday-school books. It was strange, but still it was true that this one was called Jim.

He didn't have any sick mother either—a sick mother

who was pious and had the consumption, and would be glad to lie down in the grave and be at rest but for the strong love she bore her boy, and the anxiety she felt that the world might be harsh and cold towards him when she was gone. Most bad boys in the Sunday-books are named James, and have sick mothers, who teach them to say, "Now, I lay me down," etc., and sing them to sleep with sweet, plaintive voices, and then kiss them good-night, and kneel down by the bedside and weep. But it was different with this fellow. He was named Jim, and there wasn't anything the matter with his mother—no consumption, nor anything of that kind. She was rather stout than otherwise, and she was not pious; moreover, she was not anxious on Jim's account. She said if he were to break his neck it wouldn't be much loss. She always spanked Jim to sleep, and she never kissed him good-night; on the contrary, she boxed his ears when she was ready to leave him.

Once this little bad boy stole the key of the pantry, and slipped in there and helped himself to some jam, and filled up the vessel

with tar so that his mother would never know the difference; but all at once a terrible feeling didn't come over him, and something didn't seem to whisper to him, "Is it right to disobey my mother? Isn't in sinful to do this? Where do bad little boys go who gobble up their good kind mother's jam?" and then he didn't kneel down all alone and promise never to be wicked any more, and rise up with a light, happy heart, and go and tell his mother all about it and beg her forgiveness, and be blessed by her with tears of pride and thankfulness in her eyes. No; that is the way with all other bad boys in the books; but it happened otherwise with this Jim, strangely enough. He ate that jam, and said it was bully, in his sinful, vulgar way; and he put in the tar, and said that was bully also, and laughed, and observed "that the old woman would get up and snort" when she found it out; and when she did find it out, he denied knowing anything about it, and she whipped him severely, and he did the crying himself. Everything about this boy was curious—everything turned out differently with him from the way it does to the bad Jameses in the books.

Once he climbed up in Farmer Acorn's apple-tree to steal apples, and the limb didn't break, and he didn't fall and break his arm, and get torn by the farmer's great dog, and then languish on a sick bed for weeks, and repent and become good. Oh! no; he stole as many apples as he wanted and came down all right; and he was all ready for the dog too, and knocked him endways with a brick when he came to tear him. It was very strange—nothing like it ever happened in those mild little books with marbled backs, and with pictures in them of men with swallow-tailed coats and bell-crowned hats, and pantaloons that are short in the legs, and women with the waists of their dresses under their arms, and no hoops on. Nothing like it in any of the Sunday-school books.

Once he stole the teacher's pen-knife, and, when he was afraid it would be found out and he would get whipped, he slipped it into George Wilson's cap—poor Widow Wilson's son, the moral boy, the good little boy of the village, who always obeyed his mother, and never told an untruth, and was fond of his lessons, and infatuated with Sunday-school. And when the knife dropped from the cap, and poor George hung his head and blushed, as if in conscious guilt, and the grieved teacher charged the theft upon him, and was just in the very act of bringing the switch down upon his trembling shoulders, a white-haired, improbable justice of the peace did not suddenly appear in their midst, and strike an attitude and say, "Spare this noble boy—there stands the cowering culprit! I was passing the school-door at recess, and unseen myself, I saw the theft committed!" And then Jim didn't get whaled, and the venerable justice didn't read the tearful school a homily, and take George by the hand and say such a boy deserved to be exalted, and then tell him to come and make his home with him, and sweep out the office, and make fires, and run errands, and chop wood, and study law, and help his wife do household labors, and have all the balance of the time to play, and get forty cents a month, and be happy. No; it would have happened that way in the books, but it didn't happen that way to Jim. No meddling old clam of a justice dropped in to make trouble, and so the model boy George got thrashed, and

Jim was glad of it. Because, you know, Jim hated moral boys. Jim said he was "down on them milksops." Such was the coarse language of this bad, neglected boy.

But the strangest thing that ever happened to Jim was the time he went boating on Sunday, and didn't get drowned, and that other time that he got caught out in the storm when he was fishing on Sunday, and didn't get struck by lightning. Why, you might look, and look, and look, all through the Sunday-school books from now till next Christmas, and you would never come across anything like this. Oh no; you would find that all the bad boys who go boating on Sunday invariably get drowned, and all the bad boys who get caught out in storms, when they are fishing on Sunday, infallibly get struck by lightning. Boats with bad boys in them are always upset on Sunday, and it always storms when bad boys go fishing on the Sabbath. How this Jim ever escaped is a mystery to me.

This Jim bore a charmed life—that must have been the way of it. Nothing could hurt him. He even gave the elephant in the

menagerie a plug of tobacco, and the elephant didn't knock the top of his head off with his trunk. He browsed around the cupboard after essence of peppermint, and didn't make a mistake and drink aqua fortis. He stole his father's gun and went hunting on the Sabbath, and didn't shoot three or four of his fingers off. He struck his little sister on the temple with his fist when he was angry, and yet she did not linger in pain through long summer days, and die with sweet words of forgiveness upon her lips that redoubled the anguish of his breaking heart. No; she got over it. He ran off and went to sea at last, and didn't come back and find himself sad and alone in the world, his loved ones sleeping in the quiet church-yard, and the vine-embowered home of his boyhood tumbled down and gone to decay. Ah! no; he came home as drunk as a piper, and got into the station-house the first thing.

And he grew up, and married, and raised a large family, and brained them all with an axe one night, and got wealthy by all manner of cheating and rascality; and now he is the infernalest wickedest scoundrel in his native village, and is universally respected, and belongs to the Legislature.

So you see there never was a bad James in the Sunday-school books that had such a streak of luck as this sinful Jim with the charmed life.

The Origins of Snowball & Little Snookums

• Like dogs, bears, and raccoons, the entire cat family developed more than 50 million years ago from a small, weaselly animal called *Miacis.*

• Ancient Egyptians tamed an African wildcat called *Felis libyca* about 2500 B.C. Crusaders brought some back to Europe, and bred them with small European wildcats. That's how we got the modern shorthaired housecat.

• Longhaired cats, on the other hand, descended from the Asian wildcat *(Felis manul)*, domesticated in India, also in about 2500 B.C.

• Unlike most domesticated animals, the size of cats has remained pretty much unchanged during its association with people.

•In ancient Egypt, the penalty for killing a cat was death, and cats were worshiped as gods. There was a practical reason: The Egyptians subsisted largely on grains in bread and beer, and cats kept rodents in check.

• Ancient Egyptian cat owners would shave their eyebrows in mourning and lovingly transport the cat carcass to one of the cities devoted to mummifying cats for their journey to the next world.

• The cats apparently didn't make it. In 1888, about 300,000 cat mummies were discovered still lounging around this world in a burial ground at the ancient city of Beni Hassan.

• The Jewish Talmud (about 500 B.C.) encourages people to adopt cats "to help keep their houses clean." On the other hand, the cat is the only domesticated animal not mentioned *even once* in the Bible.

The Devil's Dictionary: T–Z

More of The Devil's Dictionary by Ambrose Bierce (1842–1914?)

TAKE, *v.t.* To acquire, often by force but preferably by stealth.

TARIFF, *n.* A scale of taxes on imports, designed to protect the domestic producer against the greed of his consumer.

TELEPHONE, *n.* An invention of the devil which abrogates some of the advantages of making a disagreeable person keep his distance.

TELESCOPE, *n.* A device having a relation to the eye similar to that of the telephone to the ear, enabling distant objects to plague us with a multitude of needless details. Luckily it is unprovided with a bell.

TRICHINOSIS, *n.* The pig's reply to proponents of porcophagy.

TRUTHFUL, *adj.* Dumb and illiterate.

TSETSE FLY, *n.* An African insect (*Glossina morsitans*) whose bite is commonly regarded as nature's most efficacious remedy for insomnia, though some patients prefer that of the American novelist (*Mendax interminabilis*).

UGLINESS, *n.* A gift of the gods to certain women, entailing virtue without humility.

ULTIMATUM, *n.* In diplomacy, a last demand before resorting to concessions.

UN-AMERICAN, *adj.* Wicked, intolerable, heathenish.

VALOR, *n.* A soldierly compound of vanity, duty, and the gambler's hope.

VANITY, *n.* The tribute of a fool to the worth of the nearest ass.

VOTE, *n.* The instrument and symbol of a freeman's power to make a fool of himself and a wreck of his country.

WAR, *n.* A by-product of the arts of peace.

WHEAT, *n.* A cereal from which a tolerably good whisky can with some difficulty be made, and which is used also for bread.

WITCH, *n.* (1) Any ugly and repulsive old woman, in a wicked league with the devil. (2) A beautiful and attractive young woman, in wickedness a league beyond the devil.

YANKEE, *n.* In Europe, an American. In the Northern States of our Union, a New Englander. In the South the word is unknown. (See DAMNYANK.)

YEAR, *n.* A period of 365 disappointments.

ZEAL, *n.* A certain nervous disorder afflicting the young and inexperienced.

"BE MINE"

SWEET TALES OF CANDY HEARTS

COAX ME, HUG ME, KISS ME ... you can say a mouthful with candy hearts, the Valentine's Day icon. There's a lot we learned about them. Be our Valentine, and we'll tell you more.

ABOUT 10 BILLION candy message hearts are sold each year. Eighty percent of those are made by the New England Confectionery Company (NECCO) of Cambridge, Massachusetts, founded in 1848.

• You can buy the hearts only from January 1 to Valentine's Day. Still, the company keeps three separate plants pumping them out, 18 hours a day, year-round, to keep up with the seasonal demand. Unless Valentine's Day falls on a Sunday, the machines keep making candy hearts for the next year even through the holiday.

• Every minute of the work day, each candy machine makes 12,640 hearts. That's about 45 bags a minute.

• Hearts with messages was the idea of Daniel Chase, brother of NECCO founder Oliver Chase, in the late 1860s. He first put messages *inside* heart-shaped candies that cracked open like fortune cookies. A new process in 1902 made it possible to imprint the messages on candy hearts with food dye.

• Not surprisingly, considering its name, the company also makes Neccos, those coin-sized chalky candies that come in rolls of many colors. The hearts use the Necco recipe rolled extra thick.

• Originally, NECCO Valentine's hearts (called Motto Hearts) were much bigger than today's version. They were big enough to feature sayings like "Oh my dear, do not squeal, you're safe with me in the automobile."

• The maximum inscription length for the small hearts nowadays is two lines, six letters per line.

• Today, dough for the hearts (sugar, corn syrup, corn starch, xanthan gum, pecan syrup, color, and flavor) is made in batches weighing 550 pounds. The dough is then rolled into yard-wide sheets, stamped with red sayings, and cut into heart shapes.

• Don't like the message you've gotten? There are 125 different phrases. Each year, the company replaces a handful of old phrases with new ones.

• Retired phrases over the years include HUBBA HUBBA, GROOVY, HANG TEN, DIG ME, BUZZ OFF, STOP, HOT STUFF, TRY ME, BAD BOY, SAY YES, and R-U GAY?

• NECCO rolls with the times, though. New phrases today include MEGABYTE, GO GIRL, YOU ROCK, BE MY ICON, FAX ME, TRES CHIC, WHAT'S UP, VOGUE, and URA QT. Spanish language hearts are also available (BELLIA, AMOR, ADIOS).

• The company gets requests from people year 'round, desperate to find a MARRY ME heart to propose marriage. They try to oblige, says a spokesperson—"How could we refuse?"

"My advice to you is get married: if you find a good wife you'll be happy; if not, you'll become a philosopher." —Socrates

"Only choose in marriage a woman whom you would choose as a friend if she were a man." —Joseph Joubert

Escape Artist

How to Escape an Encounter with a Bear

Bear encounters are on the rise. Bears would rather get a good meal from you than hunt one for themselves. So how do you survive an encounter with a bear? We'll show you.

FOLLOW THESE RULES, and you've got a good chance of coming out okay. First, it's best not to encounter bears at all. Black bears, brown bears, and grizzlies all love leftovers. No food should be stored in or near your tent. Food should be hung away from your sleeping area, high enough to keep bears from reaching it. Leftover scraps should always be burned.

1. If a bear comes into your camp, let it have anything you've got and get out of the way. Humans don't taste that good; the bears aren't looking to eat you.

2. If you're hiking alone, attach something loud to your pack. If you're with a group, talk loudly as you walk. This should keep most bears at bay.

3. If a grizzly approaches you, drop your pack and climb a tree, if possible—preferably one without branches for the bear to climb. If you encounter a black or brown bear, though, don't bother. They're both expert climbers.

5. Otherwise, drop your pack and back slowly away. Bears can outrun you—and will. Step well clear away from your pack, and drop to your knees. Curl up in a ball with your legs under you and your hands protecting your head and neck.

6. Play dead and stay completely inert if the bear sniffs you and checks you out. This has worked more often than not. Bears really aren't interested in eating you; they simply feel threatened easily and will fight.

Get a Job!

MORE JOBS YOUR GUIDANCE COUNSELOR NEVER MENTIONED

Funabulist: Walks tightropes.
Virginalist: Plays a virginal (harpsichord-like instrument).
Bowdler: Smelts iron ore.
Nagelschmiedmeister: Makes nails.
Gaffer: (1) Lights movie sets. (2) Shapes glass-blown bottles.
Brailler: Makes girdles.
Necker: Feeds cardboard into box machines.
Buddleboy: Maintains the vats for washing metal ores.
Vogler: Catches birds.
Rockman: Places explosives in mines.
Secret Springer: Makes watch mainsprings.
Egg Breaker: Separates yolks from whites for food industry.
Bullwhacker: Drives oxen.
Gatward: Keeps goats.
Busker: (1) Street entertainer. (2) Hair dresser.
Paling Man: Sells eels.
Gaunter: Makes gloves
Hacker: Makes hoes.
Carnifex: Butchers animals for meat.
Peruker: Makes wigs.
Gelder: Castrates animals.
Lingo Cleaner: Maintains looms.
Cod Placer: Puts pottery into a kiln.
Hoggard: Drives pigs.
Pigman: Sells crockery.
Lump Inspector: Monitors quality of bulk tobacco.
Honeydipper / Jakes Farmer: Cleans out port-a-potty sewage.
Deathsman: Executes prisoners.
Playderer: Weaves plaid cloths.
Masher: Runs mash tub in beer making.
Gandy Dancer: Tamps gravel between newly laid railroad ties.
Toe Puncher: Runs machine that flattens knitted sock seams.

Ben's Naughty Advice

Founding Father Fulminates on Flatulence

Some of Benjamin Franklin's writings were perfect for perusing in the privy, including this satire in which he uses farts to make a pungent point about scientific societies.

To the Royal Academy of Brussels

Gentlemen:

I have perused your late mathematical Prize Question, proposed in lieu of one in natural Philosophy for the ensuing Year. I was glad to find that you esteem *Utility* an essential point in your Enquiries, which has not always been the case with all Academies. Permit me then humbly to propose one of that sort for your Consideration, for the serious Enquiry of learned Physicians, Chemists, etc., of this enlightened Age.

It is universally well-known, that in digesting our common food, there is created in or produced in the Bowels of human Creatures a great quantity of Wind.

That the permitting this Air to escape and mix with Atmosphere, is usually offensive to the Company, from the fetid smell that accompanyes it.

That all well bred People therefore, to avoid giving such offense, forcibly restrain the Efforts of Nature to discharge that Wind.

That so retained contrary to Nature, it not only gives frequently great present pain, but occasions future Diseases such as habitual Cholics, Ruptures, Tympanies, etc., often destructive of the Constitution, and sometimes of Life itself.

Were it not for the odiously offensive smell accompanying such escapes, polite People would probably be under no more

Restraint in discharging such Wind in Company than they are in spitting or blowing their Noses.

My Prize Question therefore should be: To discover some Drug, wholesome and not disagreeable, to be mixed with our common food, or sauces, that shall render the natural discharges of Wind from our Bodies not only inoffensive, but agreeable as Perfumes.

That this is not a Chimerical Project & altogether impossible, may appear from these considerations: That we already have some knowledge of means capable of *varying* that smell. He that dines on stale Flesh, especially with much Addition of Onions, shall be able to afford a Stink that no Company can tolerate; while he that has lived for some time on Vegetables only, shall have that Breath so pure as to be insensible to the most delicate Noses; and if he can manage so as to avoid the Report, he may anywhere give vent to his Griefs, un-noticed. But as there are many to whom an entire Vegetable Diet would be inconvenient, & as a little quick Lime thrown into a Jakes will correct the amazing Quantity of fetid Air arising from the vast Mass of putrid Matter contained in such Places, and render it rather pleasing to the Smell, who knows but that a little Powder of Lime (or some other thing equivalent) taken in our Food, or perhaps a Glass of Lime Water drank at Dinner, may have the same Effect on the Air produced in and issuing from our Bowels? This is worth the experiment. Certain it is also that we have the Power of changing by slight means the Smell of another Discharge, that of our Water. A few stems of Asparagus eaten, shall give our Urine a disagreeable Odour; and a Pill of Turpentine no bigger than a Pea, shall bestow on it the pleasing smell of Violets. And why should it be thought more impossible in Nature, to find means of making a Perfume of our *Wind* than of our *Water*?

"Musk, rose, or lily?"

For the encouragement of this Enquiry (from the immortal Honour to be reasonably expected by the Inventor) let it be considered of how small importance to Mankind, or how small a Part of Mankind have been useful those Discoveries in Science that have heretofore made Philosophers famous. Are there twenty men in Europe this day the happier, or even the easier for any knowledge they have pick'd out of Aristotle? What Comfort can the Vortices of Descartes give to a man who has Whirlwinds in his Bowels! The knowledge of Newton's mutual *Attraction* of the particles of matter, can it afford ease to him who is racked by their mutual *Repulsion,* and the cruel distentions it occasions? The Pleasure arising to a few Philosophers, from seeing, a few times in their lives, the threads of light untwisted, and separated by the Newtonian Prism into seven colours, can it be compared with the ease and comfort every man living might feel seven times a day, by discharging freely the wind from Bowels? Especially, if it be converted into a Perfume; for the pleasures of one Sense being little inferior to those of another, instead of pleasing the *Sight,* he might delight the *Smell* of those about him, and make numbers happy, which to a benevolent mind must afford infinite satisfaction. The generous Soul, who now endeavours to find out whether the friends he entertains like best Claret or Burgundy, Champagne or Madeira, would then enquire also whether they chose Musk or Lily, Rose or Bergamot, and provide accordingly. And surely such a Liberty of *expressing one's scent-iments, & pleasing one another,* is of infinitely more importance to human happiness than that Liberty of the Press, or of abasing one another, which the English are so ready to fight & die for.

In short, this Invention, if completed, would be, as Bacon expresses it, Bringing Philosophy home to Men's Business and Bosoms. And I cannot but conclude, that in comparison therewith for universal and continual Utility the Science of the Philosophers abovementioned, even with the addition, Gentlemen, of your mathematical prize, are, all together, scarcely worth a *Fart-hing.*

Your most obedient
humble Servant
B Franklin

Barrymorisms III

It can't be easy being the third generation of a great Hollywood family, but here's Drew, doing her best.

ON WISDOM

"I aspire to be a voice of reason one day."

ON HAPPINESS

"I don't want to be stinky poo-poo girl, I want to be happy flower child."

ON GOD'S WILL

"God made a very obvious choice when he made me voluptuous; why would I go against what he decided for me? My limbs work, so I'm not going to complain about the way my body is shaped."

ON FLORA

"Daisies are like sunshine to the ground."

ON FAUNA

"I've been a vegetarian for years and years. I'm not judgmental about others who aren't, I just feel I cannot eat or wear living creatures."

ON METAMORPHOSIS

"Everyone is like a butterfly, they start out ugly and awkward and then morph into beautiful graceful butterflies that everyone loves."

ON LIVING

"If you're going to be alive and on this planet, you have to, like, suck the marrow out of every day and get the most out of it."

ON FATE

"I've always said that one night, I'm going to find myself in some field somewhere, I'm standing on grass, and it's raining, and I'm with the person I love, and I know I'm at the very point I've been dreaming of getting to."

ON HOBBIES

"I am obsessed with ice cubes. Obsessed."

Anty Matters

How Uncle Milton Put the Ants in Ant Farm

Ants are maddening when running free in a quest for crumbs and butter. However, ants imprisoned in little prison farms allow us to relax and enjoy them again and again.

THE IDEA FOR THE ANT FARM struck Milton Levine in 1956, when Levine was at an Independence Day picnic at his sister's house. He was thirty-two at the time, and looking to expand his line of mail order novelties like spud guns and rubber shrunken heads. "The kids were more interested in lying around and watching ant hills than swimming in the pool. And it came to me. When I was a kid, we used to put ants in a Mason jar with a little dirt and watch 'em dig when they got to the sides. I thought, why not make one that was flatter, that people could see most of the tunnels?"

His first farms were 6 by 9 inches, the familiar solid-colored plastic frame holding a thin layer of sand between two sheets of transparent plastic. It featured a plastic farm scene—barn, silo, farmhouse, and windmill (about the same as they are now), and sold for $1.98.

Levine bought a 2-inch ad in the *Los Angeles Times*, inviting the curious to "watch the ants dig tunnels and build bridges" in their own Ant Farms. Levine got loads of orders, but that was just the beginning.

Not that selling ants was always a picnic. In the beginning, ants were dropping like flies—the result of either booze on the breath of the guy who assembled the kits (Levine's theory) or glue fumes (Levine's partner's theory). Whichever, the problem was eventually solved.

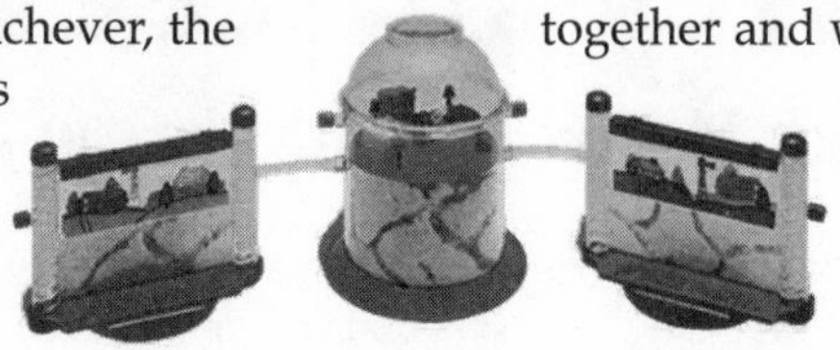

Uncle Milton's Ant Farm Village

The Ant Farm has been an enduring product, to say the least. Sales began two years before the Hula-Hoop and are still going strong. More then 20 million Ant Farms have been sold, populated by more than 360 million ants. The company, now managed by Milton's son, Steven Levine, gets about 12,000 letters each year from Ant Farm owners (often former childhood owners reporting they had bought one for a child or grandchild). Not that there isn't an occasional complaint letter—one kid was mad that his ants weren't wearing top hats like some shown on the box.

Except for the price, the basic product is just about the same today as back then. You get a certificate that you have to mail in to get your ants, and the *Ant Watchers Manual,* which gives you information about your new livestock (Do ants talk? Yes. Do they take baths? Yes). One improvement from the early days: connectors for plastic tubes so you can string Ant Farms together and watch the ants crawl from one to another.

Why is he called "Uncle Milton"? "Everyone always said, 'You've got the ants, but where's the uncles?' So I became Uncle Milton."

INSECT ASIDES

• Coincidence? You decide: The Ant Farm was invented in the same year as Raid insecticide.

• All the ants supplied for the Ant Farm are female. In the ant world, there aren't many males, and all they do is mate and die (an anty-climax, if you will). Since the company can't legally ship queen ants, your colony can't reproduce and will eventually dwindle to nothing.

• Out of thousands of varieties of ants, the harvester ant was chosen to work on the Ant Farm because it's big and is one of the few varieties that will dig in daylight.

• The leading cause of death for ants is overfeeding. If you exceed the recommended ration of one birdseed or a single corn flake every two days, the food gets moldy, and your ants "buy the farm."

• The next leading danger is too much sunlight (baked ants). Shaking the farm has been known to cause mass death by shock (it's too darn frustrating to spend all those hours digging, only to have your work reduced to nothing in a few seconds).

• At a funeral, the ant graveyard detail always carries the dead ant to the northeastern corner of the farm. If the farm is rotated to a new direction, the pallbearers march into action again, digging up the dead ants and reburying them in the northeast. Why? Nobody knows.

• The technical name for an ant farm (or any ant habitat) is *formicarium.*

• Every Ant Farm is completely American-made. assembled and packaged in Southern California by disabled workers.

A Great Way to Start Your Day—with Cereal Trivia

• The original name for Cheerios was "Cheeri Oats" when it hit shelves in 1942. But Quaker Oats had a different idea about the use of the term "oats" and tried to sue. Cheeri Oats quickly changed their name to Cheerios, the matter was dropped, and the cereal became a big hit.

• In the 1930s, it wasn't a baseball or football star, but a wild animal trainer named Maria Rasputin who appeared on a box of Wheaties.

• It happened to "Raisin Bran," "Shredded Wheat," and "Corn Flakes," but so far, the name "Grape Nuts" has not gone generic.

• Ah, the golden years of "free inside this box" cereal promotions: In the 1950s, Kellogg's offered a baking-powdered powered atomic submarine inside a box of cereal. General Mills gave away miniature license plates at around the same time. Quaker Oats, though, beat them both. It gave away a deed to a square inch of Yukon Territory.

• Cartoon geniuses Bill Scott and Jay Ward, of *Rocky and Bullwinkle* and *George of the Jungle* fame, were responsible for a cereal great, too. Ward and Scott were asked to come up with a fun ad campaign with animation, which they did with Captain Crunch. It wasn't until afterward that General Mills then designed the cereal to put in the boxes.

One More Little Yiddish Quiz

Animal, Vegetable, or Mineral?

Circle the correct category for each Yiddish term.

1. Shikse	Animal	Vegetable	Mineral
2. Kvetsh	Animal	Vegetable	Mineral
3. Shmutz	Animal	Vegetable	Mineral
4. Kishkes	Animal	Vegetable	Mineral
5. Shvitz	Animal	Vegetable	Mineral
6. Shnapps	Animal	Vegetable	Mineral
7. Gelt	Animal	Vegetable	Mineral
8. Smontzess	Animal	Vegetable	Mineral
9. Pupik	Animal	Vegetable	Mineral
10. Tsatske	Animal	Vegetable	Mineral
11. Knubble	Animal	Vegetable	Mineral
12. Latkes	Animal	Vegetable	Mineral
13. Fleyshik	Animal	Vegetable	Mineral
14. Knaiydleach	Animal	Vegetable	Mineral
15. Tsibele	Animal	Vegetable	Mineral

Answers: 1. Animal: A female gentile; 2. Animal: A complainer; 3. Mineral: Dirt—usually moral dirt; 4. Animal: Guts; intestines; 5. Mineral: A steam bath; 6. Vegetable: Liquor; 7. Mineral: Money; 8. Mineral: Gadgets; 9. Animal: A bellybutton; 10. Mineral: A knickknack; 11. Vegetable: Garlic; 12. Vegetable: Potato pancakes; 13. Animal: Meat products; 14. Vegetable: A matzo ball; 15. Vegetable: An onion

Ripe Ol' Corn

"Uncle Josh Rides a Bicycle"

"Uncle Josh," Cal Stewart's country bumpkin, had problems figuring out modern city life (circa 1901). Here he tries out yet another fad that was sweeping the nation—a big-wheeled bicycle.

ALONG LAST SUMMER Ruben Hoskins, that is Ezra Hoskins' boy, he come home from college and brought one of them new fangled bysickle machines home with him, and I think ever since that time the whole town of Punkin Centre has got the bysickle fever.

Old Deacon Witherspoon he's been a-ridin' a bysickle to Sunday school, and Jim Lawson he couldn't ride one of them 'cause he's got a wooden leg; but he jist calculated if he could git it hitched up to the mowin' machine, he could cut more hay with it than any man in Punkin Centre. Somebody said Si Pettingill wuz tryin' to pick apples with a bysickle.

Well, all our boys and girls are ridin' bysickles now, and nothin' would do but I must learn how to ride one of them. Well, I didn't think very favorably on it, but in order to keep peace in the family I told them I would learn.

Well, gee willikee, by gum. I wish you had been thar when I commenced. I took that machine by the horns and I led it out into the middle of the road, and I got on it sort of unconcerned like, and then I got off sort of unconcerned like. Well, I set down a minnit to think it over, and then the trouble commenced. I got on that durned machine and it jumped up in the front and kicked up behind, and bucked up in the middle, and shied and balked and jumped sideways, and carried on worse 'n a couple of steers the fust time they're yoked. Well, I managed to hang on fer a spell, and then I went up in the air and come down all over that bysickle. I fell on top of it and under it and on both sides of it; I fell in front of the front wheel and behind the hind wheel at the same time.

Durned if I know how I done it but I did. I run my foot through the spokes, and put about a hundred and fifty punctures in a hedge fence, and skeered a hoss and buggy clear off the highway. I done more different kinds of tumblin' than any circus performer I ever seen in my life, and I made more revolutions in a fifteen-foot circle than any buzz-saw that ever was invented. Well, I lost the lamp, I lost the clamp, I lost my patience, I lost my temper, I lost my self-respect, my last suspender button and my standin' in the community. I broke the handle bars, I broke the sprockets, I broke the 10 command-ments, I broke my New Year's pledge and the law agin loud and abusive language, and Jim Lawson got so excited that he run his wooden leg through a knot-hole in the porch and couldn't git it out again.

Well, I'm through with it; once is enough fer me. You can all ride your durned old bysickles that you want to, but fer my part I'd jist as soon stand up and walk as to sit down and walk. No more bysickles fer your Uncle Josh, not if he knows it, and your Uncle Josh sort of calculates as how he do.

French kings had a variety of colorful nicknames, including Louis the Fat (Louis IV), Louis the Indolent (Louis V), Philip the Amorous, Pepin the Short, Charles the Bald (Charles II), and Charles the Simple (Charles III).

Driving Passions

TALES ABOUT AUTOMOBILES

Buckle up, as *Bathroom Companion* correspondent Kathie Meyer maneuvers through some pretty weird car stories, as well as some interesting things you may not have known about the automobile.

NO TIP TO THE VALET NECESSARY

Going rate to buy a prime parking space in beautiful downtown Melbourne, Australia? Well, last time we checked, Jones Lang Wootton Company was offering them for fourteen thousand dollars. But that's nothing. The same properties company was offering spaces in Hong Kong for a half-million dollars each.

PAY YOUR PREMIUM TO ME NOW, MAKE YOUR CLAIMS TO ST. PETER

In 1994, Oklahoma City police discovered several credulous but sincere people had been sold an automobile liability insurance called "God's Insurance Policy." The policy was issued by "the Father, Son, and the Holy Ghost" and contained mostly text from the Bible. It cost $285 and stated that "God's policy" would lend better protection than the usual commercial variety. Purchasers said they'd been told that the policy complied with Oklahoma's mandatory-insurance law.

WHY VOLVO MEANS "I ROLL" IN LATIN

In April 2002, Irv Gordon proudly reached the 2 million mile mark on his 1966 Volvo P1800, a car he bought new when he was 25 years old. In the ensuing years, Mr. Gordon, 61, a retired school teacher, averaged 55,000 miles a year. He recorded his first million miles in 1987. Gordon has recovered the driver's seat twice, rebuilt the engine once at 680,000 miles, and has changed its oil 660 times. He claims the car has never broken down or failed to start. Asked how he felt to reach 2 million miles, Gordon said, "I was so happy, I couldn't get out of the car."

The 1898 Winton was the first car driven across America.

SOMEONE FORGOT TO TELL VOLKSWAGEN

In 1891, Emile Levassor and Rene Panhard of France were the first to come up with the idea of putting the engine in the front end of automobiles. This design, known as the *Systeme Panhard,* was the forerunner of modern cars. The vehicle Levassor and Panhard designed had an upright Daimler engine, a pedal-operated clutch, a change-speed gear box which drove the rear axle, a front radiator, and wooden ladder-chassis.

THE EDSEL BREATHES A SILENT SIGH OF RELIEF

According to National Public Radio's *Car Talk* listeners, the ten worst cars of the millennium were: **10.** VW Bus. **9.** Renault Dauphine. **8.** Cadillac Cimarron. **7.** Dodge Aspen/Plymouth Volare. **6.** Renault LeCar. **5.** Chevy Chevette. **4.** AMC Gremlin. **3.** Ford Pinto. **2.** Chevy Vega. **1.** Yugo!

BEATS SELLING LEMONADE

Road construction caused a traffic jam near the Jordan house in Corvallis, Oregon. Sean Jordan, out of school on summer vacation, organized his siblings and a cousin into a work crew to clear an old railroad line that ran parallel to the main road and through the Jordan property. The kids then created their own private toll road, manning the pike, and collecting 50¢ per vehicle. The kids earned $270 in an eleven-day period, despite the fact that someone stole their money the first night and some cars just sped by without paying.

WOMEN DRIVERS

After the first American automobile appeared in 1893, women contributed to its subsequent development more than people realize. In 1903, Mary Anderson invented a windshield wiper operated by using a handle inside the car. Anderson's goal was to improve safety while driving in poor weather conditions. In the next twenty years, women were granted more than 175 auto-related patents. These inventions included a carburetor, a clutch mechanism, an electric engine starter, turn signals, traffic lights, and a starting mechanism. And during the 1930s, geologist Helen Blair Bartlett used her knowledge of petrology and mineralogy to develop new insulation for spark plugs.

Ladies and cars have gone together since the beginning of car history.

TAKING THE CAR SERIOUSLY

Ohio can boast a number of firsts in U.S. transportation history. They claim the first ambulance service (1865), first automobile made by John Lambert (1891), first traffic light (1914), first full-time automobile service station (1899), the invention of the automobile self-starter (1911), and the site of the first pedestrian button for the control of a traffic light (1948). Akron is where Charles Goodyear developed the process of vulcanizing rubber in 1839, and it is widely recognized as the rubber capital of the world, thanks to the Goodrich and Goodyear plants located there.

Akron, Ohio: Rubber Capital of the World!

DRIVING UP DAISIES

Robert James Thompson, attempted to avoid tickets by claiming it was his wife who was driving two of his vans when they were caught by speed cameras three different times in 2001. Police became suspicious when they attempted to ticket Mrs. Thompson and found a notation on her record that she had died in 1998. The fifty-nine-year-old Thompson, who runs a pest control business, exhibited a mastery of the obvious when he noted: "It's just because my wife's dead that I got caught."

AMERICA'S MOST STOLEN

According to the National Insurance Crime Bureau, the most frequently stolen automobiles in 2002 are: **10.** Ford F150. **9.** Ford Taurus. **8.** Chevy Caprice. **7.** Toyota Corolla. **6.** Chevy C/K Pickups. **5.** Jeep Cherokee. **4.** Honda Civic. **3.** Oldsmobile Cutlass. **2.** Honda Accord. **1.** Toyota Camry. Frequently stolen cars follow market trends and the list varies from location to location. For instance, the Oldsmobile Cutlass was 2002's number one stolen vehicle in New Orleans and Chicago; the Chevrolet full-size pickup topped the stolen list in Fresno, California; and the Accord was number one in New York state.

UP ON THE ROOFTOP, FOUR-WHEELS PAUSE

A friend of Dave Anthony's asked him to help tear down his house, so he began by knocking down the garage with his 1984 four-wheel-drive GMC pickup truck. While ramming the garage and drinking liberally, a flash of genius struck Anthony: He decided to see if he could maneuver his truck up onto his friend's roof. He wanted a photograph of the truck to submit to a four-wheel-drive magazine. "It wouldn't be a good life without a challenge," he said. "If you don't break something, you aren't trying very hard."

Anthony's truck made it to the top, albeit with a great deal of damage. Police, called by neighbors, prevented the alcohol-besotted Anthony from driving the truck down, and so he was stuck with a hefty towing bill to add to his repair bill.

WHAT'S IN A NAME?

• The Edsel was named after Edsel Ford—Henry Ford's son, Henry Ford II's dad.

• "Diesel" means nothing in particular. It's the name of the fellow who invented the engine—Rudolph Diesel.

• The VW Bug was commissioned by Adolf Hitler, who wanted to call it *Kraft-durch-Freude Wagen* ("Strength Through Joy Car.") Luckily, marketers eventually convinced him that *Volkswagen* ("the People's Auto") sounded better.

Hog Wild!

A Pig is Worth a Thousand Words

If you're a pig lover (and who isn't?), you'll be in hog heaven with these pig facts submitted by *Bathroom Companion* correspondent Sue Shipman.

• Pigs don't sweat.

• A pig can run a 7-minute mile.

• Pigs have four toes to use on each foot, but only stand on two.

• Pigs are the source of more than forty drugs and pharmaceuticals, including insulin.

• Ben and Jerry's recycles waste from ice cream production by giving it to local Vermont hog farmers as pig slop. The farmers claim the animals enjoy all the flavors except Mint Oreo.

• Groundhogs have also been known as "whistle pigs."

• The words *hog* and *pig* are not interchangeable. It's all about poundage. A pig is a swine that weighs under 180 pounds. A hog is anything above that weight. Believe it or not, these weight class distinctions mean a lot if you're in the market for pigs.

• Some other pig terminology: *Piglet* is the name for a newborn pig until weaning (2 to 5 weeks). A *shoat* or *weaner* is a young pig; a *barrow* is a half-grown castrated male, and a *gilt* is a half-grown female. In the full-grown categories, *boars* are uncastrated males, *stags* are the castrated ones, and *sows* are all females. Remember this next time you're at a pig auction or you'll have bacon and egg on your face.

• In 1976 the swine flu vaccine caused more illness and death than did the disease itself.

• The phrase "pearls before swine" is from the Bible, Matthew 7:6—"Give not that which is holy unto the dogs, neither cast ye your pearls before swine, lest they trample them under their feet."

No matter what your big brother told you, pigs don't fly: never have; never will.

• The upper part of a pig's haunch provides the best, and therefore most expensive, cuts of meat. Hence the term, "high on the hog."

• **The Ineffective Rooter**—an Aesopian story:

> A drunken Man was lying in the road with a bleeding nose, upon which he had fallen, when a Pig passed that way.
>
> "You wallow fairly well," said the Pig, "but, my fine fellow, you have much to learn about rooting."

• Large hog farms made it necessary for the North Carolina legislature to vote $170,000 to fund a swine odor task force in 1994. The task force declined to take their measurements using machines, stating, "The human nose is the primary element in most attempts to gauge odor."

• Burger King restaurants cook up about 500,000 pounds of bacon every month.

• Ever wonder why the piggy bank? It's yet another victim of faulty translation. The term probably comes from the obscure French word *pygg*—a certain type of clay used to make money jars in the fifteenth century.

• Hickory smoked bacon takes about twenty-one days to cure.

• About half of the domestic pigs in the world live in China.

• The largest pig ever was 2,552 pounds. His name was Big Bill.

• A piglet is born at about 3.5 pounds and can double its weight in a week.

• It took forty-eight little piggies to film the title role in the movie, *Babe*. Each pig could act only between the ages of 16 and 18 weeks, for consistency. Mechanical pigs also played roles in the movie and sequel. The studio swears that none of the pigs used in the movies were turned into ham or bacon—they all went to universities, ag colleges, or farms to live out their 15–20 year natural lives.

• Columbus introduced hogs to the Americas in 1493 on his second voyage.

• Pigs can get sunburned.

• Pigs are loud! The Concorde jet was banned from New York when its jets were louder than 112 decibels at take off. A university study measuring pig squeals found the squeals averaged between 100 and 115 decibels.

• Buying a "pig in a poke" means buying something sight unseen. Unscrupulous merchants in Medieval Europe would often put a runt pig or a stray cat in the small bag (which was called a "poke") instead of the promised young pig. So when wary buyers actually looked into the poke prior to their purchase, they would often "let the cat out of the bag."

• Calling a police officer a "pig" wasn't just from the 1960s; the term has been in used commonly among the criminal element for almost two hundred years before that.

• Since Muslims shun pork and devout Hindus do not eat beef, in New Delhi India you can get a "Maharaja Mac" at McDonald's. It is made of mutton.

• Pigs eat like, well, pigs. They're omnivores and eat anything from breads, fruits, and vegetables, to rodents, lizards, and even parts of other pigs. One of their favorite meals is rattlesnake.

• Pigs kill more people each year than sharks do. Pigs, however, are not really aggressive, they're just large and persistent—sometimes fatally so, especially to small children.

• Although pigs sound the same from country to country, how we interpret those sounds varies. Here's what a pig "says" in places around the world:

"Oink, oink"—America
"Crum, crum"—Poland
"Hulu, hulu"—China
"Groin, groin"—France
"Kryoo krool"—Russia
"Ood, ood"—Thailand
"Neff, neff"—Sweden
"Hrju, hrju"—Ukrainian
"Rok, rok"—Croatia/Serbia
"Buu, buu"—Japan
"Grunz"—Germany

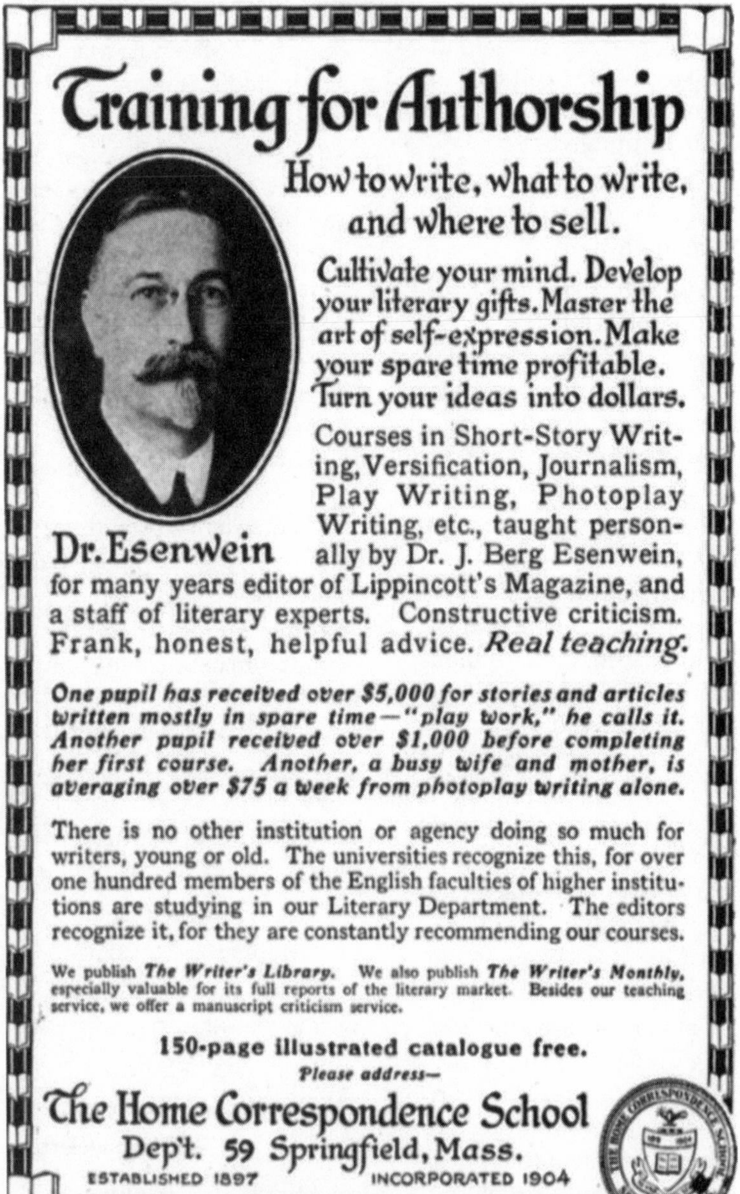

Training for Authorship
How to write, what to write, and where to sell.
Cultivate your mind. Develop your literary gifts. Master the art of self-expression. Make your spare time profitable. Turn your ideas into dollars.
Dr. Esenwein
Courses in Short-Story Writing, Versification, Journalism, Play Writing, Photoplay Writing, etc., taught personally by Dr. J. Berg Esenwein, for many years editor of Lippincott's Magazine, and a staff of literary experts. Constructive criticism. Frank, honest, helpful advice. Real teaching.
One pupil has received over $5,000 for stories and articles written mostly in spare time—"play work," he calls it. Another pupil received over $1,000 before completing her first course. Another, a busy wife and mother, is averaging over $75 a week from photoplay writing alone.
There is no other institution or agency doing so much for writers, young or old. The universities recognize this, for over one hundred members of the English faculties of higher institutions are studying in our Literary Department. The editors recognize it, for they are constantly recommending our courses.
We publish The Writer's Library. We also publish The Writer's Monthly, especially valuable for its full reports of the literary market. Besides our teaching service, we offer a manuscript criticism service.
150-page illustrated catalogue free.
Please address—
The Home Correspondence School
Dep't. 59 Springfield, Mass.
ESTABLISHED 1897
INCORPORATED 1904

W. C. Privy Wants You!

Join the **Bathroom Companions of Mr. Privy** (BCOMP)! Send an e-mail to *membership@bathroomcompanion.com* and we'll send you a printable free membership card, plus a "Go Away, I'm Reading the *Bathroom Companion*" door knob hanger for your bathroom. And don't forget to drop by our Web site at **www.bathroomcompanion.com** for bonus articles and more fun things.

Or if you prefer, write to us at Bathroom Companion, c/o St. Martin's Press, 175 Fifth Avenue, New York, NY 10010.

Send us your story ideas, photos, articles, Web links you like, or other cool stuff we'd want to know about for the next Bathroom Companion. If we use them, we'll thank you in the next book and maybe even send you cool stuff in return.

Last known photo of W. C. Privy in retirement, prematurely trying to invent the Rubik's Cube.

(For emergency use only)

(For emergency use only)

"W. C. Privy's Original Bathroom Companion—
It's not just for the bathroom anymore."

W. C. Privy's *Original* Bathroom Companion
NUMBER 2

EDITED BY ERIN BARRETT & JACK MINGO

St. Martin's Griffin *New York*

www.stmartins.com

Designed, packaged, and produced by the Univark Deconstructionists

ISBN 0-312-31580-5

First Edition: December 2003

10 9 8 7 6 5 4 3 2 1

Thanks!

To the *Bathroom Companion* staff members, our family, and our friends, for helping us keep W. C. Privy's dream alive. Without you, this book wouldn't have happened. Especially...

Heather Jackson Silverman
Elizabeth Bewley
Pam Suwinsky of Thalia Publishing Services
Kathie Meyer
Susan Shipman
Chris McLaughlin
Mary-Nell Bockman
Michele Montez
John Karle
Sarah Cocroft
Don Jollyson
Brian Marshall
Elsa Bronte
Mark Riley
Janelle Barbier
Glynne Gilmore
Cynthia Damon
Elana Mingo
Jackson Hamner
Georgia Hamner
Vera Mingo
Jerry & Lynn Barrett
Powell Hamner
Everyone at St. Martin's Press
Skip Colcord & Polaroid Corp.
Energizer
www.NJHotair.com
Gino Micheletti
The BCOMPs (members of the W. C. Privy fan club—see p. 476)
All the Univark Truckers

· "Making Eggs" and "Money Magic" originally published in *How to Spit Nickels,* by Jack Mingo, Contemporary Books,1993. Adapted with permission of author.

· "Our Favorite Disasters" adapted from *Just Curious About History, Jeeves,* by Erin Barrett and Jack Mingo, Pocket Books, 2002. Adapted with permission of authors.

· "Hand Shadows" series originally published in *Hand Shadows to Be Thrown Upon the Wall* (1859) and *Hand Shadows: Second Series* (1860), by Henry Bursill.

· "The Spirits Speak" adapted from *How to Spit Nickels,* by Jack Mingo, Contemporary Books, 1993. Used with permission of author.

· "Buttheads," "Elephants," and "Simian Says," originally published in *Just Curious About Animals and Nature, Jeeves,* by Erin Barrett and Jack Mingo, Pocket Books, 2002. Adapted with permission of authors.

· Special thanks to Aaron Trauring, Simcha Schtull, and the *Whole Pop Magazine Online* for some of the ideas and content.

Genius!

More About Mr. Privy, the Original

"There will be imitators, but no matter: 'Imitation is the sincerest form of plagiarism.' They can be nothing but pale counterfeits of the genuine Privy." —W. C. Privy

Since WE RELEASED the first volume of *W. C. Privy's Original Bathroom Companion,* we have received many questions about W. C. Privy from readers, friends, lawyers, and creditors. Ironically, the more we've discovered about this reclusive and brilliant fellow, the less we seem to know. It turns out that much of what we believed to be true turned out to be false. Much of what we believed to be false turned out to be true. And much of what we believed to be neither false nor true turned out to be neither true nor false.

So, while we may not be back to square one, we are at least back to square three or even two. Here's what we currently believe that we think we know (although we could be wrong): W. C. Privy was born on a mountaintop in Tennessee. As a child, he might have worked the coal mines in Appalachia. As a teen, he may have written marital manuals under the pen name "Dr. Hiram Cheepily." He might have founded a dollhouse factory in Maine. And after he retired from writing *Bathroom Companions,* he and his wife, Lucienne ("Loo") Donniker-Privy, may have opened some sort of museum somewhere in the Pacific Northwest.

On a more definitive note, additional, rare fragments from the original, century-old *Bathroom Companions* have begun appearing. As you recall, virtually all copies disappeared shortly after publication because it was a time when good, affordable toilet paper was hard to come by. However, a few scattered sheets of *BC #6* have appeared, giving further clues about the contents of Mr. Privy's wildly popular series. In honor of the man and his commercial good sense, we've run computer analyses of the fragments and discovered some of the original pieces they've come from, in order to reproduce them in these pages. See if you can guess which three articles came directly from the editorial mind of the great latrinographist.

We hope you enjoy Volume 2. If so, you may want to track down Volume 1 in your local bookstore or on our online site {www.bathroomcompanion.com} for yourself and your friends. (Conversely, if you *don't* enjoy it, you may want to consider buying copies for your enemies.) And we hope Mr. Privy, wherever he may be, is looking down (or, just as likely, up) at our efforts with bemusement and approval.

'Til next time,

Erin Barrett

Jack Mingo

ABOUT BARRETT & MINGO

Erin Barrett and Jack Mingo are particularly suited for the task of reviving the *Bathroom Companion*. They have written dozens of entertaining books including *Just Curious, Jeeves; Doctors Killed George Washington; Cats Don't Always Land On Their Feet; The Whole Pop Catalog;* and *How the Cadillac Got Its Fins*. Their daily column, *Random Kinds of Factness*, appears in newspapers around the country.

What's Inside...

Sweet!

How Twinkies Got Crèmed

You may be embarrassed to admit it, but you know it's true: you love Twinkies. Everyone loves Twinkies—the food of the convenience store gods.

THEY'RE GOLDEN brown, irresistibly spongy, and filled with "crème" (you don't think there's actually cream in there, do you?). And they're the Continental Baking Company's biggest seller, even beating out that other Continental food marvel, Wonder Bread. Twinkies are quite literally "the greatest thing since sliced bread," since Wonder was the first bread that came presliced and packaged.

Twinkies were invented in 1930 at the beginning of the Great Depression by the Chicago-area Continental plant manager. His name was James A. Dewar. At the time, Continental was a new company, only six years old, and Dewar wasn't completely confident in its ability to weather the new economic times. It didn't make sense to him, for example, that the plant had lots of expensive pans dedicated to a product called "Little Short Cake Fingers," which was baked for only six weeks a year. The

Fingers were designed to be made into strawberry shortcake, so they went into commission only during the strawberry season. During the rest of the year, they lay idle.

Dewar figured that the shortcake fingers could sell year-round if the company came up with something—a filling, say—to go with it. He mixed up a banana-flavored "crème" (the company switched to vanilla ten years later when, during World War II, there was a banana shortage) and figured out a way to inject it into the shortcake using three syringe-like injection tubes.

But Dewar was having trouble coming up with a name he liked until, on a business trip to St. Louis, he and a colleague drove past the Twinkle Toes Shoes factory. His friend suggested the name "Twinkle Fingers" for his new cakes; Dewar shortened it to Twinkies.

Continental started selling Dewar's new Twinkies in packs of two for 5¢. Since that time, it has made at least forty-five billion Twinkies—over two million tons. Sales records show that they sell best by far in the Midwest, and the *New York Times* has officially dubbed Chicago the "Twinkie Capital of the World" because folks in Chicago eat more Twinkies per capita than anywhere else.

Because of their success, Twinkies have had plenty of critics who call them the archetypal junk food. TV's Archie Bunker damned them with dubious praise, calling them "the white man's soul food."

In the early 1970s, they were mentioned prominently in a song called "Junk Food Junkie," and they were accused, in what was called "the Twinkie defense," of mentally unbalancing a San Francisco supervisor to the point of murder.

The company responds blandly: "We make these cakes out of the same ingredients that you'd find in a typical kitchen," says a company spokesperson. "It's a fun food. That's our position."

Dewar, before he died in 1985, was a little less soft-spoken in defending his creation, "the best darn-tootin' idea I ever had." To live 88 years like him, he advised that you should "eat Twinkies every day and smoke a pack of cigarettes." Seriously, he'd add, "Some people say that Twinkies are the quintessential junk food, but I fed them to my four kids and they feed them to my fifteen grandchildren. My boy Jimmy played football for the Cleveland Browns. My other son, Bobby, played quarterback for the University of Rochester. Twinkies never hurt them."

As to the legend that they will last forever on the grocery shelf, the company admits they do, indeed, have a long shelf life. The "crème" works to keep them moist. They're also quick to point out that unsold Twinkies are replaced in stores after only 4 to 6 days.

MORE SWEET FACTS

- There are 17 Hostess bakeries across the country.
- Five hundred million Twinkies are consumed every year across America.
- Each year it takes over a half-million chickens to lay the 160 million large eggs needed to make Hostess Twinkies.
- The bakeries at the Hostess company can put out 1,000 Twinkies every minute.
- Hostess can crème about 52,000 Twinkies in an hour.
- It takes 40,000 miles of plastic wrap a year to package Hostess Twinkies.
- When the White House put together their time capsule for the millennium, they chose the Twinkie to go in as an "object of enduring American symbolism." ☾

The T.W.I.N.K.I.E.S. Project

Tests With Inorganic Noxious Kakes In Extreme Situations, or T.W.I.N.K.I.E.S., was carried out during finals week at Houston, Texas's Rice University in 1995. The point of the tests was to determine the properties of the Twinkie snack food cake.

These tests that were conducted on Twinkies included experiments with the force of gravity, radiation, flame, electricity, water, and blender. The names of the tests were far more scientific than the actual tests themselves, including "Maximum Density Test," "Rapid Oxidation Test," "Gravitational Response Test," and "Turing Test," which was actually an extremely modified version of a real intelligence test....

Although the tests really proved very little about Twinkies in any real sense, the Web site has become a living legend. It can be found, along with haikus to Twinkies and letters to the "scientists," at *http://www.twinkieproject.com/*.

According to Mark Twain

These notations supposedly come from *Puddin'head Wilson's Calendar*, a fictitious publication that Twain "quoted" whenever he needed a maxim to head a chapter.

• "Consider well the proportions of things. It is better to be a young Junebug than an old bird of paradise."

• "Adam was but human—that explains all. He did not want the apple for the apple's sake, he wanted it only because it was forbidden. The mistake was in not forbidding the serpent; then he would've eaten the serpent."

• "Adam and Eve had many advantages, but the principal one was, that they escaped teething."

• "Why is it that we rejoice at a birth and grieve at a funeral? It is because we are not the person involved."

• "Training is everything. The peach was once a bitter almond; cauliflower is nothing but cabbage with a college education."

• "Let us to endeavor so to live that when we come to die even the undertaker will be sorry."

• "Habit is habit, and not to be flung out of the window by any man, but coaxed downstairs a step at a time."

• "One of the most striking differences between a cat and a lie is that a cat has only nine lives."

• "Whoever has lived long enough to find out what life is, knows how deep a debt of gratitude we owe to Adam, the first great benefactor of our race. He brought death into the world."

• "All say, 'How hard it is that we have to die'—a strange complaint to come from people who have had to live."

• "The holy passion of Friendship is so sweet and steady and loyal and enduring that it will last through a whole lifetime, if not asked to lend money."

• "It is easy to find fault, if one has that disposition. There was once a man who, not being able to find any other fault with his coal, complained that there were too many prehistoric toads in it."

• "When angry, count to four; when very angry, swear."

• "When I reflect upon the number of disagreeable people who I know have gone to a better world, I am moved to lead a different life."

All in the Family

Feuds, Fighting, and Other Family Fun

By digging up family dirt, contributors Chris McLaughlin and Kathie Meyer have come up with some intriguing stories and stats about life with the people we love...and who sometimes drive us crazy.

WHY WE CALL IT A FAMILY

The word *family* comes from the Latin, *famulus,* which, mothers everywhere will be interested in learning, once meant "servant." From it, the word *familia* was derived, a collective term for all of the domestic servants in the household. That's what it meant when it first entered the English language. Sometime in the mid-17th century, the word came to include the entire household—relatives and servants. Eventually, it narrowed to mean just a group of related persons.

KEEPING UP WITH THE ITURRIBERRIGORRIGOIKOERROTAKOETXEAS

According to the Guinness Book of Records, the longest English surname that's not hyphenated is Featherstonehaugh (pronounced *Fanshaw*; go figure). Two other non-English, long, and difficult surnames are Iturriberrigorrigoikoerrotakoetxea (Basque) and MacGhilleseatheanaich (Gaelic).

JUGGLING A LARGE FAMILY

Experts advise families to become expert jugglers of work, school, and other responsibilities. The Boehmer family of Iowa took this advice perhaps a little too literally. Twenty years ago, Larry Boehmer was employed as a pipeline worker, often away from his family. Instead of pining for his wife and kids at night, he bought a juggling instruction book, and learned the basics of the craft. Once home again, Larry's children saw him practicing and wanted to try, too—even little Casey, who was born without a left forearm.

Larry and three of the children gave their first family performance at an amusement park in 1989. Today, Larry and Judy Boehmer have eleven juggling children—yes, Casey, too—and lay claim to being the world's largest juggling family.

RIDING IN NASCARS WITH BOYS

Good old brother boys: gotta love 'em. Especially if you were watching the Winston Cup race at Texas Motor Speedway, Fort Worth, in 1999. Five sets of brothers ran in the Primestar 500: Geoffrey and Brett Bodine, Kenny and Rusty Wallace, Terry and Bobby Labonte, Jeff and Ward Burton, and Darrell and Michael Waltrip. Terry Labonte won: brother Bobby was third.

MY EVIL TWIN

Twins don't usually have an evil sibling and a good sibling. However, in the case of the Han twins of Irvine, California, there might be reason to believe otherwise. Jeen decided to swipe credit cards and use them to run up debts she wouldn't have to pay off. She got busted, and believed her "good" twin Sunny was responsible for ratting her out. So what did Jeen do? She conspired to murder her sister and assume her identity. She got busted for that, too.

COMING BACK FOR MOORE

What are the odds? In the early 1990s, Richard Moore had to be rescued after he became mysteriously lodged in the ceiling of a convenience store in West Haven, Connecticut. Several years later, in 1994, his brother David had to be rescued from the same convenience store when he got stuck in the chimney while attempting to burglarize it.

A Moore brother family tradition.

DADDIES & MUMMIES

Fourteen mummies, some dating back to 1,000 BC, were discovered in an ancient tomb in one of China's old cemeteries. The Shanghai office of the *Guinness Book of Records* dubbed this the world's largest family joint burial.

Archaeologists say the custom of family joint burial was quite popular in parts of China 3,000 years ago, although the customs varied slightly from family to family. The mummies were of both genders; some were old and some were children. Their faces were covered, but underneath, the various facial openings were plugged with things like gold foil, wool, and flour paste—perhaps as part of the embalming process or for religious reasons. Buried alongside were stone, wood, bronze, and iron articles, including various bits of pottery, as well as exquisite fabrics.

HAPPY FAMILY

Perhaps you've seen "Happy Family" on a Chinese menu. It's called that because it's made with a little "family member" of all kinds of meat and seafood, and its served at family events like weddings, reunions, and so on. On a similar note, the "Mother and Child Reunion" contains chicken (the "mother") and an egg (the "child").

"Our Happy Family Life Chairman Mao Gave Us," Chinese propaganda poster,1954

TWO OR MORE
According to the Statistical Abstract of the United States, in the year 2000, 85 percent of American households fall under the "family" category. The average family household has 3.24 persons.

KISS AND MAKE UP
Fed up with family squabbling during a bankruptcy trial, Florida judge Jay Cristol came up with an interesting, although probably futile, way to resolve at least some of the differences. He ordered Judith Herskowitz to send a birthday card to her estranged sister Susan Charney. He ordered that the card must have "Happy Birthday, Sister" on it, and must include Judith's signature. Just to cover all bases, he added a proviso: "The card shall not contain any negative, inflammatory or unkind remarks."

MILITARY BRATS
Within the U.S. armed forces, 55% of military personnel are married; 630,000 members have children (only 6% of these are single parents)—a collective total of 1.2 million children of military personnel. Seventy-three percent are eleven years of age or younger; 39% are below the age of six.

An ad from back in the days when birds were heavily involved in subversive politics

The Best!

The Ways We Say Something's the Greatest

From "cool" to "bad" to "boss," the slang terms that have told you, "Baby, you're tops!"

Bad: People have been using opposite words to mean "good" since the 1830s, when *nasty* meant "wonderful." The 1950s led a resurgence of the practice, leading to this exchange from "Give Him a Great Big Kiss" by the Shangri-Las (1962): "I hear he's bad!" "Well, he's *good* bad, but he's not evil."

Boss: Re-popularized in the early 1960s, *boss* first meant "the best" way back in the 1600s.

Cool: Along with *crazy, far out, real gone,* and *wild, cool* came from beatnik slang in the 1950s.

Copacetic: Popularized in the 1930s by tap dancer Bill "Bojangles" Robinson.

Cute: Came from "acute" in the 1860s.

Ducky: Now used ironically, *ducky* has meant good things since the 1830s. Before that, it was a term of endearment, and in Shakespeare's time, it was slang for female breasts.

Fabulous: Originally having to do with fables, *fabulous* has had its current meaning since about 1600. *Fantastic,* likewise, originally meant something that existed only in fantasy; in the late 1940s it attained its present meaning.

Hot: People assume that *hot* is a recent slang term, but it came to mean sexually attractive back in 1910.

Nice: When *nice* entered English from Latin in the 1290s, it meant ignorant or foolish. It took several centuries to begin meaning something good.

Nifty: Popularized in the 1860s, *nifty* might be short for *magnificent*.

Out of sight: You think "Outta sight!" first appeared in the 1960s? Nope, try the Bowery in the 1840s.

Phenom: People began shortening *phenomenon* back in the 1890s.

Spiffy: *Spiffy* started out meaning well dressed in England, and then in America in the 1870s, it came to mean any kind of stylish excellence.

Swell: The original meaning of being swollen or enlarged began in the 9th century. By the 1720s, *swelled head* came to mean pompous and stuck-up, but the word also began taking on the additional meaning of someone very well dressed by the early 1800s and general excellence not long after.

Terrific: In the 1660s, *terrific* meant *terrifying,* but by the 1880s, it had somehow become a compliment.

Stately Knowledge

12 Reasons Why Ya Gotta Love Idaho

Here are our favorite reasons to love the state of famous potatoes.

1 The state of Idaho plays host to the deepest river gorge in North America. It's Hell's Canyon, which runs along the western border of the state. It's more than 2,600 feet deeper than the Grand Canyon.

2 How can you not mention potatoes when you talk about Idaho? The state produces more than 28% of the nation's spuds. McDonald's alone uses 500,000 pounds of the state's potato crop each year.

3 In honor of all those potatoes, annual Spud Day is celebrated each year in Shelley, Idaho. Along with music and a parade are spud-specific games like Tug-O-War over a pool of mashed taters and the Potato Cook-off.

4 While we're on the topic, the World Potato Exposition is in Blackfoot. There you can see the world's largest concrete potato and the world's largest potato chip. It's a 25-inch-wide Pringle, donated by Proctor & Gamble.

5 Idaho's state capital is geothermally heated. That means hot water, naturally found about 3,000 feet underground, is pumped up and used to heat the building. We think it's pretty safe to say it's the only one of its kind in the United States.

6 Next time you're in Idaho, don't forget to visit Island Park. It's a city full of resorts, but it's laid out in a rather odd way. The resorts were all built along the same road, so when the city decided to draw boundary

lines, they stretched about 33 miles long. The results are that it's a skinny town, with a long street running through the middle of it.

7 Today it's spuds, but Idaho used to be home to a bunch of gold and silver mines. As a result, there are quite a number of ghost towns with names like Gold Dredge and Yankee Fork.

8 If you like a good fiddle, check out Weisler, Idaho. It's home to the annual National Old Time Fiddler's Contest.

9 Several more reasons to love Idaho: Ty Cobb, Mariel Hemingway, Wyatt Earp, Lillian Disney, Philo Farnsworth (inventor of TV), Paul Revere and the Raiders, Ezra Pound, Picaboo Street, Lana Turner, Edgar Rice Burroughs, and Gutzon Borglum (designer of Mount Rushmore). They're all natives of the western state.

10 Idaho has a bit of history that's not widely known. Back in the 1830s, a large influx of Hawaiian natives came to live in the state. They all came to work in the booming fur trade. As a matter of fact, most of the staff at Fort Boise during this time was originally from the Hawaiian Islands. Remnants of this era live on in Owyhee County, which got its name from an early attempt to spell "Hawaii" in honor of its newest inhabitants.

Hey, diddle-diddle: Hula, spuds, and a fiddle. It's the Idaho way!

11 Idaho is home to both the world's longest gondola (in Kellogg) and the world's longest floating bridge (in Coeur d'Alene).

12 Way back in the 1940s, a ski lodge in Sun Valley hired Larry LaPrise and his group, the Ram Trio, to entertain vacationers. To give the crowd a fun activity, Larry came up with a simple dance, and a song that told how to do it. Called the Hokey Pokey, the dance was an instant hit with the skiiers, and the song was later recorded and made famous by bandleader Ray Anthony, also famous for the Bunny Hop. €

A Boy's Life in 1890

Guns & Taxidermy, Fires & Kites

In some ways, children have really lost out in the modern age. Years ago, preteen kids were expected to run wild through woods, streams, and fields. In these days of fear, over–coddling, and lawsuits, it's amazing what was considered a normal kid's life as reflected in *The American Boy's Handy Book* by Dan Beard (1890).

Gas-bubble.

"Procure a rubber tube and force it over the gas-burner. Dip your pipe into the suds and turn the gas on; the gas will be sufficient to blow the bubble. Since the gas is lighter than the air, the bubble will rapidly ascend...."

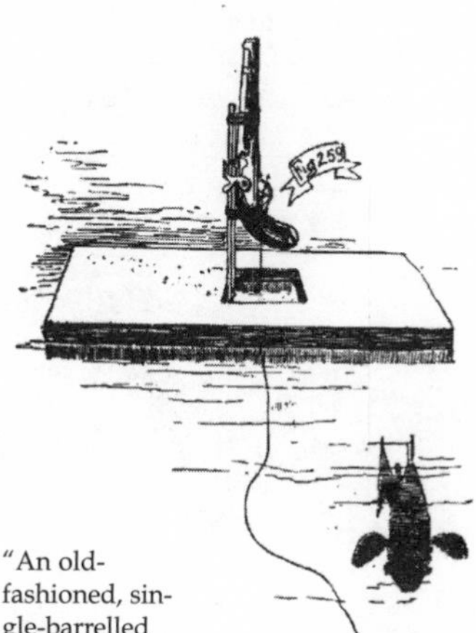

"An old-fashioned, single-barrelled pistol is securely lashed to an upright stick, and the fish-line tightly fastened to the trigger. To prevent accidents, my friend never loaded the pistol...."

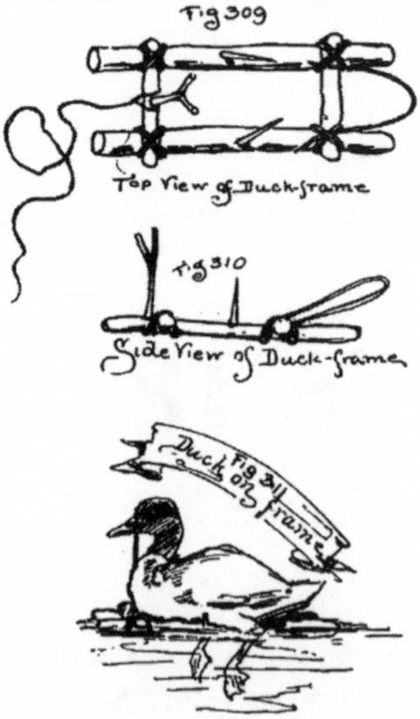

"Ducks made of wood have the usual objection—expense. You can convert dead ducks to decoys to lure their comrades to death....A **Y**-shaped stick holds the dead duck's head. Two pointed sticks keep the bird in place...."

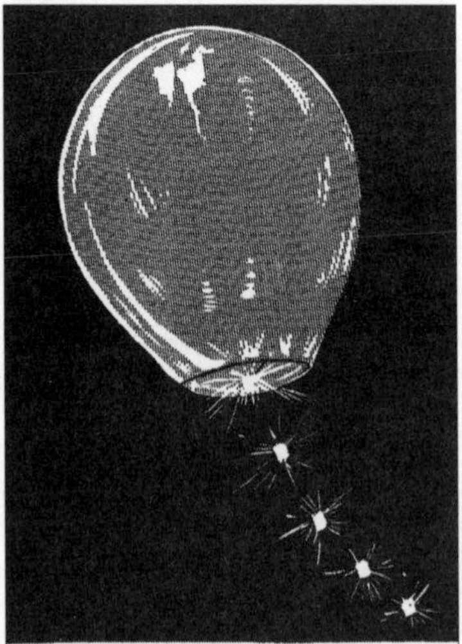

Night Balloon.

"Cut open the Roman candle and extract the powder and balls; wrap up in a piece of tissue-paper. As the fire creeps slowly along, the balloon mounts higher and higher, sending it skyward with a ball of fire for its motive power. Showers of jagged sparks fall constantly."

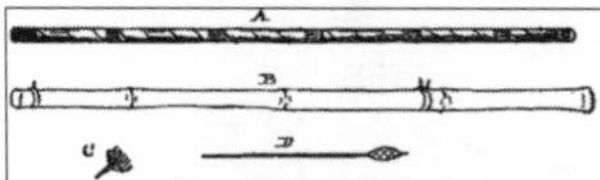

Fig. 231.—The Hunter's Blow-Gun.

"With a red-hot iron rod, enlarge the hollow in the center. The arrows must be very small, and a pin makes a simple point. You will then have a blowgun that can be used to hunt with."

"THE GOOSE FISHERMAN is a live goose with a line and spoon hook attached to one leg. As the bird swims, the spoon is jerked along and fish cannot restrain themselves. Then the fun begins. The goose feels something tugging at its leg and seeks refuge on the shore where you unhook the fish."

Position Assumed when Casting the Arrow.

"Whip-lash arrowsnappers should only be used with targets or game; they are dangerous on the play-ground."

Strap for Hawk's Leg.

"The hawk may be perfectly tamed if taken from the nest while young.... A tame hawk is very useful in keeping chickens out of the garden and as a decoy for catching other birds."

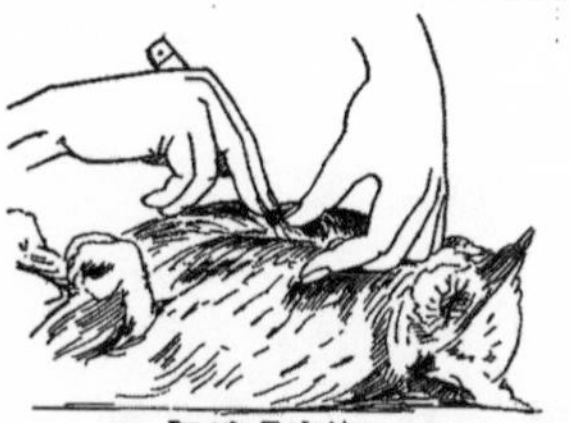

FIG. 148.—The Incision.

"He must be skinned and stuffed! Remove the eyes by breaking the bones that separate the eye orbits from the mouth....For a preservative, dissolve ten pounds soap, one pound potash, pipeclay and lime, and add ten pounds of arsenic. This preparation is, of course, very poisonous and should be so labeled."

"Fill with birdshot and bend the quill back. Allow it to fly forward — the shot from the tube can stun a small bird."

Spring Shot-gun.

FIG. 139.—Mole Trap.

"I object to deadfalls on principle, and I include this trap with some reluctance."

FIG. 90.—Cutters.

"Fasten three sharp pieces of broken glass with wax, cloth and wood. Pass twine through each apparatus. Tie to your kite's tail. To win the battle, maneuver your kite and cut your opponent's string."

"There is always a certain danger attending the use of firearms which is avoided by the crossbow....The young sportsman may shoot several times at the same bird or rabbit without frightening it away."

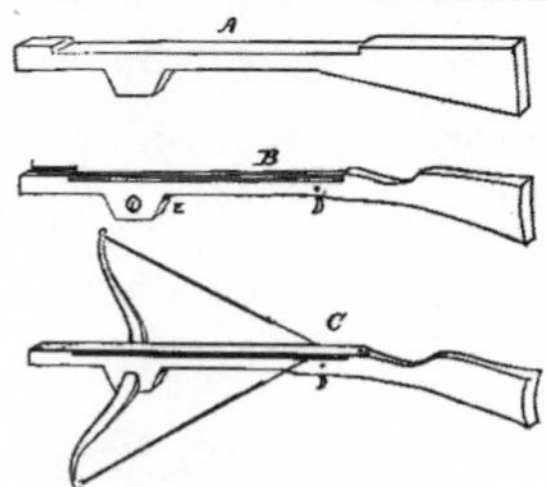

FIG. 129.—The Elastic Cross-Bow.

"To light the gas with your finger, turn it on, walk around sliding your feet on the carpet, and then touch the burner. Instantly the light will blaze up like magic."

"One end cut like a quill pen, your lance seldom injures your specimens. With a quick movement push the stick and animal both into the mud."

"Taking a long pull at a cigar, he blew the smoke into the paper box and commenced to tap the sides of it with a pencil. At each tap, a tiny but perfect smoke ring shot into the air."

Smoke-Rings.

Tom Swifties I

"Tell Me a Swifty," Tom said Punishingly

From the surreal 1960s came elephant jokes and Tom Swifties, based on bad puns and the stylistic excesses of Victor Appleton, who created the popular Tom Swift stories (see pages 53, 295 and 383).

"I can't believe I ate that whole pineapple!" Tom said dolefully.
"I dropped the toothpaste," Tom said, crestfallen.
"That's the last time I pet a lion," Tom said offhandedly.
"We don't have a homerun hitter," Tom said ruthlessly.
"I'll dig another ditch around the castle," Tom said remotely.
"I keep shocking myself," said Tom, revolted.
"I shouldn't sleep on railroad tracks," said Tom, beside himself.
"My steering wheel won't turn," Tom said straightforwardly.
"I've lost a lot of weight," Tom expounded.
"I keep banging my head on things," Tom said bashfully.
"I'll have to telegraph him again," Tom said remorsefully.
"I can't get down from the mountain!" Tom alleged.
"Let's play a C, E, and G," said Tom's band, in accord.
"You call this a musical?" asked Les miserably.
"I must make the fire hotter!" Tom bellowed.
"I have no carpet for the landing," Tom said with a blank stare.
"The girl's been kidnapped," Tom said mistakenly.
"I want a motorbike," Tom moped.
"That just doesn't add up," said Tom, nonplussed.
"Who says I have too many children?" said Mary overbearingly.
"We make a good opera duo," said Tom, callously and placidly.

Neck-rophilia

Tall Tales About Giraffes

Who doesn't love giraffes, the tallest land animal in the world? They may look absurd, but their design works in their environment. Let's take a short look at a mighty long animal.

WALK LIKE AN AFRICAN

Most animals alternate left and right feet as they walk. Giraffes walk by moving the two left feet, then the two right. Only cats and camels walk in the same way. Despite the awkward gait, giraffes can gallop at a speed of 35 mph.

NECK BONE'S CONNECTED TO ANOTHER NECK BONE....

The African plains giraffe, with a neck that extends 8 feet, has seven vertebrae in its neck, the same number as every other mammal, from man to mouse to whale.

SENSELESS BRUTALITY

The first giraffe ever seen in Europe was butchered at the Roman Coliseum for sport. It had been expected to put up a good fight against the gladiators, since the Romans thought it was a vicious cross between a leopard and a camel. Alas, the harmless herbivore was quickly slaughtered, to the cheers of the bloodthirsty Roman citizenry.

HOW'S THE WEATHER UP THERE?

A giraffe's heart would have to be quite a machine to reliably push blood up to its brain. Giraffe hearts can weigh more than 29 pounds and pump three times harder than human hearts. The blood pressure of a giraffe is the highest of any animal: 260/160. You'd think it would be in danger of blacking out when it bends down to drink and then suddenly stands up again. However, the giraffe comes with an amazing network of veins and valves in the neck to regulate and equalize blood flow.

This network has been compared to a sponge. If you watch a giraffe taking a drink, you will see that it doesn't stay down indefinitely, but raises its head now and again. When the giraffe tilts its head down to drink, the vessels in the head fill up, while valves partially close to keep the blood from rushing to the brain. The giraffe can perceive the pressure, and as the blood vessels approach full capacity, the giraffe knows it's time to right itself and reverse the process. Then, the valves partially close off and the blood vessels drain, so blood doesn't quickly rush out of the brain.

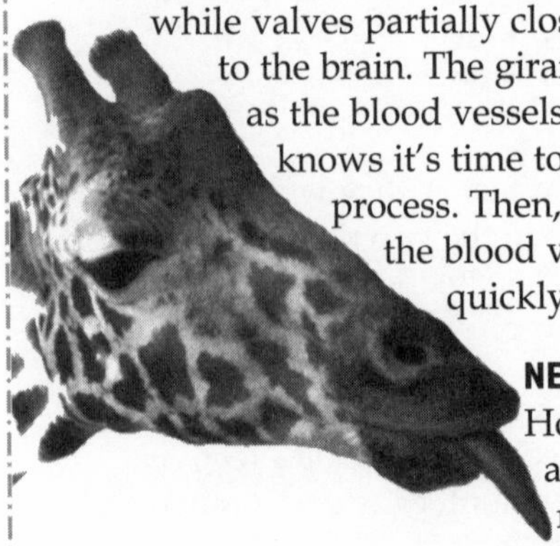

NEVER KISS A GIRAFFE

How long is a giraffe's tongue? On average, about 2 feet. It's not only really long, but black as well, which might serve the practical purpose of protecting it from sunburn...but it still looks really, really gross.

GIRAFFE NAP

Have you ever seen a giraffe lying down? It doesn't happen often. Adult giraffes would make a good supper for a lion on the African plain, so they've evolved some interesting sleep patterns. They sleep deeply a half-dozen times a day but for only a few minutes at a time, totalling about 30 minutes every 24 hours. At other times, they doze off lightly with their ears still perked and listening for predators. When a giraffe does lie down for resting, it usually will rest its head on its rump or a log so that its head stays elevated.

ALL IN THE FAMILY

There are only two separate species in the family *Giraffidae.* One is the steppe giraffe, the one we're familiar with, and the other is an okapi—also called a forest giraffe—that has a short neck and looks like a cross of a zebra, a mule, and a steppe giraffe. There are seven different subspecies of steppe giraffes, including the semi-arid savannah giraffe, the southern giraffe, and the masai giraffe. All of these have variations in their markings; however, that's not saying much because all giraffes, even members of the same subspecies and herd, have variations in their markings. Like humans' fingerprints, no two giraffes have the same spot patterns.

An Okapi, one weird-looking animal

WELCOME TO THE REAL WORLD, SPOT BOY!

A giraffe calf is welcomed into this world in a most unpleasant way. Its mother doesn't really have the ability to squat down close to the ground when it gives birth, so the newborn giraffe baby tumbles six feet to the ground. Despite the hard landing, within an hour the new baby will be standing up and trying out its spindly legs. It will also grow quickly—about half an inch an hour.

YOU THINK YOUR CHILDHOOD WAS TOUGH?

Only about a quarter of all giraffes born in the wild make it to adulthood. This is mostly because they are a favored prey among the big cats and jackals. Although the mother giraffe puts up a battle to save her baby, and can sometimes kill a lion or tiger with her kicks, the predators usually win.

HEAD–TO–FOOT NOTES

• The average male giraffe is about 17 feet tall. The average female is about 14 feet tall. This serves a very practical purpose: Unlike in most species, the two genders don't compete for food, because each reaches different levels of tree branches.

• A giraffe's digestive system is about 280 feet long. It has to be that long to extract nutrients from the high-fiber leaf diet that giraffes eat. Like cattle, giraffes chew cud that they've already swallowed and regurgitated.

• Giraffes can't swim.

• A giraffe can close its nostrils completely to keep out sand and dust.

• Giraffes have good vision, although they can't tell green from orange.

• A giraffe seldom uses its voice, though it can utter a variety of soft sounds.

• Giraffes perpetually wag their tails.

• "Camelopard" is just another name for the giraffe.

• A few African ranches raise giraffes for meat.

• Females live in groups with their young. Occasionally, they're joined by an adult male.

• Male giraffes fight each other by butting their heads against the chest and neck of their opponent. In a serious fight, you can hear their powerful head-thwacks from a distance of 100 yards. However, they rarely injure each other.

Modern Myth

"Railroad Tracks Based on Roman Chariots"

The Internet's an amazing thing—a really good myth can spread around the world instantly and linger for years afterward. Hey, did you hear that railroad tracks are based on the ruts from ancient Roman chariots? Not!

YOU HAVE TO LOVE the Internet: A piece of misinformation can get posted as a joke to a small mailing list in 1994 and take on a life of its own, accepted as gospel truth by millions as it ricochets and reverberates through cyberspace a decade later. Such is the case with the myth that modern railroad track specs came from the ancient Romans.

Here's how it began. On February 9, 1994, an R & D engineer for the military named Bill Innanen typed out a joke essay about the United States' and Britain's "exceedingly odd" railroad gauge—4 feet 8.5 inches between the tracks—and claimed that the measurement was based on the ruts left by ancient Roman war chariots.

Roman chariot

Innanen sent the mock essay to a small mailing list for other military researcher/developers. It was a group he expected would appreciate his wry point: that project specifications often live long beyond their usefulness.

Hoo boy, did they appreciate it, way beyond Innanen's wildest expectations. Members of the group sent it to their friends and coworkers, who passed it further along. The story spread and mutated as it traveled through hyperspace, and it started being reproduced in books, magazines, and news stories. The fact that it had been meant as a joke quickly got lost in the tellings and retellings. Meanwhile, Innanen sat by and watched, amused and horrified, powerless to stop his creation even if he had wanted to.

"The post was never meant to be a serious historical thesis," he explained when we tracked him down. "Never did I imagine that sending this to some friends would cause it to become a bona fide urban legend. I personally sent the message out only once. From there it took on a life of its own. Every once in a while someone would unknowingly send me a copy of whatever version was being passed around. It was like a prodigal child returning home, carrying the evidence of his travels with him (the additions and modifications). It's always fun to be able to reply to the sender on these occasions saying, 'Yes I've seen this one before. In fact, I wrote it!'"

So what's the truth? Actually, there were dozens of track sizes used by railroads, but railroads eventually standardized their equipment so that all trains could run on all tracks. But why that "exceedingly odd" gauge of 4 feet 8.5 inches? It turns out to be not so strange after all. Gauge is officially measured from the inside of the track. However, if you measured from the outside of the track, you'd find that it measures 5 feet—not a particularly odd measurement at all. ☾

Daredevils on tracks after a flood washed out a North Carolina railroad bridge, 1916

Something in Common I

It's easy, really—we'll give you a list of words and you tell us what one word goes with all of them. Answers below.

1. Street, iron, rugged, purposes, double, word
2. Baby, wicked sisters, twelve, stool, training
3. Mark, shelf, work, hand, binder, mobile
4. Big, fault, note, sewing, long, best, pounds, soldier
5. Bud, flash, head, switch, meal, housework, craft
6. Buttons, Cincinnati, Rhode Island, light, pepper, cross, hot
7. Wall, back, news, toilet, tiger, tissue, term
8. Rubber, Christmas, Easter, Navy, trained, harbor, elephant
9. Navy, string, counter, Boston, kidney
10. Quarter, porch, channel, paper, stage, diamond, street, pain
11. Quarters, hunter, shrink, board, start, hammer, potato
12. List, electrical, sheet, sighted, handed, stories, order, change
13. Forest, village, bowling, sleeves, horn, party, eggs & ham
14. High, easy, person, rocking, electric, wheel
15. Brake, wooden, running, dance, tree, tennis
16. Great, flower, street, uterine, brick, Berlin
17. Knocker, front, knob, stop, dog, revolving, screen
18. Chicago, arms, necessities, grease, brown
19. Loss, net, cut, split, grey
20. House, tennis, papers, supreme, press, people's

ANSWERS: *1.cross; 2. step; 3. book; 4. foot; 5. light; 6. red; 7. paper; 8. seal; 9. bean; 10. back; 11. head; 12. short; 13. green; 14. chair; 15. shoe; 16. wall; 17. stop; 18. bear; 19. hair; 20. court*

Potty Pourri

Random Kinds of Factness

• The largest ant in the world reaches lengths of about 41 millimeters, or a little over 1.5 inches. The smallest is only .8 millimeters long.

• The Beatles really didn't think their careers would last that long when they started. They didn't take themselves very seriously for quite some time. Ringo Starr, as a matter of fact, was planning on staying in the group to make the money he needed to open his own hair salon.

• The American flying squirrel has logged flights of more than 150 feet. But that's nothing compared to the giant flying squirrel of Asia. About four times bigger, it can fly about ten times farther.

• If it weren't for the help of a massive influx of French soldiers and sailors fighting on the American side, the British would've won the American Revolution. At the Battle of Yorktown, for example, George Washington's 11,000 soldiers turned the crimson tide of Redcoats with the help of 29,000 French troops.

• Most people could walk across Delaware in an afternoon. The narrowest part of the state is just 8 miles. The widest part isn't much bigger—35 miles.

• What's eating you, chum? There are approximately 2,250 flea species.

• Vincent Van Gogh was a late bloomer. He took up drawing at the age of twenty-seven, only after a failed attempt at being a missionary.

• Ross Bagdasarian, creator of the singing chipmunks—Alvin, Simon, and Theodore—was said to have gotten his inspiration from watching chipmunks in Yosemite, but he named his characters after the officers of his record company.

• What's that smell? *Musk* comes comes from *muschka,* the Sanskrit word for "testicle."

Raising a Führer

THE LIFE OF ADOLF HITLER

Adolf Hitler is undoubtedly one of the most puzzling personalities of our time. He was a vegetarian who loved animals and children, yet put millions to death without a second thought.

• Hitler's father, Alois Hitler, was the illegitimate son of Maria Anna Schickelgruber. Maria worked for the Frankenreithers, a Jewish family, as a servant. There has been speculation that Alois's father was the nineteen-year-old son of the family. Whether true or not, the Frankenreither family financially supported her until her son was fourteen. While postwar research casts some doubt on this story that portrays Adolf as one-quarter Jewish, Hitler himself feared that it might be true and he tried to cover up any evidence of the matter.

• Hitler's father had three wives (but only one divorce), seven or eight children, and at least one child out of wedlock. One wife was 13 years older than him, another 23 years younger, and one—Hitler's mother—was his foster daughter. Hitler's godfather was a Jew named Prinz.

Little Adolf

• At the age of eight, Hitler attended a Benedictine monastery school. He longed to become an abbot, but barely escaped expulsion when he was caught smoking. The monastery's coat-of-arms, displayed in various parts of the school, prominently featured a swastika.

• Hitler hated school, and his teachers hated his insolence. When he finally finished high school he celebrated by getting so drunk that he fell into unconsciousness. When he awoke he could not find his graduation certificate to show his mother. He returned to the school to get a duplicate. The headmaster was waiting for him with his original certificate. It had been torn into four pieces and used as toilet paper. The humiliated future Führer then made a vow never again to touch alcohol.

• Hitler once claimed that everything he knew about

Pa and Ma Hitler

America came from western novelist Karl May's books about cowboys and Indians, and that he got the idea for concentration camps from reading about American Indian reservations.

• Hitler's half-brother Alois, Jr., served time in jail for thievery on at least two occasions and was a bigamist. He was banished to a concentration camp in 1942 because he talked too much about Hitler as a youth.

• Hitler's first youthful love was Stephanie Jansten. He composed a number of love poems in her honor including one he called "Hymn to the Beloved," and apparently falsely believed from her last name that she was Jewish. In spite of his passion and his confession to his best friend that he would jump off a bridge into the Danube to commit suicide, taking Stephanie with him, he never once got up the nerve to talk to her. It wasn't until many years later that she discovered she had once been the object of Hitler's ardor.

• Unable to get into art school, Hitler moved to Liverpool, England, for a while to avoid the draft. Authorities caught up with him in Vienna. He became a message runner as World War I was breaking out. He was awarded the Iron Cross for bravery under fire, thanks to the recommendation of his Jewish commanding officer. By then, though, Hitler was already deeply anti-Semitic.

• During the 1920s Hitler took lessons in public speaking and in mass psychology from Erik Jan Hanussen, an astrologer and fortune teller. Hitler was a believer in astrology, telepathy, graphology, phrenology, and physiognomy, and usually sought supernatural advice when making decisions.

• Hitler was secretly financed by German industrialists and various German princes who believed the Nazis were the best group to stop the rising support of communism that threatened their fortunes. They contributed a reported 25 million gold marks in the years before the Nazis took over Germany. In return, Hitler discreetly changed the party platform, which had been, up to that point, against capitalists and royalists.

• Hitler was a very ordinary-looking man with a mincing walk. His strongest physical asset was his eyes, which were blue verging on violet with a depth and glint that made them almost hypnotic. In his earlier days he wore a pointed beard, often unkempt, and had broken, rotten teeth. He began wearing the famous little moustache during World War I. More of a British style than a German one, he may have adopted it in imitation of English officers, whom he grew to admire during his years at the front.

• Sister Angela's daughter was Geli Raubal, a pretty young woman in her twenties with whom Hitler lived for a number of years when he was rising to power. Nineteen years younger than Adolf, she was by all accounts the only woman he ever loved. Hitler made her pose for nude drawings, which were later stolen and bought back from a blackmailer, and reportedly whipped her with a bullwhip. She is quoted as telling a friend, "My uncle is a monster. You would never believe the things he makes me do."

• Hitler was insanely jealous of his niece. When his chauffeur confessed to him that he and Geli were lovers and wanted to marry, Hitler flew into a rage and fired him. One night, after a loud public fight, she apparently killed herself with a shot from Hitler's revolver.

• When Hitler learned of her death, he decided to become a vegetarian and made a vow never to eat meat again. He went into a deep depression and threatened suicide. An associate, Gregor Strasser, took heroic measures to keep him alive, a fact he regretted three years later when Hitler ordered his execution.

• Eva Braun, his final mistress, was a product of a convent school. She was only seventeen years old when Hitler began to take her out. Once, after seeing photographs of Hitler in the company of other women, Eva shot herself, severing an artery in her neck. She survived.

• In 1935, Eva Braun became despondent when Hitler's preoccupation with international affairs left little time for her. She again attempted suicide, this time by swallowing twenty sleeping pills. Her sister Ilse found her in a coma and saved her. Angela, Hitler's sister and Geli Raubal's mother, was his housekeeper at this time. She despised Eva, refused to shake hands with her, and referred to her as "the stupid cow." Because Hitler continued to bring Eva to his chalet, Angela gave up her housekeeper post and got married.

• Hitler did not like to be alone. He would often summon aides to sit with him in the middle of the night while he rambled on about anything that came to his mind. There was an unwritten rule among the aides that no one would ask a question lest Hitler go off on another tangent.

• By 1937, when the rest of the world didn't yet consider environmental degradation a significant problem, Hitler was mandating anti-pollution devices on factories in the Ruhr. All new factories, like that of the "Strength-Through-Joy" car (later renamed the Volkswagen), were required to install anti-pollution devices.

• Dr. Erwin Giesing treated Hitler after an aborted assassination attempt by German generals, and so was one of the few men Hitler trusted. However, Giesing wrote in his diary that he had once tried to kill the Führer by giving him a double dose of cocaine. The attempt went undetected, and Hitler remained alive.

• At the end of the war, when Hitler decided to commit suicide rather than fall into the hands of the Russians, his first act was to poison his favorite dog Wolf. €

Two Little Hitlers

During the filming of Some Like It Hot **Tony Curtis commented,** "Kissing Marilyn Monroe was like kissing Hitler," **to which she quipped,** "He only said that because I wore prettier dresses than he did."

Every Picture Tells a Story

A Friend in Need **by Cassius Marcellus Coolidge (1845-1934)**

• These poker-playing dogs have graced many a bar and rec room where men congregate. It shows two little dogs in the foreground passing a card while playing poker with the big dogs.

• Artist "Cash" Coolidge began his career as a druggist, sign painter, art teacher, and founder of a bank and small-town newspaper in upstate New York. After a trip to European museums, he decided to try his hand at painting.

• His sense of humor, love of dogs, and artistic limitations helped focus his artistry: "His paintings of people look like dogs," observed art historian Moira Harris. "I don't think his people are very good, but his dogs are wonderful."

• In the early 1900s, the Brown & Bigelow printing company recognized Coolidge's rare gift, and commissioned him to paint anthropomorphic dogs for calendars and posters. He generated sixteen scenes—including dogs in a courtroom and at a formal dance—with more than half featuring dogs playing cards.

• *A Friend in Need* seems timeless; most people don't guess that it's a century old. One clue: The cards are old-fashioned, without numbers in the upper-left corners. Many people also seem to believe that the painting's name is *Poker-Playing Dogs.*

Sports Match

MATCH THE TEAM TO THE LOCATION

Okay, sports fans. Included in this quiz are teams from the National Basketball Association, Major League Baseball, and the National Football League. See if you can correctly place them all.

1. **76ers**	New Orleans
2. **Jaguars**	Tennessee
3. **Devil Rays**	Detroit
4. **Cavaliers**	Oakland
5. **Wizards**	Cincinnati
6. **Mariners**	Texas
7. **Titans**	Anaheim
8. **Angels**	Washington
9. **Bengals**	Tampa Bay
10. **Pistons**	Baltimore
11. **Rangers**	San Diego
12. **Athletics**	Philadelphia
13. **Chargers**	Jacksonville
14. **Ravens**	Seattle
15. **Hornets**	Cleveland

Answers: *1. 76ers: Philadelphia; 2. Jaguars: Jacksonville; 3. Devil Rays: Tampa Bay; 4. Cavaliers: Cleveland; 5. Wizards: Washington; 6. Mariners: Seattle; 7. Titans: Tennessee; 8. Angels: Anaheim; 9. Bengals: Cincinnati; 10. Pistons: Detroit; 11. Rangers: Texas; 12. Athletics: Oakland; 13. Chargers: San Diego; 14. Ravens: Baltimore; 15. Hornets: New Orleans*

Arachnophile

A Tangled Web of Spider Fact

If you love spiders, this one's for you. These juicy arachnid facts, written by *Bathroom Companion* staffer Kathie Meyer, are sure to trap you in their alluring web.

HOME SWEET HOME

A Portland, Oregon, homeowner and her friend were considering the subterranean cobwebs in the basement when the friend lit one to see if it would burn. It did. In the chaos of swatting out the fire, the web-burners dislodged the dryer vent, causing built-up lint to fly, creating an even bigger fire. There were no injuries, except to the spider, but a Fire Bureau spokesman said a fire lieutenant at the scene reminded the homeowner about why it's not a good idea to use fire as a cleaning agent as well as why it's a good thing to clean lint out of the dryer vent.

WHO'S FOR DINNER?

According to some estimates, the bugs that spiders eat in one year weigh as much as all the people on Earth. These estimates, of course, include the results of the spiders' well-known habit of cannibalism. For example, as many as six Australian redback spider males may compete for the ultimate prize—having sex with the female redback spider, and usually being eaten after mating. Still, not all inmates got devoured. Research indicates that the males that got eaten were apparently the ones that most satisfied the female, usually the one with the most stamina. The eaten males' sex act lasted an average of 25 minutes, while the uneaten ones went only eleven minutes.

Australian researchers have also identified some species of baby spiders that survive by dining on their mothers still-living as they grow over a period of weeks. The scientists hypothesize that the maternal sacrifice keeps the young from eating each other.

JUST SAY NO

Government scientists tested the effects of certain drugs on a spider's ability to spin webs. A spider on marijuana tried to make a web, but gave up when it was only half-done. Spiders on Benzedrine spun webs quickly, but left huge holes in them. Spiders on caffeine spun only some random threads, while those on sleeping pills never even started in the first place.

THE CLEVELAND ARACHNOIDS

The Cleveland Indians were named in honor of Louis Cockolexis, who was the first Native American to play professional baseball. However, before they became the Indians, the team was known as the Cleveland Spiders.

The Cleveland Spiders in 1895

UP, UP AND AWAY...

How do you travel far if you're a young spider? They "balloon." They climb to the top of a plant or fence post, and spin out some lines of gossamer web silk until it catches the wind and pulls the spiderlings away. This allows them to spread out and avoid competing with their brothers and sisters. It's surprising how far spiders can go this way. For example, when the volcano Krakatoa exploded in the Java Sea over a century ago, wiping out all life on nearby islands, the first re-colonizer was a spider, which presumably got there by ballooning on the wind from another island 25 miles away.

In 1981, a Japanese weather

boat discovered that such long-distance ballooning was pretty common. Stationed 240 miles from the mainland, they collected more than a hundred young spiders in nets they had mounted 60 feet in the air.

Look out below!

KISS OF THE WOMAN SPIDER
Even though the black widow bite is the most poisonous spider in Europe and America, only about 1% of bite victims die, and most of those are the very young, the very old, or the infirm. Still, being bitten isn't a pleasant experience. Everyone bitten, though, suffers from the effects. These include a stinging bite, numbing, pain, and swelling. After a half hour or so comes severe abdominal cramping, spasms in the arms and legs, temporary paralysis of some or all parts of the body, chest constriction, and difficulty in swallowing.

ARACHNID BY ANY OTHER NAME
A harvestman, or "daddy longlegs," belongs to the class *arachnid*—like mites, ticks, scorpions, spiders, and a few other invertebrates. Although similar to a spider, it isn't technically a spider.

ENTOMOLOGICAL ETYMOLOGY
Why is it called a "cobweb"? *Cob* is from the Middle English word *coppe*. It meant "spider."

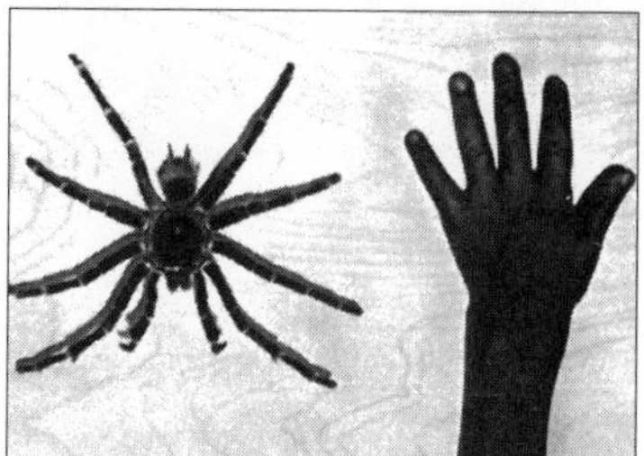

A Brazilian tarantula is about the same size as a boy's hand

BUILDING A WEB SITE
If a spider begins building her traditional-looking, round web at 6 in the morning, she'll probably have it completed before 7—just in time for breakfast. But the building phase really isn't the hard part, it's the maintenance. Between meals, a spider will spend much of her time gathering up broken threads, reweaving them, and adding a new layer of stickiness, so she can keep catching insect meals.

• A spider web consists of two types of thread: *anchor* and *snare*. Anchor threads make the basic shape and

A dew-drenched web, in need of some maintenance

aren't very sticky. Snare threads catch the flies.

• Spiders never spin webs in structures made of chestnut wood. That is why so many European chateaux were built with chestnut beams—after all, spider webs on a 50-foot beamed ceiling can be difficult to clean.

• It would take an average of 27,000 spider webs to produce a pound of web.

• Tiny, woolly bats, in West Africa, live within the large webs of colonial spiders.

• The golden orb-weaver spiders of Papua New Guinea spin the biggest, strongest webs. With supporting threads reaching up to 19 feet (6 meters), their webs can reach 5 feet (1.5 meters) across.

• Among the very rich, it was a fad in the 1800s to import thousands of spiders for special occasions. They'd have servants release them into the trees to spin webs, then sprinkle gold dust into the webs. €

The Ten Most Venomous Spiders

1. Brazilian Huntsman (Brazil)
2. Funnelweb (Australia)
3. Redback Spider (Australia)
4. Black Widow (Europe & the Americas)
5. Tarantula (Europe & the Americas)
6. Brown Recluse Spider (Americas)
7. White Tailed Spider (Australia)
8. Spitting Spider (The Tropics)
9. Woodlouse Spider (Europe)
10. Sicarius Hahnii (South Africa)

Filboid Studge

A Cautionary Tale of Art & Capitalism

In this ironic short story by Saki (Hector High Munro), a struggling artist helps his girlfriend's father save the family fortune. No good deed goes unpunished.

"I WANT TO MARRY your daughter," said Mark Spayley with faltering eagerness. "I am only an artist with an income of two hundred a year, and she is the daughter of an enormously wealthy man, so I suppose you will think my offer a piece of presumption."

Duncan Dullamy, the great company inflator, showed no outward sign of displeasure. As a matter of fact, he was secretly relieved at the prospect of finding even a two-hundred-a-year husband for his daughter Leonore. A crisis was rapidly rushing upon him, from which he knew he would emerge with neither money nor credit; all his recent ventures had fallen flat, and flattest of all had gone the wonderful new breakfast food, Pipenta, on the advertisement of which he had sunk such huge sums. It could scarcely be called a drug in the market; people bought drugs, but no one bought Pipenta.

"Would you marry Leonore if she were a poor man's daughter?" asked the man of phantom wealth.

"Yes," said Mark, wisely avoiding the error of over-protestation. And to his astonishment Leonore's father not only gave his consent, but suggested a fairly early date for the wedding.

"I wish I could show my gratitude in some way," said Mark with genuine emotion. "I'm afraid it's rather like the mouse proposing to help the lion."

"Get people to buy that beastly muck," said Dullamy, nodding savagely at a poster of the despised Pipenta, "and you'll have done more than any of my agents have been able to accomplish."

"It wants a better name," said Mark reflectively, "and something distinctive in the poster line. Anyway, I'll have a shot at it."

Three weeks later the world was advised of the coming of a new breakfast food, heralded under the resounding name of "Filboid Studge." Spayley put forth no pictures of massive babies springing up with fungus-like rapidity under its forcing influence, or of representatives of the leading nations of the world scrambling with fatuous eagerness for its possession. One huge sombre poster depicted the Damned in Hell suffering a new torment from their inability to get at the Filboid Studge which elegant young fiends held in transparent bowls just beyond their reach. The scene was rendered even more gruesome by a subtle suggestion of the features of leading men and women of the day in the portrayal of the Lost Souls; prominent individuals of both political parties, society hostesses, well-known dramatic authors and novelists, and distinguished aeroplanists were dimly recognizable in that doomed throng; noted lights of the musical-comedy stage flickered wanly in the shades of the Inferno, smiling still from force of habit, but with the fearsome smiling rage of baffled effort. The poster bore no fulsome allusions to the merits of the new breakfast food, but a single grim statement ran in bold letters along its base: "They cannot buy it now."

Spayley had grasped the fact that people will do things from a sense of duty which they would never attempt as a pleasure. There are thousands of respectable middle-class men who, if you found them unexpectedly in a Turkish bath, would explain in all sincerity that a doctor had ordered them to take Turkish baths; if you told them in return that you went there because you liked it, they would stare in pained wonder at the frivolity of your motive. In the same way, whenever a massacre of Armenians is reported from Asia Minor, everyone assumes that it has been carried out "under orders" from somewhere or another; no one seems to think that there are people who might like to kill their neighbors now and then.

And so it was with the new breakfast food. No one would have eaten Filboid Studge as a pleasure, but the grim austerity of its advertisement drove housewives in shoals to the grocers' shops to clamor for an immediate supply. In small kitchens solemn pig-tailed daughters helped depressed mothers to perform the primitive ritual of its preparation. On the breakfast-tables of cheerless parlors it was partaken of in silence. Once the womenfolk discovered that it was thoroughly unpalatable, their zeal in forcing it on their households knew no bounds. "You haven't eaten your Filboid Studge!" would be screamed at the appetiteless clerk as he turned weariedly from the breakfast-table, and his evening meal would be prefaced by a warmed-up mess which would be explained as "your Filboid Studge that you didn't eat this morning." Those strange fanatics who ostentatiously mortify themselves, inwardly and outwardly, with health biscuits and health garments, battened aggressively on the new food. Earnest spectacled young men devoured it on the steps of the National Liberal Club. A bishop who did not believe in a future state preached against the poster, and a peer's daughter died from eating too much of the compound. A further advertisement was obtained when an infantry regiment mutinied and shot its officers rather than eat the nauseous mess; fortunately, Lord Birrell of Blatherstone, who was War Minister at the moment, saved the situation

by his happy epigram, that "Discipline to be effective must be optional."

Filboid Studge had become a household word, but Dullamy wisely realized that it was not necessarily the last word in breakfast dietary; its supremacy would be challenged as soon as some yet more unpalatable food should be put on the market. There might even be a reaction in favor of something tasty and appetizing, and the Puritan austerity of the moment might be banished from domestic cookery. At an opportune moment, therefore, he sold out his interests in the article which had brought him in colossal wealth at a critical juncture, and placed his financial reputation beyond the reach of cavil.

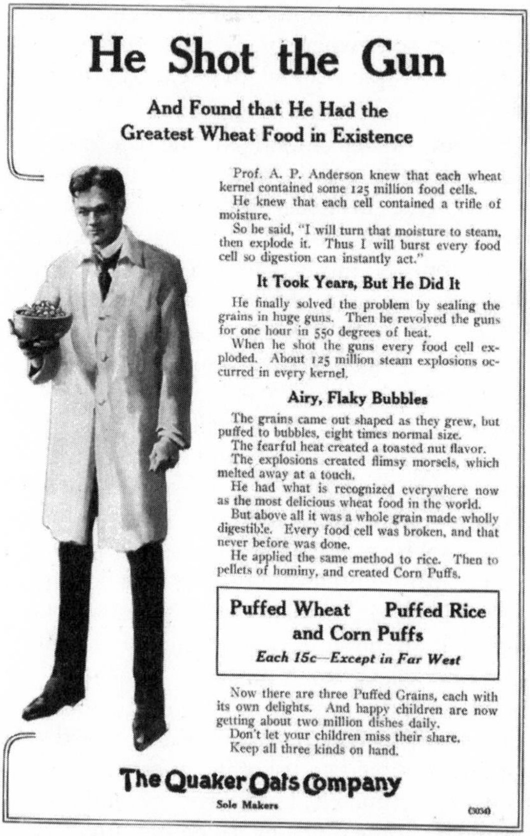

As for Leonore, who was now an heiress on a far greater scale than ever before, he naturally found her something a vast deal higher in the husband market than a two-hundred-a-year poster designer. Mark Spayley, the brainmouse who had helped the financial lion with such untoward effect, was left to curse the day he produced the wonder-working poster.

"After all," said a friend, meeting him shortly afterwards at his club, "you have this doubtful consolation, that 'tis not in mortals to countermand success."

Love & Romans

Et Tu Can Be a Latin Lover!

Love is hard in any language, but what if you end up in a Latin bar and everybody's wearing togas? Well, you know what they say: When in Rome, do as the Romans do. Here's a glossary to help you out.

LETTING SOMEONE KNOW YOU'RE INTERESTED

Here are a few good pick-up lines that just might be enough to impress that cute person in a toga across the bar:

- Seen any good movies lately? *Vidistine nuper imagines moventes bonas?*
- What's your sign? *Quo signo nata es?*
- Is that a scroll in your toga, or are you just happy to see me? *Estne volumen in toga, an solum tibi libet me videre?*
- How do you get your hair to do that? *Quomodo cogis comas tuas sic videri?*
- You know, the Romans invented the art of love. *Romani quidem artem amatoriam invenerunt.*
- Everyone is doing it! *Sic faciunt omnes!*
- Go with the flow! *Ventis secundis, tene cursum!*
- Let it all hang out. *Totum dependeat.*
- Bad kitty! Rrrr.... *Feles mala! Rrrr....*

"To fall in love you have to be in the state of mind for it to take, like a disease." —Nancy Mitford

KNOWING WHEN TO ICHTHUS OR CUT BAIT

It's pretty easy to tell if someone is interested in you, but the signs may be a bit more difficult to read if they're not. Here are a few phrases to let you or the other person know it's time to pack up your fishing nets and go home:

- As if! *Ut si!*
- Don't call me, I'll call you. *Noli me vocare, ego te vocabo.*
- Stupid cow. *Vacca foeda.*
- Gag me with a spoon! *Fac me cocleario vomere!*
- Eat my shorts. *Vescere bracis meis.*
- Men are slime. *Viri sunt Viri.*
- What a doofus! *Qualem blennum!*
- I'm outta here! *Absum!*
- I can't hear you. I have a banana in my ear. *Te audire no possum. Musa sapientum fixa est in aure.*
- I'm going to have to hurt you on principle. *Me oportet propter praeceptum te nocere.*
- Your mother was a hamster and your father smelt of elderberries. *Mater tua criceta fuit, et pater tuo redoluit bacarum sambucus.*
- I have a catapult. Give me all your money, or I will fling an enormous rock at your head. *Catapultam habeo. Nisi pecuniam omnem mihi dabis, ad caput tuum saxum immane mittam.*
- Get a life. *Fac ut vivas.*
- If Caesar were alive, you'd be chained to an oar. *Caesar si viveret, ad remum dareris.* €

Men and Women

"When a woman behaves like a man, why doesn't she behave like a nice man?" —Dame Edith Evans

"It is so many years now since Adam and Eve were first together in the garden, that it seems a great pity that we have not learned better how to please one another.... I wish that once in all the time of men and women, two ambassadors could meet in a friendly mind and come to understand each other." —Isak Dinesen

Retro-Futurism

Tom Swift's World of Tomorrow

Tom Swift was a boy inventor created by Victor Appleton almost a century ago. The breathless adventure stories are great fun, but even better are the descriptions of his inventions.

TOM SWIFT & HIS SUBMARINE BOAT (1910)

The inventor did not want to depend on the usual screw propellers for his craft. Mr. Swift planned to send *The Advance* along under water by means of electricity. Certain peculiar plates were built at the forward and aft blunt noses of the submarine. Into the forward plate a negative charge of electricity was sent, and into the one at the rear a positive charge, just as one end of a horseshoe magnet is positive and will repel the north end of a compass needle, while the other pole of a magnet is negative and will attract it. In electricity like repels like, while negative and positive have a mutual attraction for each other. Mr. Swift figured out that if he could send a powerful current of negative electricity into the forward plate it would pull the boat along, for water is a good conductor of electricity, while if a positive charge was sent into the rear plate it would serve to push the submarine along.

TOM SWIFT & HIS ELECTRIC RIFLE (1911)

"How does it work?'" asked Ned, as he looked at the curious gun. The electric weapon was not unlike an ordinary heavy rifle in appearance save that the barrel was a little longer, and the stock larger in every way. There were also a number of wheels, levers, gears and gauges on the stock.

"It works by electricity," explained Tom. "That is, the force comes from a powerful current of stored electricity."

"Oh, then you have storage batteries in the stock?"

"Not exactly. There are no batteries, but the current is a sort of wireless kind. It is stored in a cylinder, just as compressed air or gases are stored, and can be released as I need it."

"And when it's all gone, what do you do?"

"Make more power by means of a small dynamo."

"How does it kill?"

"By means of a concentrated charge of electricity which is shot from the barrel with great force. You can't see it, yet it is there. It's just as if you concentrated a charge of electricity of five thousand volts into a small globule the size of a bullet. The electric bullets will pierce anything. They'll go through a brick wall as easily as the x-rays do. You can fire through a house, and kill something on the other side."

"I should think that could very well be dangerous."

Tom took his place at the end of the range, and began to adjust some valves and levers. "Here she goes!" he suddenly exclaimed. Ned watched his chum. The young inventor pressed a small button at the side of the rifle barrel. There was no sound, no smoke, no flame and not the slightest jar. Yet, the next instant the scarecrow figure seemed to fly all to pieces. There was a shower of straw, rags and old clothes, which fell in a shapeless heap at the end of the range.

"Say. I guess you did for that fellow, all right!" exclaimed Ned.

"It looks so," admitted Tom, with a note of pride in his voice. "Now we'll try another test."

Who Was "Victor Appleton"?

The Tom Swift series was the creation of publisher Edward Stratemeyer, who also created the Hardy Boys, Nancy Drew, and the Bobbsey Twins. Stratemeyer chose the name "Victor Appleton," and hired Howard R. Garis to write the books under that name. Garis was famous under his own name as the author of the Uncle Wiggily stories.

TOM SWIFT & HIS PHOTO TELEPHONE (1914)

"It can't be done, Tom!" said Tom's dad. "To transmit pictures over a telephone wire, so that persons cannot only see to whom they are talking, as well as hear them—well, to be frank with you, Tom, I should be sorry to see you waste your time trying to invent such a thing."

"I don't agree with you. Not only do I think it can be done, but I'm going to do it. In fact, I've already started on it. As for wasting my time, well, I haven't anything in particular to do, now that my giant cannon has been perfected."

"But, Tom, this is different. You are talking of sending lightwaves—one of the most delicate forms of motion in the world—over a material wire. It can't be done!"

"Look here, Dad!" exclaimed Tom, coming to a halt in front of his parent. "What is light, anyhow? Merely another form of motion; isn't it?"

"Well, yes, Tom, I suppose it could be."

"Of course it is," said Tom. "With vibrations of a certain length and rapidity we get sound—the faster the vibration per second the higher the sound note. Now, then, light shoots along at the rate of 186,000,000 miles a second. So we have sound, one kind of wave motion, or energy; we have light, a higher degree of vibration or wave motion, and then we come to electricity—and nobody has ever yet exactly measured the intensity or speed of the electric vibrations. But what I'm getting at is this—that electricity must travel pretty nearly as fast as light—if not faster. So I believe that electricity and light have about the same kind of vibrations, or wave motion. Now, why can't I send light-waves over a wire as well as electrical waves?"

Mr. Swift was silent for a moment. Then he said, slowly: "Well, Tom, I never heard it argued just that way before. Maybe there's something in your photo telephone after all." ☾

(Interested in reading more Tom Swift theories and inventions? See pages 295 and 383.)

Tom Swifties II

"Tell Me a Swifty," Said Tom Punsively

From the surreal 1960s came elephant jokes and Tom Swifties, based on bad puns and the stylistic excesses of Victor Appleton, who created the popular Tom Swift stories.

"No need for silence," Tom allowed.
"Cobblers!" Tom said at last.
"This is where I keep my arrows," Tom said quiveringly.
"2 bdrm furn w/vu," Tom said aptly.
"This boat is leaking," Tom said balefully.
"I've swallowed a window," Tom said painfully.
"My bike wheel's badly damaged," said Tom outspokenly.
"Would you like to buy a cod?" asked Tom selfishly.
"3.14168," Tom said piously.
"Harumph!" Tom ejaculated phlegmatically.
"Are you a homosexual, too?" Tom queried gaily.
"I think I'm allergic to this fruit!" rasped Barry.
"@#$%&*!" wrote Tom in cursive.
"I'm a sloppy hot dog eater," Tom admitted with obvious relish.
"I do too know a French city and street!" Tom parried ruefully.
"So another person arrived before me?" Tom second-guessed.
"Please keep quiet about my drooling," said Tom secretively.
"I want to look at your cervix," said Dr. Tom speculatively.
"The carpet layer sneezed," explained Tom tactfully.
"I punched his stomach three times," said Tom triumphantly.
"I can't stand painting," Tom said uneasily.

Whad'ja Get?

How Cracker Jack Became a Prized Snack

Like the Ferris wheel, the ice cream cone, and Aunt Jemima pancakes, Cracker Jack premiered during Chicago's Columbia Exhibition in 1893. It never would've happened if it weren't for the Great Chicago Fire 22 years earlier.

Frederick Rueckheim was working on a farm in rural Illinois in 1871 when he heard that there were good-paying jobs in the city of Chicago cleaning up the charred ruins and debris from the Great Fire. Rueckheim, who had recently immigrated from Germany, stashed his life's savings of $200 and went.

Once Rueckheim got there, though, he discovered that the jobs weren't quite as good as promised. Instead, he opened a one-popper popcorn stand with a partner, William Brinkmeyer. Their sales were brisk enough that they expanded to more and bigger stands—and finally to popcorn wholesaling. The burgeoning company outgrew its facilities six times in the next seven years. To help out, Frederick brought his brother, Louis, over from Germany. Louis soon bought out Brinkmeyer's half of the company, but Frederick made sure Louis knew whose half was the bigger half: He named the business "F. W. Rueckheim & Brother."

In 1884, their factory burned down. The brothers quickly rebuilt, and within six months their business was popping again. They started expanding the popcorn lines, adding marshmallows and other sweet flavorings to batches. For the Columbia Exhibition, the world's first World's Fair, they decided to mix up something new and different: a molasses, peanut, and popcorn mixture. It was a huge success, garnering orders for it from retailers all over the country.

After yet another factory expansion, Frederick complained all the way to the

Bet You Didn't Know

• More than 1,200 years ago, Native Americans hybridized a special strain of dent corn that was perfect for popping. Some tribes in the New England area figured out that if they heated maple syrup and poured it over the popped corn, not only did it taste sweet, but it helped preserve the popped kernels for later consumption.

• Fast forward hundreds of years: Jack Norworth and Albert von Tilzer wrote *Take Me Out to the Ballgame* in 1908, years before either one of them had actually seen a baseball game. However, both had eaten Cracker Jack, so they included a now-famous line: "Buy me some peanuts and Cracker Jack / I don't care if I never come back...."

• During the Depression, the company came out with new products like chocolate-covered Cracker Jack and coconut-flavored corn brittle.

• Cracker Jack's largest marketing campaign, the Cracker Jack Mystery Club, lasted from 1933 to 1936. It required kids to find presidential medals hidden in a secret box compartment and return five to the company.

• Twenty dollars annually will buy you a membership into the Cracker Jack Collectors Association where you can mingle, mix, and trade with fellow Cracker Jack prize collectors.

• Since 1912, Cracker Jack gave out more than 23 billion toys, making it perhaps the biggest provider of toys in the world.

• A mint condition, full set of baseball cards from a 1915 Cracker Jack box was recently valued at $60,000.

• There are several rare Cracker Jack prizes that have been valued at $7,000 or more.

bank: "No matter how we try to plan for it, the orders always exceed our production."

"Slide, Kelly, Slide!"
"The More You Eat—The More You Want"
Now comes the open season for baseball fans and good old
Cracker Jack
America's Famous Popcorn Confection

The still-unnamed product was shipped to retailers in large wooden tubs, but there was a problem. When it arrived, due to heat and agitation, the popcorn often stuck together in one huge sticky glop. Louis went to work on the problem, and in 1896 discovered a process that kept the individual particles separate (the formula is still used by the company today and is guarded as a valuable trade secret).

But that's not all that happened in 1896. The sticky snack finally got a name. A sales rep was munching on some and he exclaimed, using Victorian slang for something very good, "That's a cracker jack!" Frederick ran down and trademarked the phrase. The rest is history. (It is sobering to realize that, had the product been born in a later decade, the caramelized corn might have been called "The Cat's Pajamas" or "Cool Stuff" or "One Groovy Thing, Man" or "Awesome, Dude.")

Now that it had a name, Cracker Jack needed a package. The brothers hired one Henry Eckstein in 1899, who developed a wax-sealed, moisture-proof, individual-serving-sized box. It was this box that made the product portable enough that it could be sold anywhere snacks could be found (including baseball games, which eventually spawned the *Take Me Out to the Ballgame* musical tribute). But that wasn't enough. Hundreds of other imitators had sprung up with names like Yellow Kid, Honey Corn, Unoit, Goldenrod, Honey Boy, Kor-Nuts, Nutty Corn, Five Jacks, Maple Jack, and Sammy Jack. The brothers decided they needed a gimmick.

Their first try were coupons that kids could collect and exchange for merchandise, a system that had recently been pioneered by Sears and Roebuck. The Rueckheims issued an illustrated catalog offering more than 300 household items, sports accessories, and toys. Cracker Jack sales picked up briefly, but leveled off again shortly afterward.

It was reportedly brother Louis who first suggested putting small toys inside the packages, figuring that kids were more likely to make repeat purchases if they received immediate gratification instead of having to save coupons. The combination of Cracker Jack's built-up name recognition and the packaged premium spurred a national craze that resulted in peak sales in 1914.

Frederick decided to add the sailor boy Jack and his dog Bingo to the package in a wartime salute to our fighting boys. (One sad footnote: The boy was modeled after Frederick's beloved grandson Robert, who often wore a sailor suit. As the first of the new packages rolled off the presses, Robert came down with pneumonia and died. So, besides Cracker Jack packages, the logo can also be seen on little Robert's tombstone in Chicago.)

Cracker Jack toys at the time were of remarkable quality: little magnifying glasses, miniature books, whistles, strings of beads, baseball cards, tops, metal trains, cars, and more. The high quality continued through two World Wars and into the 1950s, when little plastic TVs and space ships were premium items. Unfortunately, the prizes today are less than impressive—high-speed packaging and a general stinginess by corporate overlords (first Borden in 1964, then bought by Frito Lay in 1997), have reduced the prizes to little more than disappointing little pieces of paper.

Despite the downgrade in prize quality, though, Cracker Jack continues to sell without new gimmicks and/or much in the way of advertising. So much of the snack has sold over the years that, laid end to end, it could circle the globe more than 70 times. €

True Adventures

"Down the Delaware River in a Canoe"

Nowadays, weekend adventurers in indestructible crafts run white water for a lark, but there was a time when men were men and canoes were just wood and canvas. This is an excerpt from *Athletics and Manly Sport*, written by John Boyle O'Reilly in 1890.

"You can run everything on the river but the Big Foul," said the teamster at Port Jervis as he helped us launch the canoes. "It is the foulest rapid on the Delaware. You'll have to carry round."

We had before heard about this rapid with the ominous name. I had with me the notes of one of the best canoemen in the country, who had run the Delaware in the spring of last year, and found these words: "Great Foul Rift. Ran in May. Rapidity of water and danger much exaggerated."

"That's spring," said the teamster, who had heard this note read. "The river is ten feet lower now; and it's the bottom of a river that's dangerous, not the top."

Guiteras was first in his canoe. "Here goes for Philadelphia!" he cried, as he pushed off. "Are there any rapids near?"

"Listen!" and the teamster smiled. We listened and heard one, the sound coming from the bend of the river half a mile below. "It's only a little one," shouted the teamster, as we started. "Keep the left, and you'll find a channel. It's a smooth rift."

We were three, in three canoes—Mr. Edward A. Moseley in a stout boat built by Partelow of the Charles River; Dr. Ramon Guiteras, in a strong Racine; mine was a keelless, decked canoe, by the best builder in the world, Rushton, of Canton, N.Y.

It is impossible to convey the exhilarating sense of freedom one feels during the first moments in a canoe. We were silent at first, and surprised. The river was not deep—three or four feet at most; but it ran down hill like a hunted hare.

"This is superb!" said one. The others echoed the word.

TROUBLE IN THE FIRST RAPIDS

Almost before we knew, we were in the rush of the first rapid. We had not carefully followed the teamster's instructions to keep to the extreme left and had passed the narrow mouth of the channel. Before us ran an oblique bar of heavy stones, over which the river poured like a curtain. It ran clear across the river, and we found ourselves far into the closed angle. The water on the curtain to the left roared like a heavy surf, and we knew that we could not get over or through. There was no opening between the stones more than two feet wide, and below was a hundred yards of chaotic rock and roar.

We turned and paddled upstream. Inch by inch we gained, working with feverish speed, the paddle slipping back in the glancing stream as if it were in air, holding hardly any force.

But we climbed the first descent, and steered across to where the channel hugged the right bank. Guiteras went in first; he had not gone up far enough by a boat's length, and as he shot across into the narrow channel, his canoe lurched upon one side, stood a moment and swung athwart stream. He had struck; but before a thought of danger could follow, the paddle was buried, and with a lifting push, his boat slipped over the stone and rushed down the rapid like a leaf.

Greetings from the Delaware River

The other canoes followed, avoiding the buried stone. It was a vigorous little rush—about two hundred yards in length, and not fifteen feet in width. The water was deep, but its speed made it leap over every stone on the bottom, and hurl itself in all kinds of ridges and furrows and springing whitecaps.

At the bottom of the rift we plunged into the heap of boiling breakers, still running like mad. Next moment we floated into smooth water, and turned and looked back at our first rapid with much laughing and congratulation. The teamster had called it "a little one," and "a smooth rift"; what, then, was the ominous Great Foul Rift in comparison?

The Author rests between rapids.

As we gazed back at the rapid, it receded from us swiftly. We were on the quiet surface of deep water, but going down at the rate of several miles an hour. The left bank was almost black, a clean, smooth stone with round puff-holes in it, no vegetation whatever on the steep slope.

I've given too much space to our first rapid on the Delaware, which was to be only one of scores before us, and a small one—even a "smooth one." But it will save other descriptions; and it gives our first impression of the river. The Delaware is a river of extraordinary pitch, the fall from Port Jervis to Philadelphia being nearly 1,200 feet. With deep water in May or June, the river is eight to ten feet higher than it was in this last week of August. Then, a canoeman may run two hundred miles without striking a stone. But every foot of fall in the stream makes a totally new river; and he who goes down in early summer cannot imagine what the river is like at low water in late autumn.

That afternoon we pulled the canoes ashore and plunged into the delicious water, drinking it as we swam—a sensation for epicures. We lay prone in the rapid stream, our arms outspread, and our faces under water, floating quickly and looking at the yellow and white pebbles on the bottom.

At last we came to a lovely spot, a soft white sandbank on the left, the Jersey side, formed by the junction of a bright little river with the Delaware. Every paddle was laid down. Half a mile below we heard the dull roar of a rapid. Here the river was very deep and swift, and not more than eighty yards wide. On the right, a wooded but precipitous mountain rose almost straight from the water to a height of at least 800 feet. From his eyrie we had disturbed a white-headed eagle which tipped its great wings above us as it moved slowly down river.

We camped for the night. One man erected the tent; another cooked dinner; the third went in search of a farmhouse for milk, eggs, melons and peaches—the staple of our food for the next fortnight. The sun went down on the left, above the low trees, without cloud or haze. With philosophic reflection, we spread our rubber blankets on the sand of the tent, over these our woolen blankets; and then, with a big fire blazing a few feet from the tent's mouth, we lay or sat for our coffee and cigars.

Throughout our trip this quiet hour each evening with a strange scene before us was a most enjoyable part of the day.

SECOND DAY: FIDDLER'S ELBOW AND DEATH'S EDDY

We slept as if the night were an hour long, and we woke to plunge into the sweet unchilled water. The miles were long, and the river unendingly broken. It was downhill all the time, rift succeeding rift. Do what we could with careful steering, we struck again and again, and we were in constant danger of smashing boats or paddles. So common became the striking that we coined a word for it—"hung up." And we could not help laughing when one of us struck, as we swept past and saw him grimly poling his canoe over a rock, or raising his feet over the gunwale as he got out to haul her over. For this we had to be always ready; trousers tucked up, and canvas shoes on.

It came to be a jesting habit, that when one led into a rapid he would do so with a boastful shout. This was my part, at one time on this second day. I had gone into a rift with much flourish, and, a third of the way through, had been "hung up."

Down rushed the others with loud derision, avoiding the bad place. Imagine my feeling of disgust at their selfishness, as I saw their backs, leaving me there. Next moment, in the worst part of the rapid, I saw one of them strike and hold his boat with his paddle against a rock; and a second or two later the other struck just beside him. Who could help smiling? And that moment, by a fortunate lurch, my canoe floated and rushed down toward the two, who were now struggling knee-deep in the stream. They held on to let me pass, and scowled as if my laugh were in bad taste.

At ten o'clock we reached Milford, Penn. The river was a series of deep and swift reaches, and then a leaping rift, with a steep descent. In the very center of one of these rapids, my canoe struck on a covered rock and I knew in a flash that she must either get instantly over or be rolled down stream. Thought and act united. I lifted her by a vigorous push, and was whirled down, stern foremost, with my paddle broken.

Fortunately, the channel below was deep, though rough and very rapid. To meet the emergency I knelt and used the broken end of the paddle as a pole, fending off rocks, and steering occasionally with the blade end. My loss was a gain: the best way to steer down a rapid is to kneel and use a long paddle with one blade, the other end used as a pole.

The memory of that day is wholly confused with the noise of rapid water. We were no sooner through one rift than we heard another. The names of the rapids were quaint and suggestive: such as Death's Eddy, Fiddler's Elbow, Milliner's Shoe, Sambo and Mary, Vancamp's Nose, and Shoemaker's Eddy.

THIRD DAY: CALM BEFORE THE STORM

One must use colors, not words, to paint the beauty of the scene that opened before us on our third day, when we ran the upper rapid at Walpack Bend. The wooded height before us rose at least 1,200 feet. The river below was green with the immense reflection. But on the very line of union was a little flame of crimson, which held the eye and centered all the immensity. It was the small cardinal flower, a plant that grows all the way along the Delaware. The intensity of its color is indescribable, and only seen by the natives and the accidental canoe voyager.

The river affects men in a different way from the road. Never before have I seen so many quiet, contented, and gentle working people. Hundreds of farmhouses we passed, surrounded with foliage, women sitting sewing, children playing near the house, men working in the farmyard, and the bright river moving forever before their eyes.

A song sung by some country girls and boys in a boat, passing close, makes a memory as vivid as the cardinal flower. A lady in a boat, excited and joyous, holds up a splendid fish as we pass. "See! I've just caught it!" she says. A gentleman in the boat tells us that we can run all the rapids down the river—"except the Great Foul Rift!"

"Depth of mind is as safe as depth of water."

Few people are aware of the danger of rapids. To a person along a river, the rapids seem the safest spot because they are obviously the shallowest. But, as the teamster said at Port Jervis, it is "the bottom that is to be feared, not the top."

"It is just the same with humanity," says Guiteras, when this thought is spoken; "it is superficial and hasty people who make all the trouble. Depth of mind is as safe as depth of water."

We ran two or three rapids that day that tested nerves and boats, and were exasperated to hear that they were "smooth rifts," and "nothing at all to the Big Foul." Here it was again; and from this time forward, almost every one to whom we spoke warned us in about the same words. Hence grew an unexpressed desire in each of our minds to reach and run it, and have done with it.

(What happens next? Will the canoeists attempt the Big Foul Rift, or chicken out and carry their canoes around it? Does injury or death wait around the next riverbend? Turn to page 367 for the rest of the story.)

BANG!

Explosive Facts About Firecrackers

> ***"Inside the palace, the firecrackers made a glorious noise... the rumbling of which sounded like thunder."***
> **—Wu Tze-Mu, A.D. 1275**

IN CHINA, firecrackers are called *pao chuk,* which means "bursting bamboo." In ancient times, they threw segments of green bamboo into a fire to make it explode with a bang. Even after the Chinese invented black-powder firecrackers, the original name stuck.

• Who invented black powder? Historians believe that as early as the 7th century A.D., a Chinese Taoist alchemist stumbled onto the recipe while experimenting with sulfur compounds. We do know that an alchemist guide book from the A.D. 800s warned against mixing sulfur, arsenic disulfide, saltpeter, and honey: "Smoke and flames result, so that hands and faces have been burnt, and even whole houses have burned down. These things only bring Taoism into discredit, and alchemists should not do them."

• The first firecrackers to reach Europe came from the travels of Marco Polo, who sent a huge stash of them home to Italy with this (perhaps overexaggerated) description: "They burn with such a dreadful noise they can be heard for ten miles at night. Anyone who is not used to it could die, hence the ears are stuffed with cotton and clothes drawn over the head, for it is the most terrible thing in the world to hear for the first time."

• Remember the paper drives by Boy Scouts in years gone by? Until the 1970s, most of the newspapers collected were shipped to Asia and recycled into firecrackers.

• Here's how firecrackers work. The black powder inside contains saltpeter. The saltpeter releases its own oxygen so none needs to be sucked from the outside air when the powder burns, so it burns instantaneously at 3,800° C. Carbon dioxide and sulfur dioxide gases expand to fill a space 3,000 times the gunpowder's original bulk, buckling the firecracker's paper walls and exploding.

• For weddings, new year's celebrations, store openings

A Bang-Up Fourth of July

Hard to believe considering the number of casualties they've caused, but firecrackers were long encouraged as a way of making the Fourth of July a safer time. Actually, though, the standard ways of making a lot of noise were much more dangerous then. For example:

• **Guns.** Discharging pistols into the air was long considered an essential part of Independence Day. That wasn't necessarily a big problem in farmland, but in densely packed urban areas, the bullets raining down presented a grave danger to life and property.

• **Shooting the Anvil.** It was said you could hear a good anvil shoot from miles away. Celebrants put a blacksmith's anvil on the ground and placed a bag of gunpowder with a fuse on top of it. A second anvil was turned upside down on top of the bag of gunpowder. One brave (or drunk) soul lit the fuse, and everybody scattered. This was to avoid being crushed like a cartoon character.... When the gunpowder exploded, the top anvil was propelled into the air by the explosion before returning heavily, and sometimes lethally, to the ground.

and even funerals, firecrackers have been part of Chinese celebrations for more than a millennium. The firecrackers are meant to scare away unwanted bad spirits like Nian, a one-horned, mythical dragon that comes at the end of each year to savagely molest and kill people and their livestock.

• For Chinese weddings, the explosions of firecrackers are used to clear out negative *chi* and jealous *chi* (*chi* means "energy"). It's believed that if the spirits of jealousy attack during the ceremony, the bride may begin menstruating, which is a terrible omen of bad luck indicating the marriage will shortly end in death or divorce.

• Experts of *feng shui* swear that hanging firecrackers around your home will change the *chi* of your household, resulting in harmony, balance, fame, wealth, awareness, energizing of the lazy, comfort for all and the protection of the household from harm.

"Holiday in Chinatown, San Francisco" by Paul Frenzeny for *Harper's Weekly*, 1880

• Chinese Christians celebrate Christmas with firecrackers, blowing them off while waiting for the arrival of Dun Che Lao Ren ("Christmas Old Man," or Santa Claus). What's interesting is that they're following an old European and American tradition, in which the deafening sound of firecrackers and guns marked the birthday celebration of the Prince of Peace. An Englishman visiting Baltimore in 1866 wrote that he felt as though he were in the middle of a war zone.

• Poor folks who couldn't afford Christmas firecrackers

saved the bladders from slaughtered hogs. They got good explosions by inflating them and tossing them into a fire.

• Fire experts in the early 1900s suggested scattering firecrackers in rafters, studding, flooring and walls. Not for the *feng shui* benefits (*see p. 69*), but as a fire alarm, since the firecrackers going off would likely awaken the residents in time to get out safely.

• An article in the March, 1955 *Farm Journal* suggested tying firecrackers to a smoldering cotton rope in order to scare birds away from crops. "The rope will smolder away at the rate of about six inches per hour, so you can time the explosions by varying the distances between firecrackers."

• Possessing cherry bombs and M-80s became a federal felony in 1967.

• Legal firecrackers are now relatively safe, resulting in only 17 percent of all fireworks injuries. (This figure includes not just explosions, but also things like toddlers swallowing them, etc.) This compares favorably to sparklers which cause 19 percent. Illegal homemade firecrackers are responsible for 40 percent.

• In England, the big firecracker holiday is November 5—Guy Fawkes Day. The holiday commemorates an aborted plot by persecuted Catholics to blow up Parliament and the royal family in A.D. 1605. For centuries, the holiday was an excuse to make anti-Catholic speeches and burn effigies of the pope with firecrackers inside.

• In India, at the end of the five-day festival of Diwali, celebrants banish Alaksmi, the goddess of bad luck, poverty and misfortune. They do this by sweeping the house, yelling in all the rooms and setting off firecrackers.

• Although some factories use hand-powered or foot-powered rolling machines, firecrackers are still mostly assembled by hand. It's dangerous and tedious work. In China, where the bulk of the world's firecrackers are made, skilled workers get paid only 80¢ to $1 an hour. €

"Pop" Culture

Some Kernels of Truth About Popcorn

Have you ever thought about what a strange thing it is that corn can pop? And the fact that it tastes good—especially when watching movies—makes it all the more magical.

A CORNUCOPIA OF FACTS

• Popcorn grows in a variety of colors besides boring old white and yellow. The red, pink, and blue kinds are especially colorful. Unfortunately, no matter what the color of the kernel, the insides are still white when they pop.

• A German food scientist has identified twenty-three different natural compounds that contribute to the flavor and aroma of popcorn.

• Popcorn figures into a 1957 hoax that many people still believe is true. An unemployed market researcher named James M. Vicary claimed that by flashing "EAT POPCORN" for a split second on the movie screen, he subliminally convinced audiences to buy 57.5% more popcorn.

• Americans eat an average of more than 2

pounds—68 quarts—of popcorn a year.

• Maybe they should eat more. One cup of plain popcorn from a hot air popper has little fat and only 23 calories. Because of its high fiber content (15% total dietary fat), popcorn has earned recommendations from the American Cancer Society and the National Cancer Institute.

• Or, in the real world, maybe people should eat less popcorn. Because when we eat popcorn, it's usually slathered with artificial, buttery hydrogenated fat. A study in 1994 by the Center for Science in the Public Interest found that a medium-sized buttered popcorn from movie theaters contains more saturated fat than an order of bacon and eggs, a Big Mac, a medium fries, and a steak dinner, *combined*—29 grams.

An 1856 recipe for popcorn balls began with a big slather of pig fat....

• In 1996, thirty-five volunteers working 10 hours straight created the world's largest popcorn ball. At 2,225 pounds, it weighed more than a Volkswagen Beetle, and was taller—nearly 6 feet high. The superball took 1,020 pounds of sugar and 425 pounds of corn syrup to stick it all together. All this excitement took place in Sac City, Iowa, to honor the town's biggest crop.

Versatile Corn

• Only 1% of all corn grown is used for direct human consumption, and only a fraction of that is popcorn. The rest is used for animal feed or made into other products like corn starch, corn oil and alcohol.

• Besides that, cornstalks can be made into soil conditioners, building materials, paper, packing materials and even explosives.

• Corncobs are used to manufacture plastics and nylon (and rustic pipes), and corn husks can be made into cigarette paper.

READ HISTORY & BE A-MAIZED

• Ancient fossilized corn pollen from 80,000 years ago, found in Mexico City, is nearly identical to that of modern corn.

• Archeologists believe that humanity's first use of corn

was for popping. The oldest known ears of popcorn, about 5,600 years old, were discovered in Bat Cave, New Mexico.

• In ancient times, they heated sand in a fire and then stirred kernels of popcorn into the hot sand.

• Some Native Americans used the same oil-and-hot pan method often used today. Others ran a sharp stick through the cob and popped the corn kernels still attached.

• 1,000-year-old popcorn found in Peruvian graves is so well-preserved that it could still pop.

• Before Columbus, popcorn had spread from Mexico through most Native American societies in North and South America. Native Americans used it for eating, of course, but also made it into popcorn soup and beer, strung it into necklaces, and woven it into headdresses.

• When Columbus and crew

Tlaloc, Aztec god of rain, fertility... and popcorn!

first landed in the Americas, the Indians offered to sell them popcorn. Early Spanish explorers told of "a kind of corn which bursts when parched and and makes itself look like a very white flower; they said these were hail-

Why Popcorn Pops

• Popcorn has a higher moisture content than other varieties of corn. To pop, a kernel must contain at least 13.5% water, encircled inside the ring of soft starch, in order for the kernel to explode.

• If the kernel heats up quickly, the water inside the starch expands and exerts great pressure against the hard outer surface. (If heated slowly, the water escapes without popping the corn.)

• Eventually the outside cannot contain this pressure, causing the skin to burst with a loud "pop!" The softened starch inside the popcorn turns the kernel inside out and instantaneously hardens into that stiff, Styrofoam consistency.

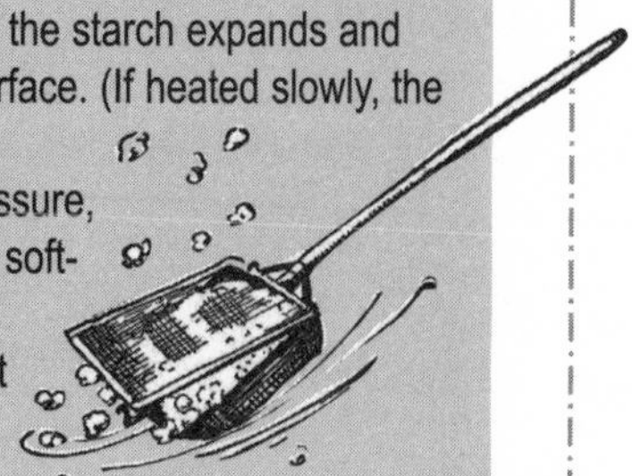

stones given to the god of water."

• While popcorn probably originated in Mexico, it was also grown in China, Sumatra and India centuries before Columbus brought it to Europe, fueling more speculation that the Chinese discovered America years before.

• Quadequina, brother of the Wampanoag chief Massasoit,

The King of Corn

• Yes, there really was an Orville Redenbacher, even though the name and the geekish bowtie-and-suspenders persona convinced many people that he was too good to be anything but an ad agency's creation.

• After graduating from Purdue University, Redenbacher and another researcher named Charles Bowman worked for decades, crossbreeding 30,000 hybrids before coming up with a strain of popcorn in 1952 that was originally branded Redbow, a combination of Redenbacher and Bowman's names. A Chicago advertising agency, realizing Redenbacher would be good at a folksy television hucksterism, suggested changing the name.

Orville Redenbacher, from a package of microwave popcorn

• Marketing his popcorn was difficult at first. Retailers didn't see a point in a higher grade of "gourmet popcorn." It wasn't until the yuppie food faddism of the 1980s that Redenbacher's popcorn came into its own. He'd sold the business to Hunt-Wesson in 1978 for $2 million before it had really taken off, yet he continued to act as its commercial front man, eventually becoming famous. When in public, he'd pass out stickers that said, "I've met Orville Redenbacher, the Popcorn King."

• The popcorn's reputation for always popping and Redenbacher's identification with it led people to complain directly to him if they ran into problems. "Every once in a while, someone will mail me a single popcorn kernel that didn't pop. They'll tape it to a piece of paper and mail it to me," he told the *LA Times* in 1984. "So I'll get out a fresh kernel, tape it to a piece of paper and mail it back to them."

• Redenbacher ate a bowl of popcorn a day.

•In 1995, he drowned in a spa after having a heart attack at the ripe old age eighty-eight.

brought a deerskin bag of popcorn to the first Thanksgiving feast of the pilgrims at Plymouth, Massachusetts. After that, colonists ate popcorn with milk and sugar for breakfast.

• A man name Charles Cretors invented the very first popcorn machine in 1885. It was pretty ingenious because of its versatility. It could be pushed on foot, pulled by horse or mounted on trucks. The Cretors family still makes machines today.

A Cretors popcorn machine

Nothing to Do with Corn at All

• When the first settlers landed in America there were about 200,000 words in the English language. Now there are more than 600,000. Most Americans know only about 10,000-20,000 of them, but actually use only about half that number. In fact, 1,500-2,000 words account for about 99% of everything we ever say.

• The most common word that's spoken in the English language is *I*. The second most common is *you*. Those two words account for almost 10% of all informal conversation.

• The third and fourth most common words are *the* and *a*.

• The ten most popular words account for about 25% of what we say, and the fifty most popular words fill about 60%.

• The fifty most popular words? Alphabetically, they are *a, about, an, and, are, be, can, do, don't, have, he, her, him, I, in, is, it, for, from, just, get, go, know, me, not, now, of, on, out, over, see, she, tell, that, them, they, thing, think, this, to, want, was, we, what, will, with, would, you.*

• *"The trouble with corporate America is that too many people with too much power live in a box (their home), travel the same road every day to another box (their office)."*

• *"Send me out into another life. But get me back for supper."*

—Faith Popcorn, U.S. Management Consultant

Typhoid, yellow fever, dysentery, cholera, malaria and hookworm all were common illnesses in parts of the United States before the arrival of sanitary, non–leaking privies.

Say "Ah"

A Closer Look at Dental History

It's hard to believe, but most Americans didn't brush their teeth until soldiers brought the Army-enforced habit back home from World War II.

ALTHOUGH IT TOOK AMERICANS a while to catch on to good oral hygiene practices, people throughout history have worked to care for their teeth, starting as far back as the ancient Egyptians. "Chew sticks"—twigs with one end frayed into soft bristles—have been found in Egyptian tombs going back to about 3000 B.C. The first toothpaste was developed about the same time—a mixture of ground pumice and wine.

POTTY MOUTHS

The ancient Romans took teeth cleaning further, including it as part of some of their religious ceremonies. The patriarchy employed certain slaves, forerunners of modern dental hygienists, to clean their teeth. They also invented the first toothpaste and mouthwash with a secret ingredient: human urine. They especially prized imported Portuguese urine for its strength, but that was probably more a function of evaporation on the long trip to Rome than any ethnic characteristics.

Urine continued to be an active ingredient in toothpastes and mouthwashes until well into the 18th century, because its ammonia was a great cleanser. In fact, ammonia continues to be an ingredient in many modern dentifrices, but now it's manufactured in the laboratory, not the lavatory. Other ingredients in toothpaste over the years included herbs, honey, ground shells, talc, mice, rabbit heads and lizard livers.

BRISTLING AT THE THOUGHT

The first toothbrush appeared in China around 1498. The bristles were plucked from hogs living in China's cold-weather provinces because their hair was stouter and firmer; the hairs were set into handles of bone or bamboo. The Chinese toothbrush traveled to Europe in the 1600s and became widely used.

The toothbrush stayed pretty much the same for several hundred years. Finally, the discovery of nylon in 1938 revolutionized the toothbrush, and just in time for World War II. The bristles of Dr. West's Miracle Tuft Toothbrush released that year were stiff enough to be a painful hazard to the gums; it wasn't until the early 1950s that a safe, soft nylon bristle became the standard. Since then, more than 2,000 toothbrushes have been patented across the world.

IT'S ELEMENTAL!

Dentists discovered the positive effects of fluoride on teeth in 1802 when they noticed that the citizens of fluoride-rich Naples, Italy, had brown mottled teeth but few cavities. By the 1840s, some Europeans sucked honey-flavored fluoride lozenges to prevent tooth decay, but the idea of adding the chemical to toothpaste was still a century away. Instead, manufacturers started adding soap in 1824 and chalk in the 1850s. In 1892, Dr. Washington Sheffield of Connecticut was the first to put toothpaste into tubes like those used for oil paint.

In 1945, Grand Rapids, Michigan, became the first U.S. city to deliberately add fluoride to city water to reduce cavities. Other cities followed suit to a point that nearly two-thirds of the U.S. population now has fluoridated water, despite warnings from right-wing fearmongers that fluoride was a communist plot to produce a generation of drugged and mind-controlled zombies. (Hmm, look around you—maybe they were right after all?)

Procter & Gamble was the first company to package fluoride into a toothpaste in 1956. In a brilliant ad campaign that's still quoted 40 years later, kids ran into the house brandishing notes from their dentist and screaming, "Look ma, no cavities!"

GOOD VIBRATIONS

Meanwhile, electric toothbrushes made their way from Switzerland, where they'd been developed immediately after World War II and tested on canines for effectiveness. They first hit the U.S. market in 1960.

The latest gimmick is an ultrasonic toothbrush that is reported to clean between teeth with high-pitched sound waves. Maybe true, but don't throw away the floss until all the results are in.

DRILLING FOR FACTS

• It's hard to imagine, but Colgate claims "Tooth Fairy" as a registered trademark. Hopefully, corporate sponsorship means the TF can leave a lot more money under the pillow. Your can fill out a form and get an e-mail from the Tooth Fairy® Itself.

• Colgate reportedly faced a big obstacle marketing toothpaste in Spanish speaking countries. Colgate translates into the command "Go hang yourself."

• Although Crest with fluoride came out in 1955, it just

sat on store shelves, to Procter & Gamble's bewilderment. P&G touted a high-profile study proving that fluoride prevents cavities and lobbied the American Dental Association for an endorsement. Both—touted in "Look ma, our group had 23% fewer cavities!" ads— finally brought Crest skyrocketing sales in the early 1960s.

• In 1959, dentists performed 34 extractions for every 100 people. Getting dentures was considered a natural step in the aging process. Today, it's half that rate.

• Saliva is a natural bacteria destroyer, and antidepressants, antihypertensives, antihistamines, decongestants and muscle relaxants can all inhibit saliva production.

• The old Listerine commercial notwithstanding, not even mouthwash really helps bad breath beyond a minute or two—in fact, alcohol and hydrogen peroxide can actually worsen the conditions. Baking soda makes your mouth more alkaline—exactly the wrong direction, because acidity decreases bad breath.

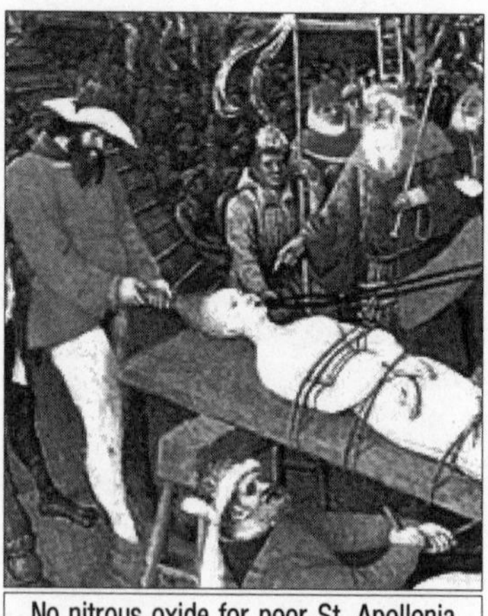

No nitrous oxide for poor St. Apollonia

• We worry about bad breath to the tune of $10 billion a year of profit to mint, gum, and mouthwash manufacturers, nearly all of it wasted.

• Regular flossing and proper brushing is the best cure for halitosis, or bad breath.

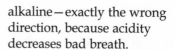

• How about a tooth tattoo? Tiny gold images of hearts, butterflies and rabbits have become popular among certain trendy subgroups. The downside is that from a distance of more than about 3 feet it just looks like you have food stuck in your teeth.

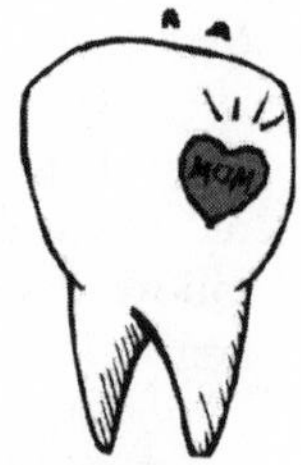

• In case you've tried brushing, flossing and regular check-ups and still have problem teeth, try religion. The patron saint of dentists is St. Apollonia, who reportedly had her teeth pulled out in A.D. 249 by an anti-Christian mob. €

Ouch!

Love Secrets of the Spiny & Hardshelled

Animal relationships can be difficult enough, but have you thought about the difficulties of animals that have prickles or shells?

PRICKLY HEAT

"How do porcupines make love?" "Very carefully!" goes the old joke, but in real life it's not quite as prickly as you'd expect. Mating is a dangerous pastime for male porcupines, but not because of the quills. They fight other males for the right to mate with a receptive female. Since the female porcupine goes into a prickly heat only once a year, the stakes are high in porcupine love. Worse, the female enjoys inciting the rivalries between males. She hangs out in a tree, urinating her sexual scents down toward them and calling saucily to the boys fighting each other below. When one man's left standing, the female crawls down the tree. The male urinates on the female to excite her with his sexual scents, and the female curls her tail over her back to expose her quill-free genital region. Male porcupine genitalia is located on his underside, too, so when they mate, there are no pointed parts for the prickly pair to be watchful of. The whole messy business takes only a minute or so.

"Hi, boys—how's every li'l prickly thing?"

A SHELLFISH KIND OF LOVE

How do lobsters mate with all that shell in the way?

Well, it turns out there's an opportunity now and again. You see, lobsters grow by molting—they get too big for their shells and shed them like a human shedding a too-tight girdle. Without a shell they grow quickly by absorbing a lot of water, and then they grow a new, bigger shell.

It's in the time just after shedding their shells that females mate. The courtship process is sweet: When the female lobster is ready to molt, she approaches a male's den and stands outside, releasing her scent in a stream of urine from just below her antennae. When the male emerges from his den, the two spar briefly, then the female signals him by placing her claws on his head that she is ready to molt and mate.

"Hey, baby, why not slip out of those wet things?"

They enter his bachelor pad and she languidly strips off her shell. He tenderly turns her limp, yielding body over onto her back with his legs and his mouth. The male, still hard-shelled and passionate, passes his sperm into her body with a rigid, grooved swimmeret. Afterward, she sinks into the soft warmth of the ocean bed and stays in the safety of his den for about a week. When her new shell is hard again, she calls a cab and goes home, never to see him again.

The sperm she receives from the male goes into a special repository where it can stay viable for two years. When she decides she's ready to settle down and have a family, she fertilizes her eggs, numbering from 3,000 to 100,000, carrying them them first in her body, then—for another 9–12 months—under the swimmerets attached to her tail.

After hatching, her microscopic larva float for a month, then settle to the bottom of the ocean to turn into lobsters proper. Still, odds are not good for them—for every 100,000 eggs hatched, only five or six will typically get up to a one-pound weight.

LOVE IN THE SLOW LANE

How do snails have sex? Well, as you'd expect, it's pretty slow; it's also complicated in the many species that are hermaphroditic (in other words, each snail is both male and female).

But that's not the weirdest thing. Snail foreplay begins with each snail jabbing the other in the head, foot or brain with a calcium carbonate "love dart" that can be as long as a centimeter (one-fifth of an inch).

"Sweet Slimer, my foot has been pierced by Cupid's dart."

People have wondered for three centuries why snails do this, but it was not until a few years ago that researchers at McGill University figured it out. They discovered that mucus covering the dart contains hormones that disable the recipient's *bursa copulatrix,* an organ near the female organs that normally digests the vast majority of received sperm. With this organ temporarily disabled, more of the donor's sperm will survive.

After this mutual piercing takes place, the snails place their slimy undersides together and exchange sperm before slowly parting company. But don't expect fond, languid farewells—snails may be slow, but they're not sentimental. They copulate frequently with many different partners, and can store other snails' sperm in their bodies for up to two years. €

Arm in Arm in Arm in Arm...

Octopuses may not have to contend with shells and prickles, but they have their own sexual idiosyncrasies to overcome. Males have a modified third arm with a groove down the edge and a leaf-shaped grasping structure at the tip. To mate, the male moves elongated sperm packages down the groove and reaches over to place them in the female's oviducts of her mantle cavity. Beforehand, some males make a vivid display of colored skin patterns and complex body movements; however, the rock pool octopuses have sex without seeing each other—while both remain hidden behind rocks, the male snakes his long arm of love over to her.

Get a Job!

WANT A CAREER CHANGE? HERE ARE SOME SUGGESTIONS

Nob Thatcher: A peruker; wig manufacturer.
Caffler: Someone who collects bones and old scraps.
Qwylwryghte: A wagon wheel mechanic.
Jouster: A fish dealer.
Accipitrary: One who works with falcons.
Eremite: A solitary soul; a hermit.
Hankyman: A magician who moves from town to town.
Perambulator: One who surveys the land.
Chiropodist: A foot and hand disease specialist.
Garlekmonger: Someone who sells garlic.
Mold Boy: Apprentice to a glass maker; helps with molding.
Scrimer: A master fencer.
Whittawer: Someone who manufactures saddles.
Costerwife: A woman who hawks fruit.
Ankle Beater: A cattle driver.
Slubber Doffer: A mill worker who changes bobbins.
Archil Maker: One who makes violet-colored dye from lichen.
Back'us Boy: A servant who works in the kitchen.
Leech: A doctor or veterinarian ("dog leech," "horse leech").
Gerund Grinder: A Latin teacher.
Vineroon: A wine maker.
Bottom Knocker: Someone who helps a potter by knocking the bottom of clay pots.
Nedeller: Someone who makes sewing needles.
Sucksmith: A plow blade manufacturer.
Fewster: One who makes the wooden parts of a saddle.
Tappiologist: A train wheel inspector; someone who taps train wheels.
Simpler: An herbalist.
Deviller: Someone who operates a machine that shreds cloth.
Owler: Ovine thief; one who deals in stolen sheep or wool.
Blemmere: One who works with pipes; a plumber.
Fustian Weaver: A corduroy manufacturer.

T.G.I. Friggas Day

WHERE THE WEEK'S DAYS GOT THEIR NAMES

The name Sunday makes sense. It's obviously a joining of "sun" and "day." But what about the other six days? Where did the names come from, anyway? Gloria Munday brings us a day by day overview.

THE IDEA OF THE SEVEN DAY WEEK came from either the Babylonians or ancient Egyptians, depending on which source you believe. Regardless, the Greeks also adopted it, and named each of the days after the five known planets, and the sun and moon. When the Greek civilization declined, the Roman Empire took much from the Greeks, including naming rights for the days of the week, substituting their own names for the planets.

As the Romans conquered Europe, they spread their names for the week's days. Today in France and Italy, for instance, the names of the days are pretty much the same as they were in ancient Roman times. England, though, had many more influences than Latin. In about A.D. 500, for instance, the Germanic tribes—the Norse, Saxons, Anglos, collectively—conquered Britain and substituted their own names in place of the Roman days of the week, and until the next conquering army, this is where we are now.

SUNDAY
Latin: *Solis dies*
Germanic: *Sonntag*

The Greeks came up with "the day of the sun," and the Romans and Germanic tribes liked it so much, they kept it. The Romans honored the god Apollo, who flew his fiery chariot through the sky each day. The Saxons changed the Roman "solis" to *sunne,* and the day to "Sonntag."

MONDAY
Latin: *Lunae dies*
Germanic: *Monandaeg*

The Romans dedicated this day to the goddess of the hunt, Diana, who was the twin sister of Apollo. Diana loved hunters, but only to a point. She once turned a hunter into a deer when she caught him spying on her, so she's often depicted with a stag.

The Saxons believed that the sun was a girl and the moon (or *mona*) a boy, and each drove chariots through the sky as wolves chased them. The legend had it that if the wolves caught them, day and night would disappear. It's no surprise, then, that eclipses caused a lot of anxiety for these early Germanic peoples.

TUESDAY
Latin: *Martis dies*
Germanic: *Tiwesdaeg*

The Romans named this day for the planet Mars, and the Roman god of war—Martius. In France, Spain and Italy, the name for Tuesday is directly descended from the Latin: *Mardi, Martes,* and *Martedi,* respectively. (*Mardi Gras,* literally means "Fat Tuesday" in French.) In Roman mythology, the god Mars was the father of Romulus and Remus, the legendary founders of Rome, who were raised by a wolf.

Years later, when the Germanic tribes rode into Britain, they gave this day to their own god of war, Tiw, hence "Tuesday." Evidence suggests that Tiw was the oldest of all the Norse gods and was long their head god. However, Odin eventually replaced him as head god, and Tiw was demoted to war god only. He's depicted dressed for battle with sword and shield.

WEDNESDAY

Latin: *Mercurii dies*
Germanic: *Wodnesdaeg*

Mercury was the ancient Roman god of messages, and Wednesday (*Mercurii dies*) was named after him.

Mercury sported a winged hat and shoes that helped him fly. He was known in mythology for being a thief. As the story goes, he stole Apollo's cows by placing shoes on their feet and having them walk backward so no one could track them. Mercury used the gut from the cows to string the first lyre, which so impressed Apollo that he forgave Mercury.

Supplanting Mercury, the Saxons decided their chief god, Odin (or Woden), deserved his own day. Odin was believed to have invented writing. He was often depicted riding on an eight-legged horse, with two ravens who served as his messengers.

THURSDAY

Latin: *Jovis dies*
Germanic: *Thorsdaeg*

Jove, god of thunder, was the Roman honoree of the day. His better-known name, Jupiter, means "Father Jove" (the Latin *pater* means "father")—a sign of respect. Jupiter was the guardian of Rome and the head of all the gods.

The Saxon's god Thor is also the god of thunder, and he lends his name to this day. Thor is usually seen depicted with a huge hammer that produces loud thunder. He was Odin's son, and is often drawn riding around on a wagon, led by two goats. He battled giants, and used his hammer to smash their heads. His sworn enemy was the hated World Snake—a snake so big and nasty, it wraps itself around the world

and bites its own tail. (You can see a drawing of the World Snake at the top of page 85.)

FRIDAY

Latin: *Veneris dies*
Germanic: *Frigedaeg*

In ancient Rome, there was the belief in a beautiful goddess named Venus who rose from the sea on a half-shell. Her legend is about competition for male attention. A man named Paris had an apple with "For the Fairest" written on it. The

goddesses Venus, Minerva and Juno offered Paris various qualities in exchange for the apple. Minerva promised Paris wisdom; Juno, power. But Venus offered him another beautiful woman—Helen. He took Venus up on her offer, and paid dearly for it with his life, the lives of his family, and his hometown of Troy. Helen, as it turned out, was a married woman. Still, the Romans were suckers for a pretty face, and Venus's day was born.

The Saxons liked the idea of a day in honor of a pretty gal, so they named this day after Frigga. She is believed to be Odin's wife, but Frigga also had affairs with his brothers. She is the goddess of marriage and fertility.

SATURDAY

Latin: *Saturni dies*
Germanic: *Saterdaeg*

The Roman god Saturn was known as Father Time, and is depicted with a sickle. A winter festival called Saturnalia was celebrated in his honor every year in ancient Rome. Schools and businesses closed; families made and ate huge banquets, and the adults showered the children with gifts. All of these traditions—including the time of year—were adopted by the early Christians to celebrate their own Christmas. They continue on today.

The Germanic tribes didn't really have a god that corresponded to Saturn, so they ended up adopting the ancient Roman Saturni day as is. ☾

Life of the Party!

A hundred years ago, with the help of a little candlelight, hand shadows were big fun at get-togethers. Today, we have much better lighting options and these cool pictures from Henry Bursill's book *Hand Shadows*. With just a little practice, you and your hand shadows can become the life of your next party.

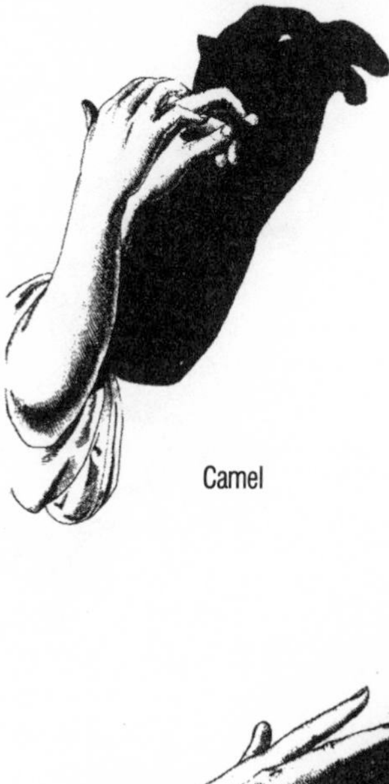

Camel

Bunny

Billy Goat

Mike

Goose

Squirrel

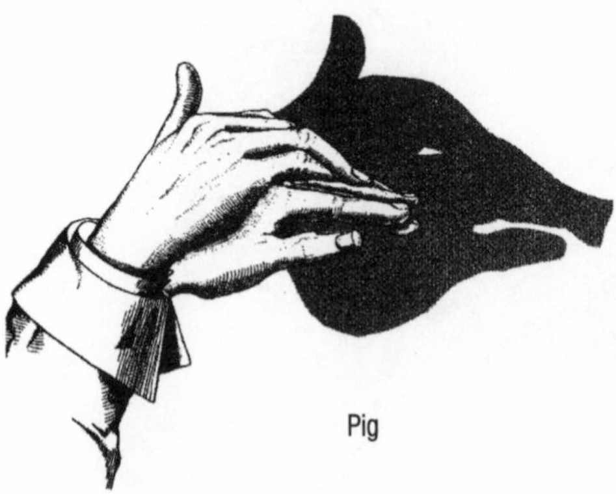
Pig

Pooh Bear

Very Little Brain, but Much Success

You can't discuss teddy bears without mentioning that Bear of Very Little Brain, Winnie the Pooh. He and the other cotton-brained residents of the Hundred Aker Woods have charmed kids for 75 years.

FOR THEIR IMPACT, it's hard to imagine that Alexander (A. A.) Milne wrote only two books about Winnie the Pooh and his friends plus two books of verse featuring his real-life son Christopher Robin Milne. For illustrations, he enlisted an artist he knew from writing for *Punch Magazine,* Ernest Shepard. Recognizing Shepard's contributions to the success of his books, Milne began giving him 20% of his royalties instead of just the normal flat rate for an illustrator.

Despite the books' huge success, Milne got tired of writing for children. He had been a moderately successful playwright who believed that his kid books were just a diversion from his "real" career. After his second Pooh book, he announced that it was to be his last, and stuck to that decision.

Meanwhile, his son Christopher got tired of media attention and being ribbed through school, military service and adult life with "Hey, where's Pooh?" and "Cwistopher Wobin is saying his pwayers." He became estranged from both father and his literary namesake, now seeking anonymity, now blasting both father and bear regularly in word and print.

His father began feeling similarly cursed by Winnie the bear as the public consistently rejected his more serious efforts. But in 1952, a few months before the stroke that eventually killed him, he seemed to have made peace with his fuzzy creation. He wrote in his memoirs: "There was an intermediate period when any reference to Pooh was infuriating; but now such a 'nice comfortable feeling' envelopes him that I can almost regard him impersonally as the creation of one of my favorite authors." Alexander's funeral in 1956 was the last time Christopher would see either parent, although his mother, Daphne, would live another fifteen years.

Daphne became busy during that time, further enraging Christopher by selling his father's original manuscripts. She also infuriated much of England by giving the original stuffed animals to Milne's American publisher, which placed them in the New York Public Library, where they still reside. Many readers, too, became exasperated because Christopher's mother sold Pooh's movie rights to the Walt Disney Corporation. Its first effort was not reassuring to Pooh fans: In *Winnie-the-Pooh and the Honey Tree* Piglet got inexplicably replaced by a gopher, and all of the characters somehow developed American accents.

Beyond the World of Pooh
Selections from the memoirs of CHRISTOPHER MILNE
Edited by A.R. MELROSE
With an introduction by LESLEY MILNE

"Billy" Milne made a career of complaining about the difficulties of being Christopher Robin

Christopher eventually came grudgingly to terms with his unwelcome notoriety over the years after writing two successful books complaining about it. He died in April 1996.

END PIECES OF THE TALE

• Through his real life childhood, Christopher Milne was usually called Bill or Billy Moon. ("Moon" because that's the closest young Billy could get to pronouncing his own last name.)

• Most of the names of characters in the stories were the real names of Billy's stuffed animals, except Owl and Rabbit, who were real animals seen in the woods behind the Milnes' house.

• Pooh was purchased at Harrod's department store in London for Christopher Robin's first birthday, August 21, 1921. He was originally called Edward.

• Christopher Milne called his toy bear "Winnie-ther-Pooh." Some people have speculated that "Winnie" may have come from Winston Churchill, like Teddy came from Roosevelt. But no—Winnie was the name of a very tame American black bear at the London Zoo that A. A. Milne and son Christopher visited regularly. Her name came from her first owner's hometown: Winnipeg, Canada.

• Why "-ther-Pooh"? Young Christopher believed that it was the masculine form of "the" that showed that Winnie was a male. "Pooh" seemed to be a name he used for other things, too, including a swan mentioned in one of his dad's *When We Were Very Young* verses.

• The Pooh stories have been translated into at least 40 languages, including Thai, Hebrew and Braille. A Latin version made history as the first non-English book to hit the *New York Times* bestseller list in 1960. *Winnie ille Pu* remained there for 20 weeks.

Pooh Sticks Game

Whether they know it or not, almost everybody's played Pooh Sticks, the game that tests the speed and agility ... of twigs. The rules are very simple:

1. You and your friends drop a stick or pine cone on the upstream side of a bridge.
2. Run to the other side and see which one emerges first.
3. Repeat indefinitely.

• The very first Kanga and Roo belonged to Christopher Robin's childhood friend, Anne Darlington. Later Milne apparently got his own. Darlington later auctioned hers off to a Teddy Bear Museum in December, 1995.

• The Bear of Very Little Brain's mindlessly mindful existence awakened Benjamin Hoff to write about Pooh-philosophy in *The Tao of Pooh* (1982). His sequel, *The Te of Piglet,* came out in 1992.

• Despite outrage from England, Winnie, Eeyore, Piglet, Kanga and Tigger are on display in the children's section of the New York Public Library's Donnell Library Center. The toys are a little worse for wear, because the Milne family dog also apparently enjoyed playing with them. And, most tragically, Roo was lost somewhere in an English apple orchard in the 1930s.

• Disney Store outlets reported in 1997 that, for the first time, sales of Winnie the Pooh merchandise beat out Mickey Mouse to become Disney's top-selling character among adult toy buyers.

Not Everyone Loved Pooh & Milne

"Tonstant Weader fwowed up." —Dorothy Parker as "Constant Reader" reviewing The House on Pooh Corner in the New Yorker

A. A. Milne responded: "No writer of children's books says gaily to his publisher, 'Don't bother about the children, Mrs. Parker will love it.'"

"We were supposed to be quite good friends, but, you know, in a sort of way I think he was a pretty jealous chap. I think he was probably jealous of all other writers. But I loved his stuff. That's one thing I'm very grateful for: I don't have to like an awful person to like his stuff." —P. G. Wodehouse, about A. A. Milne

"Some people are good with children. Others are not. It is a gift. You either have it our you don't. My father didn't....It seemed to me, almost, that my father had got to where he was by climbing upon my infant shoulders, that he had filched from me my good name and had left me with nothing but the empty fame of being his son." —Christopher Robin Milne

Ben's Money I

Advice from Franklin's Little Money Book

In 1757, Benjamin Franklin compiled a small collection of advice on money from his *Poor Richard's Almanac.* The booklet was a huge success and made Franklin wealthy. Here is some of his wisdom. "A word to the wise is enough," said Ben.

TIME MANAGEMENT

• *Dost thou love life? Then do not squander time, for that's the stuff life is made of. Wasting time must be the greatest prodigality, since lost time is never found again.*

• *If we are industrious we shall never starve; for, at the working man's house hunger looks in, but dares not enter.*

• *Industry pays debts, while despair increaseth them.*

• *Plough deep while sluggards sleep, and you shall have corn to sell and to keep.*

• *One today is worth two tomorrows.*

• *If you have something to do tomorrow, do it today.*

• *Leisure is time for doing something useful; this leisure the diligent man will obtain, but the lazy man never; so that a life of leisure and a life of laziness are two things.*

SLOTH

• *Taxes are indeed very heavy, and if those laid on by the government were the only ones we had to pay, we might more easily discharge them; but we have many others, and much more grievous to some of us. We are taxed twice as much by our idleness, three times as much by our pride, and four times as much by our folly, and from these taxes the commissioners cannot ease.*

• *Sloth, by bringing on diseases, absolutely shortens life. Sloth, like rust, consumes faster than labor wears. The used key is always bright.*

• *How much more than is necessary do we spend in sleep? The sleeping fox catches no poultry. There will be sleeping enough in the grave.*

• *Sloth makes all things difficult, but industry all easy.*

• *He that riseth late must trot all day, and shall scarce overtake his business at night.*

• *Laziness travels so slowly, that poverty soon overtakes him.*

MINDING YOUR BUSINESS

• *Drive thy business, let not it drive thee.*

• *He that lives upon hope will die fasting.*

• *There are no gains without pains.*

• *He that hath a trade hath an estate, and he that hath a calling hath an office of profit and honor; but then the trade must be worked at, and the calling well followed, or neither the estate, nor the office, will enable us to pay our taxes.*

• *Keep thy shop, and thy shop will keep thee.*

• *If you would have your business done, go; if not, send.*

• *Handle your tools without mittens; remember that the cat in gloves catches no mice.*

• *In the affairs of this world men are saved not by faith, but by the lack of it.*

• *If you want a faithful servant, and one that you like, serve yourself.*

• *Many without labor would live by their wits only, but they break for want of stock.*

• *Three moves are as bad as a fire. I never saw an oft-moved tree nor an oft-moved family, that thrived as well as those who settled be.*

ATTENTION TO DETAIL

• *A little neglect may breed great mischief.*

• *Not to oversee workmen is to leave them your purse open.*

• *The eye of a master will do more work than both his hands.*

• *Want of care does us more damage than want of knowledge.*

• *For want of a nail the shoe was lost, for want of a shoe the horse was lost, and for want of a horse the rider was lost, being overtaken and slain by the enemy, all for want of care about a horse-shoe nail.*

(Want more of Ben's advice? See page 307.)

A Suppressed Gospel

BABY JESUS' REIGN OF TERROR

The terrible twos, the fearsome fives and the perilous preteens are bad enough, but what if your petulant kid had supernatural powers? The Infancy Gospel of Thomas, excluded from the Bible by church fathers in the 4th century, fills in the missing childhood years of Jesus.

I, THOMAS THE ISRAELITE, tell you of the childhood of our Lord Jesus Christ and his mighty deeds.

THE KILLING POOL

The little child Jesus when he was five years old was playing at a brook, and he gathered together the waters into pools, and made them clean by his word alone. Having made soft clay, he fashioned thereof twelve sparrows. It was the Sabbath when he made them and there were also many other little children playing with him.

A certain Jew, when he saw Jesus playing upon the Sabbath day, departed straightaway and told his father Joseph: "Your child has taken clay and fashioned twelve little birds, and has polluted the Sabbath day." When Joseph came to the place and saw, he cried out to Jesus: "Why do you do these things on the Sabbath, which it is not lawful to do?" But Jesus clapped his hands together and cried out to the sparrows: "Go! Fly! And remember me now that you're alive!" The sparrows flew away, chirping loudly. When the Jews saw it they were amazed, and went to tell their leaders that which they had seen Jesus do.

The son of Annas the scribe was standing there with Joseph. He took a willow branch and dispersed the pools of water which Jesus had gathered together. When Jesus saw what he was doing, he became enraged and said unto him: "You evil, ungodly fool, what harm did the pools and the waters do to you? Behold, you are now going to wither like a tree, and you will never bear leaves, or root, or fruit." Immediately, the boy dried up completely, and Jesus went home to Joseph's house. The parents of the withered boy took him up, wailing about his young age, and brought his remains to Joseph. They accused him: "You are responsible for the child who did this."

WATCH IT, BUB

After that, Jesus went through the village, and a running child bumped against his shoulder. Jesus became angry and said to him: "You won't get to your destination." Immediately the boy fell down and died. When people saw what was done, they asked: "Where did this young child come from, that every word of his is an accomplished work?" And the parents of the dead child came to Joseph and blamed him, saying: "With a child like that, you cannot dwell with us in the village. Not until you teach him to bless and not to curse, because he is killing our children!"

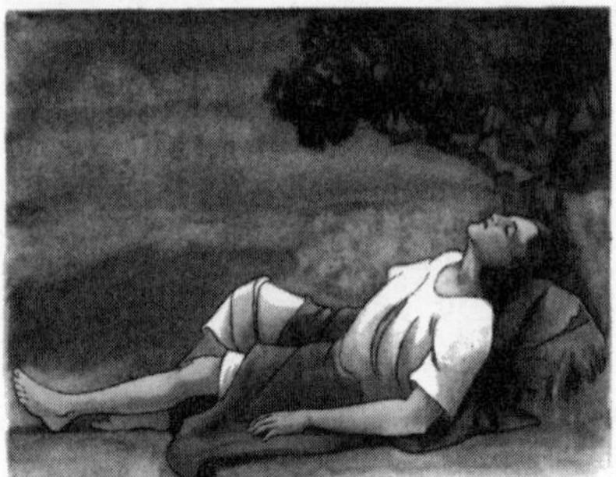

Immediately the boy fell down and died

Joseph called Jesus aside and scolded him, saying: "Why are you doing such things? The neighbors are suffering and hate us. They will cause trouble for us." But Jesus said: "I know that you don't really know what you're saying. Nevertheless for your sake I will keep my silence. However, the ones who complain will bear their punishment." Immediately after he said this, the ones that accused him were stricken blind.

When the villagers saw what Jesus had done, they became frightened and confused. They said to each other: "Every word he speaks, whether good or evil, comes true." When Joseph saw what Jesus had done, he took hold of his ear and twisted it sore. The young child became angry and said: "It's bad enough that you seek and do not find, but too much for you to act so foolishly. I'm not your child, so don't bother me."

A teacher, Zacchaeus, heard when Jesus said these things to his father. After a few days he came near unto Joseph and said unto him: "You have a wise child. Give him to me that he may learn letters and not be rebellious." Joseph replied, "Nobody but God could control this child."

[*After a disastrous first lesson, in which Jesus pointed out that he already knew more than his teacher and that "nobody understands the power of my wisdom," Zacchaeus brought the five-year-old back to Joseph, saying, "I am not able to bear his stare and tongue. This child was not born of this earth. My friend, I am going out of my mind...."*]

As the villagers were counseling Zacchaeus, Jesus laughed and said: "Now let those bear fruit that were barren and let them see that were blind in heart. I am come from above that I may curse them, and call them to the things that are above, even as he commanded which hath sent me for your sakes."

Why Were Books Left Out of the Bible?

"Many have undertaken to set down accounts [about Jesus]" wrote the author of The Gospel According to Luke. And it's true—biblical scholars have identified at least thirty–four different gospels, and have translated all or parts of nineteen. Why so many? The early Christian church was a hotbed of power struggles and competing philosophies. Believing that Jesus was going to come back within their lifetimes, eyewitnesses to his life and teachings had passed their stories along orally. (None of the known gospels was written by an eyewitness or apostle, even though names of early apostles were later attached to them.)

Finally, in the A.D. 70s, it became clear that maybe Jesus' return wasn't imminent, so people began compiling anecdotes and quotations. The plethora of competing gospels was the result of authors and factions weighing in with their version of who Jesus was. A philosopher? A revolutionary leader against the Romans? A god?

One major power struggle was between the original apostles, led by Peter and James, and the Christians in Rome, led by Paul. Early church leaders, disproportionately women, also weighed in as Paul began purging women from leadership positions. Eventually the followers of Paul and Peter merged into one unholy alliance, and immediately ruled all competing gospels as "heresy." By A.D. 400, only four were officially recognized by church authorities.

Immediately all who had come under his curse were saved. After that, nobody dared make him angry, because they didn't want to be maimed or killed.

JESUS FINALLY USES HIS POWERS FOR GOOD... NOT FOR EVIL

A few days later, Jesus was playing on the roof of a house, and Zeno, one of his playmates, fell off and died. The other children fled, and Jesus remained alone. The parents accused Jesus of pushing him off. Jesus leaped down from the roof and stood by the body of the child and cried with a loud voice and said: "Zeno, arise and tell me, did I throw you down?" And Zeno arose and said: "No, Lord, you didn't throw me down, but you did raise me up." And when they saw it they glorified God for the sign which had come to pass, and worshiped Jesus.

Later, a man was chopping wood and the axe fell and cut his foot off. Losing much blood, he was about to die. There was great tumult and Jesus forced his way through the crowd. He took hold of the young man's foot and immediately it was healed. Jesus said: "Get up, chop wood, and remember me." When the multitude saw what was done they worshiped the young child.

Jesus stretched the wood

When Jesus was six years old, his mother sent him with a pitcher to fetch water but on the way he broke it. So Jesus spread out his cloak and filled it with water. When he brought it to his mother, she kissed him, and treasured the mysteries she saw him do.

In planting season, Jesus went forth with his father to sow wheat in their land. As his father sowed, the young child Jesus planted just one kernel of wheat. From it grew an abundance; when he reaped and threshed what had grown, it had become a hundred measures. He called all the poor of the village and gave them the wheat, and Joseph took the rest. Jesus was eight years old when he wrought this sign.

Joseph was a carpenter. A rich man ordered a bed. One beam, however, was too short and Joseph knew not what to do. Jesus said to his father: "Lay down the two pieces of wood and make them even at your end." Jesus stood at the other end and took hold upon the shorter beam and stretched it to make it equal with the other. His father Joseph marvelled, saying: "Happy am I that God has given me this young child."

JESUS GOES BACK TO SCHOOL & REVERTS

Joseph saw the understanding of the child, he decided that Jesus should not be ignorant of letters; and he took him and delivered him to another teacher. Jesus said to him: "If you're really a teacher, tell me the meaning of alpha and then will I tell you the meaning of beta." The frustrated teacher smacked him on the head. Jesus got angry and cursed him, and immediately the teacher fell to the ground. Jesus returned home. Joseph was distressed and commanded to Mary: "Don't let him leave the house, because when he gets angry, people die."

"Suckle your baby and remember me."

Another teacher who was a friend of Joseph: "Bring the child to me, and maybe I can flatter him into learning." Joseph said: "If you're not afraid, my brother, take him." The teacher took Jesus with much worry and fear, but the young child followed him gladly. Going boldly into the school, Jesus found a book lying upon the pulpit and pretended to read from it, but actually delivered a sermon. A crowd gathered and marvelled at his speaking abilities. But when Joseph heard it, he was afraid, and ran unto the school thinking this teacher also was maimed or killed, but his friend said unto Joseph: "This child is full of grace and wisdom. Now I beg you, brother, take him home." When the young child heard that, he smiled at him and said: "Since you've spoken correctly, for your sake I'll heal the other teacher." The other teacher was healed, and Joseph took the young child home.

RANDOM ACTS OF KINDNESS

Joseph sent his son James to gather firewood. While in the woods, a snake bit his hand. He was close to death when Jesus came and blew on the bite. Immediately the pain ceased, the snake burst into pieces, and James continued gathering wood.

Later, a baby fell sick and died, and his mother wept inconsolably. When Jesus heard about it, he ran there quickly. Finding the child dead, Jesus touched his breast and said: "Child, live and be with your mother." Immediately, the baby looked up and laughed. Jesus said to the mother: "Suckle your baby and remember me." Bystanders marvelled, and said: "This child is either a god or an angel, for every word of his comes true." And Jesus went out to play with other children.

A year later, a house builder fell from a great height and died. Jesus took hold of his hand and said: "Mister, rise up and get back to work." Immediately the man arose and worshiped him. When the multitude saw it, they were astonished, and said: "This child is from heaven: for he has saved many souls from death, and hath power to save them all his life long."

JESUS RUNS AWAY FROM HOME

When Jesus was twelve years old, his parents went to Jerusalem for Passover. Afterward, they began the journey home. Jesus' parents assumed he was among the crowd of relatives and neighbors, but they couldn't find him and returned to Jerusalem. After three days they found him in the temple sitting

among the rabbis, who marvelled at how the young child interpreted the law and the parables of the prophets. Mary said: "Why do you do this to us? Can't you see how worried we were?" Jesus replied: "Why are you looking for me? Don't you know that I must be in my father's house?" The scribes and Pharisees asked: "Are you the mother of this child? God has blessed the fruit of your womb. For we have never seen such glory and excellence and wisdom." Jesus arose and went home with his parents. Mary kept in mind all that came to pass, and Jesus increased in wisdom and stature and grace. €

Potty Pourri

Random Kinds of Factness

• Galileo envisioned the body thermometer in the 17th century. Not long after, a scientist named Santorio Santorio invented one that worked. He called it the *thermoscope*.

• Neon is extracted from the air by *adsorption*. That involves superchilling the air to make it a liquid, collecting the neon with charcoal, then warming the charcoal to capture the evaporating neon gas. Unfortunately, the air just doesn't have that much neon in it, so you have to treat 88,000 pounds of air to get a pound of neon.

• Who attached the copper to the iron framework of the Statue of Liberty once it arrived in New York's harbor? Gustave Eiffel, the guy who built the Eiffel Tower.

• Marcel Proust was quite a character. He lined the walls of his writing room in cork to deaden sounds from outside, and when he went to work, he'd lie in bed, wrapped in scarves and blankets and wearing gloves.

• The guillotine got its name in "honor" of the French politician Joseph Ignace Guillotin, who promoted its use as more humane method of execution than the old block-and-axe method. Its inventor was a French surgeon, Antoine Lewis.

• Have you ever heard of the glass snake? Despite the fact that it has no legs and looks like a snake with ears, it's really a lizard. The glass snake's long tail breaks off very easily, which is how it got its name.

• In the Middle Ages, schools for knights didn't just teach jousting and sword fighting. The boys were also taught reading, writing and basic math, as well as chess, lute playing and chivalry.

• To your short list of famous newspaper editors, add Warren G. Harding. Prior to becoming president, Harding was with Ohio's Marion *Star*.

The Eyes Have It

William Hogarth painted *Frontis: Satire on False Perspective* in 1754. It is, perhaps, the original "What's wrong with this picture." The accompanying inscription (not pictured) reads, "Whoever makes a Design without the knowledge of perspective will be liable to such Absurdities as are shewn in this Frontispiece."

How many "What's wrong with this picture" things can you identify? Some people claim there are as many as thirty.

Heads Will Roll!

A Ghost Tale from Old Japan

In this story, another ancient Japanese legend collected by Lafcadio Hearn in 1903, a samurai-priest struggles hard... to get a head.

NEARLY 500 YEARS AGO there was a samurai named Isogai Taketsura, in the service of the Lord Kikuji, of Kyushu. But when the house of Kikuji came to ruin, Isogai found himself without a master, so he cut off his hair, and became a traveling priest, taking the Buddhist name of Kwairyo. But always, under the robe of the priest, Kwairyo had within him the heart of the samurai. He journeyed to preach the good Law in places where no other priest dared to go. For that age was an age of violence; and on the highways there was no security for a solitary traveler, even if he happened to be a priest.

One evening, as he was traveling through the mountains of Kai, darkness overcame him miles from any village, so he resigned himself to pass the night under the stars. Scarcely had he lain down when a woodcutter came along the road and said in a tone of great surprise: "What kind of a man can you be, good sir, that you dare to lie down alone in such a place as this? There are haunters about here, many of them. Are you not afraid of Hairy Things?"

"My friend," answered Kwairyo cheerfully, "I am only a wandering priest, and I am not in the least afraid of 'Hairy Things,' if you mean goblin-foxes, or goblin-badgers, or any creatures of that kind. Lonesome places are suitable for meditation, and I have learned never to be anxious about my life."

"This place has a bad name and I must assure you, sir, that it is very dangerous to sleep here. Although my house is only a wretched hut, let me beg of you to come home with me at once. There is a roof at least, and you can sleep without risk."

Kwairyo, liking the man's kindly tone, accepted this modest offer. The woodcutter guided him to a small thatched cottage, cheerfully lighted from within. As Kwairyo entered, he saw four men and women warming their hands at a little fire. They bowed low in the most respectful manner. Kwairyo wondered that persons so poor, and dwelling in such a solitude, should be aware of the polite forms of greeting.

"From your speech and manners, I imagine that you have not always been a woodcutter," he said. "Perhaps you formerly belonged to one of the upper classes?"

The woodcutter smiled, "Sir, you are not mistaken. I was once a person of some distinction. My story is of a life ruined by my own fault. I used to be in the service of a master and my rank was not inconsiderable. But I loved women and wine too well; and under the influence of passion I brought about the ruin of our house, and caused the death of many persons. Retribution followed me; and I now I try to overcome the karma of my errors by repentance and helping those who are unfortunate."

Kwairyo said to the woodcutter, "My friend, it is written in the holy sutras that those strongest in wrong-doing can become the strongest in right-doing. I do not doubt that you have a good heart. Tonight I shall recite the sutras for your sake, and pray that you may overcome the karma of past errors."

Kwairyo's host showed him to a very small side-room, where a bed had been made ready. All went to sleep except the priest, who began to read the sutras by the light of a paper lantern. Into the night Kwairyo read and prayed. After a time he felt thirsty and decided to tiptoe out for a drink of water. Very gently he pushed apart the sliding-screens that separated his room from the main apartment; and he saw, by the light of the lantern, five recumbent bodies—without heads!

For one instant he stood bewildered, imagining a crime. But quickly he saw that there was no blood, and that the headless necks did not look as if they had been cut. Then he thought to himself: "I have been lured into the dwelling of a Rokuro-Kubi, a goblin that can remove its head! Now, if these be Rokuro-Kubi, they mean me no good. It is written that if one finds the body of a Rokuro-Kubi without its head and removes it to another place, the head will never be able to join itself again to the neck. When the head comes back and finds that its body has been moved, it will bounce like a ball upon the floor three times, then pant in great fear, and then die."

He seized the body of the woodcutter by the feet and dragged it out the window. While outside, he heard voices in a grove, so he stole from shadow to shadow. From behind a tree, he caught sight of the five heads flitting about, and chatting as they ate worms and insects that they'd found.

After a while the head of the woodcutter stopped eating and said: "Ah, that fat traveling priest! When we eat him, our bellies will be well filled. I was foolish to talk to him as I did—it only set him to reciting the sutras on behalf of my soul! To go near him while he is reciting or praying would be difficult, but as it is now nearly morning, perhaps he has gone to sleep. One of you go to the house and see what the fellow is doing."

Immediately, the head of a young woman flitted to the house, lightly as a bat. After a few minutes it came back, and cried out in a tone of great alarm: "That priest is gone! But that's not the worst of the matter. He has taken the body of our *aruji*, our housemaster, and I do not know where he has put it."

At this announcement the head of the aruji—distinctly visible in the moonlight—became frightful: its eyes opened monstrously; its hair stood up bristling; and its teeth gnashed. Then a cry burst from its lips; and—weeping tears of rage—it exclaimed:

"Since my body has been moved, to rejoin it is not possible! Then I must die! And all through the work of that priest! Before I die I will get at that priest! I will tear him! I will devour him! AND THERE HE IS—hiding behind that tree! The fat coward!"

In the same moment the head of the aruji, followed by the other four heads, sprang at Kwairyo. But the samurai-turned-priest had already armed himself by plucking up a young tree; and with that tree he struck the heads as they came, knocking them from him with tremendous blows. Four of them fled away. But the head of the aruji, though battered again and again, desperately continued to attack the priest, and at last caught him by the left sleeve of his robe. Kwairyo, however, quickly gripped the head by its topknot, and repeatedly struck it. It did not release its hold; but it uttered a long moan and ceased to struggle. In death its teeth still held the sleeve; for all his great strength, Kwairyo could not force open the jaws.

With the head still hanging to his sleeve he went back to the house, and there caught sight of the other four Rokuro-Kubi with bruised and bleeding heads reunited to their bodies. But when they saw him at the back-door, they screamed, "The priest! The priest!" and fled out into the woods.

The sky was brightening; day was about to dawn. Kwairyo knew that the power of the goblins was limited to the hours of darkness. He inspected the head clinging to his sleeve—its face fouled with blood, foam, and clay—and he laughed aloud as he thought to himself: "What a great souvenir, the head of a goblin!" before descending the mountain to continue his journey.

Into the main street of Suwa he solemnly strode with the head dangling at his elbow. Women fainted, and children screamed and ran away; and there was a great clamor until lawmen seized the priest and took him to jail. Kwairyo only smiled and said nothing when brought before the magistrates of the district. He was ordered to explain why he, a priest, had the head of a man fastened to his sleeve, and why he had shamelessly paraded his crime before people.

Kwairyo laughed long and loudly at these questions. "Sirs, I did not fasten the head to my sleeve: it fastened itself there, much against my will. And I have not committed any crime. For this is the head of a goblin, and I was simply taking precautions to assure my own safety." And he laughed as he proceeded to tell of his encounter with the five heads.

But the magistrates did not laugh. They judged him to be a hardened criminal and his story an insult to their intelligence. Therefore, they decided to order his immediate execution, all of them except one, a very old man. After having heard the opinion of his colleagues, he said: "Let us first examine the head carefully. If the priest has spoken truth, the head itself should bear witness for him. Bring the head here!"

So the head, still holding in its teeth the robe from Kwairyo's shoulders, was put before the judges. The old man discovered that the edges of the neck nowhere presented the appearance of having been cut by any weapon. On the contrary, the line of severance was smooth as the line at which a falling leaf detaches itself from the stem. Then said the elder: "I am quite sure that the priest told us the truth. This is the head of a Rokuro-Kubi. It is well known that such goblins have been dwelling in the mountains of Kai from very ancient time.... But you, sir," he exclaimed, turning to Kwairyo,—"what sort of sturdy priest may you be? You have the air of a soldier rather than a priest. Perhaps you once belonged to the samurai class?"

"You have guessed rightly, sir," Kwairyo responded. "Before becoming a priest, my name was Isogai Taketsura of Kyushu: there may be some among you who remember it." At the mention of that name, a murmur of admiration filled the courtroom. for there were many present who remembered it. And Kwairyo immediately found himself among friends instead of judges. When Kwairyo left Suwa, he was as happy as any priest is permitted to be in this transitory world. As for the head, he took it with him, jocularly insisting he intended it for a souvenir.

And now it only remains to tell what became of the head.

A day or two after leaving Suwa, Kwairyo met with a robber, who tried to rob him until he saw the goblin head hanging from his sleeve. "You!" he shouted, jumping backward. "What kind of a priest are you? Why, you are a worse man than I am! It is true that I have killed people; but I never walked about with anybody's head fastened to my sleeve." Deciding he could use the head to scare people, the bandit asked to buy it.

Kwairyo answered: "I shall let you have the head; but I must tell you that this is a goblin's head. So, if you have any trouble in consequence, please to remember that you were not deceived by me." And Kwairyo, loudly laughing, sold his robe with the goblin head and went upon his way.

Thus the robber got the head and the robe; and for some time he played goblin-priest upon the highways. But when his travels took him to the neighborhood of Suwa, he learned the true story of the head; and he then became afraid that the spirit of the Rokuro-Kubi might give him trouble. So he buried the head by itself in the grove behind the cottage; and he had a tombstone set up over the grave, and a funeral service performed on behalf of the Rokuro-Kubi's spirit. And that was the end of that. ℭ

Kitchen Scientist

How to Make Rock Candy

Homemade rock candy is easy, fun and illustrates the scientific concept of crystallization. It also teaches patience, because you have to wait a long time before you can actually eat the stuff.

1 Tie a cotton string to a pencil and prop the pencil over the mouth of a jar so the string hangs down straight into the jar with no loops or curls.

2 Attach a nontoxic weight to the bottom of the string (say, a stainless steel paper clip) so that it hangs straight down. Heck, since you're going to the trouble, you might want to prepare several jars and double or triple the recipe below.

3 In a saucepan, bring about a cup of water to boil. Slowly stir in two cups of sugar, adding half a cup (or less) at a time and waiting for it to dissolve completely before adding the next scoop.

4 When all of the sugar has been dissolved into a thick, clear syrup, pour the mixture into your empty jar. Make sure the string is submerged into the hot liquid. Put the jars in a place where they won't be disturbed or tipped over.

5 Because the water mixture was supersaturated with sugar, the two couldn't stay mixed except when very hot. As the mixture cools, the sugar will begin to glom onto the string, creating cool crystal patterns. As the water evaporates further over the coming weeks, the crystals will grow bigger and bigger.

6 If you want to play a sadistic practical joke on someone at the same time, make a special batch of similar-looking "rock candy" by using salt instead of sugar. ☾

Word Thieves

Terms We've Borrowed From Native Americans

When Europeans landed in America, they came across things they didn't have names for. Luckily there were people living here already who could tell them what's what.

bayou: From Choctaw *bayuk,* which means "creek."

caribou: From Micmac *maccaribpoo* ("he who paws the ground").

chipmunk: From the Chippewa word for squirrel, *atchitamon* ("head first").

moose: From a Passamaquoddy observation, *moosu* ("he trims [bark] smoothly").

opossum: From Powantan *aposoum* ("white animal").

persimmon: From the Cree for "dried fruit," *pasiminan.*

powwow: The word originally had to do with gatherings for drug-enhanced religious ceremonies by the Indians. It comes from an Algonquian word *powwaw* ("he dreams").

skunk: From the Algonquian phrase, *skekakwa squnk,* which means "animal that pees" (sprays).

raccoon: The Algonquian word is *arakunen,* which means "scraper, scratcher."

squash: Shortened from Algonquian *asquatasquash* ("eaten raw").

toboggan: From Algonquian *tabakun* ("drag, small sled").

wigwam: Teepee was a western plains name for a dwelling, so until Europeans moved that far west in the 1830s, Indian dwellings were called wigwams, from the Ojibwa *wigwaum.*

woodchuck: From several similar languages, including the Algonquian word *wejack* and the Cree word *otchek,* both of which mean "fisher." Europeans turned the name into woodchuck, even though it doesn't chuck wood.

place names: Chicago ("place of bad smell"); Ohio ("beautiful water"); Shenandoah ("daughter of the skies"); Wisconsin ("beaver place"); Winnebago ("people of the filthy water").

Potty Pourri

Random Kinds of Factness

• Lead was once commonly used to sweeten wine. Some historians think it might have contributed to the fall of the Roman Empire. Although the dangers of lead were understood as early as the 17th century, its use in wine wasn't banned for another 200 years.

• Remember to stop and watch the insects. Mathematician René Descartes did. A fly walking across the ceiling gave him the idea for coordinate geometry in order to trace the fly's walking path.

• Long before the Druids came along, Stonehenge existed. Ancient folks built it in three main phases from 2800 to 1500 B.C. Researchers estimate that it took about 30 million work hours and hundreds of years to complete.

• "Hedgehopper" is British slang for a pilot. A one-hit British Invasion group from the 1960s named itself Hedgehoppers Anonymous because its members met while serving in the Royal Air Force.

• The educational system in ancient Sparta seemed fairer than most: both girls and boys were educated. But the curriculum wasn't particularly well rounded: The boys were taught fighting skills, while the girls were taught what they needed to mother future soldiers.

• Lobsters are not red when alive. Because the red pigment in their shells is the most heat resistant, it remains colorful even as the natural browns, grays and greens cook away.

• The term "B.O." for body odor was coined by an advertising man in 1919 to sell Odo-Ro-No, an early deodorant. The product may be gone, but the ad campaign lingers in the air.

• "Acid rock," "country rock," and "hard rock" were all geological terms years before they became musical genres. Likewise, "heavy metal" came first from chemistry.

Stately Knowledge

12 Reasons Why Ya Gotta Love Michigan

Who needs to be reminded that Michigan's cool? Just in case, though, here are some of our favorite facts about this two-part state...

1 The very first Elvis sighting following his death occured at a Burger King in Kalamazoo. Be on the lookout; he was driving a red Ferrari.

2 Detroit is the home of motors and music, but it's also the birthplace of the Kiwanis Club. When founding members were looking for a name, someone suggested an Otchipew Indian phrase, "Nunc Kee-wanis." Members believed it meant "We trade." Actually, it translates to "We have a noisy good time." That works, too.

3 Grand Rapids was the first U.S. city to fluoridate its water supply to reduce cavities.

4 DomiNick's Pizza opened in Ypsilanti, Michigan, in 1960. Maybe you know it better by its current name, Domino's Pizza.

5 What's that extra bit of land there, above the mitten-shaped mainland of Michigan? That's called the Upper Peninsula. Literally attached to Wisconsin, it was given to Michigan as a consolation prize when they lost Toledo to Ohio in the Toledo War of 1836.

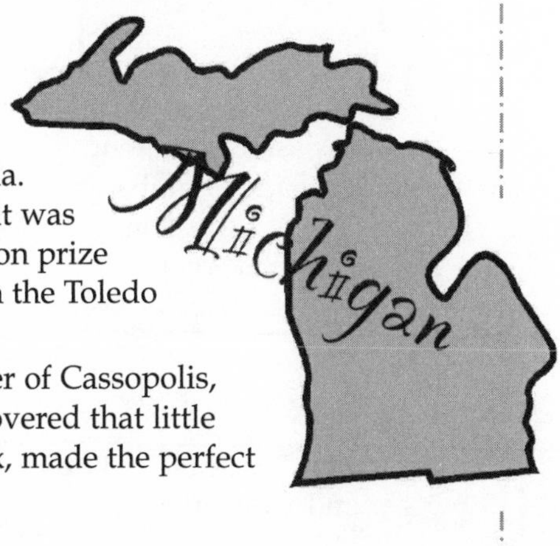

6 Three meows for Kay Draper of Cassopolis, Michigan. In 1948, she discovered that little dried bits of clay, placed in a box, made the perfect litter for a kitty.

Domino's, Post, Kellogg's, KMart, and Kiwanis ...all natives of Michigan

7 In 1907, America saw its first mile of paved road. It was a stretch of Woodward Avenue in Detroit, between Six and Seven Mile Roads.

8 About 1,500 years ago, a fungus spore somehow found its way underground in part of the forest of Michigan, and took root. Today, the fungus colony covers at least 40 acres of area underneath the ground. All in all, the fungus weighs at least 110 tons. It's the largest living organism known in the world.

9 Besides the underground fungus, famous Michiganders past and present include Charles Lindbergh, Henry Ford, Tim Allen, Eminem, Robin Williams, Francis Ford Coppola, Steven Seagal, Lily Tomlin, Ellen Burstyn, Earvin "Magic" Johnson, Diana Ross, Madonna, Ted Nugent, Bob Seger and Stevie Wonder.

10 Our favorite Michigan native, though, has got to be veterinarian and animal-lover Timothy England of Jackson, Michigan. When a stray rooster lost its legs to frostbite on a cold Michigan winter night, England fitted the cock with artificial legs.

11 Battle Creek, Michigan, is the breakfast cereal capital of the world—home to both Post cereals and Kellogg's. In the Kellogg's parking lot you can take a gander at corporate spokestoons Tony the Tiger and Tony, Jr. They both have statues erected to them, greeting visitors at the company headquarters.

12 Michigan's known as the Wolverine state; mind you, not because of a plentiful wolverine population. Truth be told, Michigan has absolutely no wolverines (little badger-like animals) whatsoever within its borders, and probably never did. So why the misnomer? During the days of Canadian fur trading, wolverine hides were shipped through the state on their way to Europe, so people indelibly associated the state with the animal. €

Many Happy Returns

How to Make & Throw a Boomerang

Make your own boomerang? Why not? It's not hard, says *The American Boy's Handy Book* by Daniel Beard (1890). The instructions even come complete with Western cluelessness, common at the time, about the Australian aborigines.

THE BOOMERANG, or bommerang as it is sometimes called, is one of the most mysterious weapons known. Evolved by slow degrees from a simple war club

by the ignorant and savage Australians, this instrument excites the interest and astonishes the civilized man by its strange and apparently unaccountable properties. To all appearances it is a simple, roughly-hewn club, yet its movements when thrown by an expert hand are so eccentric as to make it a curious anomaly even to persons educated in natural philosophy.

HOW TO MAKE A BOOMERANG

1 With boiling water, scald a piece of well-seasoned elm, ash or hickory plank that is free from knots. Allow the wood to remain in the water until it becomes pliable enough to bend into the form indicated by the figure below.

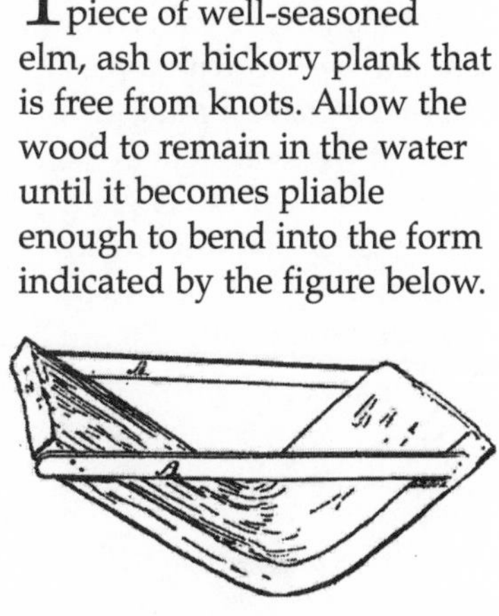

When it has assumed the proper curve, nail on the side pieces to hold the wood in position until it is thoroughly dry; after which the side pieces may be removed, with no fear that the plank will not retain the curve imparted.

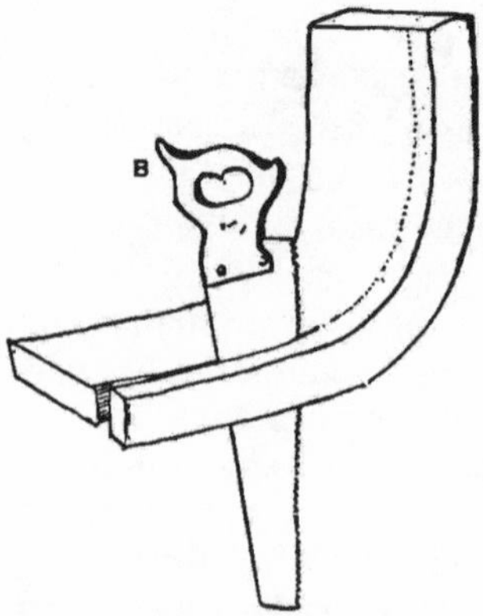

2 Saw the wood into as many slices as it will allow. Each piece will be a boomerang in the rough.

3 Your rough boomerang only needs to be trimmed up with a pocket knife, and scraped smooth with a piece of broken glass to make it a finished weapon. A large wood-rasp or file is of great assistance in shaping the implement. Figure C shows a finished boomerang. Figure D shows a cross section of the same.

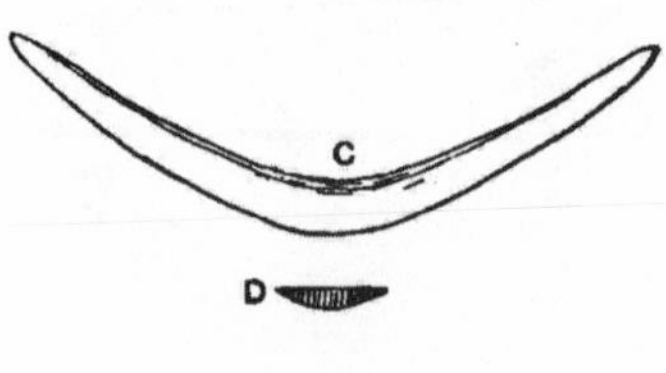

The curve in two boomerangs is never exactly the same; some come round with a graceful sweep, while others bend so suddenly in the middle that they have more the appearance of angles than curves. Just what makes a good boomerang is hard to discover, although as a rule, the one that appears to have the best balance and feels as if it might be thrown easily is the best.

GOES AROUND, COMES AGROUND

To throw a boomerang, grasp the weapon near one end and hold it as you would a club; be careful to have the concave side, or inside curvature, pointed away away from you and the convex side toward you. Take aim at a stone, tuft of grass or other object on the ground about a hundred yards in front of you, and throw the weapon at the object. The weapon will in all probability not go anywhere near the mark, but, soaring aloft, perform some of the most extraordinary maneuvers then starting off again with apparently renewed velocity, either return to the spot from where it was thrown or go sailing off over the fields like a thing possessed of life.

"FORCE ENOUGH TO CUT A DOG"

A boomerang cast by a beginner is very dangerous in a crowd, for there is no telling where it is going to alight, and when it does come down it sometimes comes with force

Duck, Dingo, duck!

enough to cut a small dog almost in two.* Select a large open field where the ground is soft and there is no one around to be hurt. In such a field, you may amuse yourself by the day throwing these curious weapons, and in this manner learn how to make the boomerang go through all manner of the most indescribable movements seemingly at your bidding.

BABY BOOMERANG

The miniature boomerang here represented is cut out of a card. The shape represented here in the illustration is a very good one, but it may be varied to an almost unlimited degree. Card boomerangs over an inch or so in length do not work well, but they may be made much smaller.

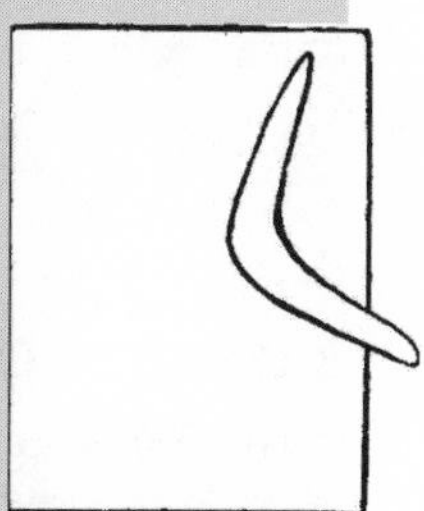

These tiny instruments cannot be grasped by the hand. Instead, the toy should be laid flat upon a card or table, allowing one end to project, as pictured. Using your forefinger, strike it a quick, smart blow with your fingernail and the little missile will sail away, going through almost the same maneuvers that a large wooden boomerang does.

* "I have seen a dog killed on the spot, its body being nearly cut in two by the boomerang as it fell." —Rev. J. G. Wood

Pasters' Choices

What Toothpaste Stuff Really Works?

To drum up business, toothpastes make a lot of claims, but what's true and what's not? Here's what dentists and consumer advocates have reported so far about the most common toothpaste additives.

WHITENING TOOTHPASTES: They work only in the very loosest sense. You know, in the same way a dishrag will whiten your dishes...if you actually have white dishes. *Consumer Reports* found no whitening toothpaste that really worked. Why? Because with age natural yellowing happens below the surface. If you go that low, you destroy the enamel. Bleaching by dentists has shown to work slightly better; it cleans stains off the surface. But it still won't whiten the tooth underneath.

TARTAR CONTROL: It works, in that sorta-kinda kind of way. It doesn't take existing tartar off, but it absorbs minerals in your saliva that could collect on your teeth and become tartar.

DESENSITIZERS: They work sometimes—particularly for pain or sensitivity from receding gums. But if you have pain from cavities or tooth-grinding forget about it. Unfortunately, most dental pain is caused by cavities or tooth-grinding.

HYDROGEN PEROXIDE: It doesn't do any good. In fact, it may give you more problems with decay and bad breath by drying the mouth. The same applies to alcohol in mouthwashes.

BAKING SODA: This folk remedy doesn't do anything at all.

TRICLOSAN: Found in Colgate Total and other pastes, triclosan appears to keep killing decay germs for hours after brushing. There are some concerns about whether it has bad environmental effects, however.

FLUORIDE: Fluoride really works. It helps lay down protection where enamel is eroding. There's also evidence that it attracts calcium in the body to do the same thing. It really hardens teeth and prevents cavities. Buy it; use it. ₵

Up, Up, & Away!

How Goodyear Got Its Blimp in the Air

The Goodyear blimp seems to be ubiquitous, drifting lazily in the sky above every major outdoor event from the World Series and Superbowl to outdoor concerts. Hard to believe that Goodyear management once nearly retired it as "a waste of money."

Despite the Goodyear name, the company was not founded by Charles Goodyear, the man who discovered how to vulcanize rubber in 1839. Charles Goodyear didn't get rich from his process—in fact, he died penniless in 1860. But when Frank A. Seiberling started a rubber company in Akron, Ohio, in 1898, he decided to name it after the unsung inventor. This was nice, but also likely a ploy to confuse consumers who were familiar with the long-established B. F. Goodrich Co.

Seiberling hired a recent graduate of the Massachusetts Institute of Technology, Paul W. Litchfield, and paid him $2,500 a year to be factory supervisor, tire designer, rubber compounder and head of personnel. Like his boss, Litchfield had turn-of-the-century confidence in technology and American know-how, and kept an eye open for any new application for Goodyear's rubber products. Goodyear began manufacturing airplane tires in 1909, only six years after the Wright Brothers' first flight, at a time when there were fewer than 100 airplanes in the United States.

This interest in the potential of aeronautics blossomed into a full-scale obsession. When Litchfield visited the North British Company in Scotland, which had developed a process for spreading rubber over fabric, he traded the specifications to Goodyear's straight-sided tire for the process's equipment and American rights. North British also threw in two technicians to run the machines.

Blimp Facts

• The word *blimp,* as one tale has it, came from Lt. A. D. Cunningham of Britain's Royal Navy Air Service. In 1915, he whimsically flicked the inflated wall of an airship and verbally imitated the sound—"Blimp! Blimp!"

• Another version of the word comes from a military requisition form that read "Airship B, Limp."

• The Goodyear blimps' light display consists of 7,650 blue, green, red and yellow auto tail lights connected to a computer by 80 miles of wiring. The computer is programmed on the ground, using a light-beam "pencil" to draw on a computer screen.

• Each blimp can carry nine passengers. The seats have no seat belts.

• The blimps' skin is only about as thick as a shirt collar, but it's made of Neoprene-impregnated Dacron and is quite tough. It's a good thing, too, since the company reports that their blimps are shot at about 20 times a year. In 1990, a man was arrested and accused of deliberately punching a 3-foot hole in the blimp with a radio-controlled model airplane. The blimp sagged, but made it safely home.

• The blimps are 192 feet long, 59 feet high, and hold 202,700 cubic feet of helium. The helium doesn't leak out quickly like a balloon, but it does have to be "topped off" every four months or so. The blimps have a traveling range of about 500 miles and cruise at 45 miles per hour. Each blimp has a crew of five pilots, 17 support members and one public relations representative.

• The blimps' first TV sports event was an Orange Bowl game in the mid-1960s. Since then, they have been used in about 90 televised events a year. Goodyear doesn't charge TV networks, figuring the publicity generated makes the free service worthwhile. Camera operators shoot through an open window from about 400 yards up where they can see everything, read the scoreboard and hear the roar of the crowd. On a calm day, a pilot can hold the blimp virtually still in the air by facing into the wind and idling. The hardest sport for the pilots is golf because they have to be careful not to disturb a golfer's shot with engine noise or a sudden shadow over the green.

• The company is secretive about how much the blimps cost, but acknowledged a few years ago the annual cost of operating and maintaining each blimp is about $2 million.

Within months, the Wright Brothers had signed on to use Goodyear's rubberized cloth for their airplanes. (This was back when airplanes were based on kite designs and made of mostly wood and cloth). Within a few years, most U. S. airplanes used Goodyear's cloth.

The same rubberized fabric turned out to be useful for lighter-than-air craft. Not that there weren't some glitches in the process, though. Goodyear's first dirigible, *The Akron,* was scheduled to make the first intercontinental flight from America to Europe. Its flight began from Atlantic City at daybreak, July 2, 1912, but ended 23 minutes later when the ship exploded mysteriously over the ocean. The crew of five was never seen again.

But Goodyear management was still convinced that there was a future for lighter-than-air craft, and World War I gave them a chance to prove it. Goodyear produced about 1,000 balloons and 60 dirigibles and blimps for observation and reconnaissance.

Blimps, smaller and lighter with flexible walls, were particularly useful for moving low over coastal waters and searching out enemy submarines. Dirigibles, bigger and with rigid walls to keep their shape better, were better for moving large objects and groups of people.

After the war, the Navy pressed ahead with dirigible research. Having seen how well the enemy's dirigibles carried heavy loads, it commissioned the Zeppelin works in Germany to build a dirigible in 1921. They christened it the *U.S.S. Los Angeles.* The Navy was further impressed when it flew from Germany to New Jersey in 81 hours. They asked Goodyear to buy the American rights to the Zeppelin design. The result was the Goodyear-Zeppelin Corporation. In 1926, the Germans finished the Graf Zeppelin which, over the next nine years, transported 13,110 passengers and covered more than a million miles in 544 trips, including 144 ocean crossings.

Unfortunately, not all Zeppelins were so reliable. A British dirigible crashed in France, killing most of the people aboard. Goodyear's two Zeppelins, *The Akron* and *The Macon,* also went down in tragedy. *The Akron,* like its blimp namesake years earlier, crashed off the New Jersey coast. A month earlier, *The*

Macon set course for its home base near San Francisco, but hit a storm and plunged into the sea. The final blow to dirigibles occurred on May 6, 1937, when the German Zeppelin *Hindenburg* burst into flames just seconds before landing in New Jersey. Actually, fewer people died than in the previous disasters, but since it took place in front of a pack of reporters and newsreel photographers, the image of the disaster was splashed all over the world.

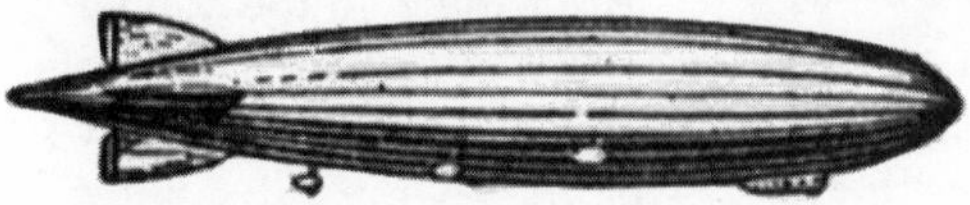

A dirigible is different from a blimp in that it has a frame with material stretched across it

(For half a century, people have wondered why the Germans used flammable hydrogen in the Hindenburg instead of fire-proof helium. They had no choice. Helium is actually a fairly rare natural gas, found in abundance only in America. Wary of the Nazis that ruled Germany, the U.S. government had refused to sell them helium.)

The world pretty much gave up on dirigible travel, but Goodyear continued making blimps, which they used for research and promotion. In 1929 they had four small ones traveling around the country, each capable of carrying four passengers and a pilot. Goodyear called them the *Pilgrim, Puritan, Mayflower,* and *Vigilant*.

When World War II started, the company built dozens more for military use. One blimp was the center of a mystery that has never been solved. In the early hours of August 16, 1942, the airship *Ranger* took off from Treasure Island in San Francisco Bay with a crew of two. It carried two anti-sub depth bombs. That afternoon, residents of Daly City, down the peninsula from San Francisco, were surprised to see a blimp coming in for a perfect landing in the middle of a residential street.

The blimp was well-stocked with fuel and helium, the batteries were charged, the radio was operating, the emergency life raft and parachute were on board. Everything was fine except for a few small details: The door was open; one depth charge was gone; and both members of the crew were missing. The Navy never came up with a satis-

A blimp, like the *Stars and Stripes* above, has no frame. It keeps its shape by the helium inside; it's sort of like a big balloon with a motor.

factory explanation, and neither man was ever seen again.

After the war, Goodyear bought five of its blimps back from the military and began using them for promotional purposes. But the company's executives didn't seem to know the value of what it had—in 1958, its board of directors considered grounding the blimps permanently to save operating and maintenance expenses. The plan was stalled by a last-minute plea by Goodyear's publicity director, and a blimp tour generated enough favorable press that the company was convinced to keep them.

The current blimps in the United States are the *Spirit of America,* based in Carson, California, the *Spirit of Goodyear,* based near Akron, Ohio, and the *Stars and Stripes,* based in Pompano Beach, Florida. €

If the Blimp is Rockin', Don't Come Knockin'

At least one child was reportedly conceived in a Goodyear blimp—Jim Maloney, whose father was a member of the blimp's ground crew in the 1940s. Apparently it had an effect, because Maloney grew up and became one of Goodyear's blimp pilots.

Potty Pourri

Random Kinds of Factness

• The crack of a whip is a small sonic boom that occurs as the lash breaks the sound barrier.

• Art imitates life: A cuckoo clock reproduces nearly exactly the sound of the European cuckoo bird.

• How fast something falls depends on its weight, shape and size. A Ping-Pong ball dropped from a mile up would reach a maximum speed of about 20 mph. A baseball, 95 mph. And a bowling ball? About 350 mph.

• The average kitten weighs 3.5 ounces when it's born, about the same as a bar of soap.

• On the Colosseum's opening day in A.D. 80, 5,000 animals were killed to entertain the masses. Procuring exotic animals to slaughter in gladiator spectacles in Rome became a major undertaking. Several species were rendered extinct by the slaughter, including the North African elephant.

• There are five flamingo species, ranging in color from nearly white to deep pink.

• J. Alfred Wight wrote some of the best stories about animals and veterinarians. Perhaps you know him better by his pen name James Herriot, author of *All Things Bright and Beautiful*.

• Log cabins seem like they're the essence of Americana, but they originally came from Finland and Sweden. In the 1630s, Finns and Swedes began settling in and around Delaware, and spread the practical home design to the New Land.

• If an octopus released its ink inside an aquarium, it would kill everything inside the glass walls...including the octopus.

• If you've got *chrematophobia,* you've got a deep, unreasonable fear of money. Send us a blank check, and we'll quickly cure your problem for you.

Money Magic

Tricks You Can Do with a Dollar

Here are some easy tricks that show the magic of the Almighty Dollar.

PAPERCLIP LINK

ALTHOUGH THE PROPS are modest, the effect is pretty mind-boggling: two paperclips fly into the air and link together before your very eyes.

1 Fold a one-dollar bill into a flattened **S** shape. (Although, keep in mind that using a five for this trick gives you a wonderfully awful punch line. Read on.)

2 Take a paperclip and clip it over the two thicknesses at the end of the bill closest to you (see illustration).

3 Take the other paperclip and clip it over the two thicknesses on the other side.

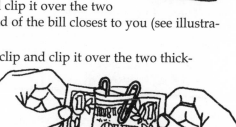

4 Grab each end of the bill. Pull your hands away from each other, straightening the bill.

5 The two clips will fly into the air—and in the process, they'll have linked themselves together.

Awful punch line: If you use a $5 bill: "Why do the paper-clips link together? That's because of the guy on the bill: it's Abraham Linkin'."

Variation: If you also loop a rubber band around the bill, the paperclips will again end up linked . . . and hanging from the bill by the rubber band.

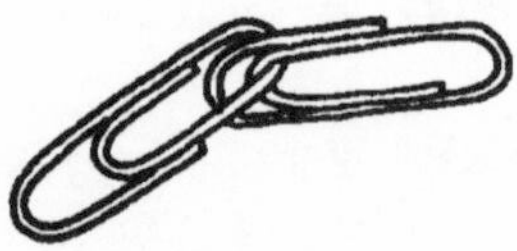

STUPID MONEY TRICKS

Breaking Bread

Hold a breadstick between your hands and challenge your tablemates to break it with a dollar bill folded in half. They can hack at it repeatedly and nothing will happen.

When it's your turn, sneak your index finger into the fold. The breadstick will break cleanly.

Double Your Money

Ask a spectator for a dollar bill. Say: "I can show you how to double your money." Fold the dollar solidly in half. Say: "I've doubled your money. Look—you can see it *in creases.*"

Turn a One into a Five

If the last trick doesn't satisfy, say that you can guarantee that you can turn a one-dollar bill into a five.

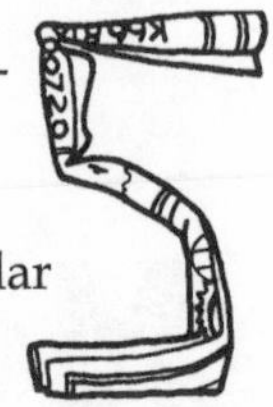

Take the dollar bill, roll it up lengthwise into a rope, and bend it into the number 5 (see picture).

Uncatchable Dollar

If you can catch it, you can keep it. That's the challenge you give when you pull out a dollar bill.

To demonstrate, you dangle a bill with your right hand. With your left hand, you hold your thumb and forefinger one inch apart at George Washington's head. When you let go with the right hand, you easily catch it with your left.

It looks simple. But it isn't. Have another person try to catch it from that position. They'll find it's virtually impossible. They don't have enough time to react before the dollar slips away...sort of a metaphor for real life.

STRONG DOLLAR

Is a dollar strong enough to hold up a water glass without the support of the International Monetary Fund?

What You'll Need

- A crisp, new dollar bill
- 3 water glasses

How You Do It

1 Place two glasses about 4 inches apart and challenge onlookers to place a dollar bill across them in a way that it will support a third glass.

2 After they pronounce it impossible, take the dollar and fold it lengthwise in tiny accordion folds.

3 Place it across the two glasses. It should now support the weight of your third glass.

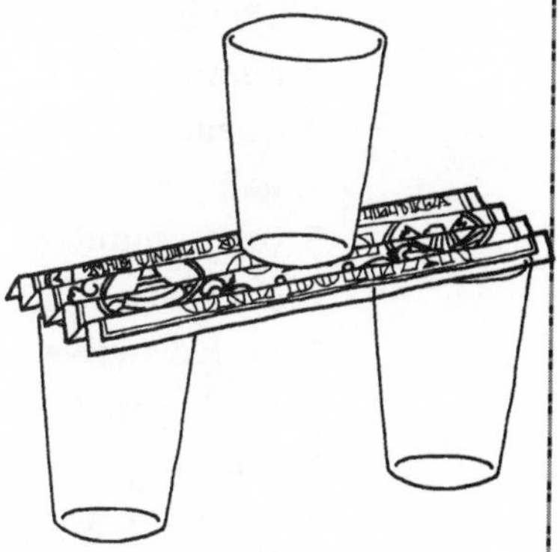

Rubber and Booze Don't Mix

A drug treatment for alcoholism is *tetraethylthiuram disulfide*, sold as the drug Antabuse. During the 1930s, workers in rubber manufacturing plants discovered that they got violently ill whenever they consumed even small quantities of alcohol. Scientists investigating the phenomenon discovered that the nausea was caused by tetraethylthiuram disulfide, a chemical used in rubber manufacturing. Apparently the drug changes the way that the body metabolizes alcohol, breaking much of it down into a chemical called acetaldehyde, which produces symptoms similar to that of a hangover: flushing, throbbing head, nausea and vomiting. Since it's nonlethal and works even when only a little bit of alcohol is consumed, doctors began using the substance in the treatment of alcoholism.

Speak English?

Translate These British Terms into American

Sometimes it seems like the British and Americans don't even speak the same language. How are you at translating? Translate these old and new British terms into American. (Answers below.)

1. aerodrome	**a. dashboard**
2. perambulator	**b. car horn**
3. queue	**c. cotton candy**
4. hair grip	**d. battery**
5. turf accountant	**e. eggnog**
6. chucker out	**f. bookie**
7. boiled sweets	**g. bouncer**
8. fascia panel	**h. baby buggy**
9. hooter	**i. diaper**
10. accumulator	**j. drug store**
11. pantechnicon	**k. checkers**
12. lorry	**l. moving van**
13. transport cafe	**m. truck**
14. draughts	**n. truck stop**
15. candy floss	**o. line**
16. nappy	**p. hard candy**
17. chemist's	**q. bobby pin**
18. egg flip	**r. airfield**

Answers: *1. aerodrome = r. airfield; 2. perambulator = h. baby buggy; 3. queue = o. line; 4. hair grip = q. bobby pin; 5. turf accountant = f. bookie; 6. chucker out = g. bouncer; 7. boiled sweets = p. hard candy; 8. fascia panel = a. dashboard; 9. hooter = b. car horn; 10. accumulator = d. battery; 11. pantechnicon = l. moving van; 12. lorry = m. truck; 13. transport cafe = n. truck stop; 14. draughts = k. checkers; 15. candy floss = c. cotton candy; 16. nappy = i. diaper; 17. chemist's = j. drug store; 18. egg flip = e. eggnog*

Witches' Loaves

A Story of Good Intentions Gone Bad

In this ironic short story by O. Henry, a romantic bakery owner finds that there are limits to charity.

MISS MARTHA MEACHAM kept the little bakery on the corner (the one where you go up three steps, and the bell tinkles when you open the door).

Miss Martha was forty, her bank-book showed a credit of two thousand dollars, and she possessed two false teeth and a sympathetic heart. Many people have married whose chances to do so were much inferior to Miss Martha's.

Two or three times a week a customer entered in whom she began to take an interest. He was a middle-aged man, wearing spectacles and a brown beard trimmed to a careful point. He spoke English with a strong German accent. His clothes were worn and darned in places, and wrinkled and baggy in others. But he looked neat, and had very good manners.

He always bought two loaves of stale bread. Fresh bread was five cents a loaf. Stale ones were two for five. Never did he call for anything but stale bread.

Once Miss Martha saw a red and brown stain on his fingers. She was sure then that he was an artist and very poor. No doubt he lived in a garret, where he painted pictures and ate stale bread and thought of the good things to eat in Miss Martha's bakery.

Often when Miss Martha sat down to her chops and light rolls and jam and tea she would sigh, and wish that the gentle-mannered artist might share her tasty meal instead of eating his dry crust in that drafty attic. Miss Martha's heart, as you have been told, was a sympathetic one.

In order to test her theory as to his occupation, she brought from her room one day a painting that she had bought at a sale, and set it against the shelves behind the bread counter.

It was a Venetian scene. A splendid marble palazzio (so it said on the picture) stood in the foreground—or rather forewater. For the rest there were gondolas (with the lady trailing her hand in the water), clouds, sky, and *chiaro-oscuro* in plenty. No artist could fail to notice it.

Two days afterward the customer came in.

"Two loafs of stale bread, if you blease....You haf here a fine bicture, madame," he said while she was wrapping up the bread.

"Yes?" says Miss Martha, reveling in her own cunning. "I do so admire art and" (no, it would not do to say "artists" thus early) "and paintings," she substituted. "You think it is a good picture?"

"Der balance," said the customer, "is not in good drawing. Der bairspective of it is not true. Goot morning, madame."

He took his bread, bowed, and hurried out.

Yes, he must be an artist. Miss Martha took the picture back to her room.

How gentle and kindly his eyes shone behind his spectacles! What a broad brow he had! To be able to judge perspective at a glance—and to live on stale bread! But genius often has to struggle before it is recognized.

What a thing it would be for art and perspective if genius were backed by two thousand dollars in bank, a bakery, and a sympathetic heart to—But these were daydreams, Miss Martha.

Often now when he came he would chat for a while across the showcase. He seemed to crave Miss Martha's cheerful words.

He kept on buying stale bread. Never a cake, never a pie,

never one of her delicious Sally Lunns.

She thought he began to look thinner and discouraged. Her heart ached to add something good to eat to his meagre purchase, but her courage failed at the act. She did not dare affront him. She knew the pride of artists.

Miss Martha took to wearing her blue-dotted silk waist behind the counter. In the back room she cooked a mysterious compound of quince seeds and borax. Ever so many people use it for the complexion.

One day the customer came in as usual, laid his nickel on the showcase, and called for his stale loaves. While Miss Martha was reaching for them there was a great tooting and clanging, and a fire-engine came lumbering past.

The customer hurried to the door to look, as any one will. Suddenly inspired, Miss Martha seized the opportunity.

On the bottom shelf behind the counter was a pound of fresh butter that the dairyman had left ten minutes before. With a bread knife Miss Martha made a deep slash in each of the stale loaves, inserted a generous quantity of butter, and pressed the loaves tight again.

When the customer turned once more she was tying the paper around them.

When he had gone, after an unusually pleasant little chat, Miss Martha smiled to herself, but not without a slight fluttering of the heart.

Had she been too bold? Would he take offense? But surely not. There was no language of edibles. Butter was no emblem of unmaidenly forwardness.

For a long time that day her mind dwelt on the subject. She imagined the scene when he should discover her little deception.

He would lay down his brushes and palette. There would stand his easel with the picture he was painting in which the perspective was beyond criticism.

He would prepare for his luncheon of dry bread and water. He would slice into a loaf—ah!

Miss Martha blushed. Would he think of the hand that placed it there as he ate? Would he—

The front door bell jangled viciously. Somebody was coming in, making a great deal of noise.

Miss Martha hurried to the front. Two men were there. One was a young man smoking a pipe—a man she had never seen before. The other was her artist.

His face was very red, his hat was on the back of his head, his hair was wildly rumpled. He clinched his two fists and shook them ferociously at Miss Martha. *At Miss Martha.*

"Dummkopf!" he shouted with extreme loudness; and then *"Tausendonfer!"* or something like it, in German.

The young man tried to draw him away.

"I vill not go," he said angrily, "else I shall told her."

He made a bass drum of Miss Martha's counter.

"You haf shpoilt me," he cried, his blue eyes blazing behind his spectacles. "I vill tell you. You vas von *meddingsome old cat*!"

Miss Martha leaned weakly against the shelves and laid one hand on her blue-dotted silk waist. The young man took the other by the collar.

"Come on," he said, "you've said enough." He dragged the angry one out at the door to the sidewalk, and then came back.

"Guess you ought to be told, ma'am," he said, "what the row is about. That's Blumberger. He's an architectural draftsman. I work in the same office with him.

"He's been working hard for three months drawing a plan for a new city hall. It was a prize competition. He finished inking the lines yesterday. You know, a draftsman always makes his drawing in pencil first. When it's done he rubs out the pencil lines with handfuls of stale bread crumbs. That's better than India rubber.

"Blumberger's been buying the bread here. Well, today—well, you know, ma'am, that butter isn't—well, Blumberger's plan isn't good for anything now except to cut up into railroad sandwiches."

Miss Martha went into the back room. She took off the blue-dotted silk waist and put on the old brown serge she used to wear. Then she poured the quince seed and borax mixture out of the window into the ash can. ☾

Potty Pourri

Random Kinds of Factness

• Both a 30-caliber bullet and a person rolled up in a tight ball fall at about the same speed: 200 mph.

• The snowy tree cricket is a white little bugger that lives in trees. Of all insects, it is the most accurate temperature gauge. If you count its chirps for 14 seconds and add 42, you'll get the temperature in Fahrenheit. This, of course, doesn't work in winter.

• For more than 4,000 years, the Great Pyramid of Egypt stood as the tallest structure in the world. No other structure has ever come close to holding the record for that long. Its reign ended in 1886, when Gustave Eiffel built a metal monstrosity in Paris.

• Edmond Rostand, the guy who wrote *Cyrano de Bergerac,* liked to write while in the bathtub.

• Some lizards come with cartilage in their tails that allow them to lose the tail without losing their life. It's simple self-preservation. Some of these lizards can regenerate new tails, but the new tail comes at great cost to the lizard's overall health.

• When Aristotle opened his school, he named it the Lyceum. People nicknamed it the Peripatetic School. *Peripatetic* means "walking around"—the teachers taught while leisurely strolling the grounds.

• Francis Cleveland, wife of Grover, was the only First Lady to deliver a baby in the White House. However, Thomas Jefferson's daughter, Martha "Patsy" Jefferson Randolph, was the first woman to give birth there.

• Wine was mighty important to the ancient Egyptians. Take King Tut as an example. The young king was entombed with 36 jars of wine to help smooth his transition into the afterlife.

• A cow that sports a black-and-white splotched face is called a *brockie*. The word can also mean a person with a dirt-smudged face.

Zen Masters

The Wisdom of Frank Zappa

Mind-altering quotes from the late musician/philosopher Frank Zappa.

• "Art is making something out of nothing and selling it."

• "There are more love songs than anything else. If songs could make you do something, we'd all love one another."

• "The United States is a nation of laws: badly written and randomly enforced."

• "Without deviation, progress is not possible."

• "Communism doesn't work because people like to own stuff."

• "Some scientists claim that hydrogen, because it is so plentiful, is the basic building block of the universe. I dispute that. I say that there is more stupidity than hydrogen, and that is the basic building block of the universe."

• "In the fight between you and the world, back the world."

• "Fact of the matter is, there is no hip world, there is no straight world. There's a world, you see, which has people in it who believe in a variety of different things. Everybody believes in something and everybody, by virtue of the fact that they believe in something, use that something to support their own existence."

• "All the good music has already been written by people with wigs and stuff."

• "One of my favorite philosophical tenets is that people will agree with you only if they already agree with you. You do not change people's minds."

• "You can't be a real country unless you have a beer and an airline. It helps if you have some kind of a football team, or some nuclear weapons, but at the very least you need a beer."

Chews Carefully

Some Ruminations on Gum

Americans chew a lot of gum—an average of about 300 sticks per person every year. Our correspondent Elsa Bronte ruminated and masticated on the subject of gum before tucking it into our pages.

WRIGLEY FINDS HIS FIELD

William Wrigley, Jr., the father of American chewing gum, worked as a soap salesman for his father's Philadelphia business, and at age 29 moved to Chicago and started his own soap business with a total of $32 in his pocket. With an acute sensitivity to his customers' whims, Wrigley used premiums to boost his sales. When he noticed that a baking soda premium helped sell his soap, he started selling baking soda. And when a chewing gum premium proved beneficial to his sale of baking soda, he moved into the chewing gum business. His first gum flavors—Lotta Gum and Vassar—came out in 1892, followed by Juicy Fruit and Wrigley's Spearmint the following year. Wrigley was a tireless promoter—for example, in 1915, Wrigley promoted a new brand by sending a piece of it to each of the 1.5 million people listed in U.S. phone books—and it made him rich enough to branch out. In 1919, he bought the Chicago Cubs and built them Wrigley Field; next he bought Catalina Island off the coast of southern California and developed it into a lucrative pleasure resort.

THE ART & LITERATURE OF GUM

• Sculptor Les Levine immortalized gum in 18-karat gold. He cast tiny sculptures from actual pieces of chewed gum, and displayed them in his Greenwich Village Museum of Mott Art in New York City.

• Besides the immortal "Close cover before striking," this phrase may be the instruction that has been most published (and unfortunately, most ignored) in the world: "Save this wrapper for disposal after use."

IT'S THE REAL THING?

• Back in the early days of the gum industry, even Coca-Cola got in on the action. From 1911 to 1920, the company hawked "Coca-Cola Chewing Gum." Today, sticks of this gum are so rare that a piece sold for $8,000 a few years back.

GUMMING UP THE WORKS

• Liquid gum base (it hardens into chewing gum only after cooking and cooling) has been used as an organic pesticide: Insects drawn to its sweetness find their jaws stuck together and they soon starve to death.

• Gum Alley: It has no official name, but it's the alley right next to 733 Higuera Street in San Luis Obispo, California. People have been depositing their chewed gum on the side of the old brick building there for more than a decade. A wonderfully tacky mural—in every sense of the word.

• New York Central Railroad once employed a full-time gum removal man to clean discarded gum from Grand Central Station. He harvested an average of seven pounds a night, with the wad growing to fourteen pounds on holiday weekends.

LOVE & GUM

• Sharing someone's ABC (already been chewed) gum is a sign of true love, as Tom Sawyer proved when he shared a piece with Becky Thatcher. The following is a selection from Mark Twain's *The Adventures of Tom Sawyer,* Chapter VII:

> **...Then they sat together, with a slate before them, and Tom gave Becky the pencil and held her hand in his, guiding it, and so created another surprising house. When the interest in art began to wane, the two fell to talking. Tom was swimming in bliss.**
>
> **He said:**
>
> **"Do you love rats?"**
>
> **"No! I hate them!"**
>
> **"Well, I do, too — LIVE ones. But I mean dead ones, to swing round your head with a string."**
>
> **"No, I don't care for rats much, anyway. What I like is chewing-gum."**
>
> **"Oh, I should say so! I wish I had some now."**
>
> **"Do you? I've got some. I'll let you chew it awhile, but you must give it back to me."**
>
> **That was agreeable, so they chewed it turn about, and dangled their legs against the bench in excess of contentment.**

"'I-LOVE-YOU!'"

A section or two later, the two youngsters got engaged.

A MEMBER OF THE CHAIN GANG

Remember spending all your allowance on gum so you could have the longest wrapper chain in the entire neighborhood? It takes 50 wrappers to make a chain one foot long. On March 11, 1965, Gary Duschl of Virginia Beach,

Gum by Any Other Name

German: kaugummi
Japanese: gamu
Norwegian: tyggegummi
Russian: zhevatelnaya rezinka
Spanish: goma de mascar
Chinese: heung how chu
Portuguese: pastilka elastica
Swiss: chaetschgummi
Arabic: elki
Greek: tsikles

Gary Duschl and his record-breaking gum wrapper chain. Find out more at http://www.gumwrapper.com/.

Virginia, began a gum wrapper chain. Thirty-eight years later, he was the world record holder for the longest gum wrapper chain, with a chain of 1,000,000 wrappers that reached 42,908 feet. The chain weighs 588 pounds and is made solely from Wrigley's gum wrappers—a total of about $50,000 worth of gum.

On his Web site, Gary draws comparisons in order to help people understand the length his obsession goes. He points out that 42,908 feet actually is about eight miles.

In case you want to challenge Gary's record (or at least have a modest-sized gum chain you can wear or display), here's how to get

started: Get a pack of flat stick gum. Remove and fold the individual paper wrapper lengthwise into thirds. Fold

in again, in half, crosswise. Fold each end in toward the center; this becomes the first link in the chain. Repeat with remaining wrappers to create many links. To assemble the

chain, slip the ends of the second link into the **V** of the first link. Add to the chain by feeding the ends of link #3 through the ends of link #2, and so on, in a zig-zag pattern.

Eyewitness

I Watched the *S.S. Titanic* Go Down

Margaret Graham, the 19-year-old daughter of W. T. Graham, a financial backer of the Dixie Cup Corporation, and Elizabeth Shutes, her governess, were passengers on the maiden voyage of the *Titanic*. Of the 2,227 aboard, they were two of the 375 that survived.

THE TITANIC left Southampton, England, on April 10, 1912, and headed for New York. On the night of April 15, it struck an iceberg and went down. Here's Shutes's account:

"Suddenly a queer quivering ran under me, apparently the whole length of the ship. Startled by the very strangeness of the shivering motion, I sprang to the floor. With too perfect a trust in that mighty vessel I again lay down. Someone knocked at my door, and the voice of a friend said: 'Come quickly to my cabin; an iceberg has just passed our window; I know we have just struck one.'

"No confusion, no noise of any kind, one could believe no danger imminent. Our stewardess came and said she could learn nothing. Looking out into the companionway I saw heads appearing asking questions from half-closed doors. All sepulchrally still, no excitement. I sat down again. My friend was by this time dressed; still her daughter and I talked on, Margaret pretending to eat a sandwich. Her hand shook so that the bread kept parting company from the chicken. Then I saw she was frightened, and for the first time I was too, but why get dressed, as no one had given the slightest hint of any possible danger? An officer's cap passed the door. I asked: 'Is there an accident or danger of any kind?' 'None, so far as I know,' was his courteous answer, spoken quietly and most kindly. This same officer then entered a cabin a little distance down the companionway and, by this time distrustful of everything, I listened intently, and distinctly heard, 'We can keep the water out for a while.' Then, and not until then, did I realize the horror of an accident at sea. Now it was too late to dress; no time for a waist, but a coat and skirt were soon on; slippers were quicker than shoes; the stewardess put on our life-preservers, and we were just ready when Mr Roebling came to tell us he would take us to our friend's mother, who was waiting above....

The *S.S. Titanic* was the biggest luxury liner of its time. So large, that designers added an extra smokestack, just so it would sport an even number. The last smokestack was non-functional; it served only as ventilation.

"No laughing throng, but on either side [of the staircases] stand quietly, bravely, the stewards, all equipped with the white, ghostly life-preservers. Always the thing one tries not to see even crossing a ferry. Now only pale faces, each form strapped about with those white bars. So gruesome a scene. We passed on. The awful good-byes. The quiet look of hope in the brave men's eyes as the wives were put into the lifeboats. Nothing escaped one at this fearful moment. We left from the sun deck, seventy-five feet above the water. Mr Case and Mr Roebling, brave American men, saw us to the lifeboat, made no effort to save themselves, but stepped back on deck. Later they went to an honoured grave.

"Our lifeboat, with thirty-six in it, began lowering to the sea. This was done amid the greatest confusion. Rough seamen all giving different orders. No officer aboard. As only one side of the ropes worked, the lifeboat at one time was in such a position that it seemed we must capsize in mid-air. At last the ropes worked together, and we drew nearer and nearer the black, oily water. The first touch of our lifeboat on that black sea came to me as a last good-bye to life, and so we put off—a tiny boat on a great sea—rowed away from what had been a safe home for five days.

The *Titanic* voyage was supposed to be Capt. Edward John Smith's final working stint as head of a ship. It ended up being his last journey of any kind.

"The first wish on the part of all was to stay near the Titanic. We all felt so much safer near the ship. Surely such a vessel could not sink. I thought the danger must be exaggerated, and we could all be taken aboard again. But surely the outline of that great, good ship was growing less. The bow of the boat was getting black. Light after light was disappearing, and now those rough seamen put to their oars and we were told to hunt under seats, any place, anywhere, for a lantern, a light of any kind. Every place was empty. There was no water—no stimulant of any kind. Not a biscuit—nothing to keep us alive had we drifted long....

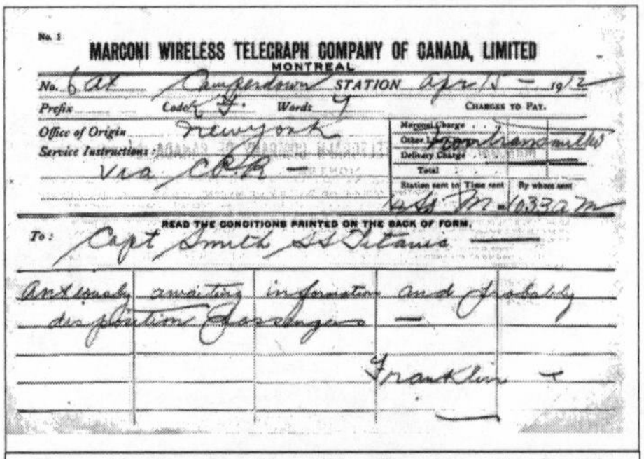
No. 1

MARCONI WIRELESS TELEGRAPH COMPANY OF CANADA, LIMITED
MONTREAL

No. 6 AX Camperdown STATION April 15 1912
Prefix Code F Words 7 CHARGES TO PAY.
Office of Origin New York
Service Instructions: via CBK

READ THE CONDITIONS PRINTED ON THE BACK OF FORM.

To: Capt Smith SS Titanic

Anxiously awaiting information and probably disposition passengers

Franklin

"From: Mr. Franline, The White Star Line, To: Captain Smith, The Titanic, Date: April 15, 1912. 'Anxiously awaiting information and probably disposition passengers.'" There was no reply.

"Sitting by me in the lifeboat were a mother and daughter. The mother had left a husband on the Titanic, and the daughter a father and husband, and while we were near the other boats those two stricken women would call out a name and ask, 'Are you there?' 'No,' would come back the awful answer, but these brave women never lost courage, forgot their own sorrow, telling me to sit close to them to keep warm.... The life-preservers helped to keep us warm, but the night was bitter cold, and it grew colder and colder, and just before dawn, the coldest, darkest hour of all, no help seemed possible....

"The stars slowly disappeared, and in their place came the faint pink glow of another day. Then I heard, 'A light, a ship.' I could not, would not, look while there was a bit of doubt, but kept my eyes away. All night long I had heard, 'A light!' Each time it proved to be one of our other lifeboats, someone lighting a piece of paper, anything they could find to burn, and now I could not believe. Someone found a newspaper; it was lighted and held up. Then I looked and saw a ship. A ship bright with lights; strong and steady she waited, and we were to be saved. A straw hat was offered as it would burn longer. That same ship that had come to save us might run us down. But no; she is still. The two, the ship and the dawn, came together, a living painting." ☾

Grandville

Kids' Illustrator, Father of Surrealism

Jean Ignace Isidore Gerard (1803–1847), who went by the name "Grandville," was a French illustrator who drew the most peculiar things. A century later, surrealist artists adopted him as a forerunner of their movement. **For the rest of the story, see page 247.**

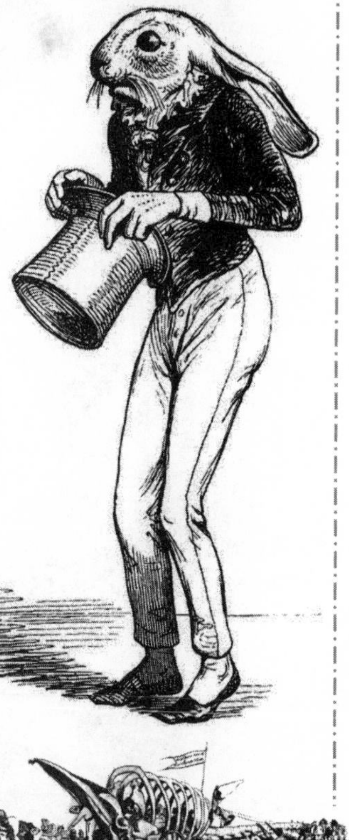

THE BIBLE

1841
I·I·G

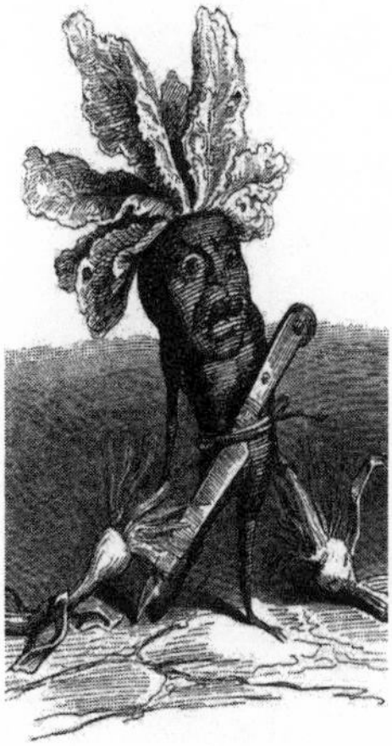

The Spirits Speak

HOW TO PERFORM A PHONY SEANCE

When Houdini tried to find a genuine psychic to talk to his beloved dead mother, he discovered only frauds. You can be a fraud, too—here's a method used by professional paranormals of the past.

THE BEST THING about seances is that everything takes place in the dark. There's a reason, as you'll see when you set up your own visitation by the spirits.

WHAT YOU'LL NEED

- Table big enough for you and your unsuspecting friends
- Cigarette lighter
- Candle
- 2 pieces of cardboard
- Pen
- 2 rubber bands
- Ambient music (optional)

HOW YOU DO IT

1 Get everything ready. Black out windows and door cracks —your room must be made completely dark.

2 Have your friends sit around the table, lit candle in center. Say: "We are here tonight in a circle to see if the spirits are among us and whether they will communicate to us from the Other Side."

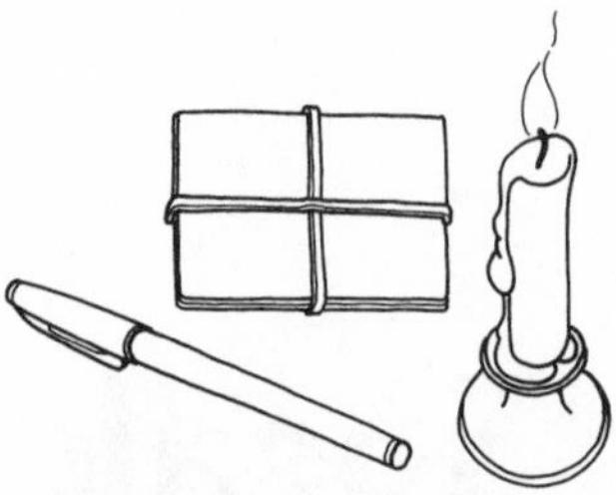

3 Show that the sides of both sheets of cardboard are blank. Wrap rubber bands around each end and put the package on the table with the pen on top of it. Say: "This is in case anybody from the Other Side wants to send us a message."

4 Have everyone place their hands palms down on the table. As you talk for a few moments about the spirits and the Other World, casually slide your hands to within a few inches of each other.

5 Tell everyone to reach over with their right hand and grasp the left wrist of the person to their right. Say: "This ensures that everybody can be trusted not to interfere with the process."

6 You announce that you are now going to extinguish the candle. Take your right hand from your neighbor's wrist and reach toward the candle. In the movement of leaning forward, you'll casually pull your left hand toward the center. Snuff the flame with your fingers, and lean back in the darkness.

7 Here comes the trick: Pull your left hand over and use *it—not* your right hand—to grip your neighbor's wrist. Now, unbeknownst to either of your neighbors, you have your right hand free.

8 Encourage everyone to concentrate on the spirits. As you talk about how to feel the presence of spirits (this is to mask any sounds you make), feel around gently for the pen. Write "I AM WITH YOU" in ghostly letters on the cardboard. Turn the package over so the writing is on the bottom.

9 After a short, meditative silence, say: "We have been in the dark long enough; let us see if there has been a message. I shall light the candle." This gives you a reason to take your "right" hand from your neighbor's wrist.

10 Actually, you slip your *left* hand off your neighbor's wrist. Use your right hand to find your

lighter and light the candle, using the movement of leaning forward to slide your left hand back toward your left neighbor.

11 Take the rubber bands from the cardboard without showing the writing on the bottom. Lift the top piece and show it. Say, with a sigh of resignation and subtle reproach: "Apparently we didn't all have our energies fully focused on reaching the spirits. Let's try again."

12 When you put the rubber band back, lift the piece of cardboard with writing on the bottom and slide the blank piece *underneath,* so the writing is now inside. Put the rubber bands back around.

13 Say: "I think we need more direct psychic energy. Let us all lay our hands directly on the piece of cardboard."

14 Snuff the candle again. Tell everyone to focus all of their energies on receiving a message from the Other World. After a short while, say: "I sense that perhaps we have waited long enough." Light the candle once more.

15 Ask: "Will somebody please open the package again to see if we received a message?"

16 Keep a blank, unsurprised face when people gasp at the sight of "I AM WITH YOU." Explain nothing.

GETTING IN THE SPIRIT

Use your imagination. You can do a lot more with that free right hand. For example, you can create a noisy spirit manifestation by tossing something to the far side of the room. You can also move things around the table, wave a white silk over the table for a ghostly visual manifestation or just about anything to create an eerie mood. ☾

Sports Match 2

Match the Team to the Location

One more time: See if you can match these NBA, MLB, and NFL teams to their correct home location.

1.	Diamondbacks	Utah
2.	Timberwolves	Florida
3.	Marlins	Toronto
4.	Rams	Arizona
5.	Grizzlies	Montreal
6.	Padres	Arizona
7.	Jazz	Milwaukee
8.	Raptors	Carolina
9.	Buccaneers	San Diego
10.	Saints	New Orleans
11.	Expos	Minnesota
12.	Cardinals	Colorado
13.	Rockies	St. Louis
14.	Panthers	Memphis
15.	Bucks	Tampa Bay

Answers: 1. Diamondbacks: Arizona; 2. Timberwolves: Minnesota; 3. Marlins: Florida; 4. Rams: St. Louis; 5. Grizzlies: Memphis; 6. Padres: San Diego; 7. Jazz: Utah; 8. Raptors: Toronto; 9. Buccaneers: Tampa Bay; 10. Saints: New Orleans; 11. Expos: Montreal; 12. Cardinals: Arizona; 13. Rockies: Colorado; 14. Panthers: Carolina; 15. Bucks: Milwaukee

Tom Swifties III

"Some You Lose," Said Tom Winsomely

From the surreal 1960s came elephant jokes and Tom Swifties, based on bad puns and the stylistic excesses of Victor Appleton, who created the popular Tom Swift stories. Here are some more.

"I've found Moby Dick!" Tom wailed.

"Does Heisenberg have principles?" asked Tom uncertainly.

"How long before my table's ready?" Tom asked reservedly.

"I don't want to die intestate," said Tom unwillingly.

"Ever hear a lion catapulted?" asked Tom over the uproar.

"How do you stop a horse?" Tom said woefully.

"I've had some ventricles removed," Tom said halfheartedly.

"My specialty is milking cows," Tom uttered.

"Anyone know a rebel army leader?" Tom asked generally.

"Got any Velveeta?" asked Tom craftily.

"This is leftover calf meat," Tom revealed.

"I can hear a member of that hive in pain!" Tom bemoaned.

"I cut too much off my toenails," Tom said quickly.

"I've forgotten the guitar part," Tom fretted.

"You brought cheese I can't shred," Tom said ungratefully.

"Unclog the drain with a vacuum cleaner," said Tom succinctly.

"I forgot to buy perma-pressed clothes," Tom said ironically.

"I come from the Dog Star," Tom said seriously.

"I think I pulled a tendon," Tom insinuated.

"I hate metal on my teeth," said Tom abrasively.

"I'd give that honey-gatherer an 80 out of 100," Tom berated.

Speak English? 2

Translate These British Terms into American

Sometimes it seems like the British and Americans don't even speak the same language. How are you at translating? Translate these old and new British terms into American. (Answers below.)

1. power point	**a. french fries**
2. lift	**b. mailbox**
3. dust bin	**c. installment plan**
4. rubbers	**d. electrical outlet**
5. chargehand	**e. molasses**
6. chips	**f. grab bag**
7. crisps	**g. merry–go–round**
8. lucky dip	**h. hassock**
9. pouffe	**i. foreman**
10. ironmonger	**j. long–distance call**
11. solicitor	**k. elevator**
12. never–never	**l. parka**
13. trunk call	**m. lawyer**
14. pillar box	**n. hardware store**
15. loud hailer	**o. megaphone**
16. roundabout	**p. garbage can**
17. treacle	**q. potato chips**
18. anorak	**r. erasers**

Answers: *1. power point = d. electrical outlet; 2. lift = k. elevator; 3. dust bin = p. garbage can; 4. rubbers = r. erasers; 5. chargehand = i. foreman; 6. chips = a. french fries; 7. crisps= q. potato chips; 8. lucky dip = f. grab bag; 9. pouffe = h. hassock; 10. ironmonger = n. hardware store; 11. solicitor = m. lawyer; 12. never-never = c. installment plan; 13. trunk call = j. long–distance call; 14. pillar box = b. mailbox; 15. loud hailer = o. megaphone; 16. roundabout = g. merry-go-round; 17. treacle = e. molasses; 18. anorak = l. parka*

Ripe Ol' Corn

"The Punkin Centre & Paw Paw Valley Railroad"

"Uncle Josh," Cal Stewart's country bumpkin, tells a story about the coming of one of those newfangled railroads.

WONDERS will never cease—we've got a railroad in Punkin Centre now; oh, we're gettin' to be right smart cityfied. I guess that's about the crookedest railroad that ever was built. I think that railroad runs across itself in one or two places; it runs past one station three times. It's so durned crooked they hav to burn crooked wood in the ingine.

Cal Stewart

Well, the first engine they had on the Punkin Centre was a wonderful piece of machinery. It had a five-foot boiler and a seven-foot whistle, and every time they blowed the whistle the durned old engine would stop.

Well, we've got the railroad, and we're mighty proud of it; but we had an awful time a-gettin' it through. You see, most everybody give the right of way 'cept Ezra Hoskins, and he didn't like to see it go through his meadow field, and it seemed as though they'd have to go 'round for quite a ways, and maybe they wouldn't come to Punkin Centre at all.

Well, one mornin' Ezra saw a lot of fellers down in the meadow most uncommonly busy like; so he went down to them and he said, "What be you a-doin' down here?" And they said, "Well, Mr. Hoskins, we're surveyin' for the railroad." And Ezra

said, "So we're goin' to have a railroad, be we? Is it goin' right through here?" And they said, "Yes, Mr. Hoskins, that's where it's a-goin', right through here." Ezra said, "Well, I s'pose you'll have a right smart of plowin' and diggin', and you'll just about plow up my meadow field, won't you?" They said, "Yes, Mr. Hoskins, we'll hav to do some gradin'."

Ezra said, "Well, now, let me see, is it a-goin' just the way you've got that instrument pointed?" They said, "Yes, sir, just there." And Ezra said, "Well, near as I can calculate from that, I should judge it was a-goin' right through my barn." They said, "Yes, Mr. Hoskins, we're sorry, but the railroad is a-goin' right through your barn."

Well, Ezra didn't say much for quite a spell, and we all expected there would be trouble; but finally he said, "Well, I s'pose the community of Punkin Centre needs a railroad and I hadn't oughter offer any objections to its goin' through, but I'm goin' to tell you one thing right now, afore you go any further. When you get it built and a-runnin', you've got to get a man to come down here and take care of it, because it's a-comin' along hayin' and harvestin' time, and I'll be too durned busy to run down here and open and shut them barn doors every time one of your pesky old trains wants to go through." ℭ

Simian Says

A Barrel of Apes & Monkeys

Climbing up the human family tree, you'd be surprised at what you'll find swinging from its branches. Here are feats and tales of some of our closest living relatives.

MONKEYS MOCK US FOR THIS

What does *Homo sapiens* mean? The name we human apes have modestly given ourselves means "wise person."

THE PRIMATE COLORS

Apes and monkeys pretty much see the same colors we do. However, many of the New World monkeys don't see reds quite as well.

Orangutan

PRIMATE COLORS II

Many people assume that the orangutan got that name because of its color, but they're wrong. *Orangutan* means "person of the forest" in the Malay language.

GORILLA WARFARE?

Chimps have been known to murder, steal and rape. They are also very human in their capacity for war. In clashes with other chimpanzee groups, they will brutalize and kill their enemies. And, although the practice is uncommon, chimpanzees have been known to eat other chimps.

MUTILATED MONKEY MEAT

How many primates are major meat eaters? Besides humans,

only chimpanzees eat any quantity of meat. About 75% of the chimps' meat consists of red colobus monkey babies ripped from the arms of their mothers. Researchers found that a chimp's major motivation for hunting monkeys is sex—if members of a hunting party offer fresh meat to a female in heat, most or all of them are likely to get lucky.

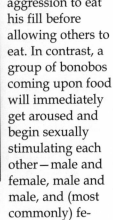

Don't be fooled by the chimp's innocent face

MONKEY LOVE

If chimps share humans' most violent attributes, bonobos are the flip side.

Even though bonobos and chimps are humans' closest relatives, sharing 98.4% of our genes, the bonobos are not as well known. They weren't even discovered by Westerners until 1929. Coincidentally, local natives along the Zaire River, where the bonobos live, have many myths about how humankind and bonobos were once brothers.

Bonobos are most interested in making love, not war—they've developed a female-led, cooperative, and egalitarian society in which promiscuous sex is a powerful substitute for aggression.

Compare bonobos with chimpanzees: If a group of chimps come upon food, the dominant male claims it as his own, using a display of aggression to eat his fill before allowing others to eat. In contrast, a group of bonobos coming upon food will immediately get aroused and begin sexually stimulating each other—male and female, male and male, and (most commonly) female and female, rubbing their genitals against each other while grinning and making cooing sounds. After about five minutes, the bonobos go ahead and feed as a community without regard to rank. A similar orgiastic thing happens when something threatens to disturb the peace. For example, when researchers in a zoo dropped a cardboard box into the chimp compound, the dominant chimp threatened violence in order to be the first to explore it. The bonobos, in contrast, engaged in a brief orgy and then approached the box together.

Unlike most simians, bonobos

often copulate face to face, looking deeply into each others' eyes. Humans once thought that they were unique in this especially intimate activity. They were wrong.

WHAT'S THE WESTERN LOWLAND GORILLA'S LATIN NAME?

Gorilla gorilla gorilla.

RELATIVE HUMILITY

Humans and gorillas are closer relatives than are gorillas and monkeys.

IN THE BLOOD OF RHESUS

The *rh* in "rh factor" stands for "rhesus," the monkey that was once widely used in medical research. When Dr. Karl Landsteiner discovered properties of blood in 1940, he decided to honor the rhesus monkeys that were deprived of their freedom, blood and lives to make his discovery.

WON'T YOU BE MY NEIGHBOR?

Koko the signing gorilla went positively ape over *Mr. Rogers' Neighborhood.* When Mr. Rogers came to visit Koko, her first response was to wrap her powerful arms gently around him. Then, as she had seen him do hundreds of times on TV, she reached down and took off his shoes.

Monkeys, Apes & Gorillas—What's the Difference?

WHAT'S A MONKEY and what's an ape? To clear up confusion, let's do a quick list. Primates have two main groups: **anthropoids** and **prosimians**.

1. **Anthropoids** include:

Monkeys. New World monkeys include marmosets, tamarins, capuchins, howlers, squirrel monkeys, woolly monkeys, spider monkeys and even woolly spider monkeys. Old World monkeys include baboons, colobus monkeys and macaques.

Apes. Chimpanzees, gibbons, gorillas, orangutans and humans. Apes have no tails and are smarter than monkeys. Apes walk in an upright position instead of on four feet like monkeys. If there's a tree to be scaled, apes climb it; monkeys take a leap into it. Excluding humans, these are known as **simians**.

2. **Prosimians** include a number of lesser-known animals like aye-ayes, galagos, lemurs, lorises, pottos and tarsiers. *Prosimian* means "pre-monkey" because they are more primitive than monkeys and actually resemble monkey ancestors. Prosimians are not as strong or smart as the anthropoids, and survive competition with them by hunting at night as their smarter cousins sleep.

Ring-tailed lemur, a prosimian

HAND GESTURES OF BIG APES

Gorillas aren't the only simians to learn sign language—so have chimps and orangutans. Washoe, the most accomplished chimpanzee, has a vocabulary of at least 240 words—nowhere near the claims for Koko that she can understand 2,000 spoken words and respond with a vocabulary of up to 1,000 signs.

ARMS OF DESTRUCTION

Gorilla arms are longer than their legs. The record gorilla arm span is 9 feet, 2 inches; a more typical adult male arm span is about 8 feet.

NOT A HEAVY DRINKER

Gorillas don't drink water. They get all the moisture they need from the leaves, tubers, flowers, fruit, fungus and insects they eat—roughly 50 pounds of food a day.

GORILLA WARFARE

What should you do if charged by a gorilla? First of all, complain to your credit card company. Okay, so it's an old joke.... The good news is that gorillas are normally very shy and amiable; the bad news is that if you wander into their territory, the male leader will charge at you beating his chest and growling. So what do you do?

You must not do the apparently rational thing of running for your life. Intruders who run are often chased and killed. Instead, screw up your courage, stand up straight, and hold your ground. Expert say that those who stand their ground are almost never harmed.

CAPPUCCINO MONKEYS

Do capuchin monkeys have anything to do with cappuccino? More than any reasonable person could expect. Both were named after the robes worn by Capuchin monks. The coffee drink is the same distinctive brown color. The monkey has a distinctive marking that looks like a monk's hood on top of its head.

EURO-MONKEY INSOUCIANCE

Few people know about the wild monkeys of Europe. Barbary apes live in Gibraltar, the British colony south of Spain. Despite its name, this "ape" is really a monkey related to rhesus monkeys of India. There are only 5,000 worldwide, with most in remote areas of Morocco and Algeria.

SEA MONKEYS?

Gorillas don't swim. A pursuing gorilla won't follow you into the water. But some monkeys do swim. For example, the proboscis monkeys of Borneo are as graceful gliding through the water as they are swinging from the trees.

SMALL AND LOUD

Smallest monkey is the pygmy marmoset. It's the size of a small squirrel, and it weighs as much as a Quarter Pounder, bun and all.

Pygmy marmoset there'd be days like this

Loudest monkey is the howler. A small band can make as much noise as a stadium full of people. They can be heard 3 miles away.

WE WOULDN'T TRUST ANY OF THEM WITH NO. 2 PENCILS

If you gave animals an IQ test, primates would rule in the smartness scale. Of the top ten, seven are primates. Here's how they stack up:

1. Humans
2. Chimpanzees / Bonobos
3. Gorillas
4. Orangutans
5. Baboons
6. Gibbons
7. Monkeys
8. Small-toothed whales
9. Dolphins
10. Elephants

RHESUS PIECES

Not many things hunt tree monkeys, but eagles do, swooping down with powerful talons to grasp and crush. Still, tree-dwellers are better off than monkeys that spend a lot of time on the ground. All of the meat eaters from lions to hyenas seem to want rhesus pieces.

Potty Pourri

Random Kinds of Factness

• President Millard Fillmore never had any formal education. Oxford University once offered him an honorary doctorate of Civil Law. He turned it down, saying, "No man should accept a degree he cannot read."

• Some archeologists claim that the soup ladle was the first single-use kitchen utensil invented.

• *Raash* is another name for the electric catfish—an African catfish that grows up to 3 feet in length. The name means "thunder," although its effects are far more like lightning.

• J. R. R. Tolkien was a procrastinator, it's safe to say. It took him fourteen years to write *The Lord of the Rings*. Granted, the epic ran about a thousand pages, and included complex histories and cultures that he made up out of thin air. But still, he averaged fewer than 100 words per day. (To compare, this paragraph uses 60 words.)

• Teachers' salaries have always been bad, but Confucius didn't complain. Once he said that he would never turn away a prospective student, "even if he came to me on foot, with nothing more to offer as tuition than a package of dried meat."

• Mark Twain was one of the first people to own the newly invented Remington typewriter. Its success convinced him to sink a lot of his hard-earned money into an early typesetting machine. That investment didn't pan out, and years later he traded his Remington for a $12 saddle.

• President Calvin Coolidge was sworn in as president by his own dad, who happened to be a justice of the peace.

• Until they got smart in 200 B.C., the French didn't make their own wine. They bought it from the Italians. The going price was one slave for a large jug of wine.

Ol' Smokey

WHERE THERE'S FIRE, THERE'S SMOKEY

Forest fire prevention goes back decades before the introduction of Smokey the Bear, but no publicity campaign has ever been anywhere near as successful as the Smokey campaign. Here's how it happened.

EARLY FOREST FIRE PREVENTION ads used Uncle Sam. In a campaign in 1937, initiated by President Franklin D. Roosevelt, the bearded old guy reminded us: "Your Forests; Your Fault; Your Loss." It was a powerful message that people took seriously at first, but after several years of use, the United States Forestry Service decided it was in need of a new approach.

In 1943, the Foote, Cone & Belding advertising agency took over the Forest Service account and decided it was a time for an aggressive, hard-sell campaign. Tying the effort to Japanese bombing of Pearl Harbor and an oil field near the Los Padros National Forest in California, the firm pumped out slogans like "Careless Matches Aid the Axis," to play up Americans' fears that the nation's forests were in danger from alien forces. The pictures accompanying the message showed stereotypical Japanese and Nazis leering menacingly at us, their faces illuminated as if gleefully watching a forest burn.

Early Forest fire prevention posters. Top: Uncle Sam, 1937. Left: Anti-Japanese, anti-Nazi, and pro-Bambi campaign. Right: "Careless matches aid the Axis" campaign

ALAS, ALL TASTELESS THINGS MUST COME TO AN END

As the war ended, however, it became clear that the old approach wouldn't work any more. Foote, Cone & Belding managed to get permission to use Bambi, the Disney deer, in one ad—but after that, Disney didn't want to grant further permissions. Next they tried using squirrels as a spokes-animal but after one poster, they decided that the cute little creatures didn't have sufficient seriousness and authority.

Finally, the ad agency convinced the Forest Service that a bear would best represent the authoritative yet gruffly lovable image the U.S. Forest Service wanted to project.

The first Smokey the Bear poster came out in 1945 from an illustration by New York artist Albert Staehle. In 1947 a copywriter penned the slogan "Remember, only YOU can prevent forest fires." Not long after, announcer Jack Weaver put his head into a barrel for resonance and gave a voice to Smokey in his first radio spots.

MYTHMAKING

Smokey the Bear actually became flesh, fur and blood in 1950, when a state game protector rescued a scorched bear cub from a New Mexico forest fire. The Forest Service quickly named the cub Smokey, created an after-the-fact story which claimed that the little charred cub was the inspiration for the Smokey ad campaign, instead of vice versa, and transferred the cub to the National Zoological Park in Washington, D.C.

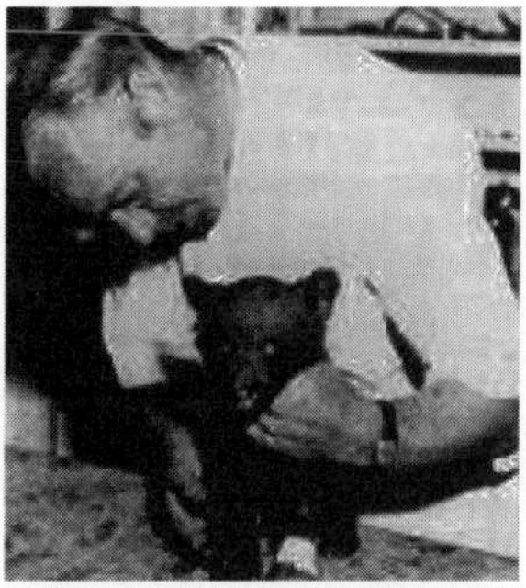

The first living Smokey, rescued in 1950

Ben Michtom, chairman of the Ideal Toy Company and son of the original creators of the teddy bear, won permission to market a toy Smokey in 1952. Ideal produced millions of the ranger-hatted bears and included a certificate with each, which children could fill out and send to the Service to become Junior Forest Rangers. More than 5 million kids enlisted.

The original living Smokey the Bear mascot died in 1967. Another bear, Smokey II, died in 1990.

Snoopy stepped in to help in 1972, and the Forest Service brought back Bambi again in 1982

MORE SMOKEY FACTS

• The Koochiching County Keep Minnesota Green Committee in International Falls, Minnesota erected a 26-foot wooden Smokey the Bear in 1954.

• Smokey was given his own zip code number in 1964, in recognition of the large volume of mail he receives. Smokey's zip: Washington, D.C., 20252.

• In 1969, Smokey the Bear appeared in his own weekly half-hour animated comedy adventure. The show ran for two years on the ABC-TV network. ☾

SMOKEY THE BEAR
By STEVE NELSON and JACK ROLLINS

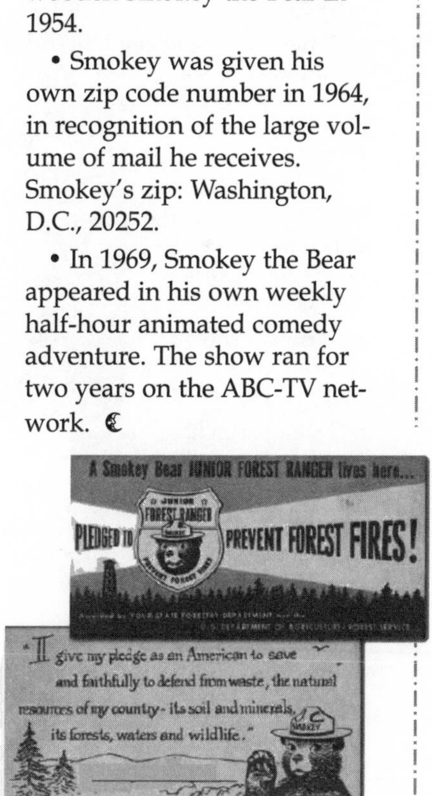

According to Mark Twain

More from *Puddin'head Wilson's Calendar*, a fictitious publication that Twain "quoted" from whenever he needed a maxim.

• "Each person is born with one possession which outvalues all his others—his last breath."

• "It takes your enemy and your friend, working together, to hurt you to the heart: the one to slander you, and the other to get the news to you."

• "If the desire to kill and the opportunity to kill always came together, who would escape hanging?"

• "Grief can take care of itself; but to get the full value of a joy, you must have somebody to divide it with."

• "Wrinkles should merely indicate where smiles have been."

• "Don't part with your illusions. When they are gone, you may still exist, but you have ceased to live."

• "Often the surest way to convey misinformation is to tell the strict truth."

• "In the first place God made idiots. This was for practice. Then he made school boards."

• "Everyone is a moon, and has a dark side which he never shows to anybody."

• "The ink with which all history is written is merely fluid prejudice."

• "When people do not respect us we are sharply offended; yet deep down in his private heart, no man much respects himself."

• "Let us be thankful for the fools. But for them, the rest of us could not succeed."

• "We begin to swear before we can talk."

• "The autocrat of Russia possesses more power than any other man in the earth, but he cannot stop a sneeze."

• "Let me make the superstititions of a nation and I do not care who makes its laws or its songs, either."

• "There are two times in a man's life when he should not speculate: when he can't afford it, and when he can."

• "Be careless in your dress if you must, but keep a tidy soul."

• "There is no such thing as 'the Queen's English.' The property has gone into a joint stock company and we own the bulk of the shares."

Quakes, Floods, and Fire

Some of Our Favorite Disasters

Based on the question-savvy virtual butler's book *Just Curious About History, Jeeves*, here's a little Q & A about famous disasters.

ASH FROM A HOLE IN THE GROUND

How many people did Vesuvius kill?

Which time? Mount Vesuvius, the active volcano on the coast of Italy, has erupted more than 50 times since burying Pompeii and Herculaneum in A.D. 79. That first reported eruption killed about 3,400 people, it's estimated, mostly by burying them in thick pumice deposits. From that date, and probably before that date, Mount Vesuvius erupted every 100 years until about 1037, when it went quiet. Almost 600 years later, however, in 1631, it surprised nearby inhabitants by erupting and causing more than 4,000 deaths in the area. It was during this eruption's cleanup that the ruins of Pompeii were uncovered.

Was Vesuvius the worst volcano in history?

No. The deadliest-volcano-in-history award goes to Mount Tambora, Indonesia, in 1815. Judith Coan in Discovery.com described it like this:

> **The largest eruption during the last two centuries, as well as the deadliest volcano in recorded history, Mount Tambora exploded April 10–11, 1815. It killed an estimated 92,000 people. Almost 80,000 of the victims died of starvation brought on by the agricultural devastation in the volcano's wake. The eruption and the resulting massive clouds of dust and ash affected most of the Northern Hemisphere, causing unusually cool temperatures and failed crops in 1816—sometimes referred to as "the year without a summer."**

Mt. Pelee blows its top

How many people survived the 1902 Mount Pelee volcanic eruption in Martinique?

Two, one of whom was saved because he was in a windowless jail cell. The other 29,000 inhabitants living nearby were wiped out.

Had Mount St. Helens ever had a larger eruption than the one in 1980?

According to those who study these things, the Washington volcano erupted more violently about 2000 B.C. Mount St. Helens has been an active volcano for over 40,000 years, and scientists have predicted that another eruption could happen in the next 20 or 30 years.

ANOTHER BIG GAS BAG GOES DOWN IN FLAMES

What's listed on the official report as the cause of the fire that destroyed the* Hindenburg *in 1937?

St. Elmo's Fire—or, to a lay person, static electricity.

WIPE OUT!

What was the name of the dam at Johnstown, Pennsylvania that broke loose and flooded the town?

It shares a name with J. R. Ewing's homestead: South Fork.

Has a tidal wave ever hit the U.S.?

"Tidal waves"—or, more accurately, tsunamis—have hit the U.S. several times, most often in Hawaii and Alaska. California has been hit a couple of times this century as well. The most deadly tsunami to strike the contiguous U.S. happened in 1964. A record-shattering earthquake in Alaska was the catalyst for a series of huge waves that crashed into America's west coast. One in Shoup Bay, Valdez Inlet, measured 67 meters high. All in all, 120 people lost their lives throughout Canada, Alaska, Oregon, Washington and California. The deaths included 106 Alaskan residents, four campers on a beach campground in Newport, Oregon, and eleven people in the city of Crescent City, California, which was engulfed.

In 1946, Hawaii was also caught unaware by a devastating tsunami and 173 people were killed, prompting the foundation of the Pacific Tsunami Warning System (PTWS), for all U.S. regions in the Pacific, which watches for tsunamis in the hope of giving timely warnings of their approach.

SHAKE, RATTLE AND ROLL

Which San Francisco earthquake was more costly: the 1906 or 1989 one?

In dollars and cents, the 1989 Loma Prieta quake was the costliest at $5.9 billion, whereas the 1906 San Francisco quake totaled $400 million. In 1989 money, that would equal just over $5 billion—close but no cigar.

How many people were killed in the 1906 San Francisco earthquake?

From both the quake and the burning aftermath, about 3,000 people. The San Francisco city government at the time deliberately under-reported the numbers and blamed most of the deaths on the fire, because they figured that tourists and newcomers would be less frightened of death by a familiar danger like fire than a terrifyingly unfamiliar one like an earthquake.

Was the 1906 San Francisco earthquake the deadliest U.S. natural disaster?

No. Hurricane Frederick, which pounded Galveston, Texas, in 1900 holds that honor. It left over 6,000 dead.

What's the worst earthquake in recorded history?

On January 23, 1556, in Shansi, China, a quake killed over 830,000 people. Other "big ones" in history:

- **Tangshan, China**, 1976: officially 255,000 dead; unofficial estimates put it at around 600,000
- **Aleppo, Syria,** 1138: 230,000 dead
- **Xining, China**, 1927: 200,000 dead
- **Messina, Italy**, 1908: 70,000 - 100,000 dead
- **Peru**, 1970: 66,000 dead

The Mississippi quake of 1811 ranks up there with "biggest," as well. The quake was so strong that it changed the course of the Mississippi River. However, there's no record of any human life lost. Next time, though....

A STICKY SWEET ENDING

What was the great Boston Molasses Flood?

That's exactly what it was: a flood of molasses. Don't laugh--people and horses died in it.

Just after noon on January 15, 1919, a fifty-eight-foot-tall, 90-feet wide steel structure burst open. It held 2.5 million gallons of hot molasses on the grounds of the United States Alcohol Company. Metal flew everywhere and a wave of sticky, boiling goo spewed up and out. The wave washed through a loading pit in the factory, boiling and smothering those standing nearby, and continued down on, washing freight cars off the tracks and pulling the front off a neighboring house. killing its inhabitants. Molasses poured through the nearby Public Works Department, boiling and smothering workers who were casually eating lunch around a table. Meanwhile, the town fire station was washed off its foundation and down toward the ocean.

When all was said and done, 21 people and numerous horses had come to a sticky end. The lawsuits that followed cost the molasses factory about a million dollars in damages.

A lengthy investigation decided that the tank hadn't been strong enough to hold that much molasses. In addition, a heat wave for several days in Boston had significantly increased the pressure inside the tanks.

Hunt and Peck

The Secret Lives of Typewriters

From the keyboard of regular contributor Kathie Meyer comes little-known facts about typewriters.

THE TYPEWRITER—an invention initially thought up to help blind people communicate—eventually became an enormous aid for sighted people as well. Although Christopher Latham Sholes is often credited as the inventor of the first typewriter, the honor should actually go to Englishman Henry Mill who patented a kind of type-writing machine in 1714. Actually, dozens of typewriters are known to have been designed prior to the Sholes model. Some were built with piano keyboards and had names like "writing harpsichord" and "piano printer." Others had names such as "machine kryptographique" (1833), "cembalo scrivano" (1837), "machine tachygraphique" (1839), "universal compositor" (1840), "chirographer" (1843), "rapigraphe" (1843), "clavier imprimeur" (1850), "stéréographe" (1814), "phonetic writer & calico printer" (1850), "mechanical typographer" (1852), "printing machine" (1857), and "the pterotype" (1866).

TYPEWRITER MIGHTIER THAN THE GUN

In 1874, gunmaker E. Remington & Sons Arms Company came out with "The Sholes & Glidden Type Writer." Remington entered the typewriter market because the demand for guns decreased after the Civil War ended and the Wild West was tamed. Remington had also branched into the farm equipment and sewing machine markets, which explains why the Sholes & Glidden ended up looking uncannily like a sewing machine. In fact, two of Remington's mechanics, William Jenne and Jefferson Clough, had been assigned the job of making the Sholes & Glidden device suitable for producing on the sewing machine assembly line.

The typewriter diversification didn't pan out that well for Remington—the retail price was a whopping $125 ($1,800 in today's money), but they managed to sell 5,000 of them. Still, the Sholes & Glidden goes down as the first production line-manufactured typewriter, and it did sell better than any other machine on the market at the time.

The Sholes & Glidden typewriter (right) was the same boxy shape of the Sholes & Glidden sewing machine (left).

UNDONE BY A TYPEWRITER

In the famous 1924 Chicago murder trial of teenagers Nathan F. Leopold, Jr., and Richard Loeb, a typewriter was the clinching piece of evidence eliciting confessions from both Leopold and Loeb. A fourteen-year-old boy, Bobby Franks, had been brutally murdered, but the killers attempted to extract $10,000 in ransom money from the boy's wealthy father anyway. Neither of the killers needed the money, for Leopold was the son of a wealthy manufacturer and Loeb, the offspring of the vice president of Sears Roebuck & Co.

Experts determined the ransom note, supposedly composed by "George Johnson," was typed on a specific brand of portable typewriter. Leopold's classmates recalled that he had once owned a portable typewriter, and provided specimens of typewriting done on the machine. They were a match to the Johnson ransom letter. In his confession, Leopold led police to the spot where he'd dumped the machine off of a bridge. Although other damning pieces of material evidence also materialized, the typewriter (which, incidentally, had been stolen from a University of Michigan classmate) was regarded as the most important.

The young ages and wealthy background of both the perpetrators and the victim made for a sensational investigation and trial. The two killers were defended by Scopes' Monkey Trial defender Clarence Darrow, who successfully argued for long-term incarceration instead of the death penalty.

Sometimes endings are a mix of tragedy and happily-ever-after. During their time in prison, Loeb and Leopold met distinctly separate fates. After expressing intense remorse, Leopold was released from prison in 1958. During his years in prison, he had mastered 28 languages and fulfilled a vow to become a full time volunteer for various social causes. Loeb, however, was never released—he had been killed by his cellmate.

EARLY ADOPTER

Mark Twain quickly realized that the typewriter could be a writer's tool. It has been claimed (even by Twain himself) and widely accepted that *Tom Sawyer* was the first novel written on a typewriter. This fact is in dispute by historians, but regardless, the manuscript of *Life on the Mississippi,* written in 1883, proves that Twain was the first author to submit a typewritten manuscript to a publisher.

TINS OF THE TIMES

After George K. Anderson of Memphis, Tennessee, patented the typewriter ribbon on September 14, 1886, they came in colorful tin containers. Some from the Art Deco period were quite pretty. Considered "poor relations" among antique collectors compared to tobacco, coffee and talc tins, ribbon tin collectors are a relatively small group, but they make up for that with their enthusiasm.

IT TAKES A CERTAIN TYPE

The Underwood typewriter was the creation of German-American inventor Franz X. Wagner, but the name comes from John T. Underwood, an entrepreneur who bought the company early in its history. The Underwood family was already a successful manufacturer of ribbons and carbon paper under contract with Remington. When Remington decided to produce its own line of ribbons, Underwood retaliated by building typewriters designed by Wagner. Underwood quickly grabbed a large share of the market.

QUICK FACTS & TRIVIA

• Pellegrine Tarri invented carbon paper in 1808.

• The echoing sounds of typewriter keys striking paper in the opening scenes of the movie *All the President's Men* were created by layering gunshots and whiplashes over typewriter sounds. It was meant to illustrate the film's theme that words could be powerful weapons against official skullduggery.

• The Blickensderfer Co. made the first electric typewriter in 1902.

• In 1944, IBM designed the first typewriter with proportional spacing.

GO AHEAD, TRY THIS AT HOME

• ***Typewriter*** is one of the longest words that can be made using the letters on only one row of the standard typewriter keyboard.

• ***Europe*** is the only name for a continent that can be typed using a single row of letters.

• There are no vowels in the bottom row. The only word that can be typed using it is *Zzz* (to indicate sleeping).

• ***Aftercataracts*** (a condition that sometimes follows cataract surgery), ***tesseradecades*** and ***tetrastearates*** are the longest words that can be typed using only the left hand in touch-typing.

• ***Deeded*** is the longest word that can be typed using just one finger.

• ***Johnny-jump-up*** (the name of a flower) is the longest word that can be typed using only the fingers of the right hand.

ONE MAN'S JUNK

Most old gadgets, especially typewriters, have little antique value, but sometimes you can get lucky. Irene Martin sure did. While at a tag sale, Irene spied a typewriter with an ornate copper nameplate with "FORD" cast in the center.

Martin paid $50 for the machine, and assorted parts and attachments. As she carried it back to the car, her husband, Marty, joked, "What pile of junk did you buy now?"

It turned out the "pile of junk" was designed in 1895 by a New Yorker named E. A. Ford (no known relation to Henry Ford). Only 12 or so are known to exist. When the Martins put the typewriter up for auction on eBay, the winning bidder paid $15,500 for the prize. ℭ

"I'm all in favor of keeping dangerous weapons out of the hands of fools. Let's start with typewriters." — Frank Lloyd Wright

Pot Shots

Privy's favorite privy shots. Send us yours! (See page 476.)

(Left) Sent in by BCOMP member Alan Levy, this was the outhouse that serviced his camping area in the snowy mountains of Australia's Broken Dam Hut. For perspective, Alan says there was about a meter of snow on top from a recent snowfall.

An open privy (right) in New Haven, Connecticut, in 1917. This photo was part of a Yale study on public health in the New Haven area. Nearly 400 privies were inspected by a Mr. O'Brian, Special Inspector. Two-thirds of them were exposed to rats, flies and other vermin.

This iron-shaped outhouse (above) is an engineered toilet serving dune shacks in Provincetown, Cape Cod, Massachusetts. Photo donated by Linda Coneen of Cape Cod & Islands Appraisal Group.

This permanent toilet (below, left), cemented on this desert island, serves a several-hundred-mile area in the South Pacific, including Suvarov Atoll, Anchorage Island and the Cook Islands group.

The privy opens into the sea below, where, at low tide, hermit crabs await what's dropped....

Photo courtesy of Matt Sponer. Thanks Matt!

Every Picture Tells a Story

***George Washington: Unfinished Portrait* by Gilbert Stuart (1755–1828)**

• This is the most famous painting of George Washington, the one reproduced in schools, governmental offices and on the dollar bill. So why didn't Gilbert Stuart ever finish it?

• Artist Stuart was a deep-in-debt alcoholic. He'd painted Washington twice before. Each time, he secretly dashed off a dozen quick copies to sell before delivering the originals.

• Martha Washington, who commissioned this painting, was wise to Stuart's way. She got the artist to agree that he would surrender the painting the moment he finished it.

• George hated posing, but Stuart was able to get the general to stop scowling by discussing horses with him. Also, a new set of false teeth rounded out his face. Stuart quickly knew he had the best portrait ever painted of Washington. He started working on a plan to keep the painting long enough to make copies.

• This was his solution: he deliberately left it unfinished. Over time, he dashed off more than 200 replicas, calling them his "hundred dollar bills." Martha never got the original.

J. P. Morgan

Straight Shooter or Man of Low Caliber?

Sometimes a company undergoes a dramatic change during its years of operation. That was true for the J. P. Morgan Company, as correspondents Eddie Fein and Billy Rubin found out.

J. P. MORGAN and Company and its subsidiary, the Morgan Guaranty Trust Company of New York, are respected institutions. They were founded by the man is still immortalized in their names, John Pierpont ("I owe the public nothing") Morgan, who amassed a mammoth fortune before he died in 1913. Not bad, considering that Morgan's first big financial deal—a wartime swindle against the U.S. government that involved a cache of dangerously defective guns—probably should have landed him in jail.

When America's Civil War broke out, 24-year-old Morgan successfully evaded serving in it. This was not too unusual; many sons of the affluent discovered that they could buy themselves out of the draft. It's also not surprising that the young financier would try to make a profit out of the war. But how he did it—well, judge for yourself.

Before the war started, the commander of the Army arsenal in New York City decided he wanted to unload some outdated and dangerous guns that were prone to backfire in such a way that they occasionally blew a soldier's thumb off. He arranged to sell them for scrap, cautioning potential buyers that they were "thoroughly unserviceable, obsolete, and dangerous."

Young J. P. Morgan

Knowing that weapons of any kind would be a hot commodity in the upcoming war, Morgan teamed up with a speculator named Simon Stevens to bid $3.50 each on the guns.

After a Union loss at the Battle of Bull Run, the commander of the U.S. Army in St. Louis put out a desperate call for rifles. When Stevens and Morgan telegraphed him an offer of "5,000 new carbines in perfect condition" for $22 each, the commander accepted the offer, sight unseen. Morgan and Stevens didn't have the money to buy the guns from the New York arsenal, but with the Army's purchase order in hand as collateral, Morgan had no trouble arranging a loan.

So the U.S. Army bought its own unusable rifles from itself at a mark-up of about 500%. To save shipping costs, the partners even arranged to have the defective rifles shipped directly from the arsenal in New York to the one in St. Louis.

That took chutzpah—not to mention stupidity. The Army suddenly figured out what was happening and refused to pay for the rifles. Morgan sued. The government tried to settle out of court, offering $13.31 per rifle, but Morgan demanded full payment. When the case went to court, the judge—incredibly—ruled in Morgan's favor, setting an unfortunate precedent for thousands of so-called "dead horse claims" in which shady suppliers were paid in full for dying animals, putrid meat, moldy bread, leaky ships, flimsy tents, dangerous weapons and breakaway shoes.

A year later, a congressional committee investigation recommended that the Army's purchasing procedures needed tightening up. It reported: "The government not only sold one day for $17,486 arms which it had agreed the day before to repurchase for $109,912—making it a loss to the United States of $92,426—but virtually furnished the money to pay itself the $17,486 which it received." The committee also ruled that Morgan and Stevens had knowingly conspired to defraud the U.S. government. Despite that, the partners were not prosecuted for the actions.

Did Morgan learn his lesson? You bet. He stopped dealing in weapons. Instead, he spent the rest of the war speculating in gold and currency. At one point in 1863 he and a partner, Edward Ketchum, quietly bought up a large amount of gold and then conspicuously shipped half of it overseas so that the price of their remaining stash went way up. They quickly made a profit of $160,000, but the effect was to suddenly and precipitously devalue the dollar in a time of national crisis. Ketchum later went to jail for other price-fixing schemes, but Morgan continued flying high.

After the war, decrying the "waste" inherent in free enterprise competition, he made it his life's work to stamp out "wasteful' competition wherever he could profitably do so, allowing him to set monopolistic rates he wanted.

Morgan was not the only robber baron of the time. Many of them through the haze of time are now thought of as philanthropists, like John D. Rockefeller and William Vanderbilt, thanks in no small part to the efforts of their P.R. folks at the time.

At the same time, these business lords came up with some business ideology that continues to live on today. One of Rockefeller's philosophical contributions was "Silence is golden" (meaning "no explanation or is apology to the public is necessary"). William Vanderbilt weighed in with an infamously crass flip-off line, "The public be damned!"

A political cartoon depicting the Vanderbilt railroad monopoly

In context, Morgan, believe it or not, was considered a softy to some, despite his famous, "I owe the public nothing" line.

Until his death in 1913, Morgan created powerful monopolies and trusts in the fields of manufacturing, steel and railroads. His spirit, for better or worse, lives on.

Cheers!

What's in This Drink, Anyway?

This one's easy: In Column A, we give you the names of some beverages. In Column B, we give you a list of main ingredients. Match them, and then (if you want) mix them.

1. Gin	a. Licorice & anise
2. Vermouth	b. Juniper berries
3. Rum	c. Honey
4. Whiskey	d. Wormwood
5. Sake	e. Flavored beer
6. Mead	f. Grapes
7. Champagne	g. Coffee
8. Vodka	h. Potatoes
9. Ouzo	i. Cactus
10. Absinthe	j. Barley, rye & corn
11. Kahlua	k. Molasses
12. Tequila	l. Rice
13. Zima	m. Wine with herbs

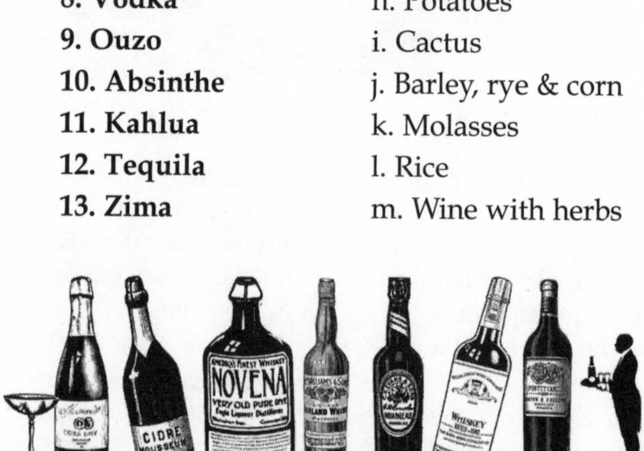

ANSWERS: 1b, 2m, 3k, 4j, 5l, 6c, 7f, 8h, 9a, 10d, 11g, 12i, 13e

The Corpse Eater

A Ghost Tale from Old Japan

In this story, another ancient Japanese legend collected by Lafcadio Hearn in 1903, a wandering priest discovers the horrifying secret of a small village.

Muso Kokushi was a priest of the Zen sect. One day, when he was journeying alone, Muso lost his way in a remote mountain-district. For a long time he wandered helplessly; and he was beginning to despair of finding shelter for the night, when he saw, on the top of a hill lit by the last rays of the sun, one of those little hermitages called anjitsu, which are built for solitary priests. It seemed to be in ruinous condition; but he hastened to it eagerly, and found that it was inhabited by an aged priest, from whom he begged the favor of a night's lodging. This the old man harshly refused; but he directed Muso to a hamlet in a nearby valley where lodging and food could be obtained.

Muso found his way to the hamlet and he was kindly received at the village leader's dwelling. Forty or fifty persons were assembled in the principal apartment, but Muso was shown into a separate room and supplied with food and bedding. Being very tired, he lay down to rest, but a little before midnight he was awakened by loud weeping in the next apartment. Soon, the sliding-screens were gently opened and a young man carrying a lantern respectfully saluted him.

"Reverent sir," he began, "it is my painful duty to tell you that I am now the head of this house. Yesterday I was only the eldest son. But when you came here, tired as you were, we did not wish that you should feel embarrassed in any way: therefore we did not tell you that father had died only a few hours before. The people assembled here are going to another village, about three miles off—for by our custom, we make the proper offerings and prayers, then we leave the corpse alone. No one may remain in this village during the night after a death has taken place, because strange things always happen, so we think that it will be better for you to come away with us. But perhaps, as you are a priest, you have no fear of demons or evil spirits. If so, you will be very welcome to use our poor house. However, I must tell you that nobody, except a priest, would dare to remain here tonight."

Muso responded: "For your kind intention and your generous hospitality I am deeply grateful. But I am sorry that you did not tell me of your father's death when I arrived, so I could have done my duty as a priest before your departure. As it is, I shall perform the service after you have gone away; and I shall stay by the body until morning. I am not afraid of ghosts or demons, so please feel no anxiety on my account."

The young man expressed his gratitude in fitting words. Then the assembled villagers came to thank him, after which the master of the house spoke. "Now, reverent sir, much as we regret to leave you alone, we must bid you farewell. We beg, kind sir, that you will take every care. And if you happen to hear or see anything strange, please tell us when we return in the morning."

All then left the priest, who went to the room where the dead body was lying. The usual offerings had been set before the corpse; and a small lamp was burning. The priest performed the funeral ceremonies, after which he entered into meditation. So meditating he remained through several silent hours. But, when the hush of the night was at its deepest, there noiselessly entered a Shape, vague and vast; and in the same moment Muso found himself without power to move or speak. He watched the Shape lift the corpse, as with hands, and devour it more quickly than a cat devours a rat: beginning at the head, and eating everything—the hair and the bones and even the shroud. And the monstrous Thing, having thus consumed the body, turned to the offerings, and ate them also. Then it went away, as mysteriously as it had come.

When the villagers returned next morning, they found the priest awaiting them at the door of the dwelling. All in turn saluted him; and when they looked about the room, no one expressed any surprise at the disappearance of the corpse and the offerings. "Reverent sir," said the master of the house, "you have probably seen unpleasant things during the night. All of us were anxious about you. But now we are very happy to find you alive and unharmed. Gladly we would have stayed with you, but whenever the village law has been broken, some great misfortune has followed. Whenever it was obeyed, the corpse and the offerings disappear during our absence. Perhaps you have seen the cause."

Then Muso told of the dim and awful Shape that had entered the death-chamber to devour the body. No person seemed to be surprised by his narration; and the master of the house said: "What you have told us, reverent sir, agrees with what has been said about this matter from ancient time."

"Does not the priest on the hill sometimes perform the funeral service for your dead?" asked Muso.

"What priest?" the young man asked.

"The priest who yesterday evening directed me to this village," answered Muso. "I called at his anjitsu on the hill yonder. He refused me lodging, but told me the way here."

The listeners looked at each other in astonishment; and the master of the house said: "Reverent sir, there is no priest and there is no anjitsu on the hill. For the time of many generations there has not been any resident-priest in this neighborhood."

Muso said nothing more on the subject; for it was evident that his kind hosts supposed him to have been deluded by some goblin. But after bidding them farewell, he decided to look again for the hermitage on the hill. He found the anjitsu without any difficulty; and, this time, its aged occupant invited him to enter. When he had done so, the hermit humbly bowed down before him, exclaiming: "Ah! I am very much ashamed! I am exceedingly ashamed!"

"You need not be ashamed for having refused me shelter," said Muso. "You directed me to a village where I was very kindly treated, and I thank you for that favor."

"I can give no man shelter," the recluse said, "and it is not for the refusal that I am ashamed. I am ashamed only that you should have seen me in my real shape—for it was I who devoured the corpse and the offerings last night before your eyes. Know, reverent sir, that I am a jikininki, an eater of human flesh. Have pity upon me, and suffer me to confess the secret fault by which I became reduced to this condition.

"A long, long time ago, I was a priest in this desolate region. There was no other priest for many miles around, so the bodies of the mountain-folk who died were brought here, sometimes from great distances, in order that I might repeat over them the holy service. But I repeated the service and performed the rites only as a matter of business—I thought only of the food and the clothes that my sacred profession enabled me to gain. And because of this selfish impiety I was reborn, immediately after my death, into the state of a jikininki. Since then I have been obliged to feed upon the corpses of the people who die in this district: every one of them I must devour in the way that you saw last night. Now, reverent sir, let me beseech you to perform a cleansing ritual for me: help me by your prayers, I beg you, so that I may escape from this horrible state of existence."

When the hermit uttered this prayer he disappeared; and the hermitage also at the same instant. And Muso Kokushi found himself kneeling alone in the high grass, beside an ancient and moss-grown tomb, which seemed to be that of a priest. ℭ

MARK TWAIN WRITES TO THE GAS COMPANY

Hartfield, February 12, 1891

Dear Sirs;

Some day you will move me almost to the verge of irritation by your chuckle-headed God-damned fashion of shutting your Goddamned gas off without givng any notice to your Goddamned parishioners. Several times you have come within an ace of smothering half of this household in their beds and blowing up the other half by this idiotic, not to say criminal, custom of yours. And it has happened again to-day. Haven't you a telephone?

Yours,
S. L. Clemens

Stately Knowledge

12 Reasons Why Ya Gotta Love Washington

Who needs more reasons to love the state of Washington? Well, in case you do, here are a dozen of our favorites.

1 Our favorite Washingtonian? Roxann Rose of Pullman, Washington, who used a hula hoop for 90 hours in a marathon display of stamina on April 2–6, 1987.

2 Or, if you prefer, businessman and pilot Kenneth Arnold, who said he was flying a small plane over Washington's Cascade Mountains and saw nine circular objects flying in formation at hyper-fast speed. He told reporters that the mysterious objects "flew like a saucer would if you skipped it across water." The reporters reported that Arnold had seen "flying saucers" and the name stuck.

3 Here's a place you might not want to stay. Kitsap County, Washington, was originally called Slaughter County, and the first hotel there was called the Slaughter House. Another place to avoid? Quillayute, Washington. It's the wettest city in the United States.

4 Washington is the only state to be named after a president. When the state was being considered for statehood, the people wanted to name it "Columbia." However, the United States Congress was afraid there'd be confusion with the new District of Columbia,

so they made them change it to Washington. Only one problem, the District of Columbia became more popularly known as Washington D.C., so the state was *still* confused with the District. They would've done better sticking with Columbia.

5 You thought it was just apples and cherries? Heck no! Washington also leads the nation in producing red raspberries, spearmint oil, dry peas, lentils, pears and hops—the stuff that beer's made from.

Ice-cream, hoops, and hops. It's a Washington thing.

6 King County, Washington, was originally named after William R. King, who was Franklin Pierce's vice president. In 1986, it was named King County *again*. The only difference was that this time, the name honored Martin Luther King, Jr.

7 The longest floating bridge in the world is the Evergreen Point Bridge, connecting Seattle and Medina across Lake Washington.

8 Firsts and oldest: Not only does Seattle hold the title of the first city to open a revolving restaurant (the Space Needle), but Olympia boasts the Dairy Queen that was the site of the first soft-serve ice cream machine ever. And Zillah, Washington, has the oldest still-operating gas station.

9 Father's Day was originated by Sonora Louise Smart Dodd, a woman with too many names who hailed from Spokane, Washington. It was first celebrated on June 19, 1910.

10 Under the Aurora Bridge in Seattle lives a troll. Well, not a real one, but huge one created out of concrete by four Seattle artists.

11 Next stop, the corner of Bing and Maraschino! There's a city named George, Washington. That's funny enough, but another odd thing is that it has streets named after all the different kinds of cherries.

12 Washington is the smallest state west of the Mississippi River, but it's larger than any state east of the Mississippi River.

Tricky Dick

The Lowdown on Richard Nixon

Richard Milhous Nixon, the 37th President of the United States, was the second president to seriously risk impeachment and the first to actually resign from office.

• Richard Nixon was a mass of contradictions: He was raised a pacifist Quaker, yet became the U.S. president who ordered more bombs dropped than any man in history. He made a career out of the fear of communism, yet was the first to try rapprochement with China. He hated how he appeared on TV, yet, apparently, won because of it. He managed to get re-elected in 1972 by a landslide, yet before his death he was rated among the least popular politicians in recent history.

• His earliest memory was falling out of a horse-driven buggy that his mother was driving, splitting his scalp in a long cut. From that point until his death he combed his hair straight back to hide the scar, even "when the vogue of parting hair on the left side came along," he said regretfully in a later interview.

• In first grade, his mother made a point of telling his teacher, "Never call him Dick—I named him Richard." Every day he wore a freshly starched white shirt with a black bow tie and knee pants, and his teacher was quoted as saying later that she could not remember him ever getting dirty. He took great pains in brushing his teeth, and before he left for school asked his mother to smell his breath to make sure he would not offend anyone on the bus. He didn't like to ride the school bus, saying the other children smelled bad.

• He was a very solemn child who rarely ever smiled, and nobody can recall him ever really laughing. When the older boys made fun of him, Nixon cried bitterly. "I was the biggest crybaby in Yorba Linda," he admitted decades later. "My dad could hear me even with the tractor running."

• He was uncoordinated, and too small for football, but his father wanted him to play so that nobody would think Richard effeminate.

• For three summers Richard was a barker at the local fair. He was quite good at it.

• His father lent him the money for his years at law school, but Richard had to pay back every penny. At school, Nixon lead a monastic life in an abandoned tool shed in a heavily wooded area near the campus. It was an eight-by-twelve-foot shed, lined with corrugated cardboard for warmth. He did not date any girls for the entire three years. His nickname was "Gloomy Gus."

• In a foreshadowing of his future, he once broke into the dean's office to get an advance look at the grades.

• After he graduated and passed the bar exam, he bungled his first court case in a way that looked as if he were unethically trying to gain a financial advantage. The case wound up costing the firm $4,800 in an out-of-court settlement. In the course of the proceedings, he was threatened with disbarment by a judge, who said, "Mr. Nixon, I have serious doubts whether you have the ethical qualifications to practice law in the state of California. I am seriously thinking of turning this matter over to the Bar Association." Nixon thought of abandoning the United States and setting up a law practice in Havana, Cuba. He traveled there to check out the possibilities before World War II interrupted his law career.

• After the war, Nixon attempted to pass himself off as a veteran who had seen actual combat while stationed on Green Island in the Pacific. There's more data available on Nixon's poker playing—he made a great deal of money—than on any other single aspect of his war experience. Nixon also opened "Nixon's Snack Shack" near the airstrip, where SCAT pilots and their crews were able to get basic food, munchies and liquor.

• After the war, he considered going back to practicing law. Instead, he decided to become a politician. Through a series of outrageous, mean-spirited, but brilliantly opportunistic campaigns, he made a successful career of accusing opponents of being communists. He rose quickly in California politics and ended up in the House of Representatives, where he served on the House UnAmerican Activities Committee—a red-hunting group of dangerous buffoons, including proudly anti-Semitic John Rankin of Mississippi and John Wood, an active member of the Ku Klux Klan. "It was," said George Reedy, covering the committee for United Press, "the worst collection of people that have ever been assembled in the entire history of American politics." With publicity from this job, during an era of anti-communist hysteria, Nixon was soon elected to the Senate in time to make a name for himself on Joseph McCarthy's witch-hunts, and then became the premiere candidate for vice president, placating the extreme right wing which was unhappy with comparatively moderate Dwight Eisenhower.

• Long before Watergate, Nixon counseled a friend,

"You don't know how to lie. If you can't lie, you'll never go anywhere."

• Truman called Nixon "a shifty-eyed goddamn liar." Nixon was for the war in Korea, until it became unpopular. Then he blamed Truman for incurring American casualties.

• In 1958, Nixon traveled to Hong Kong and met Marianna Liu, a tour guide. They became inseparable and there were rumors of an affair—rumors that eventually ended up in J. Edgar Hoover's personal files. It became one of the bits of information that Hoover later used to keep his job when Nixon was threatening to replace him.

• Nixon had a terrible temper and a salty vocabulary, which he almost always succeeded in keeping under control in public. Once though, during the 1960 campaign, he was sitting in the back seat behind his aide, Air Force Maj. Don Hughes, during a long car ride between cities. Frustrated and impatient, Nixon suddenly went into a tantrum, swearing and repeatedly kicking the back of Hughes's seat with both feet, refusing to stop. Hughes had the car stopped and got out to walk until aides got Nixon quieted down again.

• After a meeting with a group of young college editors at Cornell University who had thrown some tough questions at him, he screamed at his aide, Ted Rogers, "You son of a bitch, you tried to destroy me in front of thirty million people!"

• After losing the 1962 race for California governor and telling the press that they "won't have Nixon to kick around any more," he joined the firm of Mudge, Stern, Baldwin and Todd and signed on Pepsi, long a backer of GOP causes.

• A "new Nixon" came back in 1968 and got elected to the presidency.

• Nixon was a bit strange, even before the pressures of the Watergate investigations reportedly drove him near to the brink of paranoia and insanity. He instructed the members of the White House staff not to talk to him or to his wife, even when greeted by them. He would not let the *Washington Post* be delivered to his home, so his teenage daughters wouldn't see the political cartoons about him.

• Nixon's brother, Donald, was suspected to have had shady business dealings. Because journalist Tom Braden questioned Donald's practices, Nixon had Braden audited by the IRS every year he was in the White House. To avoid further embarrassments, though, Nixon put Donald under surveillance. There was evidence that the Watergate break-in was an attempt to find out what the Democrats knew about his brother's questionable business dealings.

• Nixon authorized secret investigations into the habits of his political rivals and others on his "enemies list." He ordered surveillance on Edward Kennedy, telling his chief of staff Bob Haldeman, "Catch him in the sack with one of his babes." However, when his own conduct was questioned, he answered indignantly, "A candidate's personal life and that of his family are not fair subjects for discussion unless they somehow bear directly on his qualifications for office."

How They Work

Hidden Stories Behind Gadgets We Love

From DVDs to inkjet printers, there's an explanation behind everything, as Brian Marshall tells us in this piece.

HOW DOES A CD PLAY MUSIC?

The "groove" on a compact disc isn't really a groove, but a path of microscopic bumps stretched over a 3 mile path. The bumps reflect light from a laser beam differently than the flat parts do, shining back into a sensor that interprets the flashing reflections as shining either "on" or "off." The electronics of your CD player interpret these signals as either a 1 or a 0, and come up with a number that reflects a fragment of wavelength that takes up 1/44,100 of a second of music.

A CD player varies its speed as it plays, so that the speed of the bumps below stays constant. Beginning at the disc's inside groove, the CD spins at 500 revolutions per minute (RPM) and gradually slows to 200 RPM as the laser beam approaches the outside edge.

HOW DO THEY GET MORE ON A DVD THAN ON A CD?

Part of the solution was making the data bumps smaller and jamming them closer together, making the "groove" of a DVD 7.5 miles long, more than twice what you get on a CD. But wait, there's more. The designers managed to double that capacity to 15 miles per side, because the DVD uses a sandwich of two different levels of

bumps. Like a CD, the DVD has a reflective aluminum base behind the inner layer. However, on top of that is a semi-reflective gold layer, also containing data bumps. The result is that the laser can read the top layer of bumps, then shine through it and read the inner layer, too. The cumulative effect is that a typical DVD stores 7.5 gigabytes of information.

HOW DOES A GPS FIGURE OUT WHERE YOU ARE?

A Global Positioning System (GPS) receiver is a pretty cool little gadget. There are 24 GPS satellites orbiting the Earth, so that wherever you are in the world, your GPS receiver can pick up at least four of them. A cluster of three satellites is the bare minimum for locating your latitude and longitude, but if you also want to know your altitude, you need a fourth one as well.

Each satellite broadcasts an identifying signal and a timing code that allows your GPS to measure the time it took the signal to get there, and thereby figure out how far away the satellite is. By comparing the distance from several satellites, your GPS can tell exactly where you are (give or take a few feet).

HOW DO INKJET PRINTERS SPRAY LETTERS SO PRECISELY?

Have you ever noticed that when bubbles pop, a little of the liquid gets propelled outward? Sure you have—think of the misty feeling you get when you put your nose up to ginger ale.

Popping bubbles inspired the inkjet printer. Its designers wanted to be able to propel microscopic dots of ink quickly and accurately onto a piece of paper without actually touching it. A tiny amount of ink waits inside each nozzle, and as the print head jerks quickly along the page (so quickly that it seems like a continuous motion), jolts of electricity heat up a resistor in the nozzle. This heat instantaneously boils the ink, vaporizing it into a bubble and launching ink from the print head to dot neatly onto the surface of the paper. How small are these neat little splatters? A bubble jet print head typically has 300 to 600 microscopic nozzles that fire ink simultaneously onto the page. It can take dozens of them, precisely fired, to make up a single letter on the page.

HOW ABOUT A LASER PRINTER?

Inside the printer is a large metal roller (called the "photoreceptive drum"). As it rotates past an electrified wire ("the corona"), the surface of the drum gets a positive electrical charge.

Next, the computer guides a laser beam that scans text and images onto the photoreceptive drum. Metal hit by the laser gets a negative electrical charge. The toner powder, a mix of positively charged plastic and pigment dust, sticks to the parts of the drum zapped by the laser, but is repelled from the parts of the drum that carry the negatively charged image, so that the drum looks like a mirror image of the page being printed.

But not for long, because the drum immediately makes contact with the paper. An electric wire under the paper (the "transfer release corona") zaps the paper with negative electricity, which pulls the powdery pattern off the roller and onto the page.

The ink, held by gravity, gets melted onto the paper with the "fuser," a pair of hot metal rollers. Which is why laser-printed paper comes out toasty warm.

WHY DOES A MICROWAVE OVEN HEAT FOOD, BUT NOT PLASTIC?

Microwaves are radio waves that have a very high frequency, which makes them very short (that's why the *micro* is in microwave). On your radio dial, you'd hear your microwave oven broadcasting at 2500 megahertz, if your radio dial actually went that high. (It doesn't—108 megahertz is the highest a standard radio picks up.) Microwaves have a powerful effect on water molecules, twisting them back and forth rapidly. As they rub against each other, the molecules heat up rapidly from the friction. Luckily, nearly all foods have at least a little moisture in them—otherwise they wouldn't heat up. Which explains why the plastic doesn't heat up, while the frozen lasagna does.

Judged by Its Cover

A Bookshelf Full of Strange Books

Can you tell a book by its title? If so, these have got to be some of the most fascinating books on the shelves, indeed. Gleaned from *Bizarre Books* by Russell Ash and Brian Lake (St. Martin's, 1985).

Queer Shipmates—Archibald Bruce Campbell (1962)
The Gay Boys of Old Yale!—John Denison Vose (1869)
The History of the Self-Winding Watch (1770–1931)—Alfred Chapuis & Eugene Jaquet (1952)
The Ups & Downs of Lady Di—Annette Lyster (1907)
Scouts in Bondage—Geoffrey Prout (1930)
The Onion Maggot—Arthur L. Lovett (1923)
Harnessing the Earthworm—Thomas J. Barrett (1949)
100 Proofs That the Earth Is Not a Globe!—W. Carpenter (1871)
How to Abandon Ship—Phil Richards & John Banigan (1942)
Manhole Covers of Los Angeles—Robert & Mimi Melnick (1974)
A Toddler's Guide to the Rubber Industry—D. Lowe (1947)
Who's Who in Cocker Spaniels—Marion Mangrum (1944)
Cool It or Lose It: Dale Evans Rogers Raps with Youth—Dale Evans Rogers (1971)
Constipation & Our Civilization—James C. Thomson (1943)
Animals as Criminals—J. Brand (1896)
Swine Judging for Beginners—Joel Simmons Coffey (1915)
The Romance of Proctology—Charles Elton Blanchard (1938)
How to Be Plump—Thomas Cation Duncan (1878)
!!!—George H. Hepworth (1881)

Whitewash

How Colgate's Blackface Turned Red

Here's an embarrassing bit of Colgate history the company would rather just forget.

DARLIE TOOTHPASTE is a popular brand in much of Asia. Its dark secret is that it used to be called Darkie, complete with a stereotyped logo of a minstrel man. Apparently the company's founder had come to the United States in the 1920s and seen Al Jolson in his blackface show, and had been impressed with how white Jolson's teeth looked.

Stereotypes of this sort were not unusual before World War II. What was unusual about Darkie was that its racist name and logo were still intact in 1985, when Colgate bought the brand from Hong Kong's Hawley & Hazel Chemical Company.

Here's where the story gets a little twisted. According to Alecia Swasy in her book *Soap Opera,* Colgate's arch-rival Procter & Gamble learned about the sale and immediately went to work to use it to their advantage. Both companies were releasing a tartar-control formula that year, and P&G was happy to have the opportunity to portray its rival as racist. It hired a public relations firm to surreptitiously slip information to activists and newspapers about Colgate's disreputable Asian brand.

The strategy worked. There was a storm of uproar: stories and editorials in major newspapers, threats of boycotts and even Eddie Murphy expressing his outrage on David Letterman. Colgate was unfairly attacked for a brand it had just purchased; however, the attacks became more and more justified as the toothpaste giant dragged its feet on changing the brand, fearing a loss of business. Finally, nearly four years later,

Before and After shots

it announced that it was changing the name to Darlie and making the man on the package an abstraction of indeterminate race.

The name change placated Western critics, who pointed out that the toothpaste actually sold better after the name change. What they didn't know, and apparently still don't, is that only the English was changed. The Cantonese name ("Haak Yahn Nga Gou") stayed the same, and the Chinese-language ads reassured users that, despite a cosmetic change to placate those inscrutable Westerners, "Black Man Toothpaste is still Black Man Toothpaste."

WHAT'S IN A NAME?

One of the nice things about the toothpaste industry is that there are still some local brands out there, despite the best efforts of Colgate, Lever and Procter & Gamble to make every country dance to the tune of Crest and Pepsodent.

The healthiest indigenous industry seems to be in Asia. Shanghai Toothpaste Company is one such manufacturer. Besides a brand called Evafresh, they've got White Jade ("Your teeth will be health and no usual oral disease can occur....It does no harm to animal, it for smok-

ers quite well") and Bulb Poll brand for children ("With fresh melon flavour...brushing teeth would be of interest for children and they can easily get into good habits"). The significance of the names? Nobody seems to know. Supirivicky brand, an herbal toothpaste developed in Ceylon, promises to relieve "obnoxious odours, spongy gums, cough, vomiting, gripe,

colic, and paralysis of tounge." (Original spelling left intact.)

Heibao toothpaste from Hong Kong goes several steps beyond that. For a mere $96 per tube, Heibao promises an even more profound rejuvenation: "You will find your hair loss to be reduced by up to 90%. You will look younger, move younger and feel younger TEN to FIFTEEN years back because your hair becomes darker (as your good old days) and thicker and most important of all, your organic systems will function at their best!...Suitable for all ages, sex and race without any bad side effect."

Pasta Medicinal Couto is "a completely natural toothpaste" from Portugal. However, given the historical record of completely natural toothpastes from Portugal (see page 77), we're a little cautious, despite the company's assurance that this one is made from plant extracts.

Other brands of note include Pooneh and Nassim from Iran, Babool and Karma from India, and Vademecuum from Sweden. None of these are particularly weird, but we like the names.

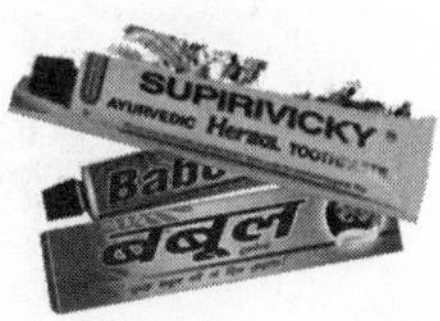

Finally, coming full circle back to the purely tasteless, Taiwan has a brand that's a real winner called White Men Toothpaste.

OTHER FISH IN THE SEA

"Bill's Best Places," a personal Web site, that critiques "Bill's" favorite places to visit, reports as follows:

> **There you are, in the South Pacific, diving in sandy-bottomed, coral-ringed waters, just off the island nation of Fiji. The water is teeming with life—some of it benign, some of it deadly, all of it beautiful. You head for a tiny crevice where a pair of cleaner shrimp live and you dive down for a closer look. You remove your mouthpiece and open your mouth wide. A shrimp spies your pearly teeth and comes over for a closer look. You hold still. It pokes and prods between them, expertly**

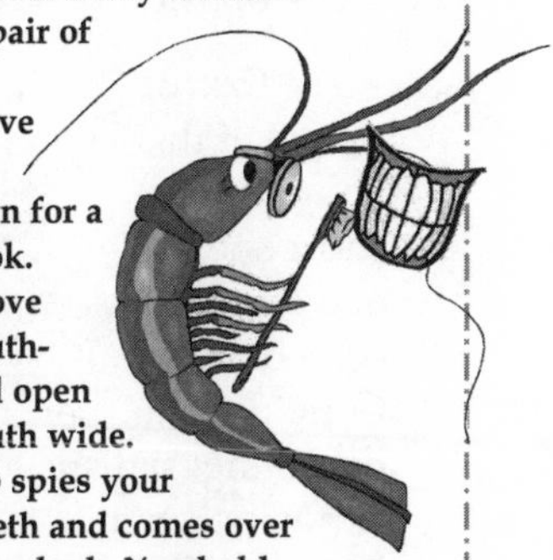

removing bits of food and plaque. This is no joke—you really can find shrimp that will clean your teeth, on the ship, Nai'a in Fiji....

D.D.S. ON 35MM

They're only there to help you keep your gums and teeth healthy, but dentists don't get much respect in movies—they're portrayed, often as not, as sadists and sometimes worse (nitrous oxide abusers, unrepentant Nazis, that sort of thing). We'll show you what we mean:

• *Little Shop of Horrors* (1960, musical; 1986, movie): Dentist as drug-abusing, woman-abusing, laughing gas sniffer who deserves to be fed to a large mutant carnivorous plant. In the movie, the dentist was played by a maniacal Steve Martin.

• *The Dentist* (1932): The first movie of this name was a short one, and featured comedian W. C. fields as a bumbling, sadistic tooth extractor. (Available in a collection of five short features called *A Fifth of Fields.*)

• *The Dentist* (1996): A campy horror film in which a deranged dentist goes on a drilling spree.

• *The Marathon Man* (1976): Sadistic Nazi dentist drills excruciatingly through Dustin Hoffman's front tooth.

• *Eversmile, New Jersey* (1989): This one is unusual—about a wacky traveling dentist who preaches the benefits of dental health. ☾

Oral Advice

Dentists are now recommending this brushing method, to be used after flossing: Place the toothbrush at the gums at a 45-degree angle. Brush down and away to remove plaque from gum and tooth. Brush each tooth individually, inside and out, then brush chewing surfaces horizontally.

But be aware. Two out of three people brush too hard, says Dr. Trucia Drommond of Chicago, causing damage to gums and teeth. His prescription? Soft bristles, a loose grip between thumb and forefinger, just a smidgen of toothpaste and 2–5 minutes of oh-so-gentle caressing instead of 1 minute of scrubbing.

Modern Myth

"Spontaneous Human Combustion"

For centuries, people have marveled at mysterious stories of victims apparently going up in flame with nothing else burning in the room. We hate to ruin a good story, but...

SPONTANEOUS COMBUSTION stories of people mysteriously going up in flames have appeared in legend, fiction and even Temperance tracts. Novelist Frederick Marryat in *Jacob Faithful* (1834) wrote about a character's disreputable mother who "perished in that very peculiar and dreadful manner, which does sometimes occur to those who indulge in an immoderate use of spirituous liquors.... She perished from what is termed spontaneous combustion, an inflammation of the gases generated from the spirits absorbed into the system."

Herman Melville recounted an incident in *Redburn* (1849) in which a drunken sailor spontaneously combusts in front of his shipmates. And in *Bleak House* (1853) Charles Dickens wrote a gruesome description of drunkard Mr. Krook's fiery demise:

Mr. Krook's fiery demise in *Bleak House*

> **"There is a smouldering, suffocating, vapour in the room and a dark, greasy coating on the walls and ceiling....Here is a small burnt patch of flooring; here is the tinder from a little bundle of burnt paper, but not so light as usual, seeming to be steeped in something; and here is—is it a charred log of wood**

sprinkled with white ashes, or is it coal? Oh, horror, he is here! Call the death by any name, it is inborn, inbred, engendered in the corrupted humours of the vicious body itself—Spontaneous Combustion."

Most 19th-century stories blamed alcohol in the body for a victim going up in flames. (Not surprisingly, the Temperance movement also often played up this angle in its literature.) Strangely enough, that's a recurring theme in more modern stories as well. Purported victims of spontaneous combustion are typically heavy drinkers (or sedative users), smokers, overweight, and elderly. They're found thoroughly burned, sometimes with a part of their body—for example, a foot or hand—strangely unscathed. Oftentimes nearby furnishings remain unburnt, and a peculiar greasy soot covers walls and ceiling.

Scientists have looked into the phenomenon, and have found that abusers of alcohol, tobacco and other drugs are disproportionately victims of the phenomenon. But not for the reasons that 19th-century chroniclers put forth.

One scientist dressed dead pigs in night clothes and placed them in chairs, beds and couches. He managed to replicate the effect, common to most "spontaneous combustion" stories, of burning with a hot, greasy fire that consumed flesh and bones without burning nearby combustibles.

Another scientist went through 200 mysterious cases and did not find one that couldn't be explained by more likely causes. Here's what he found in common for a large number of the cases: A smoker alone at home becomes unconscious from alcohol, sleeping pills, or a heart attack, and drops a cigarette. It begins smoldering in the smoker's clothes and eventually starts them on fire. The fat of the person, deeply unconscious, begins melting and gets wicked into the clothes like wax from a candle. This wicking keeps the clothes from burning away, yet burns with a continuous, smoky flame. Like a candle, the flame is contained and controlled. The heat flows upward toward the ceiling, covering it with a greasy soot, but keeping the flame from spreading.

So, the good news is that research shows no evidence that "spontaneous human combustion" has ever really happened. If you're afraid of ending your life in that way, you can stop worrying... and instead strive to lose weight, drink in moderation and avoid smoking. €

Mascot Miracles

How the Bunny Saved Energizer's Battery

He's a shades-wearing, drum-beating, hot pink cultural icon that almost never was. Here's his story.

Did you know that the Eveready battery line is the oldest in existence? In 1896, the National Carbon Company produced the first commercially marketed dry-cell battery. Two years later, the American Electric Novelty and Manufacturing Corporation produced a novelty flashlight and called it the "Eveready." When the two companies merged and became the Union Carbide Corporation, it decided to expand the Eveready name to the battery line as well.

Years later, Union Carbide decided to market a line of alkaline batteries. They decided that the alkalines needed to be differentiated from their line of normal batteries, so they downplayed the Eveready name and came up with a new one, the "Energizer." But Union Carbide's advertising was uninspired, bordering on awful: In one ad, tough-guy actor Robert Conrad dared us to commit assault on a battery by knocking it off his shoulder; in another, Olympic star Mary Lou Retton compared her high-energy routines to high-energy Energizers.

FROM BAD TO WORSE

In 1986, cereal and pet food company Ralston-Purina bought the Eveready line from Union Carbide. Ralston had a good reputation for marketing its products well. On the other hand, it never tried to sell a battery before. It made a huge mistake.

Its name was Jacko. Mark "Jacko" Jackson, to be exact—a wildly popular Australian Rules Football player. If the ads with Conrad and Retton were mediocre, though, Jacko's were horrible. Even though his commercials were a big hit Down Under, Americans found him loud and uncouth; he grated on everybody's nerves. The company received a dozen hate letters a day. Sales started dropping. Eveready stuck with Jacko for a year, even ludicrously trying to soften his obnoxious image with a sweater and easy chair, but it was a disaster.

Meanwhile, Duracell started a line of commercials that implied that its alkaline batteries lasted longer than those of its main competitor, Eveready. A viewer had to pay close attention to understand that the ads were comparing Duracell with Eveready's "ordinary" (carbon-zinc) batteries, not its alkalines. The commercials featured a group of battery-operated toys, each of them grinding to a stop until only the Duracell toy was still running.

The Energizer Bunny

WHEN OPPORTUNITY KNOCKS

Energizer decided to hit back. Their ad agency, D. D. B. Needham, set up a battalion of stupid-looking mechanical bunnies playing cymbals, looking similar to those in the Duracell ads. But the demonstration was interrupted by the ultra-cool pink Energizer Bunny wearing shades and playing a marching-band bass drum. The voice-over complained that Duracell had "never even invited us to your party."

It was an attention-getting spot, but what to do next resulted in "creative differences" between the agency and client. "We said, 'We think there's a campaign idea here. Let's do more of these,'" Eveready CEO J. Patrick Mulcahy told *Advertising*

Age. "But Needham said, 'We don't think so. We don't think we can campaign this out. We think it's a one-shot deal, a limited tactical vehicle. We should put it on the air for a while and then go back to something else.'"

The client, of course, is always right. Eveready went shopping for a new agency. In February 1989, they found Chiat/Day/Mojo, which came up with the electrifying jolt Eveready was looking for. "We kind of started the way we always do, by saying 'Let's assume people don't like advertising, and they have the means to zap us with their remote control,'" said C/D/M vice president Dick Sittig in an interview in *AdWeek*. "Given that, what are you going to do to grab people's attention for 30 seconds? We decided that since the battery business is kind of a low interest category, we'd have to do something pretty out there to get people's attention. The main idea is 'How do you demonstrate long-lasting batteries?' Our notion was that you couldn't do it in just one thirty-second spot, so that's where we came up with our idea."

Keeps going...

SERIAL BUNNY STRIKES AGAIN, AND AGAIN, AND AGAIN....

C/D/M decided to begin with the spot that Needham had done, but with a different ending. In the new commercial, the bunny runs amok and escapes from the studio. "It was just a simple idea based around the fact that the Energizer keeps going and going," said C/D/M CEO Bob Kuperman. "So it became the unstoppable bunny. And we thought not only will it escape from the commercial that we had done for it, but it would continue going through other commercials for other products. From there we decided to actually use the other commercial forms that we've all grown up with. The key was to make them believable and have people immediately see them as part of the real world of commercials. It had to be instantly recognizable as a coffee or nasal spray commercial."

The agency did extensive research on different types of

...and going...

commercials in order to stay true to the genre of each. Staff members found the components of each type of commercial that made them unique and distinctive: a certain editing rhythm, type of actor, copy and delivery style, lighting, film vs. video and so on. The hard part for the directors, they discovered, was trying to exactly emulate the style they were making fun of and not add any of their own individual stylistic flourishes.

A SMASHING SUCCESS

The cleverness of the approach got a lot of positive attention from the press and the people sitting on their couches. And there was another element as well: "People would rather not see those commercials anyway," said Sittig. "That's what makes the bunny a hero. If he interrupts your favorite commercial, you don't like him. But if he interrupts something you don't like, he's a hero."

HOP, HOP, AND AWAY!

The Energizer Bunny has another claim to fame. He's the tallest hot air balloon in the world, the company claims. The Energizer "Hot Hare Balloon" is 15 feet taller than the Statue of Liberty.

So what, exactly, are his other measurements?

- **Ears.** The Hot Hare's ears are about the size of the average hot air balloon, which equals the height of one of the presidents' faces on Mt. Rushmore.
- **Glasses.** A bunny this cool demands a monstrously cool set of glasses. This pair measures 32 feet across.
- **Drum.** His drum's about 45 feet in diameter, and 20 feet wide.
- **Nose.** His shnoz is 16 feet wide.
- **Tail.** His tail measures 20 feet across.
- **Shoe Size.** This Hot Hare wears a 98 EEEEE shoe size.

The company says he's so big, 550,000,000 double-A batteries could fit inside. On the outside, he took 5,000 yards of 60-foot-wide material, and 84 miles of thread. ☾

...and going...

Triumph of the Egg

A Tale Both Hardboiled & Scrambled

Eggs embodied the dreams of a family...and end up being its downfall in this funny yet touching story by Sherwood Anderson, author of *Winesburg, Ohio.*

MY FATHER WAS, I am sure, intended by nature to be a cheerful, kindly man. Until he was 34 years old he worked as a farmhand near Bidwell, Ohio. He on Saturday evenings drove into town to spend a few hours in social intercourse with other farmhands. Songs were sung and glasses thumped on the bar. At ten o'clock father drove home and went to bed, quite happy in his position in life. He had at that time no notion of trying to rise in the world.

It was in the spring of his thirty-fifth year that father married my mother, then a country schoolteacher, and in the following spring I came wriggling and crying into the world. Something happened to the two people. The American passion for getting up in the world took possession of them.

It may have been that mother was responsible. Being a schoolteacher she had no doubt read of how Garfield, Lincoln, and other Americans rose from poverty to greatness, and dreamed that I would someday rule men and cities. She induced father to give up his place as a farmhand and embark on an independent enterprise of his own. For herself she wanted nothing. For father and myself she was incurably ambitious.

The first venture turned out badly. They rented ten acres of poor stony land and launched into chicken raising. I grew into boyhood on the place and got my first impressions of life there. If I am a

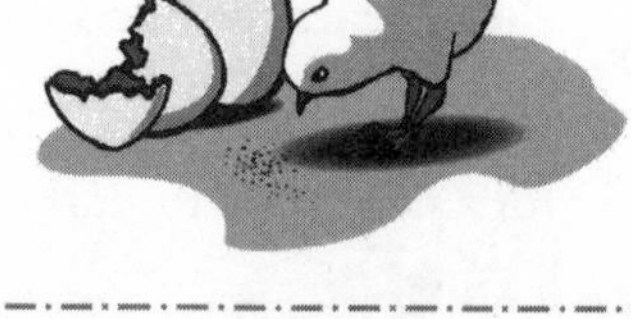

gloomy man inclined to see the darker side of life, I attribute it to the fact that what should have been for me the happy joyous days of childhood were spent on a chicken farm.

One unversed in such matters can have no notion of the many and tragic things that can happen to a chicken. It is born out of an egg, lives for a few weeks as a tiny fluffy thing such as you see on Easter cards, then becomes hideously naked, eats quantities of corn and meal bought by the sweat of your father's brow, gets diseases called pip, cholera, and other names, stands looking with stupid eyes at the sun, becomes sick, and dies. It is all unbelievably complex. Most philosophers must have been raised on chicken farms. One hopes for so much from a chicken and is so dreadfully disillusioned. Vermin infest their youth, and fortunes must be spent for curative powders.

In later life I have seen literature on the subject of fortunes to be made out of the raising of chickens. Do not be led astray by it. Go hunt for gold on the frozen hills of Alaska, put your faith in the honesty of a politician, believe if you will that the world is daily growing better and that good will triumph over evil, but do not believe the literature concerning the hen.

For ten years my father and mother struggled to make our chicken farm pay and then they gave up that struggle and began another. They embarked in the restaurant business. Packing our belongings on a wagon, we drove a tiny caravan of hope looking for a new place to start on our upward journey through life.

Father rode on top of the wagon. He was then a bald-headed man of 45, a little fat and from long association with mother and the chickens he had become habitually silent and discouraged. Mother and I walked the entire eight miles—she to be sure that nothing fell from the wagon and I to see the wonders of the world. On the seat of the wagon beside father was his greatest treasure. I will tell you of that.

Where thousands of chickens come out of eggs, surprising things sometimes happen. The accident does not often occur—perhaps once in a thousand births. A chicken is born that has four legs, two pairs of wings, two heads or what not. They go quickly back to the hand of their Maker. The fact that the poor little things could not live was one of the tragedies of life to father. He had some notion that if he could but bring into henhood or roosterhood a five-legged hen or a two-headed rooster his fortune would be made. He dreamed of taking the wonder to county fairs and of growing rich by exhibiting it.

At any rate he saved all the little monstrous things, preserved in alcohol in its own glass bottle. These he carried on the wagon seat beside him. All during our days as keepers of a restaurant, the grotesques in their little glass bottles would sit on a shelf back of the counter. Mother sometimes protested but father was a rock on the subject of his treasure. The grotesques were, he declared, valuable. People, he said, liked to look at strange and wonderful things.

Pickleville once had a cider mill and pickle factory near its railroad station, but both had gone out of business. The restaurant business was mother's idea. Buses came down to the station from the hotel on the main street of Bidwell. Traveling men, she said, would be waiting around to take trains out of town and town people would come to await incoming trains. They would come to the restaurant to buy pie and coffee.

I went to school in the town and was glad to be away from the presence of discouraged, sad-looking chickens. Still I was not very joyous.

Mother decided that our restaurant should remain open at night. At ten in the evening a passenger train went north past our door followed by a local freight. The freight crew came to our restaurant for hot coffee and food. In the morning at four they

returned. A little trade began to grow up. Mother slept at night and during the day tended the restaurant while father slept. While mother and I slept, father cooked meats that were to go into sandwiches for the lunch baskets of our boarders.

Then an idea in regard to getting up in the world came into his head. The American spirit took hold of him. He became ambitious.

In the long nights when there was little to do father had time to think. That was his undoing. He decided that he had in the past been an unsuccessful man because he had not been cheerful enough and that in the future he would adopt a cheerful outlook on life. In the early morning he came upstairs and got into bed with mother. She woke and the two talked. From my bed in the corner I listened.

It was father's idea that both he and mother should try to entertain the people who came to eat at our restaurant. When young people from the town of Bidwell came into our place, as on very rare occasions they did, bright entertaining conversation was to be made. It was father's notion that a passion for the company of himself and mother would spring up in the breasts of the younger people of Bidwell. In the evening bright happy groups would come singing with joy and laughter into our place.

For weeks this notion of father's invaded our house. We in our daily lives tried earnestly to make smiles take the place of glum looks. Mother smiled at the boarders and I, catching the infection, smiled at our cat. Father became feverish in his anxiety to please. He did not waste his ammunition on the railroad men but seemed to be waiting for a young man or woman from Bidwell to come in to show what he could do.

On the counter was a basket filled with eggs, and there was something pre-natal about the way eggs kept themselves connected with the development of his idea. At any rate an egg ruined his new impulse in life.

Late one night I was awakened by a roar of anger. Both mother and I sat upright in our beds. Downstairs the door of our restaurant shut with a bang and in a few minutes father tramped up the stairs. He held an egg and there was a half-insane light in his eyes. As he stood glaring I was sure he intended throwing the egg at either mother or me. Then he laid it gently on the table and dropped on his knees beside mother's bed. He began to cry like a boy and I, carried away by his grief, cried with him. It is ridiculous, but I can remember only that mother's hand continually stroked the bald path that ran across the top of his head.

As to what happened downstairs, I know the story as well as if I had been a witness to my father's discomfiture. On that evening young Joe Kane, son of a merchant of Bidwell, came to Pickleville to meet his father, who was expected on the ten o'clock evening train from the south. The train was three hours late and Joe came into our place to loaf about and to wait for its arrival, alone in the restaurant with father.

From the moment he came into our place the young man must have been puzzled by my father's actions. It was his notion that father was angry at him for hanging around. He thought of going out. However, it began to rain and he did not fancy the long walk to town and back. He bought a five-cent cigar and ordered a cup of coffee. He had a newspaper in his pocket and took it out and began to read. "I'm waiting for the evening train. It's late," he said apologetically.

For a long time father remained silently gazing at his visitor. He was no doubt suffering from an attack of stage fright. As so often happens in life he had thought so often of the situation that now confronted him that he was somewhat nervous in its presence. For one thing, he did not know what to do with his hands. He thrust one of them nervously over the counter and shook hands with Joe Kane. "Howde-do," he said. Joe Kane put his newspaper down and stared at him. Father's eye lighted on the basket of eggs that sat on the counter and he began to talk. "Well," he began hesitatingly, "you have heard of Christopher Columbus, eh?" He seemed to be angry. "That Columbus was a cheat," he declared emphatically. "He talked of making an egg stand on its end, then he went and broke the end of the egg."

Columbus cheats and stands an egg

My father seemed to his visitor to be beside himself at the duplicity of Christopher Columbus. He muttered and swore. He declared it was wrong to teach children that Columbus was a great man when, after all, he cheated: when his bluff had been called he had done a trick. Still grumbling at Columbus, father took an egg from the basket and rolled the egg between the palms of his hands. He smiled genially. He declared that without breaking its shell he could stand the egg on its end. He explained that the warmth of his hands and the gentle rolling movement gave the egg a new center of gravity, and Joe Kane was mildly interested. "I have handled thousands of eggs," father said. "No one knows more about eggs than I do."

He stood the egg on the counter and it fell on its side. He tried the trick again and again, each time rolling the egg between his hands. When after a half hour's effort he did succeed in making the egg stand, he looked up to find that his visitor was no longer watching. By the time he had succeeded in calling Joe Kane's attention to the success of his effort, the egg had again rolled over on its side.

Afire with the showman's passion and disconcerted by the failure of his first effort, father now took the poultry monstrosities down from the shelf. "How would you like to have seven legs and two heads like this fellow?" he asked, exhibiting the most remarkable of his treasures. A cheerful smile played over his face. He tried to slap Joe Kane on the shoulder as he had seen men do when he was a young farmhand in town on Saturday evenings. His visitor was made a little ill by the sight of the terribly deformed bird floating in the alcohol and got up to go. Father took hold of the young man's arm and led him back to his seat. He grew a little angry and had to force himself to smile. In an outburst of generosity he compelled Joe Kane to have a fresh cup of coffee and another cigar at his expense. Then he declared himself about to do a new trick. "I will heat this egg in this pan of vinegar," he said. "Then I will put it through the neck of a bottle without breaking the shell. The egg will resume its normal shape and the shell will become hard again. Then I will give the bottle to you. People will want to know how you got the egg in the bottle. Don't tell them. Keep them guessing. That is the way to have fun with this trick."

Father grinned and winked at his visitor. Joe Kane decided that the man was mildly insane but harmless. He drank the cup of coffee and began to read his paper again. When the egg had been heated in vinegar, father got an empty bottle. He was angry because his visitor did not watch him, but nevertheless went cheerfully to work. For a long time he struggled, trying to get the egg to go through the neck of the bottle. He put the pan of vinegar back on the stove to reheat the egg and burned his fingers. The shell had been softened a little but not enough. A spirit of desperate determination took possession of him. When he thought that at last the trick was about to be consummated, the delayed train came in at the station and Joe Kane started to go nonchalantly out at the door. Father made a last desperate effort to conquer the egg and establish his reputation as one who knew how to entertain guests. The egg broke under his hand. When the contents spurted over his clothes, Joe Kane turned and laughed.

A roar of anger rose from my father's throat. He danced and shouted inarticulate words. Grabbing another egg from the basket on the counter, he threw it, just missing the head of the young man as he dodged through the door and escaped.

Father came upstairs to mother and me with an egg in his hand. I imagine he had some idea of destroying it, of destroying all eggs, and that he intended to let mother and me see him begin. When, however, he got into the presence of mother something happened to him. He laid the egg gently on the table and dropped on his knees by the bed as I have already explained. He blew out the light and after much muttered conversation both he and mother went to sleep. I awoke at dawn and for a long time looked at the egg that lay on the table. I wondered why eggs had to be and why from the egg came the hen who again laid the egg.

The question got into my blood. It has stayed there, I imagine, because I am the son of my father, and the problem remains unsolved in my mind. And that, I conclude, is but another evidence of the complete and final triumph of the egg—at least as far as my family is concerned.

The Eyes Have It

Optical illusions go way back. Here are some enjoyed by our great-grandparents.

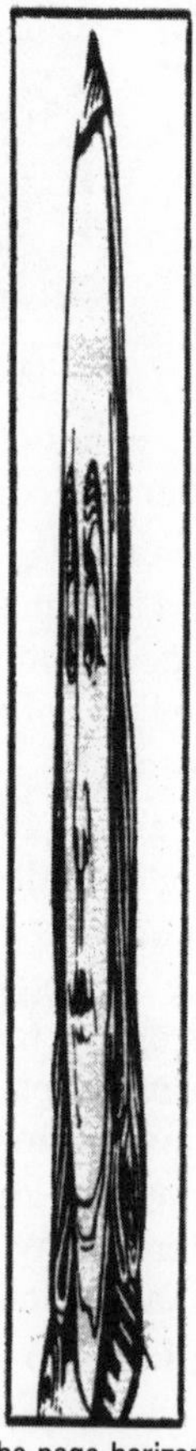

Hold the page horizontal at eye-level.

A good optical illusion is an eye-catching way to sell your products. Notice how the wheel looks like it's turning.

Rappers' Delite

WHERE DID RAP MUSIC COME FROM?

Yo, it's not just clueless adults who don't know the story of rap—neither do most of its biggest fans.

RAP IN THE 1960s meant to talk seriously about something. At the time, "rap lines" sprung up for troubled teens to dial into; black militant H. "Rap" Brown got his nickname from his abilities at public speaking and persuasion. The term all but disappeared for more than a decade, until a hybrid of talk and music revived it. A subculture called "hip-hop" (a term used in the very first successful rap record) emerged around the music, featuring stylized graffiti, break dancing, gang-inspired clothing styles and a bad-guy attitude.

• Ad-lib rhyming over a beat had a history in the black culture long before rap. For example, competitions in good-natured rhyming insults and brags were a feature of the "dozens" in the 1940s and '50s. African American radio DJs from the 1940s into the 1970s made a practice of it, as did black poets in the 1960s like the Last Poets and the Watts Prophets. And Jamaican "toasters" or "dub artists" made an art of the same wordplay traditions.

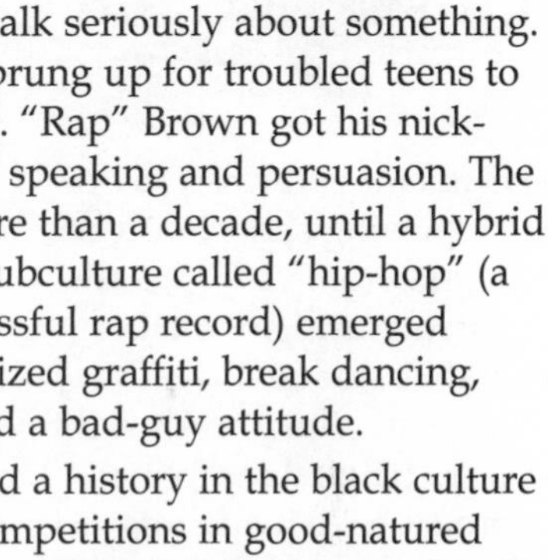

• Jamaican influence most directly spurred rap in the 1970s. Its earliest practitioners were of Caribbean descent. One of them, Kool Herc, who left Jamaica for the South Bronx in 1967, is credited as the first

DJ to buy two copies of the same record because he liked a 15–second instrumental segment in the middle. With two turntables, Herc could repeatedly switch between them to create an endless rhythm track to rap over.

• It's hard to imagine that in the earliest days of rap, the

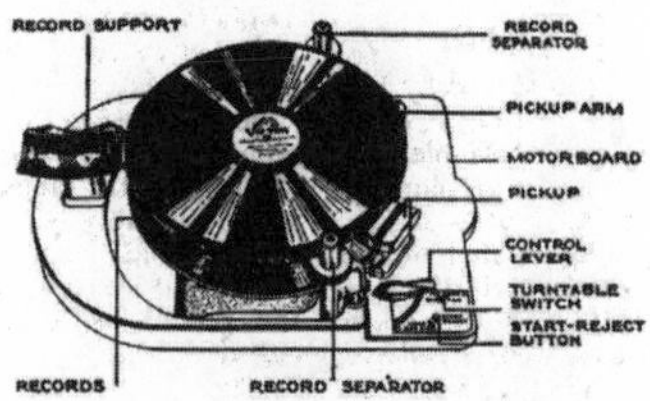

instrumentation was provided by playing short music segments from vinyl records repeatedly using two DJ turntables, manually cuing and starting the records right on beat. (Digital sampling recorders have made this process easier, so that tracks can be easily programmed before the fact instead of performed "live.") According to rap pioneer Kurtis Blow, it was largely a matter of economics: "Gifted teenagers with plenty of imagination but little cash began to forge a new style from spare parts. Hip-hop was a product of pure streetwise ingenuity; extracting rhythms and melodies from existing records and mixing them up with searing poetry."

• As with punk rock in the white teen culture, rap was largely a homemade reaction against the slickness of disco, which had taken over much of black culture.

• While "cutting" with his two turntables, Herc also joked and boasted into the microphone in Jamaican "toasting" style. It was a time when carrying a blaring boombox everywhere was *de rigueur*; fans recorded Herc's live performances on them, then used the boomboxes to spread the music through the Bronx, Brooklyn and uptown Manhattan.

• Herc's sound inspired imitators, including Afrika Bam-

baataa, a Black Muslim who got good enough to engage Herc in direct competitions at clubs, parties and in city parks (where they powered their sound systems with hot-wired street lamps). While Herc primarily used sounds from funk and disco, Bambaataa added rock music and even TV themes into the mix, inspiring other rap DJs to

plunder samples from Third World folk recordings, spoken-word tapes, bebop music and anything else that suited their fancy. (Bambaataa reportedly owned more than 25 crates of records that he could choose from.) "It became a little like 'Name That Tune,' trying to figure out what snippet came from which record," remarked one observer of the scene.

• In 1976, Grandmaster Flash (Joseph Saddler) introduced "quick mixing," using dozens of short sound bites combined for a sound-collage effect, and "backspinning," in which the record was spun quickly backward to repeat a snippet of sound. Shortly after, his partner and "MC" (master of ceremony), Grandmaster Melle Mel, added the next important component to rap—real words. Before that, rappers improvised simple rhymes on the spot, often referring to what was going on at the club or party (for example, this early Herc couplet: "Davey D is in the house / An' he'll turn it out without a doubt"). Mel composed the first pre-planned, full-length rap song.

• In 1978, either Grandmaster Flash or thirteen-year-old

Grandmaster Flash and his turntables

Grand Wizard Theodore (there's some controversy about this) introduced the technique called "scratching"—manually turning a record back and forth so the needle would make a rhythmic *fwheet-fwheet* sound.

• In 1979, the first two rap records appeared: "King Tim III (Personality Jock)," by the

Fatback Band, and "Rapper's Delight" by the Sugarhill Gang, a band manufactured by the owners of Sugarhill Records, who had heard the

new sound and decided it had commercial possibilities. The producers bypassed the DJs that had been the backbone of rap: They hired studio musicians to replicate the basic groove of the disco hit "Good Times" by Chic, and then hired three employees of a New Jersey pizza parlor and coached them in performing a rap song that stole heavily from the style and lyrics of more genuine rappers. Still, the song became the first rap record to hit the top 40. Another successful record that year was Kurtis Blow's "Christmas Rappin'."

• Ironically, the next rap record to hit the charts was "Rapture" in 1980, by the New Wave band Blondie.

• In 1982, Afrika Bambaataa's "Planet Rock" became the first rap record using synthesizers and a drum machine, starting a trend away from depending on others' prerecorded backing tracks.

• In 1986, rap became assimilated into mainstream pop culture with "Fight for Your Right (to Party)" by the Beastie Boys and "Walk This Way" by Run-DMC and Aerosmith. It began rivaling rock as the dominant musical form among young people.

Rap goes commercial: Run-DMC action figures "walk this way."

• Still, sampled sounds from pre-existing tracks continued to be the rule, to the consternation of much-sampled artists like George Clinton and James Brown, who found their work appearing on other people's hit records without compensation. Finally, by the early 1990s, threats of legal action established a standard practice of compensating for samples. The effect was that Clinton and others released CDs containing dozens of sound bites for the express purpose of facilitating sampling by others.

• Through the 1990s, rap moved from being just party and bragging songs into politics, and then mutated into subcategories, including the most controversial: "gangsta rap," with lyrics glorifying guns, drugs and misogyny. Feuds and vendettas among the self-proclaimed gangsters resulted in several prominent rappers being shot, maimed and killed.

• Other spinoffs, inspired by the "black science fiction" of Bambaataa's "Planet Rock" and using many of the same techniques, include electronic–heavy house and techno music. €

London Bridge Isn't *Really* Falling Down

Did London Bridge really ever fall down? Yes, once. Back in 1014, when the Danes controlled London. Their enemies, the Saxons and Norwegians, rowed their warships up the Thames to the then-wooden bridge, hitched cables around the bridge's pilings, and rowed away at full speed, pulling the bridge down.

What do the people in London do, now that Arizona has London Bridge? The bridge over Lake Havasu in Arizona is the third of four London Bridges in history, and it was quickly replaced by another. After the first was torn down by the Danes, city leaders wanted the next London Bridge to be more durable, so in 1176, the city built the first stone London Bridge, a drawbridge that lasted 600 years. This was the most famous London Bridge, the one where heads of executed criminals, from common thieves to Oliver Cromwell, were displayed on poles in groups of up to 30 at a time.

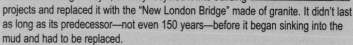

But all good things must come to an end. In 1823, the city tore down the aged structure. There was no rich American waiting to buy it, so they recycled it into building projects and replaced it with the "New London Bridge" made of granite. It didn't last as long as its predecessor—not even 150 years—before it began sinking into the mud and had to be replaced.

In 1962, the city sold the "New London Bridge" to an American developer for $2,460,000. He rebuilt it over an artificial lake in Arizona. (Rumors at the time had it that he thought he'd bought the picturesque London Tower Bridge instead of the ordinary-looking bridge he got.) The fourth London Bridge continues to stand.

(To Be Tacked Inside of the Privy and NOT Torn Down.)
Sanitary Privies Are Cheaper Than Coffins
For Health's Sake let's keep this Privy CLEAN. Bad privies (and no privies at all) are our greatest cause of Disease. Clean people or families will help us keep this place clean. It should be kept as clean as the house because it spreads more diseases.
The User Must Keep It Clean Inside. Wash the Seat Occasionally
How to Keep a Safe Privy:
1. Have the back perfectly screened against flies and animals.
2. Have a hinged door over the seat and keep it CLOSED when not in use.
3. Have a bucket beneath to catch the Excreta.
4. VENTILATE THE VAULT.
5. See that the privy is kept clean inside and out, or take the blame on yourself if some member of your family dies of Typhoid Fever.
Some of the Diseases Spread by Filthy Privies:
Typhoid Fever, Bowel Troubles of Children, Dysenteries, Hookworms, Cholera, some Tuberculosis.
The Flies that You See in the Privy Will Soon Be in the Dining Room.
Walker County Board of Health

A line at the top cautions *NOT* to remove this poster from the side of the privy. The National Library of Medicine Web site states that incidences of both typhoid fever and hookworm were lowered as a result of sanitary education campaigns like this one in the 1920s.

I See London, I See France

Here's One All About Underpants

Rifling through the drawers from the Indies to the Andies, *Bathroom Companion* regular Kitty Martindale's found some pretty risqué facts and stories on undies.

EQUAL RIGHTS TO UNDIES

In 1991, the Texas chapter of the American Civil Liberties Union threatened to sue the Dallas County Sheriff's Department because, while male inmates were routinely issued underwear, female inmates had to supply their own. Only indigent women could apply for free underwear. The female prisoners were further limited to plain white, not colorful or frilly.

AND THE CHEST, THEY SAY, IS HISTORY....

The brassiere is a twentieth-century invention, but ancient Greek women strapped cloth or leather around their breasts to minimize them under their clothes. Even earlier, women of Crete used a device to push their breasts up and out of their tops. Archeologists think a solid gold breastplate resembling a bra from around 1000 B.C. was used by a Greek woman to cover her breasts.

But who invented the modern bra? It's hard to say. A "bust improver" made of wire and silk, looking something like two tea strainers hooked together, first appeared in 1886. Hermione Cadolle, a French seamstress is credited for designing a version in 1889, and Paul Poiret, a couturier from Paris, began to build similar underpinnings into his clothes a bit later. The garment gained enough notoriety for *Vogue* magazine to coin the term "brassier" in 1907. Prior to this, the bra was called a *soutien-gorge,* translating to "throat support" or "breast support."

In 1914, an American socialite, Mary Phelps Jacobs, patented a bra-like garment made from two silk hankies and some pink ribbons. She eventually sold the patent for $1,500 to the Warner Corset Company which, in turn, became very well-endowed from sales of the item.

William Rosenthal, an immigrant from Russia, patented the first "uplift" bra in 1927. Rosenthal's wife, Ida, and her business partner, Enid Bassett, owned a dress store called Enid Frocks in Manhattan. They were of the mind that dresses looked better when worn over a natural bosom instead of the flattened chest that was the popular look at the time. This innovative idea led Enid and Ida to create cup sizes for women of all shapes, and ultimately led to the Maidenform Bra. Its advertising campaign, "I dreamed I [did just about anything] in my Maidenform Bra," had a memorable run from 1949–69.

NAMES FOR UNMENTIONABLES

Bra. An abbreviation of the French word *brassiere,* "bra" first appeared in English in the 1930s. In 17th century France, *brassiere* simply meant "bodice" and was an alteration of an earlier, Old French word *braciere,* meaning a "piece of armor for the arm or wrist."

Garter. The word "garter" probably came from a Gaulish word meaning "leg," related to the Welsh *gar*. Adopted into Old French it was used as the basis for the noun *garet* meaning "place where the leg bends; knee." *Garter* then means "band just above or below the knee." Legend even has it that while the Countess of Salisbury danced with King Edward III, her garter slipped off. The king bent down, retrieved it, and saucily put it on his leg. It was this incident, some say, that inspired name given to the order of knighthood Edward founded, the British Order of the Garter. Incidentally, the garter snake is named for its resemblance to the undergarment.

Girdle. The modern use of the word "girdle" was first seen in 1925. Although today we think of girdles as a ladies' underthing, that was not the case for much of history. The name comes from the Old English *gyrdel,* which meant a belt, worn around the waist. *Gyrdel* came from Old Germanic prefixes *gurd-*, *gard-*, or *gerd-* meaning "surrounding."

Through history, a belt-like girdle has been more than just a fashion statement for men, but also a means of carrying small articles such as a money purse or weapon. The "military girdle" was worn as a piece of armor.

Made of metal, leather, fabric or cord, a girdle was usually worn with one or two hanging ends—particularly the ones worn by women. The dangling strings were used to tote essentials like a mirror or book.

In the tenth century, a colored girdle was quite common. Priests took to wearing golden ones. Not long after, the girdle became a symbol of status and wealth. To keep the extravagance in check, a law was decreed: Squires were forbidden from wearing any girdle with gold or silver, and knights who made under a certain amount of money couldn't wear bejeweled girdles. Still, the girdles of this time period were very beautiful and expensive, often bequeathed upon death to favored family members. Others, though, took their girdles to the grave. They were so valued that stealing a girdle could mean a sentence of death.

STICKY SITUATION

A lawyer, after wearing his new J. C. Penney skivvies for the first time, found the tag "Inspected by No. 12" firmly stuck to his delicate parts. After a failed attempt at removing it himself, he sought medical help. A doctor managed to remove the tag, but the treatment left the lawyer with a nasty rash. Eventually, it cleared, but a scar in the shape of the sticker remained. The lawyer sued (surprise!) and was awarded $3,000 for the time in which he lost work and marital comfort.

UNDERNEATH, WE'RE PRETTY MUCH THE SAME

King Tut of Egypt was buried with 145 loincloths. Thousands of years later, World War II Japanese soldiers wore something similar to loincloths under their uniforms. Most clothing historians agree that modern men's briefs evolved pretty directly from early loincloths.

Even though the garment is universal, not all cultures wear them. Traditionally, Arabs are pretty modest, and cover themselves from head to toe. But underneath their robes, they don't wear any undergarments (it's hot enough with the robes!). The Scottish, too, traditionally wear nothing under their kilts. Samoans are pretty immodest, and enjoy loose clothing to go with the intense island heat, but their historical dress included underthings, and they believed that something should cover the navel—but not necessarily the female breasts—at all times.

Keep those legs down, boys!

FOR YOUR EYES ONLY

In 2002, Germany's spy agency, the Federal Intelligence Agency (or BND), announced that it would begin offering BND Brand underwear in its public shop in Berlin. The underwear will be imprinted with phrases like "Not for Public Use" and "Top Secret."

"It's not just fun and games," insisted a spokesperson for the agency. "It's all part of our plans to inform the public more about who we are and what we do."

"PATHETIC!"

What do you call one who steals women's underwear? Technically, he's a *melcryptovestimentaphiliac*. Personally, we can think of a dozen other names to call him....

GOLF BUFFS

Harpo Marx and George Burns once nearly got kicked out of Hillcrest Country Club in Beverly Hills when they played a round of golf in their underwear.

AIRING DIRTY LAUNDRY

During an MTV interview with Bill Clinton during the 1992 presidential campaign, the democrat was asked what type of underwear he wore. After a long silence, he answered, "Boxers."

Curses!

Jeffrey Racirk, author of the *Long Lost Insults Knowledge Cards,* has compiled an extensive list of long-forgotten English slurs. Tested on our siblings and friends, here are some of our favorites.

PREGNANT SCHOLAR: "One who was drunk by the middle of the morning." —*University Slang,* Morris Marple, 1950

MAMMOTHREPT: "A spoilt child." —*Dictionary of Obsolete and Provincial English,* Thomas Wright, 1857

SPATHERDAB: "A chatterer, gossip, scandal-monger who goes from house to house dispensing news." —*Leicestershire Words, Phrases and Proverbs,* A. Benoni Evan, 1881

WINDY-WALLETS: "A noisy fellow; one who romances in conversation." —*Dictionary of Archaic and Provincial Words,* James Halliwell, 1855

COUNTER-CASTER: "Contemptuous name for an arithmetician." —*Oxford Shakespeare Glossary,* C. T. Onion, 1911

PILGARLICK: "A poor, ill-dressed person; an object of pity or contempt." —*Sheffield Glossary of Words,* Sidney Addy, 1888

BEARD-SPLITTER: "An enjoyer of women." —*Dictionary of the Canting Crew,* B. E., 1699

KEYHOLE-WHISTLERS: "Persons who sleep in barns or outhouses from necessity, or in preference to sleeping in lodging houses." —*Slang Dictionary,* J. C. Hotten, 1887

SNOKER: "One who smells at objects like a dog." —*Etymological Dictionary of the Scottish Language,* John Jamieson, 1808

Bearing It All

THE INNER WORKINGS OF THE TEDDY BEAR

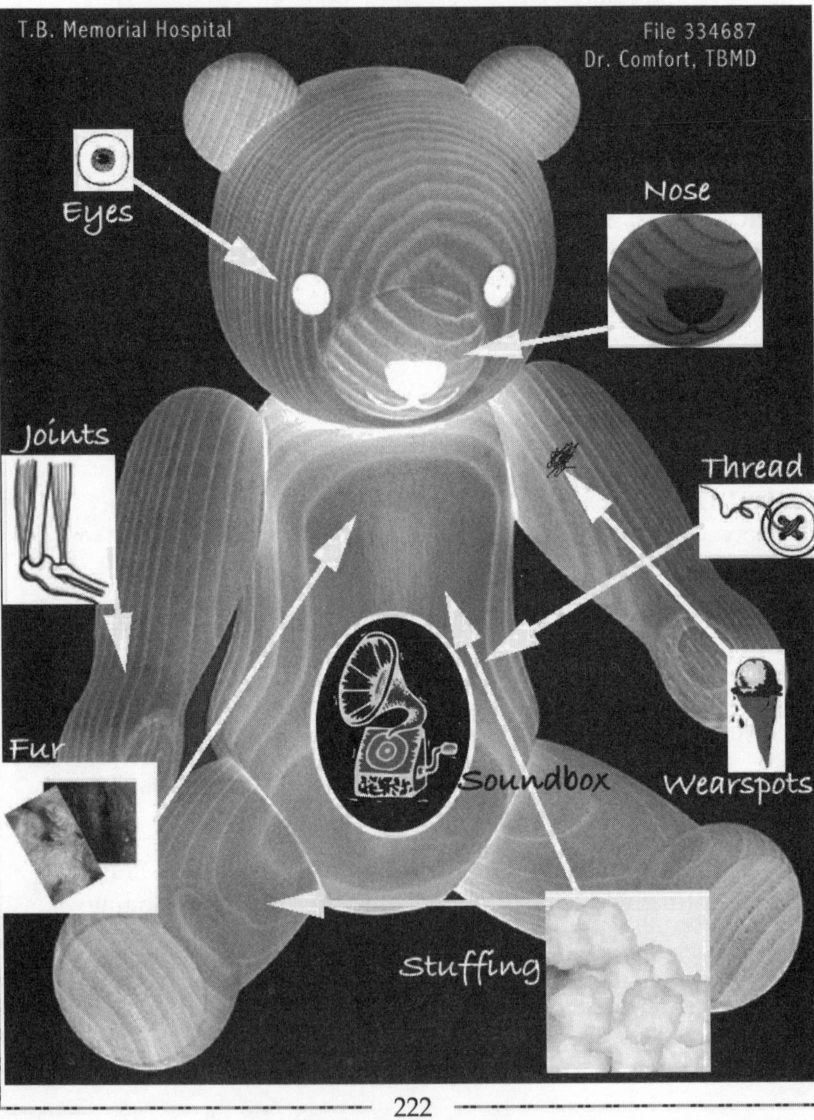

Eyes: The best eyes are glass, made specifically for this purpose. In the bad old days, they were attached to a long, sharp hatpin and just thumbtacked into the head; concerned parents would routinely remove these and sew on buttons. Nowadays, eyes are safely sewn in with extra-strong nylon "eye-floss," and the really good ones come in several lifelike colors from Germany.

Paws & Nose: On some bears, just more plush of a different color. Classically, though, it's virgin wool felt. Some modern bear artists use ultrasuede.

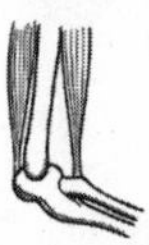

Joints: Some inexpensive teddies don't have joints; they are merely sewn permanently sitting or reclining. Bears with "fully articulated" joints use a two-disks-on-one-axle assembly on arms, legs and head so they can turn; the really sophisticated ones have "Loc-Line" armatures that look like little Dixie Cups nestled into each other that allow the bear to bend and flex naturally. Some very early bear makers used metal rods and wires to get arms and legs to pose, but sharp ends sometimes wore through the fabric.

Thread: Colored pearle cotton.

Fabric: Mohair is the fabric of choice for quality bears, but not for a bear that you might actually give a real kid to love and play with. Kid-gunk and dirt easily sponge off synthetic fake furs; some are even machine washable. Other popular bear fabrics include silk and rayon plush...and, in the bad old days, real fur from real bears.

Soundboxes: Electronic voice boxes exist for bears, but most use mechanical voices. Bears were traditionally either "squeakers" (squeeze them) or "growlers" (turn them upside down and then right side up). Wind-up bears with music-box parts playing lullabies came later. The sound mechanism is shielded from the stuffing material with muslin (earlier bears) or plastic (later).

Stuffing: Excelsior (very fine wood shavings) was long the preferred stuffing for its solid-packing and heft. While some stubborn hand-sewers still use wood shavings, fire safety laws be damned, most modern bears contain fire-safe polyester fill, sometimes augmented with tiny plastic beads (made from recycled milk cartons) to add a heft that collectors love.

Wear Spots: Most collectors like antique bears in mint condition, but some actually like to see evidence that they've been well-loved by a real kid. Typical signs? Bare spots near the center belly seam from the fingers of children falling asleep. Missing or weak ears once used as handles. Mashed and threadbare hands and feet from being grasped and chewed. Dirt marks from backyard bear dens, food stains from tea parties...well, you get the idea.

The Right to Bear Arms, Legs and Torsos

An arctophile is a person who loves bears. It comes from *arko,* which in Greek means "bear," and *philo,* which means "friend." While kids have known for decades that teddy bears offer therapeutic comfort, the professionals are finally catching on:

• Six out of ten adults surveyed for *Emotional Health* magazine said that they own or wish they owned a teddy bear.

• Some police, fire and paramedic departments routinely issue teddy bears to their officers because they're a useful tool in reaching scared, lost and traumatized children.

A firefighter lays out his comforting bears

• Following the lead of a famous old Norman Rockwell painting, several years ago the Children's Museum in Boston helped calm kids' fears of hospitals by having them bring in their teddy bears for a free checkup by trained medical professionals.

• To provide therapeutic comfort to someone suffering from illness or trauma, let the patient hold a Teddy WarmHeart that emits four hours of "human-like warmth," after being popped for a few minutes into a microwave oven (the teddy bear, that is, not the traumatized person).

Pick 'n' Chews

TAKE THE CHEWING GUM CHALLENGE

We have a pop quiz for you. If you read about gum on page 135, it'll help. Not much, but some.

1 Gum made from the resin of the mastic tree was popular

A. in Greece about A.D. 50

B. in Macedonia in the second century

C. in ancient Egypt

D. from the Middle Ages in Europe

2 British settlers in the New World were introduced to chewing spruce resins by

A. fellow settlers from Holland

B. William Wrigley, Jr.'s grandfather

C. Native Americans

D. the inventor, Thomas Adams, Sr.

3 Chewing gum as we know it today is made from chicle,

A. a plant with blue, pink or white flowers

B. the dried sap of the sapodilla tree

C. a stiff, prickly shrub that grows in alkaline regions

D. a common weed with small white flowers

4 Chicle was introduced to the Americans

A. by Mexican laborers working in California in the early 20th century

B. by a Prussian general in the late 19th century

C. by Native Americans in the early 19th century

D. by a Mexican general after the Civil War

5 The "Nostalgia Gum program" was an advertising campaign in the 1980s

A. to reintroduce 100-year-old chewing gum brands

B. to introduce sugarless gum to conservative gum chewers

C. launched by the Gum Wrappers Collectors Association

D. launched by an aggressive

new gum company in an attempt to grab some of Wrigley's market.

D. horrible color (no one wanted to chew or blow mucky green gum)

6 The initial problem with bubble gum when invented in the early part of the century was its

A. over-stickiness

B. high manufacturing cost

C. unreliable bubble-blowability (the bubbles burst too early)

7 Liquid gum base has been used

A. as an organic pesticide

B. to seal tiny parts in airplane engines

C. in the manufacture of super-adhesive glue

D. in the manufacture of rubber shoe soles

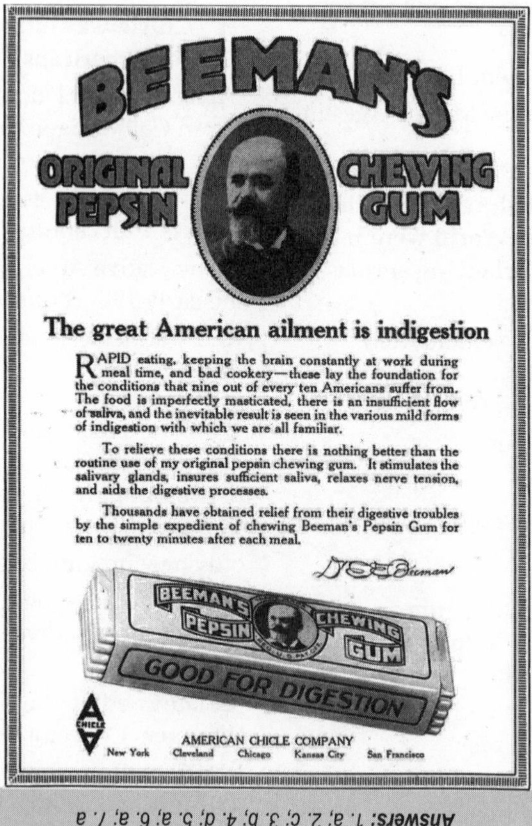

Answers: 1. a; 2. c; 3. b; 4. d; 5. a; 6. a; 7. a

Grudge Match

WHY COKE HATES PEPSI (PART I)

Few competitors have gone after each other with the battle-scarred, no-holds-barred, take-no-prisoners fervor of Coke and Pepsi. How and when did it start? It depends on who you ask. But to understand it, you have to go back to the beginning.

IN SPRING OF 1886, Atlanta was still smarting and depressed by its defeat in the Civil War. The South turned en masse for solace to religion and patent medicines. The cure-all "snake oils" of the North tended to be heavy on alcohol—an unacceptable ingredient for most Bible-thumpin', anti-demon rum Southerners. Under pressure from Temperance groups, patent medicine makers in the South began replacing alcohol with another active ingredient that was believed to be safe, healthy and morally pure...cocaine.

Coca leaves—the source for cocaine

Atlanta druggist John Styth Pemberton had been reformulating his "French Wine Coca—Ideal Brain Tonic" to remove the alcohol, yet replace it with something that would give a nice kick. He had found it in the African kola nut—a stimulant with the reputation of being a wonder hangover cure. He blended it with coca extract, bringing together the two strongest stimulants known at the time. The concoction was indeed a potent "brain tonic." Unfortunately, it tasted terrible. So the gray-bearded druggist spent spent six months hunched over a 30-gallon brass kettle in his backyard mixing up dozens of concoctions, before finally settling on what he decided was the ideal mixture to mask the flavor of the potently psychoactive mix.

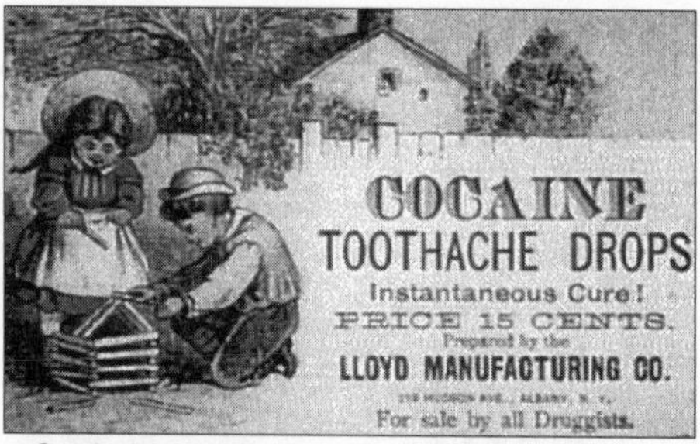

Cocaine was a common ingredient in many 19th and early 20th century remedies, including this toothache medicine for children

The result was Coca-Cola, a thick, sweet, brown syrup, packaged in reused beer bottles. Pemberton sold it to other Atlanta drugstores for 25¢ a bottle. The druggists would sell the entire bottle, or administer individual doses of the "Intellectual Beverage and Temperance Drink," often mixed into a glass of tap water to make it a little easier to get down. It became moderately successful as a pick-me-up and hangover remedy.

That summer an earthshaking event occurred in one of Coke's outlets in Atlanta, Jacob's Drug Store. A customer came in complaining of a severe hangover. Handed a bottle of Coca-Cola syrup, he asked Willis E. Venable, the soda fountain man, to open it and mix it with water right there so he could get immediate relief. Rather than walk to the tap in the back, Venable asked if the man minded soda water. The distressed customer wasn't particular. He gulped the fizzing mixture and said, "Say, this is really fine. Much better than using plain water like the label says." Word got around, and people started requesting the bubbly version all over town.

Pemberton had been marketing Coca-Cola as a medicine "for all nervous afflictions—Sick Headache, Neuralgia, Hysteria, Melancholia, Etc." He hadn't even considered that it might be drunk for refreshment recreation. But he saw the opportunity and jumped. His ads changed to "Coca-Cola makes a delicious, exhilarating, refreshing, and invigorating beverage" in addition to touting its medicinal qualities.

That same summer, Atlanta passed its first "dry laws," making alcohol illegal. Coke syrup sales jumped from 25 gallons that year to 1,049 gallons the next, largely through the marketing efforts of Pemberton's associate and financial backer Frank M. Robinson, who coined the name and drew the script "Coca-Cola" logo that is still used today. Robinson was Coke's real "secret ingredient" in its early years. He was a shrewd salesman and promoter.

Meanwhile, despite consuming large quantities of his "health tonic," Pemberton's health began to fail in 1887. Coke sales were still not brisk enough to make him financially solvent, so for a very modest amount of money, he sold two-thirds of his interest in the business to Willis Venable, the man who first brought the fizz to Coke. Pemberton's inventory, which he drew up at the time of the transfer, gives a clue to Coca-Cola's closely guarded "secret ingredients": oil of spice, oil of lemon, oil of lime, oil of nutmeg, fluid extract of nutmeg, fluid extract of coca leaves, vanilla, citric acid, orange elixir, oil of neroli, and caffeine.

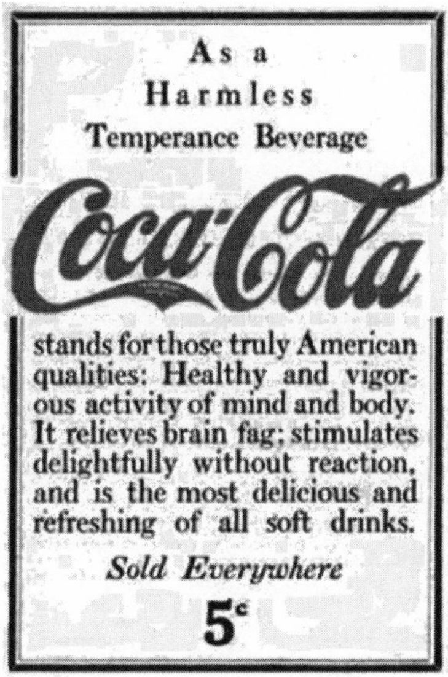

As a
Harmless
Temperance Beverage
Coca-Cola
stands for those truly American qualities: Healthy and vigorous activity of mind and body. It relieves brain fag; stimulates delightfully without reaction, and is the most delicious and refreshing of all soft drinks.
Sold Everywhere
5c

Pemberton died destitute on August 16, 1888, and was buried in an unmarked pauper's grave. Before he died, he sold the last of his stock to Asa Candler, a more prosperous fellow druggist. With the help of two partners, Candler quietly bought up all the rest of the stock in Coca-Cola from Venable and other investors. Full ownership of the company—lock, stock and secret formula—cost Candler a grand total of $2,300.

Candler was a devout Christian and teetotaler, and he wholeheartedly believed that Coke was the ideal Temperance drink and all-purpose medicine. He and Frank Robinson immediately set to work reformulating Pemberton's original recipe to improve the taste and shelf life while keeping the same heart-pounding jolt of coca leaves, kola nuts and caffeine.

Candler reformulated Coke again a few years later when anti-cocaine hysteria hit a peak. Newspapers carried shameless stories about crazed blacks rampaging with insatiable lust, superhuman strength, and even enhanced marksmanship as a result of cocaine. Slang terms for an order of Coca-Cola quickly expanded from "a Coke" to "a cold dope" and "a shot in the arm"; soda fountains became "hop joints" and "dope stores." In 1903, Coca-Cola quietly switched to a new recipe that used coca leaves that had already been stripped of cocaine. (Coca-Cola continues to use spent coca leaves. It obtains them from the Stepan Chemical Company in New Jersey, the only legal processor of medical cocaine in the United States.)

Memorable (or Not!) Coca-Cola Ad Campaigns

"Coca-Cola Revives and Sustains" (1905)
"The Great National Temperance" (1906)
"Three Million a Day" (1917)
"Thirst Knows No Season" (1922)
"Six Million a Day" (1925)
"Around the Corner from Everywhere" (1927)
"The Pause that Refreshes" (1929)
"When you think of Refreshment, think of ice-cold Coca-Cola" (1942)
"The only thing like Coca-Cola is Coca-Cola itself. It's the Real Thing" (1942)
"The Cold, Crisp taste of Coke" (1958)
"Things go Better with Coke" (1963)
"I'd Like to Buy the World a Coke" (1971)
"Coke Adds Life" (1976)
"Coke is It!" (1982)
"Always Coca-Cola" (1993)
"Real" (2003)

Right about this time, a soldier named Benjamin Franklin Thomas, stationed in Cuba during the Spanish-American War, saw the Cubans drinking something called Piña Fria from bottles. Suffering from Coke withdrawal, he wondered: Why not bottle it premixed in fizzy water and make it available everywhere? When Thomas got back to the U.S., he and a partner named Joseph Whitehead called on Candler who, seeing little profit in the venture, signed over bottling rights to them. Thomas and Whitehead immediately began selling regional bottling franchises.

Candler, in a mixture of Southern Methodist piety and good business sense, began lobbying aggressively for anti-alcohol laws all over the South. By 1907, 825 of the 994 counties in the former Confederacy had gone "dry." Sales of Coca-Cola soared.

AFTER A TIRING JOURNEY
DRINK Coca-Cola
The SATISFACTORY BEVERAGE
It satisfies the thirst; pleases the palate. Relieves fatigue quickly and naturally. Puts vim and go into tired brain and bodies. Delicious—cooling—refreshing.
Sold everywhere 5 cents

Its success spawned dozens of imitators. In 1916 alone, busy Coke attorneys went after 153 wannabes with names like Cafe Cola, Afri-Cola, Charcola, Co-Co-Colian, Dope, Kola Kola, Pau-Pau Cola, King Kola, Fig Cola, Sola Cola, Candy Cola, Toca-Cola, Cold Cola, Kos Kola, Cay-Ola, Coke Ola, Koca-Nola, Kel Kola, Kaw-Kola, Co Kola, Kola-Nola, Caro-Cola and Coca-Kola. By 1926, Coke attorney Harold Hirsch had run more than 7,000 competitors out of business.

The company began searching for a unique bottle design —one, as Thomas put it, "a person will recognize as a Coca-Cola bottle even when he feels it in the dark. The bottle should be so shaped that, even when broken, a person could tell at a glance what it was."

Coke's famous "hobbleskirt bottle" was named after a short-lived 1914 fashion

After a succession of rejected designs, the bottlers adopted the now-classic bottle designed by the C. J. Root Company of Terre Haute, Indiana. The alternately tapered and bulging shape was brilliant artistry, but astoundingly lousy botany: The bottle designers, thinking they were copying the shape of the *coca* bean, mistakenly copied the *cacao* bean, from which chocolate is made.

The bottle was a huge success. The bottlers liked it because its extra-thick glass gave a heft that disguised how little Coca-Cola was actually in it (6.5 ounces). The company liked it because it gave them a potent weapon that would kill all infringers. Or so they thought.

(For the rest of the story, see page 335)

Zen Masters

The Wisdom of Michael Jackson

Mind-bending quotes from the self-described "King of Pop."

• "I never smile when I dance."

• "It hurts to be mobbed. Not mentally, but physically. Your body feels like a noodle...."

• "People think they know me, but they don't. Not really. Actually, I am one of the loneliest people on this earth. I cry sometimes, because it hurts. It does. To be honest, I guess you could say that it hurts to be me."

• "Ours developed into a real close relationship. I fell in love with her (Tatum O'Neal), and she with me, and we were very close for a long time. Eventually the relationship transcended into a good friendship."

• "Me and Janet really are two different people."

• "When I'm not onstage, I'm not the same. I'm different. I think I'm some kinda stage addict. When I can't get onto a stage for a long time, I have fits and get real crazy. I start crying, and I act weird and all freaked out. No kiddin', I do. I start to dancin' round the house."

• "There are fans who actually have pieces of my hair. I could go to England right now, and they'd show me and say, 'This is your hair from three years ago.' I'd say, 'Oh my gosh.' And it's sitting in their wallet. They collect hair."

• "Most people don't know me, that is why they write such things in which most is not true. I cry very very often because it hurts and I worry about the children. All my children all over the world, I live for them.... Animals strike not from malice, but because they want to live, it is the same with those who criticize, they desire our blood, not our pain. But still I must achieve. I must seek truth in all things. I must endure for the power I was sent forth, for the world, for the children. But have mercy for I've been bleeding a long time now."

Potty Pourri

RANDOM KINDS OF FACTNESS

• Unless you're an exceptional monkey, you are likely *ecaudate*. It means "tailless."

• Anthropologist James Schaefer studied how music affected the drinking in bars. He found that people listening to country music drank more than those listening to pop or rock.

• In the wine-making process, it can take up to 2 years to remove all the solids (grape skins, dead yeast cells, and other debris). This step, called "racking," consists of letting the wine sit and draining out the gunk at the bottom now and again.

• Throwing a penny off the Empire State Building in New York won't really slice open a car or make a crater in the sidewalk. The fastest a penny can flutter from a height is only about 80 mph. In theory, a person below could catch it with baseball mitt. But don't try it.

• The dog days of summer come between July 3 and August 11. The Egyptians coined the term, believing that Sirius, the Dog Star, helped the sun warm the Earth during that time.

• The Greek Parthenon was wrecked by much more than time or weather. In 1687, the Turks battled the Venetians for control of the city, and stored their gunpowder in the ancient temple. It exploded, knocking over pillars and blowing the roof clean off. Renovations are currently underway.

• The original Rin Tin Tin— dog star of the silent screen—was picked up in Germany by U.S. Army corporal Lee Duncan during World War I.

• Wall-climbing lizards don't have suction cups on their feet. They have grooves with microscopic bumps that can get a toehold on the tiny imperfections on all surfaces, even glass.

"I'm Two with Nature"
QUOTES FROM WOODY ALLEN

An acting, directing, writing comedian: Woody Allen's done it all. Here are a few things he's had to say along the way.

• "If only God would give me some clear sign! Like making a large deposit in my name at a Swiss Bank."

• "To *you* I'm an atheist; to God, I'm the Loyal Opposition."

• "I'm not afraid of dying, I just don't want to be there when it happens."

• "I was thrown out of N.Y.U. my freshman year...for cheating on my metaphysics final. I looked into the soul of the boy sitting next to me."

• "I am two with nature."

• "I don't want to live on in my work, I want to live on in my apartment."

• "My success has allowed me to strike out with a higher class of women."

• "I sold my memoirs of my love life to Parker Brothers—they're going to make a game out of it."

• "I took a course in speed reading and was able to read *War and Peace* in twenty minutes."

• "I was the best I ever had."

• "And how can I believe in God when just last week I got my tongue caught in the roller of an electric typewriter."

• "If you want to make God laugh, tell him about your plans."

• "Showing up is 80% of life."

• "What if everything is an illusion and nothing exists? In that case, I definitely overpaid for my carpet."

• "What if nothing exists and we're all in somebody's dream? Or what's worse, what if only that fat guy in the third row exists?"

• "Some men are heterosexual, and some are bisexual, and some men don't think about sex at all.... They become lawyers."

• "I think a relationship is like a shark. It has to constantly move forward or it dies. Well, what we have on our hands here is a dead shark."

• "Basically my wife was immature. I'd be at home in the bath and she'd come in and sink my boats."

• "The prettiest women are almost always the most boring, and that is why some people feel there is no God."

• "It seemed the world was divided into good and bad people. The good ones slept better... while the bad ones seemed to enjoy the waking hours much more."

• "My brain is my second favorite organ."

• "The lion and the calf shall lie down together but the calf won't get much sleep."

• "It is impossible to travel faster than light, and certainly not desirable, as one's hat keeps blowing off."

• "More than any time in history, mankind now faces a crossroads. One path leads to despair and utter hopelessness, the other to total extinction. Let us pray that we have the wisdom to choose correctly."

• "I don't want to achieve immortality through my work. I want to achieve immortality through not dying."

• "There are worse things in life than death. Have you ever spent an evening with an insurance salesman?"

• "I don't think my parents liked me. They put a live teddy bear in my crib."

• "Human Beings are divided into mind and body. The mind embraces all the nobler aspirations, like poetry and philosophy, but the body has all the fun."

• "Love is the answer, but while you're waiting for the answer, sex raises some pretty interesting questions."

Potty Pourri

Random Kinds of Factness

• If you're looking for a career change to an area with a cool name, try becoming a colporter. It has nothing to do with the famous songwriter. Instead, it's another name for a Bible salesman.

• The surface of the moon has more than 30 trillion craters that measure at least a foot wide. Of those a mile or more wide, there are at least half a million, many overlapping.

• We remember that Benedict Arnold was a traitor, but history also records that he was a great general. He nearly captured Canada and won a major battle at Saratoga for the revolutionaries, then won battles for the British in Richmond, Va., and New London, Conn. After the war, he moved to London, England.

• Pluto, Venus and Uranus all spin in the opposite direction as Earth.

• Besides being a renowned American writer, John Dos Passos invented the Soap Bubble Gun.

• Despite what you've heard, it's not true that a cow has four stomachs; it has one stomach with four compartments for the different stages of digestion. The compartments are called the rumen, the reticulum, the omasum and the abomasum.

• Rudolph Valentino was the stage name that the silent-screen actor whittled down from his real name. The original was a little too difficult to work into movie credits: Rodolfo Alfonzo Raffaelo Pierre Filibert Guglielmi di Valentina d'Antonguolla.

• One out of seven Continental soldiers in the Revolutionary War was black.

• The longest running newspaper still published in the United States is the *Hartford Courant*. It was established in 1764.

Big Mac

How It Became the Hottest Thing Between Buns

The Big Mac was an idea "borrowed" from another restaurant chain. When it ended up on the McDonald's menu in 1968, it wasn't because of the company's top management, but despite it.

IN THE EARLY 1950s, the McDonald brothers of San Bernardino, California, created the first genuine fast food restaurant. They came up with an assembly-line formula that they called the Speedy Service System, dishing out low-cost burgers, fries and shakes in a fraction of the time of most drive-ins.

KROC'S EMPIRE

When entrepreneur Ray Kroc began franchising McDonald's outlets a few years later, he refined the Speedy System further, making it even more regimented. Each worker was assigned only one function, which worked out fine because the menu featured only a few items. Kroc hired only team-oriented, college-aged men, and dressed them in white military-style uniforms. (Kroc wouldn't hire women workers for more than a decade because he was afraid their presence would disrupt the military-like efficiency and attract loitering male admirers. When McDonald's finally stopped this blatant gender discrimination in 1968, the unwritten directive at the time was to hire only "flat-chested, unattractive women.")

Unfortunately, the military-like efficiency was a curse as well as a blessing. It forced Kroc to resist adding any new menu items, fearing they would slow down the system. Instead, he concentrated on perfecting the products he had, spending, for example, more than $3 million to research the secret of consistently perfect french fries. After a while, customers naturally started getting tired of the same old thing every time, and McDonald's profits began leveling off. McDonald's franchisees began griping—loudly—about the lack of variety.

KROC'S FLOPS

Kroc tried his best. He test-marketed a series of new products that he thought could be fit into the Speedy Service System. Unfortunately, he didn't have the same genius for developing new products that he did for selling franchises. All of his new products were disasters. For example, he decided in the late 1950s that the menu needed a dessert. He tried selling brownies and strawberry shortcake. When they failed to sell, he tried miniature pound cakes at 15¢ a loaf. Nobody bought them. In desperation, he tried offering *kolacky*, a Bohemian pastry his mom used to bake for him. No luck.

Frustrated, Kroc gave up on desserts. He decided that what McDonald's really needed was a non-meat burger for Catholics on Fridays. He went into the kitchen and concocted a product that he called a "Hulaburger": two slices of cheese and a grilled pineapple ring on a toasted bun. Not surprisingly, it bombed, and was ultimately replaced with a fish sandwich.

For the next decade, Kroc would fly into a rage whenever franchisees suggested new menu items. Finally, a desperate franchisee willing to risk Kroc's wrath introduced McDonald's most popular product.

Jim Delligatti was one of Kroc's earliest franchise holders. He operated a dozen stores in and around Pittsburgh. When he noticed his customer base was dwindling, he began lobbying McDonald's managers to allow him to broaden the menu.

STOLEN GOODS MAKE GOOD

His idea? He wanted to sell a double-decker hamburger with "special sauce" and all the trimmings—an idea that he unabashedly stole from the Big Boy hamburger chain. He badgered Kroc until he received reluctant permission in 1967 to test-market what was to become the Big Mac. Kroc forced some conditions. Delligatti had to agree that the product would be offered in only one marginal suburban store. He also had to promise to use the standard McDonald's patty and bun—a promise he quickly reneged on when it became clear that the standard bun was too small, making the sandwich impossible to eat without it falling to pieces. He quietly ordered oversized sesame seed buns from an independent baker and had them sliced into thirds.

The Big Mac—a fat & calorie behemoth—is featured prominently on this McDonald's nutrition flier

Within a few months, the new Big Mac had increased Deligatti's store's sales volume by a healthy 12%. He started serving it in his other stores. Other franchisees saw what was happening and began clamoring for their own Big Macs. McDonald's quickly tried the Big Mac in other test markets. The Big Mac increased sales by at least 10% in each market. At the end of 1968, it was put into nationwide distribution.

TONGUE-TIED TWISTER

The commercials that McDonald's created featured a recital of the Big Mac's ingredients. Max Cooper, a retired McDonald's publicist who owned several franchises in Birmingham, Alabama, thought the ads were boring and ineffectual. So he took matters into his own hands and held a contest in his stores: Anyone who could correctly recite the ingredients of the Big Mac in 4 seconds got one free. An ad agency recorded his customers' attempts at "Two all-beef patties special sauce lettuce cheese pickles onions on a sesame seed bun" and eventually produced radio spots using botched recitals by real customers.

The ads were an instant hit in Birmingham. Within weeks, radio stations were co-sponsoring "Recite the Big Mac" contests. Schoolkids all over town practiced the slogan at home and recess. Sales of Big Macs soared 25%. Other franchises in the South followed. Finally, McDonald's national marketing department took notice and spread the same strategy nationwide.

ONE THING LEADS TO ANOTHER

The Big Mac's success opened a floodgate of innovation among franchise holders. In 1969, Litton Cochran in Knoxville got permission to try a variation on the deep-fried apple pie his mother used to make for him. His idea was a success and spread to the national menu.

Another franchise holder discovered that customers wouldn't normally buy two orders of fries, but many would buy a double order if it were disguised as a single order. Thus was born the now-popular Large Fries, offering 60% more product for 75% more money. Another franchisee invented the McDLT; another, the Egg McMuffin, ensuring McDonald's domination of breakfast sales among fast food restaurants for many years to come. €

The Big Mac Super Sized Extra Value Meal: What You're Getting Besides the Deal

The Big Mac: One sandwich contains 590 calories—over a quarter of what you need in a day if you eat a 2,000-calorie diet. It also has 34 grams of total fat, or 53% of your Daily Value, 11 grams of saturated fat (57% D.V.), 85 milligrams of cholesterol (29% D.V.), 1,090 milligrams of sodium (45% D.V.), 8 grams of sugar and only 3 grams of dietary fiber (12% D.V.).

The French Fries: One order of Super Sized Fries has a whopping 610 calories. These same fries have 29 grams of total fat, 5 grams of saturated fat, 390 milligrams of sodium and 7 grams of dietary fiber.

The Soft Drink: One Super Sized Coke contains 410 calories, 40 milligrams of sodium and 113 grams of sugar.

Thinking of topping off your meal with a Vanilla Shake? Add 570 calories, 16 grams of fat (11 of which are saturated fat), 65 milligrams of cholesterol, 400 milligrams of sodium, 76 grams of sugar and 0 grams of dietary fiber.

To stay healthy, you'll need to not eat anything else for the rest of the day: this Super Sized™ meal gives you more calories, fat and saturated fat than you need in a 24-hour period.

Elephants

A Trunkful of Unforgettable Facts

They're smart, they're big, and on the beach they walk around with their trunks down. Who could not love elephants?

ELEPHANT HITS & MYTHS

No, elephants aren't really deathly afraid of mice. Nor is there an "elephants' graveyard" where all pachyderms go to die. And despite their intelligence, elephants *do* sometimes forget. Still, Westerners aren't the only ones who have spun elephant tales. The people of India—who live with elephants and should know better—have come up with some whoppers. For example, elephants show up in the Indian creation story (the earth sits on an elephant's head and when the head moves, an earthquake happens). Elephants were said to have appeared in the sky at the birth of Buddha. The Indians even explain why elephants no longer fly today. Here's the story:

Elephants used to have wings. One day an elephant was flying and grew tired. Spotting an old banyan tree below, he thought it looked like a good resting place. As he settled on a branch, it snapped and he plummeted toward the ground. Unfortunately for him, he landed on a meditating hermit named Dirghatapas, who was as grouchy as he was magical. Dirghatapas cursed the oafish winged beast to walk on his legs from that day on. The wings disappeared, and the elephant was henceforth forever earthbound.

BUT CALLING THEM "DUMBO" JUST TEES THEM OFF

An elephant's big, floppy ears can be 6.5 feet long and are nearly as wide. The ears have several functions, but helping the elephant hear better is not one of them. One thing the ears are good for is to make the elephant look bigger than it is when it defends or attacks (as if they aren't already big enough). Another is to wave away flies. But the primary use for the elephant's big ears is unexpected: they keep the animal cool. No,

not by waving them like a fan, but because the ears are thin, yet rich in blood vessels. Heat escapes easily into the air when you have ears like that—when elephants wave them around, the blood inside cools by as much as 9° F.

African elephants live in a hotter, sunnier climate, so it makes sense that their ears are bigger than those of Asian elephants.

TUSK A LOOSA

Elephants love sweets. Alas, they are susceptible to tooth decay, so it's a good thing that most elephants don't have many sugar-saturated foods available in the wild. Even without excessive sugar in their diets, elephants suffer from natural tooth loss in old age, which can result in starvation. Most zoos try to prevent the problem by forbidding visitors from feeding elephants. However, at least if a captive elephant loses its teeth, keepers can feed it soft foods.

SING LOW, SWEET PACHYDERM

Elephants communicate in low-frequency nasal tones that humans can't hear. Herds of elephants actually sing to each other over distances of up to 5 miles.

Elephants' natural musical ability is what inspired the Elephant Conservation Center in Thailand to create the Thai Elephant Orchestra, featuring larger, sturdier versions of Thai instruments—gongs, xylophones and percussion instruments.

GRAND OLD PACHYDERM

The elephant became the symbol for the Republican Party in 1874, thanks to political cartoonist Thomas Nast. Nast was in need of a way to depict the Republicans' policies that he considered nothing but random destructiveness. When a hoaxster reported that animals were breaking free at the New York Zoo, the image of rampaging elephants was too good for Nast to pass up.

Despite Nash's intention, the Republicans became so associated with the elephant that they eventually embraced the insulting icon while laying claim to the animal's positive traits.

The Blind Men & the Elephant

Interpretation by John Godfrey Saxe (1816–1887) of an old tale from India

It was six men of Indostan
To learning much inclined,
Who went to see the Elephant
(Though all of them were blind),
That each by observation
Might satisfy his mind.

The First approached the Elephant,
And happening to fall
Against his broad and sturdy side,
At once began to bawl:
"God bless me! but the Elephant
Is very like a wall!"

The Second, feeling of the tusk
Cried, "Ho! what have we here,
So very round and smooth and sharp?
To me `tis mighty clear
This wonder of an Elephant
Is very like a spear!"

The Third approached the animal,
And happening to take
The squirming trunk within his hands,
Thus boldly up he spake:
"I see," quoth he, "the Elephant
Is very like a snake!"

The Fourth reached out an eager hand,
And felt about the knee:
"What most this wondrous beast is like
Is mighty plain," quoth he;
"'Tis clear enough the Elephant
Is very like a tree!"

The Fifth, who chanced to touch the ear,
Said: "E'en the blindest man
Can tell what this resembles most;
Deny the fact who can,
This marvel of an Elephant
Is very like a fan!"

The Sixth no sooner had begun
About the beast to grope,
Than, seizing on the swinging tail
That fell within his scope.
"I see," quoth he, "the Elephant
Is very like a rope!"

And so these men of Indostan
Disputed loud and long,
Each in his own opinion
Exceeding stiff and strong,
Though each was partly in the right,
And all were in the wrong!

Moral:
So oft in theologic wars,
The disputants, I ween,
Rail on in utter ignorance
Of what each other mean,
And prate about an Elephant
Not one of them has seen!

GOOD THING ELEPHANTS DON'T FLY ANYMORE

African forest elephants spend about 16 hours a day eating. Each consumes up to 500 pounds of leaves and grasses every day, and 50 gallons of water. Of that, about 165 pounds of solids return to the soil as poop. It's good for the forest, and it contains lots of seeds that sprout in the nutrient-rich excrement.

PACK A TRUNK

The elephant's trunk is an extremely versatile organ, good for trumpeting, pulling down branches, caressing elephant babies, drinking and smelling. Using fingerlike lobes on its end and the sucking action of its nostrils, elephants can pick up small objects, including such hard-to-get items as a coin on the ground. The trunk's capacity? 1.5 gallons of water.

When elephants greet each other, they place the tips of their trunks in each other's mouths. Young males play-wrestle with their trunks. (In a true fight, elephants protect their trunks by curling them under their chins.)

HOW DO YOU MAKE AN ELEPHANT FLOAT?

An elephant can't gallop, jump or leap, but it can swim for miles at a time. If you weighed as much as an elephant, you'd probably rather float and kick than walk, too: An Indian elephant weighs in at 11,000 pounds; an African elephant, at more than 15,400. Yes, despite the elephant's weight, its body displaces enough water to float quite nicely. Even in rough water, it can hold its trunk out of the water to use as a snorkel.

SOME ELEPHANT FACTS TO NEVER FORGET

• During the Ice Age, elephants roamed every continent but Australia and Antarctica.

• Besides humans, the Asian elephant is the only animal that is able to stand on its head.

• Elephants are the heaviest living land animal. They are second only to the giraffes in the tallest animal competition.

• An elephant's gestation period is a whopping 22 months. Imagine the relief for the mom when birth finally takes place, since an elephant calf can weigh 250 pounds at birth.

• Elephants live about as long as humans. One difference: Their last permanent tooth comes in when they're about forty.

• Elephant herds number from 15 to 40 members, and they're a matriarchy, led by an aged female.

• Elephants were used as work animals in Asia as early as 2000 B.C. Working elephants have learned to recognize as many as forty voice commands.

• Thick foot pads and a rolling gait allow elephants to walk almost soundlessly. They normally walk at a speed of about 4 mph, but can get up to 25 mph when charging.

• The earliest known elephant ancestor was the *moeritherium,* a pig-sized animal with a snout like a tapir's, which lived about 60 million years ago in Africa.

• The earliest use of elephants in war was recorded in 331 B.C., when Persian soldiers riding elephants lost to the Macedonian army led by Alexander the Great. In 218 B.C., Hannibal of Carthage used war elephants more successfully when he crossed the Alps and invaded Italy.

• *Pachyderm* means "thick skin" in Latin. An elephant's skin is 1.5 inches thick in places, but is tender enough that mosquitoes and flies can penetrate it.

• Elephants have no sweat glands. They keep cool by submerging themselves in water and by covering themselves with mud.

• Besides rumbling, elephants use at least twenty-five different calls to communicate specific messages to each other.

• Elephants can knock down trees of up to 2 feet in diameter.

• Elephants have few natural enemies because of their size. A big cat could kill a baby, but that rarely happens because an elephant herd surrounds the babies in a circle when attacked, and anything that threatens them will get gored with tusks or fatally stepped on. ☾

Word Thieves

Terms We've Borrowed from the Germans

After a potato blight hit Germany in 1845, followed by a revolution in 1848, a tide of German emigrants hit America's shores, and their language added scores of words to the national vernacular.

bum: From German *bummler* ("loafer") and *bummelm* ("waste time").

check: The restaurant term came from the German *zeiche,* which means a bill for drinks. (However, all of the other kinds of checks come from the British word *cheque.*)

cookbook: From *kochbuch.*

dachshund: Germans thought the wienery dog looked like a badger, so called it *dachshund,* which means "badger dog."

delicatessen: The German word comes from *delicatesse* ("good things to eat").

dumb: Although the English used the word to mean "unable to speak," Americans got the "stupid" meaning from the German *dum.* The word *dumkopf* means "stupid head."

ecology: From the German *okologie* ("home" or "habitat").

frankfurter and **hamburger:** Both of these delicacies get their names from German cities (Frankfurt and Hamburg, of course).

gesundheit: "To your health."

hoodlum: Originally *hodalum.*

kindergarten: Literally, "children's garden."

klutz: From *klotz* ("block of wood").

nix: From the German *nichts* ("nothing").

ouch!: From *autcsch*!

pumpernickel: From *pumpen nickel* ("fart of the devil") because the coarse bread was hard to digest.

shyster: Probably from the German word *scheisse* ("shit").

spiel: From *spielen* ("play a musical instrument").

yesman: A literal translation of *jaherr.*

zwieback: This favorite of teething infants has a name that literally means "twice-baked."

More Grandville

Kids' Illustrator, Father of Surrealism

Jean Ignace Isidore Gerard (1803–1847), who went by the name "Grandville," became quite successful, illustrating *Gulliver's Travels* and other books. Unfortunately, that surrealistic genius apparently came with a price: He died insane in a mental institution.

Man of Steel

All About Joseph Stalin

In 1880, Yekaterian and Vissarion Dzhugashvili became parents to a son who would become one of the world's most feared personalities; his name was Iosif, nicknamed "Soso." To the world, he would be known as Joseph Stalin—the post-Lenin leader of the USSR.

• Joseph Stalin had a rather humble and uneventful childhood in the Georgian village of Gori. His two brothers, Mikhail and Georgii, died before reaching the age of one. Joseph's father Vissarion, a shoemaker, was an alcoholic who abused his wife and child. His mother was supportive, ensuring that he was educated first in a theological school and later in seminary in Tiflis. As he progressed in the Russian Communist Party, however, Joseph evidently did not feel a strong bond with her; when she died in 1937, he had not visited her for two years.

• Stalin was expelled from seminary in 1899 and became politically active shortly before Lenin and Martov began their revolutionary newspaper *Iskra* (*The Spark*). In 1901, Stalin became an elected member of the Tiflis Social Democratic Committee. This began his "career" as a political activist.

• Tsarist officials kept an eye on him between the times when he was either imprisoned or exiled. This physical description was circulated among the police at that time:

– 5′4″ male

– sunken hazel eyes

– soft voice

– birthmark on left ear

– pock-marked face

– thick black hair and mustache (but no beard)

– withered left arm

– second and third toes of left foot grown together.

• Stalin escaped the Tsarist prisons a record five times. The prisons weren't as bad as you would imagine—they were thought of as universities of sorts because the prisoners had access to vast libraries. Stalin vowed that "his" prison system would neither allow escapes nor be an educational system. It would, he said, become a grim exercise in survival.

Stalin when he took over as head of the Bolshevik party—sometime around 1912

• In June 1904, Stalin married Yekaterina "Kato" Svanidze. He had no real career, and they were forced to live "on the run." He became known as a Robin Hood of sorts, taking part in robberies to assist the Party. (He was eventually expelled for these "expropriations.") His son, Yakov, was born in 1905. In 1907, his wife died of typhoid.

• In 1912, he officially changed his name to Stalin, meaning "man of steel," and made an aggressive entrance into Bolshevik politics. After escaping deportation in Western Siberia, Stalin visited with Lenin in Cracow and proceeded to Vienna, where he met Trotsky and began writing political tracts. Stalin was selected for the Bolshevik Central Committee at a Party Conference in Prague.

• Stalin avoided being drafted into the World War I service of Russia because of his withered arm and deformed foot. During the war, he was exiled for four years to Turukhansk.

• When the Bolsheviks seized power from the temporary revolutionary government after the assassination of the Tsar, Stalin became Commissar of Nationalities. Following this revolution, there continued to be unrest in Russia and neighboring states, which would later be defeated by the Red Army to form the Union of Soviet Socialist Republics. In 1922, Stalin was elected General Secretary of the Party, positioning himself to take over as

Lenin's health failed.

• In 1924, Lenin died and Stalin seized power. The only real opposition to Stalin's power grab came from Leon Trotsky, whom Lenin had trusted and valued. However, Trotsky was more of a revolutionary thinker and philosopher, and he did not pay close attention to politics, allowing Stalin to easily gain the support and power needed to lead the Party from the General Secretary's position. Trotsky was expelled from the Party, later permanently exiled from the USSR, and eventually assassinated in Mexico.

• Stalin pretty much lived to rule. Although he remarried and was the father of more children, his personal life hardly existed as he rose in power. Stalin's second wife and mother of two of his children, Nadezhda, committed suicide on November 8, 1932. Stalin did not appear to blame himself for her death (as most others around him secretly did); instead he viewed her action as treachery on her part. He did not attend the funeral.

Stalin loved vodka, and Russians still remember that. A bottle of Stalin's Tears vodka (left), and an inset of Stalin's face featured on another Russian brand.

• His relationship with his children was so distant as to be virtually nonexistent, and his children did not lead happy lives. Stalin's eldest son, Yakov, attempted to shoot himself, but the bullet missed vital organs and he survived after a long recuperation. Shortly after this suicide attempt, Stalin reportedly greeted his son with, "Ha! You missed!" Yakov later joined the Army and became a commander; he was killed while attempting to escape from a prison camp during World War II. Stalin's other son, Vasili, was also in the Army, but he finished life an invalid from alcoholism.

• Stalin did appear to have a closer relationship with his daughter, Svetlana, but that faded quickly as she grew older and he grew more paranoid. The relationship became seriously strained when he had her first boyfriend, Alexander Yakovlevich

Kapler, sentenced, on a trumped-up charge, to ten years in a prison camp.

• Meanwhile, Stalin focused on ferreting out or "unmasking enemies of the people." He made accusations against friends and even family members who were previously regarded as allies, and he did nothing to assist those who might have been unjustly accused. Instead, he grew more intensely suspicious.

• By the time Stalin began his infamous Five-Year Plans, he was far removed from the people, and he had little regard for the human difficulties associated with collectivization. The *kulak* (farming peasant class) became desperate as their properties were confiscated. The agricultural life of the USSR was in turmoil: half to two-thirds of all livestock was slaughtered by 1933 to feed hungry people; the amount of cultivated land fell sharply; and families torn from their land became homeless. Hunger and desperation led to petty thievery of food and basic supplies, which was punishable by an unconditional ten-year imprisonment. By 1933, more than 50,000 people had been sentenced to the concentration camps.

• During this time, Stalin was trusting aides and colleagues less and less, preferring to direct Soviet life personally. He purged anyone who seemed to threaten his power. The relationship between Stalin and the rest of the Party became so strained in the early 1930s that almost a quarter of the Party delegates voted against Stalin in a leadership vote. After that, Stalin no longer took the chance of putting himself up for re-election. He directed that Party and state documents stop listing him as General Secretary, an elected position, and he continued ruling without an official title.

• Toward the latter 1930s, Stalin became more hard-lined and paranoid. Anyone could be accused of "Trotskyism" and sentenced to death. In a two-year period, 30,514 people were sentenced to be shot for disloyalty to the State. The NKVD, Stalin's police force, rounded up thousands of people suspected of capital crimes; Stalin and the chief of NKVD signed orders for their executions without considering circumstance or proof.

• By the end of the 1930s, the purges began tapering off. Party membership had understandably declined, so that

Stalin seemed less inclined to purge and more inclined to work on filling the ranks with properly dogmatized young Stalinists.

• The USSR entered the war, joining the allies against Germany, but after, the wary allies quickly split again. Stalin continued his hard-line tactics, and continual unrest was in the Party. Military standards thrived while living standards suffered.

• When Stalin died in 1953, an inventory of his possessions revealed only a government-issue piano; there were no valuable furnishings of any kind. Stalin's clothes were largely inexpensive and included a marshal's uniform. His linens consisted of Army-issued blankets. The only original art he owned was a photo of himself and Lenin together in a friendly pose at Gorky Park. This was later determined to be a carefully constructed photo montage—a fake rendition of a scene that never happened. ℭ

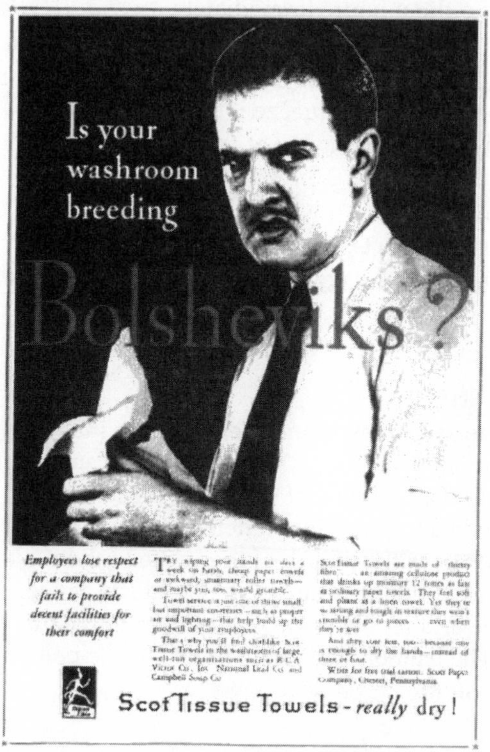

Thanks to Stalin's reign of terror, hating Bolsheviks became America's favorite pastime, as evidenced by this old ScotTissue ad

Kitchen Scientist

Baking Soda Bombs Away!

Mixing baking soda and vinegar is probably the best-known kitchen science combo around. Try this one and you'll see why.

1 Start with a leak-proof Ziploc bag, vinegar, warm water, a tissue and a carton of baking soda.

2 Place about a half-cup of vinegar and a quarter cup of warm water into your Ziploc sandwich bag. Carefully zip the bag halfway closed.

3 Pour the baking soda into the tissue and twist the top. This will prevent the baking soda from spilling into the mixture immediately when it's added.

4 Insert the baking soda tissue baggie into the bag, but don't let it fall into the liquid yet. Squeeze it from the outside while you completely seal the baggie. Let the tissue fall into the liquid and run.

5 When the baking soda, which is a base, hits the vinegar—an acid—the mixture reacts, creating carbon dioxide. The carbon dioxide fills the Ziploc baggie pretty quickly, causing it to burst open with a bang. Oh wait, did we forget to mention that this experiment is best done in a bathtub or outside? Sorry!

VARIATION ON THE THEME

Here's another, quieter, less messy, and therefore less interesting way of exploiting the same reaction. Get a soda bottle and pour a half-inch of water and a half-inch of distilled vinegar into it. Take some baking soda and put it into a deflated balloon. Fit the end of the balloon over the mouth of the bottle without letting the baking soda spill into the liquid yet. Hold the balloon securely on the bottle and let the baking soda drop down into the liquid mixture. The balloon will likely inflate to the point of exploding, or flying off the bottle. ☾

Stately Knowledge

12 Reasons Why Ya Gotta Love New York

There are so many reasons to love New York, but we've somehow managed to pick out our 12 favorites.

1 Want to stand at the most crowded street corner in the United States? Get yourself to the corner of 59th and Lexington in New York City. New York also hosts the busiest highway in the nation: the George Washington Bridge.

2 The Statue of Liberty's index finger is 8 feet long. If you plan to buy her a ring, keep in mind that her finger joint is almost 3.5 feet around.

3 Grace Bedell, an eleven-year-old from Chautauqua, New York, convinced Abraham Lincoln to grow his beard while campaigning for president in 1860 by writing him in a letter: "You would look a great deal better for your face is so thin. All the ladies like whiskers and they would tease their husbands to vote for you." It seems to have worked, because he won.

4 We love LeRoy! LeRoy, New York, that is—the birthplace of Jell-O.

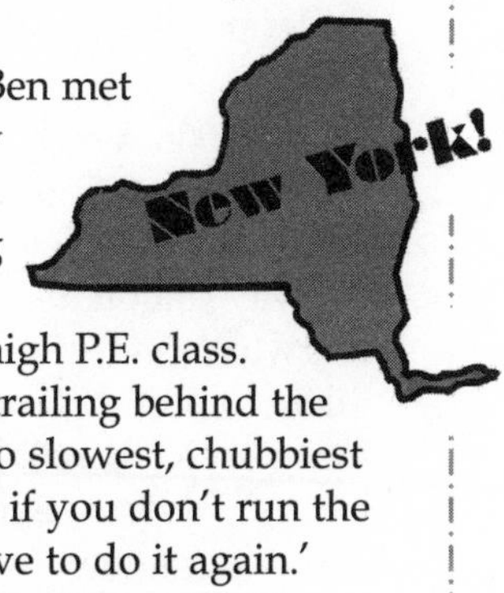

5 Want to know where ice cream maker Ben met Jerry? In 1963, Bennett Cohen and Jerry Greenfield were "smart, nerdy, fat kids" at Merrick Avenue Junior High School in Long Island, New York, undergoing humiliations that come with being overweight in junior high P.E. class. They ended up on the same running track, trailing behind the other guys. Recalled Jerry: "We were the two slowest, chubbiest guys in the class. Coach yelled, 'Gentlemen, if you don't run the mile in under 7 minutes, you're going to have to do it again.' And Ben yelled back, 'Gee, coach, if I don't do it in under 7 minutes the first time, I'm certainly not going to do it in under 7 minutes the second time.' To me this was brilliance. This was a

guy I wanted to know." Years later, when they decided to go into business together, they decided it should be food-related because they were into eating.

6 Created by Arthur Wynn, the first crossword puzzle appeared in the pages of the *New York World* newspaper on December 21, 1913. A national crossword puzzle craze ensued.

7 In the 1860s, some guys from the drinking society, "The Jolly Corks," visited Barnum's Museum in New York City and spied a stuffed elk. Thereafter, they decided to call themselves the Benevolent and Protective Order of Elks, aka the Elks Club.

8 In 1908, a sign reading "Baseball Today—Polo Grounds" in a New York City subway station inspired Jack Norworth and Albert von Tilzer to write a song. They'd never seen a baseball game, but they'd heard enough about it to know it was popular, so they penned "Take Me Out to the Ballgame."

9 The teddy bear was first created in Brooklyn, New York, in 1902.

10 In 1853 at the Moon Lake Lodge in Saratoga Springs, New York, a snack industry was born. A picky patron—Commodore Cornelius Vanderbilt—kept complaining that his fried potatoes were too thick. The restaurant's chef, George Crum, finally sliced them paper-thin as a joke. Vanderbilt's loved them, and Crum eventually opened a specialty shop dealing only in potato chips.

11 Peekskill, New York, is the place where Edwin Binney and C. Harold Smith invented "dustless" blackboard chalk and Crayola crayons in 1903.

12 Skyscrapers in New York were going up so fast in the 1930s that the director of *King Kong* had to change his script three times before filming ended. Kong was to climb the world's highest building, so the script first read, "the N.Y. Life," then, "the Chrysler," and finally, "the Empire State."

Spooky Tales

3 Short Ghost Stories from Old Japan

More ancient Japanese legends collected by Lafcadio Hearn in 1903, about ducks, decapitation and faces like eggs....

THE MANDARIN DUCK

There was a falconer and hunter named Sonjo. One day at Akanuma he saw a pair of mandarin ducks swimming together in a river that he was about to cross. To kill a mandarin duck is not considered good luck at all, but Sonjo happened to be very hungry, and he shot at the pair. His arrow pierced the male: the female escaped into the rushes of the further shore, and disappeared. Sonjo took the dead bird home, and cooked it.

That night he dreamed that a beautiful woman came into his room, stood by his pillow, and began to weep. So bitterly did she weep that Sonjo felt as if his heart were being torn out. The woman cried to him: "Oh! why did you kill him? What harm did he ever do you? Of what wrong was he guilty? We were so happy together, and you killed him! Me too you have killed, for I will not live without my husband!"

Then again she wept so bitterly that her crying pierced into the marrow of the listener's bones, and she sobbed out a poem: "At the coming of twilight I invited him to return with me. Now to sleep alone in the shadow of the rushes—Oh, what misery unspeakable!"

After reciting these verses, she exclaimed: "You do not know, you cannot know what you have done! But tomorrow, when you go to Akanuma, you will see, you will see...." And weeping very piteously, she went away.

When Sonjo awoke in the morning, this dream remained so vivid in his mind that he was greatly troubled. And he resolved to go to Akanuma at once, that he might learn whether his dream was anything more than a dream.

So he went to Akanuma; and there at the riverbank he saw the female mandarin duck swimming alone. The bird looked up and saw Sonjo; but, instead of trying to escape, she swam straight towards him, looking at him all the while in a strange fixed way. Then, with her beak, she suddenly tore open her own body, and died before the hunter's eyes.

Sonjo shaved his head and became a priest.

ON THE AKASAKA ROAD

On the Akasaka Road, in Tokyo, there is a slope called Kii-no-kuni-zaka. On one side of this slope you see an ancient moat with high green banks rising up to gardens; on the other, long walls of an imperial palace. Before the era of street-lamps, this neighborhood was very lonesome after dark; and many pedestrians would go miles out of their way rather than climb the Kii-no-kuni-zaka, alone, after sunset.

One night long ago, an old merchant was hurrying up the Kii-no-kuni-zaka, when he saw a woman crouching by the moat, all alone and weeping bitterly. Fearing that she intended to drown herself, he stopped to offer her assistance or consolation. She appeared slight and graceful, handsomely dressed; and her hair was like that of a young girl of good family. "Young lady," he exclaimed, approaching her. "Do not cry like that. Tell me what the trouble is. I would be glad to help you." (He really meant what he said, for he was a very kind man.) But she continued to weep, hiding her face from him with one of her long sleeves. "Young lady," he said again, as gently as he could, "please, please listen to me! This is no place for a young lady at night! Do not cry, I implore you! Only tell me how I may be of some help to you!" Slowly she rose up, but turned her back to him, and continued to moan and sob behind her sleeve. He laid his hand lightly upon her shoulder, and pleaded: "Young lady, listen to me, just for one little moment!"

The young woman slowly turned around, and dropped her sleeve. She stroked her face with her hand…and the man saw that she had no eyes or nose or mouth. He screamed and ran away. Up Kii-no-kuni-zaka he ran, and all was black and empty before him. On and on he ran, never daring to look back; and at last he saw a lantern, so far away that it looked like the gleam of a firefly; and he made for it.

It proved to be only the lantern of an itinerant noodle-seller, who had set down his stand by the roadside; but any light and any human companionship was good after that experience; and he flung himself down at the feet of the noodle-seller, crying out, "Ah!—aa!!—aa!!!"

"Hey now!" exclaimed the soba-man roughly. "What is the matter with you? Anybody hurt you?"

"Nobody hurt me," panted the merchant, "only...Ah!—aa!"

"Only scared you?" queried the peddler, unsympathetically. "Robbers?"

"Not robbers—not robbers," gasped the terrified man. "I saw—I saw a woman—by the moat—and she showed me.... Ah! I cannot tell you what she showed me!"

"Well! Was it anything like THIS that she showed you?" cried the noodle-man, stroking his own face—which was also smooth and featureless, like an egg. And, simultaneously, the light went out.

DEATH, WHERE IS THY BITE?

An execution was about to take place in the garden of an important samurai. The condemned man was made to kneel down in a wide sanded space with arms bound behind him. Retainers and servants packed rice-bags around the kneeling man, wedging him in that he could not move. The master came, and observed the arrangements. He found them satisfactory, and made no remarks.

Suddenly the condemned man cried out to him. "Honored sir, the fault for which I have been doomed I did not wittingly commit. It was only my very great stupidity that caused the fault. Having been born stupid, by reason of my Karma, I could not always help making mistakes. But to kill a man for being stupid is wrong—and that wrong will be repaid. So surely as you kill me, so surely shall I be avenged. Out of the resentment that you provoke will come the vengeance, and evil will be rendered for evil."

It's believed that if any person is killed while feeling strong resentment, his ghost will be able to take vengeance upon the killer. The samurai knew this, and he replied very gently, almost caressingly: "We shall allow you to frighten us as much as you please—after you are dead. But it is difficult to believe that you mean what you say. Will you try to give us some sign of your great resentment—after your head has been cut off?"

"Assuredly I will," answered the man.

"Very well," said the samurai, drawing his long sword. "I am now going to cut off your head. Directly in front of you there is a stepping-stone. After your head has been cut off, try to bite the stepping-stone. If your angry ghost can help you to do that, some of us may be frightened. Will you try to bite the stone?"

"I will bite it!" cried the man angrily. "I will bite it! I will—"

There was a flash, a swish, a crunching thud: the bound body bowed over the rice sacks—two long blood-jets pumping from the shorn neck—and the head rolled upon the sand. Heavily toward the stepping-stone it rolled: then, suddenly bounding, it caught the upper edge of the stone between its teeth and clung desperately for a moment. Then it dropped off and stood still.

None spoke; but the retainers stared in horror at their master. He seemed to be quite unconcerned. He merely held out his sword to the nearest attendant, who, with a wooden dipper, poured water over the blade from haft to point, and then carefully wiped the steel with soft paper. And thus ended the ceremonial part of the incident.

For months thereafter, the retainers and the domestics lived in ceaseless fear of ghostly visitation. None of them doubted that the promised vengeance would come; and their constant terror caused them to hear and to see much that did not exist. They became afraid of the sound of the wind in the bamboos, afraid even of the shadows in the garden. At last, after taking counsel together, they decided to petition their master to have an exorcism service performed on behalf of the vengeful spirit.

"Quite unnecessary," the samurai said, when his chief retainer uttered the general wish. "I understand that the desire of a dying man for revenge may be a cause for fear. But in this case there is nothing to fear."

The retainer looked at his master beseechingly, but hesitated to ask the reason of the alarming confidence.

"Oh, the reason is simple enough," declared the samurai,

divining the unspoken doubt. "Only the very last intention of the fellow could have been dangerous; and when I challenged him to give me the sign, I diverted his mind from the desire of revenge. He died with the set purpose of biting the stepping-stone; and that purpose he was able to accomplish, but nothing else. All the rest he must have forgotten. So you need not feel any further anxiety about the matter."

And indeed the dead man gave no more trouble. Nothing at all happened. ☾

Chatty Letter from a Salem "Witch" Persecutor

To John Cotton, Jr.
August 5, 1692

Reverend Sir,

Our good God is working of miracles. Five witches were lately executed, impudently demanding of God a miraculous vindication of their innocency. Immediately upon this, our God miraculously sent in five Andover witches, who made a most ample, surprising, amazing confession of all their villainies, and declared the five newly executed to have been of their company, discovering many more, but all agreeing in Burroughs being their ringleader, who, I suppose this day receives his trial at Salem. Since those, there have come in other confessors; yea, they come in daily. About this prodigious matter my soul has been refreshed with some little short of miraculous answers of prayer, which are not to be written: but they comfort me with a prospect of a hopeful issue.

The whole town yesterday turned the lecture into a fast, kept in our meeting-house; God give a good return. But in the morning we were entertained with the horrible tidings of the late earthquake at Jamaica, on the 7th of June last. When, on a fair day, the sea suddenly swelled, and the earth shook and broke in many places, and in a minute's time, the rich town of Port-Royal, a very Sodom for wickedness, was immediately swallowed up, and the sea came rolling over the town. No less than seventeen-hundred souls of that one town are missing, besides other incredible devastations all over the island, where houses are demolished, mountains overturned, rocks rent, and all manner of destruction inflicted. Behold, an accident speaking to all our English America.

I live in pains, and want your prayers. Bestow them, dear Sir, on your,

Cotton Mather

Something in Common 2

It's easy, really—we'll give you a list of words and you tell us the one word that goes with all of them. Answers below (don't cheat!).

1. Job, holy, judgment, camp, opening, earth, arbor
2. Main, chicken, water, fever, silent, hot, cleaning
3. Eye, looking, fiber, wine, drinking, stained
4. Cloth, chalk, gold, moon, bin, cosmic, bowl, fairy
5. Tray, wood, tree, Wednesday, volcanic, soda
6. Hair, combination, door, Soo, pad, picking, bike
7. Mill, ill, instrument, solar, westerly, shield
8. Fish, strawberry, naval, bean, roll
9. Gun, monkey, bear, hair, palm, elbow
10. West, board, minor, skeleton, stone, ignition
11. Pearl, traffic, session, raspberry, toe
12. Drive, backer, air, railroad, assembly, phone, sales, dotted
13. Right, out, bag, cuff, wash, made, stamp, delivery, puppet
14. Lunch, ears, car, cardboard, soap, match
15. Club, mail, site, ceiling, dancer, exhaust, tail, window, belt
16. Frost, tire, car, hi, lumber, hammer, Monterey
17. Seven, cheer, beat, chuck, speed, end, town, wind
18. Fighter, wild, forest, place, starter, pit, alarm, Chicago
19. Two, up, smiley, clock, rock, off, facts, powder
20. Finger, penny, hob, file, finishing, rusty, polish, salon, gun

ANSWERS: *1. day; 2. spring; 3. glass; 4. dust; 5. ash; 6. lock; 7. wind; 8. jelly; 9. grease; 10. key; 11. jam; 12. line; 13. hand; 14. box; 15. fan; 16. jack; 17. up; 18. fire; 19. face; 20. nail*

Life Lessons

How to Make a 12-Foot "Teepee"

Long before log cabins, the housing of choice in North America was the tipi. Building one isn't that difficult. Here's how.

Blackfoot tipis from the 1800s

BUILDING A "TEEPEE" (tipi) can be easy or hard, depending on how authentic you want it to be. For example, if you want one in the style of some tribes, our instructions would begin: "Skin 30 bison...."

WHAT YOU'LL NEED

- 30 bison skins, or 32 yards of canvas duck fabric
- 12 lodge poles, straight and slender, 14 feet long
- 2 poles for the smoke flaps, 16 feet long
- Rope
- Strong needle and thread
- Stakes or rocks

HOW YOU DO IT

1 Cut your 32 yards of canvas into three strips 8 yards long. Sew them side by side into a rectangle 4 yards by 8 yards. As below, draw the designs on the fabric using chalk and cut them out. (Using

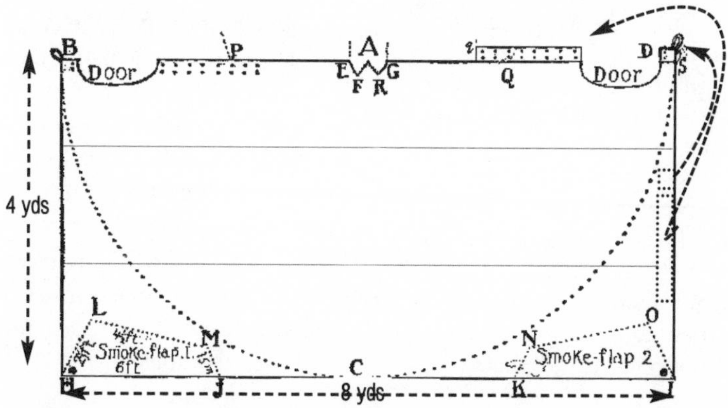

a 4-yard length of string anchored at **A** will help you draw the giant semicircle.)

2 Sew the smoke flaps and connecting strips as below. If you're a traditionalist, make reinforced holes at **B, P, Q** and **D** to lace rope through; otherwise, try using industrial-strength Velcro. Attach loops of rope or fabric strips every

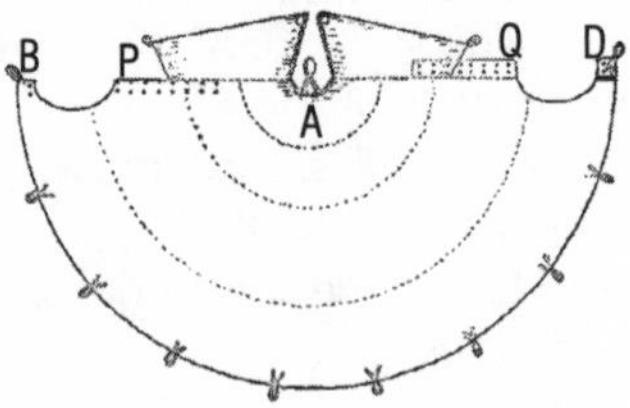

4 feet around the circle as well as one at the center point of the circle at **A** and one at the bottom of each smoke flap. Make a 2-inch hole at the top of each smoke flap.

3 About the supporting poles: using store-bought lumber is not a bad idea. For stability, you want the poles to be about 2.5 inches thick on the bottom end and 1 inch on the top. Buy 2x4s and ask a lumberyard worker to halve them lengthwise at a diagonal slant (see below). Each 2x4 will give you two poles.

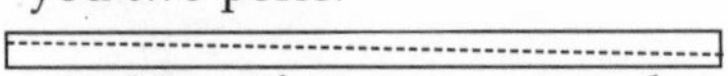

4 Now it's time to set up the tipi. Measure 12 feet from the bottom of two poles and tie them together. Tie a third pole to them to make a tripod, and set the poles up on their feet. On the ground, draw a circle 12 feet in diameter and place the bottoms of the poles equal distances around it.

5 Take all the rest of the support poles but one and lean them up against the three, spacing them as regularly as you can around the circle. Lash them all together at the top by walking around the circle with a rope two or three times. Decide where the door will be—preferably facing away from the wind—and anchor the rope with a stake driven inside the

circle opposite the door. Leave a space for the 12th pole.

5 Attach the top of the cloth to the 12th pole using the loop at **A**. Lift the pole into place and wrap the skin around the structure, using rope, pins or Velcro to hold it together. Push the two longer poles though the smoke flap holes to hold the opening open. If necessary, reinforce with ropes and a wooden crosspiece.

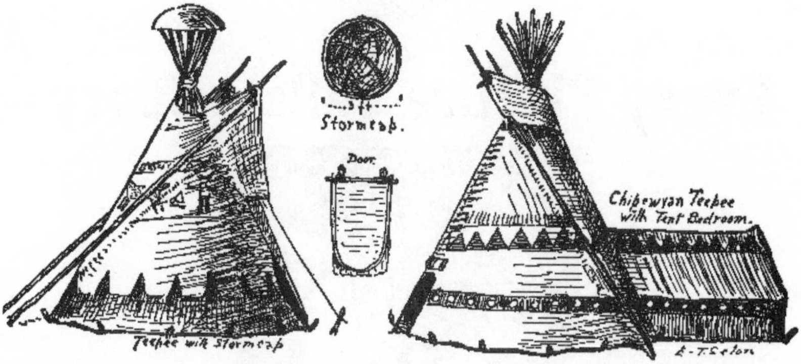

6 You can stake the tent down with the ropes at the bottom, but you won't need to unless the wind picks up substantially.

7 Using leftover fabric, make a door flap (see above).

8 In cold weather, a small fire can be set in a fire circle in the middle of the tent. In hot weather, the open top adds cooling ventilation. During rain, you can make a fabric cap to rest on top of the poles. ☾

Wigwam or Tipi?

Despite this page from an old children's book (*right*), a wigwam is not the same as a tipi. Wigwams were small, single-family domes (*below*) used as shelter in rain and bad weather.

The above is a wigwam. The picture to the right—despite the charming rhyme—is not.

W
W is for Wigwam,
that looks like a tent;
If you lived in a wigwam
would you be content?

Every Picture Tells a Story

***Nude Descending a Staircase No. 2* by Marcel Duchamp, 1912**

• Marcel Duchamp was born to a family of artists. He became a founder of Dada, an absurdist, avant garde movement. (The name doesn't come from child-speak for father, as some suppose, but from the French word for a hobbyhorse.)

• In *Nude Descending a Staircase No. 2,* Duchamp tried to show each incremental step of a moving person.

• There is also *Nude Descending a Staircase No. 1.* The main difference is that *No.* 2 has the little comic-booky curved lines and dots that indicate movement.

• After about twenty paintings, Duchamp decided he didn't want to repeat himself, so he gave it up. For a while he exhibited what he called "Readymades," which were common objects he bought and signed as if they were art.

• Eventually, Duchamp decided he was bored with art. He retired and became a champion chess player.

VW

Bugging Detroit's Autocracy

Today, they're the ultimate sign of yuppiedom, and the cost is comparable to any other car. Originally, though, the VW Beetle was a way for Americans to vote with their dollars and good sense against the excesses of Detroit.

THE BUG was designed by Ferdinand Porsche, the brilliant auto designer. He fathered a succession of high-powered yet elegant autos, including the Mercedes, for a succession of German manufacturers.

Porsche decided that his *volksauto* ("people's auto") would have to be a completely new design. He gave the car a reverse-teardrop shape to increase fuel efficiency. Brilliantly, he redesigned parts that were too heavy or expensive. Heavy wheel springs gave way to a new kind of suspension system that used torsion bars. Porsche replaced the heavy chassis with a sheet-metal floor pan, creased and corrugated for strength. He mounted a small air-cooled engine in back of the car, which improved traction, cut the expense of the drive train, and did away with the space-wasting hump in the passenger compartment.

Porsche went looking for a backer and found one in Adolf Hitler. Hitler was an auto enthusiast, even though he had never learned to drive.

He was an admirer of the Mercedes and Porsche racing cars, which were winning prestige for Germany in international races. In quick order, Porsche produced 33 cars and ran them around test tracks. They satisfactorily performed.

In 1938, the Reich built an ultramodern factory, and Hitler announced that the car would henceforth be known as the *Kraft-durch-Freude Wagen* ("Strength-Through-Joy Car").

But only 210 Strength-Through-Joy Cars were built before the factory had to be diverted to the war effort.

Staffed by slaves from the concentration camps, the factory produced some 70,000 Jeep-like *Kübelwagens* and amphibious *Schwimmkübels,* and various supplies for soldiers on the Eastern Front.

As a result, the Volksvagenwerk factory was a target of American planes and was in shambles when captured in April of 1945. The factory was scheduled for dismantling, but a few of the former car workers—hungry, having nothing much to do, and remembering the dream of Volkswagen prosperity—started coming in to see what was left of the production line. They located tools and dies, scrounged materials, and managed to hand-build a few Strength-Through-Joy Cars. These they bartered to the occupying British officers for food.

At first the plant did well, going from 1,785 cars the first year to 10,020 cars the next. Then things started sagging. In 1947, the factory produced only 8,987 cars, including the first VWs ever earmarked for export. But the plant couldn't continue building cars in an unmanaged plant that used scrounged parts.

No British car makers wanted to save the plant. They described the car as ugly, noisy, outlandish and unsalable. Henry Ford II, as well, turned down the opportunity to take over the company (Ford once described the car as a "little %#*!-box"). The Soviet Government was willing to take control if they could renegotiate the German/Soviet border to include the land the factory was on. The Allies refused the offer.

Finding no takers, the British appointed pre-war car executive Heinrich Nordhoff director of the plant. Nordhoff didn't like the VW, but he needed a job, and his family was hungry. On New Year's

Day 1948, he moved into the factory, sleeping on a cot.

Because Nordhoff had no executives looking over his shoulder, he was able to do as he saw fit. He met regularly with his workers, listening to them, and inspiring them to higher productivity and quality. All profits he plowed back into the facilities and equipment, but it became clear that the struggling company would need a larger market than postwar Germany to survive and grow. Because much of Europe was still in ruins, Nordhoff decided to go where the money was: the United States. He shipped two Beetles to his only international distributor, Ben Pon in the Netherlands.

Pon was a great car dealer. He had to be, selling German cars in the Netherlands, where residual bitterness toward Germany was still powerful. Pon took one of the Beetles to the United States. The Bug got only a little publicity, much of it negative (newspapers referred to it as "Hitler's car"). U.S. auto dealers refused to take it seriously. Finally, Pon sold his model for $800 to pay his travel costs. He returned to Holland, defeated.

It was just a temporary defeat. American vets stationed in Europe had discovered how good the cheap little cars were and began bringing them back to this country.

Their word-of-mouth praise and a write-up in *Consumer Reports* stimulated a modest demand. In 1950, 330 VWs sold in America; in 1955, 30,000; in 1957, 79,000.

Nordhoff felt vindicated in deciding not to restyle the ugly little car. "The only decision I am really proud of," he said years later, "is that I refused to change Porsche's design. It's hard to remain the same. You can always sell cars by being new. But we chose a different course."

All this stood in stark contrast to the road traveled by American manufacturers. This was, after all, the era of planned obsolescence, of fins, chrome and outlandish doodads of almost every sort, of bigger and bigger "jukeboxes on wheels." Detroit didn't know what to make of VW's success. It was the opposite of what they believed consumers wanted.

The Beetle was cheap, and American car executives were shaken to find that the people buying them weren't poor. VW customers were generally people who could afford more expensive cars but who liked the VW's no-frills design and good engineering. "The Volkswagen sells because it is, more than anything else, an honest car," noted Arthur Railton in *Popular Mechanics* in 1956.

"It doesn't pretend to be anything it is not. Being an honest piece of machinery, it is one the owner can be proud of. Wherever he looks, he sees honest design and workmanship. There are no places where parts don't fit, where paint is thin, where the trim is shoddy. There are no body rattles, no water leaks. Neither, of course, is there overstuffed, false luxury either. There is nothing about the car that is not sincere. One cannot imagine, for instance, a Volkswagen with a fake air scoop or tail fins to make it look like an airplane in flight."

Feeling pressure, GM responded with what it thought was a comparable car in 1959—the Corvair. The problem was that they thought the success of the VW had to do solely with its price, which was, at best, half-right. They cut costs on the Corvair by scrimping on key parts. Possibly the worst American car ever, the Corvair caused much unnecessary injury and death. It inspired Ralph Nader to write his best-seller, *Unsafe at Any Speed,* and spawned hundreds of product liability lawsuits.

The VW Bug and van, virtually unchanged year after year and bolstered by brilliant, honest, low-key advertising, thrived for more than a decade. Detroit's refusal (or inability) to respond in a meaningful way to the VW challenge opened the door to other low-cost, quality imports.

Modern Myth

Downward Mobility of the Upper Glass

It's a great story, often spread unknowingly by tour guides at historic sites: Pointing out that the glass is thicker at the bottom of an ancient window, they say it's because the glass is liquid and slowly flowing. But it panes us to say that it's a transparent fiction....

IS IT TRUE that windows get thicker at the bottom over years because glass is really a slow-moving liquid? Before we knock this story down, let's look at reasons why even some scientists have considered the idea plausible enough. Their reasoning goes something like this: Solids and liquids have different molecular structures. The molecules of solids occur in regular patterns, while the molecules in liquids are bonded in patterns that are irregular and haphazard. The structure of glass is irregular, so maybe it's really just a very, very thick liquid. Casting around for evidence that would fit this intriguing theory, researchers found that antique windows often had glass that was thicker on the bottom than it was on the top. Aha! they

Getting Down to Glass Facts

• How come you can see through glass if it's a solid? It's not a very dense solid. There's enough space between molecules to let light shine through.

• Glass is made of silica sand, with a little soda ash and limestone added to lower the sand's melting temperature. Humans figured out how to make glass after finding chunks of obsidian formed by lightning strikes on the beach. Early humans originally cast it like metal and then ground and polished it. In about 50 B.C., the Romans figured out how to blow glass using hollow metal tubes, which suddenly made glass inexpensive and practical for a variety of cups, bottles and other vessels.

said, here's evidence that glass slowly seeps downward with time, just like a really thick syrup would.

Well, not so fast. After a lot of shouting and bickering, it looks like the "You idiots, glass is a solid" side wins this one. Yes, glass has a different molecular structure than most solids, but it doesn't necessarily follow that it's a liquid. In fact, although scientists once called glass a "supercooled liquid," most now believe it is really an "amorphous solid," which means that it solidifies haphazardly without forming crystals.

Panes-Taking Work

MAKING GOOD glass windows long eluded human ingenuity. The ancient Romans molded glass and then ground and buffed it, but the results were cloudy and very expensive. On the other hand, their climate was such that they really didn't need windows, anyway.

In much cooler Germany, glassmakers made a giant leap in A.D. 600. They figured out how to blow a large sphere and wave it vigorously until it became a large, hollow cylinder, which the glassblower quickly sliced and flattened onto a metal table. However, this glass was thick and still hard to see clearly through.

Normandy glassmakers finally came up with a clever method of making much thinner windows that remained the state of the art until the late 19th century. Thin and transparent, these glass sheets were invariably thicker on one end, leading to the urban myth about glass oozing (*see above*). Using about 9 pounds of molten glass, a glassmaker blew a shape with a round body and straight neck on top. He'd attach a metal cap to the center of the round end, flatten the flask into a decanter shape, attach a metal rod called a "punty" to the metal cap and remove the blow pipe, leaving a hole. Now the real fun began as the glassmaker spun the punty rod inside a hot furnace. To quote an 1860 account by college professor Sheridan Muspratt:

> **The action of heat and centrifugal force combined is soon visible. The hole, caused by the removal of the blowing pipe, enlarges. The opening grows larger and larger; for the moment is caught in a glimpse of a circle with a double rim; the next moment, before the eyes of the astonished spectator, is whirling a thin, transparent, circular plate of glass.... The sound of the final opening of the piece has been compared to that produced by quickly expanding a wet umbrella. In this way a flat circular disc, sixty inches (five feet) in diameter is produced, of almost uniform thickness, except at the point of attachment to the punty, and the glass at the edge of the disc is also in some cases a little thickened.... The cutting of a circle into rectangle sheets, must necessarily be attended with waste and confined to fairly small sizes.**

Nowadays, glass manufacturers pour molten glass onto a pool of molten tin. Since tin stays melted at a lower temperature than glass, the glass can harden into a uniform thickness without coming in contact with anything solid. As a result, the process creates panes that are flawless on both sides.

Looking at other ancient glass gives better evidence than old windows do. For example, glass bottles from ancient Rome show no sign of seeping. Telescope lenses that were precision-ground centuries ago show no distortions. And arrowheads from prehistoric times made of obsidian (a glass made when lightning struck sand on the beach) are still symmetrical and razor-sharp—something that wouldn't be the case if glass droops, seeps and weeps over time.

Okay, you ask, then how do they explain away the bottom-heavy windows on ancient buildings? Simple. In the old days, glassmakers didn't use the modern technique of floating liquid glass on molten tin, which provides a pane of uniform thickness. They hand-blew and spun window glass, a technique that all but guaranteed that each pane of glass would have varying thickness.

If you were putting a fragile, heavy pane of glass into a window frame, would you place the thicker edge or the thinner edge at the bottom where all the weight of the pane would be resting? Right, the thicker side. So rather than provide evidence of glass seepage, the bottom-heavy windows merely prove that glaziers in the past weren't fools. ℭ

Words from the Wise

Things to Never, Never Do

"Never put anything on paper...and never trust a man with a small black mustache." —P. G. Wodehouse

"Never get a mime talking. He won't stop." —Marcel Marceau

"Never underestimate the power of human stupidity." —Robert Heinlein

"Never send a man to do a horse's job." —Mr. Ed

"Never lend books, for no one ever returns them; the only books I have in my library are books that other folks have lent to me." —Anatole France

"Never trust a man with short legs—brain's too near their bottoms." —Noel Coward

"Never say anything on the phone that you wouldn't want your mother to hear at your trial." —Sydney Biddle Barrows

"Never drop your gun to hug a bear." —H. E. Palmer

"Never steal anything so small that you'll have to go to an unpleasant city jail for it instead of a minimum-security federal tennis prison." —P. J. O'Rourke

"Never put off until tomorrow what you can do the day after tomorrow." —Mark Twain

"Never date a girl named 'Ruby.'" —Tom Waits

"Never offend people with style when you can offend them with substance." —Tony Brown

"Never put a razor inside your nose—even as a joke." —Jake Johansen

Tom Swifties IV

"The PH Is Low," Said Tom Acidly

From the surreal 1960s came elephant jokes and Tom Swifties, based on bad puns and the stylistic excesses of Victor Appleton, who created the popular Tom Swift stories. Here are more.

"What a grand dam," said Tom cooly.
"May I introduce the Family Stone?" Tom asked slyly.
"I'd like to teach the world to sing..." Tom began coaxingly.
"*Niña, Pinta, Santa Maria* and *Titanic,*" Tom said forebodingly.
"Add three cans water," said Tom with great concentration.
"I still haven't struck oil," said Tom boringly.
"I'm dying," Tom croaked.
"Your embroidery is terrible," Tom needled cruelly.
"The woodland goat-boy is no more," Tom deadpanned.
"Mink-lined coats are cruel," Tom deferred.
"I can't hear," Tom said deftly.
"Speak, or I'll emasculate you!" Tom demanded.
"All we brought was gold and frankincense," the magi demurred.
"They canceled my doctor's visit," said Tom, disappointed.
"Hey Egyptians, I'm drowning!" Tom said, deep in denial.
"You look like Venus de Milo," Tom said disarmingly.
"Out, damned spot," said Lady Macbeth disdainfully.
"It's June," said Tom, dismayed.
"I lost someone who can't speak," said Tom dumbfoundedly.
"Emily's put on weight," said Tom emphatically.
"I have an alternate personality," said Tom, being frank.

Zen Masters

MODELING ZEN

Here's something to meditate on: words from some of the world's top fashion models—Tyra Banks, Niki Taylor and more.

"I don't know what to do with my arms. It just makes me feel weird and I feel like people are looking at me and that makes me nervous." —Tyra Banks

"I haven't seen the Eiffel Tower, Notre Dame, the Louvre. I haven't seen anything. I don't really care." —T.B.

"I liked college guys but they could tell I was just a skinny girl." —T.B.

"I love the confidence that makeup gives me." —T.B.

"It was God who made me so beautiful. If I weren't, then I'd be a teacher." —Linda Evangelista

"All my doctors said I should become a model." —Niki Taylor

"I wish my butt did not go sideways, but I guess I have to face that." — Christie Brinkley

"In the studio, I do try to have a thought in my head, so that it's not like a blank stare." —Cindy Crawford

"It's a huge change for your body. You don't even want to look in the mirror after you've had a baby, because your stomach is just hanging there like a Shar-Pei." —C.C.

"You start out happy that you have no hips or boobs. All of a sudden you get them, and it feels sloppy. Then just when you start liking them, they start drooping." —C.C.

"Flying is awful, there's nothing to do when you're up in the air. I bloat up, my skin gets dry, and when we hit turbulence, I'm terrified. I was coming back from Tel Aviv recently, and we had forty minutes of bumps. I got so scared I grabbed a paper and pen and put them in my pocket, just in case we crashed and I needed to write a letter from wherever we landed." —Daniela Pestova

Mascot Miracles

How Chiquita Gave Bananas Appeal

"I'm Chiquita Banana and I've come to say: Bananas have to ripen in a certain way...." Before Chiquita—a direct rip-off of a popular south-of-the-border singer—United Fruit advertised fruitlessly.

Chiquita Banana, the wacky singing Latin American banana, was the response that the United Fruit Company came up with to counteract their negative image.

In the court of world public opinion, the United Fruit Company was guilty as charged. The company had a well-deserved reputation of ruthlessness among our Good Neighbors down in South America. It bought up millions of acres of land (sometimes merely to keep it out of the hands of competitors) and as many government officials as it could. The governments it couldn't buy, it undermined and overthrew. Often, as in places like Guatemala in 1954, it received the support of the U.S. government. In fact, the term "banana republic" was originally coined as a backhanded tribute to United Fruit's ability to keep in power whatever corrupt government it wanted, by ballot or bullet.

The company had so much cheap land that it wouldn't bother with maintaining the soil—when a plantation was exhausted, the company would abandon it. They'd load everything of value onto rail cars, tearing up the railroad tracks after them, and bulldoze another plantation out of the rain forest. It was costly to the land and the company, but absolutely disastrous for its local workers, who were usually abandoned at the same time.

All of these practices engendered hard feelings and unfavorable publicity for the company. In Cuba, United Fruit lost all its holdings when two sons of a lifelong United Fruit employee, Angel Castro, led a successful revolution against the banana-corrupted government. (Years later, company executives who knew Angel couldn't help but shake their heads and wonder aloud how a couple of quiet and polite kids like Fidel and Raul Castro could have gone so wrong.) It was a revolution that even United Fruit could not undo. Not that it didn't try—the company secretly provided two freighters from its "Great White Fleet" to transport fighters and weapons into Cuba during the ill-fated Bay of Pigs invasion.

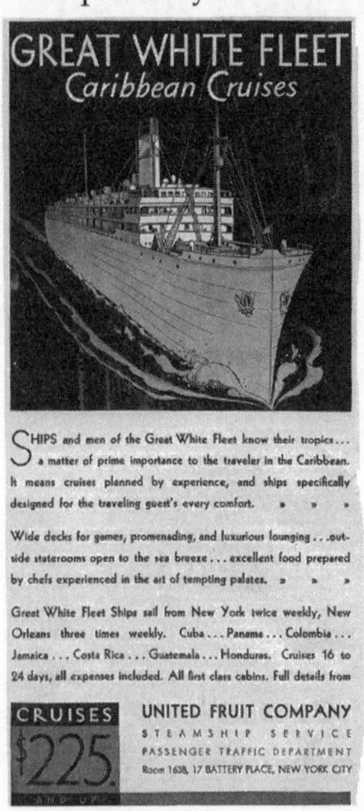

A 1931 ad for United Fruit's Great White Fleet cruise and banana line

But that was later. Lovable Miss Chiquita Banana was born two decades before Castro's revolution, as World War II began winding down. The Great White Fleet had been repainted battleship gray and pressed into emergency service by the Navy. The numbers of bananas coming into the United States turned into a trickle. United Fruit's corporate leaders had kept their plantations going even though they didn't have a way to get the bananas to market. Now they began planning a postwar blitz. As soon as they could, they once again began shipping a hundred million bunches of bananas a year.

Most Americans hadn't seen a banana since shortly after the attack on Pearl Harbor, three years earlier. United Fruit's directors decided this was a splendid opportunity to carve out a brand-new, cute and cuddly image for the company.

Carmen Miranda on the DVD cover of the 1995 documentary *Carmen Miranda: Bananas is my Business,* by Helena Solberg and David Meyer

They turned the problem over to their radio ad agency, Batten, Barton, Durstine & Osborn, which came up with the idea of a wacky but sexy female Latin American singer modeled after Carmen Miranda, even choosing a name that mimicked hers and stealing her trademark, a fruit-covered hat. BBD&O assigned two staff jingle writers, lyricist Garth Montgomery and songsmith Len MacKenzie, to write a suitable song. And indeed they did.

United Fruit pushed the "Chiquita Banana" song into the public's consciousness by insisting that it be performed on all the radio shows the company sponsored. Radio listeners heard the song rendered by such varied performers as Fred Allen, Alec Templeton, Arthur Fieldler, Bert Lahr, the King Sisters, Xavier Cugat, Charlie McCarthy, Carmen Miranda herself and even fictional detective Ellery Queen ("I'm Chiquita Banana and I'm here to say/You have to catch a criminal in a certain way/ Now here's the strategy I've tried to use/I have paid strict attention to all the clues..."). At its peak, the song was played around the country on radio 276 times in one day. Recorded on disk by Ray Bloch and the King Sisters, it became a juke box hit as well.

"Chiquita Banana" was a genuine hit, and the public began clamoring to see what she looked like. The company commissioned comic artist Dik Browne, who had just finished redesigning the Campbell Kids but had yet to create the comic strip Hägar the Horrible. He drew Chiquita as a banana with a ruffled skirt, puffy sleeves and a fruit-covered hat. She began appearing in magazine ads and in 80-second cartoon shorts where she sang her song to movie audiences in 850 movie theaters across the country.

There have been many stickers over the years. Above: A 1947 commemorative and a "Chiquita Precious" from Japan.

At first, United Fruit was happy, even delirious, about the success of Chiquita and her song. But over time they began getting uneasy. True, Chiquita sold the idea of banana consumption, which helped them—but she also helped their competitors, because consumers couldn't differentiate United Fruit bananas from the others in the store.

Jack Fox, an executive who had been hired away from Coca-Cola, called a meeting one day to complain that Chiquita was a brand name of United Fruit and all the other banana companies were getting a free ride. He announced that, somehow, they were going to start branding their bananas within 6 to 8 weeks.

The old-timers scoffed—the company had been trying to figure out how to brand bananas for years, and now this new Soft Drink Guy was going to do it in 6 weeks. Fox continued that he didn't know exactly what form the branding would take—maybe a rubber stamp or electrostatic printing (like a Xerox machine), or maybe a gummed sticker attached to every third banana.

"Stickers?" snorted one old-timer who felt secure enough in his job to challenge the vice president. "Shee-it! Do you realize how many that would be in a year? One billion stickers. You've got to be out of your mind!"

Fox, clearly taken aback by the number, asked him to repeat the number of labels he had calculated.

"One billion!"

The room erupted in nervous laughter. Fox looked at him steadily and the laughter stopped. Fox nodded his head. "That's just what I make it. One billion."

Stickers did seem like the best way to go, even though

further calculations made it clear that the company would actually need 2.5 billion stickers that year. When the company contacted its printing vendor with the order, his eyes rolled back, and he quietly fell backward in a faint.

Designing labels with the Chiquita name and drawing prominently displayed against a field of light blue was easy. The hard part was finding a way to apply the labels inexpensively. Machinery experts from around the country worked on the problem, but none of their solutions was simple and cheap enough. (Estimates for the cost of the machinery, operator and the labels came out to anywhere from 10¢ to $10 per label applied, all of which were way too expensive.)

The solution came from an unexpected source: a young worker on a Honduran plantation who came up with a simple device that had no moving parts and was powered by a squeeze of the operator's hand.

United Fruit quickly became the largest single user of pressure-sensitive labels in the world, buying more than 3 billion a year. The commercials and stickers had such an impact that the Chiquita name became much more famous than that of United Fruit. The company called itself United Brands in the 1960s, but finally got smart and changed its name to Chiquita Brands International in 1990, using the smiling banana lady as its corporate symbol.

Updated for Your Listening Pleasure

The original 1944 Chiquita Banana jingle: "I'm Chiquita banana and I've come to say/Bananas have to ripen in a certain way/When they are fleck'd with brown and have a golden hue/Bananas taste the best and are best for you/You can put them in a salad/You can put them in a pie-aye/Any way you want to eat them/It's impossible to beat them/But, bananas like the climate of the very, very tropical equator/So you should never put bananas/in the refrigerator."

1999 Update: "I'm Chiquita Banana and I've come to say/I offer good nutrition in a simple way/When you eat a Chiquita you've done your part/To give every single day a healthy start/Underneath the crescent yellow/You'll find vitamins and great taste/With no fat, you just can't beat 'em/You'll feel better when you eat 'em/They're a gift from Mother Nature and a natural addition to your table/For wholesome, healthy, pure bananas/look for Chiquita's label!"

Speak English? 3

TRANSLATE THESE BRITISH TERMS INTO AMERICAN

Sometimes it seems like the British and Americans don't even speak the same language. How are you at translating? Translate these old and new British terms into American. (Answers below.)

1. full stop
2. inquiry agent
3. mackintosh
4. wireless
5. off the peg
6. elastic
7. fitter
8. ladder
9. scribbling block
10. footway
11. sledge
12. kipper
13. plimsolls
14. minerals
15. patience
16. reel of cotton
17. tube
18. braces

a. solitaire
b. raincoat
c. sneakers
d. mechanic
e. ready-to-wear
f. scratch pad
g. period
h. spool of thread
i. smoked herring
j. rubber band
k. sled
l. soft drinks
m. run in your stocking
n. suspenders
o. private detective
p. subway
q. sidewalk
r. radio

Answers: *1. full stop = g. period; 2. inquiry agent = o. private detective; 3. mackintosh = b. raincoat; 4. wireless = r. radio; 5. off the peg = e. ready-to-wear; 6. elastic = j. rubber band; 7. fitter = d. mechanic; 8. ladder = m. run in your stocking; 9. scribbling block = f. scratch pad; 10. footway = q. sidewalk; 11. sledge = k. sled; 12. kipper = i. smoked herring; 13. plimsolls = c. sneakers; 14. minerals = l. soft drinks; 15. patience = a. solitaire; 16. reel of cotton = h. spool of thread; 17. tube = p. subway; 18. braces = n. suspenders*

Tissue, No Lies

THE ACCIDENTAL HISTORY OF KLEENEX & KOTEX

Most new products are the results of trying to solve a problem. But sometimes innovations come as a result of having too much of something and trying to find a purpose for it.

WAR AND PAPER

Kimberly-Clark had been making paper in Wisconsin since 1872. In 1914, they hired a paper technician named Ernst Mahler to develop new products. A recent graduate from the Technical University of Darmstadt, Germany, Mahler had studied cellulose chemistry. He set up a laboratory across the street from Kimberly-Clark headquarters and convinced company president J. C. Kimberly to accompany him to Germany to check out some new products that had been developed over there, including a fluffy paper wadding product that absorbed liquids better than cotton.

While Mahler and Kimberly were in Germany, World War I broke out. They cut their trip short and hurried back to the United States with enough samples and formulae to begin developing their own version of the wadding material. Mahler tested a variety of native wood pulps before deciding that spruce trees yielded the longest and most absorbent fibers.

As the war got going full swing, a cotton shortage developed, giving Kimberly-Clark a ready market for their new product. "Cellucotton," so called because it was like cotton but made from wood cellulose, was used as pads in bandages, filters in gas masks, and stuffing for emergency jackets. When America entered the war, Kimberly-Clark patriotically decided they'd sell Cellucotton to the War Department and Red Cross at no profit.

Chinese Red Cross women sew gauze together, standard practice before Cellucotton became a medical supply

When the war ended abruptly, Kimberly-Clark had partially-filled orders for 750,000 pounds of Cellucotton for the war effort. Kimberly-Clark allowed the orders to be cancelled without penalty, leaving the company with a huge surplus. Worse, the Army also had a large surplus of Cellucotton—and began selling it to civilian hospitals for a ridiculously low price, killing the market. The company floundered around for new uses for the product until two good ones dropped into its lap.

KOTEX PADS COMPANY PROFITS

One of Kimberly-Clark's grateful nonprofit wartime customers had been the American Fund for the French Wounded. An official of the organization knew that Kimberly Clark's business had been hurt by canceled war orders and passed on some helpful information: During the war, French nurses had tried using Cellucotton during their periods and found that they made excellent sanitary pads in that they didn't have to be washed but could be disposed of. Might American women be ready for a new product of this sort?

Up to that time, menstrual pads were made of felt and had to be washed after every use. They were never spoken of in public. Still, doing some extensive but very discreet market research, the company determined that women hated the felt pads and would very much welcome an alternative. So, early in 1920, Kimberly-Clark began marketing the first disposable sanitary napkin under the less-than-catchy name "Cellunaps."

MARKETING WAS A PROBLEM

Menstrual products had never been commercially displayed or advertised. Cellunaps were too sensitive to be placed in public display, and so stayed behind the druggists' counter. Company marketers found that customers were embarrassed to ask their pharmacists for Cellunaps because of the "naps" part of the name (short for "napkins"). The company decided to change the name to one that was meaningless—that would not reveal anything in a crowded drugstore. They coined the word Kotex.

The first Kotex ads appeared in women's magazines in 1921

Even with the name change and an unrevealing package, many retailers insisted that the company take the extra step of wrapping the box in unprinted brown paper so that even the Kotex name would be hidden.

While Kimberly-Clark could see the need for discreet marketing, officials at the company refused to wrap the product. They were spending millions of dollars for advertising in women's magazines and felt that the product should be treated like any other consumer product. They encouraged retailers to take Kotex out from behind the counters and put it on display. It took a few years, but eventually most retailers got with the program.

Meanwhile, letters to the company poured in, mostly favorable. Some women, however, asked questions that showed a deep ignorance of their bodies and the menstrual process. Kimberly-Clark beefed up its Education Division and began mailing out information packs, including a pamphlet called "Marjorie May's 12th Birthday," which met with a torrent of criticism from religious leaders, self-styled moralists and others who believed that too much knowledge was a dangerous thing. Several states specifically banned "Marjorie May" and other similar mailings as being too sexually explicit. But women, unable to get the information elsewhere, continued ordering them, and

eventually, the bans were lifted. Kimberly-Clark also worked with the Disney Co. to create a color movie, *The Story of Menstruation* for schools, which has been seen by over 70 million kids.

NEW but tried and proved, Kotex enters universal service from a romantic background. For, although a woman's article, it started as Cellucotton—a wonderful sanitary absorbent which science perfected for use of our men and allied soldiers wounded in France.

With peace came an idea suggested in letters from nurses in France, regarding a new use for this wonderful absorbent, and early in 1919 our laboratory made the first sanitary pads of Cellucotton enclosed in gauze and placed them on sale in various cities. Requests for more followed every sale, and we devoted two years to perfecting the new article—named KOTEX from "cotton-like texture"—and to the building of machinery which makes and seals it hygienically without contact of human hands. Kotex are now ready for every woman's use.

The gauze envelope is 22 inches long, thus leaving generous tabs for pinning. The filler, thirty-six layers of finest Cellucotton, is 3½ inches wide by 9 inches long. Kotex are cool, more absorbent, and of lasting softness. Kotex are cheap in price and easy to throw away.

CELLUCOTTON PRODUCTS CO.
208 South LaSalle Street, Chicago, Illinois

The text that ran with the first Kotex ad in 1921

By 1939, use of the reusable felt pads was down to 20%. During World War II, large numbers of women entered the labor pool. Kimberly-Clark, in the spirit of patriotism and good marketing, made it a highest priority—despite war shortages—that war plants were well-equipped with Kotex feminine napkins. By 1947, use of old washable felt pads was down to less than 1%.

SOMETHING TO SNEEZE AT

Meanwhile, Kimberly-Clark decided to try manufacturing Cellucotton in thin sheets. Kleenex was the result. But they misjudged the market and almost had a flop.

Printed on the first boxes, each containing a hundred Cellucotton sheets, was "Kleenex Sanitary Cold Cream Remover." Kimberly-Clark thought that it had found a niche market as a disposable cloth for removing makeup and cold cream. It hadn't even occurred to them that the soft little sheets might have more universal uses as well.

One problem was the price: 65¢ per box—high at the time. Marketers then aimed for an upscale crowd, associating the Kleenex with wealth, glamour and the theatrical crowd. The company sent promotional samples to makeup artists in Hollywood and then tried to capitalize on the fact that the best Hollywood stylists used the new "scientific way to remove cold cream." Company advertisements showed movie stars using the tissues after a long day of shooting movies. Despite the hype, the tissues achieved only lukewarm sales.

FIND A NICHE AND SCRATCH IT

The Kimberly-Clark marketing people kept trying. They invented a way to make tissues pop up automatically by shuffling two piles of overlapping tissues together like a deck of cards. They introduced colors. But whatever they did, the marketplace yawned, and sales stayed flat.

In 1930, a desperate marketing department decided to go and see why Kleenex was not playing in Peoria. In fact, they literally went to Peoria, Illinois, with clipboards and a series of questions, asking people if they had any suggestions, comments, ideas, hints—anything. They were surprised to discover that nearly two-thirds of the people in Peoria who bought Kleenex used them as disposable handkerchiefs, not as make-up removers.

The marketers headed back to the main office and immediately changed their advertising to reflect this newly discovered use. "Don't put a cold in your pocket!" said one ad. "During colds, smother sneezes with Kleenex Tissues! Use once, then destroy, germs and all." The same ad also suggested using Kleenex tissues as a filter in the coffee maker. "Now my coffee's clearer—my husband's happier!" Within two years, sales increased four-fold. Kleenex—appropriately considering all the tears and sniffling in the genre—became the sponsor of the first radio soap opera, *The Story of Mary Marlin*.

HISTORICAL ADDENDUM

Although Kleenex was the first commercial tissue, they weren't the first use of paper for noses. The 17th century Japanese used *hanagami* ("sneezing paper"), which was just regular paper that they crumpled repeatedly until soft. In 1637, an English visitor wrote, "They blow their noses with a certain soft and tough kind of paper which they carry about them in small pieces, which having been used, they fling away as a filthy thing."

Judged by Its Cover

More Strange Book Titles

Can you tell a book by its title? If so, these have got to be some of the most fascinating books on the shelves, gleaned from *Bizarre Books* by Russell Ash and Brian Lake (St. Martin's, 1985).

The Muck Manual: A Practical Treatise on the Nature and Value of Manures—F. Falkner (1843)

Frog Raising for Pleasure and Profit—Dr. Albert Broel (1950)

Full Revelations of a Professional Rat-catcher After 25 Years' Experience—Ike Matthews (1898)

Onania; or The Heinous Sin of Self-Pollution, and All Its Frightful Consquences, in Both Sexes, Considered—Anonymous (1725)

Colon Cleanse the Easy Way!—Verna Burnett and Jennifer Weiss (1979)

Let's Make Some Undies—Marion Hall (1954)

Eleven Years a Drunkard; or, The Life of Thomas Doner, Having Lost Both Arms through Intemperance, He Wrote This Book With His Teeth As a Warning to Others—Thomas Doner (1878)

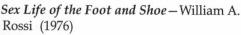

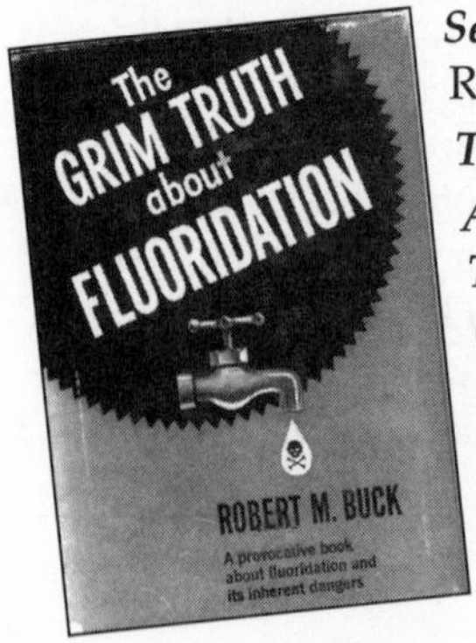

Sex Life of the Foot and Shoe—William A. Rossi (1976)

Teach Yourself Alcoholism—Meir Glatt (1843)

Amputation Stumps: Their Care and After-Treatment—Sir Godfrey Martin Huggins (1918)

The Grim Truth About Fluoridation—Robert M. Buck (1964)

Living Without Eating—Herbert Thurston (1931)

Inventing Champagne

A Short & Bubbly Primer

That glass of bubbly you toast the new year with...making it is both an art and a science. Here's the story.

Dom Pèrignon was a Benedictine monk in Hautvillers, near Reims in France. To his annoyance, he accidentally invented champagne in the 1660s, while trying to improve the abbey's white wine.

Pèrignon had been making a batch late in the season and thought that the fermentation had stopped, so he bottled it. However, some yeast remained alive and became active again when the weather warmed up, causing a second fermentation inside the bottle. When he opened a bottle, he was disgusted to find that it had gone "bad" but drank some anyway. His reaction? According to legend, he blurted out, "I'm drinking stars!" Still, he considered the bubbles were an unwelcome "impurity"—that is, until people tried the wine and asked him to try to repeat the accident. With experimentation, Pèrignon came up with the process still used today.

Although sparkling wine in America is often called "champagne," it is not technically that. By definition, true champagne comes from the Champagne district of France. The varietal can be Chardonnay, which is white, Pinot Noir or Pinot Meunier (red), or some combination thereof.

RIDDLE ME THIS, YOU BRUT

Most wines only go through one fermentation, but sparkling wine goes through two. The first takes place in big

"Riddling" the bottles

vats for two to three weeks. After that, the winemaker puts the wine in its bottle for the second fermentation and adds a sugar-yeast syrup to it before "corking" it with a temporary crown cap, like those used on soda pop bottles. Inside the sealed bottle, carbon dioxide can't escape and gets trapped in the wine, waiting for a release in the pressure to make its escape.

It then waits a long time—six months to two years. Only one problem: Over time, the yeast dies and sinks to the bottom of the bottle, making an ugly sediment.

How do you get it out without losing the carbonation? By "riddling." For six to eight weeks, winemakers rack the bottles upside-down and occasionally turn them so the yeast settles against the caps. When it's time to disgorge the sediment, the upside-down bottles go into a super-cold brine. The sediment freezes in the neck, forming an icy plug. When the winemaker pries off the bottle caps, pressure inside ejects the frozen plug.

Since there's now some wine missing from the bottle, the winemaker determines how sweet to make the champagne by topping the bottle off with a blend of sugar syrup, white wine and sometimes brandy. A little sugar makes a *brut*; increasing amounts of sugar make a *sec*, a *demi-sec*, or a *doux*.

EXPLODING BOTTLES

For centuries, champagne was a nightmare for glassblowers. With all that pressure building up inside, a good proportion of bottles exploded in wine cellars. Winemakers began the practice of closely inspecting every bottle upon arrival. The ones that were clearly irregular were set aside for uncarbonated red wine. The others were tested by smartly banging them together. Any that broke were charged to the glassblower; the ones that survived were deemed strong enough. Still, this was a less than foolproof method.

The exploding bottle crisis hit its peak with the vintage of 1828. Weather conditions

Put a Cork in It

• The Romans had first used corks in wine bottles before A.D. 200, but the practice fell out of favor for some reason and was forgotten for about fourteen centuries. During the medieval era, bottlers used a twisted cloth, leather or sealing wax.

• Finally, wine corks were reinvented in the early 16th century, soon enough for Shakespeare to write in *As You Like It,* "Take thy cork out of thy mouth, that I may drink thy tidings." Still, many winemakers preferred glass stoppers because they found, as one complained, that "much liquor is being absolutely spoiled by the defect of the cork." Cork-induced spoilage is still a big headache, with about 8 percent of all corked wine being damaged to some degree.

• Bottlers pushed corks only halfway in to make it possible to get them out again. Uncorkers wouldn't be invented for many more decades. The first mention of "bottlescrews" was recorded in 1681; they weren't called "corkscrews" until 1720.

• Corks are very elastic because they're filled with more than 300 million tiny air-filled cells. A cork can be compressed enough to get it into a bottle, yet it will immediately spring back to fill any gaps around the edge. They keep their structural integrity for up to fifty years before going brittle and crumbly.

• About 75 percent of the wine corks in the United States come from Portugal—over 360 million a year. They're made from the four-inch-thick, fire-resistant bark of the cork oak, a slow-growing evergreen. Every ten years, the trees are almost completely stripped of bark, leaving only enough to ensure that the tree will survive. A tree can be stripped twelve to fifteen times during its natural life span.

• The sheets of cork are stacked to dry for three months. They're then boiled in fungicides, dried again and cut into bottle-sized tapered cylinders that cost wine bottlers about 20 to 40 cents each.That's sometimes more than the wine itself cost to make.

• Screw tops are better and cost only a nickel each. Synthetic corks are also better at sealing bottles than corks. However, many consumers have resisted both, wrongly believing that a cork somehow indicates a good bottle of wine.

that year resulted in extra sugar in the grapes, supercharging the fermentation process. It was a booming, bang-up year for champagne makers as 80 percent of the vintage burst its bottles.

How explosive can a champagne bottle be, you ask? Ever have a blowout on a ten-speed bicycle? The pressure inside a champagne bottle is *normally* 90 pounds per square inch, about the same as a high-pressure bike tire—however, in 1828, the pressure was even higher than that. With shards of jagged, wine-soaked glass flying in all directions, spending time in a wine cellar became more dangerous than going to war.

As a result of the 1828 fiasco, a French chemist invented the *sucre-oenometre,* an instrument that measures sugar content in grapes. With its use, the champagne bottle breakage rate went way down. But "way down" is a relative thing: 15–20 percent of all champagne bottles continued to explode in storage. Wine stewards adapted their own strategies. They began storing champagne in isolated nooks and routinely wearing wire masks when in the cellar. Nowadays, that's not usually a problem.

DRINKING IT

Does champagne get you higher faster than unbubbly wine? Yes, and there are two reasons for it. The first is chemical: The carbon dioxide in the bubbles of the wine speeds the alcohol into your bloodstream quicker. The second reason is contextual: People don't usually drink champagne unless they're celebrating something, and the giddiness of the moment can have them half-drunk even without the direct effects of the alcohol.

One last thing: Although it's fun to pop the cork, it's not a great idea. Every year, popping corks blind eyes, knock out teeth and do damage to valuable furnishings. Furthermore, you lose a lot of wine and carbonation. The best way to open champagne is to hold the cork firmly and release the gas not with a bang, but with a whisper.

Retro-Futurism

More of Tom Swift's World of Tomorrow

Tom Swift was a boy inventor created by Victor Appleton almost a century ago. The breathless adventure stories are great fun, but even better are the descriptions of his inventions.

TOM SWIFT & HIS BIG TUNNEL (1916)

As soon as Tom had received the samples of the rock he had begun to experiment. First he tried some of the explosive that was so successful in the giant cannon. As he had feared, it was not what was needed. It cracked the rock, but did not disintegrate it, and that was what was needed. The hard rock must be broken up into fragments that could be easily handled. Merely to crack it necessitated further explosions, which would only serve to split it more and perhaps wedge it fast in the tunnel.

So Tom tried different mixtures, using various chemicals, but none seemed to be just right. The trials were not without danger, either. Once, in mixing some ingredients, there was an explosion that injured one man, and blew Tom some distance away. Fortunately for him, there was an open window in the direction in which he was propelled, and he went through that, escaping with only some cuts and bruises. Another time there was a hang-fire, and the explosive burned instead of detonating, so that one of the shops caught, and there was no little work in subduing the flames.

But Tom would not give up, and finally, after many trials, he hit on what he felt to be the right mixture. A day after receiving Tom's message Mr. Titus came in and a demonstration was given of the powerful explosive. "Tom, that's great!" cried the tunnel contractor. "Our troubles are at an end now."

TOM SWIFT & HIS WAR TANK (1918)

The visitors entered the great craft through the door by which Tom had emerged. At first all they saw was a small compartment, with walls of heavy steel, some shelves of the same and a seat which folded up against the wall made of like powerful material.

"I don't see how you ever thought of it!" exclaimed the girl.

"Well, I didn't all at once," Tom answered, with a laugh. "I first got the idea when I heard of the British tanks. I concluded that with a bigger tank—one capable of more speed and crossing bigger excavations—more effective work could be done against the Germans."

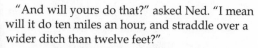

"And will yours do that?" asked Ned. "I mean will it do ten miles an hour, and straddle over a wider ditch than twelve feet?"

"It'll do both," promptly answered Tom. "I think we straddled one about fourteen feet across back there, and we can do better when I get my grippers to working."

"Grippers!" exclaimed Mary.

"And what does your tank do except travel along, not minding a hail of bullets?" asked Mr. Nestor.

"Well," answered Tom, "it can demolish a good-sized house or heavy wall, break down big trees, and chew up barbed-wire fences as if they were toothpicks. I'll show you all that in due time. Just now, if the repairs are finished, we can get back on the road—"

TOM SWIFT & HIS WIZARD CAMERA (1912)

Work went on rapidly on the Wizard Camera. Briefly described it was a small square box, with a lens projecting from it. Inside, however, was complicated machinery, much too complicated for me to describe. Tom Swift had put in his best work on this wonderful machine. It could be worked by a storage battery, by ordinary electric current from a dynamo, or by hand. On top was a new kind of electric light. This was small and compact, but it threw out powerful beams. With the automatic arrangement set, and the light turned on, the camera could be left at a certain place after dark, and whatever went on in front of it would be reproduced on the moving roll of film inside.

In the morning the film could be taken out, developed, and the pictures thrown on a screen in the usual way, familiar to all who have been in a moving picture theatre.

A number of rolls of films could be packed into the camera, and they could be taken out, or inserted, in daylight. Of course after one film had been made, showing any particular scene, any number of films could be made from this "master" one. Just as is done with the ordinary moving picture camera. Tom had an attachment to show when one roll was used, and when another needed inserting.

"I'll tell you what I'll do !" Mr. Period went on eagerly. "After you make the camera, and take a lot of films, showing strange and wonderful scenes, I'll put at the end of each film, next to my picture, your name, and a statement showing that you took the originals. How's that? Talk about being advertised! Why you can't beat it! Millions of people will read your name at the picture shows every night."

"I am not looking for advertisements," said Tom, with a laugh. ☾

(Interested in reading more Tom Swift theories and inventions? See page 383.)

In the Future Year A.D. 2000

"In 2000, commuters will go to the city, a hundred miles away, in huge aerial buses that will hold 200 passengers. Hundreds of thousands more will make such journeys twice a day in their own helicopters." —*Popular Mechanics*, 1950

"Computers are multiplying at a rapid rate. By the turn of the century, there will be 220,000 in the U.S." —*Wall Street Journal*, 1966

"By the end of this century, we're going to put a man on Mars." —Spiro Agnew, 1969

"Housewives in 50 years may wash dirty dishes right down the drain. Cheap plastic will melt in hot water." —*Popular Mechanics*, 1950

"Dishwashing will be a thing of the past. Disposable dishes will be made from powdered plastic for each meal by a machine in the kitchen...for a few pennies a meal." —The Philco Corporation, 1967

"Using wonderful new materials much lighter than aluminum, houses will be able to fly....Whole communities may migrate south in the winter, or move to new lands whenever they feel the need for a change of scenery." —Arthur C. Clarke, 1966

"Keeping house will be a breeze by the year 2000. Sonic cleaning devices and air-filtering devices will just about eliminate dusting, scrubbing, and vacuuming.... Electrostatic filters will be installed in entrances to remove dust from clothes with ultrasonic waves." —*Wall Street Journal*, 1966

"By 2000, housewives will probably have a robot 'maid.'" —*New York Times*, 1966

The Eyes Have It

These illusions don't come free. Both have to be fiddled with a bit

This is one frame from Gustave Verbeek's New York Herald cartoon series. Which way's the right way: Upside down or right side up?

This goose looks hungry! Slowly bring the girl and the goose closer and closer to your face.

What's in a Name?

We wondered where some of our favorite products got their names, so we did a little digging. Here's what we found.

• When Cheerios came out in 1941, they were called Cheery Oats. But in 1946, Quaker Oats threatened to sue, claiming that it had exclusive trademark rights to the name "Oats." Rather than fight it, General Mills changed the name to Cheerios.

• Fritos Corn Chips were named by ice cream salesman Elmer Doolin. He stopped in a Mexican restaurant and started eating tortilla chips for the first time. He liked them so much that he bought the factory from the owner. He named the chips "Fritos"—Spanish for "fried."

• Borden's Häagen-Dazs and Kraft's Frusen Glädjé were artifacts of the 1980s, when people were led to believe that imported beer, cars and ice cream were better than domestic ones. Both made-in-America ice creams were given names that sounded Scandinavian. Although Frusen Glädjé roughly translates to "Frozen Joy," Häagen-Dazs can be found in no known language. Possibly the first known case of "artificially Swedened" ice cream?

• In a similar impulse, the name Atari was chosen so that people would think the company was Japanese.

• Would it surprise you to know that Chun King isn't really Chinese? Probably not. The company was founded by an Italian American named Jeno Paulucci in mostly Scandinavian-American Duluth, Minnesota.

• Kool-Aid was originally named Kool-Ade until bureaucrats in the Food & Drug Administration banned the use of "ade" in the name because it means "a drink made from…" (take note, Gatorade!). In response, inventor E. E. Perkins simply changed the spelling to "aid," in the sense of "help."

• Fig Newtons were invented by Kennedy Biscuits (now part of Nabisco) in Cambridgeport, Massachusetts. The plant manager, to make it easier to keep track of as-yet-unnamed products, gave each of them a temporary name chosen from nearby towns. One neighboring town is Newton, and his makeshift name for the new fig cookie eventually stuck. Similiarly-named products like the Beacon Hill, the Quincy and the Brighten didn't survive.

• The Gap stores were named in the hopes that their clothes would be able to bridge (ready for a 1960s flashback?) "the Generation Gap."

• Sony, Kodak and Exxon were all coined for the same reason: They were easy to say and remember, and are not closely related to any words in any known language.

The Book I Was Born to Write, by Ima Writer

Some say fate dictates most of our actions. After receiving this list of reportedly genuine book titles and their authors, we're beginning to believe....

- *A Treatise on Madness,* by William Battie, M.D. (1768)
- *Riches and Poverty,* by L. G. Chiozza Money (1905)
- *The Boy's Own Aquarium,* by Frank Fin (1922)
- *How to Live a Hundred Years or More,* by George Fasting (1927)
- *Diseases of the Nervous System,* by Walter Russell Brain (1933)
- *Causes of Crime,* by A. Fink (1938)
- *Your Teeth,* by John Chipping (1967)
- *The Cypress Garden,* by Jane Arbor (1969)
- *Running Duck,* by Paula Gosling (1979)
- *Motorcycling for Beginners,* by Geoff Carless (1980)
- *Writing with Power,* by Peter Elbow (1981)
- *Crocheting Novelty Potholders,* by L. Macho (1982)
- *Illustrated History of Gymnastics,* by John Goodbody (1983)

The poet e.e. cummings did have a real name with capital letters and everything. He was born Edward Estlin Cummings.

Antiquated Etiquette

Learning Civility Through History

In today's fast-paced world, politeness seems scarce. But being rude has been a problem since time began, as you can see from these rules of etiquette from days gone by.

DUTCH PHILOSOPHER Erasmus of Rotterdam authored "On civility in children" in 1530. He originally wrote it for a young prince. When that prince grew up he became King Henry II, at which time the whole Western world had become familiar with Erasmus's guide.

• "Turn away when spitting lest your saliva fall on someone. If anything purulent falls on the ground, it should be trodden upon, lest it nauseate someone."

• "You should not offer your handkerchief to anyone unless it has been freshly washed. Nor is it seemly, after wiping your nose, to spread out your handkerchief and peer into it as if pearl and rubies might have fallen out of your head."

• "To lick greasy fingers or to wipe them on your coat is impolite. It is better to use the table cloth or the serviette."

• "Some people put their hands in the dishes the moment they have sat down. Wolves do that."

• "Keep your two 'pinkies' out of the serving pot. Three fingers are enough to get what you want."

• "Take the first thing you touch; do not fish around in the pot for a bigger piece."

• "If you cannot swallow a piece of food, turn around discreetly and throw it somewhere."

• "Do not be afraid of vomiting if you must; for it is not vomiting but holding the vomit in your throat that is foul."

• "Do not move back and forth on your chair. Whoever does that gives the impression of constantly breaking or trying to break wind."

• "Retain the wind by compressing the belly."

• "If your friend uses bad manners, point it out kindly and when you are alone."

Universal Truths

The Dutch weren't the only ones to get in on laying down the rules of etiquette.

• *"Use silver-tipped chopsticks; if your food has been poisoned, the silver will turn black and serve as a warning to you."* —400 B.C., China

• *"If you are not using your knife to eat, keep it in its sheath."* —A.D. 1200, France

• *"Wash your hands before you dip them into the serving pot."* —A.D. 1200, France

• *"Use a thick piece of bread for a plate; when you're finished eating, give your gravy-soaked "trencher" to the poor for their dinner."* —A.D. 1200, France

• *"Do not dip your meat into the salt bowl; instead, use your little finger to sprinkle salt on your food."* —A.D.1400, England

• *"Take your own knife, fork, and spoon when you travel because inns do not provide tableware."* —A.D.1400, England

• *"Wait until you are finished eating to scratch yourself."* —American Pilgrims

• *"Never laugh at your own jokes."* —19th-century America

• *"Never use nicknames in public."* —19th-century America

• *"Children must wait to eat until all the adults are served."* —19th-century America

• *"Children must not eat greedily, cram their mouths full, smack their lips, tilt their chairs back, or drop their knives on the tablecloth."* —19th-century America

• *"At the table, do not cough or breathe into your neighbor's face, fidget in your seat, whisper secrets, or drum the table with your fingers."* —19th-century America

The Mouse

Caught Naked with a Stranger on a Train

In this short story by Saki (Hector High Munro), a nervous young man finds himself in a compromising position with a stranger.

THEODORIC VOLER HAD been brought up, from infancy to the confines of middle age, by a fond mother whose chief solicitude had been to keep him screened from what she called the coarser realities of life. When she died she left Theodoric alone in a world that was as real as ever, and a good deal coarser than he considered it had any need to be. To a man of his temperament and upbringing even a simple railway journey was crammed with petty annoyances and minor discords, and as he settled himself down in a second-class compartment one September morning he was conscious of ruffled feelings and general mental discomposure.

He had been staying at a country inn, the inmates of which had been certainly neither brutal nor bacchanalian, but their supervision of the domestic establishment had been of that lax order which invites disaster. The pony carriage that was to take him to the station had never been properly ordered, and when the moment for his departure drew near, the handyman who should have produced the required article was nowhere to be found.

In this emergency Theodoric, to his mute but very intense disgust, found himself obliged to collaborate with the innkeeper's daughter in the task of harnessing the pony, which necessitated groping about in an ill-lighted outbuilding called a stable, and smelling very like one—except in patches where it smelled of mice. Without being actually afraid of mice, Theodoric classed them among the coarser incidents of life, and considered that Providence, with a little exercise of moral courage, might long ago have recognized that they were not indispensable, and have withdrawn them from circulation.

As the train glided out of the station Theodoric's nervous imagination accused himself of exhaling a weak odor of stable yard, and possibly of displaying moldy straw on his unusually well-brushed garments. Fortunately the only other occupation of the compartment, a lady of about the same age as himself, seemed inclined for slumber rather than scrutiny; the train was not due to stop till the end of the line was reached, in about an hour's time, and the carriage was of the old-fashioned sort that held no communication with a corridor, therefore no further traveling companions were likely to intrude on Theodoric's semiprivacy.

And yet the train had scarcely attained its normal speed before he became reluctantly but vividly aware that he was not alone with the slumbering lady; he was not even alone in his own clothes. A warm, creeping movement over his flesh betrayed the unwelcome and highly resented presence, unseen but poignant, of a strayed mouse, that had evidently dashed into its present retreat during the episode of the pony harnessing.

Furtive stamps and shakes and wildly directed pinches failed to dislodge the intruder, and the lawful occupant of the clothes lay back against the cushions and endeavored rapidly to evolve some means for putting an end to the dual ownership. It was unthinkable that he should continue for the space of a whole hour in the horrible position of a house for vagrant mice (already his imagination had at least doubled the numbers of the alien invasion). On the other hand, nothing less drastic than partial disrobing would ease him of his tormentor, and to undress in the presence of a lady, even for so laudable a purpose, was an idea that made his ear tips tingle in a blush of abject shame.

He had never heen able to bring himself even to the mild exposure of openwork socks in the presence of the fair sex. And yet—the lady in this case was to all appearances soundly asleep; the mouse, on the other hand, seemed to be trying to crowd a year's sabbatical into a few strenuous minutes. If there is any truth in the theory of reincarnation, this particular mouse must certainly have been in a former state a member of the Alpine Club. Sometimes in its eagerness it lost its footing and slipped for half an inch or so; and then, in fright, or more probably temper, it bit.

Theodoric was goaded into the most audacious undertaking of his life. Crimsoning to the hue of a beet and keeping an agonized watch on his slumbering fellow traveler, he swiftly and noiselessly secured the ends of his railway rug to the racks on either side of the carriage, so that a substantial curtain hung athwart the compartment. In the narrow dressing room that he had thus improvised he proceeded with violent haste to extricate himself and the mouse from the surrounding casings of tweed and wool.

As the unraveled mouse gave a wild leap to the floor, the rug, slipping its fastening at either end, also came down with a heart-curdling flop, and almost simultaneously the awakened sleeper opened her eyes. With a movement almost quicker than the mouse's, Theodoric pounced on the rug and hauled its ample folds chin-high over his dismantled person as he collapsed into the farther corner of the carriage. The blood raced and beat in the veins of his neck and forehead, while he waited dumbly for the communication cord to be pulled. The lady, however, contented herself with a silent stare at her strangely muffled companion. How much had she seen, Theodoric queried to himself; and in any case what on earth must she think of his present posture?

"I think I have caught a chill," he ventured desperately.

"Really, I'm sorry," she replied. "I was just going to ask you if you would open this window."

"I fancy it's malaria," he added, his teeth chattering slightly, as much from fright as from a desire to support his theory.

"I've got some brandy in my hold-all, if you'll kindly reach it down for me," said his companion.

"Not for worlds—I mean, I never take anything for it," he assured her earnestly.

"I suppose you caught it in the tropics?"

Theodoric, whose acquaintance with the tropics was limited to an annual present of a chest of tea from an uncle in Ceylon, felt that even the malaria was slipping from him. Would it be possible, he wondered to disclose the real state of affairs to her in small installments?

"Are you afraid of mice?" he ventured, growing, if possible, more scarlet in the face.

"Not unless they came in quantities. Why do you ask?"

"I had one crawling inside my clothes just now," said Theodoric in a voice that hardly seemed his own. "It was most awkward."

"It must have been, if you wear your clothes at all tight," she observed. "But mice have strange ideas of comfort."

"I had to get rid of it while you were asleep," he continued. Then, with a gulp, he added, "It was getting rid of it that brought me to—to this."

"Surely leaving off a small mouse wouldn't bring on a chill," she exclaimed, with a levity that Theodoric accounted abominable.

Evidently she had detected something of his predicament, and was enjoying his confusion. All the blood in his body seemed to have mobilized into one concentrated blush, and an agony of abasement, worse than a myriad of mice, crept up and down over his soul. And then, as reflection began to assert itself, sheer terror took the place of humiliation. With every minute that passed the train was rushing nearer to the bustling terminal, where dozens of prying eyes would be exchanged for the one paralyzing pair that watched him from the farther corner of the carriage. There was one slender, despairing chance, which the next few minutes must decide. His fellow traveler might relapse into a blessed slumber. But as the minutes throbbed by that chance ebbed away. The furtive glance which Theodoric stole at her from time to time disclosed only an unwinking wakefulness.

"I think we must be getting near now," she presently observed.

Theodoric had already noted with growing terror the recurring stacks of small, ugly dwellings that heralded the journey's end. The words acted as a signal. Like a hunted beast breaking cover and dashing madly toward some other haven of momentary safety he threw aside his rug, and struggled frantically into his disheveled garments. He was conscious of dull suburban stations racing past the window, of a choking, hammering sensation in his throat and heart, and of an icy silence in that corner toward which he dared not look. Then as he sank back in his seat, clothed and almost delirious, the train slowed down to a final crawl, and the woman spoke.

"Would you be so kind," she asked, "as to get me a porter to put me into a cab? It's a shame to trouble you when you're feeling unwell, but being blind makes one so helpless at a railway station." ☾

Ben's Money 2

Advice from Franklin's Little Money Book

In 1757, Benjamin Franklin compiled *The Way of Wealth* from his aphorisms about money in *Poor Richard's Almanac.* The booklet was a huge success and made Franklin wealthy. Here is some of his wisdom.

THRIFT

- *If he knows not how to save as he gets, a man may keep his nose all his life to the grindstone, and die not worth a penny.*
- *If you would be wealthy, think of saving as well as of getting: the Indies have not made Spain rich, because her outgoes are greater than her incomes. Away then with your expensive follies, and you will not have so much cause to complain of hard times and heavy taxes.*
- *What maintains one vice, would bring up two children.*
- *Beware of little expenses; a small leak will sink a great ship.*

- *Fools make feasts, and wise men eat them.*
- *Buy what thou hast no need of, and before long thou shall sell thy necessaries.*
- *You call them "goods," but if you do not take care, they will prove to be "evils" to some of you.*
- *Silks and satins, scarlet and velvets, put out the kitchen fire. These are not the necessaries of life; they can scarcely be called the conveniencies, and yet only because they look pretty, how many want to have them. The artificial wants of mankind thus become more numerous than the natural; and, for one poor person, there are an hundred indigent.*
- *A child and a fool imagine twenty shillings and twenty years can never be spent.*

DEBT

- *If you would know the value of money, go and try to borrow some.*
- *Creditors have better memories than debtors.*
- *He that goes a borrowing goes a sorrowing, and indeed so does he that lends to such people.*
- *Think what you do when you run in debt; you give to another power over your liberty. If you cannot pay at the time, you will be ashamed to see your creditor; you will be in fear when you speak to him, you will make poor pitiful sneaking excuses, and by degrees come to lose your veracity and sink into base downright lying.*
- *Poverty often deprives a man of all spirit and virtue: 'tis hard for an empty bag to stand upright.*
- *Better to go to bed supperless than rise in debt.*

OSTENTATION

- *Pride is as loud a beggar as want, and a great deal more saucy.*
- *When you have bought one fine thing you must buy ten more, that your appearance may be all of a piece. 'Tis easier to suppress the first desire than to satisfy all that follow it.*
- *'Tis as truly folly for the poor to ape the rich, as for the frog to swell in order to equal the ox.*
- *Pride breakfasts with plenty, dines with poverty, and sups with infamy.*
- *Of what use is this pride of appearance, for which so much is risked, so much is suffered? It cannot promote health; or ease pain; it makes no increase of merit in the person, it creates envy, it hastens misfortune.*

GOOD ADVICE

- *For age and want, save while you may; no morning sun lasts a whole day.*
- *'Tis easier to build two chimneys than to keep one in fuel.*
- *A ploughman on his legs is higher than a gentleman on his knees.*
- *Get what you can, and what you get, hold; 'tis the stone that will turn all your lead into gold.*
- *Be not uncharitable to those that at present seem to want it, but comfort and help them.*
- *They that won't be counseled, can't be helped.*
- *If you will not hear Reason, she'll surely rap your knuckles.* ₵

Fore Bears

How the Teddy Bear First Got Stuffed

Some people never get over teddy bears. And why should they? Teddy bears are about security, comfort and non-judgmental friendship.

BELIEVE IT OR NOT, the teddy bear coincidentally sprung up on two different continents in the same year. In Germany, art student Richard Steiff had gone to work for the family business which was run by his aunt, Margaret Steiff. Confined to a wheelchair, Margaret had taught the zither to music students until she saved enough to buy a sewing machine to make dresses until 1889. Her dressmaking became popular among the stylish people, and she quickly built up the business. By 1897, she had 40 people working for her, including her brother, Richard's father. Richard went to work on the sales force, but got tired of selling dresses. In 1902, he started lollygagging around the Stuttgart Zoo, sketching monkeys and bears with the idea of designing a series of jointed stuffed animals that the company could make and sell.

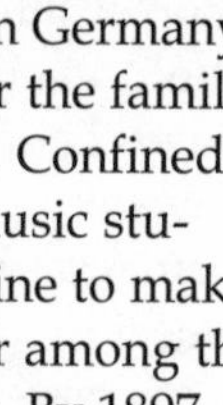

Meanwhile, back in the States, President Theodore Roosevelt traveled to Mississippi to settle a border dispute. While there, he decided to engage in a peculiar but common recreation of the time—killing wild animals for fun. After several hours, however, the president was frustrated that he hadn't found anything worth wasting a bullet on. An advance team came upon a bear cub, and knowing of the president's frustration, they tied it to a tree so Roosevelt could shoot it and have a trophy to show off when he got home. When the president came upon the scene, though, he couldn't bring himself to shoot the helpless creature.

Clifford Berryman's "Drawing the Line in Mississippi"

Today, of course, to consider shooting a bear—especially a cub and tied up, no less!—would likely get Roosevelt impeached. At that time, however, sport killing was a normal pastime, and his refusal to kill a captive cub was apparently considered an unusually kindhearted act. The moment was immortalized in a newspaper cartoon by Clifford Berryman called "Drawing the Line," and the story spread around the country. It gave Brooklyn candy store owner Morris Michtom a marketing idea.

He and his wife sketched out a pattern and made a stuffed bear that he put in his store window with a copy of the famous cartoon and a handpainted sign that said, "Teddy's Bear."

Making money in a bear market can be hard, but Michtom sold so many of the toys that he closed his candy store and founded the Ideal Toy Co.

In Germany, the Steiff Company was unaware that bear mania was growing like a tree in Brooklyn. That spring, the company debuted Richard's designs at the Leipzig Toy Fair. None of the European buyers were interested, but just as they were packing up at the end of the fair, an American toy buyer, perhaps knowing of the bear mania going on at home, ran up and ordered 3,000 bears.

In a consumer frenzy that foreshadowed fads throughout the 20th century of our own time both companies rode a bear craze in the U.S. and Europe. By 1907, Steiff had sold nearly a million bears, while Michtom had begun manufacturing a million bears a year. Steiff stuck to it and still makes very pricey stuffed toys; Ideal diversified into a variety of popular toys in the 1950s and '60s, but no longer makes stuffed bears. ☾

Stately Knowledge

12 Reasons Why Ya Gotta Love Maine

Scouring the vaults, we've come up with a dozen things to love about the state of Maine.

1 Misnomer du jour: Maine is host to the most easterly point of land in the United States. It's a small peninsula near Lubec, Maine, called, for some reason, West Quoddy Head.

2 Necessity is the mother of invention. Chester Greenwood from Farmington, Maine, invented earmuffs back in 1873 when he was only fifteen. He patented them a year later, then mass-produced them in a local factory. Chester is still honored for his important contribution to society. Every winter, folks from all over come to Farmington for a parade and festivities to celebrate—what else?—Chester Greenwood Day.

3 Ever accused of being too picky? Then Maine's the state for you—it gets the vote for being the pickiest state in the Union. More wooden toothpicks are manufactured here than in any other state.

4 Clap it out! It's easy to do because "Maine" is the only state with just one syllable.

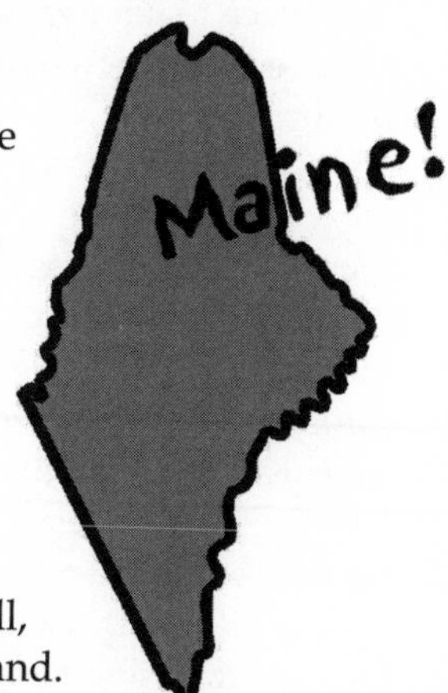

5 Hey sports fans! Oh, sorry. Maine has no major sports teams. But it does have moose. The moose is the official state animal.

6 Do you know the muffin man? About 98% of the nation's low-bush blueberries come from Maine.

7 Isn't that spatial? Maine is pretty small, but it's the biggest state in New England.

The other five New England states, put together, would almost fit inside it.

8 Strange, but true. Even though Maine is about 89% forest, there's a desert there, too. About 200 years ago, a 40-acre area of farmland near Freeport, Maine, was ruined when its protective layer of grass was destroyed. Sand dunes swept over it and stayed there. If you choose to visit this attraction, aptly named the Desert of Maine, check out the Sand Museum where you can observe sand samples from the far reaches of the globe.

9 Our favorite Mainer is author Stephen King. King wrote his first story when he was seven, sold his first piece to a magazine at eighteen and at twenty-six, published *Carrie,* his first novel. It sold over 4 million copies and became a motion picture. More success has followed with other works including *The Shining, Christine* and *Misery.* At one time, King was on the same *New York Times* best-seller list for five books. Ever hear of author "Richard Bachman"? He's actually just King writing under a pseudonym.

10 Something's fishy about Maine. Not only do the waters around Maine's coast give the nation up to 90% of its lobsters, they also produce more tins of sardines than any other place on Earth—about 75 million little cans each year.

11 Downtown Rockport, Maine, has a bronze plaque of one Hanson Gregory, who in 1847 allegedly invented the hole in the doughnut. Townspeople still argue about whether he was a sea captain or a fifteen-year-old when it happened; other historians say that other people (including the Pennsylvania Dutch and some southwestern Indians) invented holey pastry long before Gregory was born.

12 We love Maine's sense of humor. The Roadkill Café in Greenville, Maine, claims all of its dishes are made from animals that are squashed by cars on the nearby highway, with dishes like "Bye Bye Bambi Burgers" and "The Chicken That Didn't Make It Across the Road." It's all tongue in cheek, of course. Isn't it?

Elvisaurus?

GENUINE DINOSAURS WITH GREAT NAMES

Though Elvisaurus left the building millions of years ago, he lives on in paleontology. And so do the dinosaurs named after Godzilla, Bambi, a member of Monty Python and the cast of *Jurassic Park*....

ABAVORNIS was a primitive bird from about 85 million years ago. Its name means "great-great-grandfather bird."

AMBULOCETUS NATANS means "walking whale that swims," as this sea lion-sized beast had limbs that did both.

ARTHURDACTYLUS CONAN-DOYLENSIS, a pterodactyl, was named for Sir Arthur Conan Doyle, who wrote a dinosaur-heavy science fiction novel, *The Lost World*.

ATLASCOPCOSAURUS was named for the Atlas Copco, a company that provided mining tools for the expedition that discovered this Australian plant eater.

BAMBIRAPTOR was the name given a young coelurosaur found in Montana in 2000, named after the fictional young fawn of Disney fame.

Thank you...
thank you very much!

BELLUSAURUS was a dinosaur with spoon-shaped teeth. Its name means "beautiful lizard," which may only be true to a lonely paleontologist far from home.

BOROGOVIA was named for the borogoves, creatures in Lewis Carroll's poem, "Jabberwocky."

CAMELOTIA, an ancient vegetarian found in England, was named for legendary Camelot.

CHUNGKINGOSAURUS was not named for prepackaged supermarket chow mein, but for the city in China.

DEINOGALERIX means "terrible hedgehog."

ELVISAURUS ("Elvis lizard") is a paleontological nickname for cryolophosaurus, which has a crest that looks like the now-extinct singer's hairdo.

EMAUSAURUS was named after good ol' E.M.A.U., Germany's Ernst-Moritz-Arndt University.

ENIGMOSAURUS was a huge meat-eating dinosaur. Little is known about it, hence its name ("mystery lizard").

ERECTOPUS was a meat-eater with big hands, which somehow translated to a name that means "upright foot."

ERIC is a specific leptocleidine pliosaur, discovered in Australia, and named after Monty Python's Eric Idle.

GALLIMIMUS was an ostrich-like dinosaur about 17 feet long. Its name means "like a rooster."

GARGOYLEOSAURUS was an armored dinosaur from the late Jurassic period. Its name means "gargoyle lizard."

GASOSAURUS ("gas lizard") got its name because it was discovered during construction by a natural gas company.

GOJIRASAURUS was a meat-eating dinosaur discovered in New Mexico in 1997. Its name means "Godzilla lizard."

HADROCODIUM was a shrew-like mammal ancestor about the size of a paperclip that ate bugs. Its name means "heavy head."

HALLUCIGENIA, a spiky worm with tentacles, was named "delusional dream" in honor of its strangeness.

HALTICOSAURUS jumped about on two legs. The name—

Artist's rendering of Ichabodcraniosaurus

probably not inspired by Little Orphan Annie—means "leaping lizard!"

ICHABODCRANIOSAURUS was the name given a specific headless velociraptorine skeleton found in Mongolia. The detached head was later discovered, leading to the "Ichabod Crane" name, inspired by *The Legend of Sleepy Hollow*.

JURASSOSAURUS NEDEGOAPEFERIMA got its name because Steven Spielberg got naming rights for donating money toward Chinese dinosaur research. He suggested *nedegoapeferima* from the names of *Jurassic Park* cast members Sam **Ne**ill, Laura **De**rn, Jeff **Go**ldblum, Richard **A**ttenborough, Bob **Pe**ck, Martin **Fe**rrero, Ariana **Ri**chards and Joseph **Ma**zzello.

MAIASAURA was a duck-billed dinosaur that cared for its young, which is how it got its name, "good mother lizard."

MASTODON, the hairy big elephant-like creature with huge tusks, has a name from Greek that means "breast tooth."

MEGARAPTOR was a large meat eater with a name that means "huge robber."

NQWEBASAURUS (pronounced N-[click with tongue]-KWE-bah-SAWR-us) means "lizard from Nqweba," the name of an African village in the Bantu language.

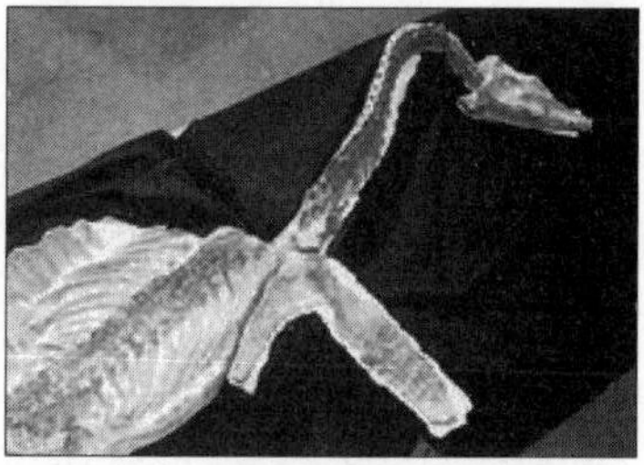

Eric, the half-leptocleidus

PROCOMPSOGNATHUS was a small theropod dinosaur with a long pointed snout. Its name means "before pretty jaw."

QANTASSAURUS was named for the Australian airline, Qantas, which provided transportation for the fossils.

SEISMOSAURUS is perhaps the longest dinosaur. Its name means "earthquake lizard."

STYGIMOLOCH had demonic-looking spikes and bumps on its skull. Its name means "demon from the river Styx."

TYRANNOSAURUS REX means "tyrant lizard king." Which brings to mind the lyric from Jim Morrison, still another extinct giant: "I am the lizard king / I can do anything." €

Zen Masters

The Zen of Einstein

He was quite a physicist. Philosophy, though, may best have been left to other thinkers. You be the judge with these mind-bending quotes from Albert Einstein.

• "The religion of the future will be a cosmic religion. The religion which based on experience, which refuses dogmatic. If there's any religion that would cope the scientific needs it will be Buddhism...."

• "We should take care not to make the intellect our god; it has, of course, powerful muscles, but no personality."

• "Nothing will benefit human health and increase the chances for survival of life on Earth as much as the evolution to a vegetarian diet."

• "Without deep reflection one knows from daily life that one exists for other people."

• "Things should be made as simple as possible, but not any simpler."

• "The faster you go, the shorter you are."

• "The wireless telegraph is not difficult to understand. The ordinary telegraph is like a very long cat. You pull the tail in New York, and it meows in Los Angeles. The wireless is the same, only without the cat."

• "I sometimes ask myself how it came about that I was the one to develop the theory of relativity. The reason, I think, is that a normal adult never stops to think about problems of space and time. These are things which he has thought about as a child. But my intellectual development was retarded, as a result of which I began to wonder about space and time only when I had already grown up."

Whatchamacallit?

What's that little bit between the lip and the nose called? A philtrum. There are all kinds of things we discovered that we didn't know had names. We thought you might enjoy them, too.

SNORKEL BOX: The name given to a drive-up mailbox, because of the projection of the drop slot.

BOTTS' DOTS: The raised bumps that mark off road lanes. Made of polyester, plastic or ceramic, they're named after their inventor, a California Department of Transportation chemist named Elbert Botts.

FUMET: Deer poop.

KEEPER: The loop on a belt that keeps the end in place after it has passed through the buckle.

COLUMELLA NASI: The bit on the lower edge of the nose that separates one nostril from the other.

FEAK: A dangling curl that hangs loose.

DRAGÉES: Tiny, little, silver candy balls that are used in cake and cookie decorating—particularly at holiday time.

FERRULE: The piece of metal that attaches a pencil to its eraser.

GRAWLIX, JARNS, QUIMP, NITTLES: These are all names for symbols that indicate a comics character is cursing.

ROWEL: The part of a cowboy spur that actually rotates. Usually, it's star-shaped.

FIPPLE: The lower lip.

SADDLE: The top, curved part of a "close-and-strike" matchbook.

FEAZINGS: The end of an unraveled rope.

Tom Swifties V

"I'm Teeing Up," Tom Forewarned

We managed to scrounge up even more weird and surreal Tom Swifty jokes. Here's the fifth and final batch. Enjoy!

"The radio jammer is working!" Tom said ecstatically.
"Let's get married," Tom said engagingly.
"I've run out of wool," said Tom, knitting his brow.
"I've gained weight," Tom said expansively.
"Elvis's daughter changed her name," Tom said expressly.
"Yes, we have no bananas today," Tom said fruitlessly.
"Love your steamroller!" Tom flattered.
"Turn 3 lefts and then go the other way," said Tom forthrightly.
"I have only diamonds, spades and clubs," said Tom heartlessly.
"Nay," said Tom hoarsely.
"The doctor removed my arm bone," Tom said humorlessly.
"Brush and floss," said Tom implacably.
"I hate that smoky sweet smell!" said Tom, incensed.
"I've borrowed my sibling's camp gear," said Tom insistently.
"I think I'm having a goat instead of a baby," Mary kidded.
"You're only average," Tom said meanly.
"I don't have a boyfriend," said Mary, guilelessly.
"I'm single, but I think I'm having a baby," said Sue, laboring under a misconception.
"This is mutiny!" said Tom bountifully.
"I should discard this low card," Tom deduced.

Ripe Ol' Corn

Uncle Josh in New York City

"Uncle Josh Weathersby," Cal Stewart's country bumpkin, had problems figuring out modern city life (circa 1901). Here are some vignettes from a visit to hustling, bustling New York City.

UNCLE JOSH'S ARRIVAL

Well, for a long time I had my mind made up that I'd come down to New York. I was ridin' along in one of them sleepin' cars, and I felt a feller rummagin' around under my bed, and I looked out just in time to see him goin' away with my boots. Well, I knowed the way that train was a runnin' he couldn't get off with them without breakin' his durned neck. In about half an hour he brought them back—guess they didn't fit him. Well, I was sort of glad he took 'em 'cause he had shined 'em up slicker 'n a new tin whistle.

Well, when I got up in the mornin' I was so crowded up like, durned if I could get my clothes on, and when I did get 'em on durned if my pants wasn't on hind side afore, and my socks got all tangled up in that little fish net along side of the bed and I couldn't get 'em out, and I got my right boot on my left foot and the left one on the right foot, and I bumped my head on the roof of the bed over me, and then some feller stepped right square on my bunion and I let out a war whoop you coulda heard over in the next county. Well, along come that durned porter and told me I was a wakin' up everybody in the car.

Well, I got my clothes on and went into a room where they had a row of little troughs to wash in, and fast as I could pump water in the durned thing it run out of a little hole in the bottom so I just had to grab a handful and then pump some more.

When I got off the ferry boat, I commenced to think I was about the best lookin' old feller what ever come to New York, because fellers down there with buggies and carriages, the minute they seen me they all hollered, "hansom—hansom!"

Folks at home said I'd be buncoed or have my pockets picked fore I'd been here more than half an hour. Well, I fooled 'em a little bit—I was here three days before they buncoed me.

JOSH IN AN AUCTION ROOM

I was walkin' along down the street lookin' at things, when some feller throwed a banana peel on the sidewalk. Well, now I don't think much of a man what throws a banana peelin' on the sidewalk, and I don't think much of a banana what throws a man on the sidewalk, neither. My foot hit that banana peelin' and I went up in the air, and come down ker-plunk, and for about a minute I seen all the stars what astronomy tells about, and some that hadn't been discovered yet.

Well, just as I was pickin' myself up a little boy come runnin' cross the street and he said, "Oh mister, won't you please do that again, my mother didn't see you do it."

I come to a place where they was auctioneerin' off a lot of things. I stopped to see what they had to sell. Well, that place was just chuck full of old-fashioned curiosities. I saw an old book there, they said it was five hundred years old, and it belonged at one time to Louis the Seventeenth or Eighteenth, or some of them old rascals; durned if I believe anybody could read it.

Well, I commenced a biddin' on different things, but it just looked as though everybody had more money than I did, and they sort of out-bid me; but finally they put up an old-fashioned sugar bowl for sale, and I wanted to get that mighty bad, 'cause I thought as how mother would like it first rate. Well, I commenced a biddin' on it, and it was knocked down to me for $3.50. I put my hand in my pocket to get my pocket book to pay for it, and by gosh it was gone. So I went up to the feller what was a sellin' the things, and I said, "Now look here mister, will you just wait a minute. When I come in here I had a pocket book in my pocket, had fifty dollars in it, and I lost it somewheres round here; I wish you'd say to the feller what found it that I'll give five dollars for it." Another feller said, "Make it ten!" another said, "Give you twenty!" and another said, "Go you twenty-five!"

Durned if I know which one of 'em got it; when I left they was still a biddin' on it.

UNCLE JOSH IN SOCIETY

Well, I didn't suppose when I come down to New York that I was a-goin' to flop right into the middle of high toned society, but I guess that's just about what I done. You see I had an old friend a livin' down here named Henry Higgins. We was boys together down home at Punkin Centre, and I hadn't seen him in a long time.

Well, I got a feller to look up his name in the city almanac, and he showed me where Henry lived, on Avenue Five. Well, when I seen Henry's house it just about took my breath away. Henry's house is bigger'n the courthouse at Punkin Centre.

Well, I mustered up my courage, and I went up and rang some newfangled door bell. Well, Henry jist come out and grabbed me by bot hands and said, "Why Josh Weathersby, come right in!" Well, he took me into the house and introduced me to more folks than I ever seen before in all my life at one time.

After that we had something to eat in the dinin' room. They had a lot of foreign dishes, somethin' what they called "beef all over mud," and another what they called "a-charlotte russia" — a little shavin' mug of cake and sweetened lather. Well, that was good eatin', though it took a lot of them, they weren't very fillin'. Then they handed me somethin' what they called ice cream, looked to me like a hunk of castile soap. Well, I stuck my fork in it, and it slipped off and got inside my vest, and in a minute I was froze from my chin to my toes. Yep, I really cut a caper at Henry's house.

JOSH IN THE DRY GOODS STORE

I'd said to mother, "I'll take a load of produce with me, and that will pay expenses of the trip." Well, I picked out a right likely lookin' store. I said to the clerk inside, "Well, be the storekeeper to home?" And presently we come to a place that had bars in front of the windows, and looked like the county jail. The clerk said, "Go in," and I said, "I hadn't done anything to be locked up for."

And that clerk commenced to laughin' though durned if I could see what he was a-laughin' about, and the storekeeper said, "Good mornin', what can I do for you?" So I said, "Do you want to buy any 'taters?" And he said, "No, sir, we don't buy potatoes here; this a dry goods store." So I said, "Well, don't want any cabbage, do you?" And he said, "No, sir, this is a dry goods store." So I said, "Well, now, I want to know; do you need any onions?" And by chowder, he got madder 'n a wet hen. He said, "Now look a-here, I want you to understand once for all, this is a dry goods store, and we don't buy anything but dry goods and don't sell anything but dry goods; do you understand me now? DRY GOODS." And I said, "Yes, I understand; you don't need to get so riled; far as I can figure, you just buy and sell dry goods." And he said, "Yes, only dry goods." So I said, "Do you want to buy some dried apples?"

THE SIGNS SEEN IN NEW YORK

I seen a good many funny things when I was in New York, but the signs on the buildins' are 'bout as funny as anything I ever seen.

I went into the restaurant and I noticed a sign'd said "Trust in the Lord," and right under it was another what said "Try our mince pies." Well, I tried one, and I want to tell you, if you eat them pies you want to put your trust in the Lord.

Well, I come to a store, they had a sign in that window that said "Frog in your throat 10¢." It tickled me 'cause I wouldn't put one of them critters in my throat for $10!

Well, up the street I seen a sign what said "Boots blacked

on the inside." Now, any one what gets his boots blacked on the inside ain't got much respect for his socks. I get mine blacked on the outside.

A little further I seen a sign what said "Cast iron sinks." Well, now, any durned fool what don't know that cast iron sinks, ought to have some one feel his head and find out what ails him.

UNCLE JOSH AT THE OPERA

Well, I got into one of your theaters, got set down and a lot of fellers come out with horns and fiddles, and they all started in to fiddlin' and tootin'. All to once they pulled the curtain up, and there was a lot of folks having a regular family quarrel. I knowed that wasn't any of my business, and I sort of felt uneasy like; but none of the rest of the folks seemed to mind it any, so I calculated I'd see how it come out, though my hands sort of itched to get hold of one feller, 'cause I could see if he would just go 'way and tend to his own business there wouldn't be any quarrel. Well, just then a young feller handed me a piece of paper what told all about the theater doings, and it said the second act takes place five years after the first. I knowed I couldn't wait that long to see the second part, so I got up and went out.

UNCLE JOSH ON A STREET CAR

Well, I paid 5¢ and got on one of them street cars. In one end of the car there was a little slim lady, and right along side of her was a big fleshy lady, and it didn't look as though the slim lady was gettin' more'n about 2¢ worth of room. Finally she turned to the fleshy lady and said, "They ought to charge by weight on this line," and the big lady said, "Well, if they did they wouldn't stop for you." Gosh, I had to snicker right out loud.

Three ladies got onto the car, and there weren't a place for 'em to set down, and so the big lady said to a little boy sitting nearby, "You oughta get up and let one of them ladies set down," and the little boy said, "If *you* get up, they can *all* set down."

Well, I got to talkin' to the nice feller steerin' the car. He showed me how every thing worked and when I got off I said, "Good bye, mister, hope I'll see you again some time," and he said, "Oh, I'll run across you one of these days." I told him by gosh he sure wouldn't run across me if I seen him a'comin' first. €

Sports Match 3

Match the Team to the Location

If you're not an absolute sports junkie, this one's going to be a little tough. Match the pro teams from the National Hockey League, Major League Soccer and the Women's National Basketball Association with the places they call home.

1.	Shock	New York
2.	Hurricanes	Ottawa
3.	Fire	Chicago
4.	Revolution	Carolina
5.	Crew	Washington, D.C.
6.	Sting	Atlanta
7.	Islanders	Detroit
8.	Fever	Sacramento
9.	MetroStars	New Jersey
10.	Liberty	Charlotte
11.	Senators	New York
12.	Penguins	New England
13.	Monarchs	Indiana
14.	Thrashers	Columbus
15.	United	Pittsburgh

Answers: 1. *Shock:* Detroit—WNBA; 2. *Hurricanes:* Carolina—NHL; 3. *Fire:* Chicago—MLS; 4. *Revolution:* New England—MLS; 5. *Crew:* Columbus—MLS; 6. *Sting:* Charlotte—WNBA; 7. *Islanders:* New York—NHL; 8. *Fever:* Indiana—WNBA; 9. *MetroStars:* New Jersey—MLS; 10. *Liberty:* New York—WNBA; 11. *Senators:* Ottawa—NHL; 12. *Penguins:* Pittsburgh—NHL; 13. *Monarchs:* Sacramento—WNBA; 14. *Thrashers:* Atlanta—NHL; 15. *United:* Washington, D.C.—MLS

Sugar Daddy

No Sucker for Commies!

What does a caramel on a stick have to do with fighting the international communist conspiracy? Plenty, mister.

Robert Henry Winborne Welch, Jr., was born in 1899 and quickly got a reputation as a child prodigy. At age twelve, he entered the University of North Carolina and was, by his own admission years later, "the most insufferable little squirt that ever tried to associate with his elders." Raised as a fundamentalist Baptist, he tried to get his fellow students to come to Bible classes in his dorm room.

After four years, he entered the U.S. Naval Academy for two years before dropping out. He then entered Harvard Law School. Already a hard-line conservative, Welch left Harvard in the middle of his third and final year, "in disgust over what Felix Frankfurter was teaching—that labor and management were enemies." While Professor Frankfurter went on to a distinguished stint on the Supreme Court, the embittered Welch went home and began a candy company, "the one field in which it seemed least impossible to get started without either capital or experience."

His Oxford Candy Company started making fudge from a recipe Welch bought from a candy store owner. He also began making caramels. One day, inspired by lollipops, he rolled out some of his caramel and stuck a stick into it. He called his new taste treat Papa Sucker. Powered by this success, the Oxford Candy Company did well enough for him to hire an employee, his brother James.

Things went along well enough for a while, but in 1925 James left and started his own candy company. Short the help, Robert made an unusual rights deal with the Brach Candy Company to manufacture Papa Suckers from its Chicago factory. Robert spent his time flying between his Brooklyn-based company and Chicago-based Brach, overseeing the production of the caramel suckers.

WHAT'S IN A NAME?

In 1932, his candy company was hit hard by the Depression and went bankrupt. However, the James O. Welch Company, founded by his brother, was doing fine. In a reversal of fortunes, James hired Robert to take charge of his company's advertising and sales.

One of the first things Robert did in his new capacity was to start making a candy identical to the Papa Sucker. To avoid legal problems with Brach, he changed its name to Sugar Daddy, hoping the new name would insinuate easy living and wealth.

His brother's company began selling Sugar Daddies along with spin-offs like Sugar Babies, Junior Mints and Pom Poms. During the next three decades, the company's annual sales increased from $200,000 to $20 million. Robert retired in 1956, a millionaire many times over.

TOO MUCH MONEY

Despite his money, Welch was very worried about holding onto it. He sensed foreign, alien philosophies floating through the land that threatened his fortune and sense of well-being. "There is no reason on Earth why we should let ourselves be infected by such diseases as socialism and communism, and other ideological cancers," he wrote. In 1958, Welch decided to start an organization to wake America up to the grave dangers that threatened from every direction. He joined with ten other men and started the ultra-conservative John Birch Society, named after an Army intelligence agent who was killed in China ten days after World War II ended. Welch decided that Birch was the first casualty in World War III, which, as far as Welch was concerned, had already begun.

Welch believed that all Americans fell into one of four categories: "Communists, communist dupes or sympathizers, the uninformed who have yet to be awakened to the communist danger, and the ignorant." He believed it was almost too late to shake Americans out of their stupor: Wasn't America was already ruled by Dwight David Eisenhower, "a dedicated, conscious agent of the communist conspiracy"? Was not democracy itself nothing more than "a deceptive phrase, a weapon of demagoguery and a perennial fraud"? It was the Birch Society, he believed, that would bring America back to "less government, more responsibility and, with God's help, a better world."

PINKOS AND PARANOIA

But, of course, it wouldn't be easy. Welch made up a map of the world, coloring each nation various shades of pink and red to indicate how "communistic" it was. The United States was a deep pink, and even the most brutal right-wing Latin American dictatorships that machine-gunned suspected communists by the carload were painted a light pink ("somewhat communistic") instead of white ("completely free of communism").

The John Birch Society achieved a surprising level of public awareness and claimed membership in the upper five figures. In the paranoid 1950s and '60s, Welch and his cronies funded scores of books, started bookstores all over the country, published a monthly called *American Opinion* and even opened a dozen summer camps to indoctrinate kids against communism. Welch used some of his Sugar Daddy earnings to buy billboards all over the country with the message "Impeach Earl Warren," referring to the Chief Justice of the Supreme Court, whom Welch believed was leading the country down the crimson path with his pro-union and civil rights rulings.

Welch was also opposed to the fluoride in the water ("a communist plot to make Americans into mongolian idiots"), Norway ("secretly communist"), the Beatles ("Their songs are written by a communist think tank"), federal aid to education, arms negotiations, foreign aid, income taxes, collective bargaining, Social Security and much more. He wasn't even particularly happy when Ronald Reagan was elected president, considering him hopelessly liberal.

As Welch's political analysis ripened to full flagrant paranoia, he eventually decided that the "International Communist Conspiracy" was itself merely a front for something even bigger and scarier. The "inner circle that has been running the show," for two centuries, he became convinced, was an ultrasecret cabal of Masons that formed in Bavaria in May, 1776, and called itself "the Illuminati."

THE END...OR IS IT?

Welch died in 1985, and his organization fell into irrelevancy and debt. The fall of the Berlin Wall and communism in Eastern Europe made it difficult for most of the world to take its message seriously (even though, the Society claimed, "the so-called fall of communism was just a clever hoax"). Even a move to Appleton, Wisconsin, to be close to the birthplace of their hero, senator and witch-hunter Joseph McCarthy, couldn't sufficiently bolster the troops.

James Welch disavowed his brother's views in 1961. He sold his candy company to Nabisco in 1963, but continued as a Nabisco director until 1978. James also died in 1985, just 27 days after his brother.

Coincidence? Or was it conspiracy...? €

Sweet Remainders

• The year was 1935. The song was *Let Me Be Your Sugar Baby.* Welch introduced Sugar Babies to the market to cash in on the popularity of the song.

• In 1963, Ann Miller and Mickey Rooney, stars of the Broadway hit *Sugar Babies,* were given the little candies by the company to toss into the audience. The promotion worked like a charm and Sugar Babies sales soared.

• Sugar Mamas were just Sugar Daddies that had been dipped in chocolate. They didn't sell well and were discontinued. No mention of them can be found in current company literature.

• Welch began including "comic cards," in Sugar Daddies in the 1940s. They were like sports trading cards, but were comic characters. In the 1970s, the company combined the two ideas and offered sports stars' heads with caricatured bodies as sort of a sports/comic trading card hybrid.

Such a Clatter

WHO WROTE "THE NIGHT BEFORE CHRISTMAS"?

Clement C. Moore has long been credited with writing the once-anonymous Christmas classic. However, some scholars now believe that the real author was probably somebody else. Here's the story.

YOU MAY NOT KNOW the title, "A Visit from St. Nicholas," but you know the poem. It's the one that begins: "'Twas the night before Christmas and all through the house...." It was an important poem in that it largely created our view of who Santa Claus is.

For centuries, Saint Nicholas had been portrayed as a stern churchman bringing whippings and punishment as often as gifts. However, in the 19th century, the image started shifting. In 1812, Washington Irving wrote about the Dutch tradition of Santa Claus "riding over the tops of the trees, in that selfsame waggon wherein he brings his yearly presents to children." In 1821, William Gilley, a New York printer, published a short poem about "Santeclaus," who drove a sleigh pulled by a reindeer. Finally, in 1823, the *Troy* (N.Y.) *Sentinel* published "An Account of a Visit from St. Nicholas," in which Santa was first depicted as a jolly fat man having eight flying reindeer and a proclivity for coming down stocking-hung chimneys with gifts.

The poem was published anonymously, and would remain so for years afterward through several reprintings. Until recently, the story that has long been accepted is that Clement Clarke Moore—a wealthy academic who dabbled in Greek and Latin, Bible studies, politics and poetry—had written it a year earlier on Christmas Eve. According to the story, a family friend had given it to the newspaper anonymously so that the ever-so-serious Moore would be spared the embarrassment of having written such a frivolous poem. Finally, 21 years later—after the

(As published in the *Troy Sentinel,* December 23, 1823)

Account of a Visit from St. Nicholas

'Twas the night before Christmas, when all thro' the house,
Not a creature was stirring, not even a mouse;
The stockings were hung by the chimney with care,
In hopes that St. Nicholas soon would be there;
The children were nestled all snug in their beds,
While visions of sugar plums danc'd in their heads,
And Mama in her 'kerchief, and I in my cap,
Had just settled our brains for a long winter's nap-
When out on the lawn there arose such a clatter,
I sprang from the bed to see what was the matter.
Away to the window I flew like a flash,
Tore open the shutters, and threw up the sash.
The moon on the breast of the new fallen snow,
Gave the lustre of mid-day to objects below;
When, what to my wondering eyes should appear,
But a miniature sleigh, and eight tiny rein-deer,
With a little old driver, so lively and quick,
I knew in a moment it must be St. Nick.
More rapid than eagles his coursers they came,
And he whistled, and shouted, and call'd them by name:
"Now! Dasher, now! Dancer, now! Prancer, and Vixen,
"On! Comet, on! Cupid, on! Dunder and Blixem;
"To the top of the porch! to the top of the wall!
"Now dash away! dash away! dash away all!"
As dry leaves before the wild hurricane fly,
When they meet with an obstacle, mount to the sky;
So up to the house-top the coursers they flew,
With the sleigh full of toys - and St. Nicholas too:
And then in a twinkling, I heard on the roof
The prancing and pawing of each little hoof.
As I drew in my head, and was turning around,
Down the chimney St. Nicholas came with a bound:
He was dress'd all in fur, from his head to his foot,
And his clothes were all tarnish'd with ashes and soot;
A bundle of toys was flung on his back,
And he look'd like a peddler just opening his pack:
His eyes - how they twinkled! his dimples how merry,
His cheeks were like roses, his nose like a cherry;
His droll little mouth was drawn up like a bow,
And the beard of his chin was as white as the snow;
The stump of a pipe he held tight in his teeth,
And the smoke it encircled his head like a wreath.
He had a broad face, and a little round belly
That shook when he laugh'd, like a bowl full of jelly:
He was chubby and plump, a right jolly old elf,
And I laugh'd when I saw him in spite of myself;
A wink of his eye and a twist of his head
Soon gave me to know I had nothing to dread.
He spoke not a word, but went straight to his work,
And fill'd all the stockings; then turn'd with a jerk,
And laying his finger aside of his nose
And giving a nod, up the chimney he rose.
He sprung to his sleigh, to his team gave a whistle,
And away they all flew, like the down of a thistle:
But I heard him exclaim, ere he drove out of sight-
Happy Christmas to all, and to all a good night.

poem had been reprinted several times—Moore stepped forward to claim credit for it.

But was he taking credit for someone else's work? According to descendents of another New York amateur poet, Moore was a fraud. They say their ancestor, Henry Livingston, a farmer and surveyor, was the true author of "A Visit from St. Nicholas." According to the recollections of Livingston's children and a neighbor, Livingston had read the poem to them in 1808, fifteen years before it was published anonymously.

The Livingstons have gotten some powerful support from Don Foster, an expert on analyzing the stylistic quirks that are every author's trademark. He is best known for identifying Shakespeare as the author of an anonymous poem and outing political writer Joe Klein as the anonymous author of *Primary Colors*. According to Foster:

• Clement Moore was a grouch whose poems were full of stern, moralistic cant. He never would've written such a playful, child-friendly poem. For example, a St. Nicholas poem he wrote for his own daughter (*see box*)

(A genuine Santa Claus poem by Clement C. Moore)

From Saint Nicholas

What! My sweet little Sis, in bed all alone;
No light in your room! And your nursy too gone!
And you, like a good child, are quietly lying,
While some naughty ones would be fretting or crying?
Well, for this you must have something pretty, my dear;
And, I hope, will deserve a reward too next year.
But, speaking of crying, I'm sorry to say
Your screeches and screams, so loud ev'ry day,
Were near driving me and my goodies away.
Good children I always give good things in plenty;
How sad to have left your stocking quite empty:
But you are beginning so nicely to spell,
And, in going to bed, behave always so well,
That, although I too oft see the tear in your eye,
I cannot resolve to pass you quite by.
I hope, when I come here again the next year,
I shall not see even the sign of a tear.
And then, if you get back your sweet pleasant looks,
And do as you're bid, I will leave you some books,
Some toys, or perhaps what you still may like better,
And then too may write you a prettier letter.
At present, my dear, I must bid you good bye;
Now, do as you're bid; and, remember, don't cry.

threatened that her "screeches and screams, so loud every day / Were near driving me and my goodies away...."

• Moore condemned "immodest verse" without a moral that had "no other recommendations that the glow of its expressions and the tinkling of its syllables, or the wanton allurement of the ideas that it conveys."

• Moore condemned tobacco as "opium's treacherous aid," yet the poem's Santa enjoyed a pipe.

• Moore's only original contribution, according to Foster, was to screw up the names of two reindeer. They had originally been named "Dunder and Blixem," a common Dutch expression meaning "thunder and lightning." Livingston spoke Dutch; Moore did not. When Clement republished the poem under his own name, he changed the names to "Donder and Blitzen."

• In 1844, Moore contacted the *Troy Sentinel* to ask if anybody could identify the author. He was told that the staff members who had known anything about the origins of the poem had died more than a decade earlier. Shortly after, Moore published the poem as his own in a collection of his poetry.

•Livingston, on the other hand, wrote lighthearted poems with some interesting stylistic quirks. One of them was that he often wrote in the anapestic meter, emphasizing every third syllable ("da da DUM da da DUM da da DUM"), as seen in "A Visit from St. Nicholas." His annual Christmas poem was always written in the anapestic form. Moore, on the other hand, used anapestic meter in only one known poem.

• Livingston's poems often had the unusual quirk of using *all* as an adverb. So does this poem, in phrases like "all through the

(A poem example by Henry Livingston)

Epithalamium
A Marriage Poem

'Twas summer, when softly the breezes were blowing,
And Hudson majestic so sweetly was flowing,
The groves rang with music and accents of pleasure
And nature in rapture beat time to the measure,
When Helen and Jonas, so true and so loving,
Along the green lawn were seen arm in arm moving,
Sweet daffodils, violets and roses spontaneous
Wherever they wandered sprang up instantaneous.
The ascent the lovers at length were seen climbing
Whose summit is grac'd by the temple of Hymen:
The genius presiding no sooner perceived them
But, spreading his pinions, he flew to receive them;
With kindest of greetings pronounced them well come
While hollidays clangor rang loud to the welkin.

Henry Livingston, we presume

house," "all snug in their beds," and "dressed all in fur."

• At a time when most people said "Merry Christmas," Livingston habitually used "Happy Christmas" in his writings. So does Santa in this poem.

Clement Moore

• Livingston tended to use an extravagant number of exclamation marks. Moore almost never used them. The use in the roll call of reindeer is "vintage Livingston," said Foster.

• Finally, Livingston was known for populating his poems with flying creatures, fairies, animals and people. He considered himself an expert on Lapland's reindeer. And his Dutch heritage gave him the legend of "Sint Nikolass" with his annual visits with gifts. €

The Roots of Christmas Traditions

JESUS WAS NOT really born on Christmas (many historians think it was more likely in autumn). In third-century Rome, though, Christianity was competing with other sects that had big winter solstice holidays. Worried that they were losing converts to the jollier sects, the early Christians began a long tradition of adopting other groups' ceremonies:

• Mithraism celebrated the birth of the sun king on that date.

• Worshipers of Saturn, god of agriculture, held feasts and parades.

• From the cult of Bacchus, the god of wine, Christians adopted lights and wreaths. Bacchus was the son of a god and mortal woman who was routinely depicted with a halo over his head. His followers ate bread and wine to symbolize his body and blood (in fact, Bacchus's blood *was* wine).

•Christmas trees? Borrowed from pagan tree worshipers in Germany.

Get a Job!

More Suggestions for a Change in Careers

Brachygrapher: A shorthand specialist.
Hello Girl: A telephone operator.
Eyer: One who puts eyes into sewing needles.
Bluestocking: A woman writer.
Shrimpschonger: A carver.
Tucker In: A bed-maker; a servant.
Castora: Salt and pepper shaker manufacturer.
Bang Beggar: One who tosses unwanted visitors out of town.
Shrieve: One who serves as sheriff.
Trepanger: A circular saw expert.
Gager: One who collects revenue from alcoholic beverages.
Todhunter: A city official paid to hunt foxes.
Apiarian: One who keeps bees.
Rhapsode: A professional epic poet reciter.
Nimgimmer: A physician.
Cambist: A bank employee.
Bodeys: One who makes bodices for dresses.
Stuff Gowsman: A barrister in training.
Fogger: A vendor.
Travers: Someone who works a bridge toll booth.
Cocus: A cook.
Sperviter: A sparrow specialist.
Pistor: A baker.
Woolen Billy Piecer: A mill worker responsible for salvaging broken pieces of yarn.
Banker: Ditch digger.
Times Ironer: One who irons the daily newspaper.
Ad Conveyancer: Someone who carries a sandwich board.
Claker: One who reads fortunes in the stars.
Scrutineer: A judge who investigates for misconduct in elections.
Grimbribber: An attorney.
Trencherman: A professional cook.
White Limer: A wall plasterer.

Grudge Match

Why Coke Hates Pepsi, Part II

Continuing the story from page 231: **Despite the new curvy Coke bottles and Coke attorney Harold Hirsch's constant lawsuits, one Coke-wannabe prevailed and thrived. Here's how Pepsi came alive.**

Pepsi-Cola, like Coke, came from the South. It was formulated by a former Confederate Army officer, pharmacist Caleb B. Bradham. His New Bern, North Carolina, pharmacy thrived because it provided a soda fountain alternative to saloons of the town. Like other druggists at that time, Bradham began tinkering with new elixirs and patent medicines, using the knowledge he picked up in medical school.

He modeled one concoction after the wildly popular Coca-Cola. Intended to relieve stomach disorders and ulcers, "Brad's Drink," as it was called, was a pleasant mixture of vanilla, exotic oils and spices, sugar and the African kola nut. It became popular with the locals. He renamed it Pepsi-Cola in 1898, and in 1902 started peddling it to other soda fountains. Two years later, he sold shares in the business and copied Coke's franchise system to begin marketing Pepsi in bottles. By 1909, Bradham had 250 bottlers in 24 states. He was getting rich.

From 1905 to 1915, Pepsi circulated free coupons to get people to try the stuff

World War I, though, changed all that. Rapidly fluctuating sugar prices and labor costs crippled the company. By 1922, the Pepsi Company was bankrupt, and Bradham went back to filling prescriptions at his New Bern drug store.

A Wall Street money man named Roy C. Megargel bought up the company's assets and started a new Pepsi-Cola company in Richmond, Virginia. When he failed to come up with enough investment capital to keep it going, though, the company went down in flames again in 1932.

Next in line came Charles Guth, president of Loft, Inc., a candy company in Long Island, New York. Guth had a grudge against the Coca-Cola company for not giving him a volume discount on the Coke syrup he sold each year at his 115 soda fountains. He decided to make his own beverage, so he took money out of Loft's till to buy up the Pepsi rights, including Megargel as a silent partner, and started still another new Pepsi Cola Company. He tinkered with the recipe to his own taste preferences and began serving it in his stores.

Coca-Cola, ever-vigilant in protecting its own market, sent its undercover agents into Loft stores, then filed a lawsuit, claiming they had fraudulently been served Pepsi-Cola when they had ordered Coca-Cola. Guth countersued, claiming that Coke was illegally harassing and maligning his stores and employees. The bitter court case would be played out in slow motion over the following decade.

Meanwhile, however, the Pepsi-Cola Company had other troubles. With Loft stores as its only outlet, the company was losing money fast, and Guth decided he wanted out. He even offered to sell Pepsi to Coca-Cola, for a modest price. In the blunder of its life, Coke turned him down. His partner Megargel, meanwhile, sued for funds Guth owed him, so Guth bought him out for $35,000, of which all but $500 came out of Loft's company funds.

Pepsi, now 91% owned by Guth, was about to go under

for a third time, when a used bottle dealer suggested that Guth start bottling his drink in used beer bottles. Even though the bottles held nearly twice as much as Coke's 6.5-ounce bottles, he decided to charge only a nickel since the Depression was on. Because Pepsi offered twice as much drink for the same price as a Coke, Pepsi's sales went through the roof. Guth's candy stores, however, were falling apart. Stockholders revolted, and he resigned his presidency.

The Loft Company board of directors sued Guth in 1939, after discovering he had taken most of the money for his Pepsi venture from their till. After a bruising battle, the court ruled that Loft, Inc., was the legitimate owner of Pepsi-Cola.

Regardless of the legal issues, Coke noted with alarm that Pepsi continued to do booming business. The battle soon escalated beyond sending undercover agents into Loft stores: Coke sued Pepsi over trademark violations, claiming proprietary rights to the name "Cola." On the first day of the trial, Coke lawyers made a big show of hauling out huge stacks of legal documents detailing its victories over trademark infringers.

From weighty precedence, it looked like an open and shut case. The widow of the victim of an earlier Coke lawsuit called on Walter Mack, the new president of Pepsi, to offer condolences. Her husband had been president of something called Cleo Cola. She casually mentioned that Coca-Cola had given her husband a $35,000 check to put him out of business.

A payoff? Mack couldn't believe his ears. Maybe Coke wasn't so sure of victory after all. The next day in court, Pepsi's lawyers asked about the check, and Coke's lawyers asked for a two-day recess to respond. That afternoon, Coke president, Robert Woodruff called Mack and invited him to meet the next morning. According to Mack the conversation went like this:

"Mr. Mack, I've been thinking about this lawsuit, and I think we ought to settle it. Is that agreeable to you?"

"It is, under one condition."

Mack took a piece of paper

and wrote, "I, Robert Woodruff, president and chief executive officer of the Coca-Cola Company, hereby agree that the corporation will recognize the Pepsi-Cola trademark and never attack it in the United States." He handed it to Woodruff, who drafted a similar agreement stating that Pepsi would recognize Coke. Both men signed and then shook hands on the deal.

The truce didn't last long. Coke, saying the agreement applied only to the U. S., dispatched attorneys to file trademark violation suits in countries all over the world. A lower judge in Canada ruled for Coke, but Canada's Supreme Court reversed that ruling. Because Canada was a member of the British Commonwealth, Coke appealed to the highest Commonwealth court, the Privy Council in England.

"It was a hell of a dirty trick," Mack observed later, "because it was during the war and they had lawyers over there. The Privy Council had set a date, and Coke figured we wouldn't be able to get anybody over there." Pepsi hired Wendell Willkie, who had just finished an unsuccessful presidential bid. Willkie was able to get the government to fly him over to England in an Air Force bomber, ostensibly to make speeches for the war effort. He got there in time to represent Pepsi in the courts. The Privy Council ruled in favor of Pepsi's claim that "cola" was a generic term and requested that both companies coexist in peace.

That, though, wasn't going to happen. Although the suits and countersuits stopped, the two companies continued to slash at each other in the marketplace. Coke managed to finagle a position as a quasi-government agency in World War II as a boost to the morale and energy levels of the fighting boys. Shipped

Pepsi Slogans Through the Ages

"Brad's Drink" (1898)
"Exhilarating, Invigorating, Aids Digestion" (1903)
"Pepsi-Cola—It makes you Scintillate" (1919)
"Peps You Up!" (1928)
"Join the Swing to Pepsi" (1938)
"Twice as Much for a Nickel" (1939)
"More Bounce to the Ounce" (1950)
"Be Sociable, Have a Pepsi" (1958)
"Now It's Pepsi for Those Who Think Young" (1961)
"Join the Pepsi People Feelin' Free" (1973)
"The Choice of a New Generation" (1984)
"Be Young, Have Fun, Drink Pepsi" (1993)
"The Joy of Pepsi" (2001)

with food and ammo as a "war priority item," the deal spread Coke's market worldwide at government expense. Also at U.S. expense after the war, fifty-nine new Coke plants were installed to help rebuild Europe. What isn't widely known, though, is that, despite Coke's wartime posture as an All-American icon, Coca-Cola continued bottling in Nazi Germany throughout the war, using syrup smuggled in through circuitous contacts in the international business community.

NO FINER DRINK...
for Salesgirl—or Sailor
PURITY...
PEPSI-COLA
IN THE BIG BIG BOTTLE

During the war, one of Coke's officers served as a consultant to the Beverage and Tobacco Board, which (according to Pepsi president Mack) he used to help Coke and hinder Pepsi. For example, one of his first directives limited sugar users to 80% of their 1941 consumption. That was acceptable for Coke's long-established bottling operation, but many of Pepsi's bottlers were not even established in 1941. After the war, Pepsi accused Coke of working to extend sugar rationing beyond necessity.

But Pepsi played dirty, too. While Coke extended its influence deeper into the Democratic executive branch, Pepsi courted Republicans, most notably Senator Joe McCarthy, who, in exchange for a $20,000 "loan," became known in the Senate as the Pepsi-Cola Kid. Two decades later, Pepsi would hire defeated presidential candidate Richard Nixon as their chief counsel. Pepsi later helped bankroll Nixon's successful presidential bid.

More legitimately, Pepsi and Coke also fought it out in the advertising world, trading slogans and marketing punches left and right. Both used elaborate advertising campaigns and giveaways. (Pepsi, for example, bought the exclusive rights to skywriting when it was new and wrote "Pepsi Cola" over nearly every city in America.) Coke's ads usually focused on cementing its image as an all-American institution; Pepsi's, on being the upstart challenger favored by youth and other non-stodgy types.

The Cola Wars continue.

Potty Pourri

Random Kinds of Factness

• Moose are lethal fighters. If one stands its ground, a wolf pack will back down and skulk away.

• Most male mammals have nipples. However, stallions and bulls don't. Zoologists speculate that's because the females have their mammary glands located between their hind legs. There simply isn't enough extra room down there on the males.

• Of course the Roosevelts were related, and the Bushes and Adamses, too, but Richard Nixon had relatives who also served in the White House. Hoover and Taft were his distant cousins.

• Although nearly all wine grapes are now machine pressed, small quantities of some of the finer ports are still pressed by foot.

• Why does "meteorology" refer to weather and not meteors? Ask Aristotle, who coined the term in 340 B.C. In Greek, *meteora* means "stuff that's up in the air," so he called snow an "aqueous meteor." Rainbows were "luminous meteors." Wind was an "aerial meteor." And he called both lightning and shooting stars "fiery meteors."

• The joystick was used in airplanes long before it was seen with computers or video games. The first reference to one goes back to 1914.

• There are lots of legends about who knocked the nose off Egypt's Sphinx. Most involve invading armies using it for target practice. Despite the legends, you can't blame Napoleon, the Germans, the British or Arab conquerors in A.D. 693. Blame the sand, wind and rain. The Sphinx is carved out of sandstone, and all of its parts have eroded over the years. The nose, being the thinnest part, has simply taken the hardest hit from it.

• Looking for sympathy? Next time you bang your elbow, tell everyone that you've developed an *ecchymosis*. That's the formal name for a bruise.

A Suppressed Gospel

Mary's Midwife Gets Her Hand Burned

Church fathers excluded the Infancy Gospel of James (attributed to Jesus' half-brother) from the Bible during the 4th century. It tells us that Jesus was born in a cave, that Mary was given to a reluctant Joseph after being kicked out of the temple...and that the midwife who examined Mary got her hand burned off.

IN THE HISTORIES of the twelve tribes of Israel it is written that there was a man named Joachim who was exceeding rich. On the day of the Lord, Reuben told him: "It is not lawful for you to give offerings because you have not had a child for Israel." Joachim was sore grieved, and did not go home to his wife, but went into the wilderness. He pitched his tent there, and fasted forty days and forty nights, saying to himself: "I will not have either food or drink until God visits me."

His wife Anna lamented, saying: "I mourn my widowhood, and my childlessness." She prayed to the Lord, saying: "God of our fathers, bless me, and answer my prayer, as you blessed the womb of Sarah and gave her a son, Isaac." And behold an angel of the Lord appeared, saying: "Anna, the Lord has heard your prayer. You will conceive and bear, and your child will be known all over the world." Anna replied: "As God lives, I will bring my child for a gift to the Lord."

Anna's months were fulfilled, and in the ninth she gave birth. She asked the midwife: "What did I have?" The midwife said: "A girl." Anna replied: "My soul is magnified this day!" After her days were fulfilled, Anna cleansed her menstrual flow, and gave her breast to the child and named her Mary. Anna made a sanctuary in her bed chamber and allowed nothing common or unclean to pass through it. And she called for the daughters of the Hebrews that were virgins, and they were the only ones who played with Mary.

MARY BECOMES TEMPLE MASCOT...BUT THEN SHE GROWS UP

When Mary became three years old, Joachim and Anna took her to the temple of the Lord. The priest kissed her and blessed her and said: "The Lord will magnify your name through all generations; the Lord will use you to redeem the children of Israel in the last days." He sat Mary on the third step of the altar, and the Lord rained grace on her. She danced, and all the houses of Israel loved her. When Mary was in the temple of the Lord, she was nurtured like a dove as a dove, and she received food from the hand of an angel.

Mary hangs out with the virgins

When Mary turned twelve years old, the priests met saying: "Behold Mary will reach puberty soon. What can we do with her before she pollutes the sanctuary of the Lord?" And lo, an angel of the Lord appeared, saying: "Go forth and assemble all the widowers in the kingdom. Have every man carry a rod. The lord will give a sign, and that man shall have Mary for his wife."

RELUCTANT JOSEPH GETS A YOUNG WIFE

And the heralds went forth over all the country round, calling all the widowers. Throwing down his axe, Joseph ran to join them, and took their rods to meet the high priest. When he had finished a prayer, a dove flew out of Joseph's rod and landed on his head. The priest told Joseph: "Take the virgin of the Lord and keep her for yourself." Joseph refused, saying: "I have sons, and I am an old man, but she is just a girl. I'll become a laughingstock to the children of Israel." The priest replied: "Hear the Lord thy God, and remember what God did to Dathan, Abiram and Korah, how the earth opened up and swallowed them because of their disobedience."

So Joseph took her to his house. He said: "Mary: I have taken you from the temple of the Lord. I must leave you in my house, because I have been contracted to build a building, but I'll be back. Until then, the Lord will watch over you."

Mary was spinning cloth for the temple, and suddenly heard a voice say: "Hail! The Lord is with you: you among all women are blessed." Mary looked to her right and her left to see where the voice came from, and behold an angel of the Lord stood before her saying: "Fear not, Mary, for you have found grace before the Lord, and you shall conceive from his word."

Hearing this, Mary was distraught. She asked, "Will I have to conceive from the Lord in the same way all women conceive?"

The angel replied: "Not like that, Mary. The power of the Lord will come over you, and the holy child born from you will be called the Son of the Highest. Name him Jesus, for he shall save his people from their sins."

"Will I have to conceive from the Lord as all women conceive?"

HOW DO YOU FORGET AN ANGEL?

Mary rejoiced and went to the house of her cousin, Elizabeth. When Elizabeth opened the door, she blessed Mary and said: "Why should the mother of my Lord come to me? See how the child within me leaps and blesses you." Mary, however, had forgotten the mysteries which the angel Gabriel had told her, and she looked to the heaven and asked: "Who am I, Lord, that all the generations of the earth do bless me?"

Mary stayed three months with Elizabeth, and then went home and hid from the children of Israel. Day by day, her womb grew. She was sixteen years old when these mysteries came to pass.

Now it was the sixth month with her, and Joseph came home from his building. He entered into his house and found her swollen with child. He struck his face and cast himself down upon the ground, weeping: "How can I face my Lord? For I received a virgin out of the temple, and have not kept her safe. Who has done this evil in my house? Has not the story of Adam repeated itself, when the serpent came and found Eve alone and deceived her, so has it not happened to me, too?"

Joseph arose and said to Mary: "Why have you forgotten the Lord your God, you who was fed by the hand of an angel?"

But she wept bitterly, saying: "I am pure and I have not had sex with a man." Joseph said: "So where did this thing in your belly come from?" She replied: "As the Lord my God lives, I don't know how it got there."

Joseph became frightened and left her alone, wondering what he should do with her: "If I hide her sin, I break the law of the Lord. But what if I expose her sin? If what is inside her is the seed of an angel, I will be delivering up innocent blood to a death penalty. What then should I do? I will send her away from me secretly."

ANGELS IN THE NIGHT

That night, an angel appeared to him in a dream, saying: "Do not fear this child, for it came from the Holy Ghost. She will bear a son you will name Jesus, for he shall save his people from their sins." When Joseph arose from sleep, he glorified God, and watched over Mary.

Mary in a cave again

Annas the scribe* came later and said to Joseph: "Why didn't you come to the assembly?" Annas turned and saw that Mary was swollen with child. He went hastily to the priest and told him that Joseph had sinned grievously. "He has defiled the virgin he received out of the temple and stolen her virginity."

[*The priest gave them "water of the Lord's wrath" and sent them out to the wilderness to meet their fate. They returned unscathed, which surprised all. The priest said, "If God didn't judge your sins, then I won't either" and released them.*]

CHRISTMAS DELIVERY

Now there went out a decree from Augustus the king that all that were in Judea should be recorded. And Joseph said: "I will record my sons, but how will I explain this child? How shall I

* *A few years later, Jesus later got his revenge – in another suppressed gospel (see page 98), the Boy Savior killed Annas's son for messing up his mud.*

record Mary? As my wife? No, I am ashamed. As my daughter? But all the children of Israel know that she is not my daughter...." As they drew within three miles of Bethlehem, Mary said unto him: "Take me down from the ass, for this child is pressing to come out." He replied: "Where can I shelter you in your labor? This place is a desert."

Joseph found a cave there, and left his sons to care for her, and he went out and returned with a midwife. As they reached the cave, a bright cloud overshadowed it. Immediately the cloud disappeared, and a bright light blinded them. When the light went out, the young child appeared and took the breast of its mother Mary.

"A bright light blinded them."

The midwife cried aloud: "This is a great day for I have seen a miracle!" She left the cave and met her friend Salome. She said to her: "Salome, a virgin has given birth, even though her body shouldn't allow it." And Salome said, "As the Lord my God lives, if I don't insert my finger and feel her hymen myself, I will not believe that a virgin has given birth."

The midwife went to Mary and said: "Position yourself for a test, because there is a disagreement here about you." Salome inserted her finger into Mary and screamed: "Woe is me for not believing the living God and insisting on a test. Look, my hand has fallen off and is burning up in fire!" And she bowed her knees to the Lord. And lo, an angel of the Lord appeared, saying: "Salome, the Lord has heard you. Lift the child, and you will get salvation and joy." Immediately Salome was healed.

There came wise men, saying: "Where is he that is born king of the Jews? For we have seen his star in the east and have come to worship him." When Herod heard this he was troubled. He said: "If you find him, tell me so I may also worship him." They brought gifts of gold, frankincense and myrrh. Being warned by an angel that they should not enter into Judea, they went into their own country by another way.

Salome gets her hand back after an unfortunate gynecological incident

When Herod figured out that he had been tricked by the wise men, he told his men to kill all children younger than two years old. When Mary heard that the children were being slain, she was afraid. She wrapped the baby in swaddling clothes and laid him in an ox-manger.

Now I, James, wrote in Jerusalem, at a time of tumult after Herod died. I withdrew myself into the wilderness until the unrest died down, glorifying the Lord God, who gave me the gift and the wisdom to write this history. €

The Secret Gospel of Mark

OF THE DOZENS of gospels written in the century after Jesus' death, one of the most intriguing is "The Secret Gospel of Mark," of which only a fragment exists that was quoted by an early church father, Clement of Alexandria, to "Theodore." Available only to advanced initiatives of the church, it was a more extensive version of the Gospel of Mark that appears in the Bible. What's in there? The surviving fragments are intriguing. The first, meant to be inserted between Mark 10.34 and 35, reads:

> **They came to Bethany. There was one woman there whose brother had died. She came and prostrated herself before Jesus and spoke to him. "Son of David, pity me!" But the disciples rebuked her. Jesus was angry and went with her into the garden where the tomb was. Immediately a great cry was heard from the tomb. And going up to it, Jesus rolled the stone away from the door of the tomb, and immediately went in where the young man was. Stretching out his hand, he lifted him up, taking hold his hand. And the youth, looking intently at him, loved him and started begging him to let him remain with him. And going out of the tomb, they went into the house of the youth, for he was rich. And after six days Jesus gave him an order and, at evening, the young man came to him wearing nothing but a linen cloth. And he stayed with him for the night, because Jesus taught him the mystery of the Kingdom of God. And then when he left he went back to the other side of the Jordan.**

The second fragment of "Secret Mark" was meant to be inserted into Mark 10:46. It reads:

> **Then he came into Jericho. And the sister of the young man whom Jesus loved was there with his mother and Salome, but Jesus would not receive them.**

Gee Man

THE STRANGE LIFE OF J. EDGAR HOOVER

America's premiere law enforcement agent for fifty years was also its chief blackmailer and unelected despot. Ironically, there's evidence that he ignored America's worst criminals because he, himself, was being blackmailed. Read on....

• By the time he was thirteen, J. Edgar Hoover had already discarded his first name, John, and begun his habit of keeping tabs on people. He began compulsively filing away accounts of the personalities and habits of his teachers and friends, and the clothing sizes of his loved ones.

• Edgar's father, Dickerson Hoover, Sr., suffered from clinical depression and was in and out of asylums for years until his death. His mother was overprotective and controlling.

• After college, Hoover used his government job to avoid being drafted into World War I. Fifty years later he would incessantly pursue Vietnam War draft resisters.

• J. Edgar lived with his mother until her death in 1938, when Edgar was forty-three.

• After his mother's death, Hoover started seeking out the company of women, notably Lela Rogers, Ginger Rogers's mother. Four years older than Edgar, Lela's ultra-conservative political views were a perfect complement to his. Marriage was never seriously considered, but Edgar and Lela remained friends until her death in 1955.

• Hoover made a career out of anti-communism, starting in 1919 while an ambitious desk jockey in the Bureau of Investigation (the "Federal" had not yet been tacked on). He began amassing files on suspected "Bolsheviks," cross-referencing half a million names at a time when the country had only

110 million people. The day after his twenty-fifth birthday, Hoover celebrated with the biggest "Red Raid" in America's history, in which 10,000 people were arrested in one day. Most of the suspects were found to be innocent and eventually released, and the Bureau took a great deal of heat for its police-state tactics. Still, the raids did the trick—Communist Party membership, 80,000 strong before the raids, dwindled to 6,000 after 1920 and continued to dwindle down to 2,800 by 1971.

• William Sullivan's job in the FBI was monitoring the Party. He suggested in 1970 that Hoover release membership figures to show that the FBI was winning the war against subversion. "How do you think I'm going to get my Appropriations out of Congress if you keep downplaying the Communist Party?" Hoover asked him angrily. Years later, after Hoover was safely dead, Sullivan announced that the "communist threat" had long been "a lie perpetrated on the American people."

• Hoover considered Supreme Court Justice Felix Frankfurter "the most dangerous man in America" for his support of civil rights. Hoover kept a file on Frankfurter for fifty years, and bugged his offices and those of at least eleven other Supreme Court justices.

• Hoover never voted in an American election. In fact, he never even registered to vote. He claimed to be apolitical, but in fact was a staunch supporter of the right wing of the Republican Party, feeding its candidates dirt on opponents.

• Hoover was apparently homosexual. He wrote hundreds of increasingly explicit and infatuated letters to his young protégé, Melvin Purvis. Things didn't work out, however—alas, the handsome younger man turned out to be heterosexual. The last straw was when Purvis started getting publicity for capturing some high-profile criminals, threatening to overshadow Hoover. Purvis was forced out of the FBI. During the next decade, Hoover used the FBI to harass Purvis, getting him fired from jobs, spying on him and spreading false stories about him to the press. Purvis committed suicide in 1960.

• Hoover's next big infatuation centered on a young, handsome FBI rookie named Clyde Tolson.

• The two men became inseparable, traveling together on taxpayer-financed junkets and even dressing alike. Every day the were in Washington, they ate the same lunch for free from the same restaurant.

• The romance between the two men was the source of a great deal of speculation. In the 1960s, agents joked regularly about "J. Edna" and "Mother Tolson."

Later on this New Year's Eve in 1936, model Luisa Stuart (right) claimed she saw Tolson (left) and Hoover (middle) holding hands in their limo

• For decades, despite evidence that was obvious to everybody else, Hoover claimed there was no such thing as "organized crime." He refused to allow the FBI's resources to be used to fight the mob, instead going after "communists" and petty criminals. Why? According to author Anthony Summers in *Official and Confidential: The Secret Life of J. Edgar Hoover,* it was because the mob had explicit photos of Hoover and Tolson having sex, and information about an arrest of Hoover in New Orleans on a morals charge in the 1920s.

• Ironically, one of Hoover's favorite smears, offered without any apparent evidence, was that somebody was gay. For example, that's how he characterized Martin Luther King, Jr., Adlai Stevenson and three top aides of Richard Nixon.

• Hoover learned his lesson from being blackmailed by the mob, wrote Summers. For four decades, he had agents collect any allegation of sexual, political or financial misconduct they could find on every politician in Washington. Every president from Roosevelt on wanted to retire Hoover but backed down when they saw what he had on them. John and Robert Kennedy, whom Hoover despised, were particularly vulnerable to the volume of information Hoover had on their womanizing. In fact, some accounts have it that Hoover used his clout to demand that JFK choose Hoover's friend Lyndon Johnson as his running mate.

• His fear of germs was legendary. He installed a special ultraviolet lighting system that he believed would kill viruses, and kept a servant on staff to swat flies in his office.

• Hoover refused to hire black agents. Robert Kennedy pressured him on this in the 1960s, so Hoover merely "promoted" his black servants on staff, calling them "agents" while they performed the same menial duties as before. When he died, the FBI had only 70 black agents out of a total of 6,000.

• Hoover absolutely despised Martin Luther King, Jr., and was enraged when King won a Nobel Peace Prize in 1965, an honor that he himself coveted. Shortly before King was to pick up his prize in Sweden, Hoover had an unmarked parcel sent to King's wife. It contained a tape of King allegedly having sex with another woman, along with an anonymous note to King threatening to expose him to the world and suggesting that suicide was the only honorable way out.

• King was demoralized for several months. The FBI stepped up the pressure, harassing King with anonymous phone calls, threats and midnight false fire alarms. Hoover gleefully reviewed the wiretap transcripts for signs that the constant badgering was having an effect; one transcript quoted King as telling a friend, "They are out to break me, out to get me, harass me, break my spirit." King fell into a period of insomnia and deep depression. Finally, he rallied and decided that the cause was just, and that "we are not going to let Hoover and the FBI turn us around."

• When King was killed three years later, Atlanta FBI agents cheered; one shouted, "We finally got the son of a bitch!" Hoover "personally" took over the investigation. The first day he spent getting his photo taken for public relations purposes. The next day, as he had the day after Kennedy's assassination, he went to the racetrack for the day. In the weeks that followed, he failed to show up for meetings with the attorney general on the subject.

• The fingerprints of James Earl Ray, small-time criminal and prison escapee, had immediately been found on the scene, as well as a radio with his prison number on it. But it took two weeks for the FBI to issue an alert for him. For two months, Ray traveled freely around the country.

• When caught, Ray was carrying a large amount of cash, the source of which was not pursued with any vigor.

• For years afterward Hoover continued to smear King as a "communist and a scoundrel," leaking information and copies of the FBI tapes. He adopted a new goal: to stop Congress from making King's birthday a national holiday. His efforts were successful for several years; King's birthday wasn't honored until 1982.

Johnny and Clyde lunched every day (for free) at the Mayflower Hotel in D.C., until Hoover's death in 1972

• Hoover felt that female criminals were far more vicious and dangerous than males. He also claimed that female criminals always have red hair—if not naturally, "she either adopts a red wig or has her hair dyed red."

• During the student unrest of the 1960s, Hoover set up the COINTELPRO program to harass lawful protesters, using everything from threatening letters and phone calls to goon squads.

• On May 2, 1972, J. Edgar Hoover was found dead next to his bed. He had been in good health, and had had no previous heart problems. The cause of death was officially "hypertensive cardiovascular disease," but no autopsy was done to validate this. When undertakers arrived shortly after, they found 15–20 men in suits on the scene, ransacking books, files and papers, and emptying out drawers.

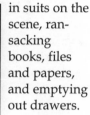

• Before his death, Hoover had somehow managed to amass millions of dollars on his civil servant's pay ($43,000 a year was his peak salary). Although he projected an air of incorruptibility, he made a lot of money from unethical and illegal dealings. Hoover received hundreds of thousands of dollars in illegal gifts, some from mob connections, and he and Tolson converted FBI Library and Recreation funds to their own uses.

• Hoover left all his earthly belongings to Clyde Tolson, bypassing relatives and other friends. Tolson died a recluse in 1975. He was buried, by mutual request, ten yards away from his former boss.

Kitchen Scientist

Cutting Fruit Inside the Peel

Your hapless victim peels a banana for morning cereal—and finds that it comes pre-sliced! What gives? Is this the result of some fiendishly clever genetic engineering?

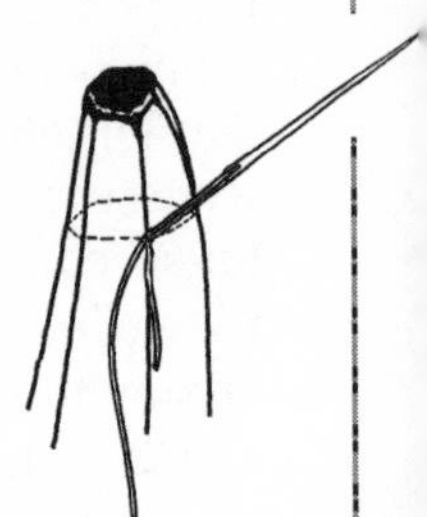

1 Get together a ripe banana, a thin needle and some thread.

2 Push the threaded needle into an unobtrusive spot on the ridge of the banana, angled along the inside of the peel. Bring it out at the next ridge, leaving a few inches of thread sticking out of the first hole.

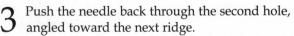

3 Push the needle back through the second hole, angled toward the next ridge.

4 Keep repeating until you have gone completely around the banana and the needle has come out of your first hole again.

5 Hold both ends of the thread and pull. The thread will pull out through the banana, slicing it cleanly in two.

6 Repeat the process in other spots until you've made several slices. Make sure your victim picks the right banana from the bowl. Peeling the banana will reveal that the fruit has been presliced.

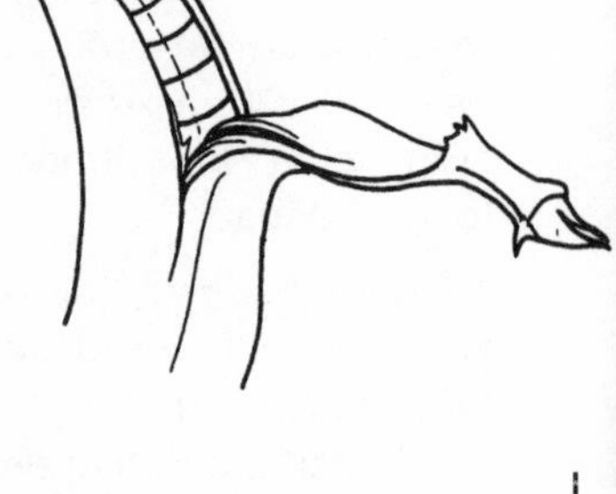

Variation: Try it with another fruit like a pear or an apple. The needle holes will be more visible, so you should take the doctored fruit this time. You'll be able to hold it in two hands and calmly twist it into neat halves. ☾

Life of the Party!

Part Two

Not just anyone can do hand shadows. So why not bone up with these from Henry Bursill's *Hand Shadows*, and become entertainer extraordinaire at your next shindig?

Sheep

Mrs. Gump

Bulldog

Eagle

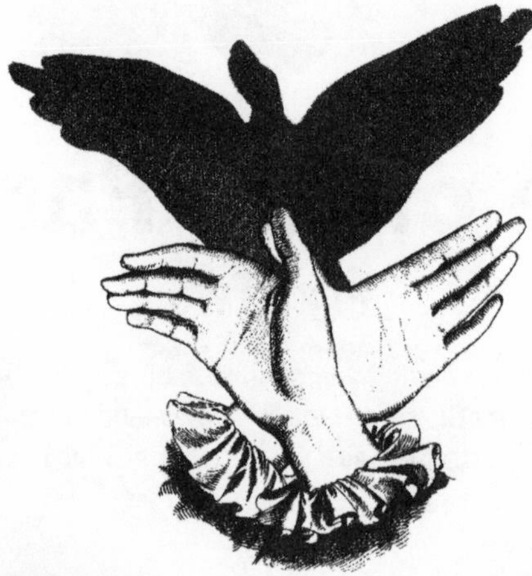

Bird on the Wing

Elephant

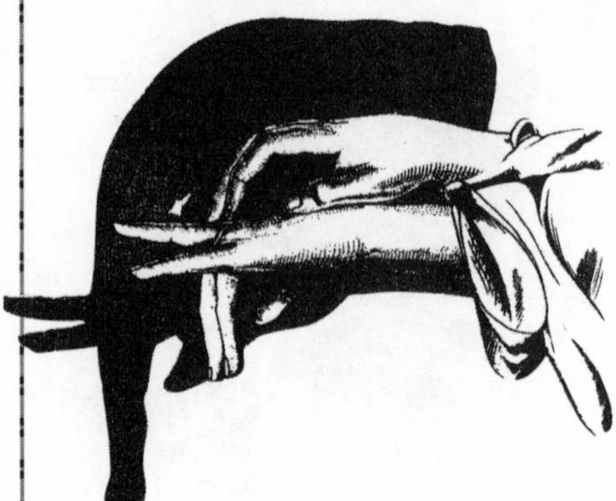

Mule

Frightened Man

Eyewitness

I Saw Vesuvius's Eruption Destroy Pompeii

Gaius Plinius Caecilius Secundus, known as Pliny the Younger, was asked to relate the story of his uncle's death. The uncle, Gaius Plinius Secundus ("Pliny the Elder"), died during the eruption of Vesuvius in A.D. 79 while trying to save others. Special thanks to Cynthia Damon of Amherst College for her translation.

My Dear Tacitus,

You ask me to write you something about the death of my uncle so that the account you transmit to posterity is as reliable as possible. I am grateful to you, for I see that his death will be remembered forever if you put it in your *Histories.*

He perished in a devastation of the loveliest of lands, in a memorable disaster shared by peoples and cities, but this will be a kind of eternal life for him.

He was at Misenum in his capacity as commander of the fleet on the 24th of August [A.D. 79]. Between 2 and 3 in the afternoon my mother drew his attention to a cloud of unusual size and appearance. He had had a sun bath, then a cold bath, and was reclining after lunch with his books.

Vesuvius erupts again in 1906

He called for his shoes and climbed up to where he could get the best view of the phenomenon. The cloud was rising from a mountain—at such a distance we couldn't tell which, but afterwards learned that it was Vesuvius. I can best describe its shape by likening it to a pine tree. It rose into the sky on a very long "trunk" from which spread some "branches." I imagine it had been raised by a sudden blast, which then weakened, leaving the cloud unsupported so that its own weight caused it to spread sideways. Some of the cloud was white, in other parts there were dark patches of dirt and ash. The sight of it made the scientist in my uncle determined to see it from closer at hand.

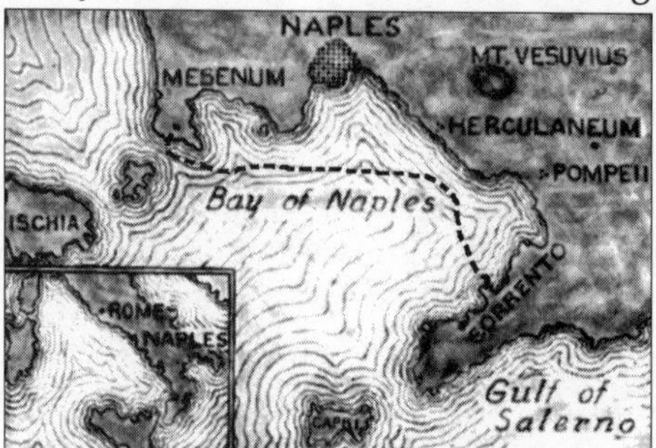

Pliny the Elder's 20-mile journey from Misenum, trying to save refugees and satisfy scientific curiosity

My uncle ordered a boat made ready. He offered me the opportunity of going along, but I preferred to study—he himself happened to have set me a writing exercise. As he was leaving the house he was brought a letter from Tascius' wife Rectina,

who was terrified by the looming danger. Her villa lay at the foot of Vesuvius, and there was no way out except by boat. She begged him to get her away. He changed his plans. The expedition that started out as a quest for knowledge now called for courage. My uncle launched the quadriremes [galley boats with four banks of oarsmen] and likewise embarked, a source of aid for more people than just Rectina, for that delightful shore was a populous one. He hurried to a place from which others were fleeing, and held his course directly into danger. Was he afraid? It seems not, as he kept up a continuous observation of the various movements and shapes of that evil cloud, dictating what he saw.

Ash was falling onto the ships now, darker and denser the closer they went. Now it was bits of pumice, and rocks that were blackened and burned and shattered by the fire. Here the sea had become like a sandbar; debris from the mountain blocked the shore. He paused for a moment wondering whether to turn back as the helmsman urged him. "Fortune helps the brave," he said. "Head for the house of Pomponianus."

At Stabiae, on the far side of the bay formed by the gradually curving shore, Pomponianus had loaded up his ships even before the danger arrived, though it was visible and indeed extremely close, once it intensified. He planned to put out as soon as the contrary wind let up. That very wind carried my uncle right in, and he embraced the frightened man and gave him comfort and courage.

To lessen the other's fear by showing his own unconcern, my uncle asked to be taken to the baths. He bathed and dined, carefree or at least appearing so (which is equally impressive). Meanwhile, broad sheets of flame were lighting up many parts of Vesuvius; their light and brightness were the more vivid for the darkness of the night. To alleviate people's fears my uncle claimed that the flames came from the deserted homes of farmers who had left in a panic with the hearth fires still alight. Then he rested, and gave every indication of actually sleeping; people who passed by his door heard his snores, which were rather resonant since he was a heavy man.

As he slept, the ground outside his room rose so high

Pompeii Rises from the Ashes

On August 24, A.D. 79, the cities of Herculaneum, Pompeii and Stabiae were covered by ashes and lava several yards deep. Pompeii had not

been a particularly remarkable city, but it became significant to historians because its location was lost for seventeen centuries. When Pompeii was rediscovered by a farmer digging in a vineyard in 1748, the ruins had remained largely undisturbed for all that time, providing a rich trove of historical artifacts that show what life was like at the time.

Graffiti and campaign posters still adorned the city walls (an election campaign had been in progress when the volcano erupted). Remains of about 2,000 of the 20,000 residents have been found; their bodies rotted away, but the lava and ash created perfect molds of their features, allowing archeologists to make replicas of the dead by pouring plaster into them.

About a quarter of the city is still unexcavated.

with the mixture of ash and stones that if he had spent any more time there escape would have been impossible. He got up and came out to be with Pomponianus and the others who had been unable to sleep. They discussed what to do, whether to remain under cover or to try the open air. The buildings were being rocked by a series of strong tremors, and appeared to have come loose from their foundations and to be sliding this way and that. Outside, however, there was danger from the rocks that were coming down, light and fire-consumed as these bits of pumice were. Weighing the relative dangers they chose the outdoors; in my uncle's case it was a rational decision, others just chose the alternative that frightened them the least.

Despite this 18th-century engraving of Pliny the Elder's death, the guy was fifty-five and quite chunky. He likely died of a heart attack.

They tied pillows on top of their heads as protection against the shower of rock. It was daylight now elsewhere in the world, but there the darkness was darker and thicker than any night. But they had torches and other lights. They decided to go down to the shore to see if it were yet possible to escape by sea, but it remained as rough and uncooperative as before.

Resting in the shade of a sail he drank once or twice from the cold water he had asked for. Then came a smell of sulfur, announcing the flames, and the flames themselves, sending others into flight but reviving him. Supported by two small slaves he stood up, and immediately collapsed. As I understand it, his breathing was obstructed by the dust-laden air, and his innards, which were never strong and often blocked or upset, simply shut down. When daylight came again two days after he died, his body was found untouched, unharmed, in the clothing that he had been wearing. He looked more asleep than dead.

Meanwhile at Misenum, my mother and I—but this has nothing to do with history, and you only asked for information about his death. I'll stop here then. But I will say one more thing: that I had written out everything while memories were still fresh. Use the important bits, for it is one thing to write a letter, another to write history; one thing to write to a friend, another to write for the public. Farewell, Pliny.

MEANWHILE, BACK IN MISENUM (LETTER #2)

My dear Tacitus,

You say that you want to know of my fearful ordeal at Misenum (where I broke off in my letter). "The mind shudders to remember...but here's the tale."

After my uncle's departure I finished up my studies, as I had planned. Then I had a bath, then dinner, and a short and unsatisfactory night. There had been tremors for many days previously, a common occurrence in Campania and no cause for panic. But that night the shaking grew stronger and people thought it was an upheaval, not just a tremor. My mother burst into my room and I got up. I said she should rest, and I would rouse her if need be.

We sat out on a terrace between the house and the sea. I sent for a volume of Livy; I read and even took notes from where I had left off, as if it were a moment of free time; I hardly know whether to call it bravery, or foolhardiness (I was seventeen at the time).

Up came a friend of my uncle's, recently arrived from Spain. When he saw my mother and me sitting there, and me even reading a book, he scolded her for her calm and me for my lack of concern. But I kept on with my book.

The day began with a hesitant and almost lazy dawn. All around us buildings were shaken. We were in the open, but it is only a small area and we were afraid—no, certain actually—that there would be a collapse. We finally decided to leave the town. A dazed crowd followed us, preferring our plan to their own (this is what passes for wisdom in a panic). Their numbers were so large that they slowed our departure, and then swept us along. We stopped once we had left the buildings behind us. Many strange things happened to us there, and we had much to fear: The carts that we had ordered up were rolling in opposite directions, though the ground was perfectly flat, and they wouldn't stay in place even with their wheels blocked by stones. In addition, it seemed as though the sea was being sucked backwards, as if it were being pushed back by the shaking of the land. Certainly the shoreline moved outwards, and many sea creatures were left on dry sand. Behind us were frightening dark clouds rent by lightning, opening to reveal huge figures of flame like lightning, but bigger.

Pliny the Younger

At that point our Spanish friend urged us strongly: "If your brother and uncle is alive, he wants you to be safe. If he has perished, he wanted you to survive him. So why are you reluctant to escape?" We responded that we would not look to our own safety as long as we were uncertain about his. Waiting no longer, he himself ran from the danger at a mad pace.

It wasn't long thereafter that the cloud stretched down to the ground and covered the sea. It girdled Capri and made it vanish, it hid Misenum's headlands. My mother begged, then urged, then ordered me to flee however I might, saying that a young man could make it, but that she, weighed down in years and body, would die happy if she escaped being the cause of my death. I replied that I wouldn't save myself without her, and then I took her hand and made her walk a little faster. She obeyed with difficulty, and blamed herself for delaying me.

Now came the dust, though still thinly. I looked back: a dense cloud loomed behind us, following us like a flood pouring across the land. "Let us turn aside while we can still see, lest we be knocked over and crushed by the crowd of our companions." We had scarcely sat down when a darkness came that was not like a moonless or cloudy night, but more like the black of closed and unlighted rooms. You could hear women lamenting, children crying, men shouting. Some were calling for parents, others for children or spouses; they could only have recognized each other by voices.

Some bemoaned their own lot, others that of their loved ones. Some were so afraid of death that they prayed for death. Many raised their hands to the gods, and even more believed that there were no gods any longer and that this was one last unending night for the world. Nor were we without people who magnified real dangers with fictitious horrors. Some claimed that one or another part of Misenum had collapsed or burned; lies, but they found believers.

Pliny's villa in Misenum

It grew lighter, though that seemed not a return of day, but a sign that the fire was approaching. The fire itself actually stopped some distance away, but darkness and ashes came again, a great weight of them. We stood and shook the ash off again and again, otherwise we would have been covered with it and crushed by the weight. I might boast that no groan escaped me in such perils, no cowardly word, but that I believed that I was perishing with the world, and the world with me, which was a great consolation for death.

At last the cloud thinned out and dwindled to no more than smoke or fog. Soon there was real daylight. The sun was even shining, though with the lurid glow it has after an eclipse. The sight that met our still terrified eyes was a changed world, buried in ash like snow. We returned to Misenum and took care of our bodily needs, but spent the night dangling between hope and fear. Fear was the stronger, for the earth was still quaking and a number of people who had gone mad were mocking the evils that had happened to them and others with terrifying predictions. We still refused to go until we heard news of my uncle, although we had felt danger and expected more.

You will read what I have written, but will not take up your pen, as the material is not the stuff of history. You have only yourself to blame if it seems not even proper stuff for a letter.

Farewell, Pliny

Pot Shots

Even *more* of Privy's favorite privy shots. Send us yours!
(See page 476.)

Each house, above, has its own sanitary privy in this 1920s neighborhood. This was a new idea to most rural folks, who were used to sharing facilities with their neighbors.

This picture (below) of the Porcupine cabin outhouse in the Crazy Mountains, Montana, is courtesy of Tom Böttger.

A camper (below) peeks into the facilities in the Samburu National Reserve, Kenya.

(Above) The childhood home privy of President Calvin Coolidge.

TV Dinners

How TV Dinners Became "Tray Chic"

Today, frozen dinners are yupscale and pretentious, and there are those who say that TV dinners of the past were best: the trays were aluminum, the choices were scanty (turkey, beef, chicken or Salisbury steak), and they weren't too proud to call it a "TV dinner."

FROZEN FOOD in your local grocery is a relatively recent thing. True, seventeenth-century scientist Sir Francis Bacon had some ideas about freezing as a preservative and even did some experiments that looked promising. (Unfortunately, he died of hypothermia after spending a cold afternoon stuffing snow into a dead chicken.) But the modern-day frozen food industry owes its existence to Clarence Birdseye, who liked to be called Bob and pronounced his name BIRD-zee.

Birdseye, a naturalist and writer of books on wildflowers, birds and mammals, had gone to Labrador in 1917 to conduct a survey of fish and wildlife for the U.S. government. While there, he noticed that the Native Canadians' meat and poultry didn't get mushy when frozen and thawed. It felt and tasted nearly fresh, unlike food he had tried freezing back in the States.

He figured that it was because of the extreme cold that the food froze quicker. When he got back, he tested the theory. He bought $7 worth of ice, salt water and an electric fan. Sure enough, he found that slow freezing allowed large ice crystals to form, bursting the food's cell walls. Fast freezing prevented that, saving the cellular integrity, texture and flavor for months on end. As a side benefit, he also found that he could entertain dinner guests by bouncing frozen steaks off the kitchen floor before cooking them for dinner.

In 1923, Birdseye gambled everything he owned designing a practical large-scale fast freezer and setting up Birdseye Foods, Inc. He nearly went broke. When the Postum Company (which changed its name to General Foods that same year) offered to buy his patented process for $22 million, Birdseye jumped at the chance.

The corporation already had a distribution system set up, which had been Birdseye's undoing. It also could afford to buy advertising to convince America that it needed frozen food. By 1934, 80 percent of the frozen food market belonged to General Food's Birds Eye Division. (They added the space in Birdseye's name and began pronouncing it like it was spelled.)

For his part, Birdseye went on tinkering, amassing over 250 patents on a range of things from recoilless harpoons to a way to turn sugar cane waste into paper. Like Bacon, he died with his inventor's boots on—in 1956, while in Peru trying to figure out how to make paper out of the agave plant, he had a fatal heart attack from the high altitude. But he lived long enough to see the preeminent use for his fast-freezing process: the TV Dinner, invented by the Swanson brothers.

Gilbert and Clarke Swanson had a problem: they were surrounded by turkeys. Real turkeys. They owned the largest turkey processing plant in the country, C. A. Swanson & Sons, and it drove them crazy that most Americans ate turkey on only one day a year: Thanksgiving. The Swansons made it their goal to insinuate more turkey meat into America's diet. First they started making frozen turkey pot pies. These became so popular that people started clamoring for more varieties. This was good news for business, but not good news for the turkey problem.

In 1951, the Swanson kitchens began experimenting with individual portion meals that could be popped into the oven and eaten without much preparation. Inspired by the segmented plates used in diners for "Blue Plate Specials," they made similar trays out of aluminum and put dinner courses in them.

TV and dinner...a perfect match!

Television was the hot new fad sweeping the country. The Swanson Company arranged to sponsor its own show, *Ted Mack's Family Hour*. Gilbert Swanson invited some friends over to have dinner and watch the premiere show.

While eating in front of Swanson's console TV, one of the guests remarked about how odd it was to see everybody balancing food trays on their laps in front of the TV. Swanson suddenly thought of the individual portion meals his company was working on. They'd be perfect for eating while watching TV, and tying them in to the TV craze couldn't hurt. In fact, if you rounded the corners of the aluminum trays, they'd sort of look like a TV screen.... Why not call them TV Dinners?

The next morning Gilbert told his brother about the idea. Clarke liked it, and suggested putting a picture of a TV on the box with the dinner coming off the screen.

In January 1952, the first Swanson's TV Dinners rolled off the line in Omaha. They contained turkey, cornbread stuffing, gravy, buttered peas and sweet potatoes in orange and butter sauce—and cost 98¢. The dinners did well. Soon the company introduced fried chicken TV Dinners, which sold quickly until consumers started noticing that the chicken tasted like bananas.

It turned out that the yellow ink on the box used a solvent that smelled like bananas, and that the smell was seeping into the food. Swanson recalled the chicken dinners and changed the ink, but one food chain in Florida complained because it said that its customers actually preferred the banana-flavored variety. Swanson pragmatically shipped its entire recalled inventory to Florida.

In the 1960s, after TV became a guilty pleasure instead of a harmless fad, Swanson's redesigned its package to downplay the TV Dinner brand name, allowing it to more or less become a generic term. In 1984, the Swanson Company replaced the aluminum tray with a microwaveable plastic one. As a sop to the health-conscious times, the company replaced the brownie with a fruit dessert in 1986, but soon reversed the decision after a deluge of customer complaints.

We can hope that with a consumer crusade they might bring back the classic aluminum tray as well. The dinner's don't quite taste the same without that faint metallic tinge to the vegetables. And if that works, maybe next we can work toward the return of that banana-flavored chicken. €

True Adventure

Canoeing the Delaware River, Part 2

When we left the intrepid canoeists on page 66, they were preparing to confront the monster rapids of the Big Foul. As the fourth day breaks, the three adventurers nervously pack their canoes....

IN THE MORNING A SWIM, a solid breakfast, and an extra careful packing of the canoes. No one spoke of it; but that morning we each paid a particular attention to the trim of the boats and the stowing of dunnage. At about noon we would reach Belvidere; and the Great Foul Rift was only a mile farther.

There was a camp of bass fishers near us, and they came to see us start. They learned our intention of going down without portage, rift or no rift. They did not dissuade us. One of them said he knew the Big Foul, and he gave us precise, too precise, instructions. All I could recall half an hour later was: "Keep to the right when you come to the big white stone—if there's water enough to float your boats."

We came to the town of Belvidere. The mill-workers came down to have a chat. "Keep to the right of the big white rock, and you will strike the channel," shouted a man as we started.

A discussion in *Forest and Stream* a few years ago directed the attention of canoemen to its alleged dangers and extreme rapidity of current. Two canoemen of East Orange, N.J., who ran the rapids in 1878 and claimed to be the first to do so, wrote:

> **"After passing through two or three small rifts, we arrived at Great Foul Rift, which is considered the most dangerous one in the river, on account of the number of rocks and the swiftness of the current. How to describe our passage through here, we hardly know; all we can say is, we saw it, we entered it, and we passed it. You can see big slate rocks on all sides, and are unable to tell what minute you will strike them. This rift is two miles long, and we passed through it in three minutes exactly, being carried that fast by the current, without using our paddles." This statement**

was received with astonishment. Two miles in three minutes, or 40 miles an hour, is not the speed of a rapid, but almost that of a waterfall.

Among the critics was Mr. A. H. Siegfried of Louisville, who had also run the Great Foul Rift. He wrote: "We were warned against Foul Rift for two days above it, and came to it determined not merely to run it, but to examine it carefully, and see if it is as dangerous as the natives think. We went through it without paddle, save for steering purposes, and were just eleven minutes from the time we entered until we left the swift water. That we thought a quick run, considering the windings of the channel, following which the distance is fully three miles, though a straight line will measure nearly one-third less. The rift is very swift and crooked, whirling among many and such recklessly distributed boulders that the speed claimed by 'F. P. and E. P. D.' would have been sure death to both boats and men if it had been possible."

Half a mile or so below Belvidere, we felt the water quicken and sweep to the right. We knew we were in the first reach of the rapid that had been roaring for us since we started.

There are two distinct rapids—the Little Foul and the Great Foul—divided by swift water of half a mile. From the moment we struck the Little Foul Rift, we knew we were in the grip of a giant. We were as much astonished as if we had never run a rapid before. We shot down the river—each one finding his own channel; and, with all our careful steering, we grazed several dangerous stones.

Moseley paddles manfully into rough water

There was no stopping at the foot of the Little Foul Rift; but we ran with the stream without paddling, and examined the entrance to the Great Rapid ahead.

There was no bar or ledge formation here, as in the minor rifts behind us. The rocks stood up like the broken teeth of a sperm whale, irregularly across the river as far ahead as we could see from the canoes. Some of the stones were twelve feet out of the water, others of lesser height, and of all shapes; some were level with the surface, and some covered with a few inches of water. These last were the dangers: to strike and get "hung up" on one of these meant certain upsetting; for no boat could stand the rush, and there was no footing for the canoeman if he tried to get out to push her over. We could steer between the teeth we saw, but we suddenly became conscious of unseen teeth that lay in wait to lacerate the boats under the waterline with irregular edges as sharp as a shattered punch-bowl.

High water marks on the Delaware bank

We were going into the Great Foul Rift all this time, at the rate of—but who can tell the rate of rapid water? The best canoeman I know says there is no canoeing-water in America over twelve miles an hour (I think he places this on the Susquehanna, below Columbia), and that eight miles is very rapid indeed. He may be right; but, were I asked how fast we went into the Great Foul Rift, I should say, at least twelve miles an hour and, in parts of the descent, much faster.

Guiteras went first, but was caught on a covered flat stone in the quick, smooth water; so Moseley led into the rapid, with Guiteras, who had floated off the stone, following. I came about fifty yards behind.

From the first break of the water, the sensation was somewhat similar to that of falling through the branches of a tree. The river was twisting downhill in convulsions. We rushed through narrow slopes of ten or twenty feet as if we were falling, and then shot round a rock, flinging the whole weight of our bodies on the steering-paddle. The tall stones ahead seemed to be rushing at us with the velocity of an ocean steamer.

All the time we were painfully conscious of the incisive edges under water, as one might feel the nearness of burglars' knives in the night. If we struck one of these stones on a downward shoot, it would rip the canoe from bow to stern.

Moseley steered skillfully, and we cleared two-thirds of the tortuous descent without a shock. A quarter of a mile ahead we saw the smooth water at the foot of the rift. Suddenly, the channel divided at a great white stone, the wider water going to the left, toward the center of the river, and a narrow black streak keeping straight down to the right.

A memory of the warning came to me, "Keep to the right of the big rock—if you can." But it was too late. A man could not hear his own shout in such an uproar. The white rock rushed past us. The canoes ahead had turned with the main stream, and were in the center of the river in a flash. Suddenly both canoes ahead were shot out of the channel, their bows in the air resting on a hidden rock; and the current, just then turning a sharp curve, swept by their sterns with a rush. Fortunately they were out of the stream, driven into an eddy, or that would have been the end of them.

I had time to profit by their mishap. Kneeling in the canoe, using the long-handled paddle, I rounded the curve within a foot of the grounded canoes, and fairly leaped downhill on a rounded muscle of water. In the rush, a thrill swept my nerves—and another—as if twice I had touched cold steel. I found later that my canoe had twice been pierced by the knife-like edges under water.

O'Boyle and Guiteras at the bottom of the Great Foul Rift

Before I realized it, the end had come, and the canoe shot across the river in a sweeping eddy. The Great Foul Rift was behind me.

A fisherman on the bank had been watching our passage. "You ought to have kept to the right of that stone," he shouted. "See, there's the channel!" And, looking up, I saw it, straight as a furrow from the big white stone, keeping swift, close to the Pennsylvania shore, unbroken, and safe. Had we kept in this straight way the Great Foul Rift would to us have been no more than an exaggerated name.

The grounded canoemen pushed free, and were down in a minute; and then we went ashore, and while Moseley photographed the Great Foul Rift, the others plunged into the delicious water, that seemed too peaceful and sweet ever to have been violent and brutal.

Half a mile below the Great Foul Rift, we came to the pastoral scene of the voyage, par excellence. It was not great or grand in any way; but simply peaceful, pastoral, lovely. It was a sloping hillside of two or three farms smothered in soft foliage. A round-arched stone bridge spanned a stream. Cows and horses stood in the shadow of trees. Children's voices at play filled the air, and a dog barked joyously in some romping game.

We laid our paddles on the canoes in front of us, and floated a full mile through the lovely picture. It can never be forgotten. In its quiet way, nothing equaled it on the whole river.

"Photograph the place," I said to Moseley.

"No," he replied. "It is too good for any thing but memory." €

Epilogue

• The rips in author O'Reilly's canoe turned out to be a problem. Although patched that night, they reopened on the river the next day, and he had to travel the rest of the way by canal boat.

• Stretches of the Delaware are officially designated as Wild & Scenic, so much of the beauty the men saw in 1890 is still there. However, the area around the Great Foul Rift is outside that designated area and is now littered with industrial sites. Still, canoeists and kayakers make the run regularly.

• Ironically, with modern boaters using crafts of nearly indestructable acrylics instead of canvas, wood and bark, the Great Foul Rift is now considered not that big a deal. Its designation from the American Whitewater Affiliation is only Class II (out of V), which means that it is suitable for even novices.

Something in Common 3

It's easy, really—we'll give you a list of words and you tell us the one word that goes with all of them. Answers below (don't cheat!).

1. House, alley, pole, walk, fish, boat, nap, call, gut
2. House, Christmas, apple, frog, surgeon, family
3. Fall, dish, melon, works, toilet, waste, fresh, salt
4. Attack, beat, break, take, burn, ache, land, candy, felt
5. Mr., wing, human, hander, whale, turn, angle, away
6. Core, road, crab, computer, pie, sauce, jack, green, butter
7. Evil, cross, lazy, candy, glass, black, lid, public, private
8. Body, stones, plaster, iron, original, off, on, away
9. Shoe, fly, around, hobby, sea, saw, dark, latitude, race, power
10. Fruit, cricket, baseball, brick, man, vampire
11. Saw, boy, rock, big, rubber, head, stand, cigar, marching
12. Horse, brake, tree, gym, platform, polish, running, lace
13. Well, big, fifth, barrow, potter's, steering
14. Port, brush, bag, craft, line, plane, hot, conditioner, raid
15. Row, gravy, river, house, fishing
16. Beef, hog, solid, wire, coffee, floor, ball, squirrel, speed
17. Lady, state, grounds, trade, practices, way, not
18. Agent, taker, movie, traffic, laundry, office, lottery, split
19. Clear, worm, measure, ticker, video, duct
20. Pin, out, contact, view, grade, spread, breaking, game

ANSWERS: *1. cat; 2. tree; 3. water; 4. heart; 5. right; 6. apple; 7. eye; 8. cast; 9. horse; 10. bat; 11. band; 12. shoe; 13. wheel; 14. air; 15. boat; 16. ground; 17. fair; 18. ticket; 19. tape; 20. point*

Life of the Party!

PART THREE

We like them enough to give you more!

Deer

Brown Bear

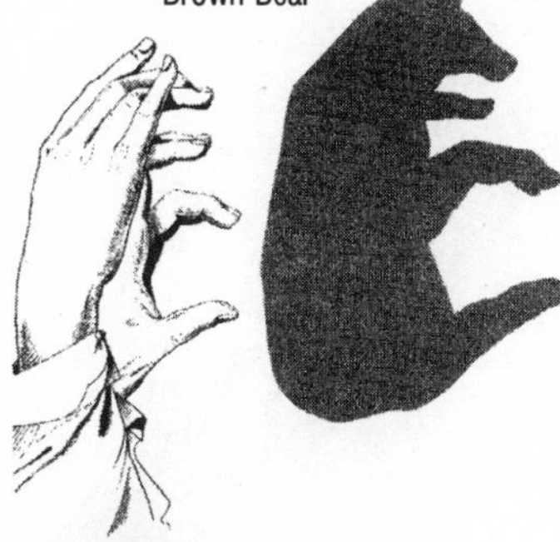

Swan

Tortoise

Greyhound

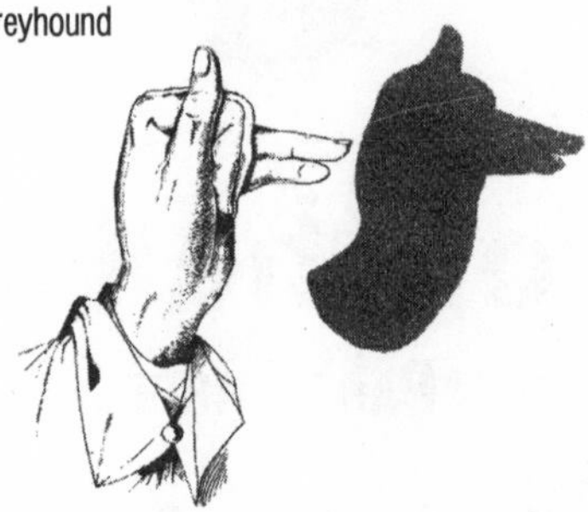

Cockatoo

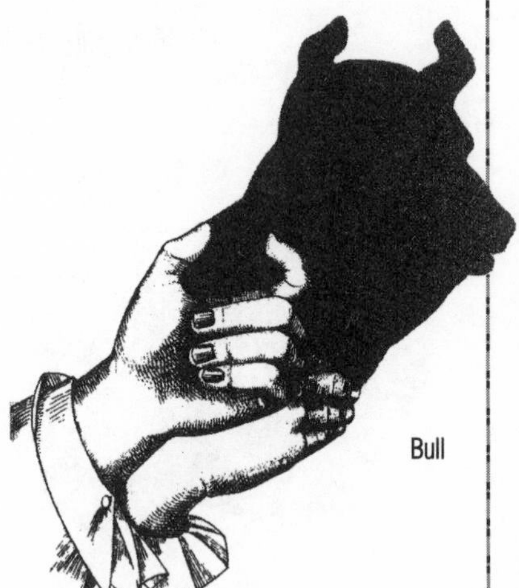

Bull

Shakespeare

Snow Business

Making a Snow Pig, Owl & French Man

All right, so maybe the French guy isn't completely politically correct, but here is a snow sculpture guide from the 1890 *The American Boy's Handy Book* by Dan Beard, one of the founders of the American Boy Scouts.

In the "land of the midnight sun," the far arctic regions where Jack Frost rules supreme, where the glistening ice and thickly packed snow covers the landscape, the hardy inhabitants live in snow.

After the first good old-fashioned snow storm has covered the playground, roads, and housetops, and while the merry jingle of the sleigh bells tinkles through the wintry air, let children busy themselves rolling huge balls of snow.

THE PIGS OF SNOW

Snow statuary may be of various kinds. It is very seldom that pigs are sculptured in marble or cast in bronze, and it would be well to make some of snow, so as to have statues not likely to be found elsewhere. An oblong mass of snow forms the body (Fig. 1); the legs, nose, and ears are

FIG. 1.—Making the Pig.

FIG. 2.—A Snow Pig.

made of sticks surrounded by snow, and a bit of rope nicely curled will make a very good tail. The various parts can be shaped and carved according to the skill of the young artist. A number of pigs, of different sizes, will give a lively and social air to the yard of a house. Fig. 2 shows a finished pig.

FRENCHY, THE FRENCHMAN

A statue of a Frenchman is also rather uncommon, and is not hard to make. The foundation of the body, head, and legs consists of several large snowballs, as seen in Fig. 3, and the arms are made of smaller balls stuck on two sticks, which are inserted in the body at proper angles.

FIG. 3.—Making "Frenchy."

When the whole figure has been "blocked out," as the artists say, it must be carved, with broad wooden knives or shingles, into the proper shape, as shown in Fig. 4. The moustache should be made of icicles, which may be stuck in the face.

FIG. 4.—Frenchy.

ARCTIC OWL

Arctic owls, which are very large and white, can also be made of snow, in the manner shown in Fig. 5 and 6. These figures can be placed on snow pedestals if they are small, but if they are monster owls, like those in the illustrations, they must be placed upon the ground. In either position, if they are fashioned properly, they will look very wise and respectable.

FIG. 5.—Carving the Owl.

When the snow is too dry to make a snowball it cannot be used to make statuary, but after a slight thaw or a fresh fall of snow it readily adheres upon a slight pressure, and can be formed or fashioned in almost any shape.

FIG. 6.—An Arctic Owl.

Many curious objects and figures may be carved out of solidly packed balls of snow. A lawn covered with a number of large snow figures presents a most grotesque appearance, and is sure to attract the attention of all passers-by. With practice not a little skill may be acquired by the young sculptor, and if the statuary be made of large proportions, they will sometimes last for weeks after the snow has disappeared from the ground and house-tops. ☾

Building a Snow House

Showing the construction of a Snow-House.

The pictures of the house show so well how it is constructed, and how it looks when it is done, that very little explanation is necessary. The walls are made of large snowballs properly placed, with snow packed between them to make the surfaces tolerably even, and then the whole shaved down with a spade, outside and inside. It will be found impossible to put one tier of balls upon the top of the others by lifting them in place, but this difficulty may be overcome by sliding the balls up an inclined plane made of a strong plank, one end of which must be placed upon the ground and the other allowed to rest upon the top of the first or foundation row of snowballs.

—The American Boy's Handy Book
by Dan Beard, 1890

A Snow-House Finished.

According to Mark Twain

More from *Puddin'head Wilson's Calendar*, a fictitious publication that Twain "quoted" from whenever he needed a maxim.

• "It could probably be shown by facts and figures that there is no distinctly native American criminal class except Congress."

• "We should be careful to get out of an experience only the wisdom that is in it, and stop there, lest we be like the cat that sits down on a hot stove. She will never sit down on a hot stove again. That is well, but also she will never sit on a cold one, either."

• "Everything human is pathetic. The secret source of humor itself is not joy but sorrow. There is no humor in heaven."

• "Truth is the most valuable thing we have. Let us economize it."

• "When in doubt, tell the truth."

• "It is better to have old second-hand diamonds than none at all."

• "Faith is believing what you know ain't so."

• "Names are not always what they seem. The common Welsh name Bzjxxllwcp is pronounced Jackson."

• "Few of us can stand prosperity. Another man's, I mean."

• "We can secure other people's approval, if we do right and try hard; but our own approval is worth a hundred of it, and no way has been found out of securing that."

• "It is by the goodness of God that in our country we have three unspeakably precious things: freedom of speech, freedom of conscience, and the prudence never to practice either of them."

• "Truth is stranger than fiction, but it is because fiction is obligated to stick to possibilities; truth isn't."

• "'Classic': A book which people praise and don't read."

• "Man will do many things to get himself loved, but he will do *all* things to get himself envied."

• "There are people who can do all fine and heroic things but one: keep from telling their happiness to the unhappy."

• "Man is the only animal that blushes. Or needs to."

• "There are several good protections against temptation, but the surest is cowardice."

Hopping to It

An Amphibious Assault of Frogs & Toads

They're slimy and bug-eyed—not unlike your last blind date, but with a lot more appeal. Frogs and toads are the stuff that myth, legend and French dishes are made of. Sue Shipman tells us more.

• Scientists estimate that a toad can catch and devour approximately 10,000 insects during one summer.

• Some large tropical frogs eat small mammals and snakes.

• No frog lives in salt water.

• There are almost 4,000 known species of frogs and toads.

• The word for frog in Sanskrit translates to "cloud" because, in India, frogs were thought to personify thunder.

• Frogs are symbols of good luck in Japan.

• The main difference between toads and frogs is that toads don't spend as much time in the water as frogs do. As a result, their skin is thicker and retains moisture better, and they tend to be stockier in build than most frogs.

• The goliath frog from Cameroon in West Africa can be a foot long and weigh as much as a large house cat.

• The smallest known frog in the southern hemisphere is the Brazilian gold frog. Its body is less than half of an inch long.

• A group of toads is called a "knot." A group of frogs is called a "chorus."

• The desert horned lizard or "horny toad" is neither a toad nor a frog. It is a reptile. It has a spiky body that it can flatten or puff up to discourage predators.

• Some toads have glands behind their ears which they can use to squirt poison at predators. The poison of the marine toad can kill a dog within minutes if the dog ingests it. These toads were introduced to Florida and other parts of the world to try to reduce sugar cane pests.

• Some of the poison in a poisonous frog comes from its diet of toxic insects.

• Although humans use frog venom to hunt, poisonous frogs don't. They use it solely as a defense mechanism against predators.

Some South American tree frogs have webs under their legs too to help them glide from tree to ground

• Chemicals secreted by the skin of poison-arrow frogs in Central and South America are some of the deadliest biological toxins in the world—so toxic that one frog's poison could kill up to eight humans.

• South American poisonous frogs can't kill a human by touching them unless there's an abrasion on the skin, or the person otherwise ingests the poison. Scientist wear thick gloves to study them.

• Most South American hunters don't risk touching a poisonous frog at all—gloved or not—but simply skewer it on the ground with a stake and roast it to drain the poison for their darts.

• Frogs are found everywhere in the world except Antarctica. Most frogs, however, are found in the tropics.

• Presumed to be extinct, the gastric brooding frog gave birth through its mouth. It's not known whether the mother swallowed the eggs or if her tadpoles swam into her mouth and into her stomach. During gestation, she fasted and her stomach did not produce hydrochloric acid. She birthed her brood of up to 30 tadpoles by opening her mouth and letting the babies swim out.

• Frogs don't chew; they swallow their food whole.

• It is believed the phrase "frog in your throat" comes from the Old English *frogga* which meant "hoarseness."

• There are at least two theories about why the term *frog* is used as a derogatory term when speaking about the French. One is that the beef-loving English were disgusted by the French appetite for frogs' legs. Another is that the term dates from the middle ages when the British mistook the gold "fleur-de-lys" on the French flag for a frog.

• Tadpole is the name given to the aquatic larval stage of all amphibians, not just frogs and toads.

• Apart from poisonous varieties, frogs and toads won't hurt you, and they don't cause warts. Although, of course, picking up a frog or toad can be harmful to it.

• Frog legs taste like chicken. Think of it as "chicken of the swamp."

• Catherine the Great's tableware sported a frog design.

• The British dish "toad in the hole" contains no frog or toad parts. Although the origins of the name and the dish are not completely clear, it's an old recipe, dating back more than 250 years, and the name is comparable to that of our sausage and roll treat, "pigs in blankets."

• Frogs don't drink with their mouths, but absorb water through their skin.

• There are some toads that don't even need standing water to hydrate. They have a pouch on their bottoms called a "seat," that can absorb three-quarters of all the water they need from the moist soil.

• The frog's tongue attaches to the front of its mouth, not the back. It's designed for shooting out and catching bugs, not for swallowing.

• A frog's eyes are big, bulgy and are located on the top of its head. Even when its body and most of its head is submerged or buried, it can still see. The area inside the body that houses these big eyeballs is also large. When the frog swallows, it closes its eyes, pushing them down into their cavities. The eyeballs actually get shoved down into the back of the frog's mouth, helping to push the wiggling bug down its throat.

• Although the cane frog lays 30,000 to 35,000 eggs at a time, the Cuban frog lays only one.

More Curses!

And more of our favorite long-forgotten, archaic insults from Jeffrey Racirk's *Long Lost Insults Knowledge Cards.*

GAMMERSTANG: "Usually applied to a female of idle, loose habits." —*Dialect of Mid-Yorkshire,* C. Clough Robinson, 1876

FUMBLER: "An unperforming husband, one that is insufficient; *fumbler's hall,* the place where such are to be put for their non-performance." —*Dictionary of the Canting Crew,* B. E., 1699

NYARGLE: "A foolish person fond of disrupting." —*Scottish Gallovidian Encyclopedia,* John Mactaggart, 1824

MOTH OF PEACE: "A mere idler; one who consumes but does not work." —*Shakespeare Cyclopædia and Glossary,* John Phin, 1902

HOGS-NORTON: "This proverbial phrase was commonly addressed to any clownish fellow, unacquainted with the rules of good society." —*Dictionary of Archaic and Provincial Words,* James Halliwell, 1855

GYLE-HATHER: "He that will stand by his master when he is at dinner, and bid him eat no raw meat, because he would eat it himself. This is a...knave that would make his master believe that the cow is wood." —*The Fraternitye of Vacabonds,* John Awdeley, 1565

QUEERE-DUKE: "A poor decayed gentleman; also a lean, half-starved fellow." —*Dictionary of the Canting Crew,* B. E., 1699

SHOOLER: "One who intrudes upon his neighbour, and forces an invitation to dinner." —*History and Antiquities of Boston,* Pishey Thompson, 1856

Retro-Futurism

More of Tom Swift's World of Tomorrow

Tom Swift was a boy inventor created by Victor Appleton almost a century ago. The breathless adventure stories are great fun, but even better are the descriptions of his inventions.

TOM SWIFT & HIS GREAT SEARCHLIGHT (1913)

"Do you notice that searchlight, and how powerful it is?"

"I do, Tom. I never knew you had one as big as that."

"Neither did I, and I haven't, really. That's one of my smallest ones, but something seems to have happened to it to make it throw out a beam like that. I'm just going to look. Come on in the shop."

The two inventors, young and old, entered, and Tom made a quick inspection.

"Look, father!" he cried. "The alternating current from the automatic dynamo has become crossed with direct current from the big storage battery in a funny way. It must have been by accident, for never in the world would I think of connecting up in that fashion. I would have said it would have made a short circuit at once.

"But it hasn't. On the contrary, it has given a current of peculiar strength and intensity—a current that would seem to be made especially for searchlights. Dad, I'm on the edge of a big discovery."

"I believe you, Tom," said his father. "That certainly is a queer way for wires to be connected."

TOM SWIFT & HIS AIRSHIP (1910)

The general idea of the airship was that of the familiar aeroplane, but in addition to the sustaining surfaces of the planes, there was an aluminum, cigar-shaped tank, holding a new and very powerful gas, which would serve to keep the ship afloat even when not in motion.

Two sets of planes, one above the other, were used, bringing the airship into the biplane class. There were also two large propellers, one in front and the other at the rear. These were carefully made, of different layers of wood "built up" as they are called, to make them stronger. They were eight feet in diameter, and driven by a twenty-cylinder, air-cooled motor, whirled around at the rate of fifteen hundred revolutions a minute. When operated at full speed the airship was capable of making eighty miles an hour against a moderate wind.

But if the use of the peculiarly-shaped planes and the gas container, with the secret but powerful vapor in it were something new in airship construction, so was the car in which the operator and travelers were to live during a voyage. It was a complete living room. There were accommodations for five persons, with sleeping berths, a small galley where food could be prepared, and several easy chairs where the travelers could rest in comfort while skimming along high in the air, as fast as the fastest railroad train.

The engine, steering apparatus, and the gas machine were within easy reach and control of the pilot, who was to be stationed in a small room in the "bow" of the ship. An electric stove served to warm the interior of the car, and also provided means for cooking the food. The airship could be launched either by starting it along the ground, on rubber-tired wheels, as is done in the case of the ordinary aeroplane, or it could be lifted by the gas, just as is done with a balloon. In short there were many novel features about the ship.

The gas test, which took place a few days later, showed that the young inventor and Mr. Sharp had made no mistake this time. No explosion followed.

TOM SWIFT & HIS GIANT TELESCOPE (1939)

"What have people on the planets got to do with the question?" asked Ned. "Huge chunks of metal break off of any heavenly body and go hurtling through space. The inhabitants don't throw them off!"

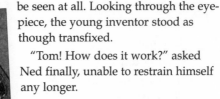

"But our meteor was no ordinary one as we have proved already," replied Tom. "I firmly believe that someone on another planet deliberately fired that missile into space, hoping it would reach this world. Since scientists agree that Mars probably is inhabited by a highly intelligent race, that planet is a reasonable guess."

"Whew!" whistled Ned. "Such ideas are beyond me."

At last Tom stepped to the giant telescope and adjusted it upon the planet Mars. He electrified the immense disk, which glowed, then could not be seen at all. Looking through the eyepiece, the young inventor stood as though transfixed.

"Tom! How does it work?" asked Ned finally, unable to restrain himself any longer.

"Look for yourself!" cried Tom, turning from the instrument. His face wore an expression of awe. Ned quickly took his place.

"Marvelous!" he exclaimed.

Before his eyes were revealed a great city, nearly seventy-five million miles distant! Peculiar people surged along the avenues, weird aircraft thronged the upper atmosphere, and gigantic buildings and palaces dotted the place. All on far-distant Mars! Ned grasped his chum's hand but could say nothing. Mr. Damon blessed the distant stars. Koku and Rad fell upon their knees. Into the eyes of Barton Swift came tears as he said: "Tom, my son, you have performed the greatest miracle of the Age!" ☾

(Interested in reading more Tom Swift theories and inventions? See pages 53 and 295.)

Speak English? 4

Translate these British Terms Into American

Sometimes it seems like the British and Americans don't even speak the same language. How are you at translating? Translate these old and new British terms into American. (Answers below.)

1. vacuum flask	a. cowcatcher
2. noughts and crosses	b. tote bag
3. sponge bag	c. zero
4. holdall	d. flashlight
5. drummer	e. tic-tac-toe
6. ex-directory	f. wrench
7. waistcoat	g. briefcase
8. spanner	h. traveling sales rep
9. nought	i. gelatin
10. courgette	j. shaving kit
11. combinations	k. hallway
12. plough	l. vest
13. wood wool	m. union suit
14. torch	n. excelsior
15. jelly	o. Thermos
16. passage	p. buddy
17. portfolio	q. zucchini
18. mate	r. unlisted number

Answers: *1. vacuum flask = o. Thermos; 2. noughts and crosses = e. tic-tac-toe; 3. sponge bag = j. shaving kit; 4. holdall = b. tote bag; 5. drummer = h. traveling sales rep; 6. ex-directory = r. unlisted number; 7. waistcoat = l. vest; 8. spanner = f. wrench; 9. nought = c. zero; 10. courgette = q. zucchini; 11. combinations = m. union suit; 12. plough = a. cowcatcher; 13. wood wool = n. excelsior; 14. torch = d. flashlight; 15. jelly = i. gelatin; 16. passage = k. hallway; 17. portfolio = g. briefcase; 18. mate = p. buddy*

Fires & Plagues

MORE OF OUR FAVORITE DISASTERS

More questions and answers about famous disasters from *Just Curious About History, Jeeves*, by Erin Barrett and Jack Mingo.

CATTLE-CLYSM IN CHICAGO

Did a cow really cause the Great Chicago Fire?

No, probably not, although the fire did start in Mrs. O'Leary's barn. There's no reason to believe the fire was anything more than the result of an extraordinarily dry spell of weather mixed with the practice of keeping dry wood chips around as a cheap source of fuel. A cigarette, a match, an ember from a burning stove nearby, or even spontaneous combustion would have been more than enough to have set the blaze going.

CLAIM TO FLAME

Why did the Chicago Fire of 1871 do so much damage?

Besides the dryness in the air and the wood chips, the houses were old, wooden and packed in tightly. There may have been little anyone could do to have prevented the disaster. However, it didn't help that the firemen were misdirected when the initial call first came in. Furthermore, they had been busy with another huge blaze the day before and were exhausted. By the time they reached the site, the blaze was way beyond control.

Was the Chicago Fire the worst fire in America's history?

Heck, it wasn't even the worst fire that *day*. A much bigger, more deadly fire happened at exactly the same evening in Peshtigo, Wisconsin, begun by railroad workers clearing a way for new tracks. As a result of the same hot, dry air as Chicago's, a small brush fire turned into a blazing inferno. Before the fire

Mrs. O'Leary's; the Chicago fire started in the barn behind the house

went out, almost a week later, it had burned more than 1.2 million acres and caused more than $169 million dollars worth of damage—about the same dollar amount of the property that was lost in the Chicago Fire blaze. On top of that, more than 1,200 people were killed by the Wisconsin fire—four times as many as in the more-famous Chicago Fire.

Which was worse: the Chicago Fire or the Great London Fire?

The 1666 London Fire burned four-fifths of the city and an additional 63 acres outside the city walls. It burned longer, covered more land and wreaked more architectural devastation, notably the Custom House, the Royal Exchange and St. Paul's Cathedral. Still, the Chicago Fire was worse in some ways. First of all, the Chicago Fire took more lives. Only 16 people died in the London fire because it burned slowly and gave enough warning for most people to escape. The fast-moving Chicago Fire claimed between 250 and 300 lives, leveling several Chicago neighborhoods—a total of 2,150 acres in less than two days. Both great fires were mass devastation with few rewards, save an architectural revitalization following the blaze and a good story about a cow.

One irrefutable bright spot came on the heels of the Great London Fire: After hundreds of years of periodic devastation, the Black Plague was finally wiped out. It had resurfaced again two years prior to the blaze, in 1664. However, after the fire, incidences suddenly declined and fizzled out, never to resurface again. It's believed, since the fire burnt everything to the ground, it took with it the old, damp breeding grounds of the plague rats, too, saving literally thousands of human lives in the long run.

PUDDING & PIE

How did the Great London Fire start?

It's reported that the 1666 fire that swept London was started by King Charles II's baker,

Thomas Farrinor, who accidentally went to bed with his oven still burning.

The phrase "from Pudding to Pie" comes directly from the great fire of London. Farrinor's house was situated on Pudding Lane. Pie Lane is located on the other side of the city where the fire finally stopped. So those clever Brits used "from Pudding to Pie" to mean the whole bloomin' city from then on.

SHOW ME YOUR BUBOES

What was the worst plague in human history?

The "Black Death" that ran through China and across to Europe in the 14th century is considered the worst plague in recorded history. Depending on the way the virus was contracted, 70–90% of those exposed to the plague died from it. During a 5-year period from 1347 to 1352, more than 25 million people in Europe alone were wiped out.

The disease was called the "Black Death" because of the color of the sores that developed on the bodies of the afflicted. However, doctors eventually figured out that there was a connection to the swollen lymph nodes called *buboes,* and "bubonic plague" seemed a better label for the affliction.

That was the world's worst plague for humanity; however, it wasn't the worst epidemic. What's the difference? A plague is a specific bacterial infection, but many of the worst diseases are caused by viruses. The worst epidemic was not a plague, but a flu in the 20th century, right after World War I in 1918-1919. The first reported case was in Kansas in 1918 and from there it spread like wildfire. After eighteen months, when the virus vanished as mysteriously as it had appeared, perhaps 37 million people worldwide had died from the disease. At no other time in recorded history have so many people died from one affliction in so little time.

How long did it take to die from the bubonic plague?

From exposure (flea bite, animal bite or exposure to mucus) to the onset of the first symptoms (headache, fever, nausea, aching and swollen buboes) took about six days. The next stage—hemorrhaging and respiratory problems stemming from severe pneumonia—came quickly, causing death within a day or two. Now, bacterial infections can usually be wiped out by antibiotics. €

Pot Shots

More of Privy's favorite privy shots. Send us yours! **(See page 476.)**

(Below, left) The privy at Alameda Beach—headquarters of the *Bathroom Companion*

A very colorful men's restroom (above), somewhere in the outback of Australia

The outhouse at Hanging Rock Raptor Observatory in Monroe County, West Virginia. At the top of Peters Mountain—elevation 3,812 feet—a cable attaches the outhouse to a tree to keep it from blowing over. Thanks fo Rodney Davis at http://www.hangingrocktower.org.

These ancient public toilets in old Ephesus could seat up to 40. An orchestra played for the crowd of users, probably to drown out sounds. Photo courtesy of Joe Garlitz.

Chicle Your Fancy

Gum Through a Bubble of History

A good chew has been touted as good for the mouth, nerves, digestion and sex appeal. But how did it all begin? Correspondent Elsa Bronte fills us in.

PEOPLE LIKE to chew. Through history, humanity has chewed everything from human gristle to synthetic rubber. As early as A.D. 50, the ancient Greeks chewed latex from the mastic tree, which they believed had curative powers. Upon arrival to the New World, the European settlers were introduced to spruce resin by the Native Americans. They had been chewing it for centuries. The discovery of well-chewed wads of various tree resins, unearthed along with bones and other prehistoric artifacts, leads archaeologists to believe the practice of gum chewing goes as far back as early civilization—even our primitive ancestors engaged in recreational chewing.

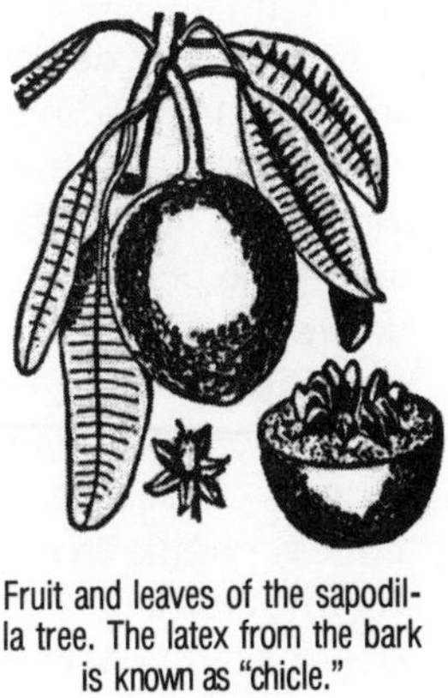

Fruit and leaves of the sapodilla tree. The latex from the bark is known as "chicle."

THE BEGINNINGS OF A BUBBLE INDUSTRY

Our more recent forebears enjoyed chewing homemade gum of spruce resin and beeswax. A man named John Curtis mixed up the first commercial batch of spruce resin chewing gum in 1848. His sales were slow at first, but at two spruce chaws for a penny, the gum became an overwhelming success within a few years. By 1852, his Curtis Chewing Gum Co. employed more than 200 workers in its brand-new three-story factory in Portland, Maine.

But that was sap gum. The chicle-based chewing gum we know today came from Mexico soon after the Civil War. General Antonio Lopez de Santa Ana, infamous for leading the Mexican siege on the Alamo, was forced out of Mexico after some political upheaval. He went into exile in New York City, bringing from his native Mexico a quantity of chewing chicle, the dried sap of the sapodilla tree. The story has it that it was Santa Ana's chewing habit that gave inventor Thomas Adams, Sr. the idea of selling a chicle gum in the United States.

1. Chemists test ingredients and flavors. 2. Chefs mix the gum dough. 3. Machines slice gum pieces from big sheets. 4. Gum wrapping gals wrap gum. Nowadays, they've been replaced with modern machinery.

In 1871, Adams received the first patent on a gum-making machine. His first gum, called "Snapping & Stretching," was pure chicle with no flavoring, but it sold enough packs to encourage Adams. He began to experiment with flavorings, beginning with sarsaparilla. In 1884, his licorice-flavored Black Jack gum premiered as the first flavored gum in America. Pepsin Tutti-Frutti chewing gum followed in 1890. Adams invented Beemans in 1898 as a cure for heartburn, and his Clove Gum got a boost during Prohibition when it was sold as a breath freshener in illegal liquor houses. (All of the gums eventually went off the market, although the current owner of Adams' gums, the

Warner-Lambert Pharmaceutical Co., irregularly reissues the century-year-old gums as a part of their "Nostalgia Gum program.")

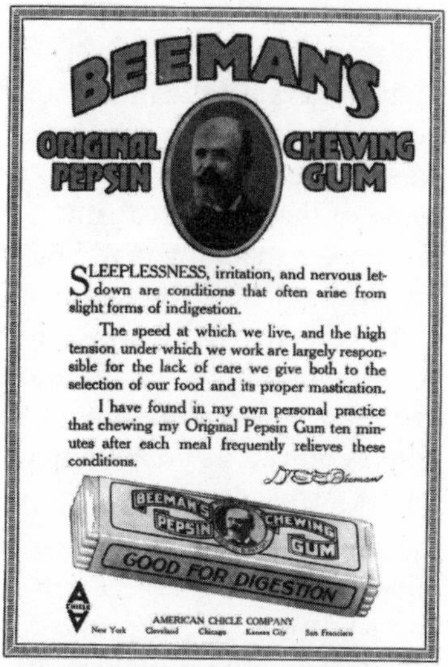

RESOLVING A STICKY SITUATION

By the turn of the century, the chewing public was gobbling up new products such as Frank V. Canning's Dental Gum and Henry Fleer's candy-coated Chiclets. Henry's brother, Frank, began to work on a gum that would be elastic enough to blow into bubbles. His first prototype, Blibber-Blubber, came along in 1906, but never made it to market—it was so sticky that the only way to remove it from skin was with vigorous scrubbing and turpentine.

Walter Diemer achieved a breakthrough in August, 1928, and he wasn't even a chemist. Although Diemer was Fleer's accountant, he was messing around in the lab and discovered, through trial and error, the magic mix of ingredients that was stiff enough to get off skin, but flexible enough to blow. Bubble gum even owes it characteristic pink hue to Diemer's serendipity, because pink was the only coloring that happened to be nearby when he mixed up his first successful batch. Not long after its introduction, Fleer's Dubble Bubble became the best-selling penny candy in the United States. Fleer sold the Chiclet business in 1909 (Chiclets are now owned by Warner-Lambert), but Dubble Bubble is still made at the Fleer plant in Philadelphia.

SWEET NOTHINGS

The next major innovation in gum production came in the early 1950s, with chemically-sweetened sugarless gum. Suddenly, gum was deemed safe to chew, and its popularity surged again as dentists began recommending sugarless gum "to their patients who chew gum." (Ironically, it's been since discovered that sugared gum really isn't bad for teeth, because the sugar goes quickly as the gum stimulates saliva, and that the sugar is probably healthier than the chemical alternatives.)

A PENNY FOR YOUR CHAW

Gum machines have been dispensing gumballs and little Dentyne-sized pieces of stick gum since before the 1880s.

The stick gum machines featured mirrors in front, a smart bit of merchandising, because most people will check themselves in a mirror, and while there, maybe drop a penny into the slot.

Early gumball machines were often quite pretty—the glass globe distorting the balls to make the multicolor balls look unearthly and slightly bigger than life, the fire-engine red base creating a three-alarm wail among kids hankering for a piece. Gumball machines were simple at first—in fact, too simple, because kids learned pretty quickly how to stick their fingers up the hole and get a free ball. After that bug was worked out, however, some of them went to gimmickry—a machine made by the Pulver Company featured a little mechanical man who held the ball in his hands and dropped it down the shoot when you put in your money.

In the 20th century, much of the gumball market was taken over by the Ford Gum and Machine Co., the only U.S. company that makes both machines and the gumballs that stock them.

CHEWS FOR JESUS

The Ford Co. was founded by a roofing salesman in 1918. Named Ford S. Mason, he used his first name instead of his last name, figuring that it couldn't hurt to have people think his machines were related to the popular Model T.

At the time, the gumballs in machines were often pretty bad, and the machines unreliable. According to *The Great American Chewing Gum Book* by Robert Hendrickson

(Scarborough, 1980), Mason's father, a Baptist minister, urged him to manufacture his own machines as well as gum so that the brand would become associated with dependable quality. ("Make your own machines, my boy," he said, "and share your profits with God.") His father believed so strongly in the machines that he took time away from his sermons to design a machine for his son, one so simple yet dependable that the basic design remains unchanged to this day. Mason worked on perfecting and branding the gumball, coming up with a stamping machine to stamp FORD on each gumball at the rate of 25,000 an hour, and figuring out a waterproof glaze so that condensation inside the machine wouldn't ruin them. (Try it: Run water over a machine-bought gumball and the color probably won't come off.)

CHARITY BALLS

In 1939, an Ohio women's charity group suggested that local merchants donate their 20% cut from Ford machines to local children's charities. The idea caught on, and now 3,500 service clubs and organizations share about $2 million a year from the Fordway Program. €

The Dentist Hall of Fame

In honor of all those cavities that bubble gum has produced over the years (actually, science now says it's less than you'd think), we honor famous people who were also dentists.

- ***Dr. Doc Holliday*** helped Wyatt Earp win the OK Corral shootout.
- ***Dr. G.W.A. Bonwill*** invented the safety pin.
- ***Dr. William Lowell*** invented the wooden golf tee.
- ***Dr. Pearl Zane Grey*** wrote best-selling Western novels.
- ***Dr. George W. Beers*** created the official rules for lacrosse.
- ***Dr. Edgar Buchanan*** appeared in *Petticoat Junction.*
- ***Dr. Allan Jones*** starred in the movie *Showboat* in 1936.
- ***Dr. Marlon Loomis*** transmitted radio signals 27 years before Marconi.
- ***Dr. Cary Middlecoff*** won the U.S. Open in 1946 and 1956.
- ***Dr. Charles Willson Peale*** painted George Washington's portrait.
- ***Dr. Paul Revere*** became a silversmith and courier for the revolution.
- ***Dr. Thomas Welch*** bottled grape juice.
- ***Dr. Painless Parker*** legally changed his first name to circumvent 1880s laws against advertising, created the first national chain of dental clinics.

Word Thieves

Some Words We Borrowed from the Aztecs

You say *tomato,* we say *tomatl.* We were surprised how many English words come from Nahuatl, the language of the Aztecs and related tribes in Central and South America. Here are some of them.

avocado: Squishy, small, round—is it any surprise that the fruit's name came from *ahucatl* ("testicle")?

axolotl: Maybe you'd only know this word if you're a salamander fancier, or a *Mad* reader in the 1960s. From Aztec times to the present, these 6–8-inch amphibians have been roasted and eaten with vinegar or cayenne pepper. The name comes from *atlxotl* ("water spirit").

Axolotl, the other white meat

chili: The dish originated with the Aztecs; the Nahuati name was *chilli.*

chocolate: Called *xoclatl* from the days when cocao beans were ground up in hot water without sugar. The name meant "bitter water."

coyote: The original word was *coyotl.*

guacamole: The word comes from *ahuacatl-molli,* which means "avocado sauce."

mescal: From *mexcalli* ("agave liquor").

mesquite: From *mezquitl.*

Mexico: From *mexihco* ("place of the Mexih.")

ocelot: From *ocelotl* ("jaguar").

peyote: From *peyutl* ("caterpillar's cocoon," which is what the peyote button's silky inside looks like).

shack: From *xacalli* ("thatched hut").

tamale: From *tamal,* another Aztec dish.

tomato: From Aztec *tomatl.*

Let's Roll!

The Nitty Gritty on Toilet Paper

Toilet paper from the bottom up, by *B.C.* regular Kathie Meyer.

FIRST ATTEMPTS GO DOWN THE TOILET

Toilet paper dates back as early as the late 1300s in China. Still, the emergence of modern toilet paper in the United States is credited to New Yorker Joseph C. Gayetty who produced the first packaged bathroom tissue in 1857. Named "the Therapeutic Paper" because it contained soothing aloe, the tissue sold in flat packs of 500 sheets. In an odd sort of egotism, it had Joseph Gayetty's name printed on every sheet. Gayetty's paper didn't do well in the marketplace, in part because it was very expensive—50¢ a pack, which is comparable to almost $10 in today's money—at a time when people were willing to use old newspaper.

GREAT SCOTT

In 1879, Walter Alcock of England invented perforated toilet tissue on a roll. In the United States, Edward and Clarence Scott began manufacturing their copy of Alcock's product. Hotels and restaurants had begun installing indoor plumbing, and the traditional wiping materials—newspapers, magazines, catalogs—were not very classy. The Scott Paper Company began finding buyers in the finest places, and capitalized on this snob appeal by naming their toilet paper "Waldorf Tissue," after a famous hotel.

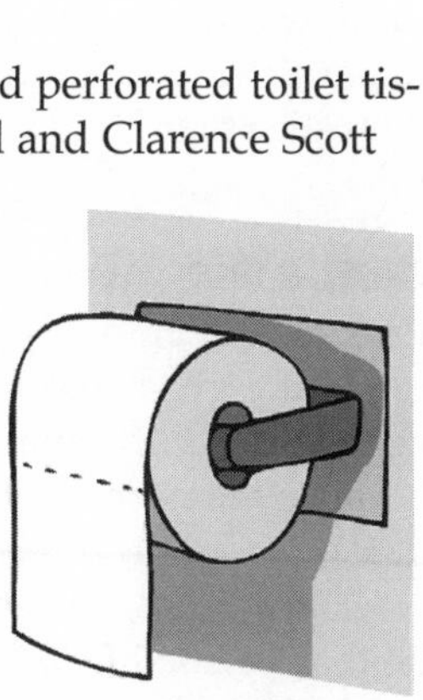

Consumers, initially resistant to the idea, quickly began succumbing to the snob appeal of having fancy, soft rolls of toilet paper in their bathrooms.

THE MOTHER OF INVENTION

Before the invention of modern toilet paper, people used just about anything on hand. For instance: newsprint, catalogue pages, a sponge at the end of a stick, discarded sheep's wool, straw, hay, grass, leaves, a corn cob, mussel shells, sand, the left hand, pages from a book, coconut shells, lace, hemp, a spritz of water from a bidet, snow, or tundra moss.

MYSTERY SOLVED

Have you ever wondered how manufacturers wind the toilet paper neatly onto those 3-inch cardboard tubes? Actually, they don't. The machines wind wide rolls of paper around long tubes, and then slice them into smaller rolls.

CRUEL & UNUSUAL PUNISHMENT

Prisoners in Florida jails have filed numerous complaints against the authorities because the normal allocation of toilet paper is one roll per week per person. That roll is all that's issued for all tissue needs, including nose-blowing. That's in the best case. Prisoners further said that the authorities used toilet paper as a "privilege" that was routinely revoked for up to a week as a punishment.

FOR WANT OF SOME TISSUE

Statistics say the average family has eight toilet paper rolls in reserve to avoid running out. Households run by folks younger than 30 run out more often than adults older than 50.

RUN ON THE MARKET

In 1973, *Tonight Show* host Johnny Carson joked during his monologue that there was a toilet paper shortage and people took him seriously. As a result, store shelves soon were out of t.p. as the nation began to hoard the product.

YOUR TAX DOLLARS AT WORK

The bathrooms at the Pentagon use an average of 666 rolls of toilet paper daily. The building also has twice as many bathrooms than necessary, a legacy of Virginia's laws that required separate bathrooms for white and black people.

TANKS FOR THE TP

Military toilet paper is camouflaged, since bright white could attract enemy fire at a vulnerable time. During America's war against Iraq in 1989, some tank crews reportedly t.p.'ed their tanks to hide them better.

A DIFFERENT KIND OF AIR BAG

Officials said a train crash in southern Mexico, where two trains collided head-on, killing five people and injuring 50, would have been much worse if it hadn't been for two freight cars loaded with toilet paper that helped cushion the impact.

REALITY SPONSORSHIP

In the Ivory Coast, manufacturers have named brands of toilet paper "Santa Barbara" and "Dallas Jumbo"to capitalize on the glamour of American soap operas.

NOT FOR LAZY BUMS

A pre-moistened toilet paper called Andrex is the most expensive brand on the market in Britain. It's very soft, and, apparently, very popular.

Price is apparently no object: it's the most popular brand of toilet paper in Great Britain, and the seventh best-selling product overall in that country.

TRADING THEIR PLY

- More consumers in the Western states prefer one-ply toilet paper than in the Eastern states.
- St. Andrew's Paper Mill in Walthamstow, London, gave the world the first two-ply toilet paper in 1942.
- Single-ply has one layer of 13-pound-thick paper. Double-ply has two layers of 10-pound-thick paper each. Single-ply is generally cheaper to use because folks use about the same amount of sheets regardless of the ply, and is recommended for toilet systems in recreational vehicles and boats, because it doesn't clog pipes as readily.

HOW MANY SHEETS?

- One cord of wood will yield 1,000 pounds of toilet paper.
- The standard size of a single sheet of toilet paper is 4.5 inches by 4.5 inches. Some manufacturers, however, have

come out with "cheater sheets" as small as 4 inches by 3.8 inches.

• According to the American Forest & Paper Association, the United States produces about 5.8 million tons of tissue-grade paper (consisting of toilet and facial tissue, paper napkins, towels, diapers and various other sanitary products) annually. In 1992, approximately 3.5 million tons of scrap paper were recycled into soft paper products.

GROSS NATIONAL CONSUMPTION

The number of days the average roll of bath tissue lasts in the most-used bathroom of a household is five. On average, consumers use 8.6 sheets per trip to the bathroom, or 57 sheets per day. That's a total of 20,805 sheets per year for the average person.

FRONT OR BACK?

Polls show that 60% of all respondents prefer the toilet paper to come out in the front of the roll while 29% prefer it to come out down the back of the roll. (A full 11% didn't care either way.) By more than 4 to 1, older folks prefer to have their toilet paper dispense over the front. Clearly, age brings wisdom—otherwise the paper is pressed against the wall, making it harder to get the end loose, eventually dirtying and scratching the paint below the toilet paper holder.

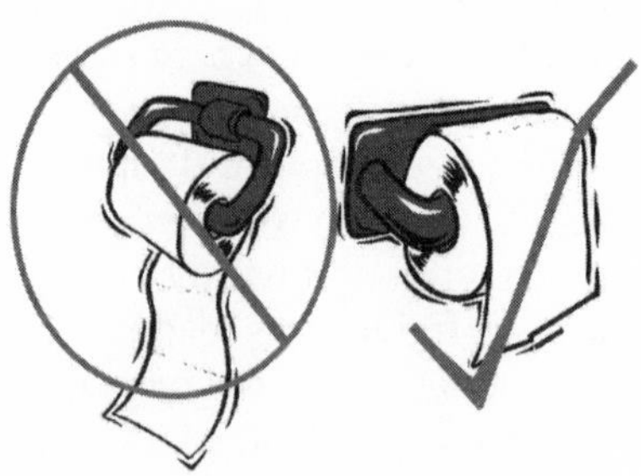

LOOSE ENDS

Why do hotels fold the loose end of the toilet paper in a **V** shape? The little nip and fold on the roll is meant to assure you that no one has used that toilet seat since it was last scoured by hotel employees. Or at the very least you know that if someone *did* use it, they didn't use toilet paper afterward. Eeew!

Every Picture Tells a Story

***The Spirit of '76* by Archibald M. Willard, 1875**

• Most people think this painting depicts America's Revolutionary soldiers. However, most people are wrong.

• The painting was meant to be a sly commentary on drunken 4th of July celebrations that were common in the late 1800s. Note the puffy faces, the unnatural exuberance, and the guy lying on a splintered wagon wheel, who's too drunk to sit up, much less stand, as he salutes his flag.

• Anticipating a market for humorous prints with the upcoming United States 1876 centennial, commercial artist Achibald M. Willard started working on this painting of lit-up musicians clowning around in a July 4 parade. He used his father, a friend and a military cadet as models.

• Willard first called it *The 4th of July Musicians* and then *Yankee Doodle.* A print dealer renamed it *The Spirit of '76* when he sold tens of thousands of copies, making both men rich.

• Willard had no formal art training. Before discovering a lucrative market for kitsch, he mostly painted designs on wagons.

• The painting was so popular that Willard painted copies of it many times. Some subsequent editions were less comical.

Couch Potato Quiz

How Addicted Are You?

Match each of the fifteen sitcom characters to their shows.

1. Sam Malone	**A.** *Rhoda*
2. Paul Buchman	**B.** *The Honeymooners*
3. Buffy Davis	**C.** *M*A*S*H**
4. Ralph Kramden	**D.** *The Beverly Hillbillies*
5. Rob Petrie	**E.** *Taxi*
6. Ricky Stratton	**F.** *ALF*
7. Alex Keaton	**G.** *Family Affair*
8. Rhoda Morgenstern	**H.** *Silver Spoons*
9. Mary Ann Summers	**I.** *Family Ties*
10. Jack Tripper	**J.** *The Dick Van Dyke Show*
11. Willie Tanner	**K.** *Cheers*
12. Jane Hathaway	**L.** *Mad About You*
13. Alex Reiger	**M.** *The Mary Tyler Moore Show*
14. Mary Richards	**N.** *Three's Company*
15. Hawkeye Pierce	**O.** *Gilligan's Island*

Answers: 1.K; 2.L; 3.G; 4.B; 5.J; 6.H; 7.I; 8.A; 9.O; 10.N; 11.F; 12.D; 13.E; 14.M; 15.C

Eyewitness

I Led the Capture of John Wilkes Booth

A gun went off, the president was shot, and John Wilkes Booth gave a short, one-line speech on stage. But what then? After fleeing the Ford Theatre, Booth went south into Virginia with one of his co-conspirators, David Herold, where they were soon surrounded.

It was April 24, 1865, when Lieutenant Edward Doherty got orders to go to a Virginia farm owned by Richard Garrett, to hunt down fugitives David Herold and John Wilkes Booth—both wanted in relation to the death of President Abraham Lincoln. According to Doherty, this is what happened:

"I dismounted, and knocked loudly at the front door. Old Mr. Garrett came out. I seized him, and asked him where the men were who had gone to the woods when the cavalry passed the previous afternoon.

David Herold

"While I was speaking with him some of the men had entered the house to search it. Soon one of the soldiers sang out, 'O Lieutenant! I have a man here I found in the corn-crib.' It was young Garrett, and I demanded the whereabouts of the fugitives. He replied, 'In the barn.'

"Leaving a few men around the house, we proceeded in the direction of the barn, which we surrounded. I kicked on the door of the barn several times without receiving a reply. Meantime another son of the Garretts had been captured. The barn was secured with a padlock, and young Garrett carried the key. I unlocked the door, and again summoned the inmates of the building to surrender.

The three Booth brothers were well-known actors. John's pictured on the left.

"After some delay Booth said, 'For whom do you take me?'

"I replied, 'It doesn't make any difference. Come out.'

"He said, 'I am a cripple and alone.' I said, 'I know who is with you, and you had better surrender.'

"He replied, 'I may be taken by my friends, but not by my foes.'

"I said, 'If you don't come out, I'll burn the building.' I directed a corporal to pile up some hay in a crack in the wall of the barn and set the building on fire.

"As the corporal was picking up the hay and brush Booth said, 'If you come back here I will put a bullet through you.'

"I then motioned to the corporal to desist, and decided to wait for daylight and then to enter the barn by both doors and over power the assassins.

"Booth then said in a drawling voice, 'Oh Captain! There is a man here who wants to surrender awful bad.'

"I replied, 'You had better follow his example and come out.'

"His answer was, 'No, I have not made up my mind; but draw your men up fifty paces off and give me a chance for my life.'

"I told him I had not come to fight; that I had fifty men, and could take him.

"Then he said, 'Well, my brave boys, prepare me a stretcher, and place another stain on our glorious banner.'

"At this moment Herold reached the door. I asked him to hand out his arms; he replied that he had none. I told him I knew exactly what weapons he had. Booth replied, 'I own all the arms, and may have to use them on you, gentlemen.' I then said to Herold, 'Let me see your hands.' He put them through the partly opened door and I seized him by the wrists. I handed him over to a non-commissioned officer. Just at this moment I heard a shot, and thought Booth had shot himself. Throwing open the door, I saw that the straw and hay behind Booth were on fire. He was half-turning towards it.

"He had a crutch, and he held a carbine in his hand. I rushed into the burning barn, followed by my men, and as he was falling caught him under the arms and pulled him out of the barn. The burning building becoming too hot, I had him carried to the veranda of Garrett's house.

"Booth received his death-shot in this manner. While I was taking Herold out of the barn one of the detectives went to the rear, and pulling out some protruding straw set fire to it. I had placed Sergeant Boston Corbett at a large crack in the side of the barn, and he, seeing by the igniting hay that Booth was leveling his carbine at either Herold or myself, fired, to disable him in the arm; but Booth making a sudden move, the aim erred, and the bullet struck Booth in the back of the head, about an inch below the spot where his shot had entered the head of Mr. Lincoln. Booth asked me by signs to raise his hands. I lifted them up and he gasped, 'Useless, useless!' We gave him brandy and water, but he could not swallow it. I sent to Port Royal for a physician, who could do nothing when he came, and at seven o'clock Booth breathed his last. He had on his person a diary, a large bowie knife, two pistols, a compass and a draft on Canada for 60 pounds."

Sergeant Boston Corbett—the man who shot John Wilkes Booth

Judged by Its Cover

Even More Strange Books

Can you tell a book by its title? If so, these have got to be some of the most fascinating books on the shelves, gleaned from *Bizarre Books* by Russell Ash and Brian Lake (St. Martin's, 1985).

Cooking with God—Lori David & Robert Robb (1978)

A Pickle for the Knowing Ones; or, Plain Truths in a Homespun Dress—Timothy Dexter (1802)

Daddy Was an Undertaker—McDill McCown Gassman (1952)

How I Know That the Dead Are Alive—Fanny Ruthven Paget (1917)

Gay Agony—H. A. Manhood (1930)

?—Sir Walter Newman Flower (1925)

Pernicious Pork; or, Astounding Revelations of the Evil Effects of Eating Swine Flesh—William T. Hallett (1903)

Beard Shaving, and the Common Use of the Razor, an Unnatural, Irrational, Unmanly, Ungodly and Fatal Fashion Among Christians—W. E. Painter (1847)

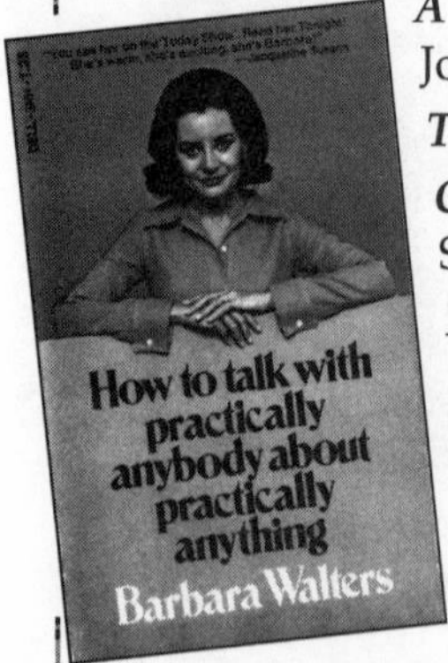

A Letter to the Man Who Killed My Dog—Richard Joseph (1956)

The Manliness of Christ—Thomas Hughes (1931)

Chancho: A Boy and His Pig in Peru—Sutherland Stark (1947)

I Was Hitler's Maid—Pauline Kohler (1940)

The Bright Side of Prison Life—Captain S. A. Swiggett (1897)

Why Bring That Up? A Guide To and From Seasickness—Dr. J. F. Montague (1936)

Armadillo

A Life on the Half-Shell

The armadillo was named by the Spanish Conquistadors; its name (pronounced arm-a-DEE-o in Spanish) means "little man in armor."

SIMPLY MARBLE-LOUS, INCREMENTALLY & EXCREMENTALLY

In Texas or Mexico, if you find what looks like clay marbles in the middle of nowhere, it's most likely armadillo poop. Their excrement is almost perfectly round. Armadillos eat insects and small snails; in the course of picking them off the ground, they also eat a lot of soil. We're not sure if anybody has thought of picking up the poop pellets and firing them in kilns, but they could make a wonderful gift for marble-playing children.

Nine-banded armadillo walking; rolled up (2½ ft. long, including the tail).

Or maybe not. This dirt-eating habit, by the way, is the reason why armadillo teeth are dark, sometimes even black.

DON'T LOOK A GIFT ARMADILLO IN THE MOUTH

Armadillo teeth are back in their mouths and designed for grinding up insects and snails, so biting is not a part of the armadillo's self-defense repertoire. Good thing, too—armadillos are the only animals besides humans that can carry leprosy.

ROW VS. WADE

Despite common folklore and the fact that they look so heavy in their armor, an armadillo can swim. The bony plates that protect it do weigh it down, but an armadillo can still maintain buoyancy for short swims by gulping air to inflate its intestines. However, it often prefers to cross small waterways by simply holding its breath and crawling along underwater.

ARMADILLOS ON THE ROAD

Armadillos are so commonly found as road kill because the armadillo's responses to danger are uniformly unsuitable for dealing successfully with cars. One of its strategies is to roll up into a protective ball completely surrounded by its armor, which can save it from a variety of natural things, but not a pickup truck. Another strategy is to dig straight into the ground, which they can do in almost any soil type with remarkable speed—but not, unfortunately, into blacktop. Still another strategy is to leap up into the air—which doesn't save the armadillo, but at least gives it a pyrrhic victory of making a dent in the car's front grill.

Adding to the problem is the fact that armadillos come out by night in hot weather, making them hard to see until drivers are right upon them. Unfortunately, they also live in areas of flat, straight highways that enable speeding...not to mention that those highways are oft-traveled by people who apparently have few qualms about banging into wildlife.

ARMADILLO PECCADILLOS

• Armadillo babies are identical quadruplets. The first fertilized cell splits into four identical cells, and each develops. That means that the four babies in a brood will always be the same gender.

• Armadillos sleep about 18.5 hours a day.

• Armadillos have a very low metabolic rate, so they have trouble maintaining their body temperature of about 90° F except in very warm climates. Armadillos don't have a lot of body fat, so they must forage on a daily basis. Just a few cold days in a row can be deadly to an armadillo. That's one reason why you don't see them much on the backroads of Ohio.

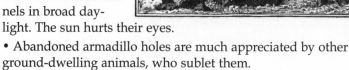

• Depending on the armadillo's species, the bands around its body will always number 3, 6 or 9.

• Armadillos can be housetrained.

• It is specifically against the law to own a pet armadillo in many states.

• Armadillos' closest relatives are sloths and anteaters.

• Armadillos don't come out of their tunnels in broad daylight. The sun hurts their eyes.

• Abandoned armadillo holes are much appreciated by other ground-dwelling animals, who sublet them.

• Armadillo meat is edible. A pound has about 780 calories.

• Fossil remains of gigantic extinct armadillos have been found in South America. This Ice Age "megadillo" was about the size of a VW bug and plated like its modern-day counterpart, but it sported a deadly cluster of spikes on the end of its tail for protection. It died out about 10,000 year ago, and we're mighty thankful for that.

• Another Ice Age armadillo is dubbed the "beautiful armadillo" (*Dasypus bellus*) for reasons unclear. It looks a lot like the not-very-pretty nine-banded armadillo of present day, although quite a bit larger. ☾

Potty Pourri

Random Kinds of Factness

• England's King George V seems to have been murdered. He was administered a fatal injection minutes before midnight by his doctor on January 20, 1936. "It was evident that the last stage might endure for many hours," wrote the doctor, Lord Dawson, in his journal. "Dignity demanded a brief final scene, so I decided to determine the end."

• Sometimes a cigar is just a cigar, and sometimes a river is just aqueous liquid. The name "Nile" means "water" in ancient Egyptian.

• Sequels never get much respect. There was a second Boston Tea Party three months after the first that got lost to history. No matter. Between the two, the British tea monopoly lost $3 million in today's money.

• There's no real difference, but a burro is a smaller, more sure-footed donkey.

• In a sense, pill bugs or roly-polies are the marsupials of the crustacean world. They carry their babies in light-colored pouches on their bellies until the little roly-polies get big enough to go off on their own.

• Not just Saturn but all of the giant outer planets have rings. Saturn has six, Uranus has eleven, Jupiter has a large one and several smaller ones and Neptune has four. Saturn's are so bright that they were discovered almost 350 years ago. The other planets' rings, too dim to be seen with primitive telescopes, were discovered in the 1970s.

• Sibling rivalry can be a real motivator: Agatha Christie began writing detective stories, not for the love of the art, but to show up her older sister Madge, who insisted that Agatha didn't have the aptitude for it.

How They Work

Hidden Stories Behind Everyday Things

From polyester threads to scratch-and-sniff perfumes, there's an explanation behind everything, and *Bathroom Companion* science correspondent Brian Marshall is here to explain them.

HOW DO THEY MAKE PLASTIC INTO CLOTHES?

Polyester chips are hard bits of plastic, so how do manufacturers make them into cloth? The process is not unlike the way a cotton candy machine turns granulated sugar into spun candy. The plastic pellets go into a hot metal cup that has tiny holes in it. The cup rotates at a high speed, sending tiny threads of molten plastic shooting out of the little holes (called spinnerets). The molten threads instantaneously harden into a cobwebby consistency when they hit the cool air.

These are heated again, stretched, and then twisted into threads. During that process, polyester is often mixed with cotton or other fibers. The polyester lessens wrinkling; the natural fibers let your perspiration wick away from the body, alleviating the Disco Fever Sweats that plagued wearers of 100% polyester clothes in the 1970s.

HOW CAN THEY MEASURE CALORIES IN FOODS?

A little device called a "bomb calorimeter" burns foods and measures the difference between how much energy went into burning the food versus how much energy came out. A calorie is defined as the amount of energy it takes to raise 1 gram of water (about a thimbleful) 1 degree Celsius.

Here's where it gets confusing: What we call a calorie is actually a *kilocalorie*—it's equal to 1,000 scientific calories. To a scientist, a doughnut doesn't have 235 calories, but 235 *kilocalories* (235,000 calories). Better start jogging....

HOW POLAROID PHOTOS DEVELOP BEFORE YOUR EYES

When you think of the requirements of developing normal photography—most notably a light-free room—it's surprising that Polaroid cameras could do the same thing in broad daylight. Instant photos seem like a magic trick, and in fact there is more than a little illusion in the "developing before your eyes" part. In fact, by the time you begin to see it, the photo has already fully developed.

Here's what happens after you snap your photo: First it passes through two stainless steel rollers that spread a blob of chemicals located at the edge of the plastic film sheet. These chemicals start developing the photo. But their action is hidden by a white layer of "opacifier," which is an opaque coating that keeps light from reaching photosensitive layers below.

With time, the photo underneath has already developed, yet you can't see it because the opaque layer is still in place. Finally, acid in the chemicals seeps up and reacts with the opacifier. It becomes translucent, then transparent, slowly revealing the photo that's fully developed below.

WHY DO PHONES WORK IN A POWER FAILURE?

Only corded ones do. Because the telephone system provides its own power through the phone lines, your basic corded phone will often work even when your lights won't. It's a pretty good system that gets messed up when you add those newfangled cordless phones that require household power to keep the handset charged and run the transmitter/receiver that plugs into your wall. Our advice is to make sure that at least one of your phones is of the corded variety. It could save your life in an emergency (or at least let you order pizza until you can get your microwave working again).

THE COOL PRINCIPLES BEHIND YOUR REFRIGERATOR

Bear with me now. Two ideas make refrigeration possible:

1. Gases heat up if you compress them and cool down when you let them expand. You may have seen compressed gas heat up if you've ever inflated a tire using a hand pump and found it surprisingly hot afterward. You may have noticed expanding gas cool when water evaporates off your skin on a hot day.

2. The other rule you likely learned while eating Popsicles: When two things of different temperatures come into contact, the hotter thing cools and the cooler thing heats up.

The coils and tubes of a refrigerator contain a gas. In the bad old days it was Freon, now discontinued because it was eating the Earth's ozone layer. Newer refrigerators use ammonia gas. The refrigerator motor runs a compressor that squeezes the gas, heating it up. Your refrigerator pushes the hot, compressed gas through coils on the back or bottom of your fridge. There the gas loses heat to the surrounding air and cools way down...so much so that the compressed gas turns into a liquid.

The high pressure generated from the compressor then forces that liquid through a tiny valve into the coils inside your refrigerator. This area has little pressure because its gas has been pumped into the high-compression area (*see above*). As a result, the cold, compressed liquid immediately vaporizes and expands with abandon, cooling down to arctic temperatures. The gas brings temperatures in your freezer to below freezing and then flows through the coils to cool the main part of your refrigerator. Finally, the compressor sucks the gas up and begins the process all over again.

HOW DO THEY GET SMELLS INTO SCRATCH-N-SNIFF?

Think of microscopic bubbles stuck to the paper. The oily odor extracts of the smells are placed in water and furiously mixed, breaking the oil into very tiny droplets. At that instant, a gelatinous mixture is dropped in, which settles around the oil droplets, encasing them. After they're dried, the bubbles are mixed with an inky adhesive and printed onto paper. Later, when you scratch it, some of the bubbles burst, releasing the smell. The process is called "microencapsulation," and it's also been used for carbonless copying paper. €

Reality Bites

Do You Remember These Toothy Slogans?

Match the ad campaign to the (mostly!) toothy brand name.

1. "Look ma, no cavities!"

2. "Kills germs by the millions."

3. "No mediciny breath."

4. "Double protection fights cavities and freshens breath."

5. "Cleans your breath while it cleans your teeth."

6. "You'll wonder where the yellow went, when you brush your teeth with..."

7. "Gives your mouth (*Ting!*) sex appeal."

8. "The taste you can feel."

9. "Cleans teeth, freshens breath naturally."

10. "You have bad breath. BAD BREATH!"

A. Listerine

B. Colgate

C. Ultrabrite

D. Scope

E. Crest

F. Milk Bone Dog Biscuits

G. Aquafresh

H. Pepsodent

Answers: 1E; 2A; 3D; 4G; 5B; 6H; 7C; 8C; 9F; 10D

Glass Eyes

How Polaroid Created an Optical Empire

There are Polaroid cameras and there are Polaroid sunglasses. Wondering how in the world these two Polaroid products are connected is enough to make you a Polaroid schizophrenic.

THE NAME *POLAROID* was coined in 1934 by a Smith College professor named Clarence Kennedy to describe a plastic material created by techno-genius Edwin Herbert Land that polarized light. But Land wasn't sure he liked the name—he was leaning toward *Epibollipol* (supposedly Greek for "sheet polarizer")—but thankfully, a friend talked him out of it.

BIRTH OF A NOTION

Land had been struck by inspiration eight years earlier at age seventeen. He was strolling down Broadway in New York City, on vacation from Harvard, and was blinded by the light of an oncoming car. The boy scientist had been reading theoretical studies about polarized light. Normally, light waves travel in a forward motion, vibrating at right angles in every direction from the direction of the forward path. Polarization makes light waves go in a parallel plane instead of vibrating every which direction. Land wondered if he could develop a polarized lens that would cut the glare from headlights—without reducing their effectiveness at illuminating the road.

Other scientists had discovered the phenomenon of polarization using crystals. One, William Bird Herapath, an English physician, actually produced polarizing material in 1852 after discovering that tiny needle-shaped crystals would "comb" light. Such crystals could be formed by combining iodine with quinine salt. He dosed a student's dog with a huge dose of quinine.

To the dog's quinine-rich urine, he added iodine. Sure enough, the tiny, very fragile crystals that formed could be seen to be polarizers when you looked at them under a microscope. Herapath spent the rest of his career fruitlessly trying to create a larger and stronger polarizing crystal (maybe if he had tried dosing an elephant?) until his death 70 years later.

A LOT OF SCIENTIFIC MUMBO JUMBO ENSUES

Land, his work cut out for him, decided that the quest to make a simple and inexpensive polarizer was a matter that was worth his time and considerable intellect. He did not go back to Harvard at the end of his vacation; he stayed in New York, settling into a small apartment to figure out the problem.

By day, Land haunted the library and read everything he could find about Herapath and polarization. By night, he worked in secrecy in a science lab building at Columbia University. There was a reason for his secrecy—he didn't belong there. He climbed the fire escape each night to a window that was usually left unlocked and took advantage of the unusually well-equipped laboratory.

"It is a curious property of research activity," Land once said, "that after the problem has been solved, the solution usually seems obvious." His solution was that Herapath had gone off on a wrong path—rather than find one large crystal to work as a filter, why not align millions of microscopic crystals in rows like a comb to form an "optical grain" that would do the same thing?

Land's parents agreed to fund his quest and even provided enough money to hire an assistant, a former dental technician named Ernest Calabro, who performed tasks of plating, cutting and polishing alloy and glass plates without having any idea of what the secretive Land was up to. For his part, Land believed he would solve the problem within a relatively short time, perhaps a few months.

EUREKA!

It was more like three years, but he finally got the solution that had eluded Herapath. In the Columbia University lab, he used a powerful electromagnet to line up millions of tiny iodine-quinine crystals in a hollow glass cylinder.

Shining a light through it confirmed that Land had succeeded. He soon figured out how to do the same thing on a plastic sheet, with 1,000 billion crystals per square inch. In 1929, at the age of twenty, he had his first major invention.

About that same time, the stock market crashed, reversing his family's fortunes. Land returned to Harvard, aware that his family was sacrificing to keep him there, and began working on his degree in dead earnest. Land also continued his research, this time using a lab provided to him by a professor. It became so compelling that he dropped out of Harvard one semester shy of graduating and never returned.

FINDING THE RIGHT NICHE

He spent the next several years trying to interest the car makers in the safety features of Polaroid windshields and headlights. To remind himself of what he was trying to accomplish, Land mounted a sign in his laboratory that said, "Every night, 50 people will die on the highway from headlight glare." But the car makers believed that styling and horsepower sold cars and that safety features actually were a mistake, because they reminded potential buyers that a car could be a dangerous thing. So even though the Polaroid materials would have added only about $4 per car and could have saved thousands of lives, Detroit turned Land down.

Other manufacturers, however, started seeing some applications for Land's new material. Out of the blue, future competitor Kodak sent a huge order for something that didn't even exist yet—a Polaroid lens to tone down glare and sky light for photos. Movie makers started looking into polarized lenses and glasses for 3-D movies. (Unfortunately, 3-D was set back for a decade when Land demonstrated it to Harry Warner of Warner Brothers. "I don't get it," said Harry after the movie. "What's the big deal?" It wasn't until several weeks later that Land found out from a Hollywood friend that Warner had a glass eye.)

With a glass eye, this was the only way Harry could ever see Bugs through any lense

Wurlitzer began using Polaroid film for light displays on its new jukeboxes. The American Optical Company bought the rights to make Polaroid sunglasses. And with war at hand, the Polaroid Company received millions of dollars in contracts to develop optical military applications. By war's end, the Polaroid Company's sales had multiplied to $17 million.

Land, shown here with one of his early model cameras

THE NAME IS FAMILIAR....

But before that, Land began getting bored and restless. He was looking for new scientific problems to take on. In 1943, while photographing vacation scenes in Santa Fe, his three-year-old daughter asked to see the pictures he just took. When he explained that she couldn't see them until they got home, she wanted to know, "Why not?"

Why not, indeed?

Land was immediately struck by the idea of instant photography. Before the day was over, he had already worked out the basic process. The developing chemicals would have to be included in the film pack, maybe in small pods that would rupture when the film traveled through a roller system like that on an old-fashioned washing machine.

Land went back to his lab and started working with a team of technicians, including Maxfield Parrish, Jr., the son of the artist. Four years later, they had a working model to demonstrate. A year later, they introduced the camera in department stores, accompanied by near-riots. People had never seen anything like this camera in 1948. They snapped it up, even at the outrageous price of $89.75—the equivalent of more than $500 today.

Maybe he had a glass ear, too:
"Who the hell wants to hear actors talk?"
—Harry Warner of Warner Brothers Studios in 1927

Akinosuke's Dream

A Spooky Tale from Ancient Japan

Who says you need a highly paid Hollywood screenwriter to get a supernatural story with a *Twilight Zone* ending? This is an ancient legend collected by Lafcadio Hearn in 1903.

In Yamato Province, there lived a farmer named Miyata Akinosuke. In his garden there was an ancient cedar tree. One warm afternoon he was sitting under this tree with two of his friends, chatting and drinking wine, when he felt all of a sudden very drowsy—so drowsy that he begged his friends to excuse him for taking a nap in their presence. Then he lay down at the foot of the tree, and dreamed this dream:

As he laid there in his garden, he saw a grand procession, more imposing than anything he had ever seen before, and it was advancing toward his dwelling. Young men, richly clothed, were drawing a great lacquered palace-carriage hung with bright blue silk. When the procession arrived within a short distance of the house it halted; and a richly dressed man advanced from it, approached Akinosuke, bowed to him profoundly, and said: "Honored sir: the king, the Kokuo of Tokoyo, commands me to greet you in his august name. Please immediately enter this carriage, which he has sent for your conveyance."

Upon hearing these words Akinosuke wanted to make some fitting reply; but he was too much astonished for speech. He entered the carriage and the journey began.

In a very short time, to Akinosuke's amazement, the carriage stopped in front of a huge two-storied gateway of a Chinese style. After some little waiting, two noble-looking men came from the gateway wearing robes of purple silk and high caps of lofty rank. They bowed to him and led him to a palace whose front appeared to extend a distance of miles.

Akinosuke was shown into a reception-room of wonderful size and splendor. Serving-maids, in costume of ceremony, brought refreshments. When Akinosuke had partaken, the two purple-robed attendants bowed before him and addressed him, each speaking alternately according to the etiquette of courts: "It is now our honorable duty to inform you...as to the reason of your having been summoned hither.... Our master, the King,

augustly desires that you become his son-in-law...and it is his wish and command that you shall wed this very day...the Princess, his maiden-daughter...."

Having thus spoken, the attendants rose together, and attired Akinosuke as befit a princely bridegroom, and conducted him to the presence-room, where the Kokuo of Tokoyo was seated upon his throne, wearing a high black cap of state, and robes of yellow silk. The king greeted him with gracious words, and then said: "The wedding shall now be performed." Joyful music played and beautiful court ladies advanced from behind a curtain to conduct Akinosuke to the room in which the bride awaited him. The room was immense; but it could scarcely contain the multitude of guests. All bowed down before Akinosuke as he took his place, facing the King's daughter, on the kneeling-cushion prepared for him. The bride appeared like a maid of heaven; her robes were beautiful as a summer sky. After the wedding the couple received the congratulations of many noble persons, and wedding gifts beyond counting.

Some days later Akinosuke was again summoned to the throne-room. On this occasion he was received even more graciously than before; and the King said to him: "In the south-western part of Our dominion there is an island called Raishu. We have now appointed you Governor of that island. You will find the people loyal and docile; we entrust you with the duty of improving their social conditions and ruling them with kindness and wisdom." So Akinosuke and his bride departed from the palace of Tokoyo.

Akinosuke entered at once upon his new duties; and they did

not prove to be hard. During the first three years of his governorship he was occupied chiefly with the enactment of laws; but he had wise counselors to help him, and he never found the work unpleasant. When it was all finished, the country was so healthy and so fertile that sickness and want were unknown; and the people were so good that no laws were ever broken.

Akinosuke dwelt and ruled in Raishu for twenty years more, during which no shadow of sorrow traversed his life. But in the twenty-fourth year, a great misfortune came upon him, for his wife, who had borne him five boys and two girls, fell sick and died. She was buried, with high pomp, on the summit of a beautiful hill; and a monument, exceedingly splendid, was placed upon her grave. But Akinosuke felt such grief at her death that he no longer cared to live.

Now when the period of mourning was over, there came from the Tokoyo palace a royal messenger with condolences. "We will now send you back to your own people and country," he added. "As for the seven children, they are the grandchildren of the King, and shall be fitly cared for. Do not, therefore, allow you mind to be troubled about them."

On receiving this mandate, Akinosuke submissively prepared for his departure. When all his affairs had been settled, he was escorted with much honor to the port. There he embarked, and the ship sailed out into the blue sea, and the shape of the island of Raishu itself turned blue, then grey, and then vanished forever.... And Akinosuke suddenly awoke, under the cedar tree in his own garden!

For a moment he was stupefied and dazed. But he perceived his two friends still seated near him, drinking and chatting merrily. He stared at them in a bewildered way, and cried aloud: "How strange!"

"Akinosuke must have been dreaming," one exclaimed with a laugh. "What did you see, Akinosuke, that was strange?" Then Akinosuke told his dream of three-and-twenty years' sojourn on the island of Raishu, and they were astonished, because he had really slept for no more than a few minutes.

His friend said: "Indeed, you saw strange things. We also saw something strange while you were napping. A little yellow butterfly was fluttering over your face for a moment or two. Then it alighted on the ground beside you, close to the tree; and a big ant seized it and pulled it down into the hole. Just before you woke up, we saw that butterfly come out of the hole again, and flutter over your face as before. And then the butterfly suddenly disappeared—we do not know where."

"Perhaps it was Akinosuke's soul," the other friend said. "I thought I saw it fly into his mouth. But, even if that butterfly was Akinosuke's soul, the fact would not explain his dream."

"The ants might explain it," returned the first speaker. "Ants are queer beings—possibly goblins.... Anyhow, there is a big ant's nest under that cedar tree...." "Let us look!" cried Akinosuke. He went for a spade.

The ground beneath the cedar tree proved to have been excavated, in a most surprising way, by a prodigious colony of ants.

The ants had furthermore built things inside their excavations; and their tiny constructions of straw, clay, and stems bore an odd resemblance to miniature towns. In the middle of a structure considerably larger than the rest there was a marvelous swarm of small ants around one very big ant, which had yellowish wings and a long black head.

"Why, there is the King of my dream!" cried Akinosuke. "And there is the palace of Tokoyo! How extraordinary! Raishu ought to lie somewhere southwest of it—to the left of that big root.... Yes! Here it is! How very strange! Now I am sure I can find the mountain, and the grave of the princess...."

In the wreck of the nest he searched, and at last discovered a tiny mound, on the top of which was fixed a water-worn pebble, in shape resembling a Buddhist monument. Underneath it he found, embedded in clay, the dead body of a female ant. €

Surgery Before Anesthesia

What did hospitals use for surgery before anesthesia? Until the mid-1800s in Europe and America, hospitals routinely used "holders down"—burly guys who pinned screaming patients to the operating table to keep them from writhing.

Viva la Revolución

TIDBITS FROM THE LIFE OF FIDEL CASTRO

Fidel Castro led a successful revolution in Cuba in 1958 and has ruled it for more than three and a half decades, despite repeated U.S. efforts to overthrow or kill him.

• Fidel Castro grew up in an affluent family, the oldest of seven children. His father, Angel Castro, worked for the United Fruit Company (which was eventually thrown out of Cuba). For decades, United Fruit executives who knew Angel couldn't help but shake their heads and wonder how his quiet, polite boy could have gone so bad.

• Besides the seven children, the Castro house had a flock of chickens living inside it.

• When Castro was a child, other children called him "Judio" (the Jew) because he wasn't baptized until he was six.

• At age ten, Castro got appendicitis and spent three months in the hospital. He wanted to work in medicine: "Some people thought I might make a good doctor, because I used to play with lizards and a Gillette razor blade," he told an interviewer. "I had been impressed by the operations like the one I'd been through and after that I would 'operate' on lizards—lizards that usually died, of course. Then I would enjoy watching how the ants carried them off, how hundreds of ants working together could carry the lizard and move it to their heap."

• Known as "El Loco Fidel," he was so competitive in basketball games that he would forget which side he was playing for, switching sides and making baskets for the other team.

• Castro organized a baseball team and was its pitcher, even though he had an out-of-control fastball. When his team wasn't winning, Fidel would simply halt the game and go home. He claimed later that a scout had tried to recruit him into the American major leagues.

Castro loved baseball. He's pictured here with the Minneapolis Millers during the 1959 Junior World Series vs. Havana.

• In 1940, as a teenager, Castro wrote a letter to Franklin D. Roosevelt. "My good friend Roosevelt: I don't know very English, but I know as much as I write to you. I like to hear the radio, and I am very happy, because I heard in it that you will be president of a new era. I am a boy but I think very much but I do not think that I am writting to the President of the United States. If you like, give me a ten dollars bill green american, in the letter, because never, I have not seen a ten dollars bill green american and I would like to have one of them." He received a letter back thanking him for his "letter of support and congratulations," but no ten dollar bill.

• For his honeymoon, Fidel and his new wife Mirta traveled to New York City for three months, courtesy of his new father-in-law. A friend of both families gave the couple $1,000 for spending money. His name? Fulgencio Batista, who would later become Cuban president and be overthrown by Castro's revolutionaries. In New York, Castro used part of the money to buy a huge white Lincoln Continental.

• The Castros' first son, Fidelito, was a healthy baby, but then he suddenly became gravely ill. Doctors were mystified until Mirta discovered that Fidel was force-feeding his son three times the recommended concentration of formula so that his son would grow bigger and stronger than other children. She stopped the overfeeding then—and a few months later when Fidel began doing it again.

• On Castro's first revolutionary attack on a military post, he forgot his glasses. As a result he could barely drive to the post, much less aim his gun accurately.

• He was jailed after the attack. His marriage began breaking up when he failed to follow a cardinal rule of prison: Don't write to your wife and your mistress on the same day. The prison censor switched the two letters when he put them back in their envelopes.

• While training his revolutionaries in mountain camps, he confiscated all shaving supplies, toothpaste and brushes and soap, saying true revolutionaries don't concern themselves with personal hygiene.

• Castro, knowing the power of the American press to mold opinions, once tricked Herbert Matthews, a *New York Times* reporter, into thinking he had hundreds of soldiers when he had only 20 by having them march into a clearing by ones and twos, and then march in again and again. One man had a shirt without a back, so he had to march sideways. Che Guevara then had a man come running into the clearing, feigning exhaustion, to report on a completely fictitious Army Number 2. Matthews wrote an article saying that Castro's band was so large that "General Batista cannot hope to suppress Castro's revolt."

• The Cuban Communist Party opposed Castro's rebellion, saying armed struggle was futile. On the other hand, it was supported by the Havana Lions Club and Rotarians.

• In those tense, pre-revolutionary times, Johnny Weissmuller, taking a break from playing Tarzan in the movies, was participating in a Cuban golf tournament. Suddenly, he was surrounded by group of Castro's soldiers who emerged from the rough near the 14th hole. Weissmuller pulled himself up to full height, beat his chest, and let out a Tarzan yell. After a shocked pause, the rebels shouted in delight, "Tarzan! Tarzan! Bienvenido! Welcome!"

• After Batista fled Cuba, mobs went around breaking up casinos as symbols of the American Mafia that had run

Weissmuller, second from left, once used his famous role to befriend Castro's revolutionaries

Cuba for so long. Tough-guy actor George Raft owned the Capri Hotel. When an angry mob began storming the front steps, he snarled at them in his famous gangster voice, "Yer not comin' in my casino!" The people stopped at the sound of the famous voice and retreated.

• After the revolution, Castro came again to New York, where he was wined and dined by all facets of American society—so much so that his brother Raul called from Cuba to ask if he were selling Cuba out to the Americans. His entourage went down in New York history as the ones who plucked chickens in the cities' hotels. At the time, it was assumed that the chickens were for eating—in fact, some of them were sacrificed in Santería rituals. Like many Cubans, Castro dabbles in the Santería religion. He has a mystical attachment to the number 26, picking the 26th day of a month for major speeches, decisions and actions.

• The Bay of Pigs invasion by the United States was such a talked-about "secret" in Miami's "Little Havana" that Cuban intelligence agents assumed it was some sort of disinformation campaign. On the morning before the invasion, Castro aide Carlos Franqui received a call from a *New York Times* reporter asking if he had any news about "an invasion of the island," but the security breach didn't do much harm—Castro had already stationed troops at the landing site.

• Castro always fancied himself quite a lady's man. In fact, there are dozens of children in Cuba who claim him as father. But his technique? One purported lover, a dancer at the Tropicana Hotel, said he read while he made love. A French actress complained that he smoked his damned cigar during the act. An American woman said he never took his boots off. Other women said he took them to romantic spots and then only talked for hours on end about things like agricultural reform.

Life Lessons

How to Make Giant "Ostrich" Eggs

These are great for displays, gifts, Easter eggs and even practical jokes. They look and feel like real eggs. Here's how to make them.

OVER THE YEARS, we've made thousands of these eggs for fun, friends, art galleries and store windows. You can make them any size, but we suggest starting small, because the bigger they are, the easier they break.

WHAT YOU'LL NEED

- Tarp and/or newspapers
- Egg-shaped balloons
- Plaster of Paris
- Water basin
- Plastic cups or Tupperware
- Stirrer
- Plastic squeeze bottle (like from shampoo or detergent)
- Small knife or scissors

HOW YOU DO IT

1 Gather your materials and fill your basin with clean water. Wear old clothes, work outdoors if you can and put down tarp and newspapers. Prepare for a mess because the balloons sometimes burst and shoot plaster in all directions.

2 Fill your cup or Tupperware container half-full with water. Begin adding plaster, stirring continuously, until it reaches the consistency of a thin milk shake. Work quickly now, because the plaster will set in 5 to 10 minutes.

3 Carefully pour the plaster into your squeeze bottle. You'll spill only a little if you approach the problem with a steady hand, an insouciant attitude and a lot of practice.

4 Put a balloon on the mouth of the squeeze bottle as if you were making a water balloon on a faucet.

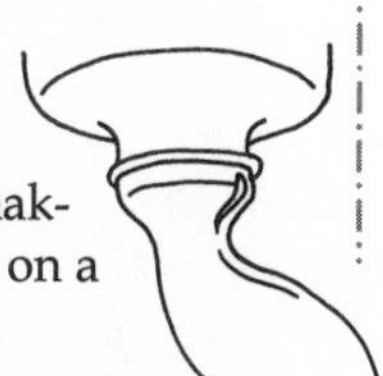

5 Turn the bottle upside down. Hold the neck of

the balloon on the bottle so it doesn't slip off. Squeeze plaster into the balloon, inflating it to about the size of a tangerine.

6 Take the balloon off the bottle, squeezing its neck so the plaster doesn't escape. Blow the balloon up the rest of the way (if you don't like the idea of plaster in your mouth, use a straw), and tie it. Float it in the water tub and gently roll it around, end over end.

7 Repeat steps 4, 5 and 6 until you run out of plaster.

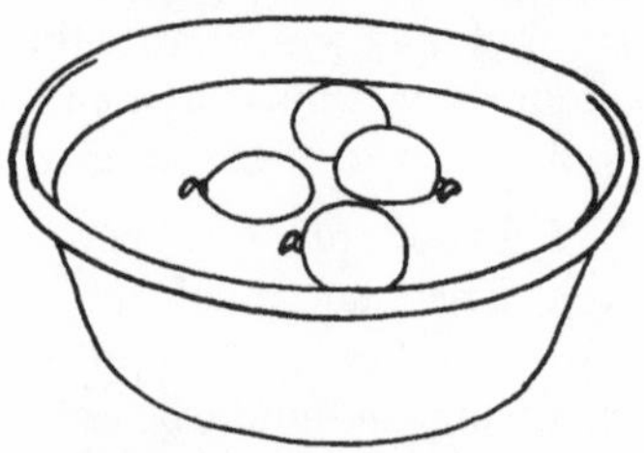

Quickly clean your bottle before the plaster residue inside hardens.

8 Gently turn each balloon end over end, smoothly coating its inside wall with plaster. Do this quickly to each balloon until the plaster inside stops moving. Immediately stop turning the balloons, and let them float untouched for at least 10 minutes.

9 When the plaster has completely hardened, cut the balloon away with your blade, being careful not to gouge the surface of the plaster.

10 Trim away the excess plaster from the "navel" where the balloon neck was. And there you have it—a giant egg!

MORE IDEAS

- You can decorate the eggs after the fact, or add pigment when you mix up the plaster.
- If they break (and many of them will), use the broken shells. You can make things "hatch" out of them, or use them as small animal houses. ☾

Mascot Miracles

How Elsie Became Borden's Cash Cow

Every consumer loves company mascots, but they're usually the last resort for ad agencies. Along with the Energizer Bunny (page 199) and Chiquita Banana (page 279), here's one of our favorites.

THE PUBLIC MAY LOVE Mr. Whipple (remember him?) and Betty Crocker and (especially) the cute spokesanimal cartoon characters like Tony the Tiger and Charlie Tuna. But most advertising agencies hate them because there's no challenge to them. Not only that, if they're successful, they lock the client into variations of the same kind of advertising for years into the future, making it hard to justify an ad agency's big, continuing "creative" costs.

Still, the use of "cute" has been especially successful with companies that realize that they are perceived as big, greedy, impersonal and heartless. That's how the Borden Co. got Elsie.

MASTER OF ALL TRADES

Before Gail Borden discovered how to condense milk, he was an inventor (see page 433 for more information). He had long been interested in condensing and preserving food. He poured his heart, soul and finances into a concoction he called the meat biscuit in which he boiled 120 pounds of beef down to 10 pounds of beef jelly, which he then mixed with flour and baked into long-lasting biscuits for travelers. His biscuits won awards at exhibitions, including the prestigious London International Exhibition in 1851. His meat biscuits were even taken along by a group of pioneers on their way to California.

There was only one problem: The meat biscuits tasted absolutely foul. Even though *Scientific American* called the biscuit, "one of the most valuable inventions that has ever been brought forward," the Army, with its notoriously low gastronomical standards, disagreed. After field tests, a board of Army officers reported that Borden's biscuits were "not only unpalatable, but failed to appease the craving of hunger—producing headache, nausea, and great muscular depression." His meat biscuit business failed, and Borden plummeted into bankruptcy.

Gail Borden

The year before, however, Borden had gotten inspiration for a new invention. On the trip home from winning his London International Exhibition award, Borden had been confronted with the sight of distraught immigrant mothers holding crying, starving babies in the steerage compartment of the ship because the two cows aboard the steamer were giving infected milk. Borden is said to have been haunted by what he saw, and decided to find a way to preserve milk for long periods of time.

Borden's perverse luck from tragedy continued: If his business hadn't failed, and if he hadn't been a penniless widower, he wouldn't have sent his four children off to live with the Shaker religious colony in Lebanon, New York, where he eventually discovered the solution to preserving milk. First, though, he began living and working in a cellar in Brooklyn. He tried boiling gallons of milk down to quarts, but the dark substance that remained tasted horrible, like burnt molasses.

SHAKE, VACUUM & BOIL

He had his stroke of luck when he visited his children at the Shaker colony. The Shakers were well known for their inventive and functional designs. Borden noticed some of them making fruit preserves with a device of their own invention: a "vacuum pan" from which most of the air had been pumped out. It worked on the principle that liquids in a near-vacuum boil at a much lower temperature.

Borden made his own vacuum pan and found that milk boiled at 136° instead of 212°, leaving its color and taste essentially unchanged. He discovered he could remove 80% of the water from milk, leaving a heavy fluid that, when preserved with sugar, could last indefinitely and didn't taste too bad.

Financial success, however, eluded him. Selling the viscous liquid was not as easy as he had hoped at first. He had to sell half of his company to keep it going. Then another stroke of his perverse luck struck: A muckraking editor of *Leslie's Illustrated Weekly* launched a lurid exposé of "swill milk" with vivid word pictures of urban milk supplies from diseased cows fed on brewery refuse, milk cans and manure being hauled on the same carts, and "milk murder!"—high infant death rates from typhoid and tuberculosis. Capitalizing on the uproar, Borden bought ads extolling the purity of his condensed "country milk." Sales picked up.

MILK WARS

In fact, the Borden Company thrived so much in following decades that in the 1930s it became the subject of controversy. People began wondering why, if milk cost so much, the dairy farmers were paid so little. In the ensuing "milk wars," the big milk wholesalers, distributors and retailers were blamed for jacking up prices and pocketing obscene profits. The Borden Company, now one of the biggest "middlemen," decided it needed to quickly change its public image from rapacious and greedy to cute and cuddly.

1950s cookbook

Company executives decided to milk their obvious assets and came up with cartoon spokescows in humorous comic strips. They tried them in medical journals first, with laugh-riot hijinks like

> **Calf: "Mama, I think I see a germ!"**
> **Cow: "Mercy, child—run quick for the Borden Inspector!"**

Doctors swamped the company with requests for reprints for their waiting room walls, so Borden began running the ads in New York newspapers. There was a herd of cartoon cows with names like Bessie, Clara, Mrs. Blossom and Elsie. Then, in

1938, a radio copywriter randomly singled out Elsie's name in a commercial for Rush Hughes, a network news commentator who was sponsored by Borden. Hughes read aloud a letter, purportedly from a cow to her mother:

> **Dear Mama:**
> **I'm so excited I can hardly chew. We girls are sending our milk to Borden now!**
> **Love, *Elsie***

The commercial so tickled Hughes's listeners that they started sending fan mail to Elsie. She quickly became Borden's one main sacred cow, and made her solo debut in national magazines like *Life* and *Saturday Evening Post.* For the New York World's Fair, the company bought a seven-year-old, 950-pound Jersey from Massachusetts, whose registered name was "You'll Do, Lobelia." They set up Elsie in an exhibit that was supposedly her bedroom. It was done up in "Barn Colonial" with churns used as tables, milk bottles as lamps, a wheelbarrow for a chaise longue and oil paintings of Elsie's ancestors. Elsie became such a media hit that the actress that played her, You'll Do, Lobelia, was asked to co-star in the movie *Little Men* with Jack Oakie and Kay Francis in 1940.

ELSIE'S CUTE CALVES

About the same time, the cartoon cow became married to Elmer and had two calves, Beulah and Beauregard (named after the Confederate General in the Battle of Bull Run). The family ruled the barnyard for nearly three decades. The company even named a glue after Elmer. (They didn't use Elsie's name because they feared that consumers would think the glue was made from over-the-hill dairy cows.)

In 1963, Borden introduced Elsie's Milkman Game, in which players delivered milk house to house. Despite Elsie's popularity, the game didn't go over so well.

A GOOD IDEA IN THE TOILET

In 1969, Borden's chairman, caught up in the conglomerate diversification fever of the time, decided that Elsie gave "an inaccurate message" about the company, forgetting that that had been the whole point in the first place. He decided that a company bent on diversifying into chemical manufacturing should downplay an animal that had long been meant to symbolize wholesome country goodness. Elsie was dropped as a corporate symbol, even though polls indicated she was among the best-known corporate mascots. Instead, the company settled on a logo that using an abstract red oval. Employees derided the abstract oval among themselves as "the toilet seat." Eventually, new management of Borden recognized the value of Elsie's image. On March 10, 1993, Borden readopted her to represent all of its dairy brands, building a new logo around her smiling cow face. €

Gail Borden Beyond "Remember the Alamo"

BEFORE GAIL BORDEN discovered how to condense whole milk in the 1850s, he was the official state surveyor for the state of Texas (among other things, he laid out the streets of Galveston) and founder of the weekly *Telegraph and Texas Register*—the newspaper that coined the phrase, "Remember the Alamo." He was also a tinkerer and inventor. We're probably fortunate that most of his inventions never amounted to anything.

• First up was a beach bathhouse that women could move around with them, and change in when out for a day in the sun.

• Borden came up with the idea for a steamboat that was self-propelled by mechanical oars.

• A special lazy susan for quick table service bombed, too.

• One of the more interesting Borden inventions had to be his "simplified method" of converting Catholics to Protestants. Something like a step-by-step guide for converters. Not surprisingly, this idea failed, too.

Battle at the Alamo

• Borden's Terraqueus Machine, although a bust, was one of his favorites. It was a contraption, made with a sail from a boat and a wagon, that could travel on both land and water. A horse would lead the wagon, equipped with the sail, to water, where the wheels and sail were supposed to take over so it could move through the sea. Unfortunately, as the story goes, Borden decided to try it out on some dinner guests with disastrous results. The contraption failed miserably once it hit the water, tipping over and dumping all his riders into the Gulf of Mexico.

Sports Match 4

MATCH THE TEAM TO THE LOCATION

Here we go again with a tough sports team match-up quiz. Match the pro teams from the NHL, MLS and the WNBA with the places they call home.

1. Storm	San Jose
2. Sharks	Dallas
3. Rapids	Minnesota
4. Sparks	Anaheim
5. Avalanche	Nashville
6. Rockers	Kansas City
7. Canucks	Phoenix
8. Burn	Colorado
9. Wizards	Seattle
10. Mighty Ducks	Cleveland
11. Earthquakes	Colorado
12. Mercury	Vancouver
13. Predators	Los Angeles
14. Galaxy	Los Angeles
15. Lynx	San Jose

Answers: 1. Storm: Seattle—WNBA; 2. Sharks: San Jose—NHL; 3. Rapids: Colorado—MLS; 4. Sparks: Los Angeles—WNBA; 5. Avalanche: Colorado—NHL; 6. Rockers: Cleveland—WNBA; 7. Canucks: Vancouver—NHL; 8. Burn: Dallas—MLS; 9. Wizards: Kansas City—MLS; 10. Mighty Ducks: Anaheim—NHL; 11. Earthquakes: San Jose—MLS; 12. Mercury: Phoenix—WNBA; 13. Predators: Nashville—NHL; 14. Galaxy: Los Angeles—MLS; 15. Lynx: Minnesota—WNBA

Ripe Ol' Corn

"Uncle Josh at a Circus"

Uncle Josh Weathersby—a country bumpkin created by Cal Stewart—tells about circus folks who came to town in this reprint from W. C. Privy's original *Bathroom Companion #4*, published in 1905.

WELL, 'LONG LAST YEAR, 'bout harvest time, there was a cirkus come to Punkin Centre, and I think the whole population turned out to see it. They come paradin' into town, the bands a-playin' and banners flying, and animals pokin' their heads out of the cages, and all sorts of jim-cracks. Deacon Witherspoon said they was a sinful lot of men and wimmin, and no one oughta go and see them, but seein' as how they was there, he allowed he'd take the children and let them see the lions and tigers and things. Si Pettingill remarked, "Guess the Deacon won't put blinders on himself when he gits there." We noticed afterwards that the Deacon had a front seat where he could see and hear purty well.

Well, I said to Ezra Hoskins, "Let's you and me go down to the cirkus," and Ezra said, "All right, Joshua." So we got on our store clothes, our new boots, and put some money in our pockits, and went down to the cirkus. Well, I never seen any one in my life cut up more fool capers than Ezra did. We got in where the animals was, and Ezra he walked around the elephant three or four times, and then he said, "By gum, Josh, that's a durned handy critter—he's got two tails, and he's eatin' with one and keepin' the flies off with t'other." Durned old fool!

Well, we went on a little ways further, and all to once Ezra he said, "Gee whiz, Josh, there's Steve Jenkins over there in one of them cages." I said, "Come along you silly fool, that ain't Steve

Jenkins." Ezra said, "Well, now, I guess I'd oughter know Steve Jenkins when I see him; I jist about purty near raised Steve." Well, we went over to the cage, and it wan't no man at all, nuthin' only a durned old baboon; and Ezra wanted to shake hands with him jist 'cause he looked like Steve. Ezra said he'd bet a peck of pippins that baboon belonged to Steve's family a long ways back.

Well, then we went into where they was havin' the cirkus doin's, and I guess us two old codgers jist about busted our buttons a-laffin at that silly old clown. Well, he cut up a lot of didos, then he went out and set down right alongside of Aunt Nancy Smith; and Nancy she'd like to had histeericks. She said, "You go 'way from me you painted critter," and that clown he jist up and yelled to beat thunder—he said Nancy stuck a pin in him. Well, ev'rybody laffed, and Nancy she jist set and giggled right out.

Well, they brought a trick mule into the ring, and the ring master said he'd give any one five dollars what could ride the mule; and Ruben Hoskins allowed he could ride anything with four legs what had hair on. So he got into the ring, and that mule he took after Ruben and chased him 'round that ring so fast Ruben could see himself goin' 'round t'other side of the ring. He was mighty glad to git out of there.

Then a gal come out on horse back and commenced ridin' around. Nancy Smith said she was a brazen critter to come out there without clothes enough on her to dust a fiddle. But Deacon Witherspoon said that was the art of 'questrinism; we all allowed it, whatever he meant. And then that silly old clown he told the ring master that his uncle committed sooiside different than any man what ever committed sooiside; and the ring master said, "Well, sir, how did your uncle commit sooiside?" and that silly old clown said, "Why, he put his nose in his ear and he blowed his head off." Then he sang an old-fashioned song I hadn't heered in a long time; it went something like this:

"From Widdletown to Waddletown is fifteen miles,
From Waddletown to Widdletown is fifteen miles,
From Widdletown to Waddletown, from Waddletown to Widdletown--
Take it all together and it's fifteen miles."

He was about the silliest cuss I ever seen.

Well, I noticed a feller a rummagin' 'round among the benches as though he might a-lost somethin'. So I said to him, "Mister, did you lose anythin' 'round here any place?" He said, "Yes, sir, I lost a ten dollar bill; if you find it I'll give you two dollars." Well, I jist made up my mind he was one of them cirkus sharpies, and when he wan't a-lookin' I pulled a ten dollar bill out of my pockit and give it to him; and the durned fool didn't know that it wasn't the same one that he lost. Gosh, I jist fooled him out of his two dollars slicker 'n a whistle.

I tell you cirkus day is a great time in Punkin Centre.

• Ever wonder why the calliope always appeared at the end of a circus parade? Besides being deafening to nearby ears, there was also the safety issue—the steam-powered contraptions would occasionally blow up.

• "Leotards" were named after Jules Leotard, the man who invented the flying trapeze. He also invented the safety net...sort of. While at the Cirque Napoleon, he worked with a pile of mattresses beneath him.

Zen Masters

The Zen of Pop Babes

Britney Spears and Christina Aguilera—bleach-blonde pop stars—sometimes have words of wisdom for their young fans. And sometimes they don't....

Britney Says: "I always call my cousin because we're so close. We're almost like sisters, and we're also close because our moms are sisters."

"I always listen to 'NSYNC's "Tearin' Up My Heart." It reminds me to wear a bra."

"I think I'm more grounded, you know, and I know what I want out of life and I'm, you know, my morals are really, you know, strong and I have major beliefs about certain things and I think that has helped me, you know, from being, you know, coming from a really small town."

"I want to be an artist that everyone can relate to, that's young, happy and fun."

"Just because I look sexy on the cover of *Rolling Stone* doesn't mean I'm naughty."

"The cool thing about being famous is traveling. I have always wanted to travel across seas, like to Canada and stuff."

Christina Says: "I don't want to be just a straight pop singer. I'm a vocalist and that's what I want to be seen as in the long run."

"I think everybody should have a great Wonderbra. There's so many ways to enhance them, everybody does it."

"I'm not really religious but very spiritual. I give money to this company that manufactures hearing aids on a regular basis. More people should really hear me sing. I have a gift from God."

Whole Lotta Shakin'

How Jell-O Got the Wiggles & Jiggles

Although today it's a staple in kitchen pantries across the globe, Jell-O hasn't always been around. We were curious about everyone's favorite dessert, so we had intrepid reporter Don Jellyson look into Jell-O's jiggly past.

IT WIGGLES. It's colorful. It's served to patients by the finest hospitals in the world. Even the Smithsonian has done a retrospective exhibit and seminar tracing its history. Like bowling and Cheez Whiz, it's so déclassé that it's hip. We're talking about Jell-O, the salad that has no vegetables, the only pork product you can eat that's certified as kosher. Gelatin is so transformed from its original forms that rabbis have ruled it kosher and pareve—neither meat nor dairy.

Gelatin appeared in Europe centuries ago (history records that Napoleon ate it with Josephine). A specialized kind, isinglass, was milky-colored and made from the air bladders of sturgeons.

Modern-style powdered gelatin was developed by the American engineer Peter Cooper, founder of the Cooper Union for the Advancement of Science and Art, who also designed and built the Tom Thumb locomotive. In 1845, he patented the process of turning animal skin, bone and connective tissue into a highly refined flavorless wiggly clear material.

Unfortunately, Cooper never quite figured out how to make a silk purse out of his sow's ear creation. His gelatin never became a commercial success. Maybe it was because he just didn't have a promoter's sense for selling the wiggle and not the steak byproducts: His advertisements described gelatin as "a transparent substance containing all the ingredients fitting it for table use in portable form, and requiring only the addition of hot water to dissolve it."

Cooper's product sat jiggling but dormant for a half-century until 1895, when all things came to a man improbably named Pearl B. Wait. Wait was a maker of patent medicines and corn plasters in LeRoy, New York. One of his most successful products was a cough syrup, so he knew something about using flavors and colors to mask the unpleasant qualities of a product.

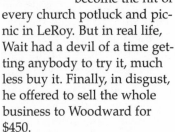

"There's always room for J-e-l-l-O!"

Wait had a neighbor with the also unlikely name of Orator Woodward, who was an inventor, too. His first invention was a pesticide-laced cement egg you could place in a chicken's nest to kill lice. Commercially, it laid an egg. However, he had more success marketing a coffee-substitute grain beverage called Grain-O.

The "-O" ending was a commercial fad at the time, similar to "-a-Rama" in the 1950s, or unrecognizable techno-gibberish names in the 1990s. May Wait, Pearl's wife, was inspired by Woodward's Grain-O when she named the powdered dessert mix "Jell-O."

In a Hollywood treatment of the story, Wait's fruit-flavored, brightly colored gelatin would quickly become the hit of every church potluck and picnic in LeRoy. But in real life, Wait had a devil of a time getting anybody to try it, much less buy it. Finally, in disgust, he offered to sell the whole business to Woodward for $450.

Woodward bought, figuring he could use the same manufacturing and distribution system he had already set up for Grain-O. He quickly found, though, that no matter how good your system is, it doesn't do much good if nobody wants your product. Packages of Jell-O piled up unsold in his warehouse. One day he was walking with his warehouse superintendent, A. S. Nico, and impulsively offered to sell him the entire Jell-O business for $35. Nico looked at him, looked at the pile of unsold goods—and refused the offer.

Nico soon had reason to regret the decision. Jell-O started finding its market. By 1902, Woodward was selling $250,000 worth of the stuff a year. He started advertising, using pictures of famous actresses and opera singers serving the delicate dessert from fluted glassware on silver trays. He hired famous artists like Maxfield Parrish and Norman Rockwell to illustrate his advertisements and recipe books. He began direct-mail ad campaigns, sending recipes directly to the consumer, and sent out a fleet of nattily dressed salesmen to appear at country fairs and women's clubs and demonstrate the ease and versatility of Jell-O.

Jell-O advertised heavily on radio and sponsored Jack Benny's show in the 1930s, but the true Golden Age of Jell-O came in the 1950s. Its ease of preparation and versatility of use in recipes brought forth the collective creative genius of American housewifery. On file at Jell-O headquarters are more than 2,200 different Jell-O recipes. They range from *Joy of Jell-O Cookbook* favorites like Gelatin Poke Cake to new wave Jell-O recipes like Primordial Aspic (green Jell-O with gummy fishes and worms suspended in it). General Foods, which owns the brand, maintains an active hotline for recipes, questions and even Jell-O wisdom. (For example, did you know that there are certain fruits like pineapple, kiwi, papaya and mangoes that should only be used canned? Canning destroys an enzyme in them that keeps the Jell-O from fully hardening.)

Jell-O started falling from its slippery state of grace in the 1960s. Part of it was general anti-establishmentarianism, part was a health-conscious backlash against artificial ingredients and empty calories, and part had to do with the Baby Bust. Jell-O became a punch line signaling a lower-class mentality in jokes by people like Archie Bunker and Fred Sanford. Jell-O's sales declined precipitously from a high of 715 million packages in 1968 to 305 million by 1986.

But Jell-O started bouncing

back in 1987, thanks to the 1980s Baby Boomlet. Jigglers, a high-density finger-food Jell-O recipe, became immensely popular with the preschool set, and a vodka-laced version appealed to the young party crowd. Bill Cosby became the recognized spokesperson in TV commercials. Even President-elect Bill Clinton dined on Bing Cherry Jell-O Salad for his first post-election Thanksgiving and Christmas.

Not bad for a food product made from artificial flavor, artificial color, fresh and frozen pork skins, cattle bones and hides, and assorted connective tissue from both animals.

Other Jell-O Facts

• 3 out of 4 American houses have at least one package of Jell-O in the pantry.

• America eats an average of eight boxes of Jell-O every second of the day.

• The current Jell-O Capital of America is Grand Rapids, Michigan, which consumes 82 percent more Jell-O per capita than average. Why? Maybe because of all the Protestant churches. Another strange, hopefully unrelated, fact: Grand Rapids is also the largest per capita buyer of rat poison.

• 30 percent of Jell-O is served, not straight-up, but in recipes.

• The most popular flavor? "Red" (strawberry, raspberry and cherry). Jell-O has grown from four flavors in 1897 (orange, lemon, strawberry and raspberry) to twenty today, including recent additions blueberry and watermelon.

• The key to hosting the ever-popular spectator sport called Jell-O Wrestling? Use an 8-foot padded box, pour in 55 gallons of powder, add boiling water, chill for two days and don't allow contestants to hold their opponents' heads under the Jell-O.

Eyewitness

I Saw Burr Kill Hamilton

Many have wondered what actually went down between Alexander Hamilton and Aaron Burr on that July morning, 1804, in Weehawken, New Jersey. There were two there who wrote about what they saw of the famous duel and its aftermath.

CONSIDERING HOW it all ended, it's not surprising to find out that Alexander Hamilton and Aaron Burr began their relationship as law partners. The animosity that was built there stoked the fires of resentment that flared up later in their careers. When Burr won a Senate seat that had belonged to Hamilton's father-in-law, though, things got really tense between the two.

Burr walked away from the vice presidency in 1804, and ran a campaign for New York governor. He was unliked by many besides Hamilton, including George Washington and Thomas Jefferson. He'd developed a reputation for being untrustworthy and had a tendency to court any political party that would put him ahead. Many people were willing to try almost anything to make sure he didn't win the New York governor's race, Hamilton among them. Burr soon became the victim of a vicious smear campaign led by Hamilton. When accused by Burr of leading the slanderous attack, Hamilton refused to acknowledge it, much less apologize for the role he played. Burr, then, challenged Hamilton to a duel.

One just didn't show up for a duel unaided. Hamilton, like any other duel participant, brought a Second—a guy who prepared the guns, tended wounds and assisted the duelers with various tasks.

Hamilton's Second, Nathaniel Pendleton, and Burr's Second, W. P. Van Ness, collaborated on a summary in the aftermath of the event. Not long after, they published this account:

> **He then asked if they were prepared; being answered in the affirmative, he gave the word present, as had been agreed on, and both parties presented and fired in succession. The intervening time is not expressed, as the seconds do not precisely agree on that point. The fire of Colonel Burr took effect, and General Hamilton almost instantly fell. Colonel Burr advanced toward General Hamilton with a manner and gesture that appeared to General Hamilton's friend to be expressive of regret; but, without speaking, turned about and withdrew, being urged from the field by his friend, as has been subsequently stated, with a view to prevent his being recognized by the surgeon and bargemen who were then approaching. No further communication took place between the principals, and the barge that carried Colonel Burr immediately returned to the city. We conceive it proper to add, that the conduct of the parties in this interview was perfectly proper, as suited the occasion.**

Accompanying Alexander Hamilton to the duel on that day was physician David Hosack. When Hamilton fell, it was Hosack who attended to his injuries. This is what he remembered:

> **When called to him upon his receiving the fatal wound, I**

found him half sitting on the ground, supported in the arms of Mr. Pendleton. His countenance of death I shall never forget. He had at that instant just strength to say, "This is a mortal wound, doctor"; when he sunk away, and became to all appearance lifeless. I immediately stripped up his clothes, and soon, alas I ascertained that the direction of the ball must have been through some vital part. His pulses were not to be felt, his respiration was entirely suspended, and, upon laying my hand on his heart and perceiving no motion there, I considered him as irrecoverably gone. I, however, observed to Mr. Pendleton, that the only chance for his reviving was immediately to get him upon the water. We therefore lifted him up, and carried him out of the wood to the margin of the bank, where the bargemen aided us in conveying him into the boat, which immediately put off. During all this time I could not discover the least symptom of returning life. I now rubbed his face, lips, and temples with spirits of hartshorn, applied it to his neck and breast, and to the wrists and palms of his hands, and endeavoured to pour some into his mouth.

When we had got, as I should judge, about fifty yards from the shore, some imperfect efforts to breathe were for the first time manifest; in a few minutes he sighed, and became sensible to the impression of the hartshorn or the fresh air of the water. He breathed; his eyes, hardly opened, wandered, without fixing upon any object; to our great joy, he at length spoke. "My vision is indistinct," were his first words. His pulse became more perceptible, his respiration more regular, his sight returned. I then examined the wound to know if there was any dangerous discharge of blood; upon slightly pressing his side it gave him pain, on which I desisted.

Soon after recovering his sight, he happened to cast his eye upon the case of pistols, and observing the one that he had had in his hand lying on the outside, he said, "Take care of that pistol; it is undischarged, and still cocked; it may go off and do harm. Pendleton knows" (attempting to turn his head towards him) "that I did not intend to fire at him."

"Yes," said Mr. Pendleton, understanding his wish, "I have already made Dr. Hosack acquainted with your determination as to that."

He then closed his eyes and remained calm, without any disposition to speak; nor did he say much afterward, except in reply to my questions. He asked me once or twice how I found his pulse; and he informed me that his lower extremities had lost all feeling, manifesting to me that he entertained no hopes that he should long survive.

The next day, Hamilton was dead. But that's not the end of the sordid tale.

Burr's "victory" meant that he was charged with murder in both New York and New Jersey. He became a social and political pariah.

Aaron Burr's treason trial

He didn't let it stop him, though.... Within a few years, Burr was caught red-handed organizing a private army so that he could go and conquer portions of both Mexico and Louisiana, probably to set up his own kingdom. Although he never officially stated his purpose, Burr wrote to his co-conspirator General James Wilkinson of his intentions, "The gods invite us to glory and fortune; it remains to be seen whether we deserve the boon." Wilkinson, in the end, ratted him out to President Thomas Jefferson, but thanks to a legal technicality, Burr escaped being convicted of treason.

Soon after, he fled to Europe, hoping to leave his reputation behind. He did so successfully, but he sound wound up in serious debt. To avoid debtors' prison there, he had to come back home to New York.

The murder charges were eventually dropped, and Burr managed to rekindle his career as a lawyer, but the legacy he built over his lifetime never really left him. He lived a life "severed from the human race," as he put it, and died forgotten in 1833 at the age of eighty. €

The Long Road to American College Football

• ***"I will not permit 30 men to travel 400 miles merely to agitate a bag of wind." —Cornell president Andrew White, forbidding an intercollegiate game of football with the University of Michigan in 1873.***

• ***"There's murder in that game!"* —Rugged boxer John L. Sullivan, upon watching a grueling Harvard-Yale football game prior to the game's near-ban in 1909.**

Rotting Grapes

A Short History of Wine

"The peoples of the Mediterranean began to emerge from barbarism when they learnt to cultivate the olive and the grape vine."
—Thucydides, fifth century Greek historian

When did wine first appear on the Earth? First, the legends. According to the Bible, Noah became the first winemaker after the flood. (Wine was important in Biblical times: In the Old Testament, all books but Jonah mention it. Isaiah even includes advice on how to plant a vineyard.)

• According to an Arabic tale recorded by Omar Khayyam in the twelfth century, a woman in a Persian king's harem discovered wine. A jar of grapes had been set aside as probably poisonous when it began foaming and smelling funny. A concubine suffering from unbearable headaches decided to kill herself with this poison. Instead, she lost her headache, she became the life of the party, and sank into a restful sleep.

• Despite the legends, though, wine dates back before history. In fact, it was probably the first alcoholic drink. Unlike beer, wine does not have to be actively fermented—it happens naturally if fruit juice is stored too long. Wine historian Hugh Johnson thinks that wine is at least 2 million years old.

Egyptians stomping grapes

• The earliest solid archaeological evidence of wine—a jar with wine residues found in Mesopotamia—dates to about 3500 B.C. The wine seems to have been made from dates.

• Egyptian wall paintings of winemaking from 3,000–5,000 years ago show that the technology of winemaking has not changed all that much since then. One of their innovations was an overhead safety grid to keep grape stompers safe from slipping and drowning or being overcome by the car-

Bacchus, Roman God of Wine & Party Guy

bon dioxide that fermenting grapes give off. Wine was important to the Egyptians—King Tut was buried with 36 jars of it to help him make a smooth transition to the Next World.

• Romans drank their wine diluted with warm water. Many preferred the salty tang of sea water to the blandness of fresh water.

• In Rome during the second century B.C., women were forbidden to drink wine. A husband who discovered his wife soaking up the Sauvignon was allowed to divorce or even kill her with impunity.

• Many Romans worshiped Bacchus, the Roman wine god who was the miracle-working son of a god and a mortal woman. Bacchus's followers ate bread and wine to symbolically ingest the body and blood of the god.

• Some ancient wine techniques were not healthy. The Egyptians added burned sulfur to wine as a preservative. The Romans "sweetened" their wine with lead. Lead poisoning may have caused the fall of the Roman Empire, yet even after 1696, when Dr. Eberhard Gockel of Germany proved that it was a deadly poison, adding lead to wine was not banned in most countries until the mid-1800s. (Even the laws didn't stop French winemakers who continued to drop lead musketballs into their vats for several decades after.)

• Before the French got the hang of making wine, around 200 B.C., they had to buy wine from the wily Italians, exchanging a French slave for every large amphora of wine.

• Jesus' first miracle was reportedly turning water into wine. He referred to wine often, calling himself "the true vine" and used wine in the Last Supper. He even talked of humanity in grape grower terms: "Every bunch in me that beareth not fruit he taketh away; and every branch that beareth fruit, he purgeth it, that it may bring forth more fruit."

• The proper use of wine in Christian ceremony, like a lot of other apparently trivial things, has set off century-long doctrinal disputes. Greek and Armenian churches split over whether the Eucharist wine should be watered, with the Armenians refusing to water their wine and the Greeks insisting that it was a spiritual necessity. The Armenians offered a compromise in 1178—they would add water as long as it didn't have to be warm water as the Greeks demanded. The Greeks refused to budge. Finally, a Muslim was brought in as a neutral arbiter. After listening to both sides, he issued his opinion: Since wine itself was an impure liquid forbidden by the Koran, they should skip the wine and serve the water, either hot or cold. Both sides rejected his advice.

• Wine had been banned by Muslim clerics years earlier, to the despair of Arabic doctors, then among the best in the world, who used wine as medicine and disinfectant.

• Not all Muslims followed the injunction. Even Mohammed's favorite wife (he had seven) quoted him as saying, "You may drink, but do not get drunk," while quaffing his *nabidh,* a date wine.

Wine by the Foot

Men, stripped of all their clothes, step into the vessel, and begin to tread down the floating mass, working it also with their hands. This operation is repeated several times if the wine does not ferment rapidly enough. The reason is that the bodily heat of the men aids the wine in its fermentation. The treaders form three separate rows of ten men each and, placing their arms on each other's shoulders, commence work by raising and lowering their feet, varying this, after a time, with songs and shoutings in order to keep the weaker and the lazier ones up to the work, which is quite irksome and monotonous. Taking part with them in the treading is a little band of musicians who strike up a lively tune. Walking over the pips and stalks, strewn at the bottom of the vat, becomes something like the pilgrimages of old when the devout trudged wearily along, with hard peas packed between their feet and the soles of their shoes. The treaders move slowly in a listless way. The fiddle strikes up anew, and the overseers drowsily upbraid. But all to no purpose. Music has lost its inspiration and authority its terrors, and the men, dead beat, raise one purple leg languidly after the other. —Description by an American winegrower visiting Spanish and French wine regions in 1877

• Muslims weren't alone in condemning wine, by the way. So did the Druids.

• Leif Ericson, who landed in America in the year A.D. 1000, named the new continent Vinland the Good, based on his impression the continent was completely covered in grapevines. He made two voyages and started a settlement, possibly near Cape Cod, where some historians believe that the first American wine was made.

• Not drinking wine can be a sign of fanaticism, believed King Louis XVI. In his last letter before losing his head in the French Revolution, King Louis blamed the savagery of the revolutionaries on the fact that its leader, Robespierre, drank only water.

• Louis Pasteur first developed pasteurization in the 1850s as a way to prevent wine spoilage. Afterward, he realized it could *also* be used on other substances like milk. Pasteurization came just in time: When the Prussians laid Paris under siege in the winter of 1870, there was little in the way of food in the city, but plenty of wine. One famous restaurant, Voisin, provided exactly one menu item for Christmas Day: "Chat flanqué de rats, accompagné d'un Bollinger frappé" ("Cat flanked with rats, with Bollinger wine, chilled").

Louis Pasteur, Oenologist

• Meanwhile, in America, the wine trade had already begun thriving on both coasts half a century earlier. Franciscan monks started both the Napa and Sonoma wine regions in 1824 at the Solano Mission in Sonoma. The wine industry they began continued to the present, interrupted only by Prohibition in the 1920s.

• Surprisingly, the first large-scale American winemaking region was not on either coast, but in Ohio, of all places. So much so that it was known in the 1850s as "The Rhine of America." In 1870, America's largest winery was located on Middle Bass Island, just off the grape-growing town of Sandusky, Ohio.

Modern Myths

Things That Just Ain't True

As we hang around the ol' debunk house, we sit and swap misinformation in order to knock it down. Here are some of the most maddening bits of misinformation that we hear over and over again.

ETERNAL LIGHT

The myth: You save energy by leaving fluorescent lights on all the time instead of turning them on and off.

The truth: There was a time that fluorescents required a hefty jolt to get them started, so it was best not to flash them continuously. However, nowadays, starting a fluorescent light takes only a tiny jolt of extra electricity, so you'll save electricity by turning the lights off when they're not needed. Even if you were turning them on and off repeatedly, you'd still save electricity over the standard filament light bulb.

BEAT ME DADDY, EIGHT TO THE BAR

The myth: The phrase "rule of thumb" came from English Common Law, dictating that men could beat their wives with a stick as long as it was no wider than a thumb.

The truth: Although the myth has been cluelessly cited as fact over and over again, there was no such law in English Common Law. Likewise, there was also no such law on the books anywhere in the United States either. (In fact, wife beating was expressly against the law in the American colonies long before the revolution, and men were often punished for breaking it.) In reality, the "rule" has to do with measuring, as in "ruler." The expression comes from carpentry--essentially using the thumb to estimate an inch.

DOUBTING THOMAS

The myth: A man named Thomas Crapper invented the flush toilet.

The truth: In 1969, a writer named Wallace Reyburn wrote *Flushed with Pride,* a far-fetched "biography" of one Thomas Crapper who he said invented the flush toilet. The book was a joke, as was Reyburn's follow-up book *Bust Up: The Uplifting Tale of Otto Titzling and the Development of the Bra.* Unfortunately, not everybody got the joke, and you will still see these "inventors" erroneously credited in books and trivia games by writers who should know better.

MR. THOMAS CRAPPER

Having said that, however, here's a twist: There is evidence that there really was a Thomas Crapper. Although he didn't invent the toilet, he manufactured toilets and accessories in the late 19th century. The evidence is actually quite convincing, consisting of old newspaper ads and so on, but one hesitates to take it unambivalently at face value considering past hoaxes and the "too-good-to-be-true" coincidence. So, to sum up: There might have been a Thomas Crapper who sold toilets; however, the flush toilet predated him by nearly 400 years. In fact, Sir John Harrington, godson of Queen Elizabeth I, created the first flush toilet in 1596. In 1775, Alexander Cumming improved Harrington's design by inventing the stink trap, which preventing odors from wafting back up from the sewers.

THOMAS CRAPPER & CO.'S
Sanitary Specialities.
IMPROVED
LAVATORY BASIN.
ELASTIC VALVE CLOSET.
IMPROVED SYPHON
Water Waste Preventer.
MARLBOROUGH ROAD, CHELSEA, LONDON, S.W.

BEAUTIFUL HAIR WITH BODY EXTRA

The myth: Your hair and nails will continue to grow after you die.

The truth: This one is wrong, but at least it's based on what appears to be true. When a person dies, the skin loses moisture and begins to get thinner. This makes the hair and nails stick out farther, so it looks like they've grown since death.

10% OF OUR BRAINS

The myth: We use only 10% of our brains.

The truth: The myth is beloved by New Agers, human potential gurus and others with seminars and books to sell. The truth is that you likely use all of your brain during a normal day, but not necessarily all at the same time (any more than you use all of your muscle groups at one time).

Our brains just aren't so big that we could afford to let that much of it lie fallow—it weighs only about 3 pounds. Coincidentally, 10% of that is comparable to the brain of a sheep. Don't give up on that other 90%--between eating, sleeping, work and finding your keys, every bit counts.

FIRST IN WAR, LAST IN TEETH

The myth: George Washington had wooden teeth.

The truth: Washington did have only one remaining tooth at the time of his inauguration. He didn't have wooden teeth, though. His four sets of dentures, one crafted by Paul Revere, were made of hippopotamus bone, elephant ivory and teeth from cows and dead people, held together with gold palates and springs. None of them worked well. Back then, though, nobody expected them to—the false teeth were not designed for eating, just for looking good. ☾

The Ups & Downs of Transportation

Elevators are about the safest form of transportation, boasting of only one fatality every 100 million miles traveled. (Stairs, in comparison, are five times more dangerous.)

Elevators owe their emergency brakes to engineer Elisha Graves Otis, founder of the elevator company that still bears his name. His invention in 1854 was a large, bow-shaped spring attached to the car and connected to the elevator cable. When taut, the cable kept the spring flexed.... However, if the cable broke, the spring would immediately flatten out, jamming its ends into notched guard rails on either side of the elevator, bringing the car to an immediate stop.

Every Picture Tells a Story

***The Scream* by Edvard Munch, 1893**

• *The Scream,* garishly colored and crudely rendered, is the first example of Expressionism, a style of painting that's meant to express the inner experience instead of external realities.

• Edvard Munch's childhood was gloomy and tragic. Growing up in a dark Norwegian landscape was bad enough, but he lost his mother at five, and a beloved sister at fourteen.

• On the day Munch painted this, he wrote, "I was walking with two friends.... The sun was setting.... The sky turned blood-red. I stopped, and leaning against the railing, deathly tired. My friends walked on. I stood there trembling with fear, and I sensed a great, infinite scream pass through nature."

• Munch later used the same bridge setting and colors for his paintings *Anxiety* and *Despair*.

• Munch's paintings were controversial. An exhibit in Berlin was closed down after critics and the public exploded in uproar.

• Success came, but so did mental and alcohol problems. Munch committed himself to a mental institution for nine months. When he emerged, he became a brilliant printmaker, and his later work explored much less disturbing themes.

• The painting was stolen in 1994, but was recovered.

Miss Snow Death

A Ghost Tale from Old Japan

In this story, another ancient Japanese legend collected by Lafcadio Hearn in 1903, a man is spared by a snow goddess of death...but the favor comes with a heavy obligation.

In a village of Musashi Province, there lived two woodcutters: Mosaku and Minokichi. At the time of which I am speaking, Mosaku was an old man; and Minokichi, his apprentice, was a lad of eighteen years. Every day they went together to a forest situated about five miles from their village. On the way to that forest there is a fast, wide river to cross; and there is a ferryboat.

Mosaku and Minokichi were on their way home one very cold evening when a great snowstorm overtook them. They reached the ferry, but they found that the boatman had gone away, leaving his boat on the other side of the river. It was no day for swimming; so the woodcutters took shelter in the ferryman's hut, thinking themselves lucky to find any shelter at all. There was no fireplace in the tiny hut, so Mosaku and Minokichi fastened the door, and lay down to rest, with their straw raincoats over them.

The old man almost immediately fell asleep; but Minokichi lay awake a long time, listening to the awful wind, and the continual slashing of the snow against the door. The river was roaring; and the hut swayed and creaked like a junk at sea. It was a terrible storm; and the air was every moment becoming colder; and Minokichi shivered under his raincoat. But at last, in spite of the cold, he too fell asleep.

He was awakened by a showering of snow in his face. The door of the hut had been forced open; and, by the snow-reflected light he saw a woman all in white. She was bending above Mosaku, and blowing her breath upon him like a bright white smoke. Almost in the same moment she turned to Minokichi, and stooped over him. He tried to cry out, but found that he could not utter any sound. The white woman bent down over him, lower and lower, until her face almost touched him; and he saw that she was very beautiful, though her eyes made him afraid. For a little time she continued to look at him. Then she smiled, and she whispered, "I intended to treat you like the other man. But I cannot help feeling some pity for you, because you are so young. You are a pretty boy, Minokichi; and I will not hurt you now. But, if you ever tell anybody—even your own mother—about what you have seen this night, then I will kill you! Remember what I say!"

With these words, she turned from him, and passed through the doorway. He suddenly found himself able to move, and he sprang up and looked out. But the woman was nowhere to be seen; and the snow was driving furiously into the hut.

Minokichi closed the door and secured it with wood. He wondered if the wind had blown it open; he thought that he might have been only dreaming, but he could not be sure. He called to Mosaku, and was frightened because the old man did not answer. He put out his hand in the dark, and touched Mosaku's face, and found that it was ice! Mosaku was dead.

By dawn the storm was over; and when the ferryman returned to his station, a little after sunrise, he found Minokichi lying senseless beside the frozen body of Mosaku. Minokichi was promptly cared for, and soon came to himself; but he remained a long time ill from the effects of the cold of that terrible night. He had been greatly frightened also by the old man's death; but he said nothing about the vision of the woman in white. As soon as he got well again, he returned to his calling, going alone every morning to the forest, and coming back at nightfall with his bundles of wood, which his mother helped him to sell.

One evening, in the winter of the following year, as he was on his way home, he overtook a girl who happened to be traveling by the same road. She was a tall, slim girl, very good-looking;

and she answered Minokichi's greeting in a voice as pleasant to the ear as the voice of a songbird. Then he walked beside her; and they began to talk. The girl said that her name was O-Yuki, a common Japanese name meaning "snow," that she had lately lost both of her parents, and that she was going to Tokyo, where she happened to have some poor relations who might help her to find a situation as a servant. Minokichi soon felt charmed by this strange girl; and the more that he looked at her, the handsomer she appeared to be. He asked her whether she was yet betrothed; and she answered, laughingly, that she was free.

By the time they reached the village, they had become very much pleased with each other. Minokichi asked O-Yuki to rest awhile at his house. After some shy hesitation, she went there with him; and his mother made her welcome, and prepared a warm meal for her. O-Yuki behaved so nicely that Minokichi's mother took an immediate fancy to her, and persuaded her to delay her journey to Yedo. And the natural end of the matter was that O-Yuki never went to Yedo at all.

O-Yuki proved a very good wife and daughter-in-law. When Minokichi's mother came to die—some five years later—her last words were of affection and praise for the wife of her son. And O-Yuki bore Minokichi ten handsome children.

The country-folk thought O-Yuki a wonderful person, by nature different from themselves. Most of the peasant-women age early; but O-Yuki, even after having become the mother of ten children, looked as young and fresh as on the day when she had first come to the village.

One night, after the children had gone to sleep, O-Yuki was sewing by the light of a paper lamp. Minokichi, watching her, said: "To see you sewing there, with the light on your face, makes me think of a strange thing that happened when I was a lad of eighteen. I then saw somebody as beautiful and white as you are now—indeed, she was very like you."

Without lifting her eyes from her work, O-Yuki responded: "Tell me about her.... Where did you see her?" Then Minokichi told her about the terrible night in the ferryman's hut, about the White Woman who had stooped above him, smiling and whispering, and about the silent death of old Mosaku. And he said: "Asleep or awake, that was the only time that I saw a being as beautiful as you. Of course, she was not a human being; and I was very much afraid of her, but she was so white! Indeed, I have never been sure whether it was a dream."

O-Yuki flung down her sewing, and bowed above Minokichi where he sat, shrieking into his face: "It was I — I — I! Yuki it was! And I told you then that I would kill you if you ever said one word about it! But for those children asleep there, I would kill you this moment! And now you had better take very, very good care of them; for if ever they have reason to complain of you, I will treat you as you deserve!"

Even as she screamed, her voice became thin, like a crying of wind; then she melted into a bright white mist that spired to the roof-beams, and shuddered away through the smoke-hole. Minokichi worked to be the best father ever, and O-Yuki was never again to be seen. ☾

Prescriptions and Second Opinions

"Nothing is more fatal to health than over-care of it." —Benjamin Franklin

"A cheerful heart is good medicine, but a crushed spirit dries up the bones." —Proverbs 17:22

"Always laugh when you can. It is cheap medicine." —Lord Byron

"Many serious illnesses are nothing but the expression of a serious dis-satisfaction with life." —Dr. Paul Tournier

"The best doctors are Doctor Diet, Doctor Quiet, and Doctor Merryman." —Jonathan Swift

"Let food be your medicine and medicine be your food." —Hippocrates

"No illness which can be treated by the diet should be treated by any other means." —Moses Maimonides of Caldova

"It requires a great faith for a man to be cured by his own placebos." —Dr. John L. McClenahan

"Early to rise and early to bed / Makes a man healthy, wealthy, and dead." —James Thurber

"Doctors are just the same as lawyers; the only difference is that lawyers merely rob you, while doctors rob you and kill you, too." —Anton Chekhov

"Don't think of organ donation as giving up part of yourself to keep total strangers alive. Think of it as total strangers giving up most of themselves to keep parts of you alive." —Anonymous

Dead Presidents

Without Looking, Who's on a $10 Bill?

When's the last time you took a good look at the money you use every day? Match the money with the person who appears on it. Get ten or more right and you're looking like a million bucks.

1. 1¢
2. 5¢
3. 10¢
4. 25¢
5. 50¢
6. $1 (coin until 1978)
7. $1 (coin 1979–99)
8. $1 (coin, after 2000)
9. $1 (bill)
10. $2
11. $5
12. $10
13. $20
14. $50
15. $100

a. Thomas Jefferson
b. Ulysses Grant
c. Andrew Jackson
d. John Kennedy
e. Abraham Lincoln
f. Millard Fillmore
g. Benjamin Franklin
h. Dwight Eisenhower
i. Susan Anthony
j. Franklin Roosevelt
k. Ronald Reagan
l. William McKinley
m. George Washington
n. Sacagawea
o. Alexander Hamilton

ANSWERS: 1e, 2a, 3j, 4m, 5d, 6h, 7i, 8n, 9m, 10a, 11e, 12o, 13c, 14b, 15g

Words from the Wise

Advice to Always, Always Live By

"I always wanted to be somebody, but I should have been more specific." —Lily Tomlin

"I always keep a supply of stimulant handy in case I see a snake—which I also keep handy." —W. C. Fields

"Always acknowledge a fault. This will throw those in authority off their guard and give you an opportunity to commit more." —Mark Twain

"Always *and* never *are two words you should always remember never to use."* —Wendell Johnson

"Arguments are to be avoided; they are always vulgar and often convincing." —Oscar Wilde

"Confusion is always the most honest response." —Marty Indik

"Always get married early in the morning. That way, if it doesn't work out, you haven't wasted a whole day." —Mickey Rooney

"Always be nice to your children because they are the ones who will choose your rest home." —Phyllis Diller

"Always read stuff that will make you look good if you die in the middle of it." —P. J. O'Rourke

"Always do sober what you said you'd do drunk. That will teach you to keep your mouth shut." —Ernest Hemingway

"Always forgive your enemies; nothing annoys them so much." —Oscar Wilde

"Therefore, from a logical point of view, Always marry a woman uglier than you." —Calypso song

"Always make water when you can." —Duke of Wellington

Oh, Henry!

The Ransom of Red Chief

One of O. Henry's best short stories is about a couple of two-bit grifters who decide to make a fortune by kidnapping the son of a prominent man. However, the plot doesn't quite work out the way they intended.

IT LOOKED LIKE A GOOD THING: but wait till I tell you. We were down South, in Alabama—Bill Driscoll and myself—when this kidnapping idea struck us. It was, as Bill afterward expressed it, "during a moment of temporary mental apparition"; but we didn't find that out till later.

There was a town down there, as flat as a flannel-cake, and called Summit, of course. It contained inhabitants of as undeleterious and self-satisfied a class of peasantry as ever clustered around a Maypole.

Bill and me had a joint capital of about six hundred dollars, and we needed just two thousand dollars more to pull off a fraudulent town-lot scheme in Western Illinois with. We selected for our victim the only child of a prominent citizen named Ebenezer Dorset. The father was respectable and tight, a mortgage financier and a stern, upright collection-plate passer and forecloser. The kid was a boy of ten, with bas-relief freckles, and hair the colour of the cover of the magazine you buy at the newsstand when you want to catch a train. Bill and me figured that Ebenezer would melt down for a ransom of $2000 to a cent. But wait till I tell you.

O Henry (William Sydney Porter)

One evening after sundown, we drove in a buggy past old Dorset's house. The kid was in the street, throwing rocks at a kitten on the opposite fence.

"Hey, little boy!" says Bill, "would you like to have a bag of candy and a nice ride?" The boy catches Bill neatly in the eye with a piece of brick.

"That will cost the old man an extra five hundred dollars," says Bill, climbing over the wheel.

That boy put up a fight like a welter-weight cinnamon bear; but, at last, we got him down in the bottom of the buggy and drove away. We took him up to the cave. After dark I drove the buggy to the little village where we had hired it, and walked back to the mountain.

Bill was pasting court-plaster over the scratches and bruises on his features. There was a fire burning, and the boy was watching a pot of boiling coffee, with two buzzard tailfeathers stuck in his red hair. He points a stick at me when I come up, and says:

"Ha! cursed paleface, do you dare to enter the camp of Red Chief, the terror of the plains?"

"He's all right now," says Bill, rolling up his trousers and examining some bruises on his shins. "We're playing Indian. I'm Old Hank, the Trapper, Red Chief's captive, and I'm to be scalped at daybreak. By Geronimo! that kid can kick hard."

Yes, sir, that boy seemed to be having the time of his life. The fun of camping out in a cave had made him forget that he was a captive himself. He immediately christened me Snake-eye, the Spy, and announced that, when his braves returned from the warpath, I was to be broiled at the stake at the rising of the sun.

Then we had supper. He made a during-dinner speech something like this: "I like this fine. I never camped out before; but I had a pet 'possum once, and I was nine last birthday. I hate school. Rats ate up sixteen of Jimmy Talbot's aunt's hen's eggs. Are there any real Indians in these woods? I want some more gravy. Amos Murray has got six toes. A parrot can talk, but a monkey or a fish can't. How many does it take to make twelve?" Every few minutes he would remember that he was a redskin. He would let out a war-whoop that made Old Hank the Trapper shiver. That boy had Bill terrorized from the start.

"Red Chief," says I to the kid, "would you like to go home?"

"Aw, what for?" says he. "I don't have any fun at home. I hate to go to school. I like to camp out. You won't take me back home again, Snake-eye, will you?"

"Not right away," says I. "We'll stay here in the cave a while."

"All right!" says he. "I never had such fun in all my life."

We went to bed about eleven o'clock. We spread down some blankets and put Red Chief between us. We weren't afraid he'd run away. He kept us awake for three hours. At last, I fell into a troubled sleep, and dreamed that I had been kidnapped and chained to a tree by a ferocious pirate with red hair.

Just at daybreak, I was awakened by a series of awful screams from Bill. They weren't yells, or howls, or whoops, or yawps, such as you'd expect from a manly set of vocal organs—they were humiliating screams, such as women emit when they see ghosts or caterpillars. It's an awful thing to hear a strong, desperate, fat man scream incontinently in a cave at daybreak.

I jumped up to see what the matter was. Red Chief was sitting on Bill's chest, with one hand twined in Bill's hair. In the other he had the knife we used for slicing bacon; and he was industriously trying to take Bill's scalp, according to the sentence that had been pronounced upon him the evening before.

"I was to be broiled at the stake at sunrise."

I got the knife away from the kid and made him lie down again. But, from that moment, Bill's spirit was broken. He never closed an eye again in sleep as long as that boy was with us. I dozed off for a while, but along toward sun-up I remembered that Red Chief had said I was to be burned at the stake at the rising of the sun. I wasn't nervous or afraid; but I sat up and lit my pipe and leaned against a rock.

"What you getting up so soon for, Sam?" asked Bill.

"Me?" says I. "Oh, I got a kind of a pain in my shoulder. I thought sitting up would rest it."

"You're a liar!" says Bill. "You're afraid. You was to be burned at sunrise, and you was afraid he'd do it. And he would, too, if he could find a match. Ain't it awful, Sam? Do you think anybody will pay money to get a little imp like that back home?"

"Sure," said I. "A rowdy kid like that is just the kind that parents dote on. Now, you and the Chief get up and cook breakfast, while I go up on the top of this mountain and reconnoiter."

I went up on the peak of the little mountain. Over toward Summit I expected to see the sturdy yeomanry of the village armed with pitchforks beating the countryside for the dastardly kidnappers. But what I saw was a peaceful landscape dotted with one man ploughing with a dun mule. Nobody was dragging the creek; no couriers dashed hither and yon, bringing tidings of no news to the distracted parents.

"Perhaps," says I to myself, "it has not yet been discovered that the wolves have borne away the tender lambkin from the fold," says I, and I went down the mountain to breakfast.

When I got to the cave I found Bill backed up against the side of it, breathing hard, and the boy threatening to smash him with a rock half as big as a cocoanut.

"He put a red-hot boiled potato down my back," explained Bill, "and then mashed it with his foot; and I boxed his ears. Have you got a gun about you, Sam?"

I took the rock away from the boy. "I'll fix you," says the kid to Bill. "No man ever yet struck the Red Chief but what he got paid for it. You better beware!"

"We've got to fix up some plan about the ransom," says I. "There don't seem to be much excitement around Summit, but maybe his folks think he's spending the night with Aunt Jane or one of the neighbors. Anyhow, he'll be missed today. Tonight we must get a message to his father demanding $2000."

Just then we heard a kind of war-whoop, such as David might have emitted when he knocked out the champion Goliath. It was a sling that Red Chief had pulled out of his pocket, and he was whirling it around his head.

I dodged, and heard a heavy thud and a kind of a sigh from Bill, like a horse gives out when you take his saddle off. He fell in the fire. I dragged him out and poured cold water on his head for half an hour. By and by, Bill sits up and says, "You won't go away and leave me here alone, will you, Sam?"

I went out and caught that boy and shook him until his freckles rattled. "I was only funning," says he sullenly. "I didn't mean to hurt Old Hank. I'll behave, Snake-eye, if you won't send me home, and if you'll let me play the Black Scout today."

"I don't know the game," says I. "That's for you and Mr. Bill to decide. He's your playmate for the day. I'm going away for a while, on business. Now, you make friends with him and say you are sorry for hurting him, or home you go, at once."

I made him and Bill shake hands, and then I took Bill aside and told him I was going to Poplar Cove, a little village three miles from the cave, and send a peremptory letter to old man Dorset, demanding the ransom.

"You know, Sam," says Bill, "I've stood by you without batting an eye in earthquakes, fire and flood—in poker games, dynamite outrages, police raids, train robberies and cyclones. I never lost my nerve yet till we kidnapped that two-legged skyrocket of a kid. You won't leave me long with him, will you, Sam?"

"I'll be back some time this afternoon," says I. "You must keep the boy amused and quiet till I return. And now we'll write the letter to old Dorset."

Bill and I got paper and pencil and worked on the letter while Red Chief, with a blanket wrapped around him, strutted up and down, guarding the mouth of the cave. Bill begged me tearfully to make the ransom fifteen hundred dollars instead of two thousand. "I ain't attempting," says he, "to decry the celebrated moral aspect of parental affection, but it ain't human for anybody to give up $2000 for that forty-pound chunk of freckled wildcat. I'm willing to take a chance at $1500. You can charge the difference up to me."

To relieve Bill, we collaborated a letter that ran this way:

Ebenezer Dorset, Esq.:

We have your boy concealed in a place far from Summit. It is useless for you or the most skilful detectives to attempt to find him. Absolutely, the only terms on which you can have him restored to you are these: We demand fifteen hundred dollars for his return; the money to be left at midnight tonight at the same spot and as your reply—as hereinafter described. If you agree to these terms, send your answer in writing by a solitary messenger tonight at half-past eight o'clock. After crossing Owl Creek, on the road to Poplar Cove, at the bottom of the fence-post opposite the third tree, will be found a small box. The messenger will place the answer in this box and return immediately to Summit.

If you attempt any treachery or fail to comply with our demand as stated, you will never see your boy again. If you pay the money as demanded, he will be returned to you safe and well within three hours. These terms are final, and if you do not accede to them no further communication will be attempted.

—TWO DESPERATE MEN.

I addressed this letter to Dorset, and put it in my pocket. As I was about to start, the kid comes up to me and says, "Aw, Snake-eye, you said I could play the Black Scout."

"Mr. Bill will play it," says I. "What kind of a game is it?"

"I'm the Black Scout," says Red Chief, "and I have to ride to the stockade to warn the settlers that the Indians are coming."

"What am I to do?" asks Bill, looking at the kid suspiciously.

"You're the hoss," says Black Scout. "Get down on your hands and knees. How can I ride to the stockade without a hoss?"

"You'd better keep him interested," said I, "till we get the scheme going. Loosen up." Bill gets down on all fours, and a look comes in his eye like a rabbit's when you catch it in a trap.

"How far to the stockade, kid? " he asks, in a husky voice.

"Ninety miles," says the Black Scout. "And you have to hump yourself to get there on time. Whoa, now!" The Black Scout jumps on Bill's back and digs his heels in his side.

"For Heaven's sake," says Bill, "hurry back, Sam. I wish we hadn't made the ransom more than a thousand. "

I walked over to Poplar Cove and sat around the postoffice and store, talking with the chawbacons that came in to trade. One says that he hears Summit is all upset on account of Eb Dorset's boy having been lost or stolen. That was all I wanted to know. I posted my letter. The postmaster said the mail-carrier would come by in an hour to take the mail on to Summit.

When I got back to the cave Bill wabbled out of the cave.

"I tell you, Sam, a human can only stand so much," says Bill. "I was rode the ninety miles to the stockade, not barring an inch." I told him that we would get the ransom and be off with it by midnight if old Dorset fell in with our proposition. So Bill braced up enough to promise the kid to play a Russian in a Japanese war as soon as he felt a little better.

I had a scheme for collecting that ransom without danger of being caught by counterplots that ought to commend itself to professional kidnappers. The tree under which the answer was to be left—and the money later on—was close to the road fence with big, bare fields on all sides. If a gang of constables should be watching for any one to come for the note they could see him a long way off crossing the fields or in the road. But no, sirree! At half-past eight I was up in that tree as well hidden as a tree toad, waiting for the messenger to arrive.

Exactly on time, a half-grown boy rides up the road on a bicycle,

WHERE DID OH HENRY! GET ITS NAME?

What's the connection between author O. Henry, and the **Oh Henry!** candy bar?

None. Zip. Nada. Absolutely no connection. At least that's what manufacturer George Williamson claimed when the bar came out in 1921. His story was that a guy named Henry used to hang around his candy shop, flirting with the female candymakers. They, in turn, began asking him to do odd jobs for them, always prefacing their requests with, "Oh, Henry!"

Sounds a little fishy, right? Somewhat reminiscent of the Curtiss Candy Company's insistence that **Baby Ruth** was *really* named after a dead president's daughter instead of the popular baseball star.

Oh well, unlike the Curtiss Company, Williamson didn't have to worry about lawsuits: O. Henry had conveniently died eleven years earlier.

locates the box at the foot of the fencepost, slips a folded piece of paper into it and pedals away again back toward town.

I waited an hour and then slid down the tree, got the note, slipped along the fence till I struck the woods, and was back at the cave in another half an hour. I opened the note, got near the lantern and read it to Bill. The sum and substance of it was this:

Two Desperate Men.

Gentlemen: In regard to the ransom you ask for the return of my son, I think you are a little high in your demands, and I hereby make you a counter-proposition, which I am inclined to believe you will accept. You bring Johnny home and pay me $250 in cash, and I agree to take him off your hands. You had better come at night, for the neighbors believe he is lost, and I couldn't be responsible for what they would do to anybody they saw bringing him back.

Very respectfully,
EBENEZER DORSET.

"Great pirates of Penzance!" says I; "of all the impudent—"

But I glanced at Bill, and hesitated. He had the most pleading look I ever saw on the face of a dumb or a talking brute.

"Sam," says he, "what's $250, after all? We've got the money. One more night of this kid will send me to a bed in Bedlam. I think Mr. Dorset is a spendthrift for making us such a liberal offer. You ain't going to let the chance go, are you?"

"Tell you the truth, Bill," says I, "this little he ewe lamb has somewhat got on my nerves too. We'll take him home, pay the ransom and make our get-away."

We took him home that night. It was twelve o'clock when we knocked at Ebenezer's front door. At the moment when I should have been abstracting $1500 from the box under the tree, according to the original proposition, Bill was counting out $250 into Dorset's hand.

When the kid found out we were going to leave him at home he started up a howl like a calliope and fastened himself as tight as a leech to Bill's leg. His father peeled him away gradually, like a porous plaster.

"How long can you hold him?" asks Bill.

"I'm not as strong as I used to be," says old Dorset, "but I think I can promise you ten minutes."

"Enough," says Bill. "In ten minutes I shall cross the Central, Southern and Middle Western States, and be legging it trippingly for the Canadian border."

And, as dark as it was, and as fat as Bill was, and as good a runner as I am, he was a good mile and a half out of summit before I could catch up with him. ℭ

Sy-Clo

TRADE MARK

The Latest Word In Sanitation

The name Sy-Clo on a closet means health insurance for your home or any building in which the closet is placed; it means freedom from all those diseases which are usually traceable to noxious odors and poisonous gases arising from ordinary closets.

Sy-Clo stands for more than mere flushing; it stands for a wonderful syphonic action of great power—an action which literally pulls the contents of the bowl into the drain, cleansing the non-reachable parts, instantly sealing the outlet channel with a water trap to an unusual depth, and absolutely preventing all danger of gas.

The Sy-Clo Closet stands for an interior cleanliness and purity impossible in an iron closet, and unknown in any closet but one made of china—like the Sy-Clo. Hand-moulded of china all into one solid piece like a vase, the Sy-Clo is without crack, joint or rough surface to collect dirt or disease germs. It is as clean inside and out as a china pitcher, being made exactly the same way and of the same material.

The surface of the Sy-Clo Closet cannot chip off, is not affected by acid, water or wear, and hence cannot rust or discolor as an iron closet does. The Sy-Clo is strong, simple, durable; it cannot get out of order and, with ordinary care, will last as long as the house in which it is placed. It costs but little more than the common closet, and when health and comfort are considered, it really costs less; in fact, *your doctor pays the bill.* Your plumber will tell you that Sy-Clo is absolutely the latest word in perfect sanitation.

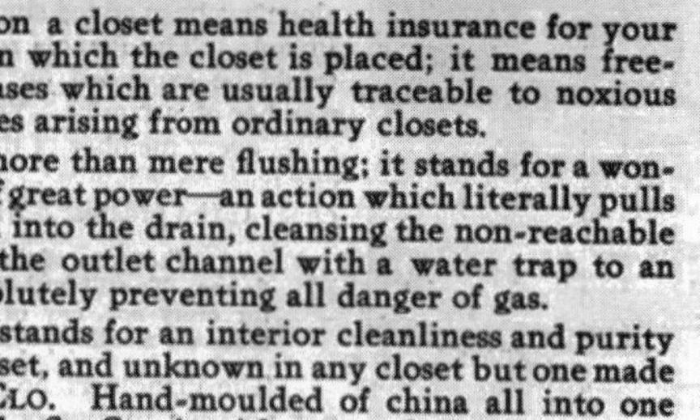

Send for booklet on "Household Health"—mailed free.

POTTERIES SELLING CO.
Trenton, N. J.

Buttheads

A Whole Herd of Goat Facts

Did you know that the term *butthead* wasn't originally an insult, but a technical term referring to goats? Most people don't know much about goats—here's your chance to be hoof and horn above the rest.

• Despite their reputation, goats don't really eat everything in sight. They do, however, explore new things with their sensitive lips, so it sometimes looks like they're chowing down on any ol' thing.

• Mohair and cashmere fabrics sound much fancier than what they really are: goat hair.

• Nanny goats have little similarity with human nannies. The name is used to denote any female goat. In England, "Nanny" was a derivative of the name *Annie*. All "billy" goats are males—it's a nickname for William. You see the same sort of naming with tom cats, and jack and jennie mules.

• Both sexes of goats have beards.

• Neutered goats are called *wethers*.

• Hey, Beavis, a "butthead" is technically any goat with horns. We kid you not.

• The most popular milk worldwide comes from goats, not cows.

• Despite a reputation for being ornery, goats are much easier to milk than cows. For one thing, they're smaller. For another, they actually like being around people. Finally, goats have only two teats instead of four like cows, cutting the work in half. (For more milking info, see next page.)

• At least four presidents had goats patrolling the White House grounds back in the days when lawnmowers were unavailable and fresh milk was hard to come by. Goat owners in the White House included Abraham Lincoln, Rutherford B. Hayes, Benjamin Harrison and Harry Truman.

• Today, a *scapegoat* is usually someone who takes the rap for something gone wrong. The name, though, originally applied only to goats. It comes from "escape goat." In Leviticus 16:10, God demanded that at Yom Kippur one goat should be killed in his honor, and another released into the desert. That "escaped goat" symbolically carried away all the sins of the Israelis. Human scapegoats nowadays serve a similar function—they get burdened with the misconduct and mistakes of others.

• Don't confuse the terminology: goats don't live in flocks, they live in herds.

• Racehorses were often given goat companions to keep them calm in strange stalls. Rivals would sometimes try to upset another's horse before a race by stealing its goat friend. Etymologists tell us that that's where "getting your goat" comes from.

• Goats are consider sexually licentious. It's where the term "old goat"—implying a dirty, old man— came from.

• Goatees were likewise named in the 1840s when sporting goat-like chin-warmers became popular.

How to Milk a Goat

• You'll need a small stool and bucket. If you milk from the side, make sure it's the same side every time. Some goat milkers prefer to milk from the rear, but that requires being fast on your feet if the goat decides to eliminate body waste.

• Tie up the goat and wash its flank and udder with warm water. Use udder cream, available at finer feed stores, on both the teats and your hands—it lubricates and acts as an antiseptic.

• Take the tops of the two teats in your two hands between your thumb and forefinger. Squeeze with those two fingers, then with the second, third and fourth fingers in fast, rolling succession.

• The milk should be creamy white. If it isn't, or if it's clotted, the goat has an easily-cured ailment called mastitis, so throw the milk away. Otherwise, keep milking. Talk to the animal gently as you milk—most goats love human attention.

• Older siblings take note: It's said that the ancient Romans used goats to tickle prisoners to insanity and death. They'd repeatedly dip the bottom of victim's feet in salt water and let salt-loving goats lick them. After several days of this the guy would die of exhaustion and shock, laughing all the way.

• The sport that requires the fastest reflexes is jai alai. The rubber-and-goatskin ball that's used in the game can be thrown at 188 miles per hour with a curved wicker basket called a *cesta*. One hit from the ball can be deadly.

• Virginia Woolf's childhood nickname was The Goat. And, of course, there was Billy the Kid. Both were called that because a perceived resemblance to the animal. Of course, if you mentioned that to Virginia, she'd write something bad about you. Billy, though, he'd just kill you.

• Credit a lost goat for the archaeological discovery of the Dead Sea Scrolls. A herdsman wandered into a cave to see if his errant animal was there, and found the scrolls rolled up in clay jars. Whether he found his lost goat, we don't know.

• Goats were probably first tamed more than 9,000 years ago in Asia and regions of the eastern Mediterranean.

• In tropical areas, goats mate throughout the year; in cooler regions, they breed only from late summer to winter as the days become shorter.

• In the wild, does and kids travel in herds of up to fifty animals. Bucks live separately, joining the herd only during the mating season.

• Just like cows, goats chew their cud.

According to Mark Twain

More from *Puddin'head Wilson's Calendar*, a fictitious publication that Twain "quoted" from whenever he needed a maxim to head a chapter.

• "October. This is one of the peculiarly dangerous months in which to speculate in stocks. The others are September, July, April, January, November, May, March, June, December, August, and February."

• "Nothing so needs reforming as other people's habits."

• "Behold the fool saith, 'Put not all thine eggs in the one basket,' but the wise man saith, 'Put all your eggs in the one basket and WATCH THAT BASKET.'"

• "If you pick up a starving dog and make him prosperous, he will not bite you. This is the principal difference between a dog and a man."

Be good & you will be lonesome.
Mark Twain

• "Even popularity can be overdone. In Rome, at first you are full of regrets that Michaelangelo died; but by and by you only regret that you didn't see him do it."

• "Few things are harder to put up with than the annoyance of a good example."

• "Some people are useless on top of the ground. They ought to be under it, inspiring the cabbages."

• "April 1. This is the day upon which we are reminded of what we are on the other 364."

• "It is often the case that the man who can't tell a lie thinks he is the best judge of one."

• "There are three infallible ways of pleasing an author: 1, to tell him you have read one of his books; 2, to tell him you have read all of his books; 3, to ask him to let you read the manuscript of his forthcoming book. No. 1 admits you to his respect; No. 2 admits you to his admiration; No. 3 carries you clear to his heart."

• "Noise proves nothing. Often a hen who has merely laid an egg cackles as if she had laid an asteroid."

• "It is easier to stay out than get out."

SPAM

Too Many Cold Shoulders

SPAM, the ultimate mystery meat. What's in it, and how did a canned meat become a beloved pop culture icon?

Margaret Thatcher ate it for Christmas dinner in 1943. Nikita Khrushchev credited it for keeping the Soviet Army alive during World War II. Monty Python wrote a song about it. GIs in World War II joked that it was "ham that flunked its physical." Its manufacturer calls it "the Rodney Dangerfield of luncheon meat—it don't get no respect."

We're talking Spam, ladies and gentlemen, also known as "mystery meat" or (to quote those Python boys) "Spam Spam Spam Spam / Lovely Spam, oh wonderful Spam...." It's much maligned, but much eaten as well, accounting for 75 percent of all luncheon meat sales in this country. It is especially popular in Hawaii, for some reason, which has the highest per capita Spam consumption rate in the nation. (And, let the record show, the highest life expectancy in the nation as well—84 and 80 years for women and men respectively. Coincidence? We think not. Perhaps all those sodium compounds preserve more than pork products.)

In Korea, Spam is an imported luxury item, a part of the good life. A can of it is often given as a present on a date, or to coworkers and business associates, and even to newlyweds. Koreans often fry it with the peppery cabbage dish, kimchi, or roll it up into kimpap, a Spam sushi-like item made with rice and seaweed.

Why was Spam invented? Because of a surplus of pig shoulders. Every meat processor runs into the problem of what to do with the parts of the animal that are less popular than others.

Pork shoulders, for example, aren't meaty enough to sell as ham, and aren't fatty enough to make bacon. Seeing pork shoulders piling up in the coolers of the George A. Hormel Company in 1937 gave one of its executives an idea. Why not chop the meat up, add some spices and ham from other parts of the pig, and form it into small ham-like loaves? Put it in a can and fill the excess space with gelatin from the pig's leftover skin and bones—you could probably keep the meat edible for months without refrigeration.

They tried it. It worked. Hormel's Spiced Ham quickly found a niche in the market. It was inexpensive, savory, convenient and it didn't need refrigeration.

Other packers, also plagued with a surplus of pig parts, began issuing their own "Spiced Hams." Hormel offered a $100 prize for a name that would differentiate its product from the imitators. A brother of one of its workers contracted the words "Spiced Ham" and got Spam.

Spam was bolstered by a memorable ad campaign that showed how it could be served morning, noon and night and by singing commercials performed live and on the radio by the 60-strong traveling Hormel Girls ("Spam, Spam, Spam, Spam / Spam, Spam / Hormel's new miracle meat in a can / Tastes fine, saves time / If you want something grand, ask for Spam..." sung awkwardly to the tune of "My Bonnie Lies Over the Ocean").

When World War II came, Spam's price, portability and shelf life made it a staple of every GI's diet. The gospel according to Spam was also spread by American aid packages to its allies. Although many GIs swore that they'd never eat the stuff again (even Dwight Eisenhower complained about too much Spam in Army messes), they apparently got a craving once they got home and out of uniform, because Spam did booming business immediately after the war. Even now, 228 cans of Spam are eaten every minute of the day. €

Join Our Club!

THERE'S NO BETTER TIME than now to join W. C. Privy's special club of special friends, the Bathroom Companions of Mr. Privy. Becoming a BCOMP member has never been easier. Simply send an e-mail note to our membership committee at *membership@bathroomcompanion.com* and receive a printable membership card and a door hanger (*see below*).

Here at Bathroom Companion Central we're busy at work putting together the next installment of the BC. If you have any suggestions for stories, feel free to send them along to *ideas@bathroomcompanion.com*. If you're interested in submitting pictures for inclusion on the Pot Shots pages, please submit them to *potshots@bathroomcompanion.com,* or send anything to The Bathroom Companion, c/o St. Martin's Press, 175 Fifth Avenue, New York, N.Y. 10010.

Once again, thank you for surporting us in keeping W. C. Privy's dream flowing!

Become a member today, and get your printable "Go Away!" door hanger, and your very own membership card to BCOMP—the W. C. Privy Fan Club.

Write to:
membership@bathroomcompanion.com

(For emergency use only)

(For emergency use only)

(For emergency use only)

(For emergency use only)